Gary Rhodes

Gary Rhodes is one of Britain's best-loved chefs. He has numerous awards to his name, including the prestigious CATEY Special Award, the catering industry's equivalent to an Oscar, for helping to revive British cookery and for his total dedication to the industry. The new presenter on BBC's long-running *Masterchef* series, Gary has also presented seven other television series. He has written nine cookery books as well, including, most recently, the bestselling *At the Table*. Gary runs two Michelin-starred restaurants in London, city rhodes and Rhodes in the Square, and two brasseries, Rhodes & Co, in Manchester and Edinburgh.

Photographs by Sîan Irvine

Gary Rhodes
NEW BRITISH CLASSICS

This book is published to accompany the television series entitled *New British Classics,* first broadcast in 1999. The series was produced by BBC Features and Events.
Executive Producer: Nick Vaughan-Barratt
Producer: Mandy Cooper

Published by BBC Worldwide Ltd,
Woodlands, 80 Wood Lane, London W12 0TT

First published 1999
Reprinted 1999 (twice), 2000 (five times)
First published in paperback 2001
Reprinted 2002, 2003, 2004, 2005
© Copyright Gary Rhodes 1999
The moral right of the author has been asserted.
Photographs by Sîan Irvine © copyright BBC Worldwide Ltd

Recipe for mincemeat in *Home-made Mincemeat and Mince Pies* on page 337 taken from *Delia Smith's Christmas* and reproduced by kind permission of Delia Smith.

ISBN 0 563 55100 3 (hardback)
ISBN 0 563 53411 7 (paperback)

Commissioning editor: Nicky Copeland
Project editor: Khadija Manjlai
Copy editor: Deborah Savage
Additional research: Susan Fleming
Art director: Lisa Pettibone
Styling by Pippin Britz
Food prepared for photography by Gary Rhodes and Jo Pratt
Thanks to Divertimenti, Thomas Goode, Villroy & Boch and The Blue Door in London for the loan of items for photography

Typeset in Classical Garamond and Syntax
Printed and bound in Singapore by Tien Wah Press
Colour separations by Radstock Reproductions, Midsomer Norton

Acknowledgements

This book is the biggest collection of recipes that I have written and put together. It's almost impossible to compile such a repertoire without the support and help of others, so I would like to take this opportunity to express my dearest thanks to all, including those not mentioned by name here.

A very special thank you to Sue Fleming for the many hours it took accumulating the vast quantity of research information required. I'd like to thank Borra Garson, Lissanne Kenyon, Gardner Merchant, my team at city rhodes restaurant, in particular Wayne Tapsfield and Michael Bedford, and the BBC books team: Nicky Copeland, Khadija Manjlai, Andrew Barron, Sarah Miles and Charlotte Lochhead. Another big thank you to the best home economist in the business – Jo Pratt, Sîan Irvine for the beautiful photography, Nick Vaughan-Barratt, Mandy Cooper and the rest of the BBC television crew for the many exciting weeks of filming the *New British Classics* series.

And, of course, my wife and sons – Jennie, Samuel and George – who've put up with me for yet another year and will, I hope, for many more to come.

Thank you – simple words that mean so much.

Contents

British cookery has gone through many changes, with different approaches to ingredients resulting in varied tastes and styles. Twenty-five years ago, the UK had a poor reputation throughout the culinary world and little respect. But then an innovative influence, *nouvelle cuisine*, burst onto the scene, affecting restaurants and home kitchens alike.
We did not fully understand its style, but it gave us light at the end of the tunnel, inspiring us to find our place in the world of culinary excellence.

It turned out to be a long journey, but we did not lose direction. Two brothers were responsible for this, showing us that classical methods and long-held traditions are the bedrock of new ideas.
They showed how to work with tastes, not overwork them, creating complements rather than conflicts.

The brothers have an aura about them: they have given me nothing but inspiration, and continue to do so. I would like to dedicate *New British Classics* to the Roux brothers, Albert and Michel, who, for me, are the godfathers of the culinary world.

Thank you.

'The discovery of a new dish is more beneficial to humanity than the discovery of a new star.'
Brillat Savarin

Introduction

New British Classics is a book of culinary stories and recipes feeding us with information of the past, carrying many flavours that have survived, with many others re-born. British cookery, as most of you know, is a long-held passion of mine. While other cuisines have had a large influence on its development, its worldwide culinary reputation has always been less esteemed than that of France and Italy. I have never quite understood how and why this was until I started to research this book. Yes, I had heard various views and held many of my own, but the origins and progress of cookery in the UK is more complicated and fascinating than one imagines, and deserves exploration. In each chapter I have outlined the history of the recipes included. I have also interspersed the chapters with features on ingredients, foods and food occasions (afternoon tea, for instance) that I think are particularly, sometimes even uniquely, British.

So, how did the history of cooking start? The first few lines from 'The Invention of Cuisine' by Carol Musk set the scene.

> Imagine a thin woman
> before bread was invented,
> playing a harp of wheat in the field.
> There is a stone, and behind her
> the bones of the last killed,
> The black bird on her shoulder
> That a century later
> Will fly with trained and murderous intent.
>
> They are not very hungry
> because cuisine has not yet been invented.
> nor has falconry,
> nor the science of imagination.
>
> All they have is the pure impulse to eat.

Out of the need to eat for survival came the instinct to put foodstuffs together and cook them for variety and taste – an impulse that developed in most countries at the same time.

The principal characteristic of British culinary tradition is the number of influences it has absorbed over the centuries. As a group of islands to the side of a great continental mass, Britain has always been open to invasion. The invaders came, bringing with them their foods and cooking techniques. The Romans were perhaps of the greatest significance, and during their 400 years of occupation, they introduced many ingredients and ideas to an essentially simple cooking style. Many vegetables, fruits and meats that we consider British-born were actually brought in by the Romans – from pheasants, guinea fowl and deer to figs, walnuts, chestnuts, parsley, mint, chervil, onions, leeks, garlic and many others. Also introduced were two vegetables I have always considered to be purely British: cabbage and turnips.

The Saxons, Angles and Vikings were also influential, as were the Normans after 1066. These 'men of the North' – Normandy was itself originally a Viking stronghold – not only brought in ideas from France, and from their own heritage, but from southern Europe too. Norman forces went on to conquer parts of southern Europe, in particular Sicily, which had been strongly influenced by Arab invaders, and food traditions from there were to filter through to northern Europe. Medieval food in England was rich in many ways that were as much Middle Eastern as northern European, in its use of dried fruits, nuts such as almonds, and a multitude of spices. Cane sugar was another introduction, brought back to England by soldiers returning from the Crusades. So rare and expensive were the blocks of refined or brown sugar that they were looked upon as a sweet spice and kept under tight lock and key.

Food for the rich can't have been boring during and after the Middle Ages, although the many fish days forced on the population by the Church must have made salt fish (most people did not have access to fresh) less than welcome. For ordinary people this simply meant salted and pickled fish, but for the rich there were many more types of seafood readily available – from basics such as plaice, haddock, herring and mackerel to the more extravagant oysters, whales, sturgeon, crabs, lobsters and even seals.

It is said that a plainer feel to British food than that of the medieval style started to creep in during the years of the Commonwealth (1649–60), when the Puritans so disapproved of the use of culinary spices, thinking they led to intemperance and lasciviousness, that they even tried to ban Christmas! I think that British food has always been plain, but not dull, to a greater extent than is often thought, because the majority of the population, denied access to expensive imported fruits, nuts and spices, cooked and ate very simply. The traditions of the yeoman's and peasant's table are as important in our culinary heritage as those of the aristocracy. Moreover, the good climate and agriculture, in England at any rate, ensured adequate grain supplies and lush pastures and thus produced good-quality meats. So, basically, for those who could afford meat, there was no need to do anything more fancy to a piece of beef than roast it. The majority of people liked foods to taste of what they were, with 'the taste of the fire', and didn't favour rich complementary sauces or tricksy combinations of foods as the French might. However, then as now, sharp and piquant garnish sauces, such as mint or horseradish, were much favoured.

Following the great world explorations of the sixteenth century, many foods were introduced to Britain from the New World, among them turkeys, tomatoes, sweet peppers, chillies and vanilla (as well as tobacco). The one that was to have the most significance, though, was the potato, which did not take long to become a dietary staple in the British Isles, particularly in Ireland.

The increasing industrialization of the country from the eighteenth century onwards, and enclosures of land, meant that many people were displaced and rural and culinary traditions began to be eroded. Those who had to seek work in the gradually expanding towns became cut off from their former ways of cooking and eating. Food, once again, became simpler. Eating took second place to work in daily life, playing a smaller part in the family budget and was of little general interest. It was at this time that cookshops became part of the culinary culture, offering some of the dishes that most characterize British cooking to many – things such as eels and mash, pies and mash and, one of the most classic, fish and chips. With the breakdown of the rural communities, some traditions were lost and others replaced with outside influences among those who had moved to the cities – notably French cuisine, which dominated 'refined' British cooking in restaurants and wealthy private houses in the eighteenth and nineteenth centuries. These dual culinary styles continued until the First and Second World Wars, when food for pleasure became difficult as rations were introduced.

Later, with the introduction of *nouvelle cuisine* – a new 'fashion' in cooking – we seemed to lose our way completely. Perhaps I should say mislay, rather than lose, because in many country districts, those parts of England, Scotland, Wales and Ireland furthest from the urban centres of influence, great traditions did manage to survive. I've personally experienced, with nothing but gustatory pleasure, large pots containing all three courses – boiled ham with lots of vegetables and potatoes cooking away with a muslin bag of leek dumpling, for instance, where the vegetables are served with the liquor for soup, followed by the ham and potatoes, and finished with a wedge of the savoury dumpling. In the last few years there has been a more generalized revival of interest in the old ways. Twenty years ago British cooking was looked upon as having nothing to offer but well-done roast beef and soggy Yorkshire puddings. It was in the mid 1980s that the image of British cookery began to change, and I am proud to have played a small part in this, re-introducing to my menus recipes that I consider to be Great British

Classics. Lancashire hotpot, faggots, fishcakes and bread and butter pudding are all part of a huge tradition, north to south and east to west, and are all honest and simple, with real, full, delicious flavours. Why did we lose these dishes? Slowly braised oxtail (returning soon, we hope, page 230) is perhaps one of the best foods in the world. It's also so exciting and encouraging to see and hear how many of my colleagues in the business are re-thinking their views on British food, and exploring complementary culinary roads.

However, nothing ever stands still, and this is undoubtedly true in cooking. Just think how flavours and tastes have changed in the last twenty years in Britain. Ingredients we hadn't even heard of, such as chillies, pasta, polenta, vanilla pods and all the fresh herbs, are now virtually commonplace. A lot of people think we are being very adventurous trying out these 'new' tastes, but it's almost a replay of what it must have been like in the Middle Ages, when these new tastes – all those spices, dried fruits, citrus fruits and so on – were making their first appearance. It wasn't the years of the Raj that introduced us to spices. We had been using them centuries before, and they were and still are an essential ingredient in British cooking. Gingerbread, for instance, with ginger as its main component, is one of our most basic and ancient cake-biscuits; the cloves in apple pie, along with the dried fruits, currants, sultanas, raisins and prunes that appear in so many of our festive cakes and puddings, are a direct survival of a medieval tradition – a British tradition. So, all these new trendy flavours are not so new after all. They have been part of British cuisine for some time and are now playing their part in the Great British revival.

I have always had a strong passion for classics – after all, every new style has been born from them – but putting this book together, taking it from its original idea and researching it, has stirred a new passion within me. Now my feelings for cooking, in particular British cooking, are 'souffléing' larger than I ever imagined. It's a soufflé that won't overcook, but will keep that gentle, soft texture inside, without allowing any flavours I work with to become abused.

The world has become a global village, providing and making accessible to us all the foods and ingredients from different corners of the Earth. With all of these items available, let's just make sure we do not forget our basic traditions and classics. I've worked to bring our traditional dishes up to a new level of eating so that they will sit more than comfortably with the best from other countries. The simplest of dishes are often the best: a plate of fish and chips executed well is just perfection to eat and can stand up to any international fish dish. British food might have taken on many of its influences from outside, but the end results – what we have today – are as good as those of any other country and this book is a celebration of that fact.

You'll discover many dishes I want to be looked at as new British classics, such as omelette thermidor, scallops with black pudding, braised beef, caramelized onions and turnip purée, and others that I've simply brought back to life, such as baked egg custard tart.

To sum up, the whole book is about taking British ideas (and there are so many) from yesterday and refining them for tomorrow – for another thousand years. These recipes, with their rejuvenated flavours, are here to be enjoyed, and to revive your feelings for good traditional cookery, as well as giving you new culinary inspirations. And, of course, recipes can be adapted to suit your own tastes – as Roger Vergé, one of the great French chefs of the world, says:

'A recipe is not meant to be followed exactly – it is a canvas on which you can embroider.'
Cuisine of the Sun (translated by Caroline Conran), 1979

General Information

I include here a few hints and tips which you might be interested in, some culinary, some about ingredients or products used in my recipes.

Blind-baking Pastry

Line the tin/ring/case with the rolled-out pastry and leave it to rest, preferably in the refrigerator, for 20–30 minutes. Now line the pastry case with baking parchment, foil or greaseproof paper, fill with baking beans (or pulses kept especially for the purpose), and bake at the suggested temperature for the recommended time. It is best, when blind-baking, to leave the excess pastry hanging over the rim of the container, because pastry shrinks as it cooks. Once it is cooked, you can trim off the excess and you will have a perfectly neat, even finish.

Butter

The butter I use most is unsalted because it gives greater control over the seasoning of a dish.

Chocolate

Chocolate basically consists of two components: cocoa solids (including cocoa butter) and sugar. Chocolate with a cocoa-solid content of 85 per cent or over is considered unpalatable because it is too bitter. Extra-bitter chocolate ranges from 75 to 85 per cent cocoa solids, but is palatable. A bitter chocolate will be in the 55–75 per cent range, when it should hold 31 per cent cocoa butter. Valrhona 'Grand Cru', which falls into this category, is probably the best for cooking. There are also bitter-sweet and semi-sweet chocolates: the bitter-sweet varieties must always include a minimum of 35 per cent cocoa butter within the solids, which makes it easier to work with.

I have always bought my cooking chocolate from Valrhona, or Callebaut, a famous Belgian company. These makes are not always easily obtainable, but Lindt, the Swiss chocolate, is readily available, is good to work with and carries a good depth of flavour. Some supermarkets also sell their own brand of good, high-cocoa-solids chocolate.

White chocolate is a blend of cocoa butter, sugar and milk, and, for a quality product, should contain no more than 50 per cent sugar.

Crème Fraîche

This is made by pasteurizing milk before the cream has formed. The milk is then separated into cream and skimmed milk. The cream is pasteurized again, to give it extra shelf life, and selected lactic cultures are added to give it acidity. It can be used to finish both sweet and savoury sauces. Double or clotted creams contain an average 48 per cent fat, crème fraîche just 30 per cent.

Eggs

All eggs used in the recipes in this book are large.

Fromage Blanc and Fromage Frais

Fromage blanc is a soft, unripened cheese, usually made from skimmed cow's milk with a culture. Fromage frais is fromage blanc, beaten to a smooth consistency. Both contain between zero and 8 per cent fat, unless they have been enriched with cream. Fromage frais can replace yoghurt in ice-creams, mousses, and so on.

Game Seasons in Britain

Grouse – 12 August to 10 December
Mallard (wild duck) – September to January
Partridge – 1 September to 1 February

Pheasant – 1 October to 1 February (best between
  December and January)
Quail – All year
Venison – March to October
Wild hare – July to February

Gas Gun/Blow Torch

Powerful butane gas canisters can be used as a blow
torch in the kitchen to give a crispy glaze to many
desserts. They are available from almost any hardware
store and can also be found in the kitchen sections of
department stores. Follow the instructions carefully,
use carefully and, of course, keep away from children.

Herbs

If you substitute dried herbs for fresh herbs,
remember to use only half the amount specified.

Ice-cream Making

I recommend using an ice-cream machine for the
best results: as it churns, the mixture becomes lighter
and the texture smoother. Fill the machine half to
two-thirds full, to leave room for the mixture to
increase in volume.

  If you don't have a machine, you can still make
ice-creams: freeze the ice-cream mix and whisk it
every 20–30 minutes until it is set. It will still taste
good, although it may be a bit grainier because of
the larger ice crystals.

Medjool Dates

These come from India and, without doubt, are the
best to eat. They are plump and meaty, and have a
natural fudge-toffee flavour that is perfect for many
dishes.

Pig's Caul and Sausage Skins

Caul is the lacy lining of a pig's stomach. It is quite
difficult to get hold of but you should be able to
order it through your butcher. It must be soaked in
cold water for 24 hours first, which makes it easier
to use, then drained. It's used almost like cling film,
rolled around meat or a meaty mixture, to which it

will cling. If caul is unavailable, cook without a
covering or use buttered foil.

  Sausage skins are the intestines of the pig, and
must be ordered from your butcher as well. They,
too, need to be soaked for several hours and rinsed
before use.

Pin Bones

These fine bones are found in round fish fillets, that
is, red mullet, trout, salmon, cod and so on. The
bones run down the centre of most of these fillets
and are easily removed with fine pliers or tweezers.
It's worth spending the time needed to remove them,
as the fish then becomes more comfortable to eat.

Seasoning

Unless otherwise stated, 'season' or 'seasoning'
simply means seasoning with salt and pepper –
preferably freshly ground white, or black.

'It may be that there are some men who seek gold,
but there lives no man who does not need salt,
which seasons our food.' Cassiodorus, AD 468–568

Soured Cream

This is single or double cream that has been treated
with a souring culture and contains about 20 per
cent butterfat. You can make soured cream at home
by simply adding a few drops of lemon juice to
either double or whipping cream.

Squeezy Bottles

Small plastic bottles with narrow spouts can be
bought in good kitchen departments. They can be
filled with something like a sauce or *coulis* (a sieved
puréed sauce, usually fruit-related), which can be
squeezed out for a neater finish on the plate or food.

Stocks, Gravies and Sauces – Alternatives

I give a number of stock and sauce recipes
throughout the book, but there are also many good
bought alternatives (fresh, dried or cubed) available
in supermarkets.

Suet

This is the hard white fat surrounding beef kidneys, and it is shredded and floured for use in the domestic kitchen. It is vital in making traditional British suet pastries and puddings. Hard vegetable oils are now prepared in the same way for use by vegetarians.

Vanilla

Vanilla pods are the fruit of a tropical vine. When you buy them, they are long, thin and black. They can be split to allow you to use the tiny seeds within, or the pods, which are very fragrant in themselves, can be used whole. Keep the pods in an airtight jar with your caster sugar, and the sugar will be infused with the vanilla flavour – giving you a constant supply of vanilla sugar for desserts and cakes.

Vegetarian Dishes

All vegetarian dishes in this book have been marked with the symbol Ⓥ.

Vinegars

I use a selection of vinegars in this book. Red-wine vinegar is a favourite. Because many of those available are thin and not very red-wine-flavoured, I urge you to spend a little more and buy a vinegar that bears the hallmark of a good wine – a Bordeaux vinegar, say, or my current favourite, Cabernet Sauvignon. Balsamic is the vinegar of the moment and, again, do spend a little more to get a good-quality product. The older it gets, the better, it tastes – and the more expensive it is to buy – but because of its strength you won't use it up too quickly. I also like to use good-quality cider vinegar.

Weights and Measures

All the recipes in the book have been tested in both metric and imperial. Do not work with a mixture of the two.

Spoon sizes: My tablespoon measurements are 15 g (½ oz) for solids and 15 ml (½ fl oz) for liquids, my dessertspoon measurements are 10 g for solids and 10 ml for liquids and my teaspoons are 5 g for solids and 5 ml for liquids. All spoon measurements are level.

Yeast

Three types of yeast are available – fresh or compressed yeast, granular dried yeast, and easy-blend dried yeast. Fresh is very perishable and should be used quickly, or frozen; the dried yeasts should be stored in a cool place, and a close eye kept on sell-by dates.

Fresh and granular dried yeasts need to be activated in lukewarm liquid before being added to a flour; easy-blend yeast doesn't need to be activated with water and can be mixed straight into the flour. Dried yeast is twice as potent as fresh yeast, so use 15 g (½ oz) dried, say, when a recipe specifies 25 g (1 oz) fresh yeast. Two level teaspoons is approximately 15 g (½ oz) dried yeast.

Yoghurt

Low-fat or skimmed milk is treated with a culture of selected lactic ferments to make natural (unsweetened and unflavoured) yoghurt. The butterfat content is between 8 and 10 per cent, making natural yoghurt healthy to eat and to cook with.

OPPOSITE
Pressed Tomato Cake with Peppered Goat's Cheese (page 66)

Soups

Once man had succeeded in making
fireproof containers (saucepans), soup
would probably have been the very
first episode in the long-running
British cookery show. Diet no longer
had to consist of individual foods such
as grains or seeds, leaves or berries, or
a hunk of meat charred over flames.
Now these ingredients could be mixed
and cooked in water to achieve
different flavours and textures.
Soup was originally known as
'pottage', a name that stuck for
hundreds of years. The principal early
vegetables or 'potherbs' used were
leeks and kale, but after the Roman
occupation of Britain, many new
ingredients became available, including
onions, cabbages and pulses such as
beans and peas.

Through the succeeding centuries, pottage remained one of the three main staple foods for all classes of British society (the other two being bread and ale). The peasant's one would consist of water with whatever else he could find, grow, or had dried for the winter – a little grain, a few root or pulse vegetables, some wild herbs or seaweed with, occasionally, a little meat. But quite often it might just be water and the local grain. A pottage was likely to be the dish of the day for a working man, either for breakfast or supper. The rich would probably include more protein or nourishing vegetable in theirs, and, often, a fine wheat version, known as frumenty, might serve as an accompaniment to meat or fish. Cereal pottage for breakfast still survives now in the oats porridge (the Scottish classic) with which many of us start our day. And pulse varieties were taken to America by early colonists, to be returned to Britain centuries later as Boston baked beans.

Often the pottage would be poured over what were called 'sops', pieces of bread or toast served in a tureen or bowl. In France the dish became known as *soupe*, and the name soon transferred, in the latter seventeenth century, to a thinner version enjoyed by the British gentry. Other French influences had crept in as well. Meat began to be cooked in and served with sauces (rather than being an integral part of pottage), and vegetables were boiled separately and buttered. The concept of a meal consisting of individual courses was gradually adopted. The new 'soup' became a course by itself at the beginning of a meal, and was known as a 'remove' dish because, after the soup was eaten, it was removed from the table to be replaced, usually by a fish dish.

Soups became even more ambitious in their ingredients. In the eighteenth century, turtle soup – made from green turtles brought live in tanks from the West Indies – became popular. On many banquet menus, it was served in several different ways – as thick, clear calipash (the part next to the upper shell), calipee (belly) and fins. (Mock turtle, an infamous English soup, was made from a calf's head simmered in stock and served in an empty turtle shell.) Meanwhile, pottage, or the thicker vegetable, meat or fish soup, remained a basic food for the poor, as it has always been in more northerly countries.

Soup is one of the very few foods that has a virtually unlimited repertoire. Flavours from everything that is edible can be cooked, mixed and mingled; and the end result can range from a clear consommé to a thick, creamed soup. This wonderful variety of consistencies suits different eating times, both of day and year. In the following chapter, you will find a 'pottage' to fit almost every category. Here are a few examples of what I would choose: for lunch, *Vegetarian Scotch Broth* (page 31) or *Cullen Skink* (page 27); at a dinner party, the *Clear Ham Soup* (page 20) or *Lobster 'Bisque'* (page 23); and for supper on a cold, slushy, winter evening, it would just have to be the *Boiled Bacon and Vegetable 'Main Course' Soup* (opposite), served with loads of bread. How's that for starters?

PAGE 14
Lobster 'Bisque' Soup (page 23)

Boiled Bacon and Vegetable 'Main-Course' Soup

Bacon and vegetables are a common combination all over Great Britain, and have been for centuries. Bacon was always available throughout the year, and vegetables would be grown at home. This is a dish I found many years ago while filming in Northumberland. I'll always remember having the vegetables served in a bowl of stock for the first course, which was then followed by slices of the bacon with pieces of potato and some of the liquor. The 'pudding' was a chunk of savoury leek dumpling, also cooked in the liquor. So, basically, all three courses were cooked in the same pot, something that has always been very traditional.

This is really a main-course soup, with the bacon served with the vegetables. If you also fancy the leek dumpling, the recipe for it is included as an optional extra.

SERVES 6–8 FOR MAIN COURSE OR 10–12 FOR STARTERS

900 g (2 lb) bacon collar, boned and tied, soaked in cold water for 24 hours
1 bay leaf
Sprig of fresh thyme
350 g (12 oz) button onions, peeled
3 large carrots, cut into 2.5 cm (1 in) dice
4 celery sticks, cut into 2.5 cm (1 in) pieces
2–3 large potatoes, peeled and cut into 2.5 cm (1 in) dice
1 large swede, cut into 2.5 cm (1 in) dice
25–50 g (1–2 oz) butter
Salt and pepper
Chopped fresh parsley, to garnish (optional)

For the Leek Dumpling

250 g (9 oz) self-raising flour
250 g (9 oz) leeks, sliced
125 g (4½ oz) shredded suet
1 dessertspoon English mustard powder
1 egg, beaten
About 100 ml (3½ fl oz) cold water
Salt and pepper

Once the bacon has been soaked for 24 hours, which removes excess saltiness, wash off well and cover with cold water again in a large saucepan. Bring to the boil and then place under cold running water to totally refresh. This will take out any remaining excess salt flavour and impurities.

Now cover again with water, adding the bay leaf and sprig of thyme. Bring to the simmer and cook for 1¼ hours. After this initial 1¼ hours' cooking time, the vegetables can be added and cooked for the last 45 minutes. The total cooking time will be approximately 2 hours. This guarantees the vegetables are cooked through completely to an over-cooked stage, when they soak up all of the bacon-stock flavour.

Once completely cooked, after 2 hours, turn off the heat and leave to rest, covered, for 15 minutes.

Remove the bacon and either just break it or carve into slices. Remove the thyme and bay leaf from the stock. Add the butter and stir in. Check the seasoning, adding pepper and salt only if necessary. Present the meat in large bowls and divide the vegetables and stock between all four. Finish with a sprinkling, if using, of chopped parsley. The one-pot meal is now ready to enjoy.

To make the leek dumpling, mix together the self-raising flour, leeks and suet. Season with salt, pepper and mustard. Mix in the egg and enough of the water to create a soft dough. Blanch a muslin cloth in boiling water, before squeezing out well until almost dry. Dust with flour. Place the dough on the muslin and tie into a dumpling. This can now be added to the bacon one hour before cooking finishes and be served with the finished dish.

Spicy Smoked Haddock and Saffron Soup

Kedgeree became a popular breakfast dish (see page 162) following the years of the British Raj in India. It's made from a blend of rice, smoked haddock and curry, and this soup brings two of these old friends together again, only omitting the rice (although cooked rice could be added at the end if preferred). The spicy flavour here comes from a medium curry powder, and the saffron adds to this taste, working well with the curry and, at the same time, enriching the colour of the soup.

SERVES 4 GENEROUSLY

Butter
1 medium leek, washed and cut into
    rough 1 cm (½ in) dice
1 medium potato, peeled and cut into
    rough 1 cm (½ in) dice
2 small garlic cloves, crushed
1 tablespoon medium curry powder
Good pinch of saffron strands
350 g (12 oz) natural smoked haddock fillet
350 ml (12 fl oz) water (or *Chicken Stock*,
    page 33, for a stronger flavour)
250 ml (8 fl oz) milk
100–125 ml (3½–4 fl oz) single cream
    (or double, for an extra-rich finish)
Squeeze of lemon juice
Salt and pepper
10–12 fresh coriander leaves, to garnish (optional)

Pre-heat the oven to 180°C/350°F/Gas Mark 4.

Melt a knob of butter in a saucepan and, once bubbling, add the chopped leeks and potatoes and crushed garlic. Cook for a few minutes on a medium heat, without letting the vegetables colour. Add the curry powder and saffron and continue to cook for a few minutes.

While the vegetables are cooking, the haddock can be poached. Lay the fillet in an ovenproof roasting pan or dish; pour the water or stock and milk on top. Add a good knob of butter, cover with foil and bring to a soft simmer. This is best finished in the oven, for 5–6 minutes.

Once it's cooked, remove the fish from the liquor and keep to one side. The cooking liquor can now be added to the soup vegetables. Bring to the simmer and cook for 15–20 minutes until all the vegetables are completely tender.

The curry soup can now be liquidized to a smooth purée. For a very smooth, silky finish, strain through a sieve. The cream can now be added, along with a squeeze of lemon juice to liven up all the flavours. Season with salt and pepper, if needed.

While the soup is cooking, the haddock fillet can be skinned and have all its bones removed; flake the flesh. Add the haddock flakes to the soup and serve. To finish, roughly chop the coriander leaves (if using) and sprinkle over.

Note: I like to eat this soup with lots of good crusty bread, to dip in and wipe the bowl clean.

Leek and Potato Broth ⓥ

Leeks were early pottage vegetables, and, even when potatoes were introduced, they tended not to be cooked in the same way. However, throughout Europe the combination has proved long-lasting – in France this soup is the famous *potage bonne femme*.

The classic recipe consists basically of leeks, potatoes and a white stock. I've added a few more ingredients to enrich the flavours – some onions, a touch of cream and butter – which will lift the soup, making it a bit more exciting. The double cream can be omitted or replaced with crème fraîche for a lighter touch, or even soured cream to give a slightly acidic finish.

SERVES 4–6

50 g (2 oz) butter
1 large onion, sliced
2 large potatoes, cut into 1 cm (½ in) dice
600 ml (1 pint) *Chicken* or *Vegetable Stock*
    (page 33 or 36)
450 g (1 lb) leeks, shredded or cut into
    1 cm (½ in) dice
150 ml (5 fl oz) double cream
Salt and pepper

ABOVE
Spicy Smoked Haddock and Saffron Soup

Melt a quarter of the butter and add the sliced onion. Cook for a minute or two, until softened. Add the potato dice and also cook for a minute or two, stirring, before adding the stock. Bring to the simmer and cook until the potatoes have become just tender. This should take 8–10 minutes of simmering.

Increase the heat until the stock is almost boiling. Add the leeks and continue to simmer for 5–6 minutes, until the leeks are tender.

Add the double cream and remaining butter. Re-warm to simmering point and season well with salt and pepper.

The leek and potato broth is now ready to serve and eats beautifully with good crusty bread.

Note: If using crème fraîche or sour cream, take a ladle of the hot liquor and whisk it into either cream to emulsify and bring it up to temperature before pouring into the pot. Crispy strips of streaky bacon also work very well in this soup.

Clear Ham Soup with Pea Pancakes

England has always been famous for her hams, and many counties have developed different cures. There are a lot of ham recipes in eighteenth- and nineteenth-century cookery books, but the combination of cured pork with peas – not quite so sophisticated as here, I must admit – is an ancient one.

In the past, such a soup would have been a thick pottage, but here I am making a liquid with the clarity of a consommé. To create this, of course, takes rather a lot of time. First, the ham stock has to be made (after soaking the hocks for 24 hours), then it has to be chilled. The next step is to clarify the stock, which leaves you with a clear soup. Making a good consommé does bring a great sense of achievement. If that's what you enjoy, then please do try this recipe. This recipe will give you a minimum of 1–2 litres (2 pints) of finished consommé.

Now all you need to do is to make the pea pancakes, which are a wonderful garnish for the soup. They can be served just floating in the consommé or as a separate garnish. It's not essential that you make them. But pea and ham is a great

British soup that I've turned around. The ham is the leader this time, with peas close behind. This quantity of mix will give you at least 14–18 small pancakes.

For the Ham Stock

1 onion, roughly chopped
2–3 celery sticks, roughly chopped
1 leek, roughly chopped
1 large carrot, roughly chopped
Butter
Sprig of thyme
1 bay leaf
Few black peppercorns
2 raw ham hocks (knuckles), soaked in
    cold water for 24 hours
450 g (1 lb) chicken wings
At least 3 litres (5¼ pints) water

For the Clarification Crust

1 large chicken breast
1 small onion, peeled and roughly chopped
1 small carrot, peeled and roughly chopped
1 celery stick, roughly chopped
1 egg white (2 for extra body and security!)
Salt and pepper

For the Pea Pancakes

225 g (8 oz) frozen peas, cooked
1 egg
1 egg yolk
3 tablespoons plain flour
3 tablespoons double cream
50 g (2 oz) unsalted butter
50–75 g (2–3 oz) ham, finely shredded
    (optional)
Oil or butter, for frying
Salt and pepper

For the stock, in a large pot, lightly soften the vegetables in a knob of butter, without letting them colour. Add the thyme, bay leaf, peppercorns, ham

OPPOSITE
Clear Ham Soup with Pea Pancakes

hocks (knuckles) and chicken wings and cover with plenty of water.

Bring to the simmer, skimming off any impurities that rise to the top. Allow the stock to simmer on the lowest possible heat, uncovered, for 2 hours. The finished quantity of stock needed for the soup is approximately 2.25 litres (4 pints): if the liquid is reducing too quickly, simply top up with extra water during the cooking time.

At the end of this cooking time, the flavour of the ham will have become quite predominant, with the chicken wings helping to create a balance between the flavours. Do not add any salt as the ham will provide enough saltiness on its own.

Strain the stock and then sit the hams in the liquor to keep them moist. Allow to cool. Once cooled, the hams can be removed and trimmed. This involves removing the skin, discarding it, and then taking the meat from the bone. Some of this can be finely shredded to add to the pea-pancake mix. Any remainder will be lovely to eat in a good home-made sandwich, with mayonnaise and crispy Iceberg lettuce.

Now it's time to make the clarification crust. Place all of the ingredients, except the egg white(s), in a food processor. This mixture can now be blitzed to a pulp. Remove and place in a bowl. Mix in the egg whites and check for seasoning, being careful not to oversalt.

Blend together the stock with the chicken mix. Place on a low heat, making sure the soup is stirred well and is not catching on the bottom of the pan. Slowly, a pad will start to form, which is the clarification mix rising to the top.

When the first stage of this appears, increase the heat and whisk quickly. Return the heat to its former temperature. The crust will now begin to form again. The soup can be allowed to cook on a gentle simmer for 1½ hours. During this time, the impurities in the original stock will be absorbed into the crust.

Usually a small gap will form at the top of the crust. It's from here you can taste the soup and test its strength. If the flavour still seems shallow after the cooking time, then just continue to simmer for another 20–30 minutes. Now it's time to strain the consommé.

For the ultimate clear soup, carefully ladle, not breaking the crust too much, through a double muslin cloth. It's best not to try and strain every last drop. The last inch of consommé is best poured into a separate pan; if this is totally clear just strain into the rest of the consommé. However, this may have taken on a slight cloudiness from the crust. If so, keep separate. Now take a look at the beautiful amber-coloured consommé you have made. Your moment of pride begins.

To make the pea pancakes, place the peas, egg, egg yolk, flour and cream in a food processor and blitz to a smooth consistency. Heat a frying-pan and add the butter, allowing it to colour to the nut-brown stage. Add the butter to the mix and season with salt and pepper. If making pea and shredded ham pancakes, stir in the shredded ham at this stage. The mix is now ready to cook.

Heat a frying-pan over a medium heat and add a trickle of oil or small knob of butter. The pancake mix can now be dropped in, a tablespoon at a time. This will spread slightly, giving you small pea pancakes; you'll probably have room to cook 3–4 together, depending on the size of your pan. Cook until golden, 3–4 minutes, and then turn over and brown the other side for 1–2 minutes. Remove and keep warm while the remaining mix is cooked.

The pancakes can be made well in advance and allowed to cool. To re-heat, take a ladleful of consommé and warm the cakes gently in a saucepan or, if serving separately, in warm melted butter. Now just re-heat the soup and garnish with the pea pancakes. The results are worth every minute of precious cooking time.

Note: The pancake mix can be spooned into small stainless-steel buttered rings in the frying-pan, for perfectly round results.

Lobster 'Bisque' Soup

From Elizabethan times onwards, many French culinary techniques and recipes were adopted by the British gentry. One of these was the bisque, a soup with a broth base and added pieces of meat and poultry, and regarded as the king of all soups. From the eighteenth century, a bisque was usually associated with puréed crustaceans, often crayfish. Lobster, then, as now, would have been the most extravagant and valued of the lot.

In order to get the maximum flavour from the shells, making bisque does take time, so it's worth making a fair quantity and freezing some (the soup freezes well). Broken lobsters can be found at a reasonable cost or, if you're a big lobster eater, simply save and freeze any cooked shells until you reach the quantity required. This recipe can also be adapted to crab, prawn, langoustine or shrimp by simply replacing the quantity of lobster shells with those of the appropriate seafood.

MAKES 1.2–1.75 LITRES (2–3 PINTS)

450 g (1 lb) lobster shells or a 675 g
    (1½ lb) lobster
1.2–1.75 litres (2–3 pints) *Fish Stock*
    (page 35)
25 g (1 oz) butter
1 tablespoon olive oil
1 large carrot, roughly diced
2–3 shallots or 1 large onion, roughly diced
2 celery sticks, roughly diced
1 small leek, roughly diced
1 fennel bulb, roughly diced
1 garlic clove, crushed
1 star anise (optional)
Strip of orange zest
Few basil leaves
Few tarragon leaves
Pinch of saffron, soaked (page 397)
50 ml (2 fl oz) brandy
4 large ripe tomatoes, quartered
1 teaspoon tomato purée
½ bottle white wine
150 ml (¼ pint) single cream (optional)
Few drops of lemon juice
Salt and pepper
Pinch of cayenne pepper

If you are using a live lobster, bring the fish stock to the boil and drop in the lobster. Cook for 3–4 minutes, then remove from the heat. Leave the lobster in the stock until completely cooled. This will help flavour the stock and keep the lobster meat moist.

Break off the claws and crack open with the back of a heavy knife to release the meat. The joints connecting the claw to the body should also be cracked open and the meat removed. Split the body and tail through the middle, lengthways, and remove the tail meat.

Reserve all of the lobster meat in a little of the cooking liquor to keep it moist. The meat can be used either as a garnish for this soup or in another recipe, such as *Lobster Omelette 'Thermidor'* (page 75). All of the shells, whether you're using ones from the live lobster or frozen/broken shells (see recipe introduction), can now be crushed as finely as possible. This can be achieved relatively easily with the use of a rolling pin, breaking the shells up in a saucepan.

To make the soup, melt the butter with the olive oil. Add the diced carrot, shallots or onion, celery, leek and fennel, with the crushed garlic, star anise, orange zest, basil and tarragon leaves. Add the pinch of saffron and allow to cook on a medium heat for 10–15 minutes, without colouring. The vegetables will now begin to soften.

Add the crushed lobster shells and cook for a further 10 minutes. Add the brandy and, if possible, flame (*flambé*) the contents of the pan. Boil until almost dry. Add the quartered tomatoes and tomato purée and continue to simmer for 6–7 minutes. Pour over the white wine and allow to reduce by half. Add 1.2 litres (2 pints) of fish stock and bring to the simmer; cook for 25–30 minutes.

The soup, with the shells and all vegetables included, can now be blitzed in a liquidizer to a smooth consistency. Strain through a fine sieve to remove any shell, pushing all the flavour through.

The bisque, if too thick, can now be loosened with extra fish stock until it reaches the correct consistency. Season with salt, pepper and a pinch of cayenne pepper. The lobster bisque soup is now ready to serve.

For a creamier finish, add the single cream, a splash at a time, to suit your taste buds. A drop or two of lemon juice can also be added, to lift the total taste (or add an extra splash of neat brandy).

Note: If making the *Lobster Omelette 'Thermidor'* (page 75) take 150–300 ml (¼–½ pint) of finished bisque and reduce by half to two-thirds. This can now be used to enhance the cheese sauce for the 'Thermidor'.

The soup can also be trickled with Lobster/Shellfish Oil (page 386).

Almond and Celery Soup ⓥ

Soups and dishes that were 'white' were a great old British speciality. They were very popular in the early Middle Ages, the white coming from pounded chicken or other pale meats, or from almonds. These nuts had been introduced from the Mediterranean, and had become an essential ingredient, added whole to dishes as a garnish, made into a milk (as we would coconut today), or pounded to use as a white thickening for a dish. In the past, cooks would have had to pound the whole shelled almonds in a mortar, but today we can buy them ready ground, so there really is no excuse for not trying the recipe.

A nice little garnish is to toast a few flaked almonds and sprinkle them on top. Using chicken stock gives a meatier flavour to the almond and celery combination, but you can of course make it vegetarian by using vegetable stock.

SERVES 4–6

25 g (1 oz) butter
450 g (1 lb) celery sticks, roughly diced
½ small onion, roughly chopped
1 small potato, peeled and roughly diced
150 ml (¼ pint) dry white wine
100 g (4 oz) ground almonds
500 ml (17 fl oz) *Chicken* or *Vegetable Stock*
    (page 33 or 36)

250 ml (8 fl oz) milk
250 ml (8 fl oz) single cream (this can be
    replaced by extra milk)
Celery salt or table salt
Pepper

Melt the butter in a large saucepan. Add the vegetables and cook on a low heat, turning them in the butter until all are coated. Simmer with a lid on top for 10–15 minutes until they begin to soften.

Add the white wine and increase the heat, leaving the lid off. This will allow the wine to reduce. Once it has all reduced, add the ground almonds, stock and milk. Season with the celery salt or table salt and pepper, bring to the simmer and cook for 20 minutes. Check that all of the vegetables are cooked through.

Add the single cream and return to the simmer; the soup can now be removed from the heat and liquidized until smooth.

For a smoother finish and no grainy texture from the almonds, strain through a fine sieve, pushing all flavours through with a ladle. Re-check for seasoning and the soup is ready to serve.

Note: A small squeeze of lemon juice will help lift all of the flavours.

Chopped fresh chives and a trickle of cream can also help the garnishing of the soup.

The soup will also eat well cold. It may be slightly too thick when it cools, so just loosen with a drop more milk.

Chunky Tomato Soup

Tomatoes, although known in England since the sixteenth century following their introduction from the New World, did not gain acceptance as a food until some two centuries later. They were usually cooked and pounded for soups, or made into an acid pickle with garlic, ginger and vinegar, so our famous Great British tomato soup and tomato ketchup (page 49) have a long history. But we were so suspicious of them that it was only in this century that we started to eat tomatoes raw.

This soup can be served as either a starter or a main course, but one of my favourites is to offer this soup warm from a large flask at picnics. Its real beauty is how easy it is to make, and its chunky nature makes it a pleasure to eat. I like to serve it with bread croûtons, fried or baked in olive oil, and Parmesan flakes sprinkled over the top. As illustrated, this soup also makes a great vegetarian dish – simply omit the bacon and replace the chicken stock with a vegetable stock.

SERVES 6–8

3 onions, chopped
3 carrots, cut into 5 mm (¼ in) dice
3 celery sticks, cut into 5 mm (¼ in) dice
50 ml (2 fl oz) olive oil

25 g (1 oz) unsalted butter
1 bay leaf
1 large garlic clove, crushed
6 smoked back bacon rashers, rinded and cut
    into strips
900 g (2 lb) ripe tomatoes, preferably plum
600–900 ml (1–1½ pints) *Chicken* or *Vegetable
    Stock* (page 33 or 36)
Small bunch of fresh basil, chopped
Small bunch of fresh tarragon, chopped
Tomato purée (optional, to taste)
Salt and pepper

Sweat the chopped onions, carrots and celery in the olive oil and butter for a few minutes. Then add the bay leaf and garlic and cook for a few more minutes.

BELOW
Chunky Tomato Soup

Add the bacon, if using, and continue to cook for about 5 minutes until the vegetables are slightly softened.

Cut the tomatoes into eight pieces. Add them to the vegetables, cover the pan and cook gently for about 15 minutes. The cooking will create its own steam and slowly cook the tomatoes. The mixture must be stirred occasionally, which will help the tomatoes to break down and start to create the soup.

When the tomatoes have softened, start to add the stock, just a ladle at a time, until you have a looser consistency. This brings us to personal choice. The soup can be as thick or as thin as you like. Leave it to cook for a further 20 minutes. Add the chopped herbs and check for seasoning; you may find that a little tomato purée will help the strength of taste. The soup is now ready to serve.

Roast Parsnip Soup, Glazed with Parmesan and Chive Cream ⓥ

Parsnips are native to Britain, and they fulfilled the function of potatoes before the latter were introduced – they were served with roast beef, and eaten with salt fish on Ash Wednesday and other fast days. It was their sweet flavour that was valued mainly and, in Elizabethan times, they were even included in sweet dishes. They could also stay in the ground over the winter without spoiling, so were an extremely useful food.

I love roast parsnips. I couldn't bear them when I was at school, but I could eat lorry loads now. The idea for this soup came from trying a wonderful Delia Smith recipe, her roast Parmesan parsnips – great as a vegetable, so why not a soup? It's packed with flavour and, when the cream is spooned over and glazed, it gives the whole dish a new look, taste and finish.

SERVES 4

50 g (2 oz) butter
450 g (1 lb) parsnips, peeled, quartered and woody centres removed

2 shallots or 1 onion, finely chopped
750 ml (1½ pints) *Chicken* or *Vegetable Stock* (page 33 or 36)
125 ml (4 fl oz) single cream (optional)
Salt and pepper

For the Parmesan Cream (optional)

1 medium egg yolk
4 tablespoons double cream
1 heaped tablespoon freshly grated Parmesan
1 teaspoon chopped fresh chives
Pinch of salt

Pre-heat the oven to 220°C/425°F/Gas Mark 7. Heat a roasting pan on top of the stove. Melt 25 g (1 oz) of the butter and, once it's bubbling, add the parsnips. Allow to reach a golden colour, turning them in the pan. The parsnips can now be roasted in the oven for 15–20 minutes.

Towards the end of roasting, melt the remaining 25 g (1 oz) of butter in a saucepan. Add the chopped shallots or onion and cook, without colour, for a few minutes, until softened. Transfer the parsnips to the saucepan. Add the stock and bring to the simmer. The soup can now be gently simmered for 15 minutes.

Now it's time to pour in the single cream, if using. Season with salt and pepper and liquidize to a smooth consistency. For a guaranteed smooth finish, push through a fine sieve. The roast parsnip soup is ready to serve.

Here's the Parmesan cream, if using, to finish the dish. Add the egg yolk to the double cream and lightly whisk until it begins to form soft peaks. Fold in the grated Parmesan with the chives and a pinch of salt.

Once the hot soup has been ladled into bowls, spoon the Parmesan chive cream over each. These can now be glazed under a pre-heated grill. The cream will become golden brown and ready to eat.

Note: Another nice garnish, if eating the soup without the glaze, is toasted French bread, topped with lots of melting Parmesan.

Cullen Skink

A Gaelic word meaning 'essence', 'soup' or 'broth', 'skink' can be made with meat or fish, and is the Scottish version of pottage. Traditionally it could feature beef or, for those who could not afford that, cereal simmered with a sheep's head. Along the coastlines of Britain, soup-stews made with fish were more common, and this is my version of one that originated in Cullen, a small village in the north-east of Scotland. How the two met and stayed together I'm not quite sure, but they have had a long-lasting relationship.

Basically, this soup simply consists of natural smoked haddock (preferably Finnan haddock), onions and potatoes cooked in milk with a knob of butter. I like to add some leek to the soup, though, which gives a fuller and fresher finish, lifting all the other flavours. Cullen skink can stand as a complete meal on its own, with just the help of some good crusty bread for dunking and mopping up.

SERVES 4–6, DEPENDING ON HOW HUNGRY YOU ARE

2 large potatoes, peeled
1 small leek (optional)
Butter
1 onion, finely chopped
250 g (9 oz) natural smoked haddock fillet
1 bay leaf
750 ml (1½ pints) milk
50 ml (2 fl oz) double cream (single for a looser finish)
Squeeze of lemon juice
Salt and pepper

The potatoes must first be chopped, along with the leek. One of the potatoes I like to cut into neat 1 cm (½ in) dice to use as a garnish. The other can be cut into rough 1 cm (½ in) dice. The leek, if using, should first be split, separating the white from green. Wash both parts well to ensure they are free of soil and grit. Chop the white part into rough 1 cm (½ in) dice. The green can now be cut into neat 1 cm (½ in) dice (*brunoise*); this will be used as part of the finished garnish.

Melt a knob of butter in a saucepan big enough to accommodate the fish. Cook the onion on a medium heat for a few minutes, without colouring it, until just soft. Sit the smoked haddock in the pan, along with the bay leaf. Pour in some of the milk, just topping the fish.

This can now be brought to the simmer and cooked for 4–6 minutes, depending on the thickness of the fish. Remove the fish from the pan and keep to one side. Add the roughly chopped potato, leek and remaining milk. Bring to the simmer and cook until the potato has cooked through. This will take 15–20 minutes.

While the skink is cooking, remove any skin and bones from the haddock fillet. This can now be flaked, revealing moist translucent flesh. The other garnishes, the potato dice and leek *brunoise*, can be blanched. Simply cook the potato in salted water until cooked completely through (10–15 minutes). The leeks will take literally a few minutes. Once cooked, drain through a sieve and keep to one side.

When the soup is ready, remove the bay leaf and liquidize to a smooth purée. Add the double or single cream and season with salt, pepper and a squeeze of lemon juice.

Add the garnishes, haddock flakes, diced potatoes and leeks and bring back to a warm temperature. Add a knob more of butter for an even richer finish. The Cullen skink is ready to enjoy.

Note: The potato and leek dice can be just roughly chopped and cooked in the soup for a thicker finished consistency, leaving just the haddock flakes for garnish.

Freshly chopped parsley is a nice finishing touch, adding lots of flavour and colour.

Crème fraîche can be added in place of double cream for less fat content.

For a real classic Cullen, use Finnan haddock. This will contain more bones, but carries a flavour other types of haddock cannot quite match. Well worth the extra work.

Creamy Bubble and Squeak Soup
with **Crunchy Bacon**

Bubble and squeak is reputed to have got its name because it echoes the sound the ingredients make when frying. Usually thought of as a nineteenth-century dish of potato and cabbage leftovers, the dish was originally made with beef and cabbage, without potato. Here, I have taken the potatoes and mixed them with onions and Brussels sprouts, the alternative to cabbage. This version has been blitzed to a smooth, creamy-soft finish, but it can, if preferred, be left in its rustic, brothy consistency. The flavours and texture can be enhanced by a last-minute addition of slivers of bacon cooked to a crisp.

This recipe is perfect at Christmas time if you have leftover sprouts, potatoes and crispy bacon rashers from Christmas lunch that you want to use up.

SERVES 4–6

Butter
2 large onions, roughly diced
2 large potatoes, peeled and cut in rough
    1 cm (½ in) dice
1 litre (1¾ pints) *Chicken* or *Vegetable Stock*,
    (page 33 or 36)
250 g (9 oz) Brussels sprouts, finely shredded
    and rinsed
125 ml (4 fl oz) single cream
6–8 rashers of streaky bacon, rinded and cut
    into thin strips
Cooking oil
Salt, pepper and freshly grated nutmeg

Melt the butter in a saucepan. Once bubbling, add the onions and potatoes. Cook without colouring for 5–10 minutes, until beginning to soften. The stock can now be added. Bring to the simmer and cook for 20–25 minutes, until the vegetables are totally cooked.

Season the soup with salt, pepper and a pinch of nutmeg. Bring to the boil and add the shredded sprouts. Allow the soup to simmer vigorously for 6–8 minutes, until the sprouts become tender.

OPPOSITE
Creamy Bubble and Squeak Soup with Crunchy Bacon

The soup can now be completely liquidized and then pushed through a sieve for a smooth, creamy finish. Add the single cream and check the seasoning.

Cook the bacon strips while the soup is being made, by heating a non-stick frying-pan with a drop of cooking oil. Begin to cook the bacon on a fairly high heat. This will seal the individual strips. After a minute or two, reduce the cooking temperature so the bacon is just bubbling. As the bacon cooks, its natural fat will melt, letting it 'deep-fry' in its own oil. Continue until the strips are a deep colour and have become very crispy, almost like crackling. Strain off the fat and sit the bacon pieces on kitchen paper to absorb any remaining oil. You now have crunchy bacon, which eats very well sprinkled over the bubble and squeak soup.

Note: For vegetarians, omit the bacon strips and cook the vegetables in vegetable stock. The soup can also be served as a bubble and squeak broth. Simply cut the onions and potatoes into neat 1 cm (½ in) dice, and follow the recipe, adding the shredded sprouts. Once all the vegetables are cooked, add 50 g (2 oz) butter in place of the single cream. The bacon can be an optional extra.

Frozen-pea Soup ⓥ

The most famous pea soup was called 'The London Particular' because it was as thick as a London fog – which was called, in its turn, a 'pea-souper'. Peas, in fact, are one of man's oldest vegetables. Dried, they were an ingredient of the earliest pottages in Britain – and of the famous pease pudding and mushy peas – but it was not until the sixteenth century, when Italian gardeners developed tender varieties, that they could be eaten fresh. For this recipe I'm using frozen peas. This will give you a version that is quicker, greener and just as fresh-tasting as the historic dish.

SERVES 4–6

1 large onion, finely chopped
Butter
450 ml (¾ pint) *Vegetable* or *Chicken Stock*,
    (page 36 or 33) or alternative (page 11)

ABOVE
Vegetarian Scotch Broth

450 g (1 lb) frozen peas
Pinch of sugar
150 ml (¼ pint) single cream (optional)
Salt and pepper

Cook the onion in the butter for a few minutes, without letting it colour, until softened. Add the stock and bring to a rapid simmer. Add the peas now and cook on a fast heat for 3 minutes. Once the peas are soft and tender, season with salt, pepper and sugar and then liquidize to a smooth consistency. For an even smoother finish, push the soup through a sieve. For a creamier consistency, add the single cream. The pea soup is now ready to eat, preferably with lots of crusty bread.

Note: A sprig or two of fresh mint can be added to the soup during the cooking of the onion, for some extra taste. The soup can be garnished with fried or toasted bread croûtons and small, crisp-cooked strips of smoked or unsmoked bacon.

Vegetarian Scotch Broth ⓥ

This is the classic pottage, a good and nourishing country soup that can be made with whatever is in season, the only essentials being barley, vegetables and a little meat, usually lamb or mutton. Traditionally, the meat would be boiled with the barley for a good hour before adding the vegetables, then cooked for another hour. It would be left overnight for the fat to set and be removed. Once re-warmed, a little butter and parsley were added and the soup was ready. However, I thought we would make a vegetarian version, with lots of vegetables and pearl barley in a good vegetable stock. The soup will take about an hour to make – no waiting overnight – and is packed with fresh flavours.

The famous Dr Johnson was rather dismissive of Scotland and the Scots, but less so about Scotch broth: his companion, James Boswell, recorded in 1776 that the great man ate several platefuls and 'seemed very fond of the dish. I said, "You never ate it before?" – Johnson, "No, sir; but I don't care how soon I eat it again." '

SERVES 4–6

50 g (2 oz) pearl barley
1.5 litres (2½ pints) *Vegetable Stock* (page 36)
2 onions, cut into 5 mm (¼ in) dice
2 carrots, cut into 5mm (¼ in) dice
1 large turnip, cut into 5 mm (¼ in) dice
1 small swede, cut into 5mm (¼ in) dice
2 celery sticks, cut into 5mm (¼ in) dice
1 potato, cut into 5 mm (¼ in) dice
1 leek, finely shredded
Butter
Salt and pepper
1 dessertspoon chopped fresh parsley

Wash the pearl barley well. Place in a saucepan with the vegetable stock. Bring to the simmer, skimming off any impurities. The barley can now be gently simmered for 30–40 minutes, until tender. At this point, add the onions and carrots and cook for a further 8 minutes.

Now it's time to add the turnips, swede, celery and potato. Return to the simmer and continue to cook for 20 minutes; check all the vegetables are cooked.

To finish, add the finely shredded leeks; the soup will just take 5 more minutes to be ready. Season with salt and pepper. Add a large knob of butter and chopped parsley.

The vegetarian Scotch broth is now ready to serve, and will be at its best with lots of crusty bread.

See also

Cheddar-cheese Soup (page 70)
Pan-fried Red Mullet with a Tomato and Leek Soup
(page 149)

Basic Stocks

Soups and stocks have always had quite an intimate relationship, the soup always needing a helping hand from the other. However, in the strictest culinary terms, the two are completely different. A soup is a finished dish, complete in itself, while stock is used as the base, or as part of, finished dishes, although, once clarified, it almost stands on its own as the ultimate clear soup, consommé.

A stock or broth is water in which meat or fish, plus vegetables, or vegetables alone, have simmered until the water takes on their flavour. This would have been an essential and daily part of British eating after the introduction of cooking pots, when the first pottages – or soups – were created and enjoyed. Very many different vegetable and herb flavourings could be added to make the liquid tastier and more interesting to the palate. As the liquid warmed, it softened the often-tough meats (if any were used), along with grains, whose starches would swell and thicken the liquid. As well as being practical and nourishing, making and eating stocks would have been economical – as it is still – in that tough pieces of meat and bone could be used, as well as trimmings, carcasses and leftovers that might otherwise have been thrown away.

From the very earliest times, throughout the Middle Ages and almost up to the present day, stocks have been made in this way, and used in pottages or soups or as the basis of sauces. Interestingly, in French culinary terms, *fond* or 'foundation' is the name for stock. In 1651, the first great French cookery book, *Le Cuisinier François* by François Pierre de la Varenne, was published, and it began with a stock – much as most cookery books, French, American or British, have done ever since. A cookbook published not much later in England mentioned a basic sauce called 'cullis', which was a stock boiled down until sticky and intense in flavour, which was used to enrich other sauces – much as meat glazes (in professional chefs' kitchens) and stock cubes are used today. (The word 'cullis' comes from the French *coulisse*, something that slides easily, possibly related to the current menu word, *coulis*.) In fact, stock or soup cubes were known in the eighteenth century. Gelatinous meat stocks would be boiled down to a 'glue' which could be chopped into squares and added to sauces, or could be carried by travellers and added to water for an instant soup.

The story goes that the cubes were even used to prevent sea-sickness.

The nutritional importance of rich stocks and broths has always been appreciated. In the late nineteenth century, however, the London-based French chef Alexis Soyer (working at the Reform Club, Pall Mall) uncovered a scandal. Famous for his social reform in the culinary field (he had designed soup kitchens and created soups for the Irish during the famine of the 1840s), he arrived in the Crimea in 1855 and found that meat for the men in hospital was being cooked in water for a set length of time, unrelated to the size of the joint. The consequent stock/broth, which would have nourished the sick more efficiently than undercooked solids, was being thrown away. What a waste! Strict instructions followed, with the man himself visiting all the hospitals, tasting the various individual broths personally.

Today, stocks still lie at the heart of the professional kitchen, but it is less easy for the domestic cook to have a huge stockpot simmering away on a back burner, the broth absorbing every scrap of flavour from bone, root and herb. It seems the three witches from *Macbeth* understood the importance of ingredients too, as we see with this recipe of theirs:

> Fillet of a fenny snake,
> In the cauldron boil and bake;
> Eye of newt, and toe of frog,
> Wool of bat, and tongue of dog,
> Adder's fork, and blind-worm's sting,
> Lizard's leg, and howlet's wing –
> For a charm of pow'rful trouble,
> Like a hell-broth boil and bubble.

If all of Shakespeare's ingredients aren't available, there are, however, some very good stock cubes on offer in supermarkets, as well as fresh stocks in cartons, which are almost as authentic as home-made (see page 11). So, you're not under any pressure to make the stocks featured in this chapter. But if you now feel inspired, the following recipes form a basic guide to the classic types and flavours.

OPPOSITE
Chicken Pot-roast (page 244) made with *Chicken Stock*

Chicken Stock

Chicken stock is one of the most important bases in the professional and domestic kitchen. It's used for most soups and many cream sauces, the latter because it is pale in colour – it is often known as 'white' (rather than 'brown') stock. It's very easy to make but you need to use raw chicken bones. Your butcher should be able to supply you with some chicken bones, or you can take the breasts off a whole chicken, saving them for another dish, and use the carcass for the stock.

Or, if you can find one, cook a whole boiling fowl with vegetables in water and you will have a quick, tasty stock and the bird to eat as well. Chicken wings also give you an equally flavoursome result.

If you do not have a large stockpot, you can easily reduce the quantities listed below. For information on ready-made alternatives, see page 11.

MAKES 2.25 LITRES (4 PINTS)

2 onions, chopped
2 celery sticks, chopped
2 leeks, chopped
25 g (1 oz) unsalted butter
1 garlic clove, crushed
1 bay leaf
Sprig of thyme
Few black peppercorns
1.8 kg (4 lb) chicken carcasses, chopped
3.4 litres (6 pints) water

In a large stockpot (about 8.5 litre/15 pint capacity), lightly soften the vegetables in the butter, without colouring. Add the garlic, bay leaf, thyme, peppercorns and chopped carcasses. Cover with the cold water and bring to the simmer, skimming all the time. Allow the stock to simmer for 2–3 hours, then drain through a sieve. The stock is now ready to use and will keep well chilled or frozen.

Veal or Beef Stock or *Jus*

This brown stock is the basis of many dishes and sauces, particularly in the professional kitchen, and often contributes the defining flavour and richness, the essence, of a good dish. It takes a long time to achieve, particularly if you make the *jus* after the stock, but it's very satisfying, and of course any left over will store well in your freezer for another day. The stock is best started in the morning so that you can allow it to cook throughout the day. Your butcher will be able to supply you with raw veal or beef bones (if available), and trimmings, if you alert him in advance.

Good, ready-made stocks and *jus* gravies can also be bought in supermarkets.

**MAKES 4.5–6 LITRES (8–10 PINTS) STOCK OR
600 ML–1.2 LITRES (1–2 PINTS) *JUS*/GRAVY**

3 onions, halved
2–3 tablespoons water
2.25 kg (5 lb) veal or beef bones
225 g (8 oz) veal or beef trimmings
    (from the butcher)
225 g (8 oz) carrots, coarsely chopped
3 celery sticks, coarsely chopped
1 leek, chopped
3–4 tomatoes, chopped
1 garlic clove, halved
1 bay leaf
Sprig of thyme
Salt

Pre-heat the oven to 120°C/250°F/Gas Mark ½. Lay the onion halves flat in a roasting tray, with the water. Place the onions in the oven and allow to caramelize slowly until they have totally softened and coloured. This process will take 1–2 hours. The sugars in the onions will cook slowly and give a wonderful taste.

Pop the onions into a large stockpot and leave on one side. Increase the oven temperature to 200°C/400°F/Gas Mark 6. Place all the bones and trimmings in the roasting tray and roast for about 30 minutes, until well coloured. Roast the chopped carrots and celery in another roasting tray (without adding any oil) for about 20 minutes, until lightly coloured.

When ready, add the roasted bones, trimmings and vegetables to the onions in the pot, along with the leek, tomatoes, garlic, bay leaf and thyme. Fill the pot with cold water – you'll need about 6–7.2 litres (10–12 pints). Bring the stock to the simmer, season with salt and skim off any impurities. Allow to cook for 6–8 hours for the maximum flavour. If it seems to be reducing too quickly, top up with cold water.

When ready, drain and discard the bones and vegetables. The liquid now remaining is your veal stock, and you can cool it and freeze it in convenient quantities.

Alternatively, make a veal or beef *jus*/gravy with the stock. Allow the liquid to boil and reduce to 600 ml–1.2 litres (1–2 pints), skimming all the time. The stock should be thick and of a sauce-like consistency. Make sure that you taste all the time during reduction. If the sauce tastes right but is not thick enough, thicken it slightly with cornflour. (Of course, I do hope that won't be necessary.) You now have a veal or beef *jus*/gravy, a classic sauce.

Game Stock

For this stock, I'm using wild (wood) pigeons. If you are going to be roasting pigeons, then the carcasses can be used for stock – taking out the backbone and removing the legs before just roasting the breasts on the bone. For this recipe I suggest that you buy frozen birds. These don't, obviously, give you the fullest flavour, but the whole birds will be used, so a good stock can be made. This will also be made with red wine, giving a good all-round flavour. Armagnac, Cognac, Madeira and port can also be used.

There are two versions here. Using chicken stock will give you a thin game stock to work with. Using the basic veal *jus* will provide an instant game sauce.

1 tablespoon cooking oil
3 wood pigeons, chopped into small pieces
1 large onion or 2 shallots, roughly chopped
1 large carrot, roughly chopped
2 celery sticks, roughly chopped
4–5 mushrooms, quartered
Bottle of red wine
1 garlic clove, chopped
Sprig of thyme
5 juniper berries, crushed
Few black peppercorns
2–3 tomatoes, chopped
1.2 litres (2 pints) *Chicken, Veal or Beef Stock or Jus* (page 33 or 34)
300 ml (½ pint) water, if using gravy/*jus*

Heat the oil in a large frying-pan. Add the chopped pigeons and cook on a medium heat until well coloured and caramelized/roasted. This will take approximately 20 minutes on top of the stove.

Transfer the pigeons to a suitably sized saucepan. Add the onions, carrot, celery and mushrooms to the frying-pan and cook until beginning to soften and colour, but do not let them get too dark as this will create too much of a bitter finish. Increase the heat and add a third of the red wine. This will lift all the flavours from the base of the pan. Transfer all to the saucepan containing the pigeons. Add the garlic, thyme, juniper berries, black peppercorns and tomatoes. Cook until the tomatoes have reduced into the red wine. Add the rest of the wine from the bottle, bring to a fast simmer and allow to reduce by three-quarters. Add the stock or *jus* (plus water, if using *jus*). Return to the simmer. If making a stock, simmer for 1–1½ hours. For the gravy, simmer for 45 minutes–1 hour. Whichever has been made, strain through a fine sieve or, for a guaranteed smooth finish, twice through a muslin cloth.

The stock/sauce is now ready to use.

Fish Stock

To make a good fish stock, white fish bones – in particular, turbot and sole bones – should always be used. These give a good flavour, and do not carry an oily texture. A friendly fishmonger will help you out in providing the bones, I'm sure, and will, I hope, not charge you for them. Using white bones will produce a strongly flavoured stock, giving a good, full taste and clear, jelly-like finish. Perfect for poaching and making fish soups and sauces.

For information on ready-made alternatives, see page 11.

1 large onion, sliced
1 leek, sliced
2 celery sticks, sliced
50 g (2 oz) unsalted butter
Few fresh parsley stalks
1 bay leaf
6 black peppercorns
1 kg (2 lb) turbot or sole bones, washed
300 ml (½ pint) dry white wine
2.25 litres (4 pints) water
Salt

Sweat the sliced vegetables in the butter, without colouring. Add the parsley stalks, bay leaf and peppercorns. Chop the fish bones, making sure there are no blood clots left on them. Add to the vegetables and continue to cook for a few minutes. Add the wine and boil to reduce until almost dry. Add the water, season with salt and bring to the simmer. Allow to simmer for 20 minutes, then drain through a sieve. The stock is now ready to use, or you can store it for a few days in the fridge, or for up to 3 months in the freezer.

Court-bouillon ⓥ

Court-bouillon is described in the new *Larousse Gastronomique* (a cookery encyclopedia) as an aromatic cooking liquor for fish, meat and vegetables. And that's exactly what it is, but it is mostly used for fish, in particular shellfish. It's quite powerful, but when cooking lobsters (as I do overleaf), crabs, langoustines and mussels, it does nothing but add flavour. It's a joy to make because in cooking it releases a wonderfully aromatic perfume. (Making a *court-bouillon* for vegetables and meats may well need a slightly different percentage of wine and vinegar.)

This recipe can be halved to fit a smaller saucepan and make a smaller finished quantity.

MAKES 2 LITRES (3½ PINTS)

1 carrot, sliced
1 onion, sliced
1–2 celery sticks, sliced
1 garlic clove, sliced
15 g (½ oz) fresh root ginger, peeled and sliced
½ teaspoon each fennel seeds and white peppercorns
1 star anise
1 tablespoon sea salt
250 ml (8 fl oz) white wine
2 tablespoons white-wine vinegar
Grated zest of 1 orange
Bouquet garni of tarragon leaves, bay leaf and
      thyme, tied in muslin or a strip of leek
2 litres (3½ pints) water
Juice of 1 lemon

Place all the ingredients in a suitably sized saucepan and bring to the boil. Cook on a fast simmer for 15–20 minutes.

Remove the pan from the heat and leave to infuse for 2–3 hours before using.

The liquid can now be used as it is or strained through a sieve. To cook live lobsters, crabs and so on, the bouillon will need to be re-boiled.

To Cook Live Lobsters in a *Court-bouillon*

If you have managed to find fresh lobsters, all you will need to cook them is a large pot of boiling *court-bouillon*. Drop the lobsters in and return to the boil. Once the stock is boiling, cook for just 3–5 minutes, depending on size. Now remove the pot, leaving the lobsters in. They will continue to cook and the meat will also become very relaxed. Once at just room temperature, they are ready to open.

Note: For even softer and only just cooked lobster, bring back to the boil and remove the pot from the heat immediately.

A quicker way to cook lobster is simply to use boiling salted water and follow the instructions above. Of course, cooked lobsters are also available from most good fishmongers and supermarkets.

Vegetable Stock Ⓥ

This is a great alternative to chicken and fish stock in many recipes, particularly if making vegetarian soups. This is a basic recipe, but it can be adapted in any number of ways: simply add or substitute other vegetable or herb flavours for a subtle difference. Never use starchy root vegetables, such as potatoes, parsnips or turnips, however, as they will make the stock cloudy.

For information on ready-made alternatives, see page 11.

MAKES APPROX. 1.2 LITRES (2 PINTS)

225 g (8 oz) carrots (optional)
2 onions
4 celery sticks
2 leeks, white part only
1 fennel bulb
1–2 courgettes
1 tablespoon vegetable oil
1 bay leaf
Sprig of thyme
1 teaspoon each coriander seeds
      and pink peppercorns
½ lemon, sliced
1.5 litres (2½ pints) water
Pinch of salt

Cut all the vegetables roughly into 1 cm (½ in) dice. Warm the vegetable oil in a pan, then add all the diced vegetables, the herbs, coriander seeds, peppercorns and lemon slices. Cook, without colouring, for 8–10 minutes, allowing the vegetables to soften slightly. Add the water, with a good pinch of salt, and bring to a simmer. Once at simmering point, cook for 30 minutes, without a lid. During this time the stock should reduce, increasing the flavour and depth.

The stock can now be strained through a sieve, leaving you with about 1.2 litres (2 pints). If you find there is more than this, simply boil rapidly to reduce. You can also reduce the stock if you find that the flavour is not full enough.

OPPOSITE
Pan-fried Red Mullet (page 149) made with *Fish Stock*

Sauces
and
Dressings

It was during the eighteenth century
that a foreign visitor directed his
criticism at English culinary traditions
with his remark that the natives had
sixty different religious sects but only
one sauce. Perhaps he did encounter
one too many white or butter sauces,
made with butter and flour alone, that
were very common at the time.
But the history of sauces in Britain
is actually of much greater depth
and interest than his remark suggests.

When the Romans held much of Europe, including England, they would have introduced their strong-tasting garnish and seasoning sauces, *liquamen* and *garum*, made from fermented salted fish. (The anchovy and Worcestershire sauces sold today are probably not unlike *garum*; the fish sauces of the East, such as *nam pla*, are very similar.) This may have created a taste in the British for strong flavours, for many medieval sauces were extremely piquant. They consisted predominantly of vinegar with other ingredients, or ale and/or wine alone. Another alternative was a sweet and sour mixture, usually consisting of vinegar or verjuice (the juice of sour grapes, sorrel or crab apples) and sugar and/or pounded dried fruits.

The earliest 'sauce' was the flavoured liquid in which soup or pottage ingredients were cooked. It would be thickened with cereal or bread (if at all), or by adding wheat flour (but this was expensive), egg yolks or cream. Breadcrumbs were popular, always finishing a sauce with a good, thick consistency and texture. This would sit perfectly on the bread trencher (a piece of bread used as a plate), without being absorbed too quickly or running off.

After the Conquest of 1066, the Normans introduced a more elaborate way of preparing foods, including sauces. These ideas were partly French, but also perhaps partly Arab, for the Normans had also conquered the Arab-ruled Sicily not long before. This might explain the Middle Eastern feel of much medieval saucing – the use of almond milk, the incorporation of ground almonds, the mixing in of dried fruits and sweet spices. Soldiers returning from the Crusades also brought back spices in the eleventh and twelfth centuries, and these were gradually incorporated into many sauces, often used to disguise meat that was tainted, too salty or simply off.

In the sixteenth century, sauces began to be thickened with 'fried flour'. This was a flour and lard liaison, a technique that has come down through culinary history as the roux (from the French for 'reddish-brown'), and which marked the beginning of our famous British gravy. In the eighteenth century, many sauces became simpler, and this is when the white or butter sauce grew in popularity. A Swiss visitor, Carl Moritz, wrote about the food he encountered in lodging houses on his travels through England in the1780s: 'To persons in my situation [it] generally consists of a piece of half-boiled or half-roasted meat; and a few cabbage leaves boiled in plain water; on which they pour a sauce made of flour and butter, the usual method of dressing vegetables in England.' Hannah Glasse, one of the century's most famous cookery writers, actually prided herself on the simplicity of many of her sauces and gravies, and was highly critical of the intricate and complicated French recipes: '. . . So much is the blind folly of this age, that they would rather be imposed on by a French booby, than give encouragement to a good English cook.'

The sauces I've chosen for this chapter are mostly accompaniments to savoury dishes, such as Cumberland sauce, salad cream and so on. You'll find the 'personal' sauces to recipes, to accompany fish or meat dishes, featured within the recipes themselves. These days I feel we have room to recognize and appreciate both the British sauce-making tradition, which has come a long way since its 'heavy' days, and the influences of the French style.

PAGE 38
Cumberland Sauce (page 42)

Classic Hollandaise Sauce ⓥ

This is a classic French sauce, listed by Escoffier as one of the five basic sauces. It is of Dutch origin, though, and was also known in England as Dutch sauce. It eats very nicely with fish. It can be bought ready-made, but I'm going to give you two ways of making it. Both taste very good.

MAKES APPROX. 300 ML (½ PINT)

225 g (8 oz) unsalted butter
2 tablespoons malt or white wine vinegar
6 white peppercorns, lightly crushed
1 tablespoon water
2 egg yolks
Salt and cayenne or pepper
Squeeze of lemon juice

Melt the butter in a pan, then leave it to cool slightly so that it is just warm when added; if it is too hot, the sauce will curdle. The butter will have separated, leaving all its solids in the base of the pan. Pour off the butter oil. This is now clarified butter. Discard the milky solids.

Boil the vinegar with the peppercorns until reduced by half. Add the cold water to cool, and strain the reduction through a sieve into a bowl. Add the egg yolks and whisk together. Place the bowl over a pan of hot water and whisk to a *sabayon*. A *sabayon* is created by the cooking and thickening of the egg yolks. As they are whisked, they increase in volume to a cream consistency. When the yolks have reached this stage, remove the bowl from the heat and continue to whisk, slowly adding the warm, clarified butter. When all the clear butter has been added and whisked, the sauce should be a thick consistency which can now be seasoned with salt and cayenne or pepper and finished with the lemon juice.

Should the hollandaise curdle, make a one-egg yolk *sabayon* and slowly whisk in the spoilt sauce. This should bring the sauce back to a nice consistency.

Note: To increase the flavours of this sauce, a pinch of dried tarragon, chopped onion or shallot can be added to the reduction. This will leave you with a sauce béarnaise flavour, which also goes well with meat dishes and even a plain grilled steak. The sauce can also be finished with freshly chopped tarragon or parsley.

Simple Hollandaise Sauce ⓥ

The classic way of making Hollandaise Sauce involves a flavoured reduction, but this quicker way tastes just as good.

MAKES APPROX. 150 ML (¼ PINT)

100 g (4 oz) unsalted butter
1 egg yolk
½ tablespoon warm water
Squeeze of lemon juice
Salt and cayenne pepper or white pepper

Make clarified butter by melting the butter in a pan and then leaving it to cool slightly so that it is just warm when added to the sauce; the sauce will curdle if it is too hot. The butter should have separated; add only the clear butter oil to the sauce, not the buttermilk that will have collected at the bottom of the pan.

Add the egg yolk to the water in a bowl and whisk over a pan of hot water until lighter in colour and thickened. Remove from the heat and slowly add the clarified butter, whisking until the sauce is thick and all the butter is used. Add the lemon juice and season with salt and cayenne or white pepper.

Note: A teaspoon of Dijon or English mustard will bring a warmth and extra body to the finished flavour.

Cider-vinegar Dressing ⓥ

We tend to think that dressings made with oil and vinegar, and oil, vinegar and eggs were imported from France, but from the very earliest times, British cooks were dressing salads and other dishes in a similar way. Cider vinegar, of course, is pretty English, cider being such a speciality of the south-west.

This dressing works very well with the recipe for *Seared, Cured Salmon Cutlets with Leeks, Bacon and a Cider-vinegar Dressing* (page 167). It will also go well with a simple tossed salad. I have included raw egg and egg yolk in the recipe. If that puts you off, I'm following it with a version using bought mayonnaise. So no excuse, you've got to try it.

MAKES 250–300 ML (8 FL OZ–½ PINT)

1 heaped teaspoon caster sugar
1½ tablespoons cider vinegar
1 egg yolk
1 egg
2 teaspoons Dijon mustard
250 ml (8 fl oz) groundnut oil
Salt and pepper

Warm the sugar with the vinegar and allow to cool. Mix the egg yolk and whole egg with the mustard and sweetened vinegar. Gradually add the groundnut oil, a drop or two at a time, and whisk vigorously until all has worked in to create the dressing. Season with salt and pepper and the dressing is made.

Mayonnaise-based Cider Dressing ⓥ

This recipe is an alternative to the one above, replacing the eggs with mayonnaise. It's always nicer to make your own mayonnaise (see page 49), but good ready-made varieties can be bought.

1½ tablespoons cider vinegar
1 heaped teaspoon caster sugar
2 teaspoons Dijon mustard
200–250g (7–9 oz) mayonnaise (bought)
Salt and pepper

Warm together the vinegar and caster sugar. Leave to cool. Mix the vinegar with the mustard and then with the mayonnaise and check for seasoning, adding salt and pepper as necessary.

If the dressing seems to be a little thick, loosen it with a few teaspoons of warm water.

Cumberland Sauce ⓥ

Queen Victoria's relative, Ernest, Duke of Cumberland, who became the last independent ruler of Hanover, is said to be the man honoured by this sauce, though nobody seems to know how or why. The sauce has become an essential and inseparable partner to all game dishes, as well as to cold meats, pies and terrines – he must have enjoyed the hunt!

There have been many variations of Cumberland sauce, but the base has always been the same – redcurrant jelly. Cumberland sauce takes on a consistency of a loose jam, usually garnished simply with orange and lemon rind. In many recipes, fresh and glacé cherries have also been used, but neither of these excite me very much, so I'm sticking to the orange and lemon rind, with the addition of chopped shallots.

Most recipes also suggest the sauce be strained through a sieve to give a smoother finish, but I prefer the coarser texture as a good balance to the accompanying dish, particularly if it's cold meat. For maximum flavour, always check the fruit content of the redcurrant jelly before you buy it. Many contain minimum fruit and lots of colour.

SERVES 6–8

Juice of 1 lemon plus 2 peeled strips of zest
Juice of 1 orange plus 2 peeled strips of zest
1 shallot, finely chopped
4 tablespoons red-wine vinegar
¼ teaspoon English mustard powder
¼ teaspoon powdered ginger
4 tablespoons port
6 heaped tablespoons redcurrant jelly (use one with
    a high fruit content – with redcurrants listed
    as the first ingredient)
Salt
Pinch of cayenne pepper

The peeled strips of lemon and orange zest should have all pith scraped away, leaving just rich, pure zest. This can now be cut into very thin strips, even thinner than matchsticks. Place the strips (both orange and lemon together) in cold water and bring to the boil. Now allow to cook for just 5 minutes before straining.

Place the chopped shallots in a saucepan along with the vinegar. Bring to the simmer and then allow to cook and reduce until almost dry.

Strain both of the fruit juices into the saucepan and reduce by half.

Mix the mustard and ginger together, adding 1 tablespoon of the port to create a paste.

Add the redcurrant jelly to the vinegar reduction, along with the remaining 3 tablespoons of port. The sauce can now be warmed on a moderate heat until the jelly has completely melted. Add the mustard and ginger paste and season with a pinch of salt and cayenne pepper.

If you prefer a smoother finish, strain the sauce through a sieve to remove the shallots before adding the blanched lemon and orange zest.

The sauce is best eaten cold. If kept refrigerated in a screw-top jar, the sauce will last up to 2 weeks.

Note: I find this sauce is best made around Christmas time, when we all have plenty of cold meats and pâtés to enjoy.

If you are not a ginger fan, simply omit it from the recipe. The mustard quantity can then be doubled for extra bite.

A splash of Worcestershire sauce can be added to sharpen all the flavours.

Tartar Sauce ⓥ

Fish and chips is a British favourite, and perfectly complemented by tartar sauce. The flavour and acidity of capers, gherkins and onions work so well with the crisp batter and succulent fish, and create a lovely dip for home-made chips. The sauce can also be used a sharp dip for crudités.

However, the sauce is not British, but a French classic. In France, it is traditionally made by pounding hard-boiled egg yolks to a fine paste before adding olive oil to make a mayonnaise consistency, then mixing in a touch of vinegar, lemon juice and chopped chives. I'm not really sure how all the extras – the capers, gherkins and so on – found their way into the sauce, but I'm glad they did. I've also added a little chopped green olive for an extra flavour, but if you're not a fan, just omit.

There is actually a British sauce that is not too dissimilar to tartar, called Cambridge sauce. Maybe we can claim the mixture is British after all.

MAKES APPROX. 300 ML (½ PINT)

300 ml (½ pint) mayonnaise (bought or see
　　page 49)
25 g (1 oz) gherkins, chopped
25 g (1 oz) capers, chopped
25 g (1 oz) green olives, chopped
25 g (1 oz) shallot or onion, finely chopped
2 teaspoons chopped fresh parsley (optional)
Squeeze of lemon juice
Salt and pepper

Simply mix all the ingredients together, seasoning with salt, pepper and a squeeze of the lemon juice.

Bread Sauce ⓥ

This is one of our oldest sauces, but I always feel it's not made as often as it used to be. Its image is of a thick, lumpy sauce with a bland flavour. In fact, it's creamy with a spiciness that lends itself very well to poultry and game dishes. Bread or breadcrumbs were used in the Middle Ages to thicken basic sauces to accompany meat, fish and game. Many were made with milk, usually almond milk, and spiced with a final sprinkling of something such as saffron, pepper or ginger. This recipe, with the inclusion of an onion spiked with cloves and a dusting of nutmeg and mace, is an echo of those medieval flavours.

It looks quite a list of ingredients for a sauce that has a bread and milk image. A lot can be omitted from the recipe. The spices are part of the infusion of milk. This will lift the complete flavour. However, the onions studded with cloves, a few black peppercorns and bay leaf will still give a good result.

The finely chopped onion will be left in the finished sauce, giving a coarser texture. Again, it can be left out if you prefer.

1 onion
2–3 cloves
½ small onion, very finely chopped (optional)
Few black peppercorns
1 bay leaf
Pinch of ground mace
Pinch of freshly grated nutmeg
1 allspice berry (optional)
300 ml (½ pint) milk
50 g (2 oz) white breadcrumbs (taken from
    bread 24–48 hours old)
2–3 tablespoons double cream
25 g (1 oz) butter
Salt and freshly ground white pepper

Stud the whole onion with the cloves and place along with the chopped onion, peppercorns, bay leaf and all the spices in a saucepan, with the milk.

Bring to a rapid simmer and then remove from the heat. The milk can now be left to infuse for 45 minutes–1 hour (longer for even more flavour). Remove the whole onion, peppercorns, allspice berry and bay leaf.

Add the breadcrumbs and return to the heat. Allow to cook on a medium heat for 15–20 minutes, until the crumbs have swollen and thickened the sauce.

Add the double cream and butter. Season with salt and pepper and remove from the heat. The sauce is ready to serve. If keeping warm, cover with greaseproof paper or cling film to prevent a skin from forming.

Apple Sauce ⓥ

In the Middle Ages, it was believed that an animal should be cooked and/or served with something that it fed on, so, as pigs are extremely fond of windfall apples, the association between sharp fruit and sweet meat was probably very early. Apple sauce was also served with goose, roast duck and game dishes. Slow-roasted duck, cooked until so well done that it's falling off the bone, eats beautifully with a cinnamon-flavoured apple sauce. (Similar matchings of meat and accompaniment, traditionally called 'tracklements', are horseradish with beef, mint sauce with lamb and redcurrant or rowan jelly with mutton and venison.) For a vegetarian option, you can serve apple sauce with a simple cheese and onion flan that's finished with a sprinkling of toasted chopped almonds.

In many old recipes, quince was also added, usually mixed with cooking apples. The apples I'm using here are Cox's, but you can go half-and-half with Bramleys. This will give a sharper edge to the finished flavour.

SERVES 8

450 g (1 lb) Cox's apples
25 g (1 oz) caster sugar
Juice of ½ lemon
4 tablespoons water
½ cinnamon stick or pinch of ground
    cinnamon (optional)

Peel, core and cut the apples into rough small dice. Place in a thick-based saucepan with all the remaining ingredients. Now cook on a medium to low heat with a lid on top for approximately 15 minutes. During the cooking time, stir to ensure even cooking.

Once cooked and tender, with some of the apple starting to purée, remove from the heat, discarding the cinnamon stick, if using. The apples can now be whisked to a sauce consistency. The more whisked, the smoother the finish. I do like to leave some texture in the apples, as this keeps more of the natural apple taste. It's also possible to blitz the sauce in a food processor or liquidizer for the ultimate smooth finish – the decision is yours. Apple sauce is best served warm for maximum taste.

Note: Once the apple sauce is cooked, a good knob of butter can be added while whisking. This will enrich the finished flavour, also giving a silky consistency.

Fresh herbs can also be added. A teaspoon of chopped sage goes very well with crispy crackling roast pork.

White Sauce Ⓥ

The base for this sauce was first introduced in the seventeenth century, becoming very popular in Britain in the eighteenth century. It goes by the name béchamel, and is made with a roux base, a combination of butter cooked with flour. This is a French influence that has become a regular British culinary term. The word roux derives from the French for 'reddish-brown'. For this recipe, however, the roux is kept at its white stage, early in its cooking process, which maintains a creamy white finish to the sauce.

Béchamel is a 'mother' sauce to many others, including parsley, mustard, capers, onions and cheese. It's important when cooking a béchamel sauce that it's on a low heat and kept moving from time to time in the pan. If left to simmer on its own for too long, the flour will stick and begin to burn. This flavour then infuses and spoils the sauce.

MAKES APPROX. 750 ML (1¼ PINTS)

1 onion
1 bay leaf
1–2 cloves (optional)
600 ml (1 pint) milk
25 g (1 oz) butter
25 g (1 oz) plain flour
150 ml (¼ pint) double or single cream (optional)
Salt, pepper and freshly grated nutmeg

BELOW
Slow-honey-roast Belly of Pork (page 184) with *Apple Sauce*

Pierce the onion with the cloves through the bay leaf. Place in a saucepan, with the milk, and bring to the simmer. Simmer for a few minutes, before removing from the heat and leaving to infuse for 1 hour. This is not essential but does give the milk some body and flavour.

Melt the butter in a thick-bottomed pan. Once completely melted, add the flour. On a low heat, stir the two together to create the roux. This can now cook for 3–4 minutes, stirring to ensure an even cooking.

While the roux is cooking, the milk can be re-heated, leaving the onion in to increase its flavour.

The milk can now be added a little at a time, stirring as it is added. This will emulsify with the roux and become very thick. Continue this process until all the milk has been added. The sauce now needs to cook on a gentle heat for a minimum of 20 minutes. During the cooking time, constant stirring or whisking will be needed to prevent any sticking. After 20 minutes, add the double cream. This will help loosen and enrich the consistency. Single cream will, obviously, make the sauce thinner than double.

Season with salt, pepper and nutmeg. Strain the béchamel through a sieve for a guaranteed smooth finish.

If not using immediately, cover with buttered greaseproof paper or cling film. This basic white sauce can quickly be turned into a parsley sauce with the addition of the freshly chopped herb, or perhaps a mustard sauce, adding English, Dijon or wholegrain to your taste.

Note: A good knob of butter will enrich any of these sauces.

Cheese Sauce (Sauce Mornay) Ⓥ

The idea of adding grated cheese to a white sauce doesn't seem to have occurred to anyone until about the eighteenth century, when vegetables and macaroni began to be topped with cheese, which was then toasted. It's a great invention, though, and the sauce has so many uses, working well with other flavours. Cauliflower, macaroni, lasagne, leeks and many more foods have all had and have a relationship with cheese sauce.

Here, I'm adding the cheese to a basic white sauce, which does make rather a lot of cheese sauce, but you can halve both the white sauce and the ingredients below. I also love to add mustard as I find it lifts the flavour of the cheese.

MAKES APPROX. 900 ML (1½ PINTS)

1 × *White Sauce* (page 45)
1 heaped teaspoon English or Dijon mustard
 (optional)
100–175 g (4–6 oz) Cheddar cheese, grated
Salt and pepper

Warm the white sauce. Add the mustard, if using, along with 100 g (4 oz) of the grated Cheddar. Stir until melted.

Now it is time to taste and season with salt and pepper. If you prefer a stronger flavour, then add the remaining cheese.

Cook for 2–3 minutes, making sure the sauce does not over-heat. Boiling any cheese sauce will separate the fat content from the cheese itself, creating an almost curdled consistency.

For a guaranteed smooth consistency, strain through a sieve.

The rich cheese sauce is ready and waiting for cauliflower, leeks, broccoli, spinach, macaroni, lasagne, etc. etc. etc.

Note: A squeeze of lemon juice will always lift the flavours.
 For a richer finish, whisk in a mixture of 2 egg yolks and 4 tablespoons of double cream once the sauce is ready. Ensure the sauce does not boil or the egg yolks will scramble.

Cumberland Apple Sauce ⓥ

This sauce – nothing to do with the Duke of Cumberland this time – is a classic accompaniment to the famous Cumberland sausage (page 368). It also eats very well with just about any sausage, ham or terrine, plus roast pork, goose, chops and poultry; you can also use it as a dressing for simple vegetarian salads or as an accompaniment to savoury tarts. The spicy flavour and the lemon juice lift the apples, giving a sweet but sharp zing. I'm using Bramleys here, as their strong flavour is just what the Cumberland sausage needs.

MAKES APPROX. 450 G (1 LB)

450 g (1 lb) Bramley apples, peeled and cored
Butter
50 g (2 oz) demerara or light soft brown sugar
(more can be added for those with a sweet tooth; caster sugar can also be used for a 'whiter' finish)
½ teaspoon ground mixed spice
Juice of ½ lemon
2–3 tablespoons water

Dice the apples into rough 1 cm (½ in) pieces. Melt a knob of butter in a saucepan. Add the apples and cook with a lid on for a few minutes over a moderate heat. The apples will now have begun to break down. Add the sugar, spice, lemon juice and water, stirring all in well. Replace the lid and continue to cook for 10 minutes. The apples will have become very tender. The 'sauce' can now be whisked to break down its texture. For a totally smooth finish, continue cooking for a few more minutes. The sauce can now be liquidized to a smooth paste.

Note: The juice from the remaining ½ lemon can be added for a slightly more acidic finish.

Basic White-wine or Champagne Fish Sauce

This is the perfect sauce for most kinds of fish – creamy, rich in flavour, but still light on the palate.

MAKES APPROX. 200–250 ML (7–8 FL OZ)

Butter
2 shallots, finely sliced
1 bay leaf
50 g (2 oz) button mushrooms, finely sliced
225 ml (7½ fl oz) white wine or champagne
225 ml (7½ fl oz) *Fish Stock* (page 35)
150 ml (¼ pint) double cream
Salt and pepper

Melt a knob of butter in a saucepan. Add the shallots and bay leaf and cook on a medium heat, without colouring, for 1–2 minutes. Add the mushrooms and continue to cook and soften for a further 2–3 minutes.

Add the white wine or champagne and, over a medium heat, bring to a rapid simmer, cooking until the wine has reduced by two-thirds. Pour in the fish stock and again reduce by two-thirds.

Add the double cream and return to a soft simmer. Allow to cook, the cream taking on all of the flavours and slightly thickening, for 6–8 minutes.

Season with salt and pepper and strain through a fine sieve.

Before serving the sauce, if you quickly blitz it with a hand-blender, the consistency will become lighter and very frothy, giving not such an intense and possibly over-cooked flavour.

Note: For a richer finish, whisk in 25–50 g (1–2 oz) of butter. It's important not to boil the sauce once the butter has been added. This will separate the fat content.

A squeeze of lemon juice will lift the flavour of almost any cream sauce.

I prefer not to make cream sauces too thick. This tends to leave a film around the palate instead of giving a fresh, light and lively flavour.

Tarragon leaves can also be added to the sauce reduction. Once the sauce is cooked and strained, a few more torn leaves can be added before serving.

Red-wine Sauce

This sauce tastes good with almost any meat – chicken, beef, pork, veal – and even eats well with baked fish.

MAKES APPROX. 1.2 LITRES (2 PINTS)

4 shallots, chopped
1 large carrot, chopped
2 celery sticks, chopped
25 g (1 oz) unsalted butter
1 garlic clove, crushed
1 bay leaf
1 sprig of fresh thyme
225 g (8 oz) beef skirt or beef trimmings (optional)
1 tablespoon olive oil (optional)
1 bottle red wine
1.2 litres (2 pints) *Veal Jus* (page 34) or bought alternative (page 11)
Salt and pepper

In a large pan, cook the chopped vegetables in a little butter with the garlic and herbs, allowing them to colour. In a frying-pan, fry the meat, if using, in the oil, colouring on all sides, then add the meat to the vegetables. Pour the red wine into the frying-pan to release any flavours from the trimmings. Scrape and stir, then pour the wine onto the meat and vegetables and boil to reduce until almost dry.

Add the veal *jus* and bring to the simmer; skim off any impurities, then simmer the sauce gently for 30 minutes. Pass through a sieve, squeezing all the juices from the vegetables and meat. Check for seasoning and you now have a rich, glistening red-wine sauce.

Home-made Salad Cream ⓥ

This is the sauce that most of us in Britain remember adding a dollop of to the side of a plate of salad, and it usually came out of a bottle. I always liked it, I must admit, and often wondered how it was made. It's not a mayonnaise, as it is a 'cooked' sauce, but has a very similar texture. After searching for, finding, cooking and tasting many recipes, this is the one I have settled for. It has a

sweet and slightly sour taste, with a creamy finish. It's worth having a go because it is so easy, and it's always nice to offer accompaniments that are home-made.

MAKES 200–300 ML (7–10 FL OZ)
DEPENDING ON THE QUANTITY OF CREAM

1 tablespoon plain flour
4 teaspoons caster sugar
1 dessertspoon English powder mustard
Pinch of salt
2 eggs
100 ml (3½ fl oz) white-wine vinegar
150 ml (¼ pint) double cream
Squeeze of lemon juice

BELOW
Home-made Salad Cream

Mix together the flour, sugar, mustard and salt. Beat in the eggs and white-wine vinegar. Place the bowl over a pan of simmering water and stir until warmed and thickened. This will take only 4–5 minutes. Once 'cooked', remove the bowl from the heat and leave to cool.

Now it is time to add the cream. With this you can be as generous as you wish. A minimum of 100 ml (3½ fl oz) will be needed. Finish with a squeeze of lemon juice and the salad cream is ready. If refrigerated, the sauce will keep for a minimum of 1–2 weeks.

Note: The salad cream is delicious served as an accompaniment to Scotch eggs – preferably the home-made ones (page 73).

Mayonnaise ⓥ

No one seems to be quite sure where this cold sauce comes from, but it may be a modern example of the medieval mixing of eggs and verjuice (the sour juice of crab apples or unripe grapes). It's more likely that it is from the Minorcan town of Mahon, which was said to have very good eggs. Whatever, mayonnaise is useful in any number of ways – in potato salad, as a base for other sauces, in sandwiches and many more.

MAKES APPROX. 450 ML (¾ PINT)

3 egg yolks
1 tablespoon malt or white-wine vinegar
1 teaspoon English or Dijon mustard
Salt and pepper
300 ml (½ pint) olive oil
1 teaspoon hot water
Few drops of lemon juice (optional)

Whisk the egg yolks, vinegar, mustard and seasonings together, then slowly add the olive oil, whisking continuously. When all the oil is added, finish with the water and correct the seasoning. A few drops of lemon juice can be added to enhance the taste.

If refrigerated, the mayonnaise will keep for up to 1 week.

Note: Groundnut oil can be used instead of the olive oil for a milder flavour.

A quick, lower-fat mayonnaise can be made as a healthier alternative. Take 140 g (scant 5 oz) of fromage frais (a really low-fat version can be found), 1 teaspoon of Dijon mustard and 1 teaspoon of lemon juice. Mix all three ingredients together, season with salt and pepper and the healthy mayo is made. An egg yolk can be added for a richer colour and flavour. This recipe can be used in place of any ready-made mayonnaise referred to throughout the book.

Home-made Tomato Ketchup ⓥ

The tomato was not really accepted as a food in Britain until the latter part of the eighteenth century, and even then it was cooked and pulped for a soup or made into a piquant pickle with vinegar and spices. The word 'ketchup' comes from the Chinese, meaning 'brine of pickled fish', and refers to a sauce such as the Thai *nam pla* we have recently become familiar with. The nearest to the original that we have in Britain would actually be our anchovy sauce or essence.

Despite this confusion, tomato ketchup, tomato sauce, and in fact tomato soup as well, have become very popular in Britain. Ketchup for me has always been that classic, bought-in one, Heinz, but there's nothing like home-made. Its flavour is fresher, with the spicy ingredients adding a new edge that just livens up the whole experience. I'm not trying to compete with that famous ketchup company, but we should try to make our own – just once.

MAKES APPROX. 600 ML (1 PINT)

1 clove
1 bay leaf
½ teaspoon ground coriander, or a few coriander seeds
½ teaspoon ground cinnamon, or ½ cinnamon stick (optional)
250 ml (8 fl oz) cider or white-wine vinegar
8 tablespoons demerara or caster sugar
1.5 kg (3 lb) net weight of ripe tomatoes after quartering and seeding

½ teaspoon sea-salt
½ tablespoon English mustard powder
1 garlic clove, crushed
Dash of Tabasco sauce
1 tablespoon tomato purée

Tie the clove, bay leaf, coriander and cinnamon stick, if using, in a piece of muslin. Place the vinegar and sugar in a heavy-based pan and bring to a simmer. Add the tomatoes and all other ingredients and bring to the boil, stirring to prevent any sticking. Once up to the boil, reduce the temperature and simmer, stirring occasionally, for 40 minutes. Be careful the mix doesn't stick to the base of the pan. Discard the muslin bag, blitz in a food processor or liquidizer and then push the sauce through a sieve.

If you find the sauce to be loose and thin once cold, then simply re-boil and thicken with a little cornflour or arrowroot mixed to a paste with water, being careful not to make it too starchy. This will prevent the tomato water separating from the sauce.

So that's the tomato ketchup made. Whether it's for dunking your sausages or topping your burger, the experience is worth every minute of preparation time.

I've also used this recipe to flavour the tomato cakes on page 66. The sauce works like a seasoning, lifting all of the flavours. A dish you just must try, so happy shaking. If refrigerated, the sauce will keep for a minimum of 1 month.

Basic Vinaigrette ⓥ

This may be a French name, but the British have been dressing their salads and vegetables with oil and vinegar for centuries. This particular dressing is very basic, but has lots of flavours, particularly from the infusion of the fresh basil, tarragon and thyme.

MAKES APPROX. 600 ML (1 PINT)

300 ml (½ pint) extra-virgin olive oil
(French or Italian)

300 ml (½ pint) groundnut oil
50 ml (2 fl oz) balsamic vinegar
Bunch of fresh basil
Small bunch of fresh tarragon
3–4 sprigs of fresh thyme
12 black peppercorns, lightly crushed
3 shallots, finely chopped
2 garlic cloves, crushed
1 bay leaf
1 teaspoon coarse sea salt

Warm the olive and groundnut oils together. Place all the remaining ingredients in a 750 ml (1¼ pint) bottle. Pour the oil into the bottle and close with a cork or screw top. For the best results, leave to marinate for a week, which will allow all the flavours to enhance the oils. To help the dressing along, shake the bottle once a day. Taste for seasoning before using.

Note: For a quick basic vinaigrette, mix 1 teaspoon of balsamic vinegar with 2 tablespoons olive oil. Season with salt and pepper and the dressing's made.

Onion Gravy

The first 'gravy' was a sweet, spicy sauce, but it had become a brown sauce, made by browning beef in fat before stewing it, by Elizabethan times. For a classic Great British onion gravy I use a good, reduced beef stock (*jus*) and the sweet-savouriness of slowly caramelized onions, capturing all of their natural flavours which do nothing but increase in strength as the gravy cooks.

This method holds a lot fewer ingredients, and at the same time carries a lot more depth and flavour, than the 'poor man's gravy' of times past, which consisted of 'A glass of small beer, a glass of water, an onion cut small, some pepper and salt, a little lemon peel grated, a clove or two, a spoonful of mushroom liquor, or pickled walnut liquor'.

This gravy is perfect with liver, sausages and mashed potatoes, *Toad in the Hole* (page 370) and *Yorkshire Pudding* (page 237), and is a vital component of my faggot recipe (see *Faggots in Onion Gravy*, page 228). A Yorkshire pudding topping version of this sauce is also outlined below.

4 large onions, thinly sliced or finely chopped
2 tablespoons water
300 ml (½ pint) *Veal* or *Beef Jus*
    (page 34) or alternative (page 11)

Place the onions in a pan with the water and cook on a very low heat. This will slowly draw the natural sugar content from the onions and, together with the juices, the two will caramelize. This is a slow process, possibly taking up to 2 hours. It is very important that the onion does not burn as this will create a bitter taste. Once a golden caramel flavour has been achieved, add the *jus*.

For a quicker caramelizing method, cook the onions to a golden brown colour in a knob of butter. Add a teaspoon of demerara sugar and cook for 1–2 minutes. Taste the onions for sweetness. If you feel they need more, repeat with the same quantity of sugar until the flavour you are after is achieved. Now just add the *jus* and cook for 6–8 minutes before serving.

BELOW
Faggots with Onion Gravy (page 228)

Green Pepper Butter ⓥ

This butter works well with almost all fish and meats, from grilled sole or roasted sea bass to grilled steak, cutlets or chicken breasts.

150 g (5 oz) butter
2 shallots, finely chopped
1 heaped teaspoon chopped green peppercorns
2 tablespoons brandy
4 tablespoons white wine
Squeeze of lemon juice
Salt

Melt a knob of butter, adding the chopped shallots and green peppercorns. Cook for a few minutes before adding the brandy. Boil and reduce until almost dry. Add the white wine and also reduce until almost dry. Allow to cool. Mix the shallots into the remaining butter, adding a squeeze of lemon juice and pinch of salt.

The butter can now be wrapped in cling film and rolled into a cylinder shape. Refrigerate or freeze until needed.

Note: Chopped parsley or onions can also be added to this recipe.

Green Lemon Butter ⓥ

This is a very old recipe that is very close to a basic parsley butter. The difference that interested me, and which does work well, is the addition of onion juice. This gives the butter a much fuller flavour. For any mustard fans, a teaspoon of toasted and lightly crushed mustard seeds can also be added. This butter recipe goes particularly well with *Grilled or Pan-fried Dover Sole* (page 141).

FOR 100 G (4 OZ) BUTTER

50 g (2 oz) parsley (100 g/4 oz for extra green)
1 medium onion, peeled
Juice of 1 lemon
100 g (4 oz) unsalted butter, at room temperature
Salt and pepper

Pour 300 ml (½ pint) of water from a boiled kettle over the parsley and leave to stand for 1–2 minutes. Drain and squeeze out any excess liquid. The parsley must now be chopped until very, very fine. This can be most easily done in a food processor or coffee grinder. It is important that the parsley is of a moist, almost puréed consistency.

The onion can now be cut into eight pieces and mashed with a potato masher. This will begin to release the natural onion juices, but finish squeezing the onion pieces by hand until all the juices have been released. The onion solids can be discarded as all their flavour has been squeezed away. Quickly boil the lemon juice and reduce by half. Leave to cool.

Mix the lemon juice with the onion and parsley. The butter can now be beaten in. This will spread the flavours throughout and turn the colour to green. Season with salt and pepper.

Now spoon on to a square of cling film and roll into a cylinder shape. The green butter can be refrigerated or frozen (this will keep for up to 3 months) until needed.

When serving, just unwrap and cut into slices to sit on top of the fish.

Note: The onion juices can be replaced by finely chopping ½ a medium onion and cooking, without colouring, to a soft stage. Now just blitz to a purée before adding.
Green lemon butter also eats very well with chicken, pork, veal and vegetarian dishes.

Basic Butter Sauce ⓥ

This sauce is better known among chefs as *beurre blanc*. It is a very simple and very buttery sauce that works with many dishes, whether they're fish, meat or vegetarian. The basic ingredients are, normally, white-wine vinegar, water, chopped shallots and butter. I have added a few more ingredients to this recipe to add a lot more flavour. I have also given four 'stocks' as alternatives, starting with water and running through fish, chicken and vegetarian. It will really depend on which dish you are serving the sauce with. Two alternative ideas for flavourings follow the basic recipe.

100 g (4 oz) butter, chilled and cubed
1 shallot or ½ small onion, finely chopped
1 bay leaf
½ star anise (optional)
2 cardamom pods (optional)
2 tablespoons white-wine vinegar
4 tablespoons white wine
6 tablespoons water or *Chicken Stock*, *Fish Stock*
    or *Vegetable Stock* (page 33, 35 or 36)
    or alternative (page 11)
2 tablespoons single cream
Salt and pepper

Melt a small knob of the butter and add the shallot or onion and bay leaf, and, if using, star anise and cardamom pods, and a twist of black pepper. Cook for a few minutes, without letting the vegetables colour, until softened. Add the vinegar and reduce by three-quarters. Add the wine and reduce by three-quarters. Pour in the water or stock of your choice and reduce again by half. Add the single cream to help emulsify the butter.

Bring the reduction to a simmer and whisk in the remaining butter, a few pieces at a time. Season with salt and pepper and strain through a sieve. If the sauce is too thick, loosen it with a few drops of water or lemon juice. The basic butter sauce is now ready to use.

Note: For a soft, creamy, frothy finish, simply blitz with an electric hand blender.

Coriander Butter Sauce ⓥ

1 quantity *Basic Butter Sauce* (page 52)
½ bunch of fresh coriander
½ teaspoon lightly crushed coriander seeds

Reserve a quarter of the coriander leaves for chopping and adding to the finished sauce. Roughly chop the remaining leaves and stalks and add to the basic butter-sauce reduction with the crushed coriander seeds. Once the sauce has been cooked and strained, add the chopped coriander just before serving.

Mustard Butter Sauce ⓥ

1 quantity *Basic Butter Sauce* (page 52)
1 tablespoon wholegrain mustard

Warm the butter sauce and then add the mustard. I like the sauce to have a fairly strong flavour, and 1 tablespoon of wholegrain mustard will give you just that. Add more if you prefer a stronger flavour.

See also

Curry Cream Sauce (page 393)
Grilled or Pan-fried Dover Sole (page 141)
Horseradish Sauce (page 55)
Mint Sauce (page 55)
Radish and French Bean Salad with Seared Scallops (page 109)
Whole Roast Sea Bass (page 160)

Herbs

Herbs can be used to influence so many flavours in a dish and to add their own. Originally many flavours were taken from plants we recognize today but which we certainly wouldn't eat. In prehistoric times, for example, a variety of native wild plants would have been used as herbs to add different flavours to foods. An onion-garlic flavour could be obtained from the leaves and shoots of hedge garlic or garlic mustard, along with the leaves and bulbs of wild garlic (ramsoms). A peppery flavour came from the wall pepper (*Sedum acre* or biting stonecrop), watercress and lady's smock (a meadow flower), a vinegary, lemony tang from sorrel, and a nutmeg-cinnamon bitterness from all parts of the tansy (a pretty plant, with a flavour that wouldn't be considered so pleasant today).

How things changed (as with so many things) when the Romans arrived, for it is believed they brought with them some 200 varieties of herb native to the Mediterranean. They would plant gardens with whatever seeds were needed, both as medicine and food flavouring. Many hardy herbs, such as dill and fennel, became naturalized, growing as escapees along the coastlines and near to houses and towns. I'm sure you've often found many herbs growing along the ancient roadsides of Britain, probably marking the routes taken by the Roman legions. These herbs include chervil, dill, fennel, rue (an aromatic and bitter perennial herb, used mainly in medicine), sage, savory (a spicy herb used in slow-cooking dishes), marjoram, lemon balm (a strongly perfumed, lemon flavour), borage (with its mild, cucumber-like flavour), hyssop (with a minty but bitter flavour, used in the making of Chartreuse), lavender, mint, parsley, rosemary and thyme. During the 400 or so years of Roman occupation, these herbs were used both in cooking and medicine, and remain familiar to this day here in Britain.

After the establishment of the Christian church, herbs were grown mainly by monks. They would have been the 'conventional' healers of the day, practising medicine from their infirmaries. But throughout the Middle Ages herbs were also grown, by rich and poor, for medicinal purposes and for use in cooking. Many early pottages (soups) were flavoured with two of today's favourite herbs – parsley and sage. Also many other herbs we now consider to be weeds, such as chickenweed (a common annual herb), nettles and easterledge (or bistort, a tannin-rich perennial plant of the knotweed family), were used not only in pottages but also in salads to purify the blood. These were particularly welcome in the early spring after a winter of eating nothing but dried and salted foods.

By Tudor times, the poet and chronicler Thomas Tusser wrote that no kitchen garden was complete unless it grew at least 40 herb varieties. Herbs were used in many ways other than the culinary. The strongest, most aromatic and antiseptic were mixed with the reeds and rushes strewn across the floor to keep rooms smelling sweet and to keep illness at bay. Many other herbs were used to flavour ales, wines, teas, scents, aromatic posies, pomanders (which consisted of aromatic substances to protect against disease) and cosmetics, and were even included in insect repellants and furniture polish.

Herbs were still being used in sauces and soups, and also in forcemeats for poultry or stuffings for beef or veal olives. Often the herbs used would have sour and strong flavours – tansy or rue, for instance – which had the strength to disguise off flavours or lift tasteless, insipid ones. Horseradish, previously used as a medicine, began to be appreciated as a condiment in the early seventeenth century, and was served with fish as well as meat, something we've continued to do – offering it with smoked salmon or our Great British classic, roast beef.

The medicinal and culinary uses of herbs reached their climax in Europe during the sixteenth and seventeenth centuries. The discovery of America and many more world explorations led to a huge interest in new plants. More people took to growing medicinal herbs themselves, particularly once the infirmaries of the monks no longer existed. The wealthy always preferred herbs of Mediterranean origin, and these were described in seventeenth-century French cookery books as 'sweet' or 'fine' (French cuisine had begun to have considerable influence on English cookery). The 'faggot of sweet herbs' (our modern bouquet garni) is said to have been adopted by English cooks at this time, along with many other flavourings that have become traditional in our cooking.

The use of herbs declined in Britain during the eighteenth and nineteenth centuries because of the

Industrial Revolution. As people were obliged to move from the countryside to the towns, the growing of herbs dwindled, along with many other traditions. From the mid nineteenth century onwards, the only herbs commonly used were the famous four, the 'parsley, sage, rosemary and thyme' of the folksong 'Scarborough Fair'.

I like to think that the new British style of cooking, and the new Great British classics in this book, will reintroduce us to some of the wonderful flavours there are in herbs. Over the last twenty years, herbs have become very fashionable, appearing in many, often too many, daily dishes. Before adding a herb to a sauce, dressing or stuffing, its full potential flavour should be understood and appreciated. Quite often, I feel, sadly, that its addition is purely to make use of its rich, usually green, colour. Remember when flavouring a sauce or oil with a herb, that it's to infuse, not to *confuse*.

Horseradish Sauce Ⓥ

Native to west and south-east Asia, horseradish is a root with quite an ancient history. It was very popular with the Egyptians and Romans, as both cultures always enjoyed and appreciated strong flavours. The hot taste was first offered from its extracted juice. Over the years the white grated root has been used instead.

Horseradish is easily recognizable – a large thick root with an outer skin of a deep yellow/bronze colour, white, hot flesh sitting underneath and a central core which is inedible and very tough. If refrigerated, the root keeps for many weeks; it also freezes well.

The strange name came about, according to Jane Grigson, because of a misspelling. The Germans, who loved the plant, called it *Meerettich*, 'sea root', because it came from across the sea. The British adopted and adapted the name, but mistakenly using the word *Mähre*, or 'mare', which sounds the same as *Meer*, thus 'horse'.

Horseradish sauce eats very well not only with beef but also with ox tongue, terrines and some fish dishes. The whipping cream used in this recipe can be replaced with crème fraîche or equal quantities of crème fraîche and natural yoghurt. Lemon juice can also replace the vinegar.

50 g (2 oz) fresh horseradish, finely grated
1 teaspoon Dijon or English mustard
1 tablespoon white-wine vinegar
1 teaspoon caster sugar
150 ml (¼ pint) whipping cream
Pinch of salt

Place all of the ingredients in a bowl and whisk together to a soft-peak consistency. The sauce is best served chilled.

Note: Using English mustard will give a hotter finish to the sauce. Dijon is slightly milder. To calm the sauce even more, omit the vinegar, replacing it with a squeeze of lemon juice and a pinch more sugar. For a slight oniony flavour, add chopped chives, especially if using crème fraîche.

Another version of this sauce can be made with part mayonnaise (page 49 or bought). This gives the sauce a good depth and also turns it into a horseradish dip that can be served with many more dishes. Follow the above quantities for *Horseradish Sauce* and stir in 2 tablespoons of mayonnaise. Add a teaspoon of English mustard with the juice of ½ lemon. Pour in 100–150 ml (3½ fl oz– ¼ pint) of whipping cream and stir to a sauce consistency.

Mint Sauce Ⓥ

One of the most famous medieval sauces was 'green sauce', which pounded together parsley, sage, a couple of mints perhaps, garlic, pepper and salt, plus breadcrumbs, vinegar or ale. This was the recommended accompaniment to fish. Often the mixture was even simpler, a herb mixed with vinegar and perhaps some sugar, and our present-day mint sauce to accompany lamb is a direct descendant of this. The association between lamb and mint is a reflection of the medieval belief that an animal's best accompaniment or 'tracklement' was a plant that it ate or that grew near where it grazed.

This is probably the easiest recipe in the book. The quantity here is more than you need for one lamb meal, but the vinegar is a preservative, so keep the jar chilled and it will last indefinitely. Apart from using this as a straight mint sauce, I also use it as an enhancer for gravies and other sauces. A teaspoon in a lamb stew or the gravy for a lamb roast will lift all the flavours.

ABOVE
Sage Broad Beans with Bacon and Tomato

150 ml (¼ pint) malt vinegar
Small bunch of fresh mint
1½–2 heaped tablespoons demerara sugar
Fresh mint leaves, chopped

The mint for the sauce needn't be picked or chopped, just left as it is.

Pour the vinegar on to the mint in a small pan. Add the demerara sugar. Using 2 tablespoons will make the sauce sweeter, which some tastebuds prefer. Simply bring to the boil and cook for a few minutes until the sugar has dissolved. Leave to cool. Once cool, it's best to leave all the mint leaves in and simply bottle or jar. This will then increase the mint flavour. In time the mint will completely discolour; this is only due to the acidity of the vinegar.

To finish the mint sauce, strain some of the vinegar through a tea strainer and add chopped fresh mint.

Sage Broad Beans with Bacon and Tomato

Sage is a herb that has always been popular in Britain, particularly in stuffings. The use of sage in stuffings dates from the seventeenth century, when Sir Kenelm Digby, a diplomat, writer and amateur man of science, proposed that a simple sage and onion stuffing would be better for wild duck than the complicated, rich stuffings common until then. His suggestion became widely accepted, the mixture being used thereafter – and up to today – for duck, turkey (see page 327) and pork.

Here I've used sage in a dish that lends itself to so many others. The sage butter flavour, helped along by tomato, makes the broad beans the perfect accompaniment to just about any lamb dish (or chicken, beef, veal, pork and game). For a good simple roast leg of lamb in search of a tasty garnish, this is it.

The best bacon for this is *Preserved (Confit) Bacon* (page 192); this has just the right texture once warmed. Or buy a piece of ham and cut into 5 mm (¼ in) dice.

100 g (4 oz) *Preserved (Confit) Bacon* (page 192)
    or bought cooked ham, diced
2–3 large tomatoes, blanched and skinned
1 teaspoon chopped fresh sage
50 g (2 oz) unsalted butter, at room temperature
350–450 g (12 oz–1 lb) broad beans, cooked and
    picked (skinned) (page 96)
Squeeze of lemon juice (optional)
Salt and pepper

It's best to warm the bacon/ham in a few tablespoons of water or stock. Simply warm gently on a low heat. This will totally soften the texture. The tomatoes, once skinned, need to be cut into 1 cm (½ in) cubes.

Mix the chopped sage with the butter. This can be made in larger quantities and then frozen, using whatever is needed, whenever needed.

Once mixed, it's best to let the butter at least set in the fridge. When added to the beans, the cold butter emulsifies with the liquor, creating an almost butter-sauce consistency. If too warm, it will simply melt like butter and the oils will separate from the solids.

Take 2–3 tablespoons of water or liquor from the bacon warming and place in a saucepan (a wok works very well with this dish). Add the broad beans and re-heat/steam for 2–3 minutes. Once hot, add the bacon dice, drained from their liquor. Stir gently before adding the tomatoes.

The butter can now be added, warming and stirring into the mix. Season with salt and pepper. The beans are ready. To lift the butter flavour, a small squeeze of lemon juice can be added just before serving.

Stuffed Herrings with Apples and Tarragon

Tarragon is a herb probably more used in French cookery than British, but it can lend its unique flavour to so many of our best-loved dishes – to chicken, to omelettes, to mushrooms, fish, sauces and salad dressings (see page 50). Here, I'm using it, along with the slight acidity of apples, in a stuffing for oily herring, a fish that has long been a British favourite, both fresh and smoked. To add extra spice, there is a touch of horseradish too. This is not essential, but does lift the dish.

I am also using pig's caul in this recipe, again not essential, but it does guarantee that the fish is held together. An alternative is to wrap the herrings in buttered foil and bake them, before finishing under a hot grill. Another important point to remember, making the fish more enjoyable to eat, is to remove as many of the fine bones as possible from the flesh itself. This can be achieved quite easily using pliers or tweezers.

Creamy *Mashed Potatoes* (page 124) and watercress salad will eat very well with this dish.

50 g (2 oz) unsalted butter
1 onion, finely chopped
1 teaspoon chopped fresh tarragon
½–1 teaspoon horseradish cream (optional)
4 apples, peeled, cored and cut into 1 cm (½ in)
    dice
50 g (2 oz) fresh white breadcrumbs
4 herrings, cleaned and filleted, with pin bones
    removed (page 11)
100–175 g (4–6 oz) pig's caul, soaked in water
    overnight (page 11) (optional)
1 dessertspoon vegetable oil
1 tablespoon plain flour
Salt and pepper
Lemon slices and watercress, to garnish

Pre-heat the oven to 190°C/375°F/Gas Mark 5.

Melt 25 g (1 oz) of the butter in a frying-pan and fry the onion for a few minutes, until softened but not browned. Add the tarragon and apples and fry for a few minutes. The horseradish cream, if using, can now be added. Mix in the white breadcrumbs and season to taste. Stir the mixture thoroughly. Remove from the heat and allow to cool.

Divide the mixture into four and place on top of four of the fillets. Cover with the remaining four fillets. Squeeze any excess water from the pig's caul, if using, and cut into four. Wrap the pig's caul, or buttered foil, around the herring parcels.

On the stove-top, heat the remaining butter and the oil in a roasting pan. Add the herring parcels, dust with flour and fry until golden. Transfer to the oven and cook for 10–12 minutes. To serve, spoon over the juices, and garnish with lemon slices and watercress.

Lemon and Thyme Dumplings

Dumplings have a long history dating back to the one-pot cooking days, when a ball of flour and fat plus some flavourings, usually herbs, were dropped into the pot along with the boiling meat or vegetable pottage. Not only did dumplings make the meal go further, but they also added considerable nutritional value and flavour – as would these dumplings to a roast chicken for Sunday lunch, to boiled bacon, and many of the braised beef or lamb dishes. So next time you are making a stew, try these.

SERVES 4

100 g (4 oz) fresh veal bone marrow for
     the best flavour, or shredded suet
100 g (4 oz) white breadcrumbs
2 tablespoons double cream
3 egg yolks
Pinch of freshly grated nutmeg
1 heaped teaspoon chopped fresh thyme
Finely grated zest and juice of 1 lemon
Salt and pepper
Chicken Stock (page 33) or water, for cooking

Mix all the ingredients together, except for the stock or water, and season to taste with salt and pepper. Shape into four large or eight small ovals between 2 tablespoons, or roll into balls. Drop these into the simmering stock or water and cook for 10–15 minutes, depending on the size. Any excess dumpling mix can be left refrigerated and used for another dish.

Sage Fritters ⓥ

Most pork dishes and many lamb and poultry ones work well with sage.

These sage fritters can be made by two methods. The first is coated and fried in a beer batter for a complete souffléd finish. The second is simply coated in milk and flour for a thinner but still crisp finish.

MINIMUM OF 6 PORTIONS

3–4 sage leaves per portion
Cooking oil, for deep-frying
100 g (4 oz) self-raising flour
150 ml (¼ pint) lager
Salt

Heat the oil to 180°C/350°F. Lightly coat each leaf in the flour. Whisk the remaining flour with the lager. Dip the leaves into the batter and carefully place in the oil. (The oil needs to be at least 2 cm/¾ in deep.) These will now just take a few minutes to become golden and souffléd. Turn over and complete the cooking.

Once completely golden, lift from the oil and season with salt. Place on the finished main-course plates.

For flour and milk frying, simply dip the leaves in milk and then into flour. Now deep-fry until golden. Remove from the fat and season with salt. These can now also be used to garnish the finished plate.

Both varieties can be fried 10 minutes before serving; they will keep their crisp finish.

BELOW
Lemon and Parsley Carrots

Lemon and Parsley Carrots Ⓥ

Lemon works very well with carrots. The natural sweetness of the vegetables, especially if you've found some babies, is delicious with the wonderful lemon acidity, but is also helped by a good pinch of sugar, which lifts all the flavours.

Parsley has been a favourite herb for the British since medieval times, when it was used as a major ingredient in a green sauce (more like today's salsa), served mostly with the fish eaten on non-meat days. It's delicious with vegetables as well, and I'm using the Continental flat variety here, which holds more flavour than the curly. Instead of chopping it, which it too works well with flat parsley – bruising as it cuts – I'm merely tearing it into pieces.

SERVES 4

450 g (1 lb) carrots, preferably baby, peeled (if using baby carrots, it's nice to leave 1 cm/½ in of stalk on top, as this gives a new colour to the dish)
1 teaspoon sugar
25 g (1 oz) butter
juice of ½ lemon, possibly the whole fruit if not very juicy
Salt and pepper
Few sprigs of fresh Continental flatleaf parsley, picked and torn

If baby carrots are not available, larger ones can be sliced 5 mm (¼ in) thick or cut into matchsticks. Baby vegetables can be split lengthways.

Whatever carrots are being used, barely cover with water. Add a pinch of salt, the sugar and half the butter and cover with a butter paper (wrapping from blocks of butter) or greaseproof paper. Bring to the simmer and cook until the carrots are just tender. This will take anything from 3 to 10 minutes, depending on size. Once tender, use a slotted spoon to remove the carrots and keep to one side.

Now bring the cooking liquor to the boil and reduce by three-quarters. This should now be approaching a syrup consistency. Add the lemon juice and increase the heat to a simmer for another minute. Check the flavour: a sweet lemony carrot, almost butter sauce, is what you should have. Return the carrots to the pan and re-heat in the sauce. Season with salt and pepper. Add the remaining butter. The carrots are now lemon glazed and waiting for the addition of torn parsley. Sprinkle and stir. The carrots are ready to serve.

See also

Calves' Liver Steak and Kidney, with Red-wine Carrots and Rosemary Butter (page 218)
Chicken Fillet 'Steaks' with Chestnut Mushrooms, Sage and Lemon Sauce (page 248)
Coriander Butter Sauce (page 53)
Grilled Lamb with 'Irish' Cabbage and Mashed Potato Sauce (page 187)
Parsleyed Cod with Mustard Butter Sauce (page 168)
Slow-roast Shoulder of Pork with Pearl Barley and Sage 'Stuffing' (page 209)
Spicy Tomato and Mint Relish (page 381)

Cheese and Eggs

Cheese and eggs are two very basic foods that have been with us for thousands of years. When primitive man settled down, one of his first tasks was to domesticate animals for food use. Among them were the ancestors of today's cows, sheep, goats and chickens, producing milk and eggs that became major foods. The milk would probably have soured fairly quickly, so much of it would have been 'eaten' as curds and whey – and this is how the idea for making cheese from soured milk was born.

Collops, or slices, of bacon with a cooked new-laid egg would have been a rare and special meal – a combination that still lives with us now as part of our Great British Breakfast.

In the Middle Ages, 'white meats' – as milk, milk products and eggs were known – were the daily basic food of the wealthier peasants. The family who had a cow, a pig and a couple of hens or geese would have enough to keep them going. The cow alone could provide milk, curds, whey (thought very nourishing), cheese, butter, soured milk and buttermilk. The pig would be killed in the autumn and salted to supply meat throughout the winter. Collops, or slices, of bacon with a cooked new-laid egg would have been a rare and special meal – a combination that still lives with us now as part of our Great British Breakfast.

These foods were also enjoyed by the rich, but had less importance in their diet, as meat was the main feature. For both the rich and the peasantry, though, cheese and eggs would have been useful foods on the many religious fast days, although eggs as well as meat were forbidden during Lent. A variety of cooking methods was soon found for eggs, with roasting in their shells in the ashes of a wood fire becoming one of the first. Next followed the basics, boiled, and fried in butter or lard. In the early fifteenth century, eggs were made into an early version of scrambled eggs, the predecessor in England of the French omelette. 'Herbolace' was a mixture of eggs and herbs, often enriched with cheese, while 'tansy' was a mixture of raw eggs flavoured with the sour juice of tansy leaves. Both were turned over heat to make a scrambled-type mixture. Eggs were also used, mostly by the wealthy, to make pancakes, fritters, nourishing caudles (drinks) and as a good base ingredient for pastry tart fillings.

Cheese was developed in a number of forms and textures during medieval times, the main ones being soft, hard, and new or 'green'. The soft would have resembled our cream cheese, the hard was a Cheddar type, made from renneted milk and firmed by pressing, and the green was a very new soft cheese. The richer and more digestible soft cheeses would have been eaten by the wealthy. The hard cheese was a fairly cheap food, which soon became a feature of the poorer man's diet. His everyday meal of bread and cheese has come down to us virtually unchanged, as the ploughman's lunch that appears on just about every pub menu.

It wasn't until the late seventeenth century, though, that the different types of local cheeses that had evolved became known to the majority of people. The fact the cheeses from the West Country were different from those in the north was only known to people who might have encountered them in their travels, or who could afford to have them brought to them. When road, sea and canal transport improved, perishable goods such as cheeses could be appreciated across the country. By the end of the century, cheese names famous today, such as Stilton,

PAGE 60
Macaroni, Artichoke and Mushroom Cheese Pie (page 64)

Gloucester, Cheddar and Wiltshire, had become familiar to many. It is interesting, too, that many foreign cheeses were known as well, at least to those in the larger cities. As early as 1577 Parmesan was highly praised, followed by Dutch and Norman cheeses, with English last.

Nearer our own time, both eggs and cheese remained important features of the diet, although cheese was slightly looked down upon because of its association with the working classes. Mrs Beeton herself, although giving many 'receipts' or recipes for cheese dishes, wrote: '… cheese, in its commonest shape, is only fit for sedentary people, as an after-dinner stimulant, and in very small quantity. Bread and cheese, as a meal, is only fit for soldiers on march or labourers in the open air, who like it because it "holds the stomach a long time".' Mrs Gaskell, in her novel *Wives and Daughters*, gently mocked the pretensions of Mrs Kirkpatrick, just before she remarried; on being told by his daughter that her husband-to-be, Dr Gibson, ate toasted cheese, she declared, 'Oh! but my dear, we must change all that. I shouldn't like to think of your father's eating cheese; it's such a strong-smelling, coarse kind of thing. We must get him a cook who can toss him up an omelette, or something elegant.' How about a perfectly cooked cheese omelette? Now that sounds very elegant to me.

In the nineteenth century, cheese – despite its coarse and indigestible reputation – was eaten mostly after dinner as a separate course, or as a savoury such as a rabbit (or rarebit, page 178). In the last twenty years, however, English cheeses have improved and moved on vastly. We may not have the variety of France, but we do have the flavours and textures, providing us with quality cheeses I feel can stand up to those of almost any other country.

Eggs gained a new pride of place in the first meal of the day at this time. Having been used very generously in sweet puddings and pies – especially after the raising power of egg whites was recognized – they became a special and unique part of the Victorian breakfast. No breakfast sideboard was complete without a little dish of boiled eggs, or a special warmer containing fried, scrambled or buttered eggs. It's eggs we have to thank for helping us develop so many dishes, whether savoury or sweet. They hold textures and flavours together, lending the silky finish of the yolk and the strength of the white to almost all other ingredients. This chapter gives you some recipes to start with, but you'll find plenty more along the way.

> It's eggs we have to thank for helping us develop so many dishes, whether savoury or sweet. They hold textures and flavours together, lending the silky finish of the yolk and the strength of the white to almost all other ingredients.

Macaroni, Artichoke and Mushroom Cheese Pie Ⓥ

Macaroni, originally known as 'macrows', was introduced to Britain from Italy in the fourteenth century. It was not until the eighteenth century, though, that the idea of toasted grated cheese was allied with vegetables and, by extension, macaroni. The macaroni was boiled, then drained and tossed in cream before being sprinkled with cheese and browned. It became a very popular supper dish in Victorian times – and is still delicious.

This vegetarian recipe takes it a bit further. The flavour and texture are extended by the addition of artichokes and mushrooms, and the whole dish is served in a pastry case – hence the name 'pie'. I've given a recipe for cooking artichokes (page 96), but if this all seems too much, then simply use tinned (many can be found in good delicatessens), or just add extra mushrooms (wild for real extravagance). I'm also using two cheese sauces. This, again, is not essential, but the classic cheese or Mornay is there to create the glaze. If just using the Parmesan cream sauce, then top with either grated Cheddar or Parmesan to give the melted finish.

SERVES 4 AS A MAIN COURSE

450 g (1 lb) *Quick Puff* or *Flaky Pastry* or *Shortcrust Pastry*, rolled 2 mm thick (page 365 or 364)
2 medium-sized globe artichokes, cooked (page 96) or 200 g (7 oz) tinned artichoke hearts
Butter
100 g (4 oz) chestnut or button mushrooms, quartered
150 g (5 oz) macaroni, cooked (follow instructions on the packet)
Salt and pepper

For the Mornay Sauce

Cheese Sauce (page 46); reduce quantities to make only ⅓ of the total amount
2 egg yolks or 150 ml (¼ pint) *Simple Hollandaise Sauce* (page 41)
2 heaped tablespoons whipped cream

For the Parmesan Cheese Sauce

300 ml (½ pint) double cream
75 g (3 oz) Parmesan cheese (preferably fresh), grated
2 tablespoons crème fraîche
Squeeze of lemon juice

Pre-heat the oven to 200°C/400°F/Gas Mark 6.

The metal pastry rings I use for this recipe are 10 cm (4 in) in diameter and 6 cm (2½ in) high. If these are unavailable, substitute with mini 10 cm (4 in) flan rings, sitting them one on top of another to get the same depth. The rings should first be buttered. Sit them on a greaseproof-paper-lined baking tray. Roll out the pastry and cut out four 10 cm (4 in) circles. Sit one in the base of each ring. Roll the remaining pastry and cut into strips wide enough to line the sides of the rings. Once in place, press the pastry along the bottom edge, so that it makes a good seal with the base, and then all the way around the sides, so that it comes a little above the ring. Line each mould with greaseproof paper or foil and fill with baking beans or rice. Leave to rest in the fridge for 20 minutes.

Bake the pastry cases blind for 15–20 minutes, cooking them to a light golden colour. This will guarantee a crisp finish.

To make the Parmesan cheese sauce, bring the double cream to the boil. Whisk in the Parmesan cheese and crème fraîche, reducing the heat. Add lemon juice to taste, some salt and pepper, and the sauce is now ready to use.

To finish the dish, warm the pie cases in a medium oven. Cut each cooked artichoke into 8 or 12 pieces. Melt a knob of butter in a frying-pan and fry the mushrooms to a golden brown. Add the artichokes and gently fry. The warm macaroni can now also be added, seasoning all with salt and pepper. Remove from the heat and bind with the Parmesan cheese sauce. This can now be divided between the pie cases.

To finish the Mornay sauce, once the pies are ready, either add the egg yolks or the quantity of hollandaise sauce, and gently fold in the softly whipped cream. To check for the perfect golden glaze, spoon a little onto a tray and colour under the grill. Add a tablespoon or so more cream if it doesn't glaze properly.

Spoon the finished Mornay sauce on top of each pie and place under a hot grill, colouring to a rich golden glaze. These wonderfully rich macaroni cheese, artichoke and mushroom pies are now ready to serve.

Note: These pies eat particularly well with a tossed green salad flavoured with *Basic Vinaigrette* (page 50), with the addition of tiny sliced red onions, watercress and chopped walnuts.

One to two tablespoons of cooked spinach can be placed in the bottom of each pastry case to create another flavour and texture in the complete dish.

Steamed Leek and Cheddar-cheese Pudding ⓥ

This is a vegetarian answer to steak and kidney pudding. It has the very rich flavours and the lovely puddingy texture. I've kept this one quite simple, with just the two main flavours of the early pottage vegetable, leek, and the very British Cheddar cheese. But the dish is also a reflection of the old English dumpling tradition which, I'm glad to say, still lives on. The dumpling has taken on many more roles, starting as a simple meal extender, moving on to an accompaniment and now, as here, a dish that will stand on its own.

Lots more ingredients can be added – mushrooms, sweet peppers, onions and so on. I also include a cream sauce that is quick and easy to make. It can be left 'plain' or finished with grated Parmesan for cheese sauce, or English or Dijon mustard for a mustard sauce.

SERVES 4

225 g (8 oz) leeks, sliced
225 g (8 oz) self-raising flour
½ teaspoon salt
100 g (4 oz) vegetarian suet
175 g (6 oz) Cheddar cheese, grated (extra can be placed in the centre of the pudding for a gooey middle)
About 150 ml (¼ pint) water
Black pepper

For the Cream Sauce

4 tablespoons double cream
4 tablespoons crème fraîche
50 g (2 oz) unsalted butter
1–2 tablespoons finely grated Parmesan cheese or 1–2 teaspoons English or Dijon mustard
1 tablespoon water
Salt and pepper

The leeks should first be blanched in boiling, salted water for just 30 seconds–1 minute. Once blanched, drain from the water and allow to cool naturally on a kitchen cloth or tea towel.

Sift together the flour and salt. Add the suet, cheese and a good twist of pepper. Mix well together. Add the leeks and enough water to give a soft dough texture.

Butter and lightly flour a 1.2 litre (2 pint) pudding basin and fill with the pudding mixture. Press down and cover with buttered foil, pleated to allow for expansion. The pudding can now be placed in a steamer in a covered pan, or stood on a trivet, and steamed for 1½–1¾ hours, until firm to the touch. Keep checking the water level to make sure it doesn't boil dry.

Meanwhile, make the sauce. Place the double cream, crème fraîche and butter in a small saucepan. Bring to the boil, whisking continuously. Sprinkle in the cheese, if using, and also whisk in. Remove from the heat and season with salt and pepper. The cheese sauce is ready. If too thick, add the water.

Repeat the same process for mustard sauce, adding a quantity to suit your taste buds.

Once the pudding is cooked, remove the foil and turn out; the pudding is ready to enjoy. Extra grated Cheddar cheese can be sprinkled on top and gratinated under a pre-heated grill.

Pressed Tomato Cake with Peppered Goat's Cheese

Although it was viewed with suspicion for hundreds of years, the tomato has become one of the most popular fruit/vegetables in the country, particularly when used in soups and ketchup. Here, I've brought together tomatoes and cheese – goat's cheese would have been much more common in the past – in a dish that makes a wonderful starter or main course. The flavour of the home-made tomato ketchup gives a good, strong lift to the finished dish. It's not essential to use the ketchup, but the flavour is so powerful that it's worth the time. (The other bonus is having the rest to eat with lots of other dishes; you won't want to buy it again.) All the flavours marry so well: the tomatoes, cheese and shallots make a classic combination, but one that gives you a totally different finish.

You will need four 8 × 5 cm (3 × 2 in) metal cooking rings.

SERVES 4 AS A STARTER

For the Cakes

12 ripe tomatoes, preferably plum, blanched and skinned, with 'eye' removed
6–8 tablespoons *Home-made Tomato Ketchup* (page 49)
Salt and pepper

For the Goat's Cheese

200–225 g (7–8 oz) soft goat's cheese, rind removed
100–150 ml (3½ fl oz– ¼ pint) whipping cream
1 teaspoon freshly ground black pepper
Squeeze of lemon juice

For the Dressing and Garnish

6 tablespoons olive oil
1 teaspoon Dijon mustard
Squeeze of lemon juice
2 teaspoons chopped fresh flatleaf parsley
4 large shallots, cut into rings, to garnish

Quarter the tomatoes, discarding the seeds. The tomato quarters can now be seasoned with salt and pepper, before being layered in the rings. After each layer has been placed in the ring, spread with a coffeespoon of tomato ketchup before adding the next layer. Once all the rings have been filled, cover with cling film and press with a baking tray and weight. These are best left refrigerated for several hours.

Beat the goat's cheese until softened. Add the whipping cream and black pepper and mix to a smooth, peppery paste. Add a good pinch of salt, along with the lemon juice. Both of these flavours will lift the complete taste of the cheese and pepper. The mix needs to be soft enough to be piped. The peppered goat's cheese is now ready to use. This can be made several hours in advance, along with the tomato cakes. When needed, just remove from the fridge and allow to soften.

BELOW
Pressed Tomato Cake with Peppered Goat's Cheese

To make the dressing, whisk all the ingredients together, except for the shallots, checking for seasoning with salt and pepper. More Dijon mustard can be added for a 'hotter' and richer finish.

The tomato cakes will simply push from the rings. Place the cakes in the centre of your plates, and garnish with shallot rings around the outside.

The best way to serve the goat's cheese cream is to pipe it from a plain 1 cm (½ in) tube and bag on top of the cakes. If you do not have a piping bag and tube, then simply shape the mixture between spoons, to make quenelles, and sit them on top.

To finish, spoon the mustard and parsley dressing over and around.

Cherry tomatoes with peppered goat's cheese

The above recipe can also be used to make 35–40 canapés. This variation is a lot easier because it uses cherry tomatoes rather than cakes. Simply cut the base of the tomatoes and spoon out all the seeds. Now just pipe in the cheese, leaving a 'spiked' finish. Just before serving, finish with a trickle of dressing. The tasty canapés are ready to serve.

Apple and Blue Cheese Tart Ⓥ

Apple pie is a Great British classic, popular all over the country. Apparently, apples used to be sent up north from Kent – the Garden of England from very early days – on the coal barges, because they loved their apple pie in Yorkshire and other northern counties. There they would serve the pie with cheese, and this recipe is an adaptation of that idea. You can use the classic Stilton, as here, or a Wensleydale, or even the Irish Cashel Blue.

It's made in the classic French *tarte tatin* style. Basically, it's just a matter of pan-frying and caramelizing the apple halves before covering them with puff pastry, baking and then glazing with a blue cheese. It's a great savoury dessert, something to suit everybody. But you could also eat it for lunch, or at a picnic, perfect with a basic green-leaf salad and a spoonful of crème fraîche or soured cream.

SERVES 4

25 g (1 oz) butter
4 medium Granny Smith apples, peeled, cored and halved crossways through the middle
25 g (1 oz) caster sugar
225 g (8 oz) *Quick Puff* or *Flaky Pastry* (page 365), rolled into a 28 cm (11 in) diameter circle
120–150 g (4¾–5 oz) Stilton or other blue cheese, thinly sliced
Pepper

Pre-heat the oven to 220°C/425°F/Gas Mark 7.

Melt the butter in a 25 cm (10 in) frying-pan with an ovenproof handle, or in a flan ring. Add the apples, flat side down, and cook slowly on the stove for a few minutes, not allowing the butter to burn. Turn the apples over and continue to cook for another minute or two.

The apples can now be turned flat side down once more. Increase the heat. The apples will begin to colour and become a rich golden brown. Sprinkle over the caster sugar. Reduce the heat slightly and allow the sugar to caramelize in the pan onto the apples. It's at this point that you might need to add one or two *drops* of water to the pan. This will help the sugar to caramelize.

Remove the pan from the stove. Arrange the apple halves neatly in it and allow to cool. Once cold, sit the pastry disc on top. Place in the pre-heated oven and bake for 18–20 minutes, until the pastry is golden. Remove from the oven once cooked and allow to rest for 2–3 minutes before sitting a plate or serving dish on top and carefully turning the whole pan over.

The tart is now sitting on its presentation plate and ready for the cheese.

Place the thin blue cheese slices on top, just enough to cover, and place under a pre-heated grill. Allow the cheese to warm and begin to melt over the apples. Finish with a twist of pepper.

The Apple and Blue Cheese Tart is ready to eat and goes very well with a glass of port or red wine.

Cauliflower Cheese with Crispy Parmesan Crumbs ⓥ

Cheese began to be used as a topping for vegetables in the eighteenth century. The cardoon, a vegetable that's a very close relative of the globe artichoke and rarely seen in Britain now, was among the first to be treated in this way, the recipe coming from France, where it was known as *chardons à la fromage*. They were covered with Cheddar or Parmesan and coloured with a hot cheese iron or under a salamander (grill). The idea was soon adopted in England for the more familiar cauliflower, the original plain grated cheese topping soon becoming the popular and versatile white or cheese sauce.

Cauliflower cheese is one of my Great British schoolday favourites. I always considered it a treat to be eating that (probably lumpy) cheese sauce with the tender cauliflower. Good dishes will always live on and this one certainly has. The crispy Parmesan crumbs are an optional extra, but do give the dish another texture and flavour to be enjoyed.

The first question always asked is – which is the best cheese to use?

Well, we have probably all been used to making it with our good old, strong Cheddar, and why not? It's a cheese that gives a good result every time. However, Cheddar can be replaced with Gruyère and Parmesan. I call this 'Continental cauliflower cheese' – the three Cs. The flavours of Gruyère and Parmesan (I use equal quantities) together are quite powerful, so 50 g (2 oz) less cheese for the recipe will be plenty.

This dish is a perfect alternative for a vegetarian Sunday lunch.

SERVES 4

1 large cauliflower, divided into florets
Butter
Salt and pepper

For the Cheese Sauce

1 clove
1 bay leaf
1 small onion
600 ml (1 pint) milk
25 g (1 oz) butter

25 g (1 oz) plain flour
150 ml (¼ pint) single cream (optional)
1 teaspoon English mustard (optional)
175–200 g (6–7 oz) Cheddar cheese (or Gruyère with Parmesan), grated
Salt, pepper and freshly grated nutmeg

For the Crispy Parmesan Crumbs (optional)

4 slices of white bread, crusts removed
Butter
1 tablespoon grated Parmesan cheese, or more to taste
Salt and pepper

To make the sauce, first stud the clove through the bay leaf and into the onion. This can now be placed in a saucepan with the milk. Warm the milk slowly; this will allow the flavours of the onion to impregnate the milk. Once up to the simmer, cover with a lid and leave to stand for 15 minutes.

Now it's time to make the roux. Melt the butter in a suitable saucepan. Once melted, add the flour and cook on a low heat for a few minutes, stirring from time to time.

The milk can now be added, a ladle at a time. As the milk and roux are warming and cooking, the two will emulsify and can be stirred to a smooth 'béchamel' sauce. This can now be cooked, adding the onion from the milk, for approximately 20–25 minutes.

The sauce will now be quite thick. Remove the onion and season the sauce with salt, pepper and nutmeg. Add the single cream, if using. This will loosen the sauce slightly, giving it a richer finish as well. Add the mustard and 175 g (6 oz) of the grated Cheddar. Once completely melted into the sauce, re-taste for seasoning and strength. It's important that the sauce does not boil as this will separate the cheese. Strain through a sieve.

To cook the cauliflower florets, bring a pan of salted water to the boil. Drop in the cauliflower and return to a gentle boil. Cook until just tender; this will take only a few minutes, leaving a slight bite. Drain off the water. Warm a knob of butter in a frying-pan and add the florets. These can now be

ABOVE
Cauliflower Cheese with Crispy Parmesan Crumbs

rolled, without colouring, in the butter and seasoned with salt and pepper. The cauliflower can be cooked ahead of time and refreshed in ice water. To re-heat, either microwave or plunge back into boiling water.

To finish, pre-heat the oven to 200°C/ 400°F/Gas Mark 6 or pre-heat the grill. Spoon a little of the cheese sauce into an ovenproof dish, arrange the cauliflower on top and coat with more of the sauce. Sprinkle the last 25 g (1 oz) of grated Cheddar on top and place under the grill or in the oven to melt and colour for 10–15 minutes.

To make the Crispy Parmesan Crumbs, the bread can either be blitzed in a food processor or broken down (rubbed) into a rough crumb. The 'rough' basically means maintaining large and small sizes throughout. These crumbs can now be pan-fried in a knob of butter to a golden colour and crisp finish. Once at this stage, add the Parmesan cheese. This will now start to melt instantly, creating a sticky consistency among the crunchy crumbs. It's now that they should be sprinkled over the finished cauliflower dish.

All you have to do now is eat it. This is superb as a complete dish on its own, accompanied by a good tossed green salad.

Note: It's not essential to glaze the cauliflower cheese under the grill or in the oven – it can be served with just the cheese sauce over and Crispy Parmesan crumbs to finish.

It's also not essential to break the cauliflower into florets. The vegetable can be kept whole and boiled. This will take approximately 10–15 minutes, depending on the size of the cauliflower. Make sure the central core/stalk has been cut away. Once cooked, cut and serve as per the florets.

Cheddar-cheese Soup ⓥ

Cheddar cheese is a great British classic, the ultimate British farmhouse cheese. It was made in and around Somerset, and was the cheese tourists ate when they visited the Cheddar Gorge – so the name stuck. It was a farmer publishing an account of how his wife made her cheese in the mid nineteenth century that brought Cheddar cheese to the world.

The word spread, and his children took the recipe and the name to Denmark, Canada, Ireland, Scotland and Australia.

Mature Cheddar eats well on its own, or helps other textures and tastes, whether as a sauce or rarebit, or as an accompaniment to fruit and nuts.

This soup is extremely moreish: it's one of those you have a spoonful of and then just can't stop. This recipe is for a vegetarian version, but I also like to serve it with flakes of smoked haddock and a diced tomato (to remind you of the *Smoked Haddock with Welsh Rarebit*, page 163), or I add some cooked macaroni for a macaroni-cheese soup.

SERVES 4 AS A STARTER

Butter
2 onions, finely chopped
2 potatoes, cut into rough 1 cm (½ in) dice
1 litre (1¾ pints) *Vegetable Stock* (page 36)
125 ml (4 fl oz) double cream (optional)
150 g (5 oz) mature Cheddar cheese (or more
    if you prefer an extra-cheesy flavour),
    finely grated
English or Dijon mustard (optional)
Salt and pepper

Melt a knob of butter and cook the onions for a few minutes on a medium heat, without colouring. Add the diced potatoes and continue to cook, keeping a lid on the pan to create steam and prevent the potatoes from colouring. Cook for a few minutes. Add the vegetable stock and bring to the simmer. The soup can now be left to cook for 20–25 minutes, until the vegetables are soft.

Liquidize and push through a sieve for a smooth consistency.

Place back on a medium heat, add the double cream, if using, and bring to the simmer. The grated cheese can now be added, stirring in well. The cheese will thicken the soup, so it's best to grate and add only 100 g (4 oz) before checking the consistency and flavour. If you prefer it to be stronger in cheese taste, then grate and add more. It's important the soup is brought only to a good, warm simmer. If boiled, the cheese will begin to separate. Season with salt and pepper and the soup is ready.

To lift the flavour even more I like to add a touch of English or Dijon mustard – this will give an extra bite.

Variations

Here are a few alternatives to give the soup different flavours.

As mentioned in the introduction, cooking some macaroni to garnish the soup gives you macaroni-cheese soup.

A little of cooked leeks also sits very well dropped into any one of the variations.

Cook 100 g (4 oz) of natural smoked haddock in 125 ml (4 fl oz) of milk and a knob of butter. The milk and butter can be added to the soup, replacing or in addition to the double cream. The cooked haddock can now just be flaked and added, along with diced tomato flesh and/or the diced leeks.

The Great British Omelette Ⓥ

Omelettes have been known in Britain since the sixteenth century, and in France many centuries before that. The name derives from the Latin *lamella*, which means 'thin plate', and that's how the omelette was first cooked, almost in pancake fashion. In Britain it was first known as 'amulet'.

Making an omelette just involves the setting of eggs with an added flavouring of your choice. It's not really a cooking process, more of a 'warming' to thicken the egg, giving you a set, scrambled effect with a soft finish and no colour.

SERVES 1

2–3 eggs (3 small or 2 large)
Butter
Salt and pepper, preferably black

It is very important to have a good non-stick, 15 cm (6 in) omelette pan.

Warm the pan on the stove. While the pan is warming, crack the eggs into a bowl and whisk with a fork. It's very important not to season the eggs until the omelette is about to be made. If eggs are salted too early, they break down and become thin, runny and slightly discoloured, giving a dull look.

The omelette pan should now be hot enough to add a knob of butter. As the butter melts and becomes bubbly, season the eggs and pour them into the pan. They will now take only 3–4 minutes to cook. To make sure they're light, keep the eggs moving by shaking the pan and stirring the eggs with a fork. This prevents them from sticking and colouring. You will soon have a scrambled look to the eggs. Now cheese or any other flavouring can be added. Allow the eggs to set on the base for 5–10 seconds; the eggs will still be moist and not completely set in the centre. Holding the pan at a downward angle, slide and tap the omelette towards the edge, folding it over as you do so.

This can now be turned out on to a plate and shaped under a cloth to give a cigar shape. The omelette is now ready. It will have no colour but be filled with an almost soufflé texture. This makes it a dream to eat, just melting in your mouth.

Omelette Arnold Bennett Ⓥ

This omelette has its own history. Arnold Bennett, the famous novelist and theatre critic, was a frequent visitor to the Savoy Hotel Grill. In his great hotel novel *Imperial Palace*, published in 1930, Bennett based his fictional chef, Rocco, on Jean-Baptiste Virlogeux, then *chef de cuisine* at the Savoy Grill. In tribute, Virlogeux created this omelette, and Bennett is said to have ordered it on each and every visit to the restaurant. The dish itself has since been immortalized, a regular feature on the Savoy Grill menu and on many other restaurant menus too.

It's simply a smoked haddock and cheese omelette. In the original recipe, the haddock was poached, flaked and mixed with Parmesan cheese. The omelette was kept flat, the haddock sprinkled over, cream poured on top and then it was glazed under the grill. The method hasn't changed too much since then, but chefs of today take the classic idea and adapt it to suit their own style, me included. My version is a basic three-egg omelette topped with flakes of haddock and then glazed with a good cheese (Mornay) sauce flavoured with English mustard. To help the glaze, I'm adding some hollandaise sauce. This does add a bit too much extra work just for an omelette (worth every minute though). As a substitute, use an egg yolk folded in with lightly whipped cream. The glaze will still work.

Otherwise, the only difference is that I serve the omelette in the pan in which it was cooked. The pans being used are small, non-stick 10 × 2–3 cm (4 × ¾–1¼ in), or, alternatively, you can make 1 or 2 large omelettes using a 20 cm (8 in) pan and 6 eggs per large omelette.

The Mornay sauce is a basic milk, flour- and butter-based sauce, with the addition of good Cheddar cheese. This, I suggest, is made in a minimum quantity of 300 ml (½ pint). Any less and you will be chasing the sauce around the pan. Once made, as per the recipe, and before adding the cheese, measure the quantity required for this recipe. The remainder can be refrigerated for up to 1 week – for your next glazed omelette.

It's for this reason that I have listed 300 ml (½ pint) of milk to poach the haddock in. Once the fish is poached, the milk can be strained off and used to make the cheese sauce recipe, following the basic method. This does nothing but add extra flavour: the slight smokiness in the milk transfers to the sauce.

Once you've made and tried this dish (and you can even have it for breakfast), you'll know why someone would want to eat it on every visit to the Savoy. So here's my own homage to both Arnold Bennett and Jean-Baptiste Virlogeux.

MAKES 1–4 OMELETTES

225–300 g (8–10 oz) smoked haddock fillet
    (50–75 g/2–3 oz per portion)
300 ml (½ pint) milk
Butter

150 ml (¼ pint) *Cheese Sauce* (page 46), made with
    the haddock-poaching milk
2–3 tablespoons *Simple Hollandaise Sauce*
    (page 41) or 1 large egg yolk
5–6 tablespoons double cream, whipped
1–2 teaspoons English mustard
3 eggs per serving
Salt and pepper
1 tablespoon olive oil, mixed with a squeeze of
    lemon juice and seasoned to serve (optional)

Stage one is to poach the fish. Pre-heat the oven to 180°C/350°F/Gas Mark 4. Grease an ovenproof dish or saucepan. Lay the smoked haddock fillet in the dish, with the skin left on, and cover with the milk, adding a knob of butter. Cover with a lid and bring slowly to a soft simmer. This can now be cooked in the oven for 4–5 minutes or very gently poached on top of the stove for just a few minutes. Remove from the heat. If the fish is particularly thick and has been protruding through the milk, turn the fillet over and leave to stand for a further 2–3 minutes.

Lift the fish from the milk. The milk can now be strained and used to make the cheese sauce.

While the cheese sauce is cooking, make the hollandaise (or use an egg yolk). When whipping the double cream, it's important not to whisk it past the thickening stage, when still light and creamy.

The fish can now be carefully flaked, saving any juices to add extra flavour to the sauce. The flakes will softly fall away from the skin, with a slight translucent centre to each one. This will tell you just how moist they are.

Once the cheese sauce is made, the English mustard can be added. Stir in 1 teaspoon and taste, before adding the other, if needed.

Before cracking the eggs to make the omelette, it's important that the sauce is ready to glaze. Fold 2 tablespoons of hollandaise sauce or the egg yolk, along with the whipped cream, into the warm cheese sauce. To test it will glaze, place a dessertspoon of sauce on a suitable tray and place under a pre-heated grill. The sauce should slightly rise under the heat and glaze with an all-round golden finish. If it appears to be taking too long and almost boiling before colouring, add more of the hollandaise sauce and cream before re-testing.

Melt a small knob of butter in an omelette pan. While melting on a medium heat, crack and fork 3 eggs together well, creating an emulsion between the yolk and white. Once the butter begins to bubble reasonably rapidly, but is not at a nut-brown stage, season the egg with a good twist of pepper and a pinch of salt. Now it's time to pour the eggs into the bubbling butter. If the eggs are seasoned too early and left out in the air, the mixture becomes very loose and takes a slight discoloration. So, for a maximum bright-yellow finish, season just before cooking.

The eggs can now be gently moved with a fork in the pan. If the pan is also kept moving, the eggs will not actually set and become over-cooked. This stage is really just a scrambling. Once thickened, but still reasonably loose and soft – which will take 2–3 minutes – remove the pan from the heat. The smoked haddock flakes can be sprinkled on top. The base of the omelette will now have set, and the eggs will continue to cook while retaining any heat.

Spoon the finished cheese sauce on top and finish under a hot grill. Within 45 seconds–1 minute a rich golden brown Omelette Arnold Bennett will be ready to serve. The olive oil and lemon juice can be mixed together, seasoned and a trickle spooned over each finished omelette.

This process can now be repeated to make the remaining omelettes.

Note: Two omelettes can always be made at the same time. Any more and they will over-cook as you won't have time to attend to each one.

The finished sauce, with the hollandaise and cream added, can be kept for a maximum 1–2 hours at room temperature, covered with cling film. After this time, the sauce tends to separate.

Scotch Eggs

It doesn't take much to work out where these were born. They are a Scottish speciality, and have become very much part of English eating habits.

They were originally part of the Great Scottish breakfast, but were also served hot at high tea with gravy. We know them today as a pub snack, a picnic feature or a cold buffet item, usually displaying that unlovely grey border surrounding the centre – as if the sausagemeat has had a row with the egg! The crumbs are often soggy as well.

I've always felt that they could be quite delicious with a flavoured, well-seasoned sausagemeat and the eggs cooked perfectly, and this is what I'm trying to give you here. These Scotch eggs eat very well as a snack, picnic, lunch or supper dish, with a good mixed salad, baked potato and lots of home-made *Piccalilli* (page 385) or *Home-made Salad Cream* (page 48).

MAKES 4

4 eggs, boiled for 7 minutes (page 81), and
    refreshed under cold running water
Butter
1 shallot or ½ small onion, very finely chopped
Finely grated zest of 1 small lemon
Good pinch of ground mace
1 dessertspoon chopped fresh sage
225 g (8 oz) pork sausagemeat
2 medium eggs, for coating
100 g (4 oz) dried white breadcrumbs, for coating
Groundnut oil or sunflower oil, for deep-frying
Salt and pepper

Peel away the shells from the eggs and keep the eggs to one side.

Melt a knob of butter in a frying-pan. Once bubbling on a medium heat, add the finely chopped shallot or onion. Cook for a few minutes, without colouring, until softened. Remove from the heat and allow to cool. Once cooled, add the grated lemon zest, mace and chopped sage. Add the cooked shallot/onion to the sausagemeat and season with salt and pepper.

Divide into four and mould around the eggs, creating an even layer. This can be made easy by lightly flouring a sheet of cling film. Place the sausagemeat on top and also lightly dust with flour. Top with another sheet of cling film and roll out.

This will ensure an even thickness. Remove the top layer of cling film and sit the egg on top of the sausage mix. Lift and wrap around the egg and, once covered, remove the film. Now, with damp hands you will achieve a perfect smooth finish. Repeat the same process for the other three.

Beat the raw eggs. Pass the 'balls' through the eggs and then roll in the crumbs. For an extra crispy finish, one I prefer, pass through the eggs and crumbs again. Refrigerate to relax and set the mix.

When ready to cook, heat the oil to 180°/350°F and cook two eggs at a time. These will take 5–7 minutes to cook and become golden and crispy.

Remove and drain on kitchen paper, and then repeat the cooking process for the last two.

These can now be served immediately or eaten cold. Simply split in two and serve.

Variation: Whisky Scotch Eggs

Follow the Scotch egg ingredients, omitting the lemon zest and sage. When cooking the chopped onions, once softened, add 1–2 measures of good Scotch whisky. Bring to the boil and reduce until almost dry. Now complete as per the Scotch Egg method.

A good sauce to serve with the whisky eggs is to take ½ teaspoon of demerara sugar and bring to the simmer with 50 ml (2 fl oz) whisky. Reduce by half and cool. Mix with 4–6 tablespoons of mayonnaise and a dot of English mustard. The whisky dip is ready.

Note: The breadcrumbs can be halved and mixed with fine oatmeal for a stronger Scottish feel.

OPPOSITE
Scotch Eggs

Lobster Omelette 'Thermidor'

This dish is certainly not British; in fact, it's very French. So why is it featured in this book? Because I would like this to become a Great British Classic of the future. After all, the best lobsters are found in Scottish waters, the sauce is flavoured with English mustard and the eggs are home-laid.

The basic idea has been taken from the French. The 'real' thermidor consists of halved lobsters, the meat presented in the shell, glazed with a cheese sauce flavoured with English mustard and bound with a sauce Bercy, a basic fish and white-wine sauce, flavoured with shallots and parsley. An outstanding dish.

This, however, is a simple three-egg omelette with poached lobster meat sprinkled on top. This is then glazed with a rich cheese sauce – enhanced by the addition of English mustard and reduced lobster bisque (soup). The sauce, lifted and strengthened by the bisque, just does nothing but pack the palate with lobster flavours.

There might seem to be too many components to the dish, but this can all be made quite simple. The hollandaise sauce to help the glaze can be replaced by an egg yolk whipped into the cream. The lobster bisque is an awful lot to make just for an omelette, but if you're making the soup to eat as a dish, then save and freeze some for future omelettes. In place of making it, good-quality tinned soup can be used. Half a tin, boiled and reduced by a third to half (about 100 ml/3½ fl oz), will give you the strength needed. An optional extra to finish the dish is the *Lobster Oil* (page 386).

The quantities of sauces in the ingredients are for a minimum of four servings.

The four omelette pans used are 10 cm (4 in) wide × 2–3 cm (¾–1¼ in) deep, as per *Omelette Arnold Bennett* (page 71). Two 20 cm (8 in) pans can also be used (using 6 eggs per large omelette). Serve larger omelettes from the pans at the table – it still looks very impressive.

SERVES 4

450 g (1 lb) cooked lobster (page 154)
Butter
3 eggs per serving

For the Sauce

150 ml (¼ pint) *Lobster 'Bisque' Soup* (page 23) or
    tinned lobster bisque
1–2 teaspoons English mustard
150 ml (¼ pint) *Cheese Sauce* (page 46)
2–3 tablespoons *Simple Hollandaise Sauce*
    (page 41) or 2–3 egg yolks
5–6 tablespoons double cream, lightly whipped
Salt and pepper
Lemon juice
Lobster or *Shellfish Oil* (page 386), to serve (optional)

The lobster meat is best kept 'whole', leaving the shell and claws as taken from the shell in some of the cooking liquor, until needed. This will keep them moist and succulent. When ready to use, simply cut into 1 cm (½ in) pieces, mixing with the lobster meat trimmings. The meat can be gently warmed, when needed, in the liquor. It's important not to boil cooked lobster – this will just toughen the texture.

Bring the lobster bisque (home-made or tinned) to the boil and allow to reduce by half. This will now have a thick consistency and very strong flavour. Add the English mustard to the cheese sauce, a teaspoon at a time, along with the bisque, a tablespoon at a time, giving a rich mustard and lobster flavour and colour. If using hollandaise, add 2 tablespoons along with three-quarters of the whipped cream (if not using hollandaise, add the egg yolk).

The sauce can now be tested by pouring a tablespoon onto a suitable tray and glazing under a hot grill. Within 1 minute, the sauce should have taken on a rich golden finish. If not, add another tablespoon of hollandaise, along with the remaining whipped cream. Check the sauce for seasoning with salt, pepper and a squeeze of lemon juice. This will now hold for 1–2 hours, at room temperature, covered with cling film.

To make the omelettes, melt a knob of butter in the pan(s). Crack and fork 3 eggs into a bowl, mixing to a smooth emulsion of yolk and white.

Once the butter is bubbling, but not at the nut-brown stage, season the eggs with salt and pepper. Pour the eggs into the butter and gently fork and move the pan over a medium heat.

The eggs should not be allowed to set on the base. They need a soft scrambling in the pan. After 2–3 minutes, when beginning to set, remove the pan from the heat. The heat in the pan itself will seal the base, without colouring the eggs. This will leave a soft, succulent base, rather than a golden brown, leathery finish. A portion of the warmed lobster can now be sprinkled on top. Spoon the sauce on top and glaze under a pre-heated grill.

The Lobster Omelette 'Thermidor' will now have the most beautiful golden shine, just waiting to be eaten. Once ready, sprinkle with a few drops of the lobster oil, if using.

Note: It's best, if making individual omelettes, to make just two at a time. Spoon the sauce on top and keep to one side while the last two are made. Once all have been sauced, glaze all four under the grill.

Eating these omelettes is a complete experience that, I promise, you will never forget.

Crab meat and soup can also be used in this recipe. Prawns will also work, making the sauce with reduced lobster bisque soup to enhance their flavour.

See also

Boiled Eggs (page 81)
Cheese Sauce (Sauce Mornay) (page 46)
Classic Scrambled Eggs (page 79)
Curried Eggs (page 394)
Egg and Bacon Salad (page 114)
The Great British Fried Egg (page 79)
Gruyère Cheese, Leek and Mushroom Flan
    (page 279)
Hollandaise Sauce (page 41)
Home-made Pancakes (page 82)
Mayonnaise (page 49)
Poached Eggs (page 82)
Simple Hollandaise Sauce (page 41)
Smoked Haddock with Welsh Rarebit
    (page 163)
Spicy Scrambled Eggs (page 81)
Yorkshire Pudding (page 237)

ABOVE
Lobster Omelette 'Thermidor'

The Great British Breakfast

The Great British Breakfast is probably one of, if not the, most famous of all our 'dishes' around the world. It's a start to the day that has become a standard feature on just about every hotel breakfast menu to be found. And I'm not really surprised. The combination of ingredients used all work together so well – pork sausages, crispy bacon, mushrooms, tomatoes, black pudding, fried bread, all balanced with the soft creamy yolk of a fried egg. This meal has become a treat. But our breakfast does offer so much more, with the famous porridge oats, stewed prunes and other cereals all playing a big part.

The novelist Somerset Maugham once said that to eat well in Britain you had to eat breakfast three times a day. He must have been referring to the lavish spreads mentioned above, introduced by the Victorians, for before then the first meal of the day was usually a rather uninspired affair. Until late in the seventeenth century, the majority of people, rich and poor, rose at dawn and broke their night's fast – hence 'break-fast' – with foods such as ale, soft cheese and bread, or some ale and salted fish, or a soup made from the local grain. The custom still survives in the north, particularly in Scotland, where many think the only way to start the day properly is with a bowl of oat porridge. Robert Burns was very flattering about his national dish, calling it 'the chief o' Scotia's food'; the Englishman, Dr Johnson, was less enthusiastic, describing oats in his *Dictionary of the English Language* as 'A grain which in England is generally given to horses, but in Scotland supports the people.'

By the beginning of the eighteenth century, the upper and middle classes preferred a lighter breakfast at a later hour, and ate spice-bread (plain bread dough enriched with spices or seeds), with one of the new drinks, chocolate or coffee. By the end of the century, they were breakfasting on plain bread or toast and butter, and were drinking the third new drink to be introduced – tea. This had been drunk at other times of the day, but when it became economical to buy, more so than coffee and chocolate, it became part of many more meals in the day (including, later, the entirely new and uniquely British ritual of afternoon tea). It had probably been drunk plain until then, but now a little cream or milk was added to the cup, along with some sugar.

It was not until Edwardian and Victorian times that the Great British Breakfast as we now know it became established. A larger meal than before was thought necessary to keep people going until the dinner hour, as most had only a snack or small meal in the middle of the day. It was Mrs Beeton herself who suggested that for 'the comfortable meal called breakfast' her readers should offer a selection of cold meats and game, potted meats, brawn and pies, along with hot fish dishes, chops and steaks, kidneys, sausages, bacon and eggs, muffins, toast, marmalade and butter. To one such lengthy listing, and just for *one* breakfast menu, she added, 'etcetera, etcetera'... I'm so glad I wasn't the breakfast chef on duty for that menu!

It was at this time that 'collops' of bacon and fried eggs – a rare treat for the working man – became a dish for the middle and upper classes. Now, too, scrambled, poached, shirred (baked), coddled and boiled eggs became an important part of the breakfast table. Queen Victoria is supposed to have eaten one small boiled egg every day, a modest meal, but it was said to have been served in a gold egg-cup and eaten from a gold spoon. Ancient and new foods were soon to appear on the breakfast menu, most of which you'll find in this book. Black puddings, made since medieval times, were enjoyed mainly in the north. Kippers – smoked herrings – were grilled, buttered, jugged or potted. Smoked haddock – Finnan haddie or Arbroath smokies – was poached in milk or flaked into rice for the new-fangled kedgeree.

The taste for hot foods introduced from the Indian subcontinent revealed itself in devilled foods, among them game, chicken legs, livers and kidneys. Toast was spread with the relatively new preserve made from bitter Seville oranges, marmalade. Potted meats and fish were also popular, and George Borrow, in his book *Wild Wales* (1862), describes a breakfast at the White Hart Inn: 'Pot of hare: ditto of trout; pot of prepared shrimps: tin of sardines; beautiful beefsteak; eggs, mutton, large loaf and butter, not forgetting capital tea. There's a breakfast for you!' And curry itself made an appearance on many an ex-colonial's table. It is said that Merchant Navy seamen were once offered a different curry for breakfast every day of the week.

With such excess, the invention of brunch at the beginning of the twentieth century, when breakfast and lunch were married together into one meal, must have appeared rather more sensible, at least to those watching their weight. Brunch is generally thought of as American, but it may well have originated at Oxford, where the students were notoriously late risers... It's a great meal for a weekend, when you can take your time and serve some Great British Breakfast Classics.

This section might not give you the lengthy variety of Mrs Beeton-style breakfast recipes, but what it does include are useful tips and hints to help you achieve the perfect breakfast.

The Great British Fried Egg ⓥ

One of the first ways people cooked eggs was by baking them whole in the ashes of the fire. Or they were fried in fat in a container of some sort, probably much as they are today. But what makes the perfect fried egg? Every book you read will give you a different recipe, some telling you just to use lard for frying, or groundnut oil, bacon fat, butter or a combination of all. Some like their eggs sunny side up, others like them turned. At the end of the day, it's up to you.

In fact, cooking a fried egg to perfection is quite scientific. If the oil or fat is not hot enough, the albumen in the egg white will not coagulate quickly enough and, consequently, the white spreads, almost covering the base of the pan. The egg is then almost poached or boiled in oil. If the fat is too hot, then the egg coagulates too quickly, giving you a very crispy base and edge, while the rest is still too raw. Apparently the perfect temperature of oil for egg frying is 124–138°C/225–280°F, which sounds great, but are we really all going out to buy electric egg fryers?

The following recipe contains butter, which will always give you better-flavoured results.

1 large egg
15 g (½ oz) of butter

It's best to use a small pan. A non-stick 15 cm (6 in) omelette pan for one egg is ideal. This will then give you a good depth of butter, not spreading it across the base. Heat the butter in the pan and bring to a good bubbling stage. This is the important point. The 'perfect' temperature will be found by not quite allowing the butter to reach a nut-brown stage. The temperature is then just right.

Another point to remember is to keep the egg in shell until the absolute last minute. Now just crack the egg in the pan and give it 30 seconds to set, before basting with the butter. This will ensure even cooking. Now just cook to your taste and lift carefully with a fish slice.

Classic Scrambled Eggs ⓥ

Eggs cooked in this basic way have been part of the British tradition since medieval times, when herbs were added to make 'herbolaces' and 'tansies': the eggs are mixed together, then 'scrambled' with butter. They are still made in virtually the same way today.

After beating yolks and whites together, there's the option of adding liquid to the eggs, which will break down the coagulating mass, giving you a softer and moister finish. Milk, water or cream can be used. The thought of water doesn't excite me at all, and cream will give you a very rich result, so milk is probably the best bet to suit everybody's tastebuds. The only problem is quantities. Too much liquid results in it bleeding from the eggs during and after cooking, leaving puddles of eggy 'cream'. The best quantity for each egg is 1 tablespoon, maximum, of liquid. But for me the perfect scrambled egg is made with no additional ingredients (apart from salt and pepper)

2 large eggs, per person
Butter
Salt and pepper

Put a good knob of butter in your saucepan and let it bubble away, making sure it doesn't reach a nut-brown stage. Put the eggs in a bowl, season and beat well, then add them to the butter. Now just turn them with a wooden spoon, fairly vigorously, capturing every corner of the pan. Once they are just starting to set and have a 'lumpy' effect but are still good and soft, remove the pan from the stove. The eggs are best left slightly under-done, as they always continue to cook, even once off the heat. The scrambled eggs are now ready to eat.

Note: Something I am very strict about when cooking scrambled eggs or omelettes is the seasoning. It's not so much the quantities – a good 'pinch and twist' is plenty – but when it's added. Eggs should always be broken at the last minute, but this rule should never be. Once the butter is bubbling in the pan and the eggs are broken and beaten, now is the time to season the eggs, and then pour them immediately into the buttery bubbles. The reason is to do with the salt itself. Freshly beaten eggs have a wonderful thick and bright yellow colour. If salt is added too quickly, the egg will become very thin and watery and at the same time lose that bright yellow, exchanging it for a dull orange tinge. Neither are the eggs as light and fluffy in texture or colour. So season at the last second.

Variations

Here are a few extras that can be added to scrambled eggs, creating completely new dishes.

Simply serve on hot buttered toast or 'French toast'. One variety of French toast is made by buttering bread and then frying it until golden on both sides, or grilling it, allowing the butter to melt through the bread. It's said that this traditional bread base for eggs is an echo of the medieval bread trencher, and is why the British – and it is only the British – eat things like baked beans and tinned spaghetti on toast.

Smoked salmon eats beautifully with scrambled eggs, either thin slices on top or strips stirred in at the last minute. For an extra taste, just as the eggs are setting, add a spoonful of crème fraîche, which gives you a lighter finish and at the same time a slightly sour cream taste. Chopped chives also eat well sprinkled in.

Try fresh oysters just lightly poached and placed on top, with soured cream.

Add Parmesan cheese, with spring onions sliced and cooked in the butter before adding the eggs.

Caviar with soured cream and toast.

The ultimate: a slice of pan-fried *foie gras* sitting on top.

OPPOSITE
Full English Breakfast with
Sautéd Potatoes (page 121)

Spicy Scrambled Eggs Ⓥ

These spiced eggs hold a lot of the flavours the British met and loved during the years of the Raj in India, and they are wonderful as a starter or snack.

SERVES 1–2

½ heaped teaspoon crushed garlic
½ heaped teaspoon crushed fresh root ginger
Unsalted butter
1 tablespoon finely chopped onion
½ teaspoon chopped fresh red chilli
½ teaspoon ground turmeric
1 tomato, seeded and diced
3 eggs, beaten
Salt and pepper
½ teaspoon chopped fresh coriander leaves
   (optional)

Pound the garlic and ginger together to a paste. Heat a frying-pan and add a knob of butter. Once the butter is bubbling, add the garlic and ginger paste, the chopped onion, chilli, turmeric and tomato. Cook for a few minutes until lightly softened. Add the beaten eggs and stir over the heat until the eggs have softly scrambled. Taste and season with salt and pepper if necessary, stir in the chopped coriander, if using, and serve.

Boiled Eggs Ⓥ

Eggs have been boiled since very early times, and were once a basic food, eaten in the hand or cut up and added to salads. They became popular as a breakfast food in Victorian times. They are very easy to do, but if you take note of the following ideas, I can guarantee you better results.

How long one boils an egg for is really up to the individual. A very, very soft-boiled egg (rare) will take only 3 minutes. A medium-rare (very soft) will take 4 minutes. And what I think most people prefer, a medium egg, with that just-soft yolk, will take 5 minutes. But what's the secret?

First, it's to have your eggs at room temperature. A cold egg cooked straight from the fridge will have such a change in pressure that it will crack. This then releases some albumen (the egg white), which creates uneven cooking. Water that is boiling will also create turbulence, jiggling the eggs around so that they could quite easily crack into one another.

For Soft-boiled Eggs

The easiest way is to bring your saucepan of water to a gentle simmer. Using a tablespoon, carefully lower the egg or eggs into the water. Once the water has returned to the same simmering point, cook for 3–5 minutes – rare to medium.

Or you can sit the eggs in a saucepan of cold water, bring to a fast simmer and then lift the pan from the heat. Place a lid on the pot and leave the egg standing in the hot water for 4–5 minutes (a minute longer for very large eggs). The egg is now ready to enjoy (with lots of toast fingers).

Alternatively you can carefully sit the egg in simmering water and cook for 1 minute. Remove from the stove and complete as for the cold water method, leaving it standing in the pot with a lid on top.

For Hard-boiled Eggs

In many recipes you're told to boil the eggs for 10–12 minutes. Surely that can leave nothing but a very dry, crumbly yolk with that 'delicious-looking' black border between yolk and white. The best way is to sit the eggs in a saucepan of boiling water and bring to a fast simmer. Cook for 7–8 minutes and then remove the eggs, running them under cold water for 1–2 minutes to calm the cooking. Now leave to cool to room temperature. Once cooled, peel and cut to reveal an egg that is totally cooked but with still a slightly soft and moist centre.

Poached Eggs ⓥ

Eggs have always been important in British cooking and eating, and poaching them would have been an early technique. You'll find a few poached eggs throughout the book. There's something about the consistency of poached eggs that can really make a dish. The warm soft yolk spilling out and mixing with and enriching other flavours is quite stunning, making the dish more enjoyable.

I'm using a cooking liquor that is two-thirds water to one-third malt or white-wine vinegar. This may sound expensive, but vinegar costs pence not pounds, and the results are worth every penny. The vinegar doesn't affect the flavour of the eggs, but what it does is make the white set instantly around the yolk, which creates a neater poached egg. If you are a bit concerned about the quantity, then simply add a few tablespoons of vinegar. The complete, round poached egg will probably not be achieved, but the egg will still poach.

4 eggs
Water
Malt or white-wine vinegar

Fill a saucepan with two-thirds water and a third vinegar. Salt should not be added because this tends to break down the egg-white consistency. Bring the water and vinegar mixture to the boil and stir. Now crack one egg at a time into the centre of the liquor and poach for 3–3½ minutes. The eggs are ready to serve, or they can be poached in advance and plunged into iced water immediately.

Trim off any excess untidy whites to give you the perfect poached egg. To re-heat, simply plunge into boiling water for 1 minute.

The eggs are now hot and ready to serve.

Home-made Pancakes ⓥ

Pancakes were among the very early enriched breads cooked on the griddle, and have become one of our favourite breakfast and afternoon tea foods. They have a long-standing yearly association with Shrove Tuesday, otherwise known as Pancake Day, which is when all the eggs must be used up before Lent.

Pancakes are a Sunday treat in our house, with my sons and me whisking away making the batter. And then I cook the pancakes, while they eat them: I'm making a mistake somewhere! But they are so easy to make and, with a dribbling of golden syrup, just delicious. They could also be served with honey, jam or ice-cream. In a savoury sense, they can be filled with ratatouille, fish stew, mussels, chicken and so on.

This quantity will make 16–24 pancakes, depending on the size of pan used. It's best to use a 20 cm (8 in) or 15 cm (6 in) frying-pan.

225 g (8 oz) plain flour
Pinch of salt
2 eggs
600 ml (1 pint) milk
50 g (2 oz) unsalted butter, melted
Vegetable oil, for frying

Sift the flour and salt into a bowl. Whisk the eggs and the milk into the flour. Add the melted butter and whisk into the mix. At this stage, the mix can be used for sweet or savoury pancakes.

For a stronger savoury flavour, chopped fresh parsley or mixed herbs can also be added.

To cook the pancakes, pre-heat the frying-pan. Lightly oil the pan and pour in some of the mixture, making sure the pan has only a thin layer of mix by tilting and rotating the pan to make the batter spread out.

Cook for 30–40 seconds, until golden brown. Turn the pancake over and cook for a further 20–30 seconds.

The pancake is now cooked. Keep warm between squares of greaseproof paper, while you cook the remainder. Two or three pancakes per portion should be plenty.

If made well in advance, the pancakes can be microwaved for 30–40 seconds to re-heat.

Breakfast Tomatoes (v)

A breakfast 'extra' that we all enjoy. Good grilled tomatoes finish a breakfast plate so nicely, giving more colour, texture and, of course, flavour. I'm not quite sure when tomatoes found their way on to the British breakfast plate, but it was probably this century. After many hours of research, the only tomato addition I found was in Mrs Beeton's *Household Management*, in a recipe for tomato sausage made from rather a lot of tomato purée, cooked rice, breadcrumbs, chopped onion and mixed herbs, all filled into skins and pan-fried. I'm not sure I'm going to try that recipe. So here's an alternative idea or two.

4 good, ripe, plum or salad tomatoes
Dribble of olive oil
25 g (1 oz) butter
Small sprinkling of coarse sea salt
Freshly ground black pepper

The tomatoes can be either pan-fried or grilled. Whichever your choice, the first job is to 'eye' them. This will be easily achieved by inserting the point of a small knife to the side of the eye and then turning and twisting the tomato while the knife cuts, angled towards the centre. The eye will simply fall out.

If using plum tomatoes (which I consider to be of a better quality and flavour, especially when cooked, than standard salad tomatoes), then cut lengthways to give two halves. Cut salad tomatoes through the middle.

To Grill

Sit the tomatoes, skin-side down, on a greased baking sheet. Divide the butter, sitting a small knob on top of each. Dribble all with a drop or two of olive oil and now season with salt (just 3–4 crystals per tomato) and a good twist of pepper. Place under a hot grill and cook to a golden finish. This should take no longer than 5–7 minutes, depending on the size of the tomato. Once cooked, arrange on the breakfast plates, pouring over any juices and liquor released from the tomatoes.

To Pan-fry

Heat a large frying-pan with a tablespoon or two of olive oil. Season the tomatoes with the sea salt and pepper. Once the pan is hot, place the tomatoes in, flesh-side down. It is important not to shake the pan. This will release juices from the tomatoes and, consequently, reduce the heat in the pan. The tomatoes then begin to boil and stew, rather than fry. After 2–3 minutes, check the stage and colour of the tomatoes. They should have begun to soften and turn golden brown. At this point, add the butter to the pan. The butter will begin to bubble. Allow to reach its nut-brown stage before turning the tomatoes over. They can now be cooked for a further 2–3 minutes, basting with the nutty butter and olive oil. The tomatoes are ready to serve, pouring excess liquor over.

Breakfast Mushrooms Ⓥ

Mushrooms became part of the breakfast plate a little earlier than tomatoes. They weren't often served on their own at breakfast but more often as part of a fish dish, such as a pie.

I serve button, chestnut, open-cup or flat mushrooms for breakfast. The flats can be either sliced 5 mm–1 cm (¼–½ in) thick if frying or left whole and grilled.

Flat Mushrooms

SERVES 4

4 large, flat mushrooms
25 g (1oz) butter, melted, or 2 tablespoons olive oil
Salt and pepper

I don't like to wash any mushrooms (apart from wild) because I always feel that I am washing away flavour and at the same time filling the vegetable with water. It's best to just wipe clean with a damp cloth. Trim any excess stalk from the mushroom. For grilling, lay the mushrooms, top-down, on a buttered baking tray. Divide the butter between them, brushing each mushroom. Season with salt and pepper. The mushrooms can now be cooked under a hot grill. They will take 6–8 minutes to cook, depending on their thickness.

To shallow fry, heat a large frying-pan and add the olive oil. Add the mushrooms and allow to cook for 1–2 minutes before turning them in the pan. Season with salt and pepper and continue to cook for a few minutes until tender.

Large flat mushrooms can also be cut into thick slices before frying.

Button and Chestnut Mushrooms

300 g (10 oz) mushrooms, stalks trimmed and
  wiped clean
2 tablespoons olive oil
50 g (2 oz) butter
Salt and pepper

Mushrooms always tend to soak up the fat used for frying. For this recipe, the butter has been doubled to account for the soaking.

Heat a large frying-pan with the olive oil. With the oil on the point of smoking, add the mushrooms. These can now be seasoned with salt and pepper and left for a few minutes, before turning them in the pan. Continue to cook, adding the butter. As this heats, it will turn to a nutty brown colour and flavour, lifting the taste of the mushroom. The mushrooms should take 6–8 minutes to fry and become tender. Large button mushrooms will take 10–12 minutes.

If you are worried about the fat content, then here's a way to dry-fry/roast, using an absolute minimum of fat. Simply heat a teaspoon of oil in a frying-pan, roasting tin or grill pan. Add the mushrooms and cook over a moderate heat, turning from time to time. As they cook they will become coloured with small burnt tinges. This gives a great bitter edge to the finished flavour.

The mushrooms tend to take longer to cook, approximately 8–10 minutes for small and 12–15 for large. They can also be roasted in a hot oven at 220°C/425°F/Gas Mark 7 for about 12–15 minutes. Season with salt and pepper and serve.

Breakfast Bacon

In early recipes for bacon and eggs – and I mean early, going back to the sixteenth century – the instructions were to take the whitest and youngest bacon and cut it into thin slices. These were placed in a dish, hot water was poured over them, and then they were left to stand for an hour or two, thus taking away the extreme saltiness. The next stage would be to take them on a long metal skewer and hold them to the heat of the fire to toast them. Today cooking bacon doesn't quite need all that preparation. However, if we were going to boil a bacon joint, most would need to be pre-soaked (gammon, gammon hock, hams and prime collar all included).

The rashers/cuts of bacon that we know for breakfast are back, streaky and middle. The middle has the back and streaky joined, giving you the best of both worlds. The back cut comes literally from the back and ribs. Streaky is found immediately below, taken from the belly. Bacon can also be bought smoked or unsmoked (known as 'green'); apart from the 'aroma', the difference can be found in the colour of the rind.

Smoking will always give the flesh a rich pink colour, with the rind taking on a golden-edged orange. As for the 'green' unsmoked, the flesh is a lot paler, with its rind more of an 'off-white'. The flavour is up to you. Smoked bacon is inevitably going to be richer and stronger, as well as saltier. The unsmoked will have a 'leaner', less salty flavour, but still be very 'bacony'.

Bacon can be bought with its rind on or off, and thinly or thickly sliced. If you are buying bacon with rind on, it's always best to trim this away before cooking, for easier eating. To achieve really crispy bacon, very thinly sliced streaky will give you the best results. And obviously for the meatier finish, it has to be back bacon.

For back bacon, use 2 rashers per portion. For streaky bacon, use 2–3 rashers per portion.

To Grill

Grill the bacon rashers, back or streaky, under a pre-heated hot grill for 2–3 minutes on each side. A little longer for extra crispness.

To Pan-fry

Heat a dry frying-pan. The bacon can now be cooked on a medium heat; this will draw the fat from the rashers, leaving crispy bacon. Frying will also take 2–4 minutes on each side, depending on the crispness required. Once cooked, lift the bacon from the pan, leaving any excess fat. The rashers can now be kept warm in a pre-heated oven. This will also help crisp the bacon.

The fat in the pan can now be used for the ultimate fried slice (*Fried Bread*, below). The taste of bacon on the bread is delicious. And if you're not using the fat for a fried slice, then how about pan-frying mushrooms in it?

Fried Bread Ⓥ

Our passion for crispy fried bread must be a hangover from the days when we ate our meals off trenchers of bread, before plates were used. I think fried bread is a must for a 'modern' full English breakfast.

Any bread can be used for frying, from our standard thin-, medium- or thick-sliced, to any flavoured and textured soft or crusty loaves. The bread will fry at its best if about 48 hours old. If the bread is too fresh, it will need an awful lot of fat to cook in. Because of the soft and absorbent texture, fresh bread tends to soak up far too much fat and, when eaten, is far too greasy. Simply make sure that the frying-pan has just enough fat to cover its base – but only just. The bread slices can then be pan-fried until golden brown, before turning and completing the frying. If the pan becomes dry, it's very easy just to add a trickle more.

Fried bread will take 2–3 minutes on each side. If it's fried too hot and quickly, the bread has burnt edges and a very patchy colour. About 2–3 minutes on each side will give you a crispy, well-coloured all round slice. A knob of butter can also be added, once the slice is turned, for a nutty flavour to finish.

For the ultimate fried bread, it's best to shallow-fry your bacon first, not too quickly, but with just enough heat to draw excess fat from the rashers, leaving you with very crispy bacon and a good pool of bacon fat to fry the bread in. The flavour is immense. Just follow the same method as frying in oil, adding a knob of butter once turned. You now have crispy bacon-flavoured fried bread – a pleasure on the plate.

Classic Porridge Ⓥ

Oats probably arrived in Britain mixed in with other seeds brought by immigrants, and became particularly useful, as they grew more comfortably in more northerly, colder and wetter parts of the country, where few other cereals would survive. Oats became – and remained – a major crop in the north of England, in Ireland and Scotland, and oatmeal pottage – porridge – still survives, as do a number of other oat dishes.

Porridge is eaten all over Scotland, and many other parts of the world. Traditional cooking of oatmeal for porridge involved boiling the water and then sprinkling in the oats with your left hand, while you stirred, clockwise, with your right. And it wasn't a spoon you would be stirring with, it was always a straight wooden stick. Some would even add the oats in stages to create different textures, leaving 'crunchy bits' in the finished dish. The pot would slowly simmer away for 30–40 minutes before it was ready. The pinch

ABOVE
Fried Bread (page 85)

of salt would be added towards the end, in order not to toughen the oats.

Porridge was often served with cold milk or cream, which you dipped your spoon into before every mouthful of porridge. Many a Scotsman would traditionally take a glass of beer to go with it.

Oats are probably the most nutritious of all cereal grains, being very rich in oils. Oatmeal comes in three grades – coarse, medium and fine – and the most commonly used for porridge is the medium. Porridge oats, the main variety sold in supermarkets, are rolled oats. These will take a maximum of 10 minutes to cook, sometimes as little as 6–7 minutes. Most porridge oats come with the cooking method printed on the pack, usually 50 g (2 oz) of oats per 300 ml (½ pint)

of milk. (Notice I say milk. Traditional porridge is all water.) Full-milk porridge will be quite rich, but can be loosened with water, half and half, for a milder flavour.

Now cream, sugar, honey, golden syrup, jams or marmalades can all be offered to spoon over.

SERVES 2, GENEROUSLY

600 ml (1 pint) water
60 g (2½ oz) medium oatmeal
Good pinch of salt

To Serve

Cold milk or cream
Sugar

Bring the water to the boil, preferably in a non-stick pan. Sprinkle the oats while stirring or whisking in, making sure to release any from the corners of the saucepan. Once all have been added to the water, continue to whisk/stir until it has returned to the boil. Cover the pan with a lid, reducing the heat to a soft simmer. The porridge can now cook for 25–30 minutes until completely tender. Add a good pinch of salt and the classic porridge is ready. Cream, milk and sugar can be offered separately or sprinkled in to taste.

Note: To guarantee the oats will not burn when returned to the boil, transfer to a bowl with a lid on top and sit over simmering water. This will now take 30 minutes to cook.

Wayne's Porridge Ⓥ

This second porridge recipe was given to me by a fellow chef and friend, Wayne Tapsfield. He often makes this for the kitchen team during the winter months, and it's now become a firm favourite. The recipe breaks every tradition, but gives loads of flavour.

SERVES 4–6

225 g (8 oz) porridge oats
600 ml (1 pint) milk
300 ml (½ pint) water (the water can be doubled and milk halved for a milder finish)
50 g (2 oz) caster or light soft brown sugar
Pinch of salt
100 ml (3½ fl oz) evaporated milk
100 ml (3½ fl oz) double cream (single for a less rich finish)
1–2 tablespoons golden syrup, to serve

Bring the milk and water to the boil. Pour in the oats, whisking continuously. Once back to the boil, add the sugar and salt, reducing the heat to a soft simmer and stirring occasionally. After 8–10 minutes, add the evaporated milk and double cream. Continue to cook gently to warm the milk and cream for the final 2 minutes.

Remove from the heat and add the golden syrup to taste. The super rich porridge is ready to enjoy. It really is worth a try and is lovely to eat. (Wayne tells me he sometimes finishes it with grated nutmeg, clotted cream and butter. I just didn't have the nerve to include them.)

Grilled Kippers

In the mid eighteenth century a mild smoke cure for herring was introduced in Yarmouth, which involved the whole herring being smoked, guts included. As the fish were only half-dried and then smoked over an oak fire, they remained plump and puffed out, for which reason they were called bloaters. They're still considered a delicacy today.

Some years after this, in the late nineteenth century, another smoke cure for herring was found. It was invented on the Northumberland coast by a Mr Woodger, who got the idea from an old system of curing salmon called kippering. Herrings were so cheap and plentiful then that another means of preserving them was very welcome. Before this, herring had been eaten fresh, salted or salted and dry-smoked; in this last form they were the means of survival of thousands of families throughout the centuries. They were soaked overnight and then boiled and served with potatoes, the potatoes taking away excessive saltiness. As the years passed, extremely salty flavours became less popular, so many of the fishing ports around the coasts of Scotland and England worked on milder cures for herring. Today the best kippers – smoked herring – come from Loch Fyne in Scotland and still use Mr Woodger's method of smoke curing.

The fish are split down the back before salting and then smoked over oak chips. A short soaking in strong salt brine is used to form a sticky solution of protein on the herring flesh, which then dries during the smoking process to give that rich, deep shine. As the years passed, the curing became lighter, keeping the fish plumper but at the same time making them more anaemic in colour. As a result, most kippers today are dyed during the curing process. There are, however, still some undyed kippers to be found, mostly in Scotland and the Isle of Man.

Kippers can be bought on or off the bone. With bone-in fish, it's always best to cut away the head and tail with scissors before cooking.

1 kipper per person
Butter

Lemon wedges
Brown bread and butter

Using a sheet of buttered foil ensures that a strong kipper smell is not left on your grill tray. Place the kipper, flesh-side up, on the foil and sit it on the grill tray. Top the kipper with a good knob of butter. Place under a pre-heated grill and cook for 4–5 minutes, until the butter is bubbling. The kipper is now ready to be enjoyed. Remove from the grill. Pull away the central bone and place the kipper on the serving plate. Pour any butter and juices left on the foil over the fish.

Serve with a wedge of lemon plus brown bread and butter to mop up the juices.

Note: Kippers also eat very well with poached or scrambled eggs.

If you feel that kippers are a little too salty, before grilling simply place them head first in a jug and pour boiling water over. Leave for 2–3 minutes before pouring the water away. This is known as 'jugging'.

Smoked Haddock

Haddock is a smaller member of the cod family. When bought fresh, it's mostly found whole, filleted or cut into haddock steaks. The reputation that has grown worldwide over the years concerns the smoked versions, and smoked haddock is one of the finest British breakfast ingredients. Naturally smoked haddock fillets, which I much prefer to the yellow-dyed versions (many of which are chemically flavoured to create the smoky taste), have even been accepted in France as a great speciality. The French name for haddock is *aiglefin*, but over the years the smoked fish has become known as 'haddock'. So if you have ever seen this listed on a French menu, it means smoked, not fresh.

In the eighteenth century, Finnan haddies, named after the village of Findon in Aberdeenshire, were haddock beheaded, split and smoked over seaweed or peat and sphagnum moss. The result was quite hard, dry and black. When the peat ran out, oak chips were introduced, and the fish took on, and have maintained, their beautiful golden lemon colour. They are cold smoked, and have a more subtle flavour than the smokies.

Arbroath smokies, which are unique, small fish, are beheaded and gutted but left whole, hung in pairs high on wooden spits or over whisky barrels, then dry salted and hot-smoked in pairs over oak or silver birch chips. It is said they originated in the early nineteenth century, when fishermen from Auchmithie moved to Arbroath, taking with them their practice of hanging fish inside the chimneys to smoke. The commercial possibilities were spotted very quickly by the locals, and Arbroath smokies were born. They have since become one of the most respected smoked fish worldwide. The skin has a lovely rich, copper colour which, once removed, reveals a golden crust working into a much paler flesh. The fish has a very savoury flavour and a creamy texture.

Smoked haddock fillets are wonderful just lightly poached in milk and butter and served with buttered toast for breakfast. I don't think that anything else is needed, apart from perhaps a poached egg. For any other meal there's plenty that can be added – a spinach and cheese sauce, eggs in an *Omelette Arnold Bennett* (page 71), or how about on a tomato salad with *Welsh Rarebit* (page 178).

Finnan Haddie

For a classic *Cullen Skink* soup (page 27), Finnan haddie should be used, bones and all, to get the maximum flavour from the fish. Once cooked in the soup, all the skin and bones are removed, and the flesh flaked and returned to the liquid. The *Cullen Skink* then has a very delicate and detailed flavour, something a straightforward smoked fillet cannot match.

To cook Finnan, just place in a dish in the oven pre-heated to 160°C/325°F/Gas Mark 3, with milk and lots of butter. This will then create a steam, softening the flesh. Serve with the bones removed and some of the rich cooking liquor poured over.

Arbroath Smokie

Split the fish and place some butter with a twist of pepper in the centre. Close the fillets. Brush the outside skin with butter as well and warm the fish under a pre-heated grill or in a low oven (160°C/325°F/Gas Mark 3). The smokie doesn't need to be cooked, as its complete smoking has already done this, so it's just a warming process. Once warmed, remove the skin, open the fish and then pull away the bones. If too cold, lightly warm again, pour the butter over and serve.

Arbroath Smokie and Cream Cheese Pâté

Pastes of fish or meat were once made as a means of preservation, and were very popular at breakfast. This is rather more sophisticated, and is good for a starter, for a snack or savoury, or in sandwiches for tea – or, of course, for breakfast.

SERVES 4–6

1 pair of Arbroath smokies, boned and skinned
Juice of ½ lemon
Pinch of cayenne pepper
250 g (9 oz) cream cheese
50 ml (2 fl oz) single cream
¼–½ teaspoon Dijon or English mustard
1 tablespoon chopped fresh chives (optional)
Salt and pepper

The smokies must first be blitzed in a food processor along with the lemon juice and cayenne pepper. Add the cream cheese, single cream and mustard and process to a smooth paste. Check for seasoning. While at this soft stage, the chopped chives, if using, can be stirred in.

The pâté can now be spooned into a suitable dish and refrigerated for at least 1 hour to set. A little melted butter can be poured over the dish to prevent a skin from forming. This pâté eats very well with hot, thick, crispy toast.

Stewed Prunes Ⓥ

At the beginning of this century, the health and daily diet of children – and of adults – was considered very seriously. In winter, children would be encouraged to eat for breakfast some porridge followed by stewed fruit; in summer they might start with some fresh fruit,

followed by one of the new-fangled cereals introduced from America, and pioneered by a man named Kellogg. Stewed prunes were considered particularly valuable, and it was at this time – perhaps to encourage reluctant small eaters? – that the 'Tinker, Tailor, Soldier, Sailor' chant originated, counting out the stones along the edge of the bowl.

Until the nineteenth century, prunes were more popular in this country than plums. The best prunes today come from Agen in France, although they are also cultivated in California. The French believe the American one can't beat theirs, and this is probably true as the French methods of drying the plum would be hard to match.

Soak the prunes before use – for flavour, the best soaking medium is tea – and do so overnight. In this recipe, the sugar can be omitted. However, without it the natural sugars from the prune will be drawn into the soaking liquid.

500 ml (17 fl oz) water
2 tea-bags
225 g (8 oz) prunes
50 g (2 oz) sugar

Bring the water to the boil and pour onto the tea-bags in a suitable bowl. Add the prunes. Stir in the sugar, cover and leave to stand for several hours, preferably overnight. Remove the tea-bags and the prunes are ready to eat.

Note: The bags can be left in just for a few hours and then removed. This will prevent the tea flavour from becoming too strong. The sugar can be stirred in, if needed, once the prunes have been soaked.

See also

Devilled Kidneys (page 178)
Orange Marmalade (page 390)
Strawberry Jam (page 387)
Smoked Eel Kedgeree (page 162)

Vegetables and Salads

One of the pleasures of cooking fresh vegetables is having so much natural flavour just waiting to be enjoyed. However, one of the most criticized aspects of British food is our general treatment of vegetables – it's said that we undervalue and over-cook them. This may have been the norm in the past but it's certainly not so now, nor was it so, perhaps surprisingly, in the more distant past, with vegetables receiving the respect they deserved.

Wild vegetables, herbs, seeds and leaves would probably have been the most important element, apart from the occasional meat kill, of prehistoric man's diet. Once cooking vessels were introduced, and after the Romans had brought in several new vegetable varieties, both wild and cultivated vegetables would have been used in the vegetable soup pottages which were so important in the diet of poor and rich alike from very early times right up to the eighteenth century. Some favourites used were early types of onions, leeks, turnips, carrots, peas, broad beans and cabbage. Possibly this close relationship between the vegetables and an over-cooked soupy consistency contributes to our bad reputation. For many centuries, vegetables were not seen as something to eat fresh, but as inevitable additions to dishes such as stews which were always cooked lengthily in plenty of water.

Another factor would have been the long association of vegetables, herbs and leaves with medicine. In addition, the agricultural year itself would have contributed to the public's view of vegetables. In the summer there would be plenty to eat, followed by feasting after the harvest before the lean months ahead. Winters would be dominated by salted meats and dried pulses, then spring would bring fresh leaves again. Even today in the north of England it is believed that easterledge (a plant with tannin-sour leaves used to counter smallpox and snake bites in medieval times), dandelion and nettle leaves should be eaten in spring to cleanse the body after the heavy diet of winter. Growers of watercress say that, despite its year-round availability now, it is most in demand in the early months of the year.

The great explorations of the sixteenth century introduced many new varieties of vegetables to Europe and eventually to Britain. Among them were potatoes, tomatoes, green beans (kidney, French, haricot, string), peppers, chillies and pumpkin. Continual trials by Continental gardeners, particularly the Italians, French and Dutch, resulted in the improvement of many wild varieties of vegetables, among them celery (developed from the wild smallage), cauliflower, Jerusalem artichoke and spinach. The wealthy started to spend lavishly on their gardens and farms, and they would grow a huge variety of vegetables for their tables. Market gardens, too, began to spring up around larger towns and cities. Those around London, at Wanstead and Blackheath, were fertilized by London 'night soil'. In the mid seventeenth century the main vegetable market in London, beside St Paul's, was moved to the roomier garden and orchard of the convent of St Peter in Westminster, a venue that became the famous old Covent Garden market (now at Nine Elms).

Many English cookery books, which began to appear in the sixteenth and seventeenth centuries, list all the new vegetables then available, and carefully detail how they thought they should be cooked and sauced. Not long after, vegetables began to be thought of as 'Vegetables', a distinct category of food to be eaten in its own right, and with respect. At this time many of the classic Great British combinations, such as boiled beef with carrots, and duck with green peas, became common currency. But there was still a general tendency to boil vegetables for far too long. They did, however, get the simple accompaniment right – melted butter (rather than the infamous 'heavy' English butter sauce). Also, because meat had established itself as the most desirable type of food, particularly in the towns, vegetables rarely found their way on to menus. After the Industrial Revolution, they were associated in many minds with poverty, and this may be another reason why so few memorable British vegetable cooking techniques and dishes developed.

The recipes featured here aim to emphasize the natural flavours of the vegetables themselves and give you perfect cooking times to achieve the best results. Whenever you cook vegetables, acknowledge what they are accompanying. For a poached/steamed piece of fish, it's best to cook the vegetables until just tender than have them fighting against the softness of the fish. After the Victorian idea of vegetables being 'good for

PAGE 90
Roasted Parsnips (page 95)

you' – a saying still used in most households – we seem in the last two decades to have rediscovered the joys of vegetables. There is a certain sense of this being the reverse as far as salads are concerned, though. We may have cooked vegetables to death in the past, but we have eaten leaves and herbs raw since at least the fourteenth century – and usually dressed with oil and vinegar. In many early books, 'salading' plants are listed which later disappeared from sight until the last few decades. Corn salad or *mâche* and rocket, for instance, were grown and enjoyed in English salads as long ago as the sixteenth century. Many of these simple leaf salads were eaten for health, but they developed over the centuries into compound 'grand salads', similar to those we associate now with America. They would often include leaves, cooked vegetables, meat, fish, hard-boiled eggs, nuts, raisins and citrus fruit, a mixture that became known as, variously, Salamagundy, Solomon Grundy, or Salmagundi. That's one of the beauties of salad-making – having an almost unlimited choice of ingredients, whether creating a one- or two-leaf, simple salad, all the way through to a great salmagundi.

A salad can appear at almost any meal, and in almost any course – as a starter, main course and even to replace a dessert. It is possibly most associated with starters because the Romans believed the milky juices of lettuce leaves lined the stomach, enabling them to drink more with their meal. But a salad can also be served as a simple accompaniment or side dish. Salads are a perfect excuse to use your culinary licence, to express your personality, but you must always remember not to over-flavour. This could lose you the beautiful fresh flavours of the leaves themselves. Various salads and dressings are featured in this book for you to choose from, but sometimes, especially for me, a trickle of good olive oil and a squeeze of lemon juice are quite enough to please the palate.

First of all, here is a list of salad garnish ingredients, followed overleaf by a selection of salad leaves.

Artichokes – bottoms or hearts
Asparagus – peeled and blanched
Broad beans – blanched and peeled
Broccoli florets – blanched
Capers – left whole or chopped
Carrots – thinly sliced, shredded or grated
Celery – trimmed and sliced
Chillies – finely chopped or thinly sliced
Cucumber – preferably peeled and de-seeded
Eggs – hard-boiled or poached
Fennel – raw and thinly sliced
Fine French beans – blanched
Fresh picked herbs – flat parsley, basil, tarragon, mint, coriander, etc.
Garlic – used in dressings or roasted
Mange-tout – blanched
New potatoes – cooked and sliced
Olives – black or green, stoned
Red onions – thinly sliced
Sesame seeds – toasted
Shallots – thinly sliced into rings
Spring onions – chopped or thinly sliced
Sweet peppers – red, green or yellow
Tomatoes – plum, salad or cherry
Walnuts, hazelnuts, almonds – shelled and peeled

And there are plenty more. Quite often, just leaves and dressing together are enough without other garnishes.

When shopping for salads you might find bags of *mesclun*. This is not an actual lettuce, but instead a name for a mixture of young tender leaves, usually consisting of baby spinach, lamb's lettuce, rocket or *mizuna* and small curly endive leaves from the heart.

Always choose good crisp leaves, not bruised ones. To store them, and keep them in the best possible condition, keep in a plastic bag, refrigerated. This will help maintain their natural crispness. Should the leaves become slightly limp, simply refresh in iced water, carefully shaking away excess water. And always pick and tear the leaves by hand – a knife will bruise the leaves. Here's a list of salad leaves, with descriptions.

Butterhead – An open, light, loose-leafed lettuce.

Cos/Romaine – Cos is the English name for this long, crisp and nutty flavoured lettuce. Romaine is the name used elsewhere in Europe and in the United States.

Curly endive – An exciting curly leaved endive that has become very trendy – but a trend that will last. As the leaves grow, they become less bitter, giving a more comforting flavour. Choose one with a good yellow heart; these leaves have a better flavour than the very crinkly, deep green leaves.

Dandelion – Known as *piss-en-lit* in France, its thin long leaves range from a yellow/white to almost deep green. Similar flavour to rocket, but must be picked young.

Escarole – Similar in flavour to curly endive and not too different in appearance. Rather than the complete curly look, escarole has more of a gathered crinkly look.

Iceberg – In the same family as Webb's Wonderful lettuce, these have to be the crispest leaves of all, and the flavour is good and fresh.

Lamb's lettuce – Also known as *mâche* or corn salad. Very much a winter salad that carries a nutty flavour in its small, deep golden leaves.

Little Gem – This is a smaller and equally crisp version of the Cos. Lovely to use in a 'standard' green salad or in the world-famous Caesar salad.

Lollo rosso – A crinkly red-and-green-leaved lettuce, which doesn't have much flavour, but which lends a nice texture and colour to a salad. Oakleaf lettuce is very similar, with a softer leaf and deeper red colour. Both of these come into the 'loose-head' lettuce category, with no heart.

Mizuna – A Japanese leaf, very attractive, small rocket-like leaves, carrying a mild pepper flavour.

Purslane – This is picked almost as small posies and then presented and served in small sprigs. It was grown and used in salads in Britain in the Middle Ages, but somehow went out of fashion, almost being looked on as a garden pest. In France it's known as *pourpier*, and is still considered an important salad item.

Radicchio – An Italian member of the chicory family. Its colour ranges from a deep ruby red through to pink, finishing with a creamy white. It comes as a round head and in a long, Cos-like shape. It carries a peppery flavour with a pleasant bitterness as well. A wonderful leaf for simply mixing with other leaves and a drop of dressing.

Rocket – Often called *arugula* or *roquette*. The long thin stalk and leaves vaguely resemble dandelion leaves. It has a good peppery, bitter flavour, sometimes almost too bitter. It is, however, a stunning leaf to use in almost any salad or as a garnish.

Spinach – Mostly associated with vegetable dishes, but young tender leaves eat beautifully in a good green salad, or with tossed bacon pieces and walnuts.

Watercress – Mostly used in garnish form, but works in salads as well. Rich, dark green sprigs will add a peppery bite to almost any leaf salad.

Roasted Parsnips ⓥ

This sweet root vegetable has been found in many recipes over the years. It was the traditional accompaniment for roast beef before the potato was introduced, and was also often served with boiled salt cod on Ash Wednesday. Its sweetness has been turned into honey, jams and even wine. It has featured in puddings, stews and soups, has been puréed for mousses and vegetable accompaniments and, the most classic of all, roasted. In Italy the pigs for Parma ham are fed on parsnips to give their flesh a rich and slightly sweet flavour. The French don't think much of parsnips, preferring turnips instead. But we once valued parsnips so highly in Britain that they were used to cure toothache, keep adders away, as an aphrodisiac for men and even to reduce swollen testicles.

Parsnips are at their best during the winter months. The smaller they are, the more tender they'll be and the less work they'll need. The root/core on baby parsnips need not be cut away, and with cooking will become very tender. They also don't need to be peeled, just well scrubbed before cooking. Larger parsnips, anything from 175–225 g (6–8 oz) upwards, will need to be peeled and definitely have the core cut away.

From roasted to creamed, the flavours are totally different, but you must give them some attention – plain boiling just isn't very exciting. Here I show you how to roast them without making them over-sweet. The addition of honey will give the parsnips a bitter–sweet edge of flavour, but I leave that option to you. As you will know by now, my style of cooking is about understanding and balancing tastes.

SERVES 6

900 g (2 lb) parsnips, peeled and quartered (if you have found good, small parsnips that do not need to be quartered, then 750 g/1¼ lb should be enough)
2 tablespoons olive or cooking oil
25–50 g (1–2 oz) butter
2 tablespoons honey (optional)
Salt and pepper

Pre-heat the oven to 200°C/400°F/Gas Mark 6). If the parsnips are large and have woody centres, cut these out before cooking.

The parsnips can be boiled in salted water for 2 minutes before roasting. I don't think this is essential; however, if you prefer them 'over-cooked' with a crispy skin and almost hollow but creamy centre, then the par-boiling will help.

Pre-heat a roasting tray on top of the stove and add the oil. Fry the parsnips in the oil until golden brown on all sides, allowing burnt tinges on the edges. The tinges will give a slightly bitter flavour that will balance the sweetness.

Roast in the oven, turning occasionally for 20–30 minutes, depending on their size. (If you want them 'over-cooked', leave in for 35–40 minutes.) Remove from the oven and season with salt and pepper. Add the butter to enrich the finished flavour, and the honey, if using. Cook for another 5–10 minutes.

Place them into a serving dish, spooning any remaining caramelized juices over.

Creamed Parsnips ⓥ

Parsnips can be prepared like mashed potato, that is, boiled, and then mashed with butter and cream. Boiling alone just gives a watery taste with the real depth and flavour of the vegetable lost. So here's a method that will retain the natural flavour of the parsnip.

Serve these creamed parsnips as a vegetable accompaniment, but they can also be eaten in other ways. I use them in *Steamed and Braised Mallard with a Parsnip Tart* (page 261) and they can also be used in a parsnip ravioli.

SERVES 4–6

450 g (1 lb) parsnips, peeled and roughly diced (core removed)
Squeeze of lemon juice
50 g (2 oz) butter
100 ml (3½ fl oz) water
50 ml (2 fl oz) double cream
Salt and pepper

Place the diced parsnips in a bowl and squeeze over the lemon juice, making sure they are spooned around to cover all with juice.

Melt the butter in a thick-based saucepan until it begins to foam. Add the parsnips and stir before adding the water.

Now they can be cooked slowly for 15 minutes or until they are completely tender and have broken down.

Place in a liquidizer. Gently boil the double cream and add to the parsnips, season with salt and pepper and blitz to a fine purée.

For an even smoother finish, push through an extra fine sieve. The creamed parsnips are now ready to enjoy.

Braised Globe Artichokes ⓥ

Although we think of them as rather exotic, globe artichokes used to be a familiar sight in British gardens, introduced from Italy (as so many vegetables were) in Elizabethan times.

They can have a variety of uses. The outside leaves can be cooked and used as garnishes or in salads. There is a small bite of flesh to be eaten at the base of them. The small, younger leaves attached to the artichoke bottoms in the centre can be cooked still attached and then used in salads, or as complete vegetarian dishes. I'm really after the artichoke bottom itself, which for me is the best and most succulent part.

To cook them and keep their natural colour, I like to make a tomato and lemon stock. The acidity from the lemon and sweetness of the tomato give the artichoke even more flavour without masking its own.

SERVES 6

6 globe artichokes
Juice of 1 lemon

For the Stock

4 over-ripe tomatoes, roughly chopped
Juice of 1 lemon

300 ml (½ pint) water
Salt
1 teaspoon coriander seeds (optional)
1 bay leaf (optional)

To make the stock, place all the ingredients together in a pan and bring to the simmer. It is now ready to use. (If cooking just 2 artichokes, then reduce the tomatoes to 2 and the coriander seeds, if using, by half.)

Remove the stalks from the artichokes and then cut around the base, removing the leaves. Now cut across about 4 cm (1½ in) from the base and cut off any excess stalk or green left on. The centre of the bottom will still be intact. Rub with lemon juice.

Place the artichoke bottoms and the remaining lemon juice in the stock and simmer for 20–30 minutes, until tender. When cooked and cooled, remove and discard the bristly centres. The artichokes are now ready to use.

Note: The artichoke-flavoured stock can be reserved, strained and refrigerated and used for cooking artichokes once more. After that it will have taken on too many bitter flavours and should be discarded.

Broad Beans ⓥ

The broad bean has been around in the West since at least the Bronze Age, and has been eaten both fresh and dried; in fact, the dried variety sustained many of our ancestors throughout the long winter months, perhaps cooked with bacon. The Egyptians had a love-hate relationship with the bean. Many loved the vegetable but priests felt that the hollow stems were used by the souls of the dead as a passageway to life after death. Despite this, the bean was soon enjoyed by the masses. In fact, until Columbus arrived in America, and the kidney bean and all its relations were introduced to the West, the broad bean was as important in daily eating as the potato is now.

We seem to ignore the broad bean nowadays, which I find difficult to understand because they are

Grilled Baby Leeks Ⓥ

so delicious, particularly when fresh. The season for fresh beans is extremely short, lasting only through the first few months of summer. You should take advantage of this and eat as many as you can – they really are superb, just lightly buttered. Also if you catch them very early in the season, you'll be able to find the small beans in 8–10 cm (3–4 in) pods. At this size they can be eaten pod and all, so no flavour is lost – and no weight either. Later, of course, you have to buy quite a load of pods to get a reasonable amount of beans.

It's best to cook broad beans as soon as they are picked. Otherwise they tend to become limp, the sugar content turning to carbohydrate, which inevitably changes the texture and flavour. This simple recipe uses the average kidney-shaped bean, which needs to be podded before it's cooked.

I insist on eating broad beans with their grey skin/shell removed. This way the deep, rich green colour is on show, and they are perfectly tender. For another recipe that uses these beans, see *Sage Broad Beans with Bacon and Tomato* (page 56).

SERVES 4

450 g (1 lb) podded broad beans
Butter
Salt and pepper

Bring a large saucepan of well salted water to the boil. Remove the lid and add the beans; it's now important the lid stays off to maintain the colour in the vegetable.

Cook medium-sized beans for approximately 1–2 minutes, 5 minutes maximum. Once tender, lift from the pan and into iced water. When the beans are cold, they can have their skins/shells removed. To re-heat, melt a knob of butter and add a tablespoon or two of water. Bring to the simmer and add the skinned, cooked beans. Season with salt and pepper. The beans will be hot within a minute or two and ready to eat.

Once cooked and skinned, they can be seasoned and rolled in the melted butter and microwaved when needed.

Baby leeks are the young, thin variety, which also carry the name 'pencil' leeks. Eating them grilled gives the young leeks quite a sweet flavour and a slightly bitter edge.

Before grilling, the leeks need to be pre-cooked in boiling salted water. This will tenderize the texture prior to cooking under a hot grill. If you are serving them as a vegetable accompaniment, 2–3 leeks per portion will be plenty.

SERVES 4

8–12 baby leeks, washed and trimmed of top and bottom
Butter, melted
Salt and pepper

Plunge the leeks into boiling salted water and cook without a lid for 2–3 minutes. If they're slightly thicker, cook for 4–5 minutes. Once tender, the leeks can be removed from the pan and left to cool naturally, or quickly plunged into iced water. If cooled in the iced water, leave in for only the same period as the cooking time: 2–3 minutes. Dry the leeks and brush with the butter. The leeks can be prepared to this stage well in advance and refrigerated until needed.

To finish, simply sit the leeks under a hot grill and cook for a few minutes, turning them over occasionally to mark and colour all around. Season with salt and pepper before serving.

Note: These leeks eat very well with most dishes, but in particular with the *Roast Loin of Pork with an Apricot and Sage Stuffing* (page 330).

Leeks with Prunes Ⓥ

The combination of leeks and prunes is an old one, both being popular pottage ingredients. Together they are a perfect accompaniment to pork and poultry dishes. Prunes have a very long relationship with duck, chicken and pork, whether in a stuffing form or, in that classic French style, with Armagnac. Leeks too have certainly had affairs with

all of those foods, so it was a question of trying to bring the two together, and they've 'married' well.

The prunes must be stoned and ready to eat. Soaking them first would create a stewed finish to the dish, with everything over-cooked and soggy. With a shredded leek, I prefer just a bite left in. A squeeze of lime is not essential but does lift all the other flavours.

SERVES 4

450 g (1 lb) leeks, split lengthways, washed and
    shredded
100 g (4 oz) ready-to-eat prunes
Butter
Salt and pepper
Squeeze of fresh lime juice (optional)

It's best to shred the leeks quite finely (2–3 mm/about ⅛ in); they will then cook very quickly. The prunes can be split lengthways and cut into sticks.

Melt a knob of butter in a large frying- or braising pan. Once bubbling fast, add the leeks. Any water from them will prevent the butter from becoming burnt. Season with salt and pepper.

Cook on a fast heat for 2–3 minutes. The leeks will now be quite tender. While still on a high heat, add the prunes and toss into the leeks. Once warmed through, add another knob of butter and a squeeze of lime, if using, and serve.

Note: The prunes can be given an almost scorched effect by throwing them into a very hot, dry pan. Stir for just 30–40 seconds and then add to the leeks. This brings out a richer prune flavour.

OPPOSITE
Leeks with Prunes

Stilton and Red-onion Salad with Peppered Beef Fillet

Basically, nothing could be more British than this combination of the very English Stilton cheese and beef. It harks back to the great compound salads of the seventeenth and eighteenth centuries. The dish is very lively, full of amazing flavours – one of those dishes you just can't get enough of.

The 'pickled' red onions are delicious in themselves and can be served as part of any salad or to accompany a 'ploughman's lunch'.

It's a great dish for a dinner party. It suits best as a starter, but I would be happy to serve just large plates of this dish for a main course, with a good bottle of red. This helps you get away from the standard three courses that give you far too much pressure, and your friends will have more than enough flavours to enjoy. A lot of the work can also be done well in advance – the beef fillet can be prepared and peppered, the red onions cooked and pickled, the Stilton broken down and the dressing made.

SERVES 4 AS A STARTER

For the Beef

350–450 g (12 oz–1 lb) beef fillet
1 tablespoon crushed black peppercorns
Oil or butter

For the Salad

3 red onions
2 tablespoons olive oil
2 tablespoons groundnut oil
2 tablespoons balsamic vinegar
Squeeze of lemon juice
10 very thin slices of French bread, halved
225–350 g (8–12 oz) mixed green leaves
100 g (4 oz) Stilton cheese, broken (more can be
    added for blue-cheese lovers, or Roquefort
    can be substituted)
Salt and pepper

For the Dressing

3 tablespoons port
2 teaspoons Dijon mustard

2 tablespoons red-wine vinegar (preferably
    Cabernet Sauvignon)
4 tablespoons walnut oil
4 tablespoons groundnut oil
Salt and pepper

First, roll the beef in the crushed black peppercorns.
The meat will start to take on the pepper flavour
and can be left until needed. The onions and
dressing can now both be prepared and kept until
you are completing the dish.

Let's start with the onions. Cut them into 6–8
wedges, keeping the root of the onion in place to
prevent them from falling apart. Bring a pan of water
to the boil, add the cut onions and cook for 2 minutes.

Warm together the oils, balsamic vinegar and
lemon juice. Drain the onions and add them to the
oil/vinegar mix. Remove this from the heat, season
with salt and pepper and leave the onions to marinate
at room temperature, turning every so often to ensure
an even flavour. The onions will eat at their best after
a minimum 1–2 hours, so these can quite easily be
prepared in the morning for an evening meal.

To make the dressing, boil and reduce the port
by half and allow to cool. Mix the mustard with the
red-wine vinegar. Whisk together the oils and pour
slowly on to the mustard and vinegar mixture, while
continuing to whisk vigorously. Once all has been
added, whisk in the reduced port and season with
salt and pepper.

BELOW
Stilton and Red-onion Salad with Peppered Beef Fillet

The French bread slices can be crisped by trickling with oil and either toasting or baking in a hot oven.

To roast the beef fillet, pre-heat the oven to 220°C/425°F/Gas Mark 7. Heat an oven-proof frying-pan and trickle with a drop of oil or knob of butter. Add the fillet and colour to a deep seared effect all round. Now finish by roasting in the hot oven for about 10–12 minutes. This will keep the beef nice and pink in the centre. Up to 20 minutes will make it medium-well to well done.

Once cooked, remove from the oven and leave to rest for another 10–12 minutes. This will totally relax the meat and also make it just warm for serving.

To finish the dish, mix the red onions (out of the marinade) with the green leaves and blue cheese. Add some of the red wine/port dressing to bind. Slice the beef, allowing three thin slices per portion, and overlap on each plate. Divide the salad, sitting it towards the top of the plate. Trickle over some more of the dressing and sit the crispy toasts on top.

Note: The port and mustard dressing can be excluded from this recipe and the marinade used to replace it. A splash or two of port can be added to the marinade, along with mustard, if preferred.

One egg yolk can be added to the vinegar and mustard before adding the oils to the dressing. This will give a creamier finish.

Bubble and Squeak Artichokes with 'Burnt' Mushrooms ⓥ

That old favourite, bubble and squeak, was originally a mixture of fried beef and cabbage, the potato addition coming much later. Here I use the basic idea of bubble and squeak in a vegetarian main course. The 'squeak' ingredients are formed into faggot shapes and then served in an artichoke bottom with the almost dry-fried 'burnt' mushrooms.

These are helped along and enriched by a red-wine dressing. Red wine and mushrooms have always had a close relationship. This is a perfect recipe for using up any leftover mashed potatoes.

I've suggested using a quantity of 350 g (12 oz), but a minimum of 225 g (8 oz) will also work.

A lovely optional extra is to finish the dish with *Hollandaise Sauce* (page 41).

SERVES 4 AS A MAIN COURSE

1 medium Savoy cabbage
2 onions, sliced
50 g (2 oz) butter
350 g (12 oz) *Mashed Potatoes* (page 124)
    (no cream added)
Oil, for frying
4 large globe artichokes, cooked (page 20)
28 small button mushrooms
150 ml (¼ pint) *Hollandaise Sauce* or *Simple Hollandaise Sauce* (page 41)
2 tablespoons olive oil
1 teaspoon chopped fresh chives
Salt and pepper
Lime juice (optional)

For the Red-wine Dressing

2 teaspoons Dijon mustard
2 tablespoons red-wine vinegar (preferably Cabernet Sauvignon)
4 tablespoons walnut oil
4 tablespoons groundnut oil

Remove four of the outer leaves from the Savoy cabbage by first cutting away some of the base stalk. The leaves will now fall away quite easily. The thick stalk veins can now be cut out from the leaves, without cutting the leaf in half. These leaves will be used to wrap the bubble and squeak faggots. A medium cabbage is the best size to buy, so that the outer leaves are large enough for wrapping. Wash them well.

Split the remaining cabbage in half and then cut one half into quarters. These two quarters should be plenty for four portions. The remaining half can be kept for another meal. Cut any stalk away from the quarters and shred the leaves very finely.

Bring a large pot of salted water to the boil. Once boiling, add the washed large leaves. Cook for a few minutes, until the leaves are very tender.

Refresh in iced water. When cold, lay them on a cloth to dry. The shredded cabbage can now also be blanched in the boiling water. Once added, return to the boil and, if finely shredded, the cabbage will then be cooked. Strain in a colander and then spread the hot cooked cabbage on a tray. Leave to cool, then refrigerate.

The sliced onions can now be cooked in 25 g (1 oz) of the butter. Fry to a rich golden caramel colour. Season with salt and pepper. Also leave to cool. The mashed potato can also be used cold.

Mix together the shredded cabbage and onions. Add enough of the potato to bind and create a good texture. Probably all will be needed. Season with salt and pepper.

Divide the mix into four and shape into balls. Season the large blanched cabbage leaves and lay them on a board, seasoning with salt and pepper. Where the stalk vein has been cut away, overlap the cabbage by 1 cm (½ in). Sit the balls in the centre and wrap the leaf around. Because the cabbage is tender it should shape easily. Once all is covered, wrap each one in cling film, twisting it firmly at the base to give a full, round, ball shape. These can now be refrigerated to set.

Melt half of the remaining butter with a trickle of cooking oil and pan-fry the artichokes. These will take 4–5 minutes to cook, acquiring a golden edge.

While these are cooking, the mushrooms can also be 'burnt'. Heat a frying-pan with a drop of

BELOW
Bubble and Squeak Artichokes with 'Burnt' Mushrooms

Cabbage

cooking oil. Add the button mushrooms and cook on a medium-hot stove until they begin to burn slightly and become tender. The mushrooms will take in total 6–8 minutes to cook. During the last minute of cooking, add the remaining knob of butter. Season with salt and pepper.

The hollandaise sauce, if using, and red-wine dressing can be made between 30 minutes and 1 hour before serving the dish.

To make the dressing, mix the mustard with the red-wine vinegar. Whisk together the oils and pour slowly onto the mustard and vinegar while whisking vigorously. Once all has been added, season with salt and pepper. The addition of 1 egg yolk or heaped teaspoon of mayonnaise to the vinegar and mustard will guarantee the emulsion of the oils.

The chopped chives can be added to the olive oil and seasoned with salt and pepper. A drop of lemon or lime juice can also be added to this oil for an extra bite.

Re-heat the bubble and squeak, preferably in a microwave. In a 750-watt machine, they will take 1 minute. They can also be placed in a steamer for 6–8 minutes to heat through.

Place an artichoke bottom in the centre of each plate. Pour a dessertspoon of hollandaise sauce into each one. Place the mushrooms, seven each, around the artichoke. Peel away the cling film and sit a bubble and squeak 'faggot' on top of each artichoke.

The red-wine dressing can now be spooned around and over the mushrooms. This can be achieved quickly and easily if piped from a squeezy bottle (page 11). The chive olive oil can now also be drizzled around the mushrooms.

A tablespoon or two of hollandaise sauce, if using, can now be spooned over each 'faggot' top.

Note: A large flat mushroom can be grilled and used to sit the faggots on. These would be used to replace the artichoke and button mushrooms.

Hollandaise sauce can, if you wish, be made with the addition of freshly grated truffles. To increase the truffle flavour, truffle vinegar can be added along with a little truffle oil.

Cabbage has a history that is actually longer than that of the potato. We have been eating it in Britain since the time of the Celts, and it was an early pottage vegetable. What we had been eating, though, was a tough, wild variety that apparently is still grown in Europe and northern Britain around the sea coasts. This was very different from the more tender cabbages we now know. It was very bitter and consequently had a bad reputation. (The bitter plant was eaten for medicinal purposes, especially while drinking – it was said to prevent you from becoming drunk.) It took the Romans to develop the plant, taking away some of that bitterness, but the vegetable was still an open-leaved kale variety, not a tight-packed ball such as we see today. It wasn't until centuries later that European gardeners mastered the art of cabbage-growing. From the Dutch came the white cabbage (and coleslaw). A late seventeenth-century gardener's book was quoted in *Food in England* by Dorothy Hartley: ''Tis scarce 100 years since we had Cabbages out of Holland, Sir Arthur Ashley of Wilburg St Giles, in Dorsetshire, being the first who planted them in England. Cabbage is not so greatly magnified by the rest of the doctors, as affording but a gross and melancholy juice. Yet loosening, if moderately boil'd. It is seldom eaten raw, except by the Dutch.' From the kingdom of Savoy (now part of France) came the Savoy cabbage, probably the most common variety in Britain today.

Over the years, the simple cabbage has developed into a very large family: green, Savoy, white, red, then spring greens, sea kale, curly kale, cauliflower, broccoli, Brussels sprouts… Most of these have become popular in Britain, particularly in Ireland, where so many traditional dishes – champ and colcannon, for instance – utilize cabbage. That these still exist and are still enjoyed demonstrates how good, simple dishes will never die.

One of the beauties of cabbage is that it is an all-year-round vegetable which can stand up very well against cold and even icy conditions. It does, however, carry one or two problems. The first is the unsavoury smell of over-cooked cabbage (from the sulphur in the leaves) that lingers in the memory from schooldays. School cabbage when cooked had a dull, almost yellow colour, as well as a bad odour. That leads me to the second problem – understanding the cooking of cabbage so that we can eat it at its best. The much earlier Roman variety needed several hours of rapid boiling before becoming tender and edible, with its bitter flavour mellowed. This cooking tradition obviously lasted hundreds of years, extending to the new, more tender variety. Cabbage, in fact, cooks to its best in just minutes, keeping all its natural tastes and colours, and giving a really inviting nose rather than odour.

The Dutch white cabbage eats at its best as sauerkraut, or raw in coleslaw (probably what it was developed for in its native country). White cabbage must be shredded or grated very finely, though, if being served raw. This prevents it from being too tough and bitter to eat. Sweet and sour cabbage can also be made. Bring 1 tablespoon of caster sugar and 4 tablespoons of white-wine vinegar to the boil and pour over the finely shredded cabbage. Season with salt and leave to cool.

Green and Savoy cabbages can also be finely shredded or grated and used in salads. It is important to serve them straight away, otherwise the acidity of vinegar or citrus fruit (lime works very well with ginger and cabbage) will discolour the leaves.

The golden rule whenever cooking any variety of green cabbage or, for that matter, any green vegetable, is to always cook in plenty of boiling salted water – and *without a lid*. Bring the water to the boil, remove the lid and add the shredded cabbage. This will take only about 1–2 minutes to cook, or until the water just begins to boil again. Drain the cabbage, re-season with salt and pepper and add a knob of butter to finish. Serve the vegetable immediately.

Cabbage can be cooked, again as soon as needed, by heating a few tablespoons of water with a knob of butter, then adding the cabbage, and stirring for a few minutes on fast heat until tender. Sliced onions and strips of bacon can be tossed in butter before adding the raw or pre-cooked shredded cabbage. This gives you a good vegetable dish or one that can be used as an accompaniment for a fish or meat dish.

If cabbage has been very quickly blanched in boiling water, just taking out the rawness, it can be sautéed to an almost golden brown tinge in butter or perhaps a flavoured oil. (Sesame oil works very well, and sesame seeds, prawns and a squeeze of lemon go with it beautifully.)

Pieces of *Pork Scratchings* (page 179) mixed with sautéed cabbage also go very well. And stir-fry dishes using all types of flavours apart from cabbage give you really tasty vegetarian starters, main courses or vegetable dishes. The cabbage must be shredded very finely, then added at the last moment when cooking with other ingredients. How about mushrooms, onions, sweet peppers, leeks, beansprouts, chillies, herbs, ginger, garlic, lemon, limes, tomatoes? – the list could go on and on.

Try *Colcannon* (page 126), *Bubble and Squeak* (page 126), *Steamed Halibut and Cabbage with a Salmon Gravadlax Sauce* (page 132), *Grilled Lamb with 'Irish' Cabbage and Mashed Potato Sauce* (page 187)… and you'll see that cabbage need never be boring.

Creamed Cabbage and Bacon

The 'creamed' in the recipe title doesn't mean puréed, but refers to the cream I have added. This collects all the bacon and onion flavours, more or less creating a sauce for the cabbage.

This creamed cabbage goes particularly well with the roast beef dishes on pages 232 and 238.

SERVES 4–6

1 Savoy cabbage
25 g (1 oz) butter
2 onions, sliced
6 rashers of streaky bacon, smoked or unsmoked, cut into strips
2 tablespoons water
6 tablespoons double cream, more if necessary
Salt and pepper

Remove the large, tough, outer leaves from the cabbage. Quarter, also cutting out the stalk. The cabbage can now be finely shredded and washed. Melt a knob of butter in a large pan. Once bubbling, add the onions. Cook on a medium heat for 6–7 minutes, until slightly softened and with tinges of golden colour. The bacon can be fried separately at the same time on a high heat until crisp.

Add the 2 tablespoons of water to the onions along with the cabbage. It's important to cook on a fairly strong heat and to keep the cabbage moving for an even cooking. Season with salt and pepper. Cook for a few minutes. Check the cooked stage of the cabbage. It should be just tender. If not, continue to cook to that stage. Add the crispy bacon and cream and bring to a simmer. During this time the cream will slightly thicken and will also take on the bacon and onion stock taste.

The cabbage will now be very tender and just right for eating. Re-check the seasoning and adjust with salt and pepper.

Note: The cabbage can first be blanched in boiling water until tender. Once drained, leave to cool. Cook the onions and bacon as above and then also allow to cool. These can now both be refrigerated until needed. To re-heat, warm the onions and bacon in a hot pan. Add the cabbage and, once warmed, add the cream. Now just finish as above. This method enables you to work ahead of time, giving you more stove space when needed.

Cabbage with Beansprouts and Onions ⓥ

In this recipe I've blanched the cabbage to take out its rawness and flavoured it very simply with olive oil. The beansprouts give a light, crunchy taste.

SERVES 4

½ green cabbage, shredded
225 g (8 oz) beansprouts
2 onions, sliced
25 g (1 oz) butter
1 tablespoon olive oil
Salt and pepper
A pinch of five-spice powder

Blanch the cabbage and beansprouts separately in boiling salted water, then refresh under cold water and drain well. Melt the butter and olive oil in a wok or frying-pan and fry the onions until softened and golden brown. Add the cabbage and beansprouts and season with salt, pepper and five-spice powder. Now stir-fry for 2–3 minutes and the dish is ready.

Curly Kale ⓥ

Curly kale is a green vegetable of the cabbage family, grown in the winter and early spring, which has been cultivated and eaten in Britain for hundreds of years. It is similar to spring greens in flavour, with a thicker and firmer texture, and it keeps both when cooked, as well as its amazing deep green colour. When raw, it has a 'curly' parsley look about it. I like to eat it just tossed in butter and seasoned. It can also be used in stir-fries (after blanching) and mixed with spices, pasta or potatoes. It also eats very well with *Pan-fried Cod with Carrots, Parsley and 'Over-cooked' Bacon* (page 143).

SERVES 4

750–900 g (1½–2 lb) curly kale
Butter
Salt and pepper

Remove the stalks from the kale, wash well and cook the leaves in boiling, salted water for 3–4 minutes with the lid off. Don't overcrowd the pot with the kale as this means it will take longer for the water to return to the boil, causing the kale to lose its rich colour. Drain well in a colander, removing excess water. Season with salt and pepper and stir through a knob of butter.

The kale can also be cooked ahead and refreshed in iced water. Season and butter it when cold and refrigerate until needed. Now all you need to do is microwave it and serve.

Broccoli ⓥ

This is an Italian vegetable, another member of the cabbage family. It was popularized in this country in the early eighteenth century by a man called Stephen Switzer, who ran a seed business, importing exotic species such as cardoons, celeriac and Florence fennel. Broccoli comes in various sizes and varieties. My favourite is calabrese. This is the broccoli that grows in individual florets with a thick stalk. These really keep their colour and are very tender to eat, needing very little cooking. There is also purple sprouting broccoli, which was apparently the original form of the vegetable. This is also very tender when cooked, but never quite keeps that rich purple colour.

SERVES 6–8

900 g (2 lb) broccoli
Butter
Salt and pepper

Boil some salted water in a deep pan. Trim off the stalks of the broccoli florets (these can be kept and also boiled to be used as another vegetable dish). Once the water is boiling, drop in the florets, making sure the lid is left off. These will take only 2–5 minutes to become tender but still with a little bite, depending on the size of the florets. Once cooked, remove from the water and, if not using immediately, plunge into iced water to stop the cooking and retain their green colour. These can simply be re-heated by dropping once again into boiling water for 1 minute, or microwaving.

The broccoli can now be seasoned with salt and pepper, buttered and served.

Variations

You could vary this basic 'buttered' recipe. Once the broccoli is cooked, you could top it with Stilton rarebit (see *Port and Stilton Cheese Toasts*, page 172) and finish it under the grill; sprinkle it with grated Parmesan and brown under the grill; fry it in some garlic butter or in butter with some flaked almonds; or finish it with some *Hollandaise* or *Simple Hollandaise Sauce* (page 41).

Buttered Brussels Sprouts ⓥ

Brussels sprouts were one of those vegetables I just couldn't enjoy at school, with their quite disgusting sulphur nose, as well as the pale green/yellow colour and soggy texture. Was it the vegetable itself or the cooking that was to blame? Of course, I blamed the vegetable, and many years passed before I realized it was in fact the cooking.

The true botanical history of this vegetable is not well documented, although it was said to be around Brussels (in Belgium) that it was first grown. A member of the cabbage family, it has become a very British vegetable, one of our favourites in the winter, but this is a comparatively recent passion. Eliza Acton was the first to include a recipe for them in her *Modern Cookery*, published in 1845. Alexis Soyer, that great chef who cooked in the Reform Club, Pall Mall, also included a recipe for them in his *Modern Housewife* of 1849. So we really only met the sprout about 150 years ago.

There are a few golden rules to choosing and buying. To appreciate the great flavour – quite different from cabbage – and the slightly nutty crunch once cooked, it's important to buy them as small and tight-leaved as possible. These signs indicate freshness and such sprouts will require minimal cooking. Never buy yellow sprouts, those whose colour is fading, or with too much loose leaf. All these will tell you they are old and they'll taste pretty old too.

Here's a very simple recipe, giving you a few alternatives to enjoy. But Brussels sprouts have many more options in cooking, and can be finely shredded raw in salads, or boiled, pan-fried or roasted.

SERVES 4

450 g (1 lb) small Brussels sprouts
25–50 g (1–2 oz) butter
Salt and pepper

The first stage is to bring a large pot of salted water, three-quarters full, to the boil.

While waiting for the water to boil, remove any damaged outside leaves (this should be very few if good, small, tight greens have been chosen). A small criss-cross incision can now be made in the base stalk of each; this will speed the cooking process.

Once the water is boiling, remove the lid of the pan and add the cleaned sprouts. It's important not to replace the lid. For perfect Brussels sprouts that keep their bite and rich green finish, cook for 2–3 minutes only. If you prefer 'well-done' sprouts, then cook for a further 2 minutes. Don't overfill the pan as this causes the temperature to drop and takes longer for the water to return to the boil, which results in the sprouts losing their rich green colour.

Once cooked, lift or drain from the pan. Melt the butter in the saucepan and roll the sprouts in it. Season with salt and pepper and serve.

Variations

Here are a few alternatives. For sautéed (pan-fried) sprouts, melt 25–50 g (1–2 oz) butter in a large frying-pan or wok. Once bubbling, add the cooked Brussels. These can now be pan-fried in the hot butter, allowing them to take on a golden edge. This method will also add a nutty flavour from the bubbling butter.

Flavoured oils can also be used for lightly coating and cooking, or pan-frying vegetables. Walnut, hazelnut or olive oil work very well.

Fry strips or dice bacon (smoked or unsmoked) before sautéing; this gives a very Christmassy finish, particularly if chopped chestnuts are also added.

Diced onions or button onions will also work very well.

Finely shred the Brussels and turn into a stir-fry. Many other ingredients can be added, creating interesting flavours, e.g. beansprouts, onions, sweet peppers, chillies and so on.

Cheese and Onion Courgettes Ⓥ

The courgette is a member of the same family as squash and pumpkin, which originated in the Americas. It is a juvenile version of the marrow, a vegetable very much associated with Britain – both in eating and in competing to see who can grow the largest. Marrows were very popular in Britain by the nineteenth century, and were grown in cottage and manor kitchen gardens alike. The courgette itself was probably not appreciated until, some say, Elizabeth David inspired us with her memories of the Mediterranean in the 1950s.

They have become part of our cooking now, though. They work very well with many other flavours, with garlic, tomatoes or just plain tossed in butter, and are superb in a ratatouille. There is a slight bitterness in their flavour. This can be drawn out by lightly salting the slices in a colander for 30 minutes, and allowing the bitter juices to be released.

This recipe can be made with good English Cheddar as listed but, for a slightly more Continental flavour, use Parmesan.

BELOW
Cheese and Onion Courgettes

SERVES 4

450 g (1 lb) courgettes
25 g (1 oz) butter
1 small onion, peeled
50–75 g (2–3 oz) Cheddar or Parmesan cheese,
    preferably finely grated
Salt and pepper

When choosing courgettes, make sure they are very firm. If they have softened, and the skin is slightly leathery, the flavour will be very bitter. Very small, baby courgettes will not need to be salted.

Top, tail and slice the courgettes. If sliced 4–5mm (about ¼ in) thick, they will cook nice and quickly while still retaining a texture. Also, if you slice at a slight angle, a good oval shape is achieved. Lightly salt the courgettes and sit, above a bowl, in a colander.

After 30 minutes, provided they are only slightly salted, they will just need to be dried on a cloth. If you are worried about the salt content, then rinse under cold water and dry.

Heat a frying-pan or wok and add the butter. Once bubbling, add the courgettes. Fry for 2–3 minutes before grating the onion on top. Season with salt and pepper. Cook on a fast heat for a further 2 minutes. Sprinkle in half the cheese and then transfer to a suitable bowl/dish. Top with the remaining cheese and gratinate under a hot grill.

The cheese and onion courgettes are now ready to serve.

Note: Chopped tomatoes can also be added with the onions. It's important that all the juices and seeds are removed. This will prevent the vegetables from stewing.

'Burnt' Mushrooms with Shallots, Crunchy Bacon and Red Wine

Mushrooms have been known as food for centuries, but have been cultivated in Europe and the USA for only about 150 years (they had been cultivated in Japan since the first century AD). All cultivated mushrooms have been developed from the wild field mushroom, *Agaricus campestris*, and, for this recipe, you can use simple button mushrooms, chestnut mushrooms with their slightly nutty flavour (hence the name), or closed-cap, open-cap or flat mushrooms. The caps and flats will give a much stronger flavour and a 'meatier' texture. Even wild mushrooms can be used.

The burnt flavour, which gives a bitter edge to the dish, is created by almost dry-frying. Mushrooms, as we know, absorb almost any quantity of fat added to a pan, resulting in a greasy finish. That doesn't happen with this dish. Instead we have a drier border holding all of the mushroom juices.

SERVES 4

4 thick rashers of streaky bacon
1 tablespoon olive oil
2 shallots, sliced
Butter
450 g (1 lb) button mushrooms, wiped
Glass of red wine
Salt and pepper

Cut the bacon rashers into small dice or strips. Heat a frying-pan or wok. Warm a tiny dribble of the olive oil, add the bacon and cook on a medium heat. This will take 7–8 minutes to fry. Once any juices have been released and then reduced in the pan, the bacon will become dry. Increase the heat and cook until totally crispy. Remove from the pan and keep to one side.

Add the shallots and fry for 1–2 minutes with a small touch of the butter. Also remove and keep to one side.

Continue heating the pan and add the remaining oil. Once hot, add the mushrooms. Cook on a medium heat. The oil will be quickly absorbed and the mushrooms will begin to 'burn' in the pan. Allow them to take on burnt tinges and continue to cook until tender. This will take 8–10 minutes. Now return the shallots to the pan. Add half of the red wine, season with salt and pepper and increase the heat, reducing until almost dry. Add the remaining wine and also reduce until almost dry. The crispy bacon, along with a knob of butter, can now be tossed into the mushrooms to finish the dish.

Note: The red wine can be omitted from this recipe. Chopped tarragon adds another flavour that works very well.

Radish and French Bean Salad with Seared Scallops

This is a lovely summer dish, which can be offered as a starter, lunchtime 'snack' or main course.

The radish is a member of the mustard family, obviously the reason for the bite they carry. There are many varieties, the most common of which are the round scarlet globe and the milder long red and white. The latter is known as the French breakfast radish, though why I'm not quite sure, as I've yet to see a Frenchman eating them for breakfast.

Scallops, despite breeding naturally around our northern coasts, have never been as readily available as oysters once were, so have always been more of a rarity – and thus a treat. Always choose fresh scallops, not frozen. Frozen scallops are soaked in water before freezing. This 'soufflés' the meat so that, once frozen, they look bigger and weigh more, giving a better deal to the seller (not the buyer). The ultimate scallops to buy are diver-collected. These have been picked by hand and just couldn't be any fresher. With all of my scallop dishes, I prefer to use large ones for a good rich, sweet and meaty texture.

SERVES 4 AS A STARTER

1 teaspoon sesame seeds
175 g (6 oz) fine French beans, preferably extra fine
12 large fresh scallops, trimmed and cleaned of roe (the roes can be made into roe butter, see Note)
1 tablespoon olive oil
Butter
12 French breakfast radishes, quartered lengthways

For the White-wine Dressing

2 shallots, finely chopped
Glass of sweet white wine, preferably Sauternes
1 heaped teaspoon Dijon mustard
Juice of 1 lime
6 tablespoons walnut oil
1 tablespoon olive oil
Salt and pepper

For the Yoghurt and Sour Cream Dressing

50 ml (2 fl oz) natural yoghurt
50 ml (2 fl oz) sour cream
Juice of ½ lime
Salt and pepper

To make the white-wine dressing, cover the chopped shallots with the sweet white wine and bring to the simmer. Cook on a medium heat until the wine has reduced almost completely. Leave to cool. Spoon the Dijon mustard into a small bowl and mix with the lime juice. Slowly whisk in the two oils. Add the shallots and season with salt and pepper. That's the first dressing made.

For the second dressing, mix the first three ingredients together and season with salt and pepper.

The sesame seeds can be quickly toasted under a hot grill, turning from time to time to give a complete golden colour.

The French beans should be cooked in plenty of salted boiling water – without a lid. Once the water is boiling rapidly, add the beans. Cook for a few minutes until the beans have become tender but still have a slight bite. Remove from the water or strain in a colander, steeping the beans in iced water. Once cold, remove from the water and drain well.

To cook the scallops, heat a frying-pan with a tablespoon of olive oil. The scallops should be dry. This will prevent them from 'poaching' in the pan. Once the oil is almost smoking, sit the scallops in the pan, making sure the maximum heat is maintained. It's important the scallops are seared, taking on a slightly burnt tinge around the edge. Cook for 1–1½ minutes and then add a knob of butter. Cook for a further 30 seconds; the scallops will now have

a rich golden colour and are ready to be turned. Once turned, cook for a further 1–2 minutes. The scallops can now be seasoned with salt and pepper and removed from the pan.

While the scallops are searing, mix together the French beans, radishes and sesame seeds. Spoon 2–3 tablespoons of the white-wine dressing into the bean mix and stir in well, making sure plenty of shallots have been included. Spoon some of the yoghurt and sour cream dressing towards the top of each plate. The bean and radish salad can now be divided between the four plates, building a 'bonfire effect' salad. Once 'built' spoon any dressing left in the bowl on top.

The scallops, three per portion, can now be arranged in a semi-circle in front of the salad. The dish is now ready to serve.

Note: I hate to throw flavours away, but very rarely use scallop roes in my recipes, so I turn them into a scallop-roe butter, simply blitzing them with an equal weight of unsalted butter to a smooth purée. For a guaranteed smooth finish, push through a sieve. Now simply wrap in cling film and freeze until needed. The butter can enhance the flavour of a fish sauce, soup or stew – literally just a tablespoon whisked into four portions of a basic fish sauce (see *Basic White-wine or Champagne Fish Sauce*, page 47) will be enough to enrich the finished taste. The butter also slightly thickens a sauce or soup. Just remember not to re-boil the liquor, as this will separate the butter.

Dandelion and Bacon Salad

A dandelion and bacon salad is a well-known French dish, but I'm sure we have been eating something similar for years in Britain. For dandelion leaves were valued in country areas as a spring green after the dried pulse diet of the winter months, and were used medicinally as a diuretic (the French name *piss-en-lit* graphically describes this property). Food writers in the seventeenth century mentioned that the leaves were good to eat and, because dandelion

is related to wild chicory, the roots have been used to make a coffee substitute. Many years ago, only the green dandelion was available, and as it had a much tougher and bitter leaf, it was cooked mostly as a vegetable, boiled for 20–30 minutes before being tossed in butter. The leaves are still quite bitter, but now they come in green or white. The white leaves have been covered before harvesting, to blanch them, which keeps them tender and less bitter to eat.

The dandelion leaves can be mixed with other leaves, but this one we'll keep as a straight dandelion salad. The bacon can be smoked or unsmoked. One more ingredient I'm adding is diced bread, which will be fried in the bacon fat. A sprinkling of finely grated Parmesan can also be added. The dressing is just a well-flavoured oil: olive, walnut or hazelnut will all complement the other flavours.

SERVES 2 AS A STARTER

2 good bunches of dandelion leaves
2 slices of thick bread (white, brown or granary)
6 rashers of streaky bacon, smoked or unsmoked, cut into 2 cm (¾ in) pieces
2–4 tablespoons olive, walnut or hazelnut oil
1 tablespoon finely grated Parmesan cheese (optional)
Salt and pepper

The dandelion leaves can first be washed and drained in a colander.

Cut the slices of bread into 1 cm (½ in) dice. Fry the bacon in a hot frying-pan; the bacon will create its own fat, cooking the pieces until very crispy. Remove the bacon with a slotted spoon and keep to one side. The bread can now be fried in the fat left in the pan until it is also golden and crispy. Return the bacon pieces, mixing them with the bread croûtons.

Place the leaves in a bowl and sprinkle over the bacon and bread. Season with salt and pepper and trickle with the oil. If using the freshly grated Parmesan, sprinkle over and serve.

Note: A squeeze of lemon or lime juice or a teaspoon of red-wine vinegar can also be added.

OPPOSITE
Radish and French Bean Salad with Seared Scallops

Gratin of Grated Turnips ⓥ

Turnips are root vegetables, members of the cabbage family, and have been around in Europe for hundreds of years; they were probably spread northwards by the Romans. Their closest relative is the swede, which only came upon the vegetable scene in the seventeenth century, the name being a contraction of 'Swedish turnip'. Before the potato was introduced, turnips were probably a staple carbohydrate food of the poor.

The turnips here are cooked using a concept vaguely like that of dauphinoise potatoes. It is a very simple dish to make, and will eat very well with many dishes featured in the book, lamb and game in particular.

SERVES 4–6

300 ml (½ pint) whipping cream
1 large garlic clove, crushed
Sprig of fresh thyme
675 g (1½ lb) peeled turnips, coarsely grated (about 850 g/1 lb 14 oz unpeeled weight)
Butter
Salt and pepper

Warm together the cream, garlic and thyme. Infuse for 10 minutes before adding the grated turnips and seasoning with salt and pepper.

Cook on a medium heat, gently simmering until the turnips are tender. This will take just 15–20 minutes. Remove the sprig of thyme and add a knob of butter to the mix. The cream will have reduced in this time and become slightly thicker.

Spoon into a greased vegetable dish and gratinate under a hot grill until golden brown.

Note: Freshly grated Parmesan cheese can be sprinkled on top before glazing. Also, a quarter or half an onion can be grated and mixed with the turnip.

Asparagus with Melted Butter or Hollandaise Sauce ⓥ

Asparagus, a member of the lily family, was eaten by the Ancient Egyptians, Greeks and Romans, and was probably introduced to Britain – as were so many vegetables – by the Romans during their 400-year-long occupation. Thereafter, it wasn't until the Elizabethan age that asparagus began to be grown again, but it was always a rare and special vegetable for a variety of reasons. An asparagus bed takes three or four years to establish, and although the shoots are available only from May to early July, the dormant vegetable monopolizes that bed for the remainder of the year. Not therefore a very practical proposition for most vegetable gardeners, but for me those two short months of English asparagus bring nothing but sheer paradise.

The accompaniments here are the most traditional – melted butter or a good hollandaise sauce. To the melted-butter version, I am adding a tablespoon or two of water, which will then emulsify the butter into a sauce consistency. I am also seasoning the spears with coarse sea salt. This is very exciting to eat with asparagus and many other green vegetables: when you bite and crunch on the salt, the flavours become even more alive.

For a starter I like to offer 6–8 medium spears per portion.

SERVES 2 AS A STARTER

12–16 medium asparagus spears

To Serve with Melted Butter

75 g (3 oz) unsalted butter
2–3 tablespoons water
Freshly ground black or white pepper
Pinch of sea-salt

To Serve with Hollandaise

150 ml (¼ pint) *Hollandaise Sauce* or *Simple Hollandaise Sauce* (page 41)

If serving with hollandaise, make the sauce first.

Trim the spiky/pointy ears from along the asparagus stalks, also cutting 2–4 cm (¾–1¼ in) of the grey/white base stalk away, keeping the spears a uniform length.

The asparagus can now be plunged into a large saucepan of rapidly boiling salted water. Twelve to

Buttered Spinach ⓥ

sixteen spears is the maximum that should be cooked at one time: any more and the water will lose its heat and begin to stew the spears.

Cook, with the lid off, for 2–3 minutes (4 is the absolute maximum), and lift from the pot.

Arrange the portions on hot plates. To glaze and shine the asparagus, lightly brush with melted butter. Sprinkle with the coarse sea-salt. While the asparagus is cooking, bring the 2–3 tablespoons water to the boil in a small saucepan. Add the butter in small knobs, whisking in vigorously. Add a twist of pepper and the sauce is ready to serve.

Hollandaise sauce, if using, can be offered separately.

Note: A squeeze of lemon juice can be added to the butter sauce, with a teaspoon of chopped fresh chives for a slight oniony bite.

BELOW
Asparagus with Melted Butter or Hollandaise Sauce

Spinach, originally from Persia, didn't reach Britain until the fourteenth century, and was one of the first vegetables to be 'cooked by itself', rather than being boiled in a pottage. It was braised simply and served with a little oil and spices or sugar sprinkled on top as a cooked salad.

Fresh spinach is one of my favourite vegetables. Cooked with a knob of butter and plenty of seasoning and eaten straight from the pan – you just can't beat it. However, it's also a vegetable that can be cooked in advance. Simply drop into boiling, salted water and cook for just a few minutes until tender; lift or drain from the pan and plunge into iced water to immediately stop the cooking process. Once cold, any excess water can be squeezed gently from the tender leaves. To have it totally ready to re-heat in a frying-pan or microwave, add a knob or two of butter along with a sprinkling of salt, pepper and freshly grated nutmeg. The spinach will keep well like this, refrigerated, until needed.

Here's the recipe if you'd rather eat this delicious vegetable straight from the pan.

SERVES 4–6

25–50 g (1–2 oz) butter
900 g (2 lb) spinach leaves, picked and washed
Salt and pepper
Freshly grated nutmeg

Heat a large saucepan with the butter. Once bubbling, add the spinach leaves. The water still clinging to the leaves after washing will create enough steam in the pan to cook the spinach. The heat can now be increased. Stir the leaves in the pan. These will begin to wilt and, within a few minutes, will have become tender. Season with the salt, pepper and nutmeg. The spinach is now ready to serve.

If a lot of excess water has collected after cooking, then drain the spinach in a colander before serving.

Spinach Dumplings ⓥ

These dumplings make a lovely vegetarian main course or a delicious starter, served with a very easy and quick tomato sauce.

SERVES 4 AS A MAIN COURSE AND 8 AS A STARTER (MAKES 16)

1 onion, finely chopped
50 g (2 oz) unsalted butter
550 g (1¼ lb) fresh spinach, stalks removed
225 g (8 oz) mascarpone or full-fat soft cheese
225 g (8 oz) plain flour
1 egg
1 egg yolk
Pinch of freshly grated nutmeg
Salt and pepper
100 g (4 oz) Parmesan cheese, grated, to serve

For the Sauce

3 tablespoons olive oil
10–12 tomatoes, blanched in boiling water for
       10 seconds and skinned, or 1 × 400 g (14 oz)
       tin chopped tomatoes
1 small garlic clove, crushed
1–2 teaspoons tomato ketchup (optional)

Sweat the chopped onion in the butter for a few minutes until softened, then allow to cool.

Wash the spinach well to remove any grit, then shake off any excess water. Blanch the spinach in boiling, salted water for about 30 seconds, then refresh in iced water. Squeeze the spinach until all the liquid is removed and then chop it finely.

Mix together the spinach and onion and then fold in the soft cheese and flour. Lightly beat the egg and egg yolk together, then add them to the mixture and season with salt, pepper and nutmeg. Leave the mixture to rest for about 30 minutes and then mould it into dumplings using floured hands.

The dumplings can now be cooked in simmering salted water for 10–15 minutes. While they are cooking, pre-heat the grill and make the tomato sauce.

Seed the tomatoes and chop the tomato flesh into a 5 mm (¼ in) dice. Heat a tablespoon of olive oil with the clove of garlic and add the tomatoes. Cook them until tender and almost reduced to a pulp, allowing the natural waters to reduce. Once reduced, season with salt and pepper and add the remaining olive oil. For a sweeter, spicy finish, add the ketchup, if using.

Arrange the dumplings in a flameproof dish and cover with the grated Parmesan. Finish under the hot grill, until the cheese is lightly browned. The dumplings are now ready to serve with the tomato sauce.

Egg and Bacon Salad

The British egg salad holds the reputation of floppy salad leaves, tomatoes, cucumber, radish and beetroot (that stains everything else), all bound with bottled salad cream. I think we've moved on from those days, but salads were once a great feature of British cookery. Hard-boiled eggs have been used in salads since Elizabethan times, in the forerunners of the great composite salads of the seventeenth century. The base of the salads would be flowers and leaves, perhaps some cucumber, dressed with oil and vinegar, then the eggs placed on top. Often slices of cold fowl or meat or pieces of fish would be added as well.

This egg salad has taken on bacon as its accompaniment, a traditional and very British marriage. Within the recipe, various cooking alternatives are mentioned: poaching or boiling the eggs, frying or grilling the bacon and toasting or frying the bread. Variety is obviously the spice of this dish. This salad is a lovely dish to have for brunch.

OPPOSITE
Egg and Bacon Salad

SERVES 4 AS A STARTER

4 slices of thick-sliced white, brown or granary
    bread, crusts removed
4 poached or 4–6 'soft' hard-boiled eggs (page 81)
4 rashers of thick-sliced back or streaky bacon
4 Little Gem lettuces, leaves separated and rinsed
    (2 small Cos can also be used; tear the leaves
    into suitable strips)
3–4 tablespoons red-wine vinegar
2–3 tablespoons olive or groundnut oil
4 spring onions, washed and finely shredded
Salt and pepper

Cut the slices of bread into 1 cm (½ in) dice, unless grilling. In this case, leave the slices whole. Cut the 'soft' hard-boiled eggs into quarters. The ingredients list suggests 4–6 eggs; 4 should be enough but 6 eggs will obviously give more generous servings.

The bacon can now be pan-fried or grilled until crispy. If pan-frying, a dry pan can be used. Any fat content will be released into the pan from the bacon. This will also happen if grilling. Whichever method you choose, keep the bacon fat for frying the bread. Once cooked, remove the bacon from the pan and keep warm. Now add the bread and fry until golden and crispy. You might need extra oil to achieve a golden finish. If the bacon has been grilled, just brush each slice of bread with the fat released, and toast. Now it can be diced.

Season the salad leaves with salt and pepper. It's best, whenever making salads, to sprinkle salt around the bowl and not directly on the leaves. This prevents the salt from falling onto wet leaves and sticking in lumps. Cut the bacon into strips and mix into the leaves, with the spring onions and fried/toasted bread. Mix together the red-wine vinegar and the olive/groundnut oil. This mixture can be spooned over the leaves, adding just enough to coat. Arrange on four plates or present as one large salad. The hard-boiled egg quarters can now also be seasoned with salt and pepper and placed among the leaves.

For poached eggs, re-heat in simmering water for 1 minute before placing on top of the salads.

Note: Extra red-wine vinegar can be mixed with olive/groundnut oil with the addition of mustard to taste. This can then be shaken in a jar ready to use.

A pinch of sugar can be added to the red-wine vinegar to sweeten the finish, slightly reducing the piquant acidity.

It's always nice to offer home-made *Salad Cream* (page 48) or *Mayonnaise* (page 49) with this dish.

Fresh Peas

Fresh peas were not really eaten in Europe until Italian gardeners developed the garden pea as opposed to the field pea (the one that was dried) in the sixteenth century. Since then, we have enjoyed them over the centuries, and they were a classic vegetable to be 'buttered' in the British vegetable tradition. I've added a few more flavourings here, making the dish more like the classic French pea dish called *petits pois à la française*.

450 g (1 lb) fresh peas, weighed out of their pods
50 g (2 oz) unsalted butter
2 onions, sliced
4 rashers of smoked streaky bacon, rinded and cut
    into strips
50–85 ml (2–3 fl oz) *Chicken* or *Vegetable Stock*
    (page 33 or 36), or water
Salt and pepper

You can cook the peas in advance and finish the dish off later. Bring a large pan of salted water to the boil. Drop in the shelled peas, return the water to the boil, and boil until tender, keeping the lid off throughout and the water boiling all the time. This takes anything from 5–15 minutes, depending on the size of the pea. If the peas are not tender by then, just keep boiling until they are ready. Drain the peas, and keep to one side. (If you are serving them straight away, simply toss in some butter and season.)

When you wish to serve the peas, melt 25 g (1 oz) of the butter and cook the onions and bacon until slightly softened. Add the stock or water and bring to the boil. Add the remaining butter and

116 VEGETABLES AND SALADS

season with salt and pepper. Quickly re-heat the peas in a microwave or in a pan of boiling water for 30 seconds, then drain. Toss the peas in the reduced bacon and onion liquor, and serve immediately.

Braised Split Peas ⓥ

The pulses that became so important in the British diet were brought in from the Continent – the small Celtic bean (of the broad bean family) and the pea, varieties of which were introduced by the Romans. The pea was particularly prized because it could be eaten fresh (although nothing like as sweet and tender as the garden peas cultivated centuries later in Italy). It could also be dried, when it was ground for a bread meal, or lengthily simmered in a meat or vegetable soup, to which it would add bulk, flavour and texture. An early Great British dish was bacon and peas, both of which were cooked in the pot together. This was popular with rich and poor alike and something that I re-introduced to my menus fifteen years ago. Later, after the invention of the pudding cloth, dried peas were boiled in the bacon pot in the cloth, resulting in the famous pease pudding. This was then cut into pieces to be served with the bacon.

I think split peas are so delicious, slowly braised until just tender. They eat well with many other dishes too, from the *Boiled Bacon with Pearl Barley* on page 224, to *Pork* or *Cumberland Sausages* (pages 367 and 368), or fish and chips. For a really mushy finish, cook for a further 10–15 minutes with an extra drop of stock.

SERVES 6–8

100 g (4 oz) carrots
2 celery sticks
2 onions
1 garlic clove, crushed (optional)
1 tablespoon olive oil
25 g (1 oz) unsalted butter
450 g (1 lb) dried green split peas

900 ml (1½ pints) *Vegetable* or *Chicken Stock* (page 36 or 33)
Salt and pepper

Pre-heat the oven to 200°C/400°F/Gas Mark 6.

Cut the carrots, celery and onions into 5 mm (¼ in) dice. Sweat with the garlic, if using, in the olive oil and butter for a few minutes in a flameproof casserole dish. Add the split peas and cook for 1–2 minutes, stirring. Cover with 600 ml (1 pint) of the stock and bring to the simmer. Cover and cook in the pre-heated oven for 20–25 minutes or until tender. The peas will need stirring during cooking and, possibly, more stock will need to be added. Season with salt and pepper before serving.

BELOW
Braised Split Peas

Green Beans and How to Cook Them

There are many varieties and sizes of green beans, which are known as haricots verts in the catering industry. The most popular type served in restaurants is the extra-fine French bean, which is considered to be a first-class vegetable. The beauty of cooking this bean is the minimum preparation needed; it simply needs topping and tailing, although I prefer to leave the spiky, pointed end attached for better visual presentation.

Another favourite of mine is the runner bean. These beans are usually found as a flat, smooth form or a coarser and fatter variety. You can cut the flat beans in two ways: either shredded at an angle to give 4–5 cm (1½–2 in) thin strips, or as larger diamonds. The coarse bean needs the sinewy string pulled away from both sides before finely shredding; a thicker cut can often result in a tough finish.

A major advantage to using these vegetables is that you can par-cook them well in advance and re-heat when needed. Once cooked, using the method that follows, simply drain from the saucepan and plunge into iced water. This immediately stops the cooking and also allows the beans to keep their rich green colour. Once cold, remove from the water and plunge back into boiling water for 30–45 seconds when you're ready to eat.

There are a few golden rules that should never be broken when cooking these or, indeed, any green vegetables. Always use a large saucepan up to three-quarters full of boiling salted water and never use a lid at any time during the cooking; even when the water has boiled and the beans are cooking, don't cover the pan with a lid. This guarantees that the rich colour is kept. One more small point: try not to cook too many green vegetables at once. If you do, the water temperature decreases and then takes too long to return to boiling point, which often results in the loss of colour.

Opposite is a guide to cooking times for beans. Having prepared them, plunge them in boiling salted water first and cook according to the times listed below:

Extra-fine beans – if they are ultra-fine beans, they should be cooked as soon as the water returns to the boil. It's best to test the beans first, which should always have a good bite to them. Extra-fine beans

should otherwise take no more than a minute to cook. *Fine French beans* (a more common size) – these should take 2–3 minutes once the water has re-boiled. *Runner beans*, finely shredded – check after 45 seconds–1 minute, by which time they should be cooked. *Runner beans*, cut into diamond shapes – they should take 1–2 minutes once the water has re-boiled.

Note: The coarser variety of runner bean will always take a little longer to cook.

Roast Mushroom and Leek Shepherd's Pie ⓥ

Shepherd's pie is such a classic of British cooking, it seemed a shame that a vegetarian variety should be left out. This is an easy recipe, which becomes almost 'meaty', using the large flat or cup mushrooms. The dish is layered like a lasagne with the mashed potato piped or forked across the top.

SERVES 4–6

Olive or cooking oil
900 g (2 lb) flat or open-cup mushrooms, wiped and stalks removed
3–4 leeks, finely shredded
Butter
1 onion, sliced
750–900 g (1½–2 lb) *Mashed Potatoes* (page 124)
Juice of ½–1 lemon
Salt and pepper
1 teaspoon each chopped fresh parsley, tarragon and basil (optional)

Pre-heat the oven to 230°C /450°F/Gas Mark 8.

Heat a frying-pan or roasting tray with a tablespoon or two of olive or cooking oil. Season the mushrooms with salt and pepper and place in the pan or tray. Fry the mushrooms on a high heat, colouring them well. After a minute, turn them in the tray and repeat the colouring (another teaspoon of oil may be needed). Now roast the mushrooms in the hot oven for 5–6 minutes. Once cooked, remove and keep to one side. Because of the fast, hot frying and roasting, the mushrooms will have kept all of their juices, giving a richer flavour.

Heat a tablespoon of olive oil with a knob of butter and add the sliced onion. Cook on a moderate heat for a few minutes, until softened but with very little colour. Increase the heat, add the shredded leeks and season with salt and pepper. Stir for 3–4 minutes, and the leeks should now be tender.

Using a buttered ovenproof vegetable or shepherd's pie dish, carve the mushrooms into slices and lay in the base of the dish. Spoon some leeks on top and then repeat with the mushrooms; continue to layer the ingredients until all are used up.

The mashed potato can now be finished with the lemon juice and chopped herbs, if using. Spread, fork or pipe the potato on top. Brush with butter and place in the hot oven for 10 minutes before serving. For an extra golden brown topping place under a pre-heated grill.

Note: If using plain mashed potato to top the 'pie', grated Cheddar or little pieces of Gorgonzola can be sprinkled over and grilled for a cheesy finish.

See also

Sage Broad Beans with Bacon and Tomato (page 56)
Breakfast Mushrooms (page 84)
Breakfast Tomatoes (page 83)
Lemon and Parsley Carrots (page 59)
Macaroni, Artichoke and Mushroom Cheese Pie (page 64)
Pressed Tomato Cake with Peppered Goat's Cheese (page 66)
Steamed Leek and Cheddar-cheese Pudding (page 65)
Vegetarian Scotch Broth (page 31)

OPPOSITE
A selection of green vegetables

Potatoes

Over the years, potatoes have become a main feature in many of my dishes, in particular the soft and creamy mashed potato, every Briton's favourite. In fact, potatoes are one of our staple foods in Great Britain, and they are much loved. But it may surprise you to know that they have been around in the West for only about 400 years.

Native to South America, the potato was discovered by the conquering Spanish in Peru, and brought to Europe in about 1536. Sir Francis Drake is thought by many to have been responsible for the potato's introduction to Britain, but Sir Walter Raleigh was probably the more likely, as it was he who first cultivated this new root vegetable at his Irish estate, Youghal (County Cork), in about 1590. Another theory maintains that potato tubers were washed ashore in western Ireland from the wrecked Armada, and began to enjoy their new home. The first recorded mention of the potato – and an illustration – was in John Gerard's *Herbal* of 1597, where it was wrongly described as being 'of Virginia, the American state'. This mistaken attribution remained in use for some time, mainly to distinguish it from *batatas* or the sweet potato (oddly enough, an earlier introduction). It wasn't until about 1710 that the potato became known as the 'common', 'English' or, more significantly, the 'Irish' potato.

The potato was disliked for centuries in Europe, for many reasons. Its appearance was unpleasant, slightly warty and scabby, and so it was thought to be related to leprosy, the dreaded skin disease of the time. The fact, too, that the potato was a relative of highly poisonous plants such as deadly nightshade was not in its favour. It was also the first plant in Europe to be cultivated from unfamiliar tubers rather than from seed.

In Ireland, however, the potato did manage to become established, and much more speedily and completely than it did elsewhere in the British Isles. In a country with an impoverished peasantry, and a soil and climate suitable for little else in an agricultural sense, the potato was ideal: it could survive in poor soil, it needed little cultivation, it could be harvested by hand, only a small plot was needed for a crop sufficient to feed a family, and it didn't need to be threshed, ground or roasted. Once planted, it just grew. From that, the potato became part of the main diet for the mass of the Irish population within about a century of its introduction, a fact illustrated by the number of Irish potato dishes. These include colcannon, boxty, champ, Irish stew and a legion of potato cakes, breads and soups, some of which you'll find in this book. And when potato blight, the killer disease, hit the whole of Europe in 1845–6, it was Ireland, the sole country reliant on this one crop, that was the most tragically devastated. It has been estimated that up to one million people died of starvation at that time, and a further million were to emigrate, principally to England and North America.

The potato was grown in Scotland and the north of England as well, welcomed where wheat was hard to grow because of climate, soil and cost, as in Ireland. The tuber's soft flesh made a change from the oats and barley commonly grown and eaten. But there was never the same enthusiasm for it as that shown by the Irish, and the fact that potatoes were the major food of the immigrant Irish didn't help either. There are a number of traditional Scottish and northern English recipes, among them the oddly named kailkenny, stelk, panhaggerty and rumbledethumps. Bubble and squeak in its present-day form is related to all these Irish and Scottish recipes – basically a mixture of mashed potato and greenery – but originally it was made with meat and cabbage leftovers, without the potato. It just can't have been the same.

Over the years, though, bad harvests and grain shortages led to the potato's gradual adoption and appreciation. By the end of the eighteenth century it was the most important vegetable crop in Britain. Potatoes became a very popular street food. They were baked (from about 1835) in the bakehouse, then sold from stalls to be eaten warm with butter and salt. Later they were sold fried to accompany fried flounder or other fish, marking the beginning of the fish and chip trade. Mashed potato with eels and parsley broth – eels and mash – was a dish sold by London's fish stalls in the later years of the nineteenth century. Gradually, potatoes were eaten at home – boiled, mashed, fried or roasted – to accompany all main courses, whether fish or meat. This was probably when the British reliance on potatoes as an integral part of a meal (meat and two veg) originated. Interestingly, had they been introduced earlier, they would probably have become a pottage vegetable, like onions or leeks; they arrived later, though, and then fell into the category of roots to be boiled and buttered or fried, to be served as a 'vegetable'.

There are hundreds of potato varieties known, but only a few are commonly available in Britain, which is a pity. My own favourites among maincrop potatoes are Maris Piper, Estima, Wilja and King Edward. All of these make a good mashed potato, the potato texture breaking down to give quite a light, creamy finish. The Maris Piper and King Edward also work well for roasting, along with Désirée, Romano and Cara. I also love to use new potatoes such as the Pink Fir Apple, Charlotte, La Ratte, Belle de Fontenay and, particularly, one that is unique to Britain, the Jersey Royal. This was discovered by fluke in about 1880 on Jersey, and grows only there; it's fertilized by seaweed, hand-planted and hand-picked, and has a thin skin and superb flavour that is unique.

Do try these recipes, and peel back the natural flavours of this wonderful vegetable.

Sautéd Potatoes ⓥ

More or less any potato can be used for sautéing, but for a perfectly shaped sauté, it's best to use a waxy variety. Dutch and Cyprus varieties will give you that waxiness, as will Charlotte, Belle de Fontenay and Pink Fir Apple.

The potatoes should always be cooked before sautéing. Some recipes will tell you to keep them slightly underdone so that during the process of pan-frying they will not break down and will keep their perfect shape.

Well, that's not really what I'm after. I like the potatoes to be boiled or steamed until almost over-cooked, then lifted from the water or steamer and allowed to cool naturally. Even standard baking potatoes can be used. These will crumble around the outside and, when peeled, will have a fluffy edge. This, when pan-fried (sautéd), will become very crispy and sometimes actually burn, giving contrasts of flavours. They might not look perfect, but they will taste sensational.

By the way, the word sauté comes from the French verb *sauter*, 'to jump' – and that's exactly what the potato pieces should be doing in the pan.

750 g (1½ lb) potatoes, cooked in their skins
Olive or groundnut oil, to give a 2 mm (thin) covering of pan
50 g (2 oz) unsalted butter
Salt
1 teaspoon chopped fresh parsley, to serve (optional)

Peel the potatoes and carefully cut into 5 mm (¼ in) slices; many potatoes will break, but don't worry – the small pieces will just crispen. If you have used new potatoes, then just halve lengthways. Warm the oil in a frying pan to a medium heat. Place the potatoes in the oil and cook for 6–8 minutes, shaking softly from time to time. The potatoes should, by now, have taken on a golden edge. Slightly increase the heat and continue to cook for 2 minutes. Unless you have a particularly large frying-pan, they are best cooked in two lots; if so, add half the butter. As this begins to bubble, turn the potatoes over and continue to shallow-fry until completely golden and crispy. These can now be kept warm in a pre-heated oven while the other half are cooked. Once all are completely sautéed, season with salt and sprinkle with chopped parsley, if using.

Note: Other fats can be used for sautéing potatoes. One of the tastiest is goose or duck fat. Both of these will give you a richer flavour. Lard or bacon fat can also be used.

Sautéd Sea-salt Potatoes ⓥ

Sautéd potatoes are thought of as a French classic, but have become very much part of British eating. How often do we have too many new potatoes cooked, and the next day halve them and sauté them in butter? This recipe is very similar, but adds sea salt along with chopped parsley.

New or jacket potatoes can be used, but both will first have to be boiled or steamed until cooked. For the very best results, these are best sautéd while still warm, which gives the potato a more flaky edge that will become golden and very crispy.

These potatoes eat very well with fish or meat. A simple grilled Dover sole (see *Grilled or Pan-fried Dover Sole*, page 141), will go very well.

450 g (1 lb) new or large potatoes, cooked
1–2 tablespoons cooking oil (olive oil can be used
　　for a richer finish)
50 g (2 oz) unsalted butter
1 teaspoon coarse sea salt
1 tablespoon chopped fresh parsley (flatleaf parsley
　　will give more flavour)
Pepper

While the potatoes are still warm, peel them. For new potatoes, this is not essential but will give a more crumbled finish. Once peeled, cut the new potatoes in half lengthways or jacket potatoes into 5 mm (¼ in) slices. When the potatoes have been peeled and sliced, shake the bowl they are in to give a slightly broken edge.

Heat a frying-pan or wok with the cooking oil. For this quantity of potatoes, it's best to fry in two lots; this will create more room to colour and not just steam.

Add half of the potatoes to the frying-pan and cook on a medium heat until golden brown on both sides. This will take 8–10 minutes.

Remove the potatoes and keep warm to one side. Repeat the frying process with the remaining half. When ready, add those set aside and toss again to completely mix and re-heat. At this point, add the butter and begin to stir/shake the potatoes in the pan. Continue to cook for several minutes, giving them a crispy edge. Add the coarse sea-salt, chopped parsley and a twist of pepper. Toss in the pan.

The potatoes are ready to serve. Some of the sea salt will have dissolved its flavour into the potatoes, while some still has a crispy texture.

Note: For an extra taste, a squeeze of lime juice brings a great finish to the potatoes, particularly if serving with fish.

Potato Cakes Ⓥ

These are discs of potato that are poached in butter. As they soften, the potatoes absorb a rich butter flavour. They can be made well in advance and kept refrigerated. To finish, the potatoes are pan-fried to a golden brown. For an alternative, I'm including a recipe for roasted potato discs. These are quickly blanched, fried and roasted.

While disc-shaped potatoes look good, they can still be cooked very simply by splitting lengthways in two and then cooking by either method.

MAKES 6 CAKES

3 medium to large potatoes
225 g (8 oz) block of butter
Salt

Pre-heat the oven to 150°C/300°F/Gas Mark 2.

Peel the potatoes and split in two. The discs can now be cut using a 7 cm (2¾ in) cutter. Trim the potato top and bottom to give a neat 1.5–2 cm (½–¾ in) deep disc.

BELOW
Sautéd Sea-salt Potatoes

Dice the block butter and sit in a suitable saucepan or small roasting tray. Place the potatoes on top in a single layer, sit over a medium heat and start to melt, bringing to a soft simmer. These can now be cooked in the slow oven for 40–45 minutes, until tender.

Once cooked, remove the cakes from the butter. The butter can be kept and strained to use again, or be used to cook other vegetables. If not using the potatoes immediately, then leave to cool. These can now be refrigerated until needed.

To finish, melt a knob of butter in a frying-pan and, once bubbling, pan-fry the potatoes until golden brown. This will take 3–6 minutes. Turn the potatoes over and finish colouring. Season with salt and the potato cakes are ready to serve.

Note: Crushed garlic, thyme and bay leaf can help flavour the potatoes. Simply add 2–3 cloves of crushed garlic, 2–3 sprigs of thyme and 1 bay leaf to the butter.

Variation: The Roast Alternative

Pre-heat the oven to 200°C/400°F/Gas Mark 6. Peel and cut the potato discs as above. Blanch in salted, boiling water for 4 minutes. Now lightly coat in plain flour. Heat 2 mm (a thin layer) of oil in a suitable pan for roasting in the oven. Place the potatoes in the oil and fry on a medium heat until rich and golden. Turn the potato discs over and continue to fry and colour. This process will take 6–7 minutes on each side. Now place the tray/pan in the oven and roast for 20–25 minutes. The potato will have a good soft centre with a crispy finish. Season well with salt before serving.

Parsnip Potato Cakes Ⓥ

This vegetarian dish can consist of many combinations. Lots of other tastes and flavours can be added, such as fresh herbs, mustard or more vegetables. Vegetable hot-pot potato cakes could also be made, cooking a selection of carrots, turnips and swedes as well as the parsnips and potatoes. This recipe can also be adapted to use up the leftover cooked vegetables and potatoes from your Sunday lunch. Mash the roast potatoes and roughly chop whatever vegetables have been left.

The parsnips are simply cooked in butter, without colouring, until tender. They can also be pan-fried until golden, for a roasted finished flavour.

The cakes can be shallow-fried or deep-fried. This recipe will give you eight cakes – two per portion – to serve as a starter or accompaniment to a main course.

SERVES 4

450 g (1 lb) parsnips
50 g (2 oz) butter
1 small shallot or ½ small onion, very finely
    chopped
225 g (8 oz) *Mashed Potatoes*, without milk, cream
    or butter (page 124)
6 fresh sage leaves, chopped
Oil, for frying
Butter
Salt, pepper and freshly grated nutmeg

For the Breadcrumb Coating

2–3 tablespoons plain flour
2 eggs, beaten with 2–3 tablespoons milk
200 g (7 oz) fresh white breadcrumbs (dried can
    also be used)

Peel and quarter lengthways the parsnips, and cut away the centre core. Now cut the vegetable into 1 cm (½ in) dice. Melt 25 g (1 oz) of the butter in a pan and add the parsnips. These can now be cooked on a medium heat with a lid on for 10 minutes. During this time, they will become tender. The steam created from having a lid on top will have created some liquor in the pan. Remove the lid and continue to cook for 2–3 minutes. The juices will now be absorbed into the pieces. Remove from the heat. Mash by hand, leaving a slightly chunky texture. For a creamier finish, blitz in a food processor. I prefer a chunkier consistency; mixing them with mashed potato will create the creaminess.

In the remaining butter, cook the shallots for 1 minute. This takes away their rawness, but still retains texture and the acidic bite.

Mix together the mashed parsnips with the potato, shallots and chopped sage. Season with salt, pepper and grated nutmeg. The mixture can now be shaped into eight disc-shaped cakes or balls. These can be laid on cling film and refrigerated for 30 minutes to set.

To breadcrumb, season the flour with salt and pepper. Lightly coat each cake with the flour. Pass the cakes, one at a time, through the egg and milk mixture and then the crumbs, shaping and patting neatly with a palette knife. To ensure a good coating, pass the covered cakes through the egg and crumbs once more. Once shaped, refrigerate again to set.

To cook, warm a tablespoon or two of cooking oil in a frying-pan. Add a knob of butter and, once bubbling, place the cakes in the pan. Shallow-fry for 6–7 minutes on each side until golden brown.

For deeper-frying, warm 5 mm (¼ in) of cooking oil in a frying-pan, over a low–medium heat. Sit the cakes in the oil and also cook for 6–7 minutes. Once golden, turn over and repeat the same cooking time. When cooked, remove from the pan and dry on kitchen paper. The cakes are ready to serve.

Note: A wedge of lemon can be offered, as with fried fish. The acidic lemony flavour goes very well.

Mayonnaise (page 49) can also be offered, flavoured with either mustard or *Horseradish Sauce* (page 55).

Simple nut-brown butter mixed with a squeeze of lemon also goes very well, particularly if finished with chopped capers, lemon segments and chopped parsley, for a nut-brown tartar finish.

Garlic Cream Potato Cakes ⓥ

These potatoes will lend themselves to many dishes. In this book they are featured with fish (see *Pan-fried Red Mullet with a Tomato and Leek Soup*, page 149), but they will also go with almost any meat dish, from sausages to roast lamb or game, stews and braised dishes.

The concept has been adapted from the French *pommes dauphinoise*, made from sliced, layered potatoes baked in the oven in a garlic cream sauce. The little oval shapes (round will also be fine), approximately 2 cm (¾ in) deep, are cooked in the garlic cream on top of the stove; 40–45 minutes later, they are ready to serve. They can also be made and cooked in advanced.

One more tip: infuse the milk and cream overnight with the garlic and thyme. This will intensify and maximize the finished flavour.

SERVES 6

3 large potatoes, peeled

For the Garlic Cream

300 ml (½ pint) double cream
300 ml (½ pint) milk
1 teaspoon coarse sea salt
1–2 thyme sprigs
2 garlic cloves, crushed

Mix together the cream, milk, sea salt, thyme and garlic. For best results, leave to infuse overnight.

Split the potatoes in half lengthways. These can now be trimmed by hand into oval shapes or cut, using an 8–10 cm (3–4 in) oval cutter.

To cook the potatoes, place in a saucepan and cover with the garlic cream. Bring to the simmer and cook on a minimal heat until the potatoes become tender; a little extra milk can be added if the sauce is becoming too thick. This cooking will take 40–45 minutes. They can now be left to stay hot until the main course is ready, or be removed from the pan, allowed to cool and refrigerated until needed. To re-heat, simply microwave.

Note: If more garlic cream is needed to cover the potatoes, top up with milk, adding an extra clove of garlic.

Mashed Potatoes ⓥ

Mashed potatoes have been around for a long time and used to be served with eels from street stalls in the nineteenth century. Soft, creamy, buttered mashed potatoes are my favourite potato dish of all time – a Great British classic that will definitely see its way through the next millennium.

Mashed potatoes are looked upon as a simple, straightforward dish, with any old potato being used for the recipe. I think very differently. During the seasons, various potatoes are available, but I have always found that Maris Piper are easily obtained and purée very well. The rest, of course, is taking care in the cooking and finishing of the dish.

The mashed potatoes can also be used as a base for a sauce (see opposite).

900 g (2 lb) large floury potatoes, preferably
    Maris Piper, peeled and quartered
100 g (4 oz) unsalted butter
120 ml (4 fl oz) single cream or milk
Salt, pepper and freshly grated nutmeg

Boil the potatoes in salted water until cooked,
approximately 20–25 minutes, depending on size. Drain
off all the water and replace the lid. Shake the pan
vigorously, which will start to break up the boiled
potatoes. Add the butter and single cream or milk, a little
at a time, while mashing the potatoes. Season with salt,
pepper and some freshly grated nutmeg according to
taste. The potatoes will now be light, fluffy, creamy and
ready to eat.

Mashed Potato Sauce

This looser and creamier version of the recipe on the
left works as a perfect accompaniment to many meat
and fish dishes, in particular the *Grilled Lamb with
'Irish' Cabbage* (page 187) and the *Slow-honey-roast
Duck* (page 268).

To achieve the 'sauce' consistency, simply double
the quantity of cream or milk. If the 'sauce' is made in
advance, when re-heating it you may well find it will
have thickened and will need more warm milk or
cream to loosen it.

BELOW
Mashed Potatoes

Hazelnut Mashed potatoes ⓥ

This alternative flavour gives the mashed potatoes a completely new face. I like to serve these rich potatoes with the *Roast Loin of Pork with an Apricot and Sage Stuffing* (page 330), but they go well with almost any of the meat dishes and with quite a few of the fish ones too.

There are two ingredients I add to the basic mash: hazelnut oil and chopped roast hazelnuts. The quantities are really down to personal taste, but a simple guide is to add 1 teaspoon each of oil and chopped nuts for every portion. For a cleaner taste, the hazelnuts should always be completely peeled of skin before chopping.

Note: Hazelnuts can be bought shelled and peeled, which will save you preparation time. These can now be 'roasted' with a trickle of oil in a frying-pan. The nuts will colour very quickly, giving a good, rich flavour.

Chopped parsley can also be added at the end.

Colcannon ⓥ

Not only did the potato became a staple food in Ireland, but cabbage did as well, and they were combined to make colcannon, a dish traditionally served at Hallowe'en. Often the mix would contain four symbols – a gold band for marriage, a sixpence for wealth, a thimble to indicate spinsterhood and a button for bachelorhood. Champ is another similar dish served at Hallowe'en, a much more buttery mixture of mashed potatoes and greenery, usually spring onions.

Colcannon is lovely as a totally vegetarian dish, perhaps with a poached egg on top, or it makes a great accompaniment to something like boiled bacon, ham or sausages. You can use kale, as is traditional in some parts of Ireland, or white or green cabbage.

SERVES 4

450 g (1 lb) potatoes, peeled
150 ml (¼ pint) milk or single cream
Pinch of ground mace
450 g (1 lb) kale or cabbage, shredded
2 small leeks or spring onion tops, chopped
150 g (5 oz) unsalted butter
Salt and pepper

Boil the potatoes in salted water until cooked, about 20–25 minutes depending on size. Drain off all the water and replace the lid. Shake the pan vigorously, which will start to break up the potatoes, then mash them until light and fluffy. Season with the salt, pepper and mace and stir in the milk or cream.

Blanch the shredded kale or cabbage in boiling water for 2–3 minutes, until softened. Drain well. Fry the chopped leeks or spring onion tops in 25 g (1 oz) of the butter for a few minutes, until softened, then add the cabbage and continue to cook for a few more minutes, before spooning into the mashed potato. Melt the remaining butter and add it to the mix. Check for seasoning, and serve.

Bubble and Squeak ⓥ

Bubble and squeak is a strange name for a vegetable dish, but it's probably so called because of the noises the vegetables make while being fried in the pan. Originally the dish was made with meat and cabbage only, but at some time potatoes were introduced, and they have stayed.

As you can see from the recipe, I have given one or two alternatives. This is because bubble and squeak can really be your own invention, and either mashed or cooked potatoes, sprouts or cabbage will do the trick. I prefer mashed potatoes as they give more of a cake consistency, but if you're using plain boiled potatoes, just peel them and cut into thick slices. The dish is usually made from leftovers, so the sprouts or cabbage should be pre-cooked.

SERVES 6–8

2 large onions, sliced
50 g (2 oz) unsalted butter
750 g (1½ lb) potatoes, cooked and sliced, or 750 g
    (1½ lb) leftover *Mashed Potatoes* (page 124)
450 g (1 lb) green cabbage or Brussels sprouts,
    cooked (page 103 or 106)
2–3 tablespoons vegetable oil
Salt and pepper

Cook the sliced onions in half the butter until softened and mix with the potatoes and sprouts or cabbage and season with salt and pepper.

Pre-heat a frying-pan (one large or two small) and add the remaining butter and the oil. Fry the bubble mix for 6–8 minutes, pushing it down with a spatula to create a cake shape. The pan should be kept hot, as this will create a crispy base.

To turn over the bubble, cover the pan with a plate or baking tray, invert the pan so the cake falls onto the plate or tray, then slip it, uncooked side down, back into the pan and repeat the cooking process.

The bubble and squeak is now ready and can be cut into six or eight wedges before serving, or left whole as a cake.

Chips and French Fries ⓥ

Fish and chips is one of our most famous national dishes, but the combination has only been around for about 150 years. Some people say that the fish was cooked and sold in the street by expatriate Italians, and that the chipped potatoes were introduced by Belgians, who, of course, are well known for their *frites* or French fries. Who knows?

Chips and French fries come in all shapes and sizes. There are many good-quality frozen fries around but I don't believe you can find any frozen chip that can beat good home-made fries. I use large potatoes, which will cool after pre-cooking and become tender without losing their potato texture. For each portion 1–1½ potatoes will be plenty. You really need a deep-fat fryer to make these and guarantee the right temperature. If you don't have one, the chips will have to be treated with even more care and attention to give you a fluffy, tender, crisp result.

SERVES 4–6

Oil, for deep-frying
4–6 large peeled potatoes, about 1.5 kg (3 lb)
Salt

Heat the oil in the deep-fat fryer or deep, heavy-based pan to 95°C/200°F for blanching.

For good large chips, trim the potatoes into rectangles. Now cut into 1 cm (½ in) thick slices, then cut again to give chips 1 cm (½ in) thick and 6–7.5 cm (2½–3 in) long. If you want French fries, then simply halve the thickness, making them 5 mm × 6–7.5 cm (¼ × 2½–3 in).

The chips now need to be blanched in the pre-heated fryer. This is very important to guarantee that the chips will be totally cooked before serving. Frying them at 95°C/200°F will cook them without colour. The large chips will take up to 10–15 minutes before becoming tender. The smaller fries will need only 6–8 minutes. Once cooked, check by piercing with a knife. When ready, remove from the oil and drain. The chips or fries can be left to cool on greaseproof paper and even chilled before finishing in the hot fryer.

To finish, pre-heat the oil in the fryer to 180°C/350°F. Once hot, place the chips in the fat. These will now take 2–3 minutes to become golden brown and crispy. Shake off any excess fat and sprinkle with salt before serving.

See also:

*Bubble and Squeak Artichokes with 'Burnt'
Mushrooms* (page 101)
Classic Roast Potatoes (page 238)
*Creamy Bubble and Squeak Soup with Crunchy
Bacon* (page 29)
Leek and Potato Broth (page 18)

Fish and Shellfish

Despite the fame of our Great British
fish and chips, it is only fairly recently
that seafood has become a British
passion again. This new feeling has
been brought on to a great extent by
chefs, who generally have a natural
passion for cooking and serving fish
and shellfish. Seafood is so versatile,
lending itself to so many different
cooking methods – the simplest most
often producing the best results.
Creating dishes with fish has become
a real challenge, an enjoyable one, in
most kitchens. Britons once virtually
survived on fish, and had to eat it
as much as, if not more than,
they did meat.

There has always been an abundance of fish and shellfish around the islands that form Britain. Very early on, fishermen were catching fish from the shore and from primitive boats; many fish bones and sea shells have been found in middens (domestic refuse dumps) attached to prehistoric sites. Because the catch could be so huge, and liable to go off, ways of preserving it had to be explored, and fish and shellfish were among the first foods to be salted and wind-dried. (Smoking is thought to have been introduced later, by the Viking invaders, and, interestingly, many of the bases of British fish-smoking – a technique for which we are famous throughout the world – are on that east coast, facing Scandinavia.) During the years of Roman rule, the Romans were hugely enthusiastic about British seafood, so much so that they transported oysters from Colchester (still the centre of the oyster industry nowadays) back to Rome. They also introduced the technique of sousing, fish 'preserved' in brine, vinegar and oil, as well as their highly flavoured fish sauces, *liquamen* and *garum*.

During the Middle Ages, it was forbidden by the Church to eat meat on several days in the week throughout the year, during Lent and on Ember days (certain Wednesdays, Fridays and Saturdays). The Church attached great importance to the effect that food had on body and soul, and meat, coming from warm-blooded animals, was thought to induce intemperance, in other words excessive self-indulgence. Fish, on the other hand, being basically cold-blooded, would have the opposite effect, promoting spirituality perhaps. This meant, literally, that on more than half the days in the year the people had to eat fish. For those living at or near the sea, this might have been no hardship, but for those inland it was less of a pleasure, for they had to rely on salted or dried fish, mainly cod and herring. Country people could have eaten freshwater fish, but often inland waters and rivers – and ponds – belonged to the wealthy or to monasteries. At this time, in attempts to find lawful 'meat', people used to eat barnacle geese and puffins (because it was said they were born at sea) and beavers (because they had a 'fishy' tail). One commentator has suggested that this medieval eating of beavers was probably responsible for the animals becoming extinct in Britain.

Until the Reformation, when the rise of Protestantism reduced the influence of the Catholic Church, fish were eaten by the wealthy in Anglo-Norman soups, heavily herbed and spiced to mask the saltiness. The poor ate them in simple stews, often with root vegetables or grains, and later potatoes, with just a few herbs as flavouring (the expression 'kettle of fish' may have developed around this time). An early relationship was that between fish and parsley, and the herb was a principal ingredient in the famous medieval green fish sauce. When available, and affordable, fresh pike, eels, oysters, and small river and sea fish were also roasted, spitted and grilled, and fried in butter. They were served upon sops or bread trenchers (plates), and later melted butter was poured over them to serve. Sharp fruit garnishes or sauces were often added – mackerel with gooseberries, for example, is an ancient combination and one that still works well. Hot and cold pies in the Great British tradition used fish, often with clarified butter poured in to make them last longer. Potting fish in butter became a popular means of preservation in the sixteenth century: the Morecambe Bay potted shrimps and potted char from Lake Windermere are still just as famous today.

PAGE 128
Lobster Casserole (page 154)

Meat, more commonly available by the seventeenth century, became the most popular protein source, although shellfish were still eaten in considerable quantities, notably cockles in Wales, and oysters, principally in southern England. There were such huge numbers of the latter that they were put in meat pies and other dishes as a means of flavouring (particularly the famous steak and oyster). It wasn't until the mid nineteenth century when the beds stopped producing, because of over-fishing and pollution, that oysters became the province of the rich. And it was at this time, too, because of faster means of transportation – steamships and the railways – and the arrival of more sophisticated ways of fishing, such as trawling, that fresh fish suddenly became much more accessible to all. Seafood became a main feature of the working classes' eating habits, particularly in Victorian London. Because plaice, mackerel, sprats, fresh and 'red' (salted and dried) herrings were cheap and quick to cook – and shellfish such as oysters, cockles and winkles hardly needed cooking at all – seafood was eaten for most meals. At this time, the smell of stale fish was said to be associated with poverty.

Salmon was now sold fresh (for years it had been available from Scotland, salted, dried or smoked), and plenty of it too – the story goes that London apprentices complained if they had to eat salmon more than once a week. (The gentler London curing and smoking of salmon would have developed at this time.) Cooked eels (with mash) and many shellfish were also sold by street vendors and from street stalls, and in the mid 1850s, this led to the establishment of shops offering fried cod or flounder along with bread or a baked potato. Some years later the accompanying potato was chipped and fried, rather than baked, and this phenomenon spread throughout the country in the form of what we now know as the famous British fish and chip shops. The recipe for *Deep-fried Cod in Batter* on page 169 will explain just why this dish became so famous.

Now, as we go into a new millennium, we have learned to love seafood again in this country, and are well aware of its health benefits, not forgetting, of course, its delicious flavours. But we are still letting most of our catch go abroad – have you ever tried to get a local langoustine or scallop in Scotland? – and we are also facing worldwide shortages because of over-fishing and polluted waters. I believe the world needs to fish – and to cook – with more care.

Here are some recipes for you to enjoy, offering a complete range of cooking methods and styles. Happy fishing …

During the years of Roman rule, the Romans were hugely enthusiastic about British seafood, so much so that they transported oysters from Colchester back to Rome.

Steamed Halibut and Cabbage
with a Salmon Gravadlax Sauce

In the nineteenth century, halibut wasn't thought much of in England, but it's certainly appreciated now. The largest of the flat fish, it is increasingly rare from the wild, but is now being farmed.

This is quite a basic recipe – steamed fish served with buttered cabbage – which sounds and is very British in concept. But I have added a few details just to lift it a little out of the ordinary. It will eat very differently with a salmon gravadlax sauce and sesame seeds to go with the accompanying cabbage. This is a classic instance of how to bring basic flavours up to date.

There are quite a few components to this recipe, but all it needs is planning ahead. All of the flavours work so well together, with the lemon oil lifting and marrying them all.

SERVES 4

4 × 175–225 g (6–8 oz) halibut fillet portions
Butter
1 small Savoy cabbage, finely shredded
1–2 teaspoons sesame seeds, toasted
4 tablespoons olive oil
1 tablespoon lemon juice
Salt and pepper

For the Salmon Gravadlax

15 g (½ oz) coarse sea salt
15 g (½ oz) caster sugar
Pepper
Splash of brandy
450 g (1 lb) salmon fillet, skinned and pin-boned

BELOW
*Steamed Halibut and Cabbage with a
Salmon Gravadlax Sauce*

Butter
2 tablespoons finely chopped shallots
2–3 tablespoons brandy
1 teaspoon demerara sugar
3 tablespoons white wine
1 dessertspoon white-wine vinegar
150 ml (¼ pint) *Fish Stock* (page 35)
150 ml (¼ pint) double cream
2–3 teaspoons Dijon mustard
1 teaspoon chopped fresh dill

The salmon gravadlax needs to be made at least 6 hours in advance. This then creates the curing process. Simply mix together the coarse sea salt, sugar and pepper and moisten with the brandy. Spread over the salmon fillet, before cling filming and allowing to cure. As the fish cures, the salt and sugar are absorbed by the fish.

Once ready, the salmon can be cut into 5 mm (¼ in) dice. You will probably find you will need no more than 100–150 g (4–5 oz) for the garnish. The rest can be thinly sliced and enjoyed with a squeeze of lemon. It's best to cure 450 g (1 lb) as a minimum to achieve the best results.

To make the sauce, melt a small knob of butter in a saucepan, along with the chopped shallots. Once melted, cook the shallots for a few minutes without colour. Add the brandy and demerara sugar and allow to boil and reduce until you have a syrupy consistency. The white wine and white-wine vinegar can also now be added, reducing to the same stage. Pour in the fish stock and boil until reduced by half. Add the double cream along with the Dijon mustard. Season with salt and bring to the simmer.

Season the halibut with salt and pepper. Sit on a buttered paper and steam above boiling water for 8–10 minutes.

While steaming, melt a knob of butter in a large pan and add the shredded cabbage. Stir well and add 1–2 tablespoons of water. This will create steam and cook the cabbage within a few minutes. Season with salt and pepper, adding the toasted sesame seeds. Divide the cabbage between four plates, sitting the halibut on top.

Add the diced gravadlax to the sauce, along with the chopped dill, and spoon over. Mix together the olive oil and lemon juice and season with salt and pepper. To finish the dish, drizzle the lemony olive oil over the halibut and around the dish. The fish is now ready to enjoy.

Steamed Turbot on Cabbage with 'Truffle' Sauce

Steamed fish with buttered cabbage couldn't be more British and simple to eat, although turbot has always been rare, highly esteemed, and very expensive. Many look upon it as the best fish in the world and I, for one, wouldn't argue with that. The natural savour of fish, in particular that of turbot, eats very well with a tasty green vegetable, but I've added a few more flavours to create another new classic.

The 'truffle' sauce couldn't be more French. The inverted commas are there because, as you'll no doubt notice, there is no truffle listed in the ingredients. Instead, the sauce is made with mushrooms and onions, which together give a truffle flavour and aroma (truffles are related to mushrooms).

However, I have included truffle oil as an optional extra. A few dots on top of the fish enhance the taste even more. This oil can be found in good delicatessens and department stores. And if you are lucky enough to have a fresh truffle (a black one from the Périgord perhaps), a fine grating added at the last moment just creates even more of an explosion in the mouth.

SERVES 4

1 small Savoy or green cabbage
Butter
4 × 175 g (6 oz) turbot fillet portions, skin left on
Salt and pepper

For the 'Truffle' Sauce

450 ml (¾ pint) Noilly Prat (French dry vermouth)
300 ml (½ pint) white wine, preferably
    Gewürztraminer
Juice of ½ lemon
175 g (6 oz) button mushrooms, finely sliced
25–50 g (1–2 oz) butter
4 large shallots, finely sliced
100–150 ml (3½–5 fl oz) double cream
Salt and pepper
Truffle oil (optional), to serve

To make the sauce: pour the Noilly Prat and white wine into two separate saucepans. Bring to the boil and reduce the Noilly by half and the wine by a third. Remove both from the heat and mix together. Squeeze the lemon juice onto the sliced mushrooms. Melt 25 g (1 oz) of the butter in a saucepan and add the sliced shallots. Cook, without colour, for a few minutes until beginning to soften. Add the sliced mushrooms and continue to cook for a further 2–3 minutes.

The alcohol from the pans can now be added. On a low heat, simmer for 10–15 minutes. Add 100 ml (3½ fl oz) of the cream, return to the simmer, and cook for a further minute before pushing through a sieve.

This is a very important stage. The sauce must be completely squeezed from the shallots and mushrooms, leaving them totally dry. This will then mean that every last drop of juice and flavour has been extracted. If you have any muslin cloth, once the shallots and mushrooms have been pushed through a sieve, take a double layer of cloth and squeeze them once more. The sauce can now be checked for seasoning with salt and pepper. The taste now has an amazing truffle edge. The remaining cream may be needed if the flavour is too acidic. Whisk in a knob or two of butter, along with a trickle of truffle oil, if using. The sauce is best blitzed with a hand blender just before serving.

Quarter the cabbage, discarding any bruised outside leaves, and cut away the core from each quarter. It's best now to pull away three or four layers of cabbage at a time before cutting. This makes the job a lot easier. Cut into 1–2 cm (½–¾ in) thick slices. Wash and drain well in a colander.

Melt a knob of butter in a large pan. Add the cabbage and cook on a medium heat, turning the cabbage carefully to ensure an even cooking. Any water from the cabbage will help create steam that will cook the vegetable. Once tender, season with salt and pepper.

While cooking the cabbage, the turbot can be steamed. Cut four butter papers or greaseproof paper into pieces of a suitable size, butter and season with salt and pepper. Place the fillets on top, skin-side up. These can now be steamed over simmering water and cooked for 6–8 minutes, depending on the thickness of the fish. The fillets should be just firm to the touch. If you do not have a steamer, then place the fillets in an oven tray. Add a knob of butter and sprinkling of white wine to the tray. Cover with foil; bring to a soft simmer and cook in a pre-heated oven (200°C/400°F/Gas Mark 6), also for 6–8 minutes.

To present the dish, divide the cabbage between four plates or bowls. The sauce can now be blitzed using a hand blender, and, if using a truffle, grate and add before spooning the sauce over and around the cabbage.

Remove the skin from the turbot; this pulls away easily, revealing a beautifully moist fillet. Present the turbot sitting on top of the cabbage. Trickle with truffle oil, if available.

Note: If fresh or tinned truffles are available, a black slice sitting on top of the turbot is a lovely garnish.
    Without any truffles or oil, it's still a beautiful dish to eat.

OPPOSITE
Pan-fried Fillet of Red Mullet with Seared Oranges
and Spring Onions

Pan-fried Fillet of Red Mullet with Seared Oranges and Spring Onions

Red mullet is one of my favourite fish. It's the most prized fish of the Mediterranean (*Mullus barbatus*), with a rich crimson skin and a delicate flavour. A variety of red mullet can also be found in the Atlantic, and around the south coast of Britain, which is not quite so delicate (*Mullus surmuletus*). Whichever fish you use, the mullet has always been prized. The Romans paid vast sums for it, and the English did too if this quote from Mrs Roundell's *Practical Cookery Book* (1898) has any truth to it: 'Fifty years ago gourmands used to spend the summers at Weymouth, on purpose to eat Red Mullet, and would give as much as two guineas for a fine fish.'

This dish is very refreshing, with the sweet acidity of the oranges and lemon working with the savoury flavour of the spring onions. The dressing can be made well in advance, which makes it a simple dish to finish. The addition of soft, creamy mashed potato balances all of these flavours and eats beautifully under crisp pan-fried red mullet fillets.

SERVES 4 AS A STARTER

Plain flour
4 fillets of red mullet from 2 × 350 g (12 oz) fish,
    scaled and pin-boned (page 11)
Butter
Drop of olive oil

Salt and pepper
250 g (9 oz) *Mashed Potatoes* (page 124, optional),
    to serve

For the Garnishes

1 large orange, segmented
Caster sugar (optional)
8 spring onions, cut into 2 cm (¾ in) sticks
Drop of olive oil

For the Dressing

3 tablespoons white-wine vinegar
3 tablespoons water
Juice of 3 oranges and 1 curl of zest
Juice of 1 lemon and 1 curl of zest
1 small shallot, chopped
2–3 coriander seeds
1 star anise
Pinch of saffron strands (optional)

To make the dressing, boil and reduce together by half the white-wine vinegar and water. The juices, zests, chopped shallot, coriander, star anise and saffron, if using, can now all be boiled together and reduced by half to two-thirds. This will increase the flavour and consistency of the liquid to a thick, rich, syrupy juice.

Mix with the white-wine vinegar reduction and then push through a fine sieve. The dressing is now ready.

Now make the garnishes. Once the orange has been segmented, it's best to allow the segments to dry on a cloth. This will soak up the excess juices; consequently, while searing, the segments will not steam and break down. You will need three segments per portion.

There are a couple of alternatives for searing. The segments can be laid on a baking tray, sprinkled with a little caster sugar and then coloured under a hot grill or with a gas gun (page 11). The gas gun can also be used with no sugar at all to give a slightly burnt tinge. Another method is to sear the segments in a very hot, dry frying-pan.

Once coloured, cut each segment into three and arrange these around the plate.

The spring onions are best cut at an angle to give 'sharp' little sticks. Quickly blanch in boiling, salted water for 1 minute before draining and allowing them to cool, refrigerated but not in iced water. Iced water will simply be absorbed and make them soggy.

To finish the cooking, heat a frying-pan until very hot. Add a splash of olive oil and pan-fry the spring onions until golden brown. Season with salt and pepper and keep warm.

To cook the fish, season the flour with salt and pepper. Lightly coat the skin of the mullet and then brush with butter.

Heat a frying-pan with a drop of olive oil. The fillets can now be laid in, skin-side down, over a medium–hot heat. Allow them to fry without shaking the pan. If the pan is shaken, it tends to reduce the heat and the fish can begin to steam rather than fry. The fillets will only take 3–4 minutes to become crisp and golden. Turn the fillets over and cook for a further minute.

The mashed potatoes are optional, but they turn this dish into a dream. The mash can either be piped or spooned into the centre of the plate, spooning the spring onions around.

Now just sit the crispy red mullet fillet on top of the mashed potatoes. Spoon or pipe, using a squeezy bottle (page 11), the citrus dressing around and scatter a few drops over the fish.

So what we have is a pan-fried fillet of red mullet, sitting on mashed potatoes with spring onions, oranges and a citrus dressing. How does that sound?

Devilled Whitebait

Whitebait are unique to Britain, in that no one else eats these tiny fish, heads, tails and guts included. Neither do whitebait really exist as fish in a distinct scientific sense, for they are tiddlers of the herring family, usually sprats or herrings, sometimes shad. Greenwich became the venue for whitebait dinners in the eighteenth century, and fashionable Londoners would go there in the summer months to eat vast plates of deep-fried fish, caught in shoals in the Thames off Blackwall.

And delicious they are still, very crispy and hot. Once you've eaten one, you suddenly want the lot. They are easily available frozen, and do cook well from the freezer, but are also in season, fresh, between February and August. They'll be scarce, but worth looking for.

This recipe is for the well-known classic – devilled whitebait, which is just deep-fried with a bite.

SERVES 4

450 g (1 lb) whitebait, fresh or frozen and
    defrosted
Oil, for deep-frying
Milk
25–50 g (1–2 oz) plain flour, seasoned with salt
    and cayenne pepper
Salt
Lemon wedges, to serve

For hot and crispy whitebait, they must be deep-fried. Heat the oil to 190°C/375°F; this will guarantee a quick, crispy cooking time. The whitebait, whether fresh or frozen, will first need to be sorted through, discarding any that are bruised or broken. Gently wash and then dry on a cloth. The fish can now be passed through milk and then lightly coated in the seasoned flour. This can be easily achieved by placing a handful into a bag with the flour and shaking. Remove the whitebait and drop into the hot fat. While cooking, the next handful can be milked and floured.

Cooking the fish at such a high temperature will crisp and colour them in approximately 1 minute. Lift with a slotted spoon and drain on kitchen paper. While still hot, sprinkle with a pinch of salt. Continue until all are cooked.

Serve with lemon wedges and the little devils are now ready to eat.

RIGHT
Devilled Whitebait

Prawn (or Lobster) Cocktail

A real Great British classic. Or is it? We have been eating this dish for decades, but where does it come from and when? It might have originated in America, but no-one is very sure. The 'history' of the prawn cocktail is only about 30 years old, dating from the beginning of the 1970s, although still very much with us today. It was so popular then that it became the most featured and eaten dish on any menu, along with its close friends – steak and chips and Black Forest gâteau. It consisted of frozen watery prawns, limp lettuce and over-ketchuped mayonnaise, not forgetting that twisted lemon slice!

All history has to start somewhere, so I like to think that we are re-writing the prawn cocktail here. This dish has more components than the original (not all essential, but they do work), each one with its own balanced flavour. And of these, the most important is the prawns. Second-rate prawns will never make a first-rate cocktail.

There are many different prawns available to use. The most basic is the small, pink, ready-cooked variety. These can be found frozen in almost any supermarket or fishmonger's. The very best of this sort can be found in marinating liquor. They are very moist and full of flavour.

There are also the large king prawns, which can be bought frozen – cooked or raw – and can also be found fresh, ready to be cooked. If they need to be cooked, lightly poach or steam for 2–3 minutes and then leave to cool naturally before peeling.

If using king prawns, 5–6 per portion will be plenty. If using small fresh or frozen prawns, allow 50–75 g (2–3 oz) per person.

Rouille is a spicy red pepper and garlic 'mayonnaise' sauce flavoured with fresh chillies. It is famous for serving with the great French 'bouillabaisse' fish stew and soups. With this recipe, it works as an enhancer to the sweet pepper discs and the total prawn-cocktail flavour. It's not essential to make but is worth it. This recipe will make approximately 300 ml (½ pint) of finished sauce. The recipe can be halved, omitting the tin of red peppers.

You will need six 6 × 5 cm (2½ × 2 in) stainless-steel cooking rings for the 'cakes'. These are available in most kitchen utensil stores. If unavailable, then plastic piping can be bought and cut to size.

SERVES 6 AS A STARTER

8 tablespoons olive oil
1 lemon, cut into quarters
4 large red peppers or 6 small ones
500–600 g (1 lb 2 oz–1 lb 5 oz) shelled, cooked
    small prawns or 30–36 large prawns
1 large iceberg lettuce, finely shredded (the finer
    the better)
12 heaped tablespoons Cocktail Sauce (recipe below)
6–8 tablespoons Rouille Sauce (recipe right)
Coarse sea salt and pepper

For the Cocktail Sauce (makes about 150 ml/¼ pint)

10 tablespoons *Mayonnaise* (page 49)
3–4 tablespoons *Home-made Tomato Ketchup*
    (page 49)

Squeeze of lemon juice
Splash (or two) of brandy
Salt and pepper

For the Rouille Sauce (makes about 300 ml/½ pint)

400 g (14 oz) tin of red peppers (optional)
2 slices of white bread, crusts removed
All red pepper trimmings from discs
2 garlic cloves, crushed
1 medium fresh red chilli, very finely sliced,
    with seeds removed
4 tablespoons olive oil
Salt

First, make the cocktail sauce. Whisk together the mayonnaise and 3 tablespoons of tomato ketchup. Add one more spoonful of ketchup if you prefer a sweeter flavour. Add a squeeze of lemon juice and season with salt and pepper.

The brandy can now be added. A dessertspoon or two will be plenty to finish the flavour. To ensure the right consistency, it's important the mayonnaise is nice and thick.

Whisk together the olive oil with the juice of 3 lemon quarters. Season with salt and pepper.

The peppers are going to be cooked, peeled and cut into discs, using the rings, to create the tops and bases for the 'cakes'.

Rub the peppers with a little olive oil and place on a baking tray. Sit the peppers under a pre-heated medium–hot grill and not too close to the heat. The peppers must now be allowed to cook, colour and start to burn. As they burn, turn them, and continue until they are coloured all around. Once cooked, remove from the heat and allow to cool for a few minutes. The skin will now pull and peel away very easily.

Once all are peeled, cut the peppers open, through one side. They will now spread into one long red strip. Carefully remove the stalk and scrape

OPPOSITE
Prawn Cocktail

Pan-fried Cod with Carrots, Parsley and Over-cooked Bacon

od has been a favourite fish in Britain for centuries. The British fishing fleet once travelled to Newfoundland to take advantage of the huge shoals of big fish they found there on the Grand Banks. They were salted on land both for the home market, and for selling on to countries enthusiastic about salt cod, primarily Spain and Portugal. In the Middle Ages, salt cod in Britain was traditionally served with mashed parsnips on Ash Wednesday. Fresh cod is probably the most popular fish battered and deep-fried in fish and chip shops.

Once again, I've combined a traditional British fish with some other familiar flavours. The 'over-cooked' bacon – which simply means very crispy – is quite important to the finished total texture of this dish. The bacon then eats like crackling and replaces the skin on the cod.

The carrots are cooked in the style of a famous French carrot dish, *à la Vichy*. Vichy is a region of France where the water is non-chalky and therefore considered just perfect for cooking vegetables. As the carrots are cooking, the water reduces with the sugar and butter, which thicken and coat the carrots with a good shine. To get as close as possible to Vichy, use bottled still water rather than that from the tap – it does make a difference.

BELOW
Pan-fried Cod with Carrots, Parsley and Over-cooked Bacon

8 rashers of streaky or back bacon
675 g (1½ lb) carrots, sliced 5 mm (¼ in) thick
Natural bottled still mineral water
75 g (3 oz) butter
1 teaspoon caster sugar
1 dessertspoon roughly chopped fresh parsley
4 × 175 g (6 oz) cod fillet portions, skinned
      (these portions have been cut from the
      fillet and not through the whole fish)
1 tablespoon plain flour
1–2 tablespoons cooking oil
Squeeze of lemon juice
Salt and pepper

The bacon can be cooked in many ways. Under a slow grill, the rashers will cook and become very crispy. The crispiness should really be at the 'snapping' stage. It can also be pan-fried until all juices have reduced into the meat, and then finished under the grill to crisp. Another way is to bake it. This will take 30–40 minutes. Pre-heat the oven to 200°C/400°F/Gas Mark 6. Lay the rashers on a baking tray and place another tray on top to keep the bacon flat. Place in the pre-heated oven and cook for 30 minutes. After the half hour, remove the top tray. Pour off any excess fat and then increase the temperature of the oven to 230°C/450°F/Gas Mark 8. Return the bacon and within 10 minutes it will have coloured and become very crispy.

Place the carrots in a saucepan and add enough bottled water just to cover. Add a pinch of salt, 25 g (1 oz) of the butter and the caster sugar. Bring to the simmer and cook for 15–20 minutes, until tender. During this time, the cooking liquor will have reduced a little. For the last 2–3 minutes of cooking time increase the heat so the liquor can reduce by half to two-thirds. Add 25 g (1 oz) butter and shake into the carrots. Add the chopped parsley and the carrots are ready.

While the carrots are cooking, the cod can be pan-fried. Season the fish with salt and a twist of pepper. The presentation side will be the skinned side. This gives a good, flat, well coloured finish, showing off the lines of the cod flakes. It's best to just salt this side, keeping it clean and not dotted with pepper. Lightly dust the skinned side with flour. Heat a frying-pan with the cooking oil and, once hot, place the fillets in, floured-side down. They can now be cooked for 5–6 minutes until golden. Add the remaining butter and cook for a further minute before turning over and continuing for 2–3 minutes.

The carrots can now be finished with a squeeze of lemon juice. Divide between four plates, sitting the cod on top. To finish the dish, place the crispy bacon rashers on top of the fish.

Note: Tarragon also works very well with this dish.

Baked Halibut with a Pumpkin Crust

This dish is certainly not one to waste flavour, and the pumpkin, seeds and all, gives a selection of tastes and textures to top the fish. The pumpkin is also helped along by wholegrain mustard. (If you're not over-keen on mustard, then simply omit from the recipe.)

Cod fillet can also be used in this recipe, but halibut is certainly first choice, having a close-flaked flesh that holds together very well while cooking.

I'm serving this dish with a white-wine cream sauce and leeks, which create a lovely base for the halibut.

1 small golden (orange-fleshed), pumpkin
      (450 g/1 lb of flesh will be needed; any
      remaining can be used for soup)
25 g (1 oz) butter
50 g (2 oz) dried pumpkin seeds
1–2 tablespoons wholegrain mustard
4 × 175–225 g (6–8 oz) halibut fillet portions,
      skinned
8 baby leeks or 3–4 medium leeks
Butter
2 tablespoons water
Salt and pepper
About 250 ml (8 fl oz) *Basic White-wine Fish Sauce*
      (page 47), to serve

Pre-heat the oven to 200°C/400°F/Gas Mark 6.

Halve the pumpkin, retaining all of the seeds. Remove the skin from 450 g (1 lb) of the vegetable and cut into rough 2–3 cm (¾–1½ in) dice.

Melt the butter in a roasting tray and, once bubbling, add the chopped pumpkin. Cook for a few minutes and, when rich and golden in colour, cover with foil and cook in the pre-heated oven for approximately 30 minutes until tender. (Leave the oven on.) Once cooked and soft, blend to a purée in a food processor. For an extra-fine smooth purée, pass through a fine sieve. Leave to cool.

While the pumpkin is roasting, the fresh seeds can be washed. Once clean, dry on a cloth. These can now be toasted until golden brown. This will give the seeds a good nutty flavour. To ensure an extra-crunchy topping, toast the bought dried seeds with the fresh ones.

These can now also be blitzed in a food processor to a fine, almost powdery, consistency. Pass through a fine sieve, to achieve a 'ground nutmeg' texture. Season with salt and pepper.

Once the pumpkin purée has cooled, add the mustard to taste and season.

Next, grease a baking tray or dish. Season the tray with salt and pepper. Each portion of the fish can now be spread, on the skinned side, with the pumpkin and mustard purée. A maximum of 4–5 mm (about ¼ in) of topping will be plenty. The fish can be topped hours in advance and kept refrigerated until needed.

If using baby leeks, cut at an angle into 1–2 cm (½–¾ in) pieces. If using larger ones, then split in half lengthways and finely shred. The leeks can now be washed and left to drain prior to cooking.

To cook the halibut, bake in the pre-heated oven for 10–12 minutes until beginning to firm. Once cooked, sprinkle the pumpkin purée top with a generous layer of the fine ground seeds. To finish, toast the halibut fillets under a hot grill for a crusty topping.

While the fish is baking, melt a knob of butter in a large saucepan. Once bubbling, add the leeks. Cook for a minute or two, without colour. Add the 2 tablespoons of water and stir. This will create a steam that will cook the shredded leeks in 2–3 minutes. If cooking the sticks of baby leek, add an extra tablespoon or two of water. These will take 3–5 minutes, depending on the size of the leeks.

The white-wine fish sauce can now also be warmed and blitzed with a hand blender, if available.

Add a few tablespoons of sauce to the leeks, ensuring any excess water has been strained off, and spoon onto four plates. Pour more sauce around and sit the pumpkin and mustard crust halibuts on top. The dish is ready to serve.

Note: The champagne version of the sauce can also be served with this dish.

Grilled Trout Fillets with Sautéd Lime Pickle Potatoes and Courgettes

Brown trout from freshwater rivers and ponds would have been one of the principal sources of fresh fish during the Middle Ages and thereafter, for those living far from the sea. Nowadays, most trout we buy are farmed, probably the imported rainbow trout, but you might also be lucky enough to come across a sea trout, a fish like the salmon, that lives and feeds in salt water and spawns in fresh.

The base for this particular, eastern-inspired trout recipe is potatoes pan-fried in butter, mixed with courgettes. The potatoes should be new potatoes, and my favourites are Pink Fir Apples, an English variety similar to smooth-skinned French varieties. Another suitable new potato is Charlotte. The potatoes and courgettes work very well together. The flavour is lifted with the sliced pickled limes and finished with a coriander butter sauce. This dish is featured here as a starter, but could also be served as a main course.

You can make the coriander butter sauce 20–30 minutes in advance and simply heat and whisk it (an electric hand-blender works very well), at the last minute, adding the chopped fresh coriander just before serving.

2 × 450 g (1 lb) trout, filleted, skin left on

350 g (12 oz) new potatoes, preferably Pink Fir
 Apple

250 g (9 oz) courgettes (2–3 medium)

6 tablespoons olive oil

Squeeze of lime juice

50–75 g (2–3 oz) butter

8–10 large fresh coriander leaves from the bunch
 for the sauce (see below), shredded

1–2 wedges of *Pickled Limes* (page 381), cut into
 thin triangular slices

2–3 handfuls of rocket leaves (other green leaves
 can also be used)

Coarse sea salt

Salt and pepper

About 150 ml (¼ pint) *Coriander Butter Sauce*
 (page 53), to serve

Make the coriander butter sauce.

The trouts are best bought filleted from your fishmonger. Season with salt and pepper and lay on a lightly buttered tray; brush the skin with butter, ready to grill.

Scrub the potatoes clean and cook in boiling, salted water. Almost any new potato should take 20–25 minutes. Once cooked, drain. If not using

BELOW
*Grilled Trout Fillets with Sautéd Lime Pickle Potatoes
and Courgettes*

immediately, leave to cool, then peel and cut into 1 cm (½ in) thick slices.

The courgettes can now be cut into a 1 cm (½ in) dice. Blanch the courgettes in boiling, salted water for 30 seconds to 1 minute. Drain and leave to cool on a cloth.

To make the lime oil, mix 4 tablespoons of olive oil with a teaspoon or two of lime juice. Season with salt and pepper.

Warm a knob of butter plus the remaining 2 tablespoons of olive oil in a frying-pan. Add the potatoes and cook on a fairly high heat to give a well-coloured golden edge. Add the blanched courgettes and also colour. Once both are golden and the potatoes are crisping, season with salt and pepper. Add the shredded coriander leaves to the potatoes.

The triangular slices of pickled limes can now be added, along with a trickle of the juices. The sharp flavour and bite of the limes is now calmed by the sautéed potato and courgette, but still gives the whole dish a more lively finish.

Place the seasoned and buttered trout fillets under a hot grill. These will take just a few minutes to begin to firm and gently cook. Arrange the lime potatoes and courgettes on four plates. Season and dress the rocket (or other green leaves) with a spoonful of the lime oil.

Re-heat and whisk the coriander butter sauce, adding the fresh coriander, and spoon some over the potatoes. Arrange the rocket leaves on top. Once the trout is just cooked, still pink in the centre, peel off the skins and sit the fillets on top of the leaves. Sprinkle with a few sea-salt granules and finish with a trickle of lime juice. The dish is now ready to serve.

Scallops with Grilled Black Pudding à l'orange

Sauce à l'orange became very much part of British eating, particularly in the 1970s, usually garnishing roast duck. The sauce may have come from France, but mixing fruits of all varieties with fish and meats had been a British habit since the Middle Ages. It became a very fashionable combination again in the 1980s, during the *nouvelle cuisine* rage that hit Britain, once again influenced by France.

Most fruit and fish/meat combinations just don't appeal to me. (Chicken and kiwi fruit just didn't work.) But citrus fruits are very different, and became traditional in British cooking as well, once the lemon and orange were introduced. Just using the juices and bittersweet tastes will often lift a dish, giving it a whole new face. Lemon is used throughout this book as an enhancer to other flavours, and lime works in a similar fashion. Orange? Well, with this dish orange is perfect. The strong flavour of black pudding takes very kindly to the taste, along with the slight bitter edge of the seared scallop. (Apparently, a dish of stewed scallops with orange sauce was very popular in the eighteenth century.)

The combination may sound and look a little 'nouvelle', but the marriage is there. I've also included a tarragon butter sauce, as tarragon and orange work together well, and the buttery, creamy consistency helps balance the total flavours.

As a garnish for this recipe, I have included candied orange peel. This is a tasty garnish to finish the dish, sitting some small dice on top of each scallop. It's not essential to make and use these – but they do give a new texture to the finished result.

SERVES 4 AS A STARTER

Cooking or olive oil
12 medium–large scallops, cleaned and trimmed
   of roe (see page 111)
12 × 5 mm–1 cm (¼–½ in) slices of black pudding
Knob of butter
Salt and pepper
Candied Oranges (page 389), cut in 3 mm (⅛ in)
   dice, to garnish (optional)

For the Orange Sauce (makes 300 ml/½ pint)

Butter
3 shallots, sliced
5–6 green peppercorns, crushed
1 small garlic clove, quartered
1 bay leaf

1 small star anise (or 2–3 broken pieces)
2 strips of orange zest
3 tablespoons brandy
Glass of white wine
150–200 ml (5–7 fl oz) orange juice
150 ml (¼ pint) *Chicken Stock* (page 33)
300 ml (½ pint) *Veal or Beef Jus* (page 34) or
    alternative (page 11)
Red-wine vinegar (optional)
Salt and pepper

For the Tarragon Butter Sauce

75–100 g (3–4 oz) unsalted butter, cubed
1 small shallot, finely chopped
Sprig of tarragon, plus ½ teaspoon chopped/torn leaves
1 tablespoon white-wine vinegar (or tarragon
    vinegar for extra flavour)

½ glass white wine
100 ml (3½ fl oz) water or *Fish, Chicken* or
    Vegetable Stock (page 35, 33 or 36)
1 tablespoon double cream
Salt and pepper

First, make the orange sauce. Melt a knob of butter in a saucepan. Add the shallots and allow to cook on a medium heat until softened, taking on a good rich caramel colour and flavour.

Add the green peppercorns, garlic, bay leaf, star anise and orange zest with the brandy. Cook until dry. Add the white wine, return to the boil and reduce by three-quarters.

Add 150 ml (¼ pint) of the orange juice. Bring to the simmer and again reduce by three-quarters.

BELOW
Scallops with Grilled Black Pudding à l'orange

Pour the chicken stock into the pan and cook until the quantity has reduced by one-third to a half. The *jus* can now also be added and reduced by a third. Then strain the sauce through a sieve.

The sauce has undertaken a lot of reductions. It's this method that increases the individual flavours, creating the finished sauce. The consistency should be just thick enough to coat the back of a spoon, without being overpowering. To loosen and enliven the sauce, if needed, add a few drops of the remaining orange juice. Season with salt and pepper. A splash or two of red-wine vinegar will also help lift the flavour of the orange sauce.

To make the tarragon butter sauce, melt a small knob of the butter and add the chopped shallot and sprig of tarragon. Cook for a few minutes, without colour, until softened. Add the vinegar and reduce until almost dry. Now add the white wine and reduce by three-quarters. Pour in the stock or water and reduce by two-thirds.

Add the double cream and, once at simmering point, whisk in the rest of the butter, a few pieces at a time. Once all has been added, season with salt and pepper. Strain through a sieve.

If the sauce is too thick, loosen with a few drops of water or lemon juice.

The butter sauce can now be blitzed with an electric hand-blender, if available, to lighten the flavour and consistency. Just before serving, add the chopped/torn tarragon leaves.

Heat a frying-pan with a trickle of olive or cooking oil. Once very hot, place the scallops in the pan. It's important not to disturb the scallops too much. This will begin to take the heat from the pan, causing the scallops to steam rather than fry.

The black pudding slices can be cooked in a separate pan or brushed with butter and placed under a hot grill. Whichever is chosen, the pudding will take approximately 1½–2 minutes on each side.

Once the scallops have been searing for 1–1½ minutes, a knob of butter can be added to the pan. Continue to cook for a further 30 seconds. The scallops will now have a deep golden colour with a slightly burnt edge. It's at this point they can

be turned in the pan, seasoned with salt and pepper and cooked for a further 1–2 minutes, depending on the size of the scallop.

Remove the scallops from the pan, along with the black pudding.

Place a scallop on top of each slice of black pudding and arrange in a line, three per portion, on the plates. If using the diced candied orange, warm in a tablespoon of the rich orange sauce and divide between the scallops, sitting 3–4 pieces on top of each. Pour a tablespoon or two of the orange sauce across each scallop with the same quantity of the tarragon butter sauce in between each pile. The dish is ready to serve.

Note: The rich orange sauce is best made in this quantity for maximum flavour. Any remaining quantity can be frozen.

Pan-fried Red Mullet with a Tomato and Leek Soup

Red mullet have been called 'the woodcock of the sea' because, like the game bird, they are traditionally cooked whole, not gutted, which lends flavour. Here, though, they are filleted, and the fillets are pan-fried, then placed on top of a potato cake, and served with tomato and leek soup. It makes a good main course.

This dish is not quite as simple as it sounds. The tomato and leek soup is made from a long, slow-cooking, mullet soup base. The ingredients are similar to those for a lobster or crab bisque, but holding a very distinctive tang of the fish's own flavour.

SERVES 6

3 × 450 g (1 lb) red mullet, filleted, scaled and
    pin-boned (page 11)
Plain flour, for coating
Butter
2–3 tablespoons olive oil
Salt and pepper
6 × *Garlic Cream Potato Cakes* (page 124), to serve

2–3 tablespoons olive oil
2 medium carrots, finely sliced
1 small fennel bulb, finely sliced
2 celery sticks, finely sliced
4 shallots, finely sliced
Red mullet bones from fillets, with heads
¼ teaspoon crushed coriander seeds
1 star anise
2 strips of orange peel
¼ teaspoon dried chilli flakes
Pinch of saffron strands
Few sprigs of basil
Few sprigs of tarragon
2 measures of Pernod
6 ripe large tomatoes, preferably plum, cut into 8
2 teaspoons tomato purée
2 glasses of white wine
1.2 litres (2 pints) *Fish Stock* (page 35)
Salt and pepper
Lemon juice

For the Soup Garnish

4 plum tomatoes, blanched and peeled
1 large leek, cut into 1 cm (½ in) dice
25 g (1 oz) butter (optional)

First, make the garnish. Once the tomatoes have been blanched and peeled, halve lengthways and remove all seeds. The flesh can now be cut into 1 cm (½ in) dice to match the leeks. Any trimmings from the tomatoes and leeks can be used in the soup.

The diced leek can now also be blanched in boiling, salted water. On boiling, drop in the leeks and cook, without a lid, for 30–45 seconds. Drain in a colander and leave the leeks to cool naturally. Once at room temperature, refrigerate, along with the tomatoes.

To make the soup, pre-heat the oven to 150°C/300°F/Gas Mark 2. Warm the olive oil in a suitable braising pan. Add the carrots, fennel, celery, shallots and any leek trimmings. On a low heat, cook for 20 minutes to soften but not colour.

Chop the mullet bones, heads included, and add to the vegetables, along with the coriander seeds, star anise, orange peel, dried chilli, saffron and herbs. Continue to cook for a further 5–6 minutes. Now add the Pernod and half of the tomatoes. Stir well, place in the pre-heated oven and cook without a lid for 1½–2 hours.

It is important during this slow cooking time that the mix is stirred every 20–30 minutes; this will ensure an even cooking.

After 1½ hours, add the rest of the tomatoes, tomato purée, white wine and fish stock. Cook for the further 30 minutes.

Remove from the oven and bring to the simmer. Season with salt and pepper and remove from the heat. The soup can now be totally liquidized (including bones), then pushed through a coarse, followed by a fine, sieve.

After being sieved, the soup will have a beautifully rich, smooth, full-flavoured finish. Re-season with salt and pepper, adding a squeeze of lemon juice, if needed, to lift the taste even more.

To pan-fry the mullet, season the fish with salt and pepper. Very lightly flour the skin side and then brush with butter.

For six portions, heat two large frying-pans with 2–3 tablespoons of olive oil. Once hot, place the fish in the pans, buttered- (skin-) side down. Cook for 3 minutes, by which time the skins will have become golden and crispy. Turn the fish over and continue to cook for 1–2 minutes.

Add the reserved leeks and tomatoes to the finished soup (butter can also be added and stirred in, if needed).

The garlic cream potato cakes, if hot, can now be placed in the bowls. If made previously, then simply microwave to heat through. Spoon the soup and garnish around generously and finish by presenting the mullet on top of the potato.

There is a lot of cooking time to reach this result, but there is even more pleasure enjoying it.

Note: You may find the quantity of soup made is greater than needed. If this is the case the soup can be frozen, keeping it ready for the next dinner party.

The soup is also lovely to serve – as a soup.

Many other fish can also be used in place of the red mullet: sea bass, sea bream or tuna fish will all eat very well.

Smoked Salmon Terrine with Warm Potato Salad

Because salmon did not travel well, the fish was more commonly available in a smoked form, and the Scottish cure was quite strong. With the arrival of the railways, salmon could be sent fresh to London, and it is probably at this time that the milder London cure was developed. Both Scottish-cured and London-cured are much-loved forms, though.

This recipe looks very expensive, as 1–1.5 kg (2¼–3¼ lb) of smoked salmon is an awful lot. But set in a 1.4 litre (2½-pint) terrine, this will give you 12–16 portions. It's the perfect starter for Christmas Day lunch, Boxing Day, and probably the day after that too. It's just thin slices of smoked salmon layered with a butter flavoured with anchovies, lemon and dill.

The anchovies used here are the marinated variety, not the tinned. The latter have too high a salt content, which just wouldn't work with smoked salmon. Marinated anchovies are available from most delicatessens and supermarket counters.

The dressing is delicious, just crème fraîche, soured cream and mustard bound around the potatoes, with a squeeze of lemon to finish, all giving flavours to complement the smoked salmon.

SERVES 12–16

For the Terrine

175 g (6 oz) butter
50 g (2 oz) marinated anchovies
Finely grated zest of 1 lemon
Juice of ½ lemon
2 tablespoons chopped fresh dill
1–1.5 kg (2¼–3¼ lb) sliced smoked salmon
Salt and freshly ground black pepper

For the Potato Salad (serves 4–6)

2 large potatoes, cut into 1 cm (½ in) dice
150 ml (¼ pint) crème fraîche
85 ml (3 fl oz) sour cream
2–3 teaspoons Dijon mustard
Juice of 1 lemon
4 tablespoons olive oil
2 tablespoons chopped fresh dill
Salt and pepper

Line a 1.4 litre (2½ pint) terrine dish or a 900 g (2 lb) loaf tin with cling film. Soften the butter. Cut the anchovy fillets into small 2–3 mm (⅛ in) dice and stir into the butter, along with the finely grated lemon zest. Add the lemon juice and season with salt and pepper. To finish, simply fold in the chopped dill. This will now need to be used at room temperature, making it easy to spread.

Place 3–4 slices of the salmon widthways in the terrine, creating a lining for the filling. It's important to make sure large slices are used, leaving a 3–4 cm (1½–1¼ in) overhang on each side.

Spread a very thin layer of butter over the base and cover with slices of salmon. Now repeat until the terrine is absolutely full.

This will have used the majority, if not all, of the sliced smoked salmon, held together with the butter. Once full, fold over the original slices to cover the top. Cover with cling film and refrigerate, using another terrine, or something similar, as a weight. This will help press the layers of the terrine together. This needs to be left for several hours, preferably overnight, until ready to turn out.

The butter when cold, will set, making the terrine a lot easier to slice.

Once set, simply turn out and, while still wrapped in cling film, the terrine can be portioned. This guarantees that the slices keep their shape. To eat this dish at its best, the terrine can be put on a plate, cling film removed, and allowed to become just lightly chilled, giving the butter spread a softer texture.

Now make the potato salad. This is best served warm, so should be cooked just 30 minutes before serving the dish.

Cook the potato dice until tender in salted water. This will take 10–12 minutes. While the potatoes are cooking, the dressings can be made.

Whisk together the crème fraîche, sour cream and Dijon mustard to taste. Add the juice of half the lemon and season with salt and pepper. Mix the 4 tablespoons of olive oil with a good squeeze of lemon juice, and season with salt and pepper.

Once the potatoes are cooked, drain the water off and place them in a bowl. Squeeze over the

remaining lemon juice and season while still warm. While the potatoes are warm, they will absorb any flavours sprinkled over.

Once the potatoes have cooled slightly but still have plenty of warmth, add the crème fraîche dressing and the chopped dill. Spoon beside the terrine slices.

To finish, drizzle a teaspoon or two of the lemon oil over the potatoes and a little around the plate.

The dish is now complete.

Note: The terrine recipe can be halved using a small terrine mould.

Sides of smoked salmon can be bought totally trimmed and cleaned of all the pin bones that run down the centre of the fillet. It's important to use a good long, sharp knife when slicing smoked salmon. This will ensure an even cut, the knife working for you.

Steamed Slice of Smoked Salmon on a Potato Cake, with Seared Lemons and a Caper Dressing

Smoked salmon has the classic reputation of just being thinly sliced across the plate and then served with a lemon wedge, or chopped, boiled egg yolk and white, shallots, capers and lemon. All work well, but steaming the fish, as here, shows the range of cooking that can actually be applied to smoked salmon.

You'll notice that some of the classic accompaniments and their flavours are being used in this dish. That's exactly what I'm trying to do with the recipe: I don't want to ignore the traditions, but instead give them a new face and identity.

The lemon dressing being used is very different to a basic lemon oil. It's made using a stock syrup, usually associated with sorbets and desserts, but the

OPPOSITE
Smoked Salmon Terrine with Warm Potato Salad

other flavours manage to calm the sweetness. The quantity of dressing made will be more than is needed immediately but, refrigerated, it will keep for up to a month. It's then a nice alternative for your mixed or green salad.

SERVES 4

4 × 75–100 g (3–4 oz) slices of smoked salmon (approx. 1 cm/½ in thick)

For the Dressing

40 g (1½ oz) sugar
100 ml (3½ fl oz) water
2 sticks of lemon grass, cut into 1 cm (½ in) pieces
1 star anise
5 pink peppercorns
Juice of 3 medium lemons (more can be added for extra bite)
Grated zest of 1 lemon
200 ml (7 fl oz) olive oil
Champagne or white-wine vinegar, to taste
Pinch of salt

For the Potatoes

4–6 peeled potatoes, preferably Cara
Groundnut oil
Salt and pepper

For the Garnish

12 lemon segments
3 tablespoons crème fraîche
3 tablespoons natural yoghurt
1 teaspoon capers, roughly chopped
1 teaspoon chopped chives
Salt and pepper

The dressing is best made 24 hours in advance to infuse all of the flavours. To make the syrup, dissolve the sugar in the water, bring to the boil and simmer for a few minutes. Allow to cool.

Place all the dressing ingredients except the vinegar in a saucepan and taste. Add 1–2 tablespoons of vinegar to increase the acidity in order to balance the sweetness. Bring to the boil. Remove from the stove and leave to cool. After 24 hours, strain.

Trim the peeled potatoes into cylinder shapes and cut into 2 mm (⅛ in) slices.

To cook the discs I'm using 10 cm (4 in) non-stick frying-pans. If only one is available, they can be 'built' and coloured one at a time, before finishing on a baking tray.

Warm a dessertspoon of groundnut oil in the pan. Before cooking the potatoes it's important they are dried on kitchen roll or a cloth. Place a slice in the centre of the warmed pan and follow by overlapping some more around the outside. Season with salt and pepper before placing a second layer around, finishing with another slice in the centre. As the potato begins to colour, lightly press. The starch from the potatoes will help stick the two layers together. Once golden, carefully turn over with a fish slice and colour the other side.

Once all four portions have been sealed and coloured, place on a buttered baking tray. This stage can be completed many hours before eating. To finish cooking and crisp the potatoes, place in a pre-heated oven at 220°C/425°F/Gas Mark 7. Cook for 10–15 minutes. The potatoes are now ready to serve.

The lemon segments can be seared quickly in a very hot dry pan, allowing them to colour on one side only, giving a burnt edge. An alternative is to colour them with a gas gun (page 11).

Mix together the crème fraîche and natural yoghurt. Season with salt and pepper. Spoon the mix between four plates, creating a circle, leaving enough room for the potato cake to sit in the centre.

Cut the lemon segments into two or three pieces and place around and on top of the crème fraîche.

Mix 8 tablespoons of the lemon dressing with the capers and chives. This mixture can now also be spooned around the plate, drizzling on the lemons and cream.

Place the smoked salmon slices on buttered greaseproof paper and steam over lightly simmering water. These will take just a few minutes to warm.

The smoked salmon is a cured fish and does not need to be cooked. If cooked through, the flavour and texture will be dry. So the steaming method is just to warm. Each slice should still have a pink look, with a lightly opaque finish.

Place the potato cakes in the centre of each plate, presenting the smoked salmon on top. Half a teaspoon of dressing can now be trickled over each slice. The dish is now complete.

Note: Fresh salmon can also be used, again steaming or pan-frying for 2–3 minutes.

Lobster Casserole

Fish and shellfish have always been cooked in pottages, the forerunners of our thick soups and casseroles, but lobster would not have been included too often, for it would always have been rare and expensive. Lobster was very popular for special occasions in Edwardian and Victorian times. They were sometimes served for breakfast, usually cold with a clarified butter, sometimes hot with a spiced sauce for a gentleman's dinner at his London club, or in rich patties or pies.

This particular lobster dish can only be described as sublime. The natural flavour of lobster is one I love, and this dish does nothing but enhance it even more. The recipe takes a little planning and work – cooking and shelling the lobsters, preparing the vegetables and so on – but the results absolutely warrant it. This dish really is a sensation and a complete meal in itself.

SERVES 4

4 × 450 g (1 lb) lobsters
50–75 g (2–3 oz) butter
3 shallots, roughly chopped
1 carrot, roughly chopped
1 small leek, roughly chopped
1 small fennel, roughly chopped
2 celery sticks, roughly chopped
1 garlic clove, crushed
1 star anise
1 bay leaf
Few fennel seeds
Sprig of tarragon
Pinch of cayenne pepper

2 teaspoons tomato purée
4 tomatoes, de-seeded and roughly chopped
4 tablespoons brandy
Glass of white wine
900 ml (1½ pints) *Fish Stock* (page 35)
1–2 tablespoons double cream (optional)
12 new potatoes
2–3 large carrots, peeled
12 small button onions, peeled
12 tarragon leaves, torn or lightly cut
8–12 flat parsley leaves, torn or lightly cut
Squeeze of lemon juice
Salt
Shellfish Oil (page 386, optional)

This dish can be prepared and almost completed several hours before cooking. The lobsters will first be blanched in boiling, salted water, then cracked from their shells. The casserole sauce/liquor can then be made from the shells. While the sauce is cooking, the vegetables can be prepared.

Bring a large pot of boiling, salted water to the boil. Drop the lobsters in the water, keeping the pot on a fast heat. Return to the boil and cook for 2 minutes. Remove the shellfish from the pan. Once cooled, the shells can be cracked and the lobster meat removed, including the meat sitting in the joints between the claws, tail and joint trimmings. Once trimmed, they can now be wrapped gently in cling film with a knob of butter. Once all are wrapped, keep refrigerated. These will later be steamed to finish the cooking and, at the same time, heat the meat through.

Cut the lobster shells (or crush) into small pieces. Melt a knob of butter in a large saucepan. Add the shallots, carrot, leek, fennel and celery. Cook for 10–15 minutes, softening with a little colour. Add the crushed garlic, star anise, bay leaf, fennel seeds, tarragon and cayenne pepper. Cook for a further 5 minutes before adding the tomato purée and chopped fresh tomatoes. The mix can now be cooked until the water from the tomato flesh has reduced. This will take another 5–10 minutes.

Add the brandy and reduce the liquid by half. Add the white wine and also reduce by half. Now it

is time to add the chopped shells, cooking them into the sauce for 5 minutes before topping with the fish stock.

Bring to the simmer and cook for 45 minutes. The sauce can now be blitzed, including shells, in a liquidizer. Then push through a coarse sieve before passing through a fine sieve.

The vegetables will have helped thicken the liquor, creating a thin sauce consistency. A few tablespoons of double cream can also be added to finish the sauce, along with 25 g (1 oz) of butter. If the sauce tastes a little shallow, a few tablespoons of tinned lobster bisque can be added. Season with a pinch of salt and cayenne pepper. Finish with a squeeze of lemon juice.

The potatoes can be boiled and left in their natural shape, peeling away the skin before serving. If this is your choice, then it is best to buy small new potatoes, allowing 3–4 per portion. Large potatoes can be 'turned', using a small knife, into barrel shapes, serving three per portion.

The carrots can also be cut to the shape of your choice – diced or sliced. I prefer to 'turn' them into barrel shapes, keeping them a similar size to the potatoes, allowing three pieces per portion. Both the potatoes and carrots can now be plain boiled until tender.

The button onions must first be blanched in boiling water for 2 minutes. Remove from the water and allow to cool naturally.

Split the onions in half and melt a knob of butter in a frying-pan. Once bubbling, place the onions in the pan, cut-side down. Cook for a few minutes, until golden brown. Turn the onions and repeat the same cooking time.

To serve the casserole, place the lobsters in a steamer, sitting over lightly simmering water; heat and cook for 5–6 minutes. In this time the lobster meat will have completely warmed through. It is very important the steaming is not too rapid; this would toughen the meat.

Warm the sauce, adding the torn herbs. The potatoes, carrots and button onions can also be added to the sauce.

Arrange the lobsters and vegetables in individual bowls, spooning the sauce over.

Once the dish is complete, I like to blitz any remaining sauce with an electric hand-blender, creating a frothy finish. The tasty froth can now be spooned over the lobsters, finishing with a drizzle of shellfish oil, if using.

Fish, Mussel and Leek Cider Pie

Fish pies were a poor man's meal. Almost any fish could be cooked and served in a liquor or sauce topped with pastry, crumble mixes or mashed potato. I prefer the mashed potato topping, which needs just to be finished under the grill for a golden top. Pastry tops, once cooked, will often lead to overcooked fish underneath.

These pies can be quite cheap to make. It really depends on what fish is happening underneath. I'm going to be extravagant here, using halibut, which is not cheap but does hold together well. Cod, haddock, hake and monkfish can be substituted, as can many other fish. The mussels can be replaced by prawns or shrimps, and the leeks by mushrooms or sweet peppers.

The sauce is made with the cidery mussel cooking liquor, which will hold all the flavours and maintain a good consistency.

SERVES 4 AS A STARTER OR 2 AS A MAIN COURSE

675–900 g (1½–2 lb) fresh live mussels, bearded, washed and scrubbed
450 g (1 lb) halibut fillet
4 baby pencil leeks, cut into 1 cm (½ in) pieces, or 2 medium leeks, split lengthways and sliced
Butter
675–900 g (1½–2 lb) *Mashed Potatoes*, including butter and cream (page 124)

OPPOSITE
Fish, Mussel and Leek Cider Pie

Mussel Cooking Liquor

Butter
1 onion, sliced
Leek trimmings (from leeks above)
1 garlic clove, peeled
Few tarragon leaves
300 ml (½ pint) cider
600 ml (1 pint) *Fish Stock* (page 35) or water

For the Sauce

35 g (1½ oz) butter
35 g (1½ oz) plain flour
Mussel cooking liquor (above)
150 ml (¼ pint) double cream (optional)
Squeeze of lemon juice
Salt and pepper

To cook the mussels, melt the knob of butter in a large saucepan. Add the onions, leek trimmings, garlic and tarragon leaves. Cook for 8–10 minutes until the vegetables have softened. Pour in the cider, boil and reduce by three-quarters. Add the mussels and fish stock, cover with a lid and cook on a fast heat. Shake the pan and stir the mussels until opened. This will take just a few minutes.

Remove all of the mussels and reduce the cooking liquor by a quarter. Any mussels unopened should be discarded; then take out the cooked mussels from the open shells, removing any shell or grit in the flesh. Strain the cooking liquor through a sieve, covering the mussels with just a ladleful to keep them moist.

For the sauce, melt the butter in a small saucepan, adding the flour. Cook for a few minutes, allowing the mix to take on a sandy colour and texture. Add the stock a ladle at a time, stirring it into the flour mix (roux), until all has been added.

Bring the sauce to a soft simmer and cook for 35–40 minutes. It is important to stir the sauce from time to time, to prevent it from sticking. The sauce can be finished with the double cream and squeeze of lemon juice for a richer finish. Extra cider can be boiled, reduced and added to give a stronger cider flavour. Check and adjust the seasoning with salt and pepper.

Pre-heat the oven to 200°C/400°F/Gas Mark 6. The halibut can now be lightly poached in some of the liquor that is keeping the mussels moist. Place the fish fillet on a buttered dish and add a few tablespoons of the cooking liquor. Cover with buttered greaseproof paper and cook in the pre-heated oven for just a few minutes to firm the fillet. Remove from the oven. The fillet can now be broken into large flakes.

Melt a knob of butter and cook the leeks for a few minutes until softened and tender.

Mix together the leeks, fish and mussels, checking the mussels have been properly bearded and no shell or grit is in the flesh.

Take half of the sauce and mix it in to bind the mussels, leeks and fish. More may be needed to loosen slightly but it is best not to make the mix too wet. (Any extra sauce can be served separately.) Spoon the mix into a suitable ovenproof dish. If preparing to eat later, then leave to cool. If not, then spoon or pipe the hot mashed potatoes on top. The pie can now be lightly brushed with butter and glazed in a hot oven at 230°C/425°F/Gas Mark 8. This will take just 8–10 minutes. The dish can also be finished by colouring under a hot grill. It is now ready to serve.

If the pie mix was allowed to cool, once cold, pipe the potato over. This can now be refrigerated until needed. To re-heat and glaze, place in a pre-heated oven at 190°C/375°F/Gas Mark 5, for 25–30 minutes. To glaze, finish under the grill.

Note: This dish will eat very well with *Buttered Spinach* (page 113). Brushed egg, or melted cheese, or white breadcrumbs can also be used to glaze the potato topping.

Mussel, Leek and Tomato Casserole, with Spinach and a Warm Poached Egg

Mussels have been eaten since prehistoric times in Britain, and a number of recipes for them exist from the fourteenth century onwards. In the very early days, they used to be baked on hot stones beside the sea, and a little butter was inserted as the shells opened. They were also cooked in pies, boiled and served with parsley, or packed into rolls or baked potatoes in Ireland.

This is quite a simple dish, with the mussel cooking liquor becoming the base to the sauce. Once everything is in the bowls, bar the egg, the sauce can be glazed to a golden finish. Sit the egg in the centre and coat with a spoon of frothy sauce, drizzle with lemon oil and it is ready to eat. Breaking into the egg yolk and eating it with the seafood and vegetables is just wonderful.

SERVES 4 AS A STARTER OR 2 AS A MAIN COURSE

1 kg (2¼ lb) fresh live mussels, bearded, washed and scrubbed
300 ml (½ pint) white wine
300 ml (½ pint) *Fish Stock* (page 35) or water
300 ml (½ pint) double cream
1 leek, cut into 1 cm (½ in) dice
3 tomatoes, blanched and peeled
Lemon juice
2 tablespoons crème fraîche
175–225 g (6–8 oz) *Buttered Spinach* (page 113)
1 large egg yolk
4 poached eggs (page 82)
2 tablespoons olive oil
Salt and pepper

When washing and scrubbing fresh mussels you will notice the beard protruding from the shell. This, using a small knife, must be pulled away.

Boil the white wine in a large saucepan, reducing it by half. Add the fish stock or water and bring to the boil. Add the mussels and cook on a fast heat, turning the mussels in the pan. After a few minutes, the mussels will open. Remove them from the pan. Reduce any mussel liquor by three-quarters. Once reduced, add 250 ml (9 fl oz) of the double cream. Cook for 10 minutes, allowing the sauce to reduce and thicken slightly. Once at this stage, strain through a fine sieve.

While the sauce is cooking, the mussels can be removed from their shells, discarding any unopened ones.

The leek can now be blanched in boiling water for 1–2 minutes until tender. Drain and spread on a tray to cool naturally. Split the tomatoes and de-seed, then cut into 1 cm (½ in) dice.

Check the mussel sauce for seasoning and add a squeeze of lemon juice along with the 2 tablespoons of crème fraîche. Separate a quarter of the sauce into a small saucepan. To the remaining sauce add the mussels, leeks and tomatoes, and warm through. The spinach can now be microwaved or pan-fried.

Divide the spinach into small piles in the centre of each bowl. Whisk the remaining 50 ml (2 fl oz) of double cream to a very soft peak. Add the egg yolk and whipped cream to the mussel sauce containing the leeks and tomatoes.

Spoon the mussels, leeks and tomatoes around the spinach, finishing with enough sauce to cover. Each plate can now be placed under a hot grill to glaze the sauce to a golden brown.

While glazing, heat the poached eggs in simmering water. Poached eggs will take 1 minute to re-heat.

Once all are glazed, sit the eggs on top of the spinach piles. Blitz the separate sauce with an electric hand blender to a frothy consistency. Spoon 1–2 tablespoons on top of each egg.

Mix the olive oil with a squeeze or two of lemon juice, season with salt and pepper and trickle around. The dish is ready.

Note: The sauce does not have to be glazed to finish. If you would prefer not to, then simply omit the egg yolk and whipped cream.

Soused Mackerel

Sousing as a means of preserving fish (and meat) dates back to Roman times, the Romans having borrowed the technique from the Greeks and introduced it to northern Europe. In the Middle Ages in Britain, many fish, usually herring, were soused in extremely powerful liquids, presumably to counter the extreme saltiness of the fish, or to disguise off-flavours.

Most fish were soused raw, but this recipe is slightly different. The mackerel is heated briefly in its spicy liquor, which is given a loose sauce consistency with the addition of butter, then served warm with potatoes.

SERVES 4 AS A STARTER OR LIGHT LUNCH

4 mackerel fillets, all bones removed
Salt and pepper
½ quantity *Mashed Potatoes* (page 124) with lemon and shallots (see Note), to serve
50 g (2 oz) butter
1 tablespoon chopped fresh parsley

For the Sousing Liquor

1 small fennel bulb, very thinly sliced
2 carrots, thinly sliced
2 celery sticks, thinly sliced
1 leek, thinly sliced
2 shallots or 1 onion, thinly sliced
Bouquet garni of 1 bay leaf, 1 star anise, a few fresh basil leaves, 2 sprigs each of fresh thyme and tarragon, tied in a square of muslin or a strip of leek leaves, or a bouquet garni sachet
6 black peppercorns
50 ml (2 fl oz) olive oil
50 g (2 oz) unsalted butter
150 ml (¼ pint) dry white wine
150 ml (¼ pint) white-wine vinegar
600 ml (1 pint) water

Cook all the sliced vegetables in a pan with the bouquet garni, peppercorns, olive oil and the butter for a few minutes. Add the white wine, wine vinegar and water and simmer for about 10–12 minutes, until the vegetables are tender. This is the sousing liquor. Allow to cool and remove the bouquet garni.

Place the fillets in a lightly buttered flameproof dish and cover with the liquor and vegetables. Season with salt and pepper. Bring slowly to the simmer then remove from the heat. The fish is now ready.

Spoon some of the hot mashed potatoes into serving bowls and sit the mackerel on top. Stir the butter and the parsley into the cooking liquor. Ladle the vegetables and sauce around the fish and serve.

Note: For mashed potatoes with lemon and shallots, fry a finely diced shallot in a knob of butter until softened, without colour. Add to the mashed potatoes, with a squeeze of lemon juice.

Whole Roast Sea Bass

Whole fresh fish would once have been roasted beside the fire, and served with a sharp or spicy sauce or relish, perhaps not too unlike the sweet pepper butter offered below and the *Green Pepper Butter* on page 52.

Roasting a whole fish and presenting it at the table is such a pleasure. Cutting through the crispy skin to find succulent, almost steamed fish

BELOW
Whole Roast Sea Bass

underneath makes you feel so hungry. As far as preparation is concerned, simply ask your fishmonger to gut, trim and scale the bass, making sure the blood clot line is scraped and washed from inside.

The fish can also be stuffed with many flavours, lemons, garlic, thyme and basil being quite common. I'll be using some of these to help enhance any juices released from the fish. And I suggest serving either buttered new potatoes or a very creamy mashed potato with the fish.

SERVES 4

1.5 kg (3¼ lb) sea bass, cleaned and scaled
25 g (1 oz) butter, softened
Coarse sea salt
Pepper
Plain flour
½ lemon
2 garlic cloves, peeled and split
Few basil leaves
Cooking oil

For the Sweet Red Pepper Butter

150 g (5 oz) butter, softened
1 large red pepper, finely diced
Pepper (or dash of Tabasco sauce)

To make the red pepper butter, melt a knob of the butter in a small saucepan. Add the sweet pepper and cook on a gentle heat for 7–8 minutes until tender. Remove from the heat and leave to cool. Mix the remaining butter with the sweet peppers, including all pepper juices and seasoning. This can now be left as a coarse butter or blitzed in a food processor or pushed through a sieve for a smooth consistency.

The butter can be rolled into cylinders, wrapped in cling film or presented in a small bowl. Refrigerate until needed.

To cook the fish, pre-heat the oven to 200°C/400°F/Gas Mark 6. Brush the inside of the fish with butter and season. Dust the outside skin with plain flour and then also brush with butter and season. Cut the lemon into four wedges and place inside the bass, with the garlic and basil leaves.

Heat a roasting tray with a few tablespoons of cooking oil.

Place the fish in the tray on a medium–high heat and fry gently to a golden brown; carefully turn the fish over and also colour. This process will take just 2–3 minutes on each side.

Place in the pre-heated oven and roast for 20–25 minutes, basting with the juices as the bass cooks.

Remove the fish from the roasting tray, allowing any juices to collect in the pan.

Present the sea bass on a large serving plate, topping it with slices of the sweet red pepper butter. Offer any accompanying vegetables separately.

Any juices left in the pan can be loosened with 3–4 tablespoons of water, strained through a sieve or tea strainer and poured over the bass.

Salmon Fish Cakes

Fish cakes were originally an economical dish, using up leftover scraps of cooked fish – nothing wasted, nothing wanted. Potatoes were the usual base, as they are here, but egg and breadcrumbs were sometimes used, particularly in a cockle fritter or fish cake, a speciality from Wales. Any fish would be suitable, but blander fish need boosting in flavour (adding a little smoked fish to it, as you might to a fish pie).

Salmon is the perfect fish for cakes, holding its moistness with a rich 'fat' content that helps spread the flavour. If salmon is unavailable, fresh cod or haddock can also be used, making sure the fish is slightly undercooked before mixing with the potatoes. This will ensure a moist rather than dry or cakey finish.

SERVES 4–6

1 tablespoon unsalted butter
2 shallots, finely chopped
450 g (1 lb) salmon, filleted and skinned
150 ml (¼ pint) dry white wine

1 tablespoon chopped fresh parsley
350 g (12 oz) *Mashed Potatoes*, without cream
    or butter (page 124)
2 tablespoons plain flour, for coating
2 eggs, beaten, for coating
225 g (8 oz) fresh or dried breadcrumbs,
    for coating
Salt and pepper
Vegetable oil, for deep-frying

For the Lemon Butter Sauce

175–225 g (6–8 oz) unsalted butter
Juice of 1 lemon
50 ml (2 fl oz) *Chicken* or *Vegetable Stock*
    (page 33 or 36)
Salt and pepper

BELOW
Salmon Fish Cakes

Pre-heat the oven to 200°C/400°F/Gas Mark 6 and use the butter to grease a baking tray. Season the tray. Sprinkle the finely chopped shallots onto the prepared baking tray, sit the salmon on top and season again with salt and pepper. Add the white wine, cover with foil and cook in the pre-heated oven for about 8–10 minutes, until the fish is just cooked. Very thick fillets may need a few minutes more. The salmon should be just firm on the outside and still pink in the middle.

Sit the salmon in a colander over a pan to collect all the cooking juices. When all the juices have been collected, boil to reduce them to a syrupy consistency.

Break up the salmon with a wooden spoon, then add the syrupy reduction and the chopped parsley. Fold in 225 g (8 oz) of the potato, and then add it a spoonful at a time until you have a binding texture. Check for seasoning, then roll into 12 to 18 balls about 4 cm (1½ in) in diameter. Three cakes per portion will be enough. Lightly pass through the flour, beaten eggs and then the breadcrumbs; repeat the process of egg and breadcrumbs once more.

The fish cakes are now ready for deep-frying. Heat the vegetable oil to 180°C/350°F, then fry the fish cakes for about 4–5 minutes until golden brown. Drain well on kitchen paper.

To make the sauce, chop the butter into 1 cm (½ in) pieces and put into a pan with the lemon juice and stock. Bring to the simmer, whisking all the time. Do not allow the sauce to boil or the butter will separate. If it's too thick, add more stock and if you like a sharper taste add more lemon juice. Season and serve immediately. To give a creamier texture, simply blitz the sauce with an electric hand blender.

To serve, just pour the warm lemon butter sauce into individual serving dishes or bowls and sit three fish cakes in the centre of each one.

Note: Lemon butter sauce is one of the simplest possible sauces, which has a silky texture and just enough acidity for the salmon fish cakes. This sauce works well with almost any fish.

Smoked Eel Kedgeree

The word 'kedgeree' is an Anglo-Indian adaptation of the Hindi *khicharhi* or *chichri*, which was a spicy dish consisting of onions, rice, lentils and fish or meat. This was encountered by the British during the years of the Raj, and brought back. It is a simpler dish now, made without lentils, and usually with smoked haddock. I have used eels here as they are so tasty, and they too have played a large part in Britain's culinary history. Eels were once virtually the only fresh fish available to those in the country; in the tenth century, live eels were used as currency to pay rents to the Abbots of Ely.

This dish could almost be called a risotto, because it's made by the risotto method, but it still holds all the flavours of a good old-fashioned kedgeree. I serve it as a starter, but it can be a total meal in itself – for breakfast or a great lunch or supper. Hard-boiled eggs are traditionally used, but having a warm poached egg sitting on top of the rice and just breaking the yolk over it is a dream. If you really cannot find smoked eel, you can make the dish with smoked haddock.

SERVES 4

450 g (1 lb) smoked eel

For the Eel Stock

1 onion, chopped
1 leek, chopped
2 celery sticks, chopped
6 mushrooms or 50 g (2 oz) mushroom
    trimmings
1 bay leaf
1 fresh thyme sprig
2 fresh tarragon sprigs
Few black peppercorns
50 g (2 oz) unsalted butter
300 ml (½ pint) dry white wine
1.2 litres (2 pints) *Fish Stock* (page 35), fish stock
    cube or water

For the Kedgeree

2 onions, finely chopped
100 g (4 oz) butter

50 g (2 oz) veal bone marrow, chopped (optional)
225 g (8 oz) arborio or long-grain rice
Approx. 300 ml (½ pint) *Curry Cream Sauce*
 (page 393), or ready-made

To Serve

4 eggs, poached (page 82)
3 tablespoons olive oil
2 teaspoons snipped fresh chives

Smoked eel is one of my favourite smoked fish. First, it has to be filleted and skinned. Hopefully, your fishmonger will do this for you but, if not, simply cut off the head and position the knife against the top half of the central bone. Carefully cut along the bone, removing the fillet of fish. Turn the fish over and repeat the same process. Now the skin can be removed: slide your finger or thumb under the skin at the head end and it should tear off all the way along. The fillets may need a little trimming down the sides to remove any excess skin.

Once skinned, turn the fillets on to their backs to show the centre. From the head end to half-way down there will be some bones. Simply position the knife under these bones and cut away from the flesh. You now have two long, clean fillets of eel. Cut these into 1.5 cm (½ in) pieces and refrigerate until needed.

To make the eel stock, chop all the bones, skin and trimmings. Place the chopped vegetables, herbs and peppercorns in a large pan with the butter and cook them gently for 10 minutes without letting them colour. Add the bones and trimmings and continue to cook for a further 5 minutes. Add the white wine and boil to reduce until almost dry. Add the fish stock, stock cube or water. (Fish stock will give you a stronger and better taste. If you are using water, ask the fishmonger to give you some fish bones as well to cook with the eel.) Bring the stock to the simmer and cook for 20 minutes. Strain through a sieve and the stock is ready.

For the kedgeree, cook the chopped onions in the butter with the bone marrow, if using, for 5–6 minutes until softened. Stir in the rice and cook for

2 minutes, then start to add the hot eel stock a ladle at a time, stirring continuously. This will create steam and help the cooking process. Wait for the stock to be absorbed before adding more, and keep adding the stock and stirring until the rice is just softening – this will take about 15–20 minutes. The rice should be tender and the mixture still moist.

When the rice is cooked, stir in half the curry sauce and taste. At this stage it becomes a matter of personal choice; some more or all of the curry sauce can be added if you want a stronger taste.

Add the pieces of chopped eel to the kedgeree and stir in to warm through. Warm the poached eggs in boiling water, then drain well. Spoon the kedgeree into four bowls and sit a poached egg on top of each one. Spoon a little olive oil over the eggs and sprinkle with the snipped chives. The dish is now ready.

Smoked Haddock with Welsh Rarebit

This has become almost my signature dish, and I must say it has remained one of my favourites. It's very British in concept, using wonderful smoked haddock – choose a natural fish, not one that has been dyed bright yellow – and a Welsh rarebit topping. Just to crown the flavours and textures, I serve it all on a good tomato salad, giving us those hot and cold tastes together. It's lovely as a starter, supper or light meal.

SERVES 4 AS A STARTER OR LIGHT LUNCH

6 ripe plum or salad tomatoes
Salt and pepper
4 × 100 g (4 oz) slices of natural
 smoked haddock
175 g (6 oz) *Welsh Rarebit* mix (page 178)
1 tablespoon finely snipped fresh chives
150 ml (¼ pint]) *Basic Vinaigrette* (page 50)

Pre-heat the oven to 180°C/350°F/Gas Mark 4 and pre-heat the grill to medium.

First remove and discard the 'eyes' from the tomatoes. Blanch the tomatoes in boiling water for 10 seconds. Cool them quickly in iced water and the skins should peel off easily. Slice the tomatoes and arrange overlapping on the centre of individual plates. You'll need about 1½ tomatoes per portion, and this should make a nice circle. Sprinkle with a little salt and a twist of pepper.

Arrange the haddock portions in a buttered flameproof dish. Split the rarebit into four pieces and pat out on your hands to about 2–3 mm (⅛ in) thick (the mix should be quite pliable and easy to use), trimming to give a neat finish. Lay the pieces on top of the haddock. Colour under the grill until golden, then finish the haddock in the pre-heated oven for 4–5 minutes.

Add the chives to the vinaigrette and spoon over the tomatoes. Sit the haddock on top and serve.

Smoked Haddock and Welsh Rarebit Tartlets

For these little alternatives it's best to buy small pastry canapé tartlet cases. This will save a lot of time and work.

This is a great recipe to try, especially if you've made the above recipe and have rarebit left over. If you have any smoked haddock fillet tails use them here. One small haddock fillet will fill a lot of tartlets, so the quantities are up to you.

¼ *Welsh Rarebit* mix (page 178)
1 small fillet (350–450 g/12 oz–1 lb) smoked
    haddock, preferably natural
300ml (½ pint) milk
Butter
2–3 large tomatoes, blanched in boiling water,
    peeled, seeded and diced into 5 mm
    (¼ in) pieces
1 heaped teaspoon chopped chives
2 tablespoons olive oil
1 teaspoon balsamic vinegar
40 canapé pastry tartlets
Olive oil, to finish (optional)

The Welsh rarebit mix can be melted into balls and patted by hand into disks 2–3mm (about ⅛ in) thick – big enough to cover the tartlet cases.

To cook the smoked haddock, place the fillet into a suitable dish. Bring the milk and a knob of butter to the boil and pour over the fish. Cover and leave to stand for a few minutes. The fish is now cooked. Break the fish into flakes and mix with the diced tomatoes and chopped chives. Mix together the olive oil and vinegar (extra vinegar can be added for a more piquant flavour) and pour over the filling. Divide among the tartlet cases and top with the Welsh rarebit discs.

Place the tartlets under a pre-heated grill and cook until golden brown. For a shiny finish, lightly brush with a drop of olive oil. The rarebit tartlets are ready to serve.

Grilled Herrings with Braised Lentils

Herrings in one form or another, but usually salted and dried, formed the staple diet of many families almost until the twentieth century. The tough and dark 'red' herring was very strong in taste but, served with potatoes after soaking, managed to keep hunger at bay. Over the years, we have continued to salt and smoke herring, but now for pleasure rather than necessity, and today the bloater (a closed herring, lightly smoked so that it is still plump and 'bloated') and the kipper (a split, brined and smoked herring) are famous British specialities.

Fresh herrings are eaten too; they are coated with oatmeal in Scotland, and fried in bacon fat. Herrings grilled whole on the bone with a separate hot English mustard sauce – a very traditional British combination – was one of the first dishes I was taught as a young chef. They were lovely to eat, but hard work. So, to simplify everything for the eater, I decided to take them off the bone and try them just with the sauce. I then needed something to eat with them, and mashed potatoes worked very well, but I find lentils even tastier.

ABOVE
Smoked Haddock with Welsh Rarebit

ABOVE
*Seared, Cured Salmon Cutlets with Leeks, Bacon and
a Cider-vinegar Dressing*

8 large herring fillets
Butter, melted

For the Braised Lentils

50 g (2 oz) unsalted butter
25 g (1 oz) carrot, finely diced
25 g (1 oz) celery, finely diced
25 g (1 oz) onion, finely diced
25 g (1 oz) leek, finely diced
1 small garlic clove, crushed
100 g (4 oz) green lentils (*lentilles de Puy*)
450 ml (¾ pint) *Chicken* or *Vegetable Stock*
　　(page 33 or 36)
Salt and pepper

For the Mustard Seed Sauce

2 shallots, finely chopped
1 celery stick, chopped
½ leek, chopped
1 bay leaf
50 g (2 oz) unsalted butter
2 glasses dry white wine
300 ml (½ pint) *Fish Stock* (page 35)
150 ml (¼ pint) double cream
2 teaspoons wholegrain mustard, to taste

Pre-heat the oven to 200°C/400°F/Gas Mark 6 and butter and season a small flameproof baking tray.

To cook the lentils, melt the butter in a small ovenproof braising pan. Add the diced vegetables and garlic and cook for a few minutes. Add the lentils, stirring well. Cover with the stock and bring to the simmer. Cover with a lid and braise in the pre-heated oven for about 30–35 minutes until the lentils are tender and all the stock has been absorbed. Make sure they are tender before taking them from the oven. Season with salt and pepper.

To make the sauce, sweat the vegetables and bay leaf in the butter for a few minutes. Add the white wine and boil to reduce until almost dry. Add the fish stock and continue to boil until reduced by three-quarters. Pour on the cream and cook slowly until the sauce is thick enough to coat the back of a spoon. Strain through a fine sieve. Stir in the

mustard a teaspoon at a time until the right taste is achieved, mustardy but not overpowering.

To cook the herring fillets, place them on the greased baking tray and brush with butter. Cook under the hot grill for about 5–6 minutes. As soon as the fillets have coloured they will be ready to serve.

To serve, spoon the lentils on to the centre of four hot plates, pour the mustard sauce around and sit the fillets on top of the lentils. The dish is now complete.

Seared, Cured Salmon Cutlets with Leeks, Bacon and a Cider-vinegar Dressing

Salmon is the king of freshwater fish – although, of course, it spends quite a lot of its life in the sea. Salmon was once eaten very much more than it is now, when the rivers up which it swam to spawn were cleaner, and pollution and overfishing were not taking their toll on the Atlantic fishing grounds. Try to use wild salmon but, if not available, many farmed fish are good value.

This particular salmon dish has lots of good British flavours, with leeks, bacon and cider amongst our classic ingredients. You'll notice that I've used the word 'cured' in the title of the recipe. This curing is an optional extra, but an absolutely beautiful one. It gives the dish and the salmon a whole new texture and flavour. It's not essential so don't be put off by it. Fresh salmon cutlets can also be used.

SERVES 4 AS A STARTER

For the Salmon

15 g (½ oz) coarse sea salt
15 g (½ oz) caster sugar
Splash of brandy or whisky
450 g (1 lb) salmon fillet, skinned and pin-boned
　　(page 11)
Pepper

6 rashers of streaky bacon, cut into very thin strips
Cooking oil
450 g (1 lb) leeks, shredded
Butter
Salt and pepper
Cider-vinegar Dressing (page 41)

Mix together the sea salt and sugar; bind with the brandy or whisky to a consistency that will hold when squeezed.

Lay the salmon fillet on cling film, big enough to wrap around, twist pepper over the salmon and then spread with the salt and sugar mix.

Wrap the cling film around, place on a tray and refrigerate. It should now be left to cure for 4–6 hours. This will give enough time for the salt to dissolve with the sugar and impregnate the salmon flesh. The salmon can be left for 24 hours. The texture will then become slightly firmer as a 'raw cooking' process takes place.

Once cured, the salmon can be cut into eight cutlet pieces, two per portion, ready to pan-fry.

For the garnish, fry the bacon lardons in a drop of cooking oil on a medium heat until completely crispy, almost like a fine bacon crackling. Other methods of cooking the bacon are to grill it, pouring off excess fat, until crisp, or bake in a hot oven, also pouring off any excess fat. These lardons can be cooked in advance; they will stay crispy and will reheat well when mixed with the hot leeks.

For the leeks, heat a knob of butter in a large pan or wok. Once bubbling, add the washed leeks. Cook on a fast heat until tender; this will only take 2–3 minutes. The slightly moist leeks will create steam, which helps cook them quickly.

Add the bacon and season with salt and pepper. Also add 2–3 tablespoons of cider dressing to bind and hold the garnish together.

Spoon the mix onto four plates. Trickle more of the cider dressing around (squeezy bottle piping can be used for a more decorative finish, see page 11).

The salmon pieces can be shallow-fried while the garnish is cooking. It's best to make the pan very hot with a drop of cooking oil. Place the 'cutlets' in the pan and cook for 1–2 minutes to colour the edges on one side until slightly burnt. Turn them over just to seal. It's important that the fish is only cooked medium-rare to medium, bearing in mind it has been cured.

The fish pieces can now be sat on top of the leek and bacon garnish.

The dish is now ready to eat.

Note: I also like to add a few drops of lemon oil. Simply mix a few tablespoons of olive oil with a teaspoon or two of lemon juice and season with salt and pepper.

Parsleyed Cod with Mustard Butter Sauce

Parsley has been associated with fish since the Middle Ages, one of the principal herbs used in the famous green sauce. I have changed this classic cod and parsley combination to give a purée of parsley mixed with spinach, which is spread over the fish, so that the parsley flavour comes through in every bite. If you serve this with some curly kale, roast potatoes and a mustard butter sauce, you will have a complete meal.

If pig's caul (page 11) is unavailable, wrap the cod in buttered foil and steam it instead of pan-frying and roasting. Or leave the parsley purée off the cod, pan-fry the cod and put it on top of the warm purée or vice versa.

I am using two varieties of parsley here because I want to put the flavour from the flat parsley – which is stronger – into the curly parsley, which has a thicker texture.

SERVES 4

Small bunch of fresh flatleaf parsley
Small bunch of fresh parsley
100 g (4 oz) spinach, picked and washed
4 × 175–225 g (6–8 oz) portions of cod fillet, skinned and boned
225 g (8 oz) pig's caul, soaked in cold water overnight

1 tablespoon cooking oil
Butter
Salt and pepper

To Serve

Curly Kale (page 105)
Butter
Mustard Butter Sauce (page 53)
'Banana' Roast Potatoes (page 239)

Pre-heat the oven to 200°C/400°F/Gas Mark 6. The two parsleys and the spinach should be plunged into salted, boiling water for 2–3 minutes until cooked and tender. Drain in a colander and refresh with cold water. Once cold, squeeze out any excess water and blitz in a food processor to a smooth purée. Season with salt and pepper.

This purée can now be spread 3 mm (⅛ in) thick on the presentation (skinned) side of the cod. Then cut the pig's caul into four pieces. Use these to wrap around the cod portions. Refrigerate until firm.

To cook the cod, warm a frying-pan with the tablespoon of cooking oil. Put the cod portions in, parsley-side down, and add a knob of butter. Cook and colour for 3–4 minutes until golden with the rich green coming through. Turn the fish over and transfer to an ovenproof dish, if necessary. Complete by cooking in the oven for 8–10 minutes.

While the cod is cooking, warm the curly kale in a little butter and season. Warm the mustard sauce and add one or two spoonfuls to the curly kale.

Once the cod is cooked, remove it from the pan and place at the front of the plate. Arrange a small pile of roast potatoes, allowing four pieces per portion, along with a few spoonfuls of curly kale. Pour the mustard sauce over and around the kale and serve.

Deep-fried Cod in Batter

This must be one of the most famous fish dishes in the whole of the British Isles, and yet it's not often cooked at home, but bought wrapped in paper from the local chippie.

Battering your own cod is not difficult at all, providing you have either a fat fryer (I always suggest using a deep-fat fryer for obvious safety reasons) or a very large saucepan. This cooking method for fish was first introduced using the batter simply to protect the fish during its cooking time. Once deep-fried and golden brown, the fish was presented on the plate and served and the eater would cut away and discard the batter to enjoy just the fish.

The batter eventually became an edible and enjoyed component of the dish and has stuck since. I have strong feelings about the purpose of the batter: yes, it's got to be flavoursome and crisp, but, equally important, it's got to be thick enough to protect the fish itself.

If a thick batter is used and it is slowly and carefully submerged into the pre-heated fat (beef dripping is the most classic cooking fat, but a good-quality cooking oil will work just as well), it will form a protective casing around the fish itself. While the fat cooks the batter, it will begin to soufflé into a crispy armour, with the heat steaming the fish.

The cod fillet will now have the most beautiful natural flavour with near-translucent flakes to enjoy, surrounded by fried, crispy, almost crackling-style batter. It really cannot be beaten.

If a very thin batter is used, it will not soufflé. Instead it will wrinkle all over the fish, sticking to the flesh and never hold a crispness (as we find in most chippies). Once removed from the fryer, the fish juices will bleed, moistening the already softening batter so that by the time you are home the fish will have stuck to the paper it's wrapped in. It's a good idea to invest in a fat fryer and, once you've made your own battered cod, I doubt you'll buy the ready-made stuff again.

A good wedge of lemon goes well with the fish along with *Tartar Sauce* (page 43) and home-made *Chips* (page 127) for the perfect supper.

SERVES 2

2 × 175–225 g (6–8 oz) cod fillet portions, boned
Squeeze of lemon juice
Salt and pepper

225 g (8 oz) self-raising flour, sieved
300 ml (½ pint) lager

Pre-heat the fat-fryer oil to 180°C/350°F.

Leaving the skin on the cod fillets holds the fillet together when it's passed through the batter and placed in the oil. Squeeze a little lemon juice over each fillet and season with salt and pepper. These can now be lightly floured before making the batter.

To make the batter, place the sieved flour into a large bowl. Whisk in three-quarters of the lager. At this point check the consistency of the batter: it should be very thick, almost too thick. If it appears to be over-gluey, whisk in a little more lager to loosen slightly. Season with a pinch of salt. The cod fillets can now be passed, one at a time, through the batter mix. It's best to hold the fillet at the thin end (in one corner) between thumb and forefinger. Coat the fish in the batter and lift from the bowl. Some of the batter will begin to fall away slowly. If the batter falls away quickly, it means it's too thin, in which case add a tablespoon or two more of flour.

Don't allow too much of the batter to fall off before placing in the deep hot oil. Submerge only an inch at a time and, once three-quarters of the fish is in, the batter will lift the fillet, floating the fish. Submerge the remaining fillet in the same way, being careful not to burn your fingers.

Allow to cook for 2–3 minutes before turning the fish over. At this point the fish will not be golden brown but the batter will have sealed and souffléd. Cook until golden brown all round. A thick slice of cod will take up to 12 minutes to cook, an average fillet 9–10 minutes.

Once cooked, remove from the oil and drain on kitchen paper. Sprinkle with salt and serve.

Note: The batter quantities can be doubled to give enough for 4–6 portions.

For an extra garnish, deep-fry curly parsley in the oil. Plunge the parsley carefully into the hot fat as the oil tends to spit. When this calms down after a minute or two, remove the parsley from the pan and lightly salt.

See also

Angels on Horseback (page 175)
Arbroath Smokie and Cream Cheese Pâté
(page 89)
Cullen Skink (page 27)
Grilled Kippers (page 87)
Lobster 'Bisque' Soup (page 23)
Lobster Omelette 'Thermidor' (page 75)
Seared Scallops with Radish and French Bean
Salad (page 109)
Smoked Haddock (page 88)
Soft Herring Roes on Caper Toasts (page 177)
Spicy Smoked Haddock and Saffron Soup
(page 18)
Stuffed Herrings with Apples and Tarragon
(page 57)

ABOVE
Deep-fried Cod in Batter

Savouries and Snacks

The savoury, when served as a separate course at a meal, is unique to Britain. Originally the word would have simply referred to a savoury rather than a sweet dish, and in the seventeenth century could have been offered before the meal as an appetizer, or at the end of the meal. In Victorian times, though, the savoury developed into a course that was only offered at the end of a meal, usually dinner, *before* the dessert. (This is when a cheeseboard, the modern equivalent of the savoury course, is correctly served.)

A savoury was considered both digestive (probably necessary after a huge Victorian meal) and as a means of cleansing the palate before the sweetness of a dessert or pudding. It is just as likely, though, that eating a little savoury mouthful or two offered a chance of finishing up the dinner wines which accompanied the main course, and this traditionally was normally up to the men. Since then the savoury has somehow become associated in our minds with men, just as sweet things are often thought to be more to the taste of women. It could simply be that women didn't have the room for a savoury – after some seven or so courses! – or that the men preferred to skip the sweet in anticipation of the port. Whatever the truth, Queen Victoria is said to have defied convention and enjoyed bone marrow on toast as a savoury each evening after dinner.

The most popular, and often the only combination contemplated, was cheese on toast. It adopted many names, and held the advantage of a base that offered so many possible variations.

It's true that cheese today is very frequently associated with savouries, but this is no surprise, for a savoury, although it should be small, needs to be strongly flavoured. Cheese usually contains a great deal of taste in itself, and was often combined with other strong flavourings. Toasted cheese – or a Welsh rabbit or rarebit (sometimes known in polite circles as *Bonne-bouche à la galloise*) – started off fairly simply. But over the years it could have added to it Worcestershire sauce, cayenne pepper, anchovy sauce, anchovies, ham, mustard, onions, horseradish or capers (when the latter is added, the rarebit is known as *Bonne-bouche à l'irlandaise*). Many mixtures for Welsh, Scottish and Irish rarebits mixed the cheese and other flavourings with ale: English rarebit soaked the bread in red wine first. I like to feel that my recipe for *Welsh Rarebit*

(page 178) has become one of our new British classics. The rarebit mix itself can simply be finished on toast, but served on top of smoked haddock sitting on a tomato and chive salad is a completely different experience (see *Smoked Haddock with Welsh Rarebit*, page 163). That dish has become probably the most popular I've ever featured on a menu. The beauty of the rarebit is how well it freezes so, once made in quantity, you can freeze the remainder for many more meals, snacks or savouries.

Other strongly flavoured favourite ingredients included anchovies, here used in what might be the most savoury of all, *Scotch Woodcock* (page 176), as well as bloaters, sardines, fish roes and smoked salmon. Chicken livers and wings, kidneys, fish roe and leftovers were 'devilled' in spicy, hot sauces which were particularly popular in the nineteenth century. Devils on Horseback, for example, another famous savoury, was given its name due to the heat of the spices rather than the 'blackness' of the central prune.

Most savouries consist of a piece of toast or fried bread spread with a topping – perhaps another reminder of the medieval bread trencher or plate. Although the popularity of the savoury course seems to have declined, many savoury recipes can be eaten as an any-time snack, as canapés (if small enough), as a light lunch if served with a salad, or as a high tea or 'supper', the latter a late-evening light meal that was most common in Georgian times (and still exists in the north).

I think we should revive the idea of savouries; if it's not a dessert you fancy then don't deprive yourself – have a savoury instead. They're easy to prepare and cook and, most importantly, they are exceedingly tasty.

Port and Stilton Cheese Toasts Ⓥ

The village of Stilton in Huntingdonshire gave its name to this most famous of English cheeses. It was not originally made there, but the recipe was acquired in the late eighteenth century by the landlord of the Bell Inn in Stilton, which was a stage on the main road from London to the North and Scotland. He sold it to the stagecoach passengers when they got out, and the cheese proved so popular that it became famous as 'Stilton' over the whole country.

ABOVE
Port and Stilton Cheese Toasts

A piece of good Stilton and a glass of rich port is a real British Classic for rounding off a meal. This recipe gives that 'classic' a totally different feel, though, serving it hot, and with both flavours working together. With every bite you have the Stilton and port experience in one. Serve as a savoury or instead of a dessert. It is also good for lunch or supper with a watercress, apple and grape salad (see Note). And for the ultimate experience with this recipe, use toasted walnut bread – the crispy nutty flavour underneath the Stilton will excite every one of your tastebuds.

This recipe will cover 6–8 slices of bread.

SERVES 6–8

1 teaspoon finely chopped shallots (optional)
50 ml (2 fl oz) port
225 g (8 oz) Stilton cheese, crumbled and at room
    temperature
15 g (½ oz) plain flour, plus extra for dusting
1 teaspoon English mustard
1 egg
Pepper
6–8 slices of bread, preferably walnut

Place the shallots (if using), in a small saucepan with the port. Bring to the simmer and reduce until almost dry. If you are not including the shallots, then simply boil and reduce the port by half. Leave the shallots to cool. The Stilton cheese should be crumbled and left out to warm to room temperature. This will make the cheese soft and workable without breaking down.

Now place all of the ingredients, bar the bread, in a food processor and blitz to a paste. The Stilton and port rarebit can now be refrigerated for at least half an hour to set.

For the finished dish, toast the walnut bread. Now the cheese paste can be spread, moulded by hand or rolled on a flour-dusted surface to a thickness of 3–4 mm (⅛ in). Top each slice and finish by toasting under a hot grill until golden.

Note: For a watercress, apple and grape salad, just pick sprigs of washed watercress and mix with halved, seeded white and black grapes. Peel, core and slice Cox's apples and add to the salad. For a quick dressing, take 2–3 tablespoons of olive oil and mix with a teaspoon or two of red-wine vinegar and a twist of pepper.

This Stilton and port mix also works well on toast and cut into squares and fingers for canapés. It can also be used to top and glaze cauliflower, broccoli, spinach, baked potatoes, chicken breasts, fish fillets and so on.

Angels on Horseback

Probably the finest of all savouries. The 'angels' are oysters, wrapped in bacon and then grilled or shallow-fried and presented on warm toast fingers. If scallops are used instead of oysters, the savoury becomes Archangels on Horseback.

There are mixed opinions about 'angels' and 'devils' (see introduction to next recipe). Some say that angels should be chicken livers instead of oysters, something I certainly do not agree with, and others that devils should be chicken livers instead of prunes. I'm sticking to what I was taught at college and most will tell you the same – oysters for angels and prunes for devils. Chicken livers can be spiced and devilled on toast, but that happens without the bacon.

Two oysters per portion of savoury are normally served, each oyster wrapped in a half-rasher of bacon. For super-plump angels, two oysters per rasher can be used.

SERVES 6

12 medium rock oysters (or 24 for super-plump angels)
6 thin rindless rashers of streaky bacon, unsmoked
Cayenne pepper
3 thick slices of white bread
Butter

For the Oyster Sauce (optional)

Oyster juice
1 heaped teaspoon finely chopped shallots
1 tablespoon double cream
25 g (1 oz) butter
Squeeze of lemon juice
Pepper

OPPOSITE
Angels on Horseback

The oyster sauce is an optional extra. It just seems such a shame, though, to waste all those tasty juices.

It's probably best to ask your fishmonger to open the oysters, making sure he saves all of the juices for you. Once opened, check over the oysters for any shell splinters. They can be quickly rinsed under cold water but, if possible, just check over.

Sit the oysters in a small saucepan with their juices. Bring to a soft simmer (this should take under 1 minute) and then remove, put on a plate and allow to cool. The juices, if making the sauce, can now be strained through a sieve. Add the finely chopped shallots and bring to the simmer. Allow to bubble and reduce by half. The double cream can now be added, returning this sauce to the simmer. Season with a twist of pepper and whisk in the butter. Add a squeeze or two of lemon juice and the sauce is ready. The acidity of lemon juice and shallots are a classic accompaniment to oysters.

Once the oysters have cooled, halve each rasher of bacon. Lightly sprinkle the oysters with cayenne pepper and wrap the bacon around. These can each be pierced with a cocktail stick to hold the bacon and then placed on a greased baking tray.

Place under a pre-heated grill and cook until golden and crispy, turning them over for an even cooking. This should take just 2–3 minutes, provided the grill is pre-heated. It's important not to cook the oysters for too long or they will become over-cooked and dry.

The bread can be just toasted, buttered and have crusts removed before cutting into large fingers or discs. Or, pan-fry in butter before cutting. Serve the angels with or on the toasts.

If you have made the sauce, simply pour around each one or offer separately.

Note: It's important to use unsmoked bacon; smoked will be too strong and salty to work with the oysters.

Devils on Horseback

No, they're not chicken livers, they're prunes. The 'devil' has nothing really to do with being the opposite of 'angel', but is a reference to the 'devil' flavour, denoting the dish has been seasoned with mustard, cayenne and/or Worcestershire sauce. It's the spice that is the devil.

The prunes are stoned and stuffed before being wrapped in the bacon. The stone can be replaced either with a roasted and skinned almond, or with a little chutney. The almond will give you a cleaner job, but I prefer to use chutney. To work with all those other flavours (mustard and cayenne) I use mango chutney, selecting the coarser pieces to stuff the prunes. However, if you're a real devil fan, a much hotter and stronger chutney can be used.

Good-quality stoned prunes can be found in abundance, and many are pre-soaked. To really plump them up, though, it's best to soak them again. For extra flavour do this in warm tea with the addition of a splash of brandy or Armagnac.

SERVES 6

12 soaked prunes, stoned
¼–½ teaspoon English mustard
25–50 g (1–2 oz) *Mango Chutney* (page 388) or
    bought chutney
6 thin rashers of streaky bacon, rind removed
6 thick slices of bread
Butter, for toast
Cayenne pepper (optional)

Once the prunes have been soaked, drain well. Mix the mustard, starting with a ¼ teaspoon, with the mango chutney. More can be added for a more 'devilish' finish.

Fill each prune with the chutney. Cut the bacon rashers in half and wrap around each prune, piercing with a cocktail stick to hold the bacon.

These are best now cooked on a buttered baking tray under a hot pre-heated grill. Grill until the bacon is golden and crispy on both sides.

While the devils are cooking, the toast can be made and buttered or pan-fried in the butter. Remove the crusts and divide into 12 triangles.

The devils can now be placed on the toast triangles and served. If using cayenne pepper, dust a little over each one.

Note: The mustard can be mixed with the butter and spread on the toasts. Prunes keep very well just soaked in neat Armagnac or Cognac.

Scotch Woodcock

This savoury was a favourite with Victorian gentlemen. It's believed the name is a sideways reference to the supposed Scottish meanness with money (!), for woodcock is one of the most expensive of game birds. Otherwise the only resemblance is that both woodcock and the savoury – traditionally consisting of scrambled eggs with anchovies (sometimes capers as well) – are served on toast.

I'm using my favourite marinated anchovies here, which are usually sold loose in delicatessen shops or counters in supermarkets. Basically I'm making anchovies on toast that are then topped with scrambled egg. There's an element of surprise as you fork through the egg and encounter the savoury fish sitting on top of the crisp toast.

SERVES 4

4 thick slices of bread (onion bread is very tasty,
    or olive)
12–16 single marinated anchovy fillets
50 g (2 oz) butter
2 tablespoons double cream (milk can also be used)
6 eggs, beaten
Salt and pepper
1 teaspoon chopped fresh chives or parsley
    (optional), to garnish

Toast the bread and remove the crusts. Sit the anchovy fillets, side by side, giving three or four a portion, on each toast.

Brush with a good knob of the butter. These can now be warmed under a pre-heated grill. Add the double cream to the eggs. Melt the remaining butter in a saucepan. Once starting to bubble, season the eggs with salt and pepper. Pour the mix into the butter and stir, preferably with a wooden spoon, until scrambled but still moist and loose.

Sit the anchovy toasts on plates and spoon the scrambled eggs on top.

The dish can be given an extra taste and colour with a sprinkling of chives or chopped parsley, if using.

Soft Herring Roes on Caper Toasts

Cod's roe with bacon used to be a popular breakfast dish in the south-west of England and in Ireland, and herring roes were eaten for breakfast and high tea. Here they are briefly fried in butter before serving on hot toast spread with a caper butter – delicious!

SERVES 4

8 soft herring roes
Plain flour, for dusting roes
50 g (2 oz) butter
½ teaspoon capers, chopped
1 teaspoon shallots, finely chopped
4 slices of toast, crusts removed
Lemon juice
Salt and pepper

Season the roes with salt and pepper and lightly flour. Melt a third of the butter and, once bubbling, add the roes. These can now be quickly pan-fried to a golden brown.

Mix the remaining butter with the capers and shallots, season with salt and pepper and spread on the hot toasts. Once cooked, arrange the roes on the toasts. Add a good squeeze of lemon to the butter the roes have been fried in (a knob more may be needed) to lift the hot butter to a bubbling finish. Now just pour over each roe toast and serve.

Peppered Mushrooms ⓥ

A favourite topping for many savouries in Victorian times, mushrooms were often devilled as well – simply spread some mustard, English or French Dijon, on top of the toast to fire up the flavour.

SERVES 4

2–3 medium cup mushrooms per portion
50 g (2 oz) butter
4 toasts, crusts removed (onion bread works well)
Salt and pepper
1 teaspoon chopped fresh chives, to garnish

Wipe and de-stalk the mushrooms. Season with salt and a good twist of black pepper, being as generous as your taste buds will allow. Melt three-quarters of the butter in a large frying-pan. Add the mushrooms and cook for 7–8 minutes until tender.

Sit the mushrooms on the toasts, pouring over any excess butter, and sprinkle with the chopped chives.

Sardine and Tomato Toasts

Sardines provide opportunities for many delicious savouries. They can be simply boned and served on toast, or grilled with grated Parmesan on top, sprinkled with chopped olives, stuffed, devilled, or deep-fried in batter. Tinned sardines can be used, but here I'm going for fresh. Ask your fishmonger to fillet them for you.

SERVES 4

8 sardines, filleted
1 small garlic clove
4 slices of onion bread (if unavailable, granary can be used)
2 plum or ripe salad tomatoes
Coarse sea salt and pepper
Olive oil

Place the 16 fillets, skin-side up, on a lightly oiled baking tray. Each portion, four fillets, can be laid top to tail and almost overlapping. Once cooked, you will be able to lift each portion with a fish slice.

Split the garlic clove lengthways and rub the fillets gently. This will just give the portions a light garlic aroma. Brush the fish with olive oil. Also brush the bread slices with olive oil and toast under a pre-heated grill on both sides. Slice the tomatoes and divide the slices, overlapping, between the toasts. Season with coarse sea-salt and a twist of pepper.

The sardines can now be lightly seasoned with salt and pepper and cooked under the grill until golden. This will only take 2–4 minutes, depending on the size of the fillets.

While the sardines are cooking, the tomato toasts can also be warmed under the grill. To serve, carefully lift the sardine portions and present them on the tomato toasts. The dish is now ready to serve.

Note: Add a squeeze of lemon juice to a teaspoon or two of olive oil. This 'dressing' can now be spooned over the savoury toasts.

Devilled Kidneys

Devilled or spiced dishes became extremely popular throughout the nineteenth century, both for breakfast and for dinner savouries. Herring roes, kidneys, chicken livers, pieces of meat and poultry were all devilled; the devil sauces were also used to add flavour to leftovers.

Devilled kidneys is one of the best-known Victorian and Edwardian breakfast dishes, often to be found sizzling gently in a silver chafing dish on a country-house breakfast sideboard.

The kidneys can be cooked in a number of ways, some shallow-fried, some grilled or even baked. Basically the idea was to zest them up with things such as cayenne, mustard, Worcestershire sauce, lemon juice and sometimes vinegar. The kidneys could also just be cooked and served with a devilled sauce. The 'devil' below is quick and easy to follow.

SERVES 4

8 lambs' kidneys
25 g (1 oz) butter, melted
1 tablespoon English mustard
1 dessertspoon white-wine vinegar
1 teaspoon Worcestershire sauce
Drop of groundnut oil, if pan-frying
Salt and cayenne pepper
4 thick slices of hot buttered toast, to serve

The outer skin of the kidneys should first be removed, cutting away any gristle.

For grilling, simply split the kidneys open, cutting three-quarters of the way through. The open shape can now be held by threading with a cocktail stick. Soak the sticks in water before using, to prevent them from catching alight. For sautéing, cut the kidneys in two, giving you four halves per portion.

To Grill

Brush the eight pieces with the melted butter and season with a pinch of salt and cayenne pepper. Sit under a pre-heated grill and cook for 3 minutes on each side.

While cooking, mix together the mustard, vinegar and Worcestershire sauce. Half of this mixture can now be brushed on the kidneys and they can be cooked for a further 1–2 minutes. Turn the kidneys and brush with the remaining mustard mix. Replace under the grill and cook for 1 minute.

The devilled kidneys can be presented on the toasts, removing the cocktail sticks before serving.

To Pan-fry

Season the kidneys with salt and cayenne pepper. Heat a frying-pan to a medium heat with the groundnut oil. Once close to smoking, place the kidneys in the pan. These will seal very quickly in the hot oil. Turn after 2 minutes and continue to fry. After approximately 3–4 minutes of cooking, add the butter. Continue to pan-fry, turning the kidneys. After 5–6 minutes the mustard, Worcestershire sauce and vinegar dressing can be added. Roll the kidneys so they are totally covered. Cook for a further minute and present them on the warm buttered toasts.

Note: If you are a kidney fan, but prefer them just grilled or pan-fried, then simply omit the mustard, Worcestershire sauce, vinegar and also the cayenne pepper. Season just with salt and pepper and then follow the cooking methods and times as for devilled.

Welsh Rarebit Ⓥ

The origin of the name 'rarebit' or 'rabbit' has been disputed for centuries. Some say the former comes from the dish's position in the meal, as a 'rear-bit' (rather as an hors d'oeuvre was known at one time as a 'fore-bit'); the latter is either a corruption of this, or reflects the patience of the Welsh huntsman's wife when he came home empty-handed from the chase, and she had to prepare cheese instead …

There are also many different recipes. Toasted cheese recipes appear in cookery books throughout the centuries, and there are English Rabbits, Welsh Rarebits, Buck Rarebits and Scotch Rabbits, all of them subtly different. This is my version, and this recipe is really the minimum amount you can make for a successful mixture. It will keep in the fridge for up to ten days and also freezes well, so can be used in plenty of other dishes, not least my favourite, *Smoked Haddock with Welsh Rarebit* (page 163). It's also delicious as a simple cheese on toast.

When I make it at home, I divide it into two and freeze the other half for use later.

COVERS 8–10 PORTIONS

SMOKED HADDOCK (PAGE 163)

350 g (12 oz) mature Cheddar cheese, grated
85 ml (3 fl oz) milk
25 g (1 oz) plain flour
25 g (1 oz) fresh white breadcrumbs
½ tablespoon English mustard powder
A few shakes of Worcestershire sauce
1 egg
1 egg yolk
Salt and pepper

Put the Cheddar into a pan and add the milk. Slowly melt them together over a low heat, but do not allow the mix to boil as this will separate the cheese. When the mixture is smooth and just begins to bubble, add the flour, breadcrumbs and mustard and cook for a few minutes, stirring, over a low heat until the mixture comes away from the sides of the pan and begins to form a ball shape. Add the Worcestershire sauce, salt and pepper and leave to cool.

When cold, place the mixture into a food processor, turn on the motor and slowly add the egg and egg yolk. (If you don't have a processor or mixer, just beat vigorously with a wooden spoon.) When the eggs are mixed in, chill for a few hours before using. After it has rested in the fridge, you will find the rarebit is very easy to handle and has so many uses.

Pork Crackling and Scratchings

Roast pork is so good to eat, but one of the best bits is the crackling – good, crunchy, salted pork flavour. Irish pubs used to serve salted pigs' trotters to increase the thirst of their customers. Nowadays, it's pork scratchings, which have much the same effect.

To get good, crispy crackling, the skin has to be scored with a sharp knife just deep enough to break through. Brush the skin lightly with cooking oil or lard, then sprinkle liberally with salt before roasting. The salt will draw any water from the skin and leave a very crisp finish.

I also like to make crackling or scratchings without any meat attached. Ask the butcher for some pork rind, preferably from the loin, and cut off any excess fat underneath. Score and salt the skin and roast in a pre-heated oven at 200°C/400°F/Gas Mark 6. The rind will take 30–40 minutes (or longer for thicker pieces) to become crunchy.

To make scratchings, instead of scoring the rind, remove the fat and cut it into 5 mm (¼ in) strips, then sprinkle with salt. Bake in the pre-heated oven, again for about 30–40 minutes.

It's nice to offer your own scratchings with pre-dinner drinks or use them in a starter for a meal.

I also like to make a pork scratching and apple salad. Simply quarter some apples and cut again into eight. Fry and toss them in butter, giving a little colour, for 2–3 minutes. Sit them around the plate with warm pork scratchings and mix some snipped fresh chives with *Basic Vinaigrette* (page 50) to spoon over. Dress the centre of the plate with mixed salad leaves tossed in dressing.

At Christmas, if you've got some roast pork and crackling left over, use up the crackling in this salad. You can also spoon some cranberry sauce into the centre of the plate, dressing the salad leaves on top.

See also

Classic Scrambled Eggs (page 79)
Coarse Pork Pâté (page 275)
Egg Sandwiches (page 372)
Poached Eggs (page 82)
Pressed Guinea Fowl Terrine with Shallots, Mushrooms and Bacon (page 260)
Roast Chicken Sandwiches (page 274)
Sausage Rolls (page 277)
Smoked Salmon Rolls (page 374)
Smoked Salmon Terrine with Warm Potato Salad (page 151)
Spicy Scrambled Eggs (page 81)
Vegetarian Cheese and Onion 'Sausage' Rolls (page 278)
Watercress and Cream Cheese Sandwiches (page 373)

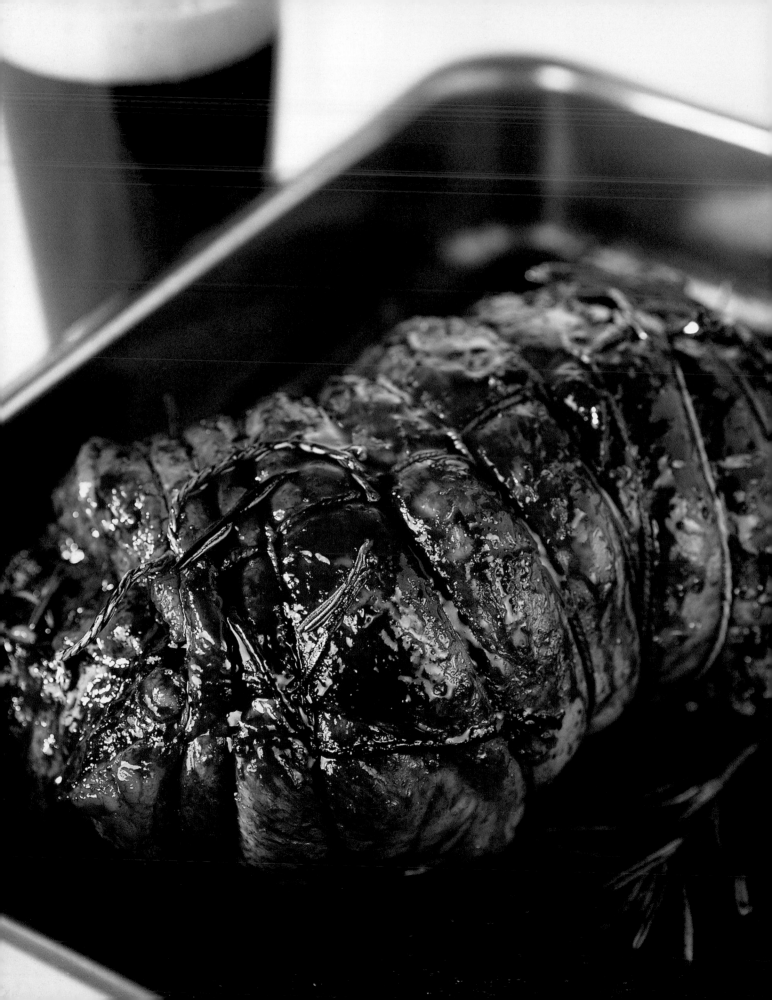

Meat

Meat is probably still the overall food favourite in Britain, with roasts, stews, casseroles, pies, steaks, chops, ribs and a lot more all being part of it. But our meat-eating habits have shocked quite a few people over the years. After a visit to England in 1748, a foreign visitor, one Per Kalm, a Swedish diplomat, recorded his surprise at the amount of meat eaten in England:

'... I do not believe that any Englishman who is his own master has ever eaten a dinner without meat.' The British association with meat-eating is so great that we actually have a corps of yeomen called Beefeaters (although the term was also applied, with little respect, to over- or well-fed servants in the seventeenth century).

With the development of salt mining, meat could be preserved with salt, and it was discovered very early that pig was the meat which required the least salt to cure it successfully, and that tasted best.

Primitive man would have eaten the meat and offal of animals which were native to the British Isles – deer, wild ox and pig, plus small animals such as hares and beavers. They would have followed the herds of meat animals, and eaten the flesh warm from the kill, roasted on a spit over a fire. The offal and innards were baked in the fire inside the gut, in much the same way as haggis and some sausages have been prepared and cooked over the centuries. The only forms of preservation would have been air-drying and basic smoking.

As man began to settle, and to cultivate crops, he could now breed the animals which he liked to eat, most of which – in Britain, the cow, goat and sheep – would also supply milk. The pig was domesticated too, although it was not an animal for milking. The fact, however, that it could find food for itself much more efficiently than the others made it extremely valuable. With the development of salt mining, meat could be preserved with salt, and it was discovered very early that pig was the meat which required the least salt to cure it successfully, and that tasted best. Our passion for this has lasted. Thin slices of cured pork, or 'collops' as they were known, usually cooked and served with eggs – our breakfast bacon and eggs – make a dish that was then and still is unique in Europe. Great traditions never die.

When the cooking pot was introduced, meat cookery changed dramatically. Now many more cuts of meat, once too tough to enjoy fresh, could be cooked in water along with other flavourings – a technique that was to lead to the great, classic Great British dishes such as boiled beef and carrots and Irish stew. During the Roman occupation, Britons learned to pen their animals, and deliberately fatten them. The Romans and later the Normans introduced many new ideas to basic British cooking, including that of sausages, smaller animal casings stuffed with meat or offal, and black puddings, made with blood (which would always have been used when an animal was killed – it was too nutritious to waste).

Until the seventeenth century, when crops began to be grown specifically for food animals, the British meat-eating year would have been dominated by the inability to feed livestock through the winter. This meant that most food animals would be killed in the autumn, with only a few kept for breeding.

PAGE 180
Roast Guinness Lamb (page 194)

Autumn, therefore, was a time of feasting, of eating offal, blood and marrow (which wouldn't keep), and perhaps some fresh meat. Most of the meat, however, would have been salted, cured or smoked as appropriate ('corned' in Ireland), to preserve it throughout the winter. For most people there would be no fresh or roast meats until after Lent and, often, the wealthier might feed a sheep or bullock throughout the winter in order to prepare a celebratory meal at Easter (lambs and calves were not usually eaten). The poor would have little to fall back on throughout the winter months but what they could catch or trap, feeding themselves on salted fish and meat, usually bacon, which they would cook in pottages with grains and pulses, and any other available flavourings.

From the Middle Ages on, fresh meat was roasted and grilled, salted and smoked. Roasting was the most popular method, especially of beef, which had been the favourite meat since at least Roman times. Preserved meat would be boiled (something we do rarely nowadays, although it is extremely traditional). Meat and offal were still boiled in the cooking pot inside animal plucks or skins (haggis, sausages, black puddings). When the pudding cloth made its appearance, animal casings could be ignored and a dough of some sort could be used – such as the suet pastry which encloses a steak and kidney pudding (although this is now cooked in a bowl).

The wealthy also baked meat in pies, enclosing it in a casing of raised pastry, known as a 'coffin'. The filling was quite often rather sweet, with dried fruit, as well as savoury and very flavourful, for the Middle Ages was the heyday of English spicing. The pastry was often not eaten, as it was considered merely a convenient wrapping for the meat and gravy in the days before the fork came into use.

Meat became more readily available, and cheaper, from the seventeenth century onwards because of improved stock and feed. Its quality improved as well, and meat became part of everyone's diet. French influences crept into the cooking of the wealthy, and meat was cooked in 'made' dishes such as fricassees and hashes. In the towns, cookshops flourished, selling pies and puddings, sheep and lamb trotters and, in the north, tripe, faggots, black puddings, brawn and haslet. With limited facilities for roasting or baking, people would take their meats to the public baker. But gradually the appetite for the 'off-falls' diminished in most parts of the country, possibly because there was so much good 'flesh' meat to enjoy, and we are only now coming back to a true appreciation of the delights and variety of offal. You'll find a few good recipes here, along with those for pies, stews, casseroles, roasts, grills...

Roasting was the most popular method, especially of beef, which had been the favourite meat since at least Roman times.

Slow-honey-roast Belly of Pork

Belly, for me, is one of the tastiest cuts of pork that we tend to forget about while we eat the prime cuts of leg and loin. The high fat content often puts people off, but I think it just adds more flavour and gives a more succulent finish. The slow roasting – over about 3 hours – helps to reduce that fat, and the juices bleed into the onions underneath the meat. The slow roasting also helps tenderize the meat – it can almost be carved with a spoon.

I like to serve a pea and potato mash with this pork dish, two traditional British vegetables together in one. The *Apple Sauce* (page 44) makes a perfect accompaniment to the pork.

SERVES 4–6

1–1.3 kg (2¼–2½ lb) piece of pork belly, boned, with rind left on
5 large onions, sliced
Cooking oil
1 teaspoon white peppercorns, crushed
Coarse sea salt
2–3 tablespoons honey
2 tablespoons water
Salt and pepper

To Serve

225–450 g (8 oz–1 lb) peas (preferably frozen)
450 g (1 lb) hot *Mashed Potatoes* (page 124)

Pre-heat the oven to 180°C/350°F/Gas Mark 4.

Score the pork belly rind with a sharp knife 1 cm (½ in) apart. Place the sliced onions in a roasting tray and sit the belly, rind-side up, on top. Trickle with a little cooking oil and lightly press on the crushed white peppercorns and a sprinkling of coarse sea salt. Place in the oven and cook for 1 hour.

After the first hour, remove from the oven and baste any fat and juices over. If the onions are dry, then add a few tablespoons of water to the pan. Continue to cook for a further 1½ hours, basting every 15–20 minutes.

The honey can now be poured over the belly and the oven temperature increased to 200°C/400°F/ Gas Mark 6. Cook for a further 30–40 minutes, basting every 5–10 minutes. As the honey becomes hotter, it will start to caramelize and leave a rich, golden glaze over the pork.

Once cooked and tender (this can be easily tested by piercing with a knife), remove the belly from the oven and leave to rest for 10–15 minutes.

While the pork is resting, heat the pan on the stove with the onions and add the 2 tablespoons of water. This will lift any residue from the pan and create a moist cooking liquor.

For the pea and potato mash, cook the peas and, while still hot, purée in a food processor. Add to the hot mashed potatoes.

Season the onions with salt and pepper and divide between four plates. The pork belly can now be cut into four portions, carved or simply broken, and served on top of the onions. Pour any remaining liquor over and serve with the pea and mashed potato purée. With this, the pork becomes a complete meal. Nothing but simplicity on a plate.

Shepherd's Pie or Cottage Pie

This dish has become as classic as our great steak and kidney pie, and began, like bubble and squeak, as a way of using up leftovers. The pieces of cooked meat – usually tough mutton – would be cut up small and pounded in the mortar to soften them before being topped with stock and mashed potato. Often, nowadays, we use cold lamb, add chopped onion, carrot and a splash of Worcestershire sauce, and then top it with mashed potato or even sliced cooked potato. Shepherd's pie is a dish I enjoy very much, reminding me of many childhood suppers.

I prefer to use raw lamb, coarsely minced, as this then spreads its flavour throughout the sauce while cooking, and doesn't totally break down as a standard mince would. I'm using some *jus* but you could replace it with *Chicken Stock* (page 33) or a bought version of either (see page 11).

For a cottage pie, use beef instead of lamb.

675 g (1½ lb) lamb, coarsely minced (shoulder will
    be a good cut for this recipe)
25 g (1 oz) lamb or beef dripping or 2 tablespoons
    cooking oil
Butter
3 onions, finely chopped
3 carrots, cut into 1 cm (½ in) dice
4 celery sticks, cut into 1 cm (½ in) dice
½ teaspoon ground cinnamon
½ teaspoon chopped fresh thyme
½ teaspoon chopped fresh rosemary
1 dessertspoon tomato purée
1 dessertspoon *Tomato Ketchup* (page 49)
2–3 glasses of red wine
25 g (1 oz) plain flour
200 ml (7 fl oz) *Veal or Beef Jus* or *Chicken Stock*
    (page 34 or 33)
Salt and pepper
2 teaspoons Worcestershire sauce
900 g (2 lb) *Mashed Potatoes* (page 124), made
    with very little butter and cream or milk

Season the minced lamb with salt and pepper. This should now be fried in the dripping or oil in a very hot pan to seal the meat and colour it, rather than stew and boil. For the best results (and it's probably quicker), fry in batches. As one lot is fried and coloured, pour off from the pan and drain in a colander.

In a separate saucepan, melt a knob of butter. Add the vegetables and season with salt, pepper and cinnamon. Then add the chopped herbs.

Allow to cook for 5–6 minutes until beginning to soften. Add the fried lamb and cook on a medium heat for a few minutes. Add the tomato purée, ketchup and Worcestershire sauce, and stir into the mix. Now it's time to add the red wine. For a really rich finish, it is best to use all three glasses, but adding only half a glass at a time, reducing by three-quarters and repeating the same process until all has been added. This method prevents the sautéed flavour of the lamb becoming boiled away in too much wine. Sprinkle the flour into the pan and cook for 2–3 minutes.

Pour in the *jus* or stock and bring to a soft simmer. This will now take, for a good rich shepherd's pie, 1–1½ hours to cook. During the cooking time, the sauce may become too thick; if so, add a little water to loosen. However, it is important to remember that mashed potatoes will be spread on top, so don't allow the sauce to become too thin.

During the last 30 minutes of the cooking time, the mashed potato can be made. Reduce the quantities of butter and cream or milk given in the recipe, to give a slightly firmer topping.

Once the shepherd's pie mince is ready, spoon into a suitable ovenproof serving dish. The mashed potatoes can now be spooned or piped on top, brushed with a little butter and finished in a very hot oven or under the grill to become golden. Another method is to allow the mince to become cold in the dish before covering with the potato. This can now be refrigerated until needed and then re-heated in a hot oven (200°C/400°F/Gas Mark 6) for 35–40 minutes.

Another popular finish is a sprinkling of grated cheese, melted and glazed on top.

Shepherd's Pie Fritters

Here's a second shepherd's pie recipe (the classic one begins on page 184), which is a combination of two ideas but quite different from both pie and conventional fritter. The main reason is the texture: the classic shepherd's pie mixture is often too loose to hold up to being rolled and deep-fried. This recipe is also slightly spicy, which suits canapé-style fritters.

If shaping into balls, the fritters will need to be egged and breadcrumbed twice to give a nice and neat finish. All they need then is to be deep-fried for a crispy golden result. A great accompaniment to go with them is *Spicy Tomato and Mint Relish* (page 381), giving you a perfect snack.

This dish is very easy and worth every minute of its cooking time.

Butter
2 onions, cut into very small dice
2 carrots, cut into very small dice
2 celery sticks, cut into very small dice
450 g (1 lb) minced lamb
Pinch of fresh or dried marjoram
Pinch of ground cumin (optional)
300 ml (½ pint) *Chicken Stock* or 150 ml (¼ pint)
    Veal Jus or *Beef Jus* (page 33 or 34)
Worcestershire sauce
275–350 g (10–12 oz) *Mashed Potatoes* (page 124),
    without milk, cream or butter
Plain flour, for rolling
1–2 eggs, beaten
8–10 slices of a fresh medium white loaf, crusts cut
    off and crumbed, or approx. 225 g (8 oz)
    ready-dried crumbs
Salt and pepper
Oil, for deep-frying

Melt a knob of butter in a saucepan. Once bubbling, add the chopped onion, carrot and celery. Increase the heat and fry quickly, allowing a golden colour to develop. Cook for a few minutes until beginning to soften.

Now the minced lamb can be added to the vegetables, along with the marjoram and cumin (if using). Cook for 5–10 minutes until the lamb is sealed. Season with salt and pepper and add half of the stock or *jus*. Cook on a low heat, allowing a slow simmer. The mince will take 30–40 minutes to become tender. As the mince is cooking it may need a slight topping up of the remaining stock or *jus* to keep the moistness.

Once cooked, increase the heat to reduce any excess liquor in the pan. It's important the mince mix is not too loose: this would make it too wet to bind or hold the mashed potatoes.

Once reduced, check for seasoning and add a dash of Worcestershire sauce to finish the spicy taste. Leave to cool.

Once cold, add the mashed potato. Adjust the seasoning with salt and pepper. The mix can now be refrigerated once more to help firm the texture – this will make it easier to work with. Dust your hands with flour and roll the mixture into balls ready to be crumbed.

Lightly re-dust with some seasoned plain flour and then pass through the beaten egg and crumbs. Once all are coated, pass through the eggs and crumbs again for a firmer finish. The shapes can now be tidied up into neat, round balls. It's best to refrigerate again, to set the shapes firmly, before frying.

To cook the fritters, heat the cooking oil to 170–180°C/325–350°F and deep-fry until golden brown. Drain well before serving.

Note: The number of fritters made will really depend on the size and shape that you have made them; if you go for just 2.5 cm (1 in) diameter balls, you'll probably be able to shape up to 30 pieces.

The fritters can be made into 'classic' fish cake shapes, giving you eight pieces, i.e. four large portions.

Boiled Leg of Lamb with Caper Sauce

Probably one of the most classic of lamb dishes, although traditionally it would have been made with mutton, the meat of a sheep that is older than a year. Mutton has a stronger flavour than lamb, is deeper red in colour, and contains less fat but, sadly, it is now difficult to find. Lamb substitutes well, though.

Capers have been a favoured accompaniment to boiled mutton since medieval times, presumably when capers were imported (they are the flower buds of a Mediterranean plant). The two strong flavours of the meat itself and the acidity associated with capers work together very well. Nasturtium seeds can be picked and used in the sauce instead of capers.

I've included potatoes and vegetables with the lamb, giving you a complete meal from one pot.

1.5 kg (3¼ lb) leg of lamb
2 litres (3½ pints) *Chicken Stock* (page 33) or water
Sprig of thyme

675 g (1½ lb) new potatoes, washed
450 g (1 lb) baby carrots, peeled
450 g (1 lb) button onions, peeled
12 baby turnips, peeled
4–6 celery sticks, cut into 5 cm (2 in) lengths
Salt and pepper

For the Sauce

25 g (1 oz) butter
25 g (1 oz) plain flour
85 ml (3 fl oz) double cream
Squeeze of lemon juice
1 tablespoon capers, chopped
Salt and pepper

Sit the leg of lamb in a large saucepan and add the chicken stock or water. Season with a pinch of salt. Bring to the boil, skimming off any impurities. Add the sprig of thyme and allow to simmer fairly rapidly, skimming from time to time, for 2 hours. During this time the lamb flavour will take over the chicken stock, almost giving you a lamb soup.

Now is the time to add the potatoes and other vegetables. Return to the simmer and cook for a further 20 minutes. The vegetables will all now be cooked and have taken on the rich taste. Turn off the heat. Now it's time to make the sauce.

Melt the butter, adding the flour. Cook on a medium heat for 3–4 minutes. While the roux is cooking, drain off 600 ml (1 pint) of the stock from the lamb. Gradually add the stock to the roux, stirring well after each addition. Once all of the liquor has been added, simmer gently for 20 minutes.

Add the double cream to the sauce and season with salt and pepper. Squeeze a drop or two of lemon juice into the sauce to lift the lamb flavour. If the sauce is smooth, simply add the chopped capers, and it's now ready.

During this sauce cooking time the lamb will have rested and relaxed, giving you a very tender finish. The vegetables will also by now be slightly overcooked, something which, in a stew, always works so well. They will have softened and absorbed even more flavour.

Now divide the vegetables between the plates. Remove the boiled lamb and carve. Its texture will be soft and it will almost tear rather than slice. Finish each portion with a spoonful or two of the caper sauce.

Note: It's not necessary to use only baby vegetables: the same weight of carrots and turnips can be cut from larger pieces. More capers can be added for a sharper flavour.

Grilled Lamb with 'Irish' Cabbage and Mashed Potato Sauce

The 'Irish' cabbage is basically taking the flavours from my version of a traditional Irish stew – onions, cabbage, carrots – and frying them all as a base for the lamb. That's one of the beauties of cooking, for me, being able to take one recipe and, using the same flavours, present it in a totally new form, introducing different cooking methods that will then give different flavours. I'm also adding a parsley purée to this recipe, which gives an extra touch (although it's not essential) and parsley, of course, is another classic with Irish stew.

The lamb tastes at its best in this recipe when cooked on a grill plate. It can, however, be pan-fried and roasted.

SERVES 4

450 g (1 lb) *Mashed Potato Sauce* (page 125)
½ bottle red wine
250 ml (8 fl oz) *Veal or Beef Jus* (page 34)
Salt and pepper
2 boned best-end loins of lamb, with fat removed,
    bones reserved
1 tablespoon cooking oil

For the 'Irish' Cabbage

1 small Savoy cabbage, finely shredded
1 large carrot, peeled and thinly sliced
Butter
2 onions, sliced
4 rashers of unsmoked streaky bacon, cut into thin
    strips
Salt and pepper

For the Parsley Purée (optional)

Small bunch flatleaf parsley, picked and washed
Small bunch curly parsley, picked and washed
50 g (2 oz) *Buttered Spinach* (page 113), omitting
    the butter
1 tablespoon groundnut oil
2 tablespoons water
Salt, pepper and freshly grated nutmeg

Pre-heat the oven to 200°C/400°F/Gas Mark 6.

For the parsley purée, blanch both the parsley leaves in boiling, salted water for a few minutes until tender. Drain both and mix with the spinach. These can now be blitzed to a purée, adding the oil, water and seasonings. Push through a fine sieve to give a smooth parsley purée. If the purée is too thick, then simply loosen with a touch more water.

Make the mashed potato sauce. The consistency, for this dish, needs to be 'saucy', so if it's still too thick, add a little single cream or milk.

The red wine needs to be boiled to reduce by three-quarters. Add the *jus* and simmer for a few minutes. Season with salt and pepper.

To cook the lamb, season with salt and pepper and brush with oil. The loins can now be grilled on a hot grill pan, turning from time to time to seal all the meat. It is best to allow the meat to colour richly, with almost burnt edges. This goes very well with

the natural sweetness of the lamb itself. The lamb will take 8–10 minutes to grill to medium stage. If pan-frying to seal and then roasting, the lamb will need 8–10 minutes' roasting for a medium finish.

Once cooked, leave the lamb to rest for 6–8 minutes before carving.

For the 'Irish' cabbage, blanch the finely shredded cabbage in salted, boiling water for 30 seconds–1 minute, until just tender. Drain. The carrots can be left raw, if very thinly sliced, or they can be blanched for a minute to take the raw edge off them.

Heat a wok or frying-pan and add the butter. Once bubbling, add the onions and carrots. Allow to fry to a light golden colour and just-soft texture. In a separate pan, fry the bacon without butter. The bacon will create its own fat and quickly become quite crisp. Add the bacon to the onions and carrots. It is now time to add the cabbage. Fry, allowing the cabbage to take on some golden-edged tinges, and season with salt and pepper.

Each loin gives two portions. Just before carving, the loins can be brushed with the red-wine sauce to give a good finished shine. Carve the lamb, allowing 4–5 slices per portion.

Spoon the 'Irish' cabbage into the centre of the plates. The mashed potato sauce can now be spooned around the outside, creating a border. Trickle some parsley purée around, along with the red-wine sauce, offering any extra separately.

Sit the lamb slices on top of the cabbage. The new Irish classic is now ready to serve.

Note: This dish has many components but it is a complete meal in itself.

The lamb can just be served with the 'Irish' cabbage, leaving out the potato sauce and parsley purée.

OPPOSITE
*Grilled Lamb with 'Irish' Cabbage and
Mashed Potato Sauce*

Corned Beef

Corned beef is one of the prepared meats we all buy, sit in a sandwich with a spoonful of pickle or sliced tomatoes (well, I do anyway), and not even think about how it's made. It's almost as if it's just a natural product that appears and is sliced.

Corned beef is basically salted beef, and the 'corning' usually refers to the large 'corns' of salt that were once used. It is particularly associated with Cork in Ireland, which supplied corned beef to England and her colonies for some 200 years up until the mid nineteenth century.

If you haven't made it before, you'll be nicely surprised to know how easy it is to make. Simple, yes, but it does take time. The beef is soaked in brine and, after three days, the texture and colour change, along with the flavour. The meat is then cooked, and it can be cut into slices straight away, but I have made the end result more like the textured meat you buy in cans. It's inexpensive, very tasty and definitely worth a try. The pig's trotters are not essential. I've added them because they help the dish to set firmly.

This is quite a big recipe that will fill a large (25–30 cm/10–12 in) terrine, enough to feed 12–15 people or more.

SERVES AT LEAST 12

2.25 kg (5 lb) beef flank
1.75 litres (3 pints) cold water
75–100 g (3–4 oz) salt
2 pig's trotters (optional)
25 g (1 oz) gelatine leaves or powder

Trim the beef flank of all visible sinews but leave it as a whole piece. Mix the water and 75 g (3 oz) of salt to create a brine. To test the strength of the brine, sit a raw new potato in the water; the potato should float. If it won't float, simply add the remaining salt or more if needed. Sit the beef in the brine and chill for 3 days.

Remove the meat from the brine and wash it, discarding the salt water. Sit the meat in a clean pan with the pig's trotters, if using. Top up with fresh water. Bring to the boil, then simmer for 2½–3 hours, skimming any impurities from the liquid.

Once cooked, remove the meat from the liquid. Drain the cooking liquid through a fine sieve and taste; it should have a good beef flavour. Discard the trotters, if using. Bring the stock to the boil and boil to reduce in volume by a third to half, and increase its flavour and jelly content. Test the stock/jelly by spooning a little onto a small plate and placing in the refrigerator. The jelly must set very firmly to enable it to hold the beef together. If it doesn't set firmly enough, or if you have not used pig's trotters, add some or all of the gelatine to the mix. Make sure you do test the setting as the dish is better if not set using gelatine. Only about 600–900 ml (1–1½ pints) of finished jelly stock will be needed.

While the beef is still warm, break it down into pieces. The meat will almost separate itself between sinew strips. Any excess sinew can be removed, but make sure that all fat content is kept. The meat can now be pushed through the large plate of a mincer (5 mm–1 cm/¼–½ in) or chopped by hand, with the fat. Mix the meat with 600 ml (1 pint) of reduced liquid and check the consistency. The meat should absorb the liquid and be left reasonably loose. If the mix is too firm, add another 300 ml (½ pint) of stock. Taste the corned beef and correct the seasoning with salt and pepper. The mix can now be pressed firmly into a terrine or bowl and set in the refrigerator overnight.

Once set, turn out the corned beef and serve with a salad and pickle, or fried for breakfast, or turn it into a corned-beef hash.

Refrigerated, this dish will keep for 5–6 days.

Rack on Black

It sounds very British and classic. Yes, it is British (if not very traditional), but classic? Well, not yet. I hope this recipe will help it to achieve that status.

This idea was shown and given to me by a butcher in Yorkshire. He was selling it as a cut to be bought and then, obviously, taken home and enjoyed. As soon as I saw the beautifully rich lamb posing intimately with a deep black pudding, I was

excited. The textures and flavours working together were racing through my mind – on a bed of parsnips, bubble and squeak, spring onions, creamy potatoes, they'd all work (although not all together, of course). Here's the recipe for the lamb and its sauce; the accompaniment is up to you.

SERVES 4

2 × 6–8 bone racks of lamb
1 × 12–16 cm (6–8 in) black pudding (2.5–3 cm/ 1–1½ in diameter), weighing 250–300 g (9–10 oz), skinned and split lengthways
2 tablespoons cooking oil
½ bottle red wine
200–250 ml (7–8 fl oz) *Veal or Beef Jus* (page 34)
Salt and pepper

The rolling and tying (see below) is best finished several hours (preferably 24) in advance, giving the joint plenty of time to 'set'.

The racks should be boned but have the flap of skin/fat still attached. The skin/fat should be trimmed to 2–3 mm (⅛ in) thickness, leaving 10 cm (4 in) to wrap around. If the fat is left too thick, it will not cook completely, consequently becoming tough. It's also best to trim away any sinews found around the lamb fillets.

Now just sit the flat side of the black pudding halves next to the lamb. Season the lamb with a twist of pepper. At this stage do not salt, or the juices will be drawn from the meat.

Fold the skin over the pudding and lamb, firmly shaping into a cylinder.

Now it's time to tie the joint with string. It's best to tie at both ends first. This then prevents the whole joint from becoming misshapen during the tying process. Once both ends are secure, tie at 1–2 cm (½–¾ in) intervals. Now wrap tightly in cling film to create an even smoother finish and refrigerate until needed.

OPPOSITE
Rack on Black

When ready to cook, pre-heat the oven to 200°C/400°F/Gas Mark 6. Season the joints with salt and pepper. Heat a roasting pan on a medium heat with the cooking oil. Place the joints in the pan and allow to colour slowly. As the fat colours it is also cooking: you'll notice more fat in the roasting pan. Continue to cook until completely coloured. The racks can now be roasted in the pre-heated oven. Pink joints will take only 8–10 minutes; for medium meat, cook for 15–18 and for well done, 20–25. Remove from the oven once roasted to your liking. As with all roasts, it is important to let the meat rest and relax.

While the lamb is resting, pour away any excess fat from the roasting pan. Heat the tray and add the red wine. This will now lift any lamb flavours (and black pudding spices). Boil and reduce by three-quarters and add the *jus*. Bring to the simmer before straining through a sieve into a clean saucepan. Skim off any impurities that have risen. Season with salt and pepper and the sauce is ready.

Remove the string from the joints. The loins can now be cut into sixes, allowing three thick slices per portion. These slices guarantee a good texture in both meats. Now just serve on plates with your chosen vegetable accompaniments and pour the sauce around.

Note: This dish eats very well with *Roast Potatoes* (page 238), *Mashed Potatoes* (page 124), *Colcannon* (page 126), *Bubble and Squeak* (page 126), *Buttered Spinach* (page 113) and plenty more featured in the book.

The *jus* can be replaced with *Chicken Stock* (page 33). This is then reduced by half with the red wine and 25–50 g (1–2 oz) of butter added, to thicken the consistency.

Preserved (Confit) Bacon

Bacon is preserved pork, and here I'm further preserving bacon, taking the idea from the French – although our potted meat is not too dissimilar. *Confit* is the French word for 'preserved', and the most usual *confit* is of duck – duck cooked and then set in its own fat. This technique allows it to be kept almost indefinitely, and that's got to be a good cooking method for working ahead of time.

But it's not the preserving I'm really after here. As the bacon cooks slowly in its own fat, the meat and fat become very tender, breaking down any sinews. I'm sure the thought of cooking any meat slowly in deep fat gives the impression that the meat will absorb the fat and just taste of it. That really couldn't be further from the truth. The meat becomes so succulent, soft and tasty, you just can't stop eating it. This confit of bacon can be used in many dishes. I include it in *Sage Broad Beans with Tomato* (page 56).

To finish the recipe, I either glaze the bacon with honey, or coat with a mixture of demerara sugar and black pepper. The perfect accompaniments to this rich dish are *Mashed Potatoes* (page 124) and preferably a buttered green vegetable – cabbage would be a real winner. Any leftover bacon pieces can be used to garnish soups, macaroni cheese or added to stews.

SERVES 4–6

1 kg (2¼ lb) streaky bacon in the piece, smoked or unsmoked, rind removed, trimmed
900 ml (1½ pints) cooking oil or pork fat
2–4 tablespoons clear honey or 50–100 g (2–4 oz) demerara sugar and freshly ground black pepper, for glazing

The joint of bacon must be soaked for 24 hours in cold water to remove excess salt flavour.

Pre-heat the oven to 180°C/350°F/Gas Mark 4. In a small roasting pan, deep enough to let the joint be immersed, put a drop of the cooking oil/fat and heat on top of the stove. This next stage of colouring the joint is not essential if using as part of a stew or, perhaps, for the broad beans (go straight to the simmering stage). If being served as a starter or main course, the flavour and finish works well. Fry the bacon, fat-side down, to a golden brown. Turn the bacon in the pan and pour on the remaining oil/fat just to cover. Bring to a soft simmer. Cover and cook in the oven for about 1–1½ hours.

After an hour, check the tenderness of the meat by piercing with a knife. The meat should feel totally tender; if it's slightly firm, continue to cook for the remaining half-hour.

Once cooked, if you're using it immediately, remove the bacon; the excess fat will drain off. If not using, transfer everything to a bowl and leave to set in the fat. The meat must be totally covered in fat. This *confit* can now be refrigerated until needed.

Whenever needed, lift from the fat and heat in a roasting pan, without the preserving fat. Place in a pre-heated oven (same temperature as when cooked), fat-side down, and heat for 20–25 minutes. The preserved bacon will now be able to return to its former glory.

To glaze the bacon with honey, once reheated, lightly dab dry the bacon, to hold the honey. On the top (fat-side down), spoon over 2–3 tablespoons of clear honey. This can now be placed under a hot grill and allowed to caramelize, to a bubbly, sticky finish.

For the peppered brown sugar glaze, mix 1 teaspoon of freshly ground black pepper with every heaped tablespoon of demerara sugar. Sprinkle well on top and sit the bacon on the grill pan. Grill the bacon so as to slowly caramelize the sugar and, at the same time, cook the black pepper. Once caramelized and rich deep golden, the bacon is ready to carve.

Baked Pork, Prune and Apple Meatballs

Finely chopped meat (raw or cooked leftovers) is used a good deal in traditional British cooking – in shepherd's pie, bubble and squeak, rissoles, and as forcemeat – but these meatballs are meatballs with a difference. The flavour of apples, always a natural with pork, works so well along with the prunes, a reminder of the many medieval British savoury dishes containing the sweetness of dried fruits. The cooking liquor takes on all of these tastes and, when reduced, leaves a good, rich, sticky finish to the meatballs.

These eat well with soft, creamy *Mashed Potatoes* (page 124) and simple buttered cabbage, peas or, perhaps, runner beans (pages 104, 116 and 118).

SERVES 4

Butter
1 large onion, finely chopped
Pinch of freshly grated nutmeg and ground
    cinnamon
6 'ready-to-eat' prunes, chopped
1 teaspoon chopped fresh sage
2 apples, peeled, cored and cut into 1 cm (½ in)
    dice
100 g (4 oz) shredded suet
1 egg, beaten
450 g (1 lb) minced pork meat

BELOW
Baked Pork, Prune and Apple Meatballs

150 ml (¼ pint) white wine or cider
300 ml (½ pint) *Chicken Stock* (page 33)
Arrowroot or cornflour, if necessary
Salt and pepper

Pre-heat the oven to 180°C/350°F/Gas Mark 4.

Melt a knob of butter in a frying-pan. Add the chopped onion and fry for a few minutes, without colour. Season with the nutmeg and cinnamon and add the prunes. Cook for 1 more minute and remove from the heat. Add the chopped sage and leave to cool. Once cooled add the diced apples, suet, egg and minced pork. Mix well, seasoning with salt and pepper.

The mixture must be well mixed to distribute all the flavours, particularly the suet. Divide into twelve meatballs. A light dusting of flour on your hands will make this job easier. These can now be shallow-fried in another knob of butter to seal and achieve a golden brown, turning gently. The meatballs can be placed in a roasting tray and put to one side.

Pour the white wine or cider into a saucepan and boil until reduced by three-quarters. Add the chicken stock. Pour the stock mixture over the meatballs and cook in the oven for 45 minutes until tender.

Lift the 'balls' from the tray and keep warm. Strain off the liquor. Once settled in a small saucepan, any fat will rise to the top. This can now be skimmed off. The liquor can now be left at its natural consistency or thickened with 1 tablespoon of arrowroot or cornflour whisked in and brought to the boil. Another method is to reduce by a third and then whisk in 25–50 g (1–2 oz) of chilled and diced butter. This will give the sauce a silky finish. Now just serve and pour the sauce over.

Note: A splash of Armagnac or Calvados can be added to the finished sauce for extra flavour.

Roast Guinness Lamb

Beer has been used as a meat-cooking liquor all over Europe for centuries, particularly in the Low Countries of Holland and Belgium. Hops were introduced from there in the early sixteenth century, and were cultivated in Kent by Flemish *émigrés*, thus initiating our Great British beer industry (as opposed to ale, which was unhopped). It may be that the concept of cooking beef in beer stemmed from that time. The idea was later adopted enthusiastically in Ireland, probably because of the unique stout, Guinness, which has been brewed in Dublin since 1759. The rich reduction of this dark malty stout gives you a good tasty base for a very powerful gravy. Finishing the lamb with a caramelizing of sugar helps counteract the bitterness of the beer.

Really good crispy *Roast Potatoes* (page 238) go well with this dish, along with most vegetables. My favourite is a bowl of *Buttered Spinach* (page 113).

SERVES 6–8

1.5 kg (3¼ lb) leg of lamb, boned, rolled and tied
1 tablespoon cooking fat or oil
Sprig of rosemary
300 ml (½ pint) Guinness or other stout
50 g (2 oz) light soft brown sugar
200–300 ml (7–10 fl oz) *Veal or Beef Jus* (page 34)
Salt and pepper

Pre-heat the oven to 200°C/400°F/Gas Mark 6. Season the lamb with salt and pepper. Place in a roasting tin with the cooking fat/oil and colour over a medium heat until totally sealed and a rich golden brown colour.

Add the sprig of rosemary and the Guinness. Place the lamb in the oven. Baste the lamb every 15–20 minutes and roast for 1 hour.

After the hour, remove the lamb from the oven and gently sprinkle with the sugar. Return to the oven, basting every 3–4 minutes for the next 15 minutes. This cooking time of 1¼ hours will leave the lamb at a medium stage. For well done, cook for a further 20 minutes. Once roasted, remove the lamb from the oven and baste once more. The roast can now be kept separate from the roasting tray.

Gently pour away any fat sitting on top of the reduced Guinness and lamb juices. Add the *jus* and bring to the simmer, skimming off any impurities. The sauce will have a very rich, slightly sweetened, caramel stout flavour. The roast lamb, which should always be left to rest and relax, leaving it a lot more tender, for at least 15–20 minutes, will have a deep, glossy colour – almost the colour of a good rich stout.

Once the roast potatoes and vegetables are ready, the meat can be carved, to reveal a pink centre surrounded by a deep glaze.

Stewed Red-wine Beef with Anchovy Scones

When cooking pots were invented, slow-cooking of vegetables, grains and less tender cuts of meat became possible, and the earliest meat soups were the forerunners of our various famous stews. This dish is a variation of two classics: the beef stew itself, which was often cooked with a few fillets of anchovies in place of salt as a seasoning, and beef cobbler. The term 'cobbler' originally described a type of pie with a thick dough lining for a filling. Over the years, the dough lining has become scones, which are baked on top of the meat, and the dish is a great alternative to that other British classic, beef stew and dumplings.

The best beef cut to use for stewing or braising is chuck steak. This has an open texture that will absorb all of the juices it has been cooked in. A close-textured cut, such as topside, will become tender, but will not absorb any liquor, therefore will have a dry bite. I'm using some *jus* in this recipe for the absolute maximum taste, but there is an alternative (see page 196).

SERVES 4

675 g (1½ lb) chuck steak, cut into 2 cm (¾ in) dice
15 g (½ oz) beef dripping or 1 tablespoon cooking oil

4 carrots, peeled and quartered lengthways
3 onions, cut into 1–2 cm (½–¾ in) dice
1 bay leaf
Bottle of red wine (½ bottle can be used, but a
    whole bottle will give a fuller flavour)
600 ml (1 pint) *Veal or Beef Jus* (page 34)
Salt and pepper

For the Scones

50 g (2 oz) butter
225 g (8 oz) self-raising flour
8–10 tinned anchovy fillets, diced
½ teaspoon chopped fresh thyme
1 egg, beaten
2–3 tablespoons milk
Pepper

Pre-heat the oven to 160°C/325°F/Gas Mark 3. Season the beef with salt and pepper. Heat the dripping or oil in a braising pan or flameproof casserole. Fry the beef, colouring and sealing on all sides.

While the beef is frying, cut the carrot quarters into 1–2 cm (½–¾ in) slices. Add the vegetables to the pan along with the bay leaf. Cook for 2–3 minutes before pouring the red wine over. This can now be cooked until reduced by half. This increases the wine flavour. Add the *jus* and bring to the simmer. It's important the meat is just covered by the liquor: add some water if needed. Once up to the simmer, skim off any impurities before covering with a lid and placing in the pre-heated oven for 1½ hours. This cooking temperature is perfect for braising. It provides a gentle heat that will not boil the meat, but instead creates a soft movement, allowing the beef to absorb all the flavours.

Check the stew after 1½ hours, skimming any impurities. If too thick, then add more water. The beef may well need another 30 minutes before you add the scones to cook on top. Return to the oven.

To make the scones, rub the butter into the flour to a breadcrumb texture. Season with black pepper. Add the diced anchovy (which will replace salt), along with the chopped thyme. Stir in the egg to create a scone dough. Milk can be added to give a dough consistency. The mix can now be divided into four and moulded into scone shapes.

Once the beef is ready, increase the oven temperature to 180°C/350°F/Gas Mark 4. Remove the lid from the beef and lay the scones on top. Return the pot to the oven. The scones will take 25–30 minutes. As the stew simmers and gently bubbles, the scones will bake, absorbing the flavour of the red-wine gravy, while becoming golden and crispy on top.

Simply serve on a plate or in a bowl, with the scones sitting on top.

Note: Other flavours can also be added to the stew – mushrooms, celery or strips of bacon all work very well.

The scones can also be flavoured with mixed herbs, bacon pieces or perhaps Parmesan or Cheddar cheese.

Alternative

This method uses water and a stock cube in place of *jus*. The ingredients list is almost identical, with 600 ml (1 pint) of water and a beef stock cube replacing the *jus* plus the addition of 1 heaped tablespoon of plain flour. The red wine should be boiled and reduced by half in a separate pan. Once all the beef has been coloured in the beef fat/oil, add the vegetables and continue to cook for 2–3 minutes. Add the flour and stir in. Cook for a few minutes before adding the water a little at a time. As it comes to the simmer, the mixture will thicken. Once all is added, sprinkle in the stock cube and pour in the red wine. Now just return to the simmer, skim, cover and cook in the oven. Continue as per the recipe. You'll still have a lovely rich finish to the dish. This technique can be used in many similar stews.

Braised Beef Olives with Black Pudding, Button Onions and Mushrooms

Beef olives have been appearing on menus since medieval times, when they were known as 'allowes' or 'aloes'. (The name 'olive' is probably a corruption of this, and virtually the first veal olive recipe appeared in a Gervase Markham book of 1660.) They were and are slices of beefsteak wrapped around a seasoned forcemeat (mutton and veal can be used as well). Whole pieces of beef can also be braised as for olives by simply filling with a stuffing. Anchovies were a regular seasoning in most forcemeats, having a strong influence on the finished flavour, but with this recipe the stuffing creates enough of a taste of its own.

The black pudding is roughly chopped and added to minced pork or chicken; helped along with red wine, these flavours work very well together. The garnish of button onions and mushrooms also lifts all of the tastes, and almost makes this a beef olive *bourguignon* dish.

SERVES 4

4 × 175 g (6 oz) slices of topside or rump of beef (smaller 100 g/4 oz slices can also be used)
½ bottle of red wine (a whole bottle can be used for a stronger taste)
600 ml (1 pint) *Veal or Beef Jus* (page 34) or water with stock granules
1 tablespoon plain flour
1 tablespoon beef dripping or cooking oil
Sprig of thyme
1 bay leaf
Salt and pepper

For the Stuffing

Butter
1 onion, finely chopped
1 garlic clove, crushed
175 g (6 oz) finely minced pork or chicken
1 egg, beaten
Salt and pepper
175 g (6 oz) black pudding, peeled and roughly chopped

For the Garnish

20 button onions, peeled
Butter
20 button mushrooms, cleaned
1 teaspoon chopped fresh parsley (optional)

Place the beef slices between two sheets of cling film; these can now be batted out with a rolling pin to a 5 mm (¼ in) thickness.

To make the stuffing, melt a knob of butter in a saucepan and, once bubbling, add the chopped onion and crushed garlic. Cook without colour for a few minutes. Once tender, remove from the heat and allow to cool.

Season the minced pork or chicken with salt and pepper. Beat in the egg. The cooked onion mix can now also be added. Add the black pudding, mixing it in well to break down the texture slightly, spreading the flavour through the forcemeat. Check for seasoning.

The stuffing can now be spread between the four steak slices. Roll up and hold together with two cocktail sticks per olive, or simply tie with string. These are best left to firm and set for at least 30 minutes, refrigerated.

While the olives are setting, the button onions can be blanched in boiling water for 2–3 minutes to release their rawness. Drain and leave to cool naturally.

Bring the red wine to the boil in a suitable sauce or braising pan. Boil and reduce by half before adding the *jus* or water and stock granules, if using. This dish can be left to simmer on top of the stove on a low heat, allowing the liquor to barely simmer, or braised in the oven at 160°C/325°F/Gas Mark 3.

Heat a frying-pan with the beef dripping or cooking oil. Sear the beef olives until golden brown. Place in a braising dish with the red wine sauce, thyme and bay leaf. If using water to make the sauce, then roll each olive in through the flour before pan-frying. Season the stuffed olives and sear, colouring on all sides in the hot pan. Once coloured, place in the red-wine gravy pot with the thyme and bay leaf. Now bring to a very gentle simmer, making sure the olives are just covered in red-wine sauce. If not, then top up with water. Cover with a lid and cook on the hob or in the oven for 1½–2 hours, skimming from time to time. The beef olives will be very tender.

Towards the end of the cooking time for the olives, melt a knob of butter in a large frying-pan.

Once bubbling, add the button onions. Cook on a medium heat and fry, allowing them to colour to golden brown and become tender. This will take 8–10 minutes. After 6–7 minutes, add the mushrooms, season and continue to cook and colour until both garnishes are ready. Keep to one side.

Remove the olives from the sauce and keep warm. Bring the sauce to the simmer and skim off any impurities. Strain through a sieve.

If the flour and water were used, the sauce will probably need to be reduced by a third to give a good consistency. The most important thing is to make sure the flavour does not become over-strong. Once at the right stage, if too thin, then thicken with a tablespoon of cornflour mixed with red wine. It's not important always to have thick, heavy sauces; just a good tasty cooking liquor will be fine.

Remove the cocktail sticks or string from the olives and divide between four plates. Pour the sauce back over, adding the button onions and mushrooms. Sprinkle each plate with chopped parsley, if using.

These beef olives will eat very well with a bowl of *Mashed Potatoes* (page 124).

Note: Pan-fried strips of bacon will also work very well with the garnish.

Pieces of Braised Beef with Slowly Caramelized Onions and Turnip Purée

Braised beef and onions served with a turnip purée certainly isn't an unusual combination in terms of British tastes. The difference in this dish, however, is that the onions are caramelized. They are halved (skin left on) and cooked, flesh-side down, for 2–2½ hours. This releases all of their natural waters and sugars which, as they cook, begin to caramelize. No extra time is needed for the caramelizing of the onions; they simply cook while the beef simmers.

The turnip purée is cooked very simply and, once made, is stuffed into the onions. Served with the beef sitting on top, the three separate components become one happy family.

SERVES 4

2 large onions, skin left on, halved through the middle
1 tablespoon beef dripping or cooking oil
4 × 175–225 g (6–8 oz) pieces of chuck steak, tied to keep shape
Salt and pepper

For the Sauce

Butter
1 onion, chopped
1 carrot, chopped

Sprig of thyme
1 bay leaf
2 tomatoes, cut into 8
Bottle of red wine
600 ml (1 pint) *Veal or Beef Jus* (page 34) or alternative (page 11)

For the Turnip Purée

450 g (1 lb) peeled turnips, cut in 2 cm (¾ in) rough cubes
200 ml (7 fl oz) milk
200 ml (7 fl oz) water
1–2 tablespoons double cream (optional)

Pre-heat the oven to 140°C/275°F/Gas Mark 1.

Place the onions, flesh-side down, in a roasting tray. These can now go towards the bottom of the pre-heated oven. They will slowly begin to caramelize and should be left alone for 30 minutes before the beef joins them.

To make the sauce, melt a knob of butter in a braising pan. Add the chopped onion, carrot, sprig of thyme and bay leaf. Cook for 5–10 minutes, allowing to slightly colour and begin to soften. Add the tomatoes and continue to cook for a few minutes. Pour on the bottle of red wine and bring to the boil. Once boiling, allow to reduce by half. Add the *jus* and bring to the simmer.

While the sauce is being put together, season the beef pieces with salt and pepper. Heat a frying-pan with the dripping or cooking oil. Once hot, add the beef. Sear and colour on all sides, before adding to the sauce in the braising dish.

Bring to the simmer, cover with a lid and place in the middle of the oven, above the onions. Increase the oven temperature to 160°C/325°F/Gas Mark 3. The beef will now take 2 hours to become totally soft and tender. During this cooking time, the onions should be checked to make sure they do not become burnt. Also, if the sauce is becoming too thick, loosen with water. This will prevent the flavour from becoming too strong.

While the meat and onions are cooking, the turnips can also be cooked. Place the turnip chunks in a saucepan and top with the milk, water and pinch of salt. If not quite covered, then top up with extra milk. Bring to the simmer and cook until tender. This will only take 10–15 minutes. Drain. Cooking the turnips in milk and water will have left them with a brilliant white finish. They can now be blitzed in a food processor or pushed through a sieve to a smooth purée. Season with salt and pepper. A tablespoon or two of double cream can also be added, if using, to enrich the creamy finish.

OPPOSITE
Piece of Braised Beef with Slowly Caramelized Onions and Turnip Purée

The meat and onions can now both be removed. Lift the meat from the dish and keep to one side, cutting away the string from the beef. Strain the sauce through a sieve, check the seasoning and pour back over the meat.

To serve the dish, remove the skin and tough outside layer of onion. Some of the centre can also be removed; this creates a caramelized onion 'case'. Season with salt and pepper.

To create a glaze for the beef, take 150 ml (¼ pint) of the sauce and boil to reduce by at least half. This will now give you a very thick, shiny finish, which can be brushed over each portion of meat.

Fill the centre of each onion with the turnip purée. Present the filled onion halves on plates, sitting the shiny, glazed portions of beef on top. Offer the remaining sauce separately. The beef pieces are ready to serve.

It's really quite a simple dish that gives a 'lot of work' impression when presented. So if you're looking to impress, as well as just create good flavours, then this is the dish for you.

The Classic Steak and Kidney Pie

This version is called 'the classic' because it's being made and cooked to the recipe we all know. The 'new classic' is on page 202 (see *Steak and 'Kidney Pie'*), which will bring you a totally different result, with the 'pie' sitting next to the steak.

In fact, the combination of steak and kidney doesn't seem to be all that old. It wasn't until about the mid nineteenth century that the essential kidney was added to a steak pie or pudding – only some 150 years ago.

Around the country, steak and kidney has many different finishes, with different pastries – shortcrust, flaky, puff or suet. Many contain flour or Worcestershire sauce, some have mushrooms and vegetables, some are without. In the West Country, or so I've heard, they pour up to 300 ml (½ pint) of clotted cream into the pie before it is served! I like to top the pie with puff pastry, but the suet paste normally used for a steak and kidney pudding (such as the one on page 200) can also be used. It does work very well baked on top and has the bonus of carrying a good beef flavour from the suet. In this recipe I'm using vegetables, mushrooms and Worcestershire sauce – hopefully keeping everybody happy.

While steak and kidney pies have often just been a combination of steak, kidneys, onions, water and Worcestershire, all mixed, topped with pastry and baked for 2–2½ hours – job done – I've never been able to understand or accept that method. It's purely cooking by chance, and to me there is no chance of the right flavours, seasonings, or any depth, texture or consistency to be found using this method. So I always stew the meat and vegetable filling first, then sit it in the pie dish and top with pastry and bake in the oven. You then know exactly what you are looking forward to. This method also carries the bonus of allowing you to make and refrigerate the filling the day before needed. Cover it the following day and bake for 45 minutes to 1 hour and dinner is ready!

BELOW
The Classic Steak and Kidney Pie

SERVES 4–6

1 tablespoon beef dripping or cooking oil
675 g (1½ lb) chuck steak, cut into 2.5 cm (1 in) dice
225 g (8 oz) ox or lamb's kidneys, trimmed and diced
350 g (12 oz) *Puff Pastry* (page 365) or *Suet Pastry* (page 204)
2 onions, chopped
3 carrots, peeled and cut into rough 1.5 cm (⅝ in) dice
Butter
4 large flat mushrooms, cut into thick slices
2 tablespoons plain flour
1 teaspoon tomato purée
1 bay leaf
600 ml (1 pint) *Veal* or *Beef Stock* (page 34) or water and stock cube or granules
Worcestershire sauce
Salt and pepper
1 egg, beaten, for glazing

Heat a large frying-pan with a little of the dripping or oil. Season the diced beef with salt and pepper. Fry in the pan until well coloured and completely sealed. Lift out the meat and transfer to a large saucepan. Add a touch more oil, if necessary, to the frying-pan. Season the kidneys and also fry quickly to seal and colour in the hot pan. Also transfer to the saucepan.

The onions and carrots can now be placed in the frying-pan along with a knob of butter; the vegetables can be cooked for 2–3 minutes. In this time they will lift any flavours left from the meats. Transfer to the saucepan. Lastly, fry the mushroom slices in a little more butter, just turning in the pan for a minute or two; keep to one side.

Place the saucepan on a medium heat. Stir the flour into the meat and vegetables and allow to cook for 2–3 minutes. Add the tomato purée, bay leaf and mushrooms. It's now time to top with the stock. Bring to the simmer, skimming off any impurities. The meat should be just covered with the stock; if not, top with a little more stock or water. Now simmer gently, not quite completely covering with a lid, for 1½–2 hours. During the cooking time, the 'stew' may need to be skimmed.

After 1½ hours check the meat for tenderness. If not quite soft enough, continue to cook for the other 30 minutes. Provided the meat is cooking gently, it will not need to be topped up with any more water. The sauce will slowly have reduced, thickening its consistency and increasing its flavour.

Once cooked, taste for seasoning. Add a dash (or two) of Worcestershire sauce to lift the beef flavour. The meat and sauce can now all be transferred to a 1.2 litre (2 pint) pie dish.

Pre-heat the oven to 220°C/425°F/Gas Mark 7.

The pastry of your choice can now be rolled out. If using puff pastry, roll 5 mm (¼ in) thick; if suet pastry, then a little thicker – approximately 8 mm (scant ½ in). Cut a strip of pastry to sit around the rim of the dish. This will guarantee the top stays on. It's best to allow the stew to have cooled to just warm, and the pastry top to rest and relax after rolling, before topping. Brush the rim of the dish with beaten egg. Sit the strip of pastry on top and brush again.

Make sure the pastry top is bigger than the dish and sit it over the top. The pastry can now be pushed down around the sides, trimmed and crimped for a neat finish. Brush with egg and place in the pre-heated oven. This will now take 30–40 minutes and is then ready to eat.

Note: It's important that the pastry has time to rest after being rolled, before topping the pie – this prevents shrinkage.

Steak and Kidney Pudding

Everybody's favourite, a rich, moist suet pastry steamed around soft, succulent and tasty chunks of beef. In this recipe I'm cooking the meat first, with carrots, mushrooms and celery included. The sweetness of the carrots really lifts the sauce.

Eliza Acton, in her *Modern Cookery* of 1845, calls a steak pie or pudding 'John Bull's Pudding' (which suggests it was thought of as a very British dish), and mushrooms were used instead of kidneys, which were introduced a little later. (Another steak and suet pudding was known as Bedfordshire Clangers, and what a clanger – it had beef at one end, fruit or jam at the other, a complete meal all in one.)

The recipe for the suet pastry recipe is on page 204. The quantity there is for a 1.2 litre (2 pint) pudding basin, as used here.

SERVES 4–6

1–2 tablespoons beef dripping or cooking oil
450 g (1 lb) chuck steak, cut into 2.5 cm (1 in) cubes
225 g (8 oz) ox or lamb's kidneys, cut into 2.5 cm (1 in) dice
2 carrots, cut into rough dice 1 cm (½ in) thick
2 onions, cut into rough dice 1 cm (½ in) thick
2 celery sticks, cut into rough dice 1 cm (½ in) thick
175 g (6 oz) button mushrooms, quartered
300 ml (½ pint) stout (optional)
600 ml (1 pint) *Veal or Beef Jus* (page 34) or alternative (page 11)
1 bay leaf
1 quantity *Suet Pastry* (page 204)
Salt and pepper

Heat a frying-pan with the dripping or oil and, in stages, fry the beef and kidneys, colouring well.

In a separate large saucepan, while the meat is being fried, the carrots, onions, celery and mushrooms can all be fried in a touch of oil. Cook for a few minutes before adding the stout, if using. Bring to the boil and reduce by two-thirds. Add the *jus* and bring to the simmer. Add the bay leaf.

The beef and kidneys can now be added and brought to a gentle simmer. Cover and cook for

1–1½ hours until just becoming tender. The meat should only be approaching its tender stage. It will finish its cooking during the steaming of the pudding. Adjust the seasoning with salt and pepper and leave to cool.

While the meat is cooking and cooling, the suet pastry can be made and the pudding basin lined as explained on page 204.

Once cool, the stewed beef and vegetables can be drained in a colander, reserving the cooking liquor. Remove the bay leaf, spoon the meat and vegetables into the pastry-lined basin and add just enough sauce to barely cover. Cover as explained. This can now be topped with folded, buttered foil, wrapping it around as you would parchment paper, and twisting to hold. Stand in a steamer (a trivet or colander with a lid will also do the trick; see Note, below) filled with hot water. This will now take approximately 1½ hours to cook the suet pastry and re-heat and finish the steak.

While the pudding is steaming, the remaining steak and kidney gravy can be brought to the simmer and strained through a sieve. This now gives you a gravy to pour over the turned-out pudding.

Remove the foil and turn the pudding out. Pour the sauce over and serve.

Note: If you do not have a steamer, a trivet or colander can be used, sitting it in a saucepan of boiling water and tightly covering with the pan lid or foil. If that's also not possible, then put a plate in the base of a large saucepan, sit the pudding on top and pour in hot water to halfway up the bowl. Now briskly simmer for the 2 hours.

Steak and 'Kidney Pie'

Steak and kidney pie, that most classic of British dishes, can be found just about anywhere in the UK. But you've never seen it quite like this. That's quite a statement because I've eaten many excellent steak and kidney pies and puddings. The reason is that this dish is made up of a piece of braised steak served with a little kidney and onion pie, so that two separate dishes are presented together to create one new British classic.

SERVES 6

6 × 175 g (6 oz) chuck 'joints' (individually trimmed and tied pieces of chuck steak)
Butter
Salt and pepper

For the Kidney Pies

225 g (8 oz) *Shortcrust Pastry* (page 364)
3 onions, sliced
Butter
Demerara sugar
150 ml (¼ pint) double cream
1 egg
8 lambs' kidneys or 225–350 g (10–12 oz) veal kidneys, cut into 1 cm (½ in) dice
225 g (8 oz) *Quick Puff Pastry* (page 365), rolled and cut into six 8–11 cm (3½–4½ in) circles
1 egg yolk, beaten, to glaze

For the Sauce

Butter
1 onion, roughly chopped
1 carrot, roughly chopped
2 celery sticks, roughly chopped (optional)
Fresh thyme sprig
3 tomatoes, roughly chopped
Bottle of red wine
900 ml (1½ pints) *Beef Stock* (not too strong, page 34), or water
3–4 lambs' kidneys, roughly diced
300 ml (½ pint) *Beef or Veal Jus* (page 34) or alternative (page 11)

To make the sauce, melt a knob of butter with the chopped vegetables and the sprig of thyme. Cook for 3–4 minutes until softened and then add the chopped tomatoes. Continue to cook for a further 3–4 minutes. Add the red wine, bring to the boil and reduce by three-quarters. This should take 5–6 minutes. Now just add the beef stock and bring to the simmer.

While the sauce is being made, season the chuck 'joints' with salt and pepper. Heat a frying-pan with a knob of butter and colour the beef joints on all sides. Add them to the simmering stock. The beef will take approximately 2½ hours to become completely tender and slightly 'overcooked'. After 2 hours, check the texture of the meat. When you press the joint, the meat should start to break away very easily; if not, continue to cook for a further 30 minutes (or more). Once completely cooked, remove the joints and cover with cling film.

To finish the sauce, sauté the roughly diced kidneys in some butter for 3–4 minutes. Add to the beef cooking liquor. Reduce the liquor by half, skimming off any impurities. This will increase the strength and flavour of the sauce, with the kidney giving an extra taste. Once reduced, add the *jus*. Bring to the simmer and then strain through a sieve. You should have a well-flavoured liquor with a sauce consistency. I now like to pour off 150 ml (¼ pint) and reduce it by at least half again to a very thick shiny consistency – it also becomes very sticky. This will be used to brush or roll the finished beef joints before serving. It leaves the meat just glistening.

Season the remaining sauce, if needed. (If the sauce is too thin but is strong in taste, it can be lightly thickened with cornflour or arrowroot.)

The pies can be made while the steaks are cooking. Pre-heat the oven to 200°C/400°F/ Gas Mark 6. Butter six 6–7 cm (2½–3 in) tartlet tins (similar to jam tart size). Roll out the shortcrust pastry, cut into large discs and use to line the tartlet tins, leaving any excess pastry hanging over the edges of the tins. Line with greaseproof paper or foil, fill with baking beans and bake blind for 15–20 minutes. Once cool, remove the greaseproof paper or foil and beans. Trim away any excess pastry to leave a neat finish.

Meanwhile, fry the onions in a knob of butter over a high heat. Fry until well softened and on the point of being burnt, which will take 5–6 minutes. The burnt tinges (and we do want some of the onions burnt) will give us the bitter side to this dish. Once softened and coloured, add a good sprinkling of demerara sugar to caramelize the onions and add a note of sweetness. Now mix together and season with salt and pepper. Reduce the heat to low. Whisk the cream and egg together and pour onto the onions while still on the stove. Stir for a few minutes

until thickened but not scrambled. Remove from the stove and check for seasoning. Taste the mix (it will be coffee-coloured) for the depth and balance of bitterness and sweetness. If you feel it is too bitter, add another small sprinkling of sugar. Leave to cool.

The 1 cm (½ in) diced kidneys can now be pan-fried very quickly in a hot pan with butter (or cooking oil). This takes about 1–2 minutes and is just to seal the kidneys. Season with salt and pepper and leave to cool. Once cool, mix some of the bittersweet onion mix with the kidneys to bind. Spoon some more onion mix into the base of the tartlet mounds and then top with the sautéed kidney mixture.

Brush around the edge of the shortcrust pastry cases with egg yolk and top with the puff pastry circles, pressing and sealing all round. Leave the pies to rest in the refrigerator for at least 20 minutes. Once set, trim off any excess pastry around the sides. Brush the tops with egg yolk.

To finish the dish, bake the pies for 15–20 minutes until golden, and warm the steaks in the finished sauce. Remove them and roll or brush with the reduced sticky sauce. To serve, sit the steaks and pies side by side in bowls or plates and pour some sauce around.

Note: The components of this dish can be made well in advance. From cold, the steaks will take 30–40 minutes to re-heat in the sauce. The pies will keep, refrigerated, for 24 hours before being baked.

Layered Steak and Onion Pudding

Another classic combination of beef and onions, in a main course that is very easy to make. Put its few ingredients in the steamer and, 2 hours later, dinner is ready. The ingredients are set in the same suet pastry used for the *Steak and Kidney Pudding* (page 201).

The basic idea can be varied in a couple of ways. Thin slices of lamb could be layered with the onions – it's best just to take thin slices from a cheap cut, breast of lamb. Add a touch of chopped mint and another dish is made. Venison also eats very well, particularly if seasoned with a pinch of crushed juniper berries and the onions lightly sweetened with redcurrant jelly (omitting the sugar).

For the beef version, a few crushed green peppercorns can be added for pudding *au poivre*. A home-made *jus* (page 34) can be made to pour over or serve with the pudding as a gravy.

SERVES 4

1 quantity *Suet Pastry* (right)

For the Filling

3 onions, sliced
50 g (2 oz) butter
1 dessertspoon demerara sugar
600 g (1¼ lb) beef chuck or skirt, cut into thin
    strips
Worcestershire sauce
Salt and pepper
Approx. 150 ml (¼ pint) water

Butter and line a 1.2 litre (2 pint) pudding basin with the pastry as explained on page 206.

The onions can now be fried in batches, using the butter. It's important to fry them well, allowing the onions almost to burn in parts; this will create a natural bitter caramelizing. As each 'load' comes to that stage, season well with salt and pepper and add a sprinkling of the sugar for a slightly sweet finish. Leave to cool.

The meat must be lean so trim it well as you cut in thin strips. One of the important stages of this dish, as with a Cornish pasty, is to season well. The good pepper bite lifts the whole dish. Once all of the beef is cut, season well and splash with a tablespoon of Worcestershire sauce.

Now the pie can be filled, spooning the onions in first. Lay thin slices of beef, not overlapping, on top. Repeat the same process until the dish has been completely filled. Pour in the water. More can be added to bring it almost level with the top layer. Brush the edge with water and cover with the pastry. Cover with buttered and folded foil. The pudding

can now be cooked in a steamer (or a colander inside a large saucepan, see Note, page 202), for 2 hours.

During its cooking time, some gravy can be prepared, if you want it.

After the 2 hours, remove the pudding from the steamer and rest for 10–15 minutes before turning out of the bowl.

The water in the pudding will have taken on the juices from the meat and onions to give a well-flavoured liquor. This dish will eat well with simple accompaniments, such as good buttered carrots and cabbage or greens.

Suet Pastry

This pastry is most famous for the part it plays in the Great British steak and kidney pudding (such as the one on page 201). It takes on all of the flavours happening inside and, when coated with a good rich gravy, is just unbelievable to eat. It can also be used as a topping for many baked dishes, *The Classic Steak and Kidney Pie* (page 199) being one of them. With this, it carries the bonus of the beef flavour contained in the suet.

Dried suet can be used, but fresh can never be beaten for its texture and flavour. If using fresh fat, simply pull away the thin outer skin and chop by hand. You could also grate it.

The quantity here will be enough to fill and top a 1.2 litre (2 pint) pudding basin. This is the size used in the steak and kidney pudding recipe. To top *The Classic Steak and Kidney Pie*, only 225 g (8 oz) of self-raising flour, 100 g (4 oz) of suet and 150 ml (¼ pint) of water will be needed.

300 g (10 oz) self-raising flour
150 g (5 oz) shredded suet
200 ml (7 fl oz) water
Salt

OPPOSITE
Layered Steak and Onion Pudding

Sieve the flour and salt together into a mixing bowl. Add the suet, breaking it into the flour as it is mixed in. Stir in the water to form a fairly firm dough. Wrap in cling film and allow to rest for 20 minutes.

The pastry is now ready to use. Lightly flour any surface before rolling. For the steak and kidney pudding, roll to about 5 mm–1 cm (¼–½ in) thick.

When lining a pudding basin, always leave 1–2 cm (½–¾ in) hanging over. When the basin has been filled, this can be folded in to create a border base to sit the lid on. Brush with water before topping with a circle of pastry for the lid.

An alternative is to leave it hanging over. Sit the lid on top of the filling, moisten with water and then fold the border in.

Note: Whichever basin you use, it must always be well buttered.

Heatproof plastic bowls work perfectly with steamed puddings. Butter well and, when cooked, just invert, squeeze and the pudding will fall out – gently.

Steak and Oyster Pie

Here, I hope, is another long-lasting, new Great British classic. Its concept is similar to that of the *Steak and 'Kidney Pie'* on page 202, with the 'pie' becoming a separate feature on the plate. The beef is cooked in red wine, and the oyster pie is finished with a glaze of red-wine béarnaise sauce.

Oysters were once a cheap food for everybody, so much so that in the nineteenth century they were actually included in steak and kidney puddings, popped under the pastry just before they went into the oven to be cooked. Since then, principally because of pollution, oysters have become very much rarer and now most are reared in fisheries.

There are two main types of oysters: rock oysters, which are farmed, or native oysters, which are wild. Rock oysters are also known as Pacific oysters, but are now more commonly and generically known by their French name *fines de claires*. Rock oysters are produced in several countries, including Ireland and France, where they are graded according

to their quality, so you'll find ones referred to as *fines de claires*, *spéciales* and *label rouge*. The seed for rock oysters are bred in hatcheries and then put out to sea on platforms called trestles. Here they grow by feeding on the plankton that grows naturally in the sea. It takes two to three years for them to reach their market size, which is 80–100 g (3–4 oz). If they are grown in inlets of the sea where there is a certain element of fresh water coming in, their flavour is sweeter.

Native oysters are produced on the south coast of England, Holland, France and predominantly in the shallow bays around the west coast of Ireland. They also feed on plankton in the sea but take four to six years to reach the same weight (80–100 g/ 3–4 oz) as rock oysters. They are fished by dredging, generally from small boats, between September and April which is the season for them (that is, any month with an 'r' in its name).

Whichever of the two types you go for and despite the cost, oysters are worth including because of their amazing flavour.

Opening oysters is not the easiest of jobs. Your fishmonger will open them for you, I'm sure, but it is important all of the juices are saved, as they will be used to spread the oyster flavour through the red-wine sauce. Here are a few tips on how to open an oyster.

1 Hold the oyster, preferably in a thick cloth. This will help grip the shell and prevent it slipping and cutting your hand.

2 The oyster must be held cup-side down. The knife (oyster knives can be easily obtained from kitchen utensil stores) can now be inserted in the 'pointed' end of the oyster. This is where the hinge holding the shell will be found.

3 Holding tightly, push the knife against and into the hinge point, twisting slightly as you do. The hinge will break, loosening the lid.

4 Lift the top lid of the shell. Be careful not to lose the juices from the cup base. Now cut away the muscle connecting the flesh to the top shell.

5 Run the knife underneath the oyster, releasing it from the base.

6 Always check that no shell splinters have been caught in the flesh before serving. For this dish, keep the oysters separate and pass the juices through a tea strainer to remove any grit.

SERVES 6

For the Pastry Cases

Butter
450 g (1 lb) *Shortcrust* or *Puff Pastry* (page 364 or 365)

For the Beef

6 × 225 g (8 oz) small chuck steak joints, trimmed of all sinews and tied
Cooking oil
1 onion, roughly chopped
1 carrot, roughly chopped
½ leek, roughly chopped
2 celery sticks, roughly chopped
1 small garlic clove
Sprig of thyme
1 bay leaf
Bottle of red wine, preferably claret
900 ml–1.2 litres (1½–2 pints) *Veal or Beef Jus* (page 34), not too thick and strong; the flavour will develop while braising
Butter
Salt and pepper
3–4 tomatoes, chopped (optional)

For the Béarnaise Sauce

100 g (4 oz) unsalted butter
Few white peppercorns, crushed
1 teaspoon chopped shallots
2 tablespoons red-wine vinegar
2 egg yolks
150–300 ml (¼–½ pint) red wine, reduced by three-quarters
Squeeze of lemon juice
1 teaspoon chopped fresh parsley
½ teaspoon chopped fresh tarragon
Salt and pepper
4–5 tablespoons lightly whipped double cream, to glaze

For the Pies

225–300 g (8–10 oz) *Buttered Spinach* (page 113), cooked weight
Butter
2–3 shallots, finely chopped
18 large rock oysters, opened, with their juices

Preheat the oven to 200°C/400°F/Gas Mark 6.

Butter six 5 × 8 cm (3 × 2 in) metal cooking rings. Roll out the shortcrust or puff pastry, cut into large discs and use to line the metal rings, leaving any excess pastry hanging over the edges of the tins. Line with greaseproof paper or foil, fill with baking beans and bake blind for 15–20 minutes. Once cool, remove the greaseproof paper or foil and beans. Slice away any excess pastry to leave a neat finish.

Turn the heat down to 180°C/350°F/Gas Mark 4.

While the pastry is baking, season the beef with salt and pepper. Heat an ovenproof braising pan on top of the stove, with some cooking oil. Once hot, seal the beef pieces, colouring the meat completely. Remove the beef and add the vegetables to the pan. Cook for 10–15 minutes until the vegetables have also taken on colour, creating a caramelization. Add the garlic, thyme and bay leaf and continue to cook for a few minutes. Pour the wine over and bring to the simmer. Cook, reducing the wine by three-quarters. The *jus* can now be added.

Return the meat to the pan and bring to the simmer. Cover with a lid and braise slowly in the oven for 2½–3 hours. The meat will now be totally soft and tender. During the cooking time, it is important to check after each hour, skimming away any impurities that collect on the surface. Also, if the sauce is becoming too thick and strong, loosen it slightly with water. Three or four chopped tomatoes can also be added to the vegetables. These will give a slight sweetness to the finished result.

Once cooked, remove the beef pieces and keep to one side. Strain the sauce through a sieve. Pour half on top of the meat, reducing the remaining amount to a good, rich red-wine sauce consistency. While it is reducing, check that the flavour does not become too strong. Once at a good level, if too thin, loosen a teaspoon of cornflour or cornstarch with red wine and add to thicken. An extra glass or two of red wine can also be reduced and added, to give an even stronger red wine flavour. The beef joints can now be kept warm in the liquor and re-warmed in it when needed. If refrigerating and re-warming at a later date, the beef will need at least 45 minutes to 1 hour of gentle simmering before it will have returned to its former glory of softness and succulence.

To create a glazed finish on the beef, reduce 100–150 ml (4–5 fl oz) of liquor by two-thirds to three-quarters. This will now be very shiny and sticky to 'paint' on the pieces before serving.

This basic recipe and method will stand as a dish completely on its own, but the pie is really delicious served with oysters, spinach and béarnaise sauce.

Make the béarnaise sauce next. Melt the butter and leave to stand. The solids will sink to the base of the pan, leaving clarified butter.

Place the peppercorns, chopped shallots and vinegar together in a saucepan. Bring to the simmer and reduce by two-thirds; leave to cool. Mix the egg yolks and vinegar reduction together in a bowl. Over a pan of lightly simmering water, whisk to a sabayon, lifting the mix to at least twice its volume. Remove the bowl from the heat and slowly add the clarified butter, whisking vigorously. The butter will now emulsify with the egg yolks, leaving a thick, creamy sauce. It is important to add the butter slowly. Once all has been added and the sauce is thick, pour in the red-wine reduction, a little at a time, until at a spoon-coating consistency. Season with salt and pepper. Strain through a sieve, adding a squeeze of lemon juice and the chopped herbs.

Once the beef is completely warmed through, add a few tablespoons of the oyster juice at a time to the finished red-wine sauce. These juices have a reasonably high salt content, so do not adjust the sauce seasoning until the oyster juice has been added.

Warm the pastry cases in a pre-heated oven. While warming, heat the spinach through and season with salt and pepper. Divide the spinach between the pastry cases. Melt another knob of butter in a hot pan, add the chopped shallots and cook for 1 minute. Increase the heat in the pan and add the oysters. Cook for literally just 20–30 seconds before placing three oysters in each pastry case on top of the spinach.

Fold the whipped cream into the béarnaise sauce. Spoon over the oysters, covering the tops of the pies. These can now be glazed to a golden brown under a pre-heated grill.

To serve, place a pie and piece of glazed steak next to one another on plates or in bowls and pour the red-wine oyster sauce around. The dishes are complete.

This really does eat like a dream, with warm oysters topped with the red-wine béarnaise. When the pie is cut into, the sauces mingle with every flavour in the dish.

White Lamb Stew

Many dishes were 'white' in medieval times, usually flavoured and 'coloured' by pounded almonds and almond milk. This dish here is similar to the French *blanquette*, which is usually associated with the 'white' meats veal, pork and chicken. It's a variation of stewed lamb, finishing in a cream sauce.

The meat I'm using is shoulder of lamb. This is quite a cheap cut and holds another bonus in that it is very flavoursome. It's best to ask your butcher if he can give you large dice of lean shoulder. Pieces of 3–4 cm (1½–1¾ in) will be just right.

Blanquettes, classically, are just garnished with button mushrooms and onions. I thought we would add some carrots too, for extra flavour and colour. This is definitely a full meal but, if you prefer to serve an accompaniment with the dish, a good bowl of buttered pasta would be ideal.

SERVES 4–6

900 g–1 kg (2–2¼ lb) shoulder of lamb, cut into 3–4 cm (1½–1¾ in) dice
1 onion, sliced

Sprig of thyme (rosemary and marjoram are good
        alternatives)
1 large garlic clove, crushed (optional)
1 bay leaf
600 ml (1 pint) *Chicken Stock* (page 33) or water
2 glasses of white wine
2 large carrots, cut into 1 cm (½ in) dice
225 g (8 oz) button mushrooms, cleaned (wiped
        rather than washed)
150 ml (¼ pint) double cream
Lemon juice
Salt, pepper and freshly grated nutmeg

To Garnish

225 g (8 oz) button onions, peeled
Cooking oil

The diced lamb should first be placed in a saucepan
and covered with cold water. This can now be
brought to the boil and then refreshed in cold water.
This method lifts any impurities from the meat.

Season the lamb with salt, pepper and nutmeg
and place in the clean saucepan with the sliced onion,
thyme, garlic and bay leaf. Pour the chicken stock and
white wine on top to cover the meat. If the two have
not quite covered it, then top up with water.

Bring to the simmer. This will now take 1½–2
hours of slow cooking, possibly even 2½ hours for
large pieces. During the cooking, skim from time to
time, keeping the liquor clean.

After 1 hour of cooking, add the carrots. The
mushrooms can be added to the stew during its final
30 minutes. This will keep their natural flavour.

To make the garnish, place the button onions in
a saucepan and cover with cold water. Bring to a
simmer and cook for 4–5 minutes. Drain and dry the
onions on a cloth. Heat a frying-pan with a drop of
cooking oil and shallow-fry until the onions are
golden brown.

Once the meat is tender and cooked, strain off
the liquor, keeping the meat with the mushrooms
and carrots covered with cling film. The sprig of
thyme and bay leaf can be discarded.

The liquor can now be brought to the boil and
allowed to reduce by half or two-thirds. This will

increase the lamb flavour. Add the double cream and
return to the simmer; cook for 4–5 minutes and
season with salt and pepper, if needed.

One or two squeezes of lemon juice can now
be added to liven up the sauce. Add the lamb and
the button onions and mushrooms and return to the
simmer. The dish is ready to serve.

Note: Adding chopped fresh parsley or torn leaves of tarragon
is a nice way to finish the dish.

Slow-roast Shoulder of Pork with Pearl Barley and Sage 'Stuffing'

Shoulder of pork is an inexpensive cut of meat.
It can be boned, rolled and tied, which is how
you'll find it in most butchers' shops. Leg or belly
can also be used. The pork will be left to cook away
for 4 hours, so if you're popping out for a while,
don't worry, your piece of pork will just be roasting
away nicely.

The 'stuffing' is actually going to be cooked
separately in an ovenproof dish. The meat cooking
time is too long for the stuffing, and would do
nothing but spoil it. A forcemeat to accompany meat
is very traditional in Britain but you don't need to
serve it. Remember that none of these recipes is
'carved in stone'. The stuffing is a great extra,
though, the pearl barley giving it a new texture and
flavour. But if you have an old sage and onion
favourite, then serve that.

The gravy I'm making here is prune-flavoured.
Again, this is not essential, but it does eat beautifully
with pork. A good *Apple Sauce* (page 44) is also a
perfect accompaniment.

I'm using quite a large joint here, so it will
probably go even further than the six portions I have
specified.

SERVES 6

1.5–1.8 kg (3¼–4¼ lb) boned and rolled shoulder
        of pork, rind scored
Cooking oil
Salt

75 g (3 oz) pearl barley
Knob of butter
2 onions, chopped
500–600 ml (17 fl oz–1 pint) *Chicken Stock*
      (page 33) or water with stock granules
      or cube
3 rashers of smoked or unsmoked back bacon,
      cut into small dice
1 dessertspoon chopped fresh sage
1 apple, peeled and chopped
1 egg, beaten
50 g (2 oz) white breadcrumbs
Salt and pepper

For the Sauce

1 heaped tablespoon tinned prunes
1–2 tablespoons prune juice from the tin
Splash of Armagnac, brandy or Calvados (optional)
300 ml (½ pint) *Veal or Beef Jus/gravy* (page 34)
      or *Chicken Stock* (page 33)

Pre-heat the oven to 160°C/325°F/Gas Mark 3.

When buying the pork, ask, if it's possible, for three or four pork bones to sit the meat on. If unavailable, then don't worry: a wire rack will do the trick. This is basically to prevent the meat from becoming burnt or dry, which it does if it's in contact with the roasting tray. Also, excess fat will just collect in the base, and can be used for basting.

Oil the pork skin and sprinkle well with salt. Sit the joint on the bones or rack and place in the middle of the pre-heated oven. This can now be left for an hour before basting with the pork fat collected. Continue to cook for another 3 hours, basting from time to time.

During that first hour the stuffing can be made. Rinse the pearl barley under a cold running tap. Melt the butter in a saucepan. Once bubbling, add the chopped onions. Cook for a few minutes until softened but without colour. Add the barley and continue to cook for 2–3 minutes. Add 500 ml (17 fl oz) of the chicken stock and bring to the simmer. Cover with greaseproof paper and gently simmer, stirring from time to time, for 45–50

minutes, until tender. If, during the cooking time, the barley becomes dry, add the remaining stock. Once cooked, remove from the heat and leave to cool.

The bacon can now be fried in a non-stick frying-pan; if the pan is hot enough it will not need any fat. Just cook for a minute or two to seal the pieces. Leave to cool.

Once all is cold, mix together the barley, bacon, sage, apple and egg. Season with salt and pepper. The breadcrumbs can now also be added to the mix. Spoon into a buttered ovenproof dish. This can now be put in the oven to bake, 40–45 minutes before the pork is ready.

After the 4 hours of roasting and basting have passed the pork will have a good crispy crackling. Take from the oven and leave to rest for 15–20 minutes. During this resting time the oven temperature can be raised to 200°C/400°F/ Gas Mark 6. The stuffing will take on a crispy topping if left for a further 10 minutes.

The gravy can also be made while the pork is resting. Pour off excess fat from the roasting tray, but leave behind any juices. Heat the tray on top of the stove. Add the prunes and the tablespoon of prune juice. Bring to the simmer, stirring them around. This will lift any flavours left behind. If using Armagnac, or one of the other spirits, then add a splash or two now, allowing to reduce in the pan. The gravy or stock can now also be added and simmered for a good 10 minutes. Strain through a sieve, pushing all of the prune flavour through. The gravy is now ready to serve.

Remove the crackling from the pork and break into pieces. Gently carve the pork; this will almost just break into slices. Arrange the meat and crackling on plates, along with a spoonful of stuffing and gravy.

Note: Classic *Roast Potatoes* (page 238), along with spring greens, *Cabbage, Kale* or *Sprouts* (page 103, 104 or 106), will all eat very well with this dish.

If made with stock, the gravy will obviously have a much looser consistency but will still have picked up all of the flavours, which is certainly the most important aspect.

Boiled and Baked Ham

Hams are the back legs taken from pigs that have been reared to become taller and leaner, and heavier and older than those used to produce pork. They are usually salted by soaking in brine and then air-dried and/or smoked. Air-dried and cold-smoked hams are raw, and hot-smoked ham is cooked. The Italian Parma ham is raw, for instance, while most of the hams we have in Britain are cooked – hot-smoked or boiled. Legend has it that the original York hams – renowned for their excellent flavour – were smoked over shavings from all the wood needed to build York Minster.

Whole brined hams can be bought cooked or uncooked, and here I'm using uncooked. It's best to order this well in advance from your butcher. The ham can then be soaked by him to reduce the salt flavour before you get it home. Even so, I still soak hams at home for 24 hours, changing the water a few times, to ensure as much salt as possible has been helped out.

You might be offered a ham that has a slight mould developing on the skin. This simply proves how well the meat has been cured. Make sure it is scraped away before boiling the leg.

Many years ago lots of flavours were added to the boiling liquid, which included chopped onions,

BELOW
Boiled and Baked Ham

carrots, celery, turnips, swedes, parsnips, as well as fresh herbs, peppercorns, cider, sugar, grated apples and black treacle. The cooking liquor must have been delicious.

In this recipe I'm using a whole ham, which weighs 5.5–7.2 kg (12–16 lb). If you decide to cook a whole ham, ask your butcher to remove the aitch bone and trotter. You'll need a large saucepan to cook the ham in. You'll probably want to cook this at Christmas or for a summer barbecue as the amount is quite large. Otherwise smaller joints of rolled ham can also be ordered: 1.4–1.75 kg (2–4 lb) pieces would be ideal. Simply follow the cooking time of 20 minutes per 450 g (1 lb).

There are several different ways of glazing hams: the traditional cloves and demerara sugar, or honey flavoured with dried English mustard, or honey and black treacle. I've even found a recipe for a ground coffee, mustard and brown sugar glaze. I'm not sure about that one, so I'm going for English mustard and demerara sugar.

If you're serving the ham hot, buttered new potatoes and fresh peas are the perfect accompaniment.

SERVES 20–25 AS PART OF A BUFFET

5.5–7.2 kg (12–16 lb) ham, soaked in cold water
    for 24 hours, changing the water occasionally
2 onions, quartered
Few cloves
Few black peppercorns
1 bay leaf
4 tablespoons English mustard
Approx. 225 g (8 oz) demerara sugar
300 ml (½ pint) *Chicken Stock* (page 33, optional)

Place the soaked ham in a large saucepan, with the onions, cloves, peppercorns and bay leaf. Cover with water and bring to the boil, skimming away any impurities. The ham can now be left to simmer, allowing 20 minutes per 450 g (1 lb).

Pre-heat the oven to 190°C/375°F/Gas Mark 5.

Once cooked, remove the ham from the stock. Leave to stand for 10–15 minutes before peeling away the skin. The fat can now be left as it is or it

can be scored, creating a diamond pattern. Brush the ham with the mustard and sprinkle well with the demerara sugar.

The ham can now be placed in the pre-heated oven and baked for 30–45 minutes. During this time, the sugar will caramelize. Any collecting in the pan should be basted back on the ham. Once golden, remove from the oven and rest for 15–20 minutes before carving and serving, or leave until cold.

The chicken stock, if using, can be poured into the roasting pan and brought to the simmer. This will lift any residue left in the pan. Simmer, allowing it to reduce by a third to a half. Strain through a sieve and offer as a loose ham gravy.

Haslet

Haslet is a faggot-type mixture, traditional in the north of England, and is still found in many butchers', delicatessens and supermarkets. It is basically a pork-based terrine/loaf that, once cold, is sliced thinly before being served. Haslet was usually made using pig's pluck mixed with minced pork belly and pork back fat. Pig's pluck contains the heart, liver and lungs. This is almost impossible to find as a complete pluck (sheep's may be easier to find, for home-made haggis), but the ingredients should be quite readily available as individual pieces. To keep this recipe quite simple, I shall be using just pig's liver and heart mixed with pork shoulder meat and back fat.

Haslet is also classically made with sage, which gives it quite a distinctive flavour.

12–16 PORTIONS

1 pig's heart
350 g (12 oz) pig's liver
450 g (1 lb) pork shoulder
225 g (8 oz) pork back fat
3 large onions, finely chopped
1 tablespoon chopped fresh sage
4 slices of white bread (crusts removed), soaked
    in milk

¼–½ teaspoon freshly grated nutmeg
Salt and pepper
50 g (2 oz) butter or pork fat, for basting

For this recipe, a buttered terrine (30 × 8 × 8 cm/ 12 × 3 × 3 in) or a 900 g (2 lb) loaf tin can be used. Pre-heat the oven to 190°C/375°F/Gas Mark 5.

All of the meat and fat can either be hand chopped or minced. If mincing, a medium blade can be used. Once chopped or minced, add the chopped onions and sage. Remove the bread slices from the milk and squeeze out. Add to the meats, with the seasonings.

Place in the terrine or loaf tin and dot with the butter or pork fat. Cover with a lid or foil before cooking in the pre-heated oven for 50–60 minutes.

The lid or foil can be removed for the last 15 minutes of cooking time; this will give the haslet a golden brown finish. To check that the haslet is cooked, with its texture firm to the touch, insert a skewer. If the terrine is cooked, this will come out clean and hot.

Once cooked, remove from the oven. The haslet will have slightly shrunk away from the sides of the mould, releasing some of its juices. Another terrine or tin can be sat on top to press it lightly, giving the loaf a firmer texture. It is important any fat and juices are kept in the terrine, as these will create a good, moist finish to the haslet.

Once cool, refrigerate until completely set.

To turn out, dip the mould in warm water, releasing the haslet. Slice thinly before serving.

A good spoonful of home-made *Piccalilli* (page 385) will go very nicely, or serve with a well-flavoured English mustard.

Calves' Liver Steak with Blue Cheese Dumplings and Blue Cheese Butter Sauce

Calves' liver, for me, is one of the most tender and tasty types of offal. The steak here is basically a slice from the whole liver, which has been more thickly cut than usual. This is not essential, as many people prefer the classic thin slice that just takes seconds to cook when flashed in a hot pan and flipped over. The difference lies in the finished texture. The thicker-cut steak, which can be cooked to your liking, will hold a lot of good succulent juices, providing it's eaten medium-rare to medium.

Dumplings are a long-established accompaniment to meat and offal in the British tradition, but these potato dumplings are more like the Italian *gnocchi*. To the potato I've simply added English Stilton, plain flour and some eggs to create a lovely accompaniment for the liver. For a classic combination, pan-fry or grill thin slices of liver and serve with creamy *Mashed Potatoes* (page 124), *Onion Gravy* (page 50) and crispy bacon.

SERVES 6

6 × 175–225 g (6–8 oz) calves' liver steaks
Plain flour, seasoned, for dusting (optional)
Cooking oil
Butter
Salt and pepper

For the Dumplings

1 kg (2¼ lb) large potatoes, with skin left on
175 g (6 oz) Stilton or other blue cheese, chopped
175–200 g (6–7 oz) plain flour, sifted
1 egg
1 egg yolk
Salt, pepper and freshly grated nutmeg
Butter and olive or cooking oil, for pan-frying
    (optional)

For the Blue Cheese Butter Sauce

100 g (4 oz) unsalted butter, chilled and diced
1 shallot or ½ small onion, finely chopped
1 bay leaf
1 tablespoon white-wine vinegar
1 glass of white wine
100 ml (3½ fl oz) water or *Chicken Stock* (page 33)
2 tablespoons single cream
50 g (2 oz) Stilton or other blue cheese, chopped
Pepper

The dumplings can be made well in advance, so let's start with these.

Cook the potatoes whole in salted, boiling water until tender (generally approximately 20 minutes, depending on size.) Peel the warm potatoes and mash to a smooth texture. At this point, the cheese can be added. While the potato is still warm, the cheese will melt and spread through the mix. Add the flour, egg and egg yolk. Season with salt and pepper, being careful with the salt as most blue cheeses have a strong, seasoned flavour. Add a touch of grated nutmeg.

The dumpling mix is now made and is ready to be rolled into 1–2 cm (½–¾ in) balls. Simply take a good tablespoon of the mix and roll with floured hands or roll on a floured surface. Once all are rolled, the dumplings are ready to poach in simmering water for 3–4 minutes; 5 minutes is the maximum they will need. It's best to cook a handful at a time. Drop carefully into the water: you'll notice, as the cooking time passes, that they will rise to the top of the pan. It's at this point that they are ready. If not using immediately, refresh in iced water. They can be made to this stage in advance.

Once cooled, refrigerate the dumplings on trays and cover with cling film. They can be re-heated by pan-frying whenever needed. To pan-fry, melt a knob of butter along with a drop of olive or cooking oil in a frying-pan. Once the butter is beginning to bubble, add the dumplings. Fry on a medium heat until golden brown. This will have created another texture in the dumplings and completely warmed them through. They are now ready to serve.

Next make the blue cheese sauce. This is a basic butter sauce flavoured with blue cheese. If the quantity of butter frightens you a little, it can be halved, but an extra 4–5 tablespoons of single cream will be needed to give the same quantity.

Melt a small knob of the butter, adding the chopped shallot or onion with the bay leaf. Cook for a few minutes without colour, until softened. Add the white-wine vinegar, allowing to simmer and reduce by three-quarters. Add the white wine and also reduce by three-quarters. Pour in the water or stock and reduce by half. The single cream can now be added. Return to the simmer. The remaining butter, best chilled, can be whisked in a little at a time. The chopped blue cheese can now also be added. Allow the sauce to simmer only slightly so as not to separate the cheese. Season with a twist of pepper and, once the cheese has melted, strain through a sieve. If the sauce is too thick, add a drop or two more of water or stock.

The sauce is now ready to serve. For a light, creamy effect and taste, blitz with an electric hand-blender. This puts air into the sauce and lightens it.

Now for the liver. If grilling or pan-frying, the liver can first be lightly coated in seasoned flour. This will create a thin, crisp texture and also helps prevent the liver from sticking to a pan or grill.

Heat a frying-pan with a little cooking oil. Once hot, place the steaks in the pan. I don't like to put salt and pepper directly onto any raw liver. The salt draws blood from the liver and also burns the meat. Cook for 3–4 minutes before adding a knob of butter. Continue to cook for another minute before turning the steaks over. Now season with salt and pepper on the seared side. Continue to cook on a medium heat for another 4–5 minutes. Season the other seared side and place on the plates. The steaks are now ready to serve.

The dumplings can just be placed next to the steak and the sauce drizzled over. It's also quite nice to offer the dumplings separately, allowing people to help themselves. If you've 'poached' the steaks, as explained below, then just pour a little of the sauce over the meat.

Note: Buttered spinach, kale, greens or leeks all eat very well with this dish. If using one of these leafy green vegetables, then why not arrange it on the plates, sitting the liver steak on top? Once quickly sealed on both sides, a calves' liver steak can be 'poached' in warm stock or *jus*. It's a 'soft' way of cooking

OPPOSITE
Calves' Liver Steak with Blue Cheese Dumplings and Blue Cheese Butter Sauce

liver steaks. Simply take some stock (perhaps flavoured with red wine) and warm to not quite a simmer. The liver can just be dropped in and allowed to warm and cook through. Literally 7–8 minutes will give you a medium-rare stage – that's for a 225 g (8 oz) steak approximately 2 cm (¾ in) thick. If poaching the liver in gravy, an extra sauce can quickly be made from it. Once the meat is cooked, some of the gravy can be reduced to a rich and shiny consistency.

Pressed Ox Tongue

Ox tongue is a substantial, soft and tasty meat. It used to be boiled, or boiled then roasted (spiked with cloves), potted and made into brawn along with ox cheeks and palates.

Most ox tongues bought these days will have been previously pickled in a sweet brine. The tongues are rubbed with salt and then left to pickle in a mixture of water, salt and sugar. This pickling process takes anything from 4–6 days. It's at this stage that you'll probably buy it. Unsalted or unpickled tongue can be used as well, but tends to take a fair bit longer to poach.

It's best to buy the tongue 48 hours before you are going to serve the dish. This will then give 24 hours of soaking in cold water and the following day for cooking and pressing. Once the tongue has been cooked and cleaned it can also be set in its own jelly. To achieve a better flavour, one or two split calves' feet can be added to the liquor. This will help the liquor with its gelling (see opposite).

Cold tongue will eat very well with many of the pickles/chutneys featured in this book or, once cooked and trimmed, could be served hot with your own home-made gravy and *Mashed Potatoes* (page 124). A *Mustard Butter Sauce* (page 53) is a traditional accompaniment.

The quantity of ox tongue will provide many thin slices for a cold buffet, but will give 6–8 generous portions for a main course.

SERVES 6–8 GENEROUSLY

1.6–1.8 kg (3½–4 lb) ox tongue, pre-soaked
    in water for 24 hours
1 large onion, thickly sliced
2 carrots, thickly sliced
4 celery sticks, thickly sliced
1 bay leaf
Sprig of thyme
8 black peppercorns

Cover the tongue well with water and bring to the boil. Cook for 6–7 minutes and then refresh under cold water. This will lift impurities from the tongue and pan.

Wipe the saucepan clean and replace the tongue. Cover with 3 litres (5½ pints) of water and again bring to the boil, skimming away any further impurities. Simmer, skim and cook for 30 minutes more before adding the vegetables, bay leaf, thyme and peppercorns. The tongue can now be gently simmered for another 3–3½ hours.

Once cooked, remove the tongue and quickly dip into cold water. This will calm its fierce heat, making it easier to peel away the skin. Once peeled, any tiny bones at the root end of the tongue can be pulled away and the meat neatly trimmed.

The tongue, while still hot, can be curled and fitted into a 15 cm (6 in) soufflé dish or a cake tin. Press with a suitable plate and a weight and leave to set overnight in the fridge.

If you would prefer to make a jelly, strain away 1 litre (1¾ pints) of the cooking liquor, boil and reduce by at least half. This will have strengthened the jelly. It's important to taste the liquor, making sure it isn't becoming too salty. If the flavour seems shallow, add 2 teaspoons of chicken or beef stock granules. This will add body. The jelly can be tested on a side plate. If it's not setting, 2–3 teaspoons or a leaf of gelatine (following instructions on packets) can be added. If using stock cubes and gelatine, strain again before pouring onto the tongue. Set, pressing lightly as above, preferably overnight.

The tongue eats very well and maintains a very moist finish when set in jelly. Simply slice and serve.

Black Pudding

Black pudding is quite an acquired taste, but what a taste that is. Good-quality black pudding is so good to eat, whether as part of your breakfast plate or working its way into any other recipe. You'll find a few recipes in this book that include the pudding, which I think demonstrates how much I love this culinary treat.

A good friend of mine, Jack Morris, runs his own butcher's shop in Bolton. He has become renowned throughout the world for his home-made black pudding, a recipe that has won many international titles, often leaving the French *boudin noir* way behind. As much as I tried to twist his arm, the famous recipe was not released (and I don't blame him), so here's a recipe that's almost as good. It contains extra flavours and ingredients, making it quite an adventurous black pudding. The recipe specifies fresh pig's blood, which cannot be used any more (dried blood is substituted), but I thought I would include an original recipe, just to give you an idea of how the puddings were once made.

A basic black-pudding recipe would, classically, be made from pearl barley, rice or groats (these are unprocessed oats, which look similar to birdseed, available from pet shops or health-food shops), fine oatmeal, pork fat, onions, pig's blood and seasonings.

Jack told me a little story of the 'other Black Beauties', as he calls them, and of how they came to England. Here's that story. The black pudding started its life in Europe. Monks, who kept their own livestock, also grew their own herbs and cereals. When the pig was slaughtered, they caught the blood, added cereal, herbs, seasonings and diced fat and mixed them together very much as we do today. The intestines were then filled and boiled in a large pan. The name was 'Blut Wurst', blood sausage. The monks travelled through Europe and then arrived in England, settling in Yorkshire, where the name was changed to 'blood pudding'. Eventually they crossed the Pennines into Lancashire, where the sausage became famous and was known as 'black pudding'.

Here's the recipe for a new 'Black Beauty', which makes a large quantity of sausages. If pig's head is unavailable, substitute with three or four pig's trotters, cooked for 2–3 hours.

MAKES 25–30 BLACK PUDDINGS

For the Pig's-head Liquor

1 boned pig's head, rolled and tied
1 onion, studded with 2 cloves
1 large carrot, chopped
Green from diced white leeks, chopped (see method)
1 teaspoon crushed black peppercorns
1 heaped teaspoon cayenne pepper
Salt
Sprig of thyme
1 bay leaf
3 litres (5¼ pints) water

For the Black-pudding Mixture

250 g (9 oz) pinhead oats
Butter
350 g (12 oz) chopped onions
350 g (12 oz) white of leek, cut into 5 mm (¼ in) dice
2 garlic cloves, crushed
350 g (12 oz) bacon, cut into 5 mm (¼ in) dice
350 g (12 oz) pork back fat, cut into 5 mm (¼ in) dice
1 tablespoon chopped fresh thyme
1 tablespoon chopped fresh tarragon
3 litres (5¼ pints) pig's blood, or dried blood equivalent
Salt, pepper, cayenne pepper and ground mace
5 metres (5 yards) sausage casing, soaked in cold water for several hours

To cook the pig's head, place all ingredients for the liquor in a large saucepan and bring to the simmer. Cook for at least 3 hours, then check the head has become tender. If not, continue to simmer for a total of 4 hours.

Remove from the heat, placing the head in a suitable container and strain the stock over. Allow to cool and the jelly to set. The head can now be removed and the meat cut into 1–2 cm (½–¾ in) dice.

Toast the pinhead oats until golden brown to achieve a nutty texture and flavour.

In a large pan, melt a knob of butter, adding the chopped onions. Cook for 5 minutes until softened before adding the dice of white leek and the crushed garlic. Add the bacon and continue to cook for 5–6 minutes. The diced pig's-head meat can now also be added, reducing the heat to a gentle warmth. Blanch the back fat in boiling water and drain. Add to the sausage ingredients. The fresh herbs and pinhead oats can now also be added to the mix.

Stir the blood well and pass through a sieve. Pour and stir into the sausage mix. It is now important to stir the blood in the pan, checking its temperature as you heat it to 40°C/104°F. At this point it will begin to coagulate and thicken. The blood must not pass this temperature or it will start to spoil. The absolute maximum it can reach is 50°C (122°F). Remove from the heat and season generously with salt, pepper, cayenne and ground mace.

The sausage casing can now be filled. This is best achieved – to ensure the fat content is equally distributed – using a funnel or piping bag with a plain nozzle, stirring the mix to maintain the even spreading of flavours. As sausages are piped tie the casings at about 15 cm (6 in) intervals, and continue.

The sausages can now be poached in the stock already made or salted water, heating to no more than 80°C (170°F). Poach for 15 minutes, then remove from the heat and leave to stand for a further 15 minutes in the liquor.

The black puddings can now be removed and, once cooled, refrigerated.

To serve, the sausages can be re-heated in warm water, split and grilled, or sliced and pan-fried or grilled.

Even if you never get the chance to make black pudding, at least you now know how this recipe is made.

Calves' Liver Steak and Kidney, with Red-wine Carrots and Rosemary Butter

Liver and kidneys together are always a pleasure to eat. This dish is a favourite with offal-lovers, the kidney roasted on top of the stove with a nugget of rosemary butter melting inside, the liver steak pan-fried and served on the red-wine carrots, topped with pan-fried spring onions. All of these ingredients give very fresh flavours.

The kidney is being presented on a roast potato disc. These are very easy to make and everybody enjoys roast potatoes.

This recipe is for four portions, but one large veal kidney, when cut, will sometimes give you five portions. I'm also wrapping these kidney portions in pig's caul. This is not the easiest product to obtain so, if unavailable, make the dish without it.

SERVES 4

1 medium-sized veal kidney
100 g (4 oz) pig's caul, soaked for several hours
    (page 11, optional)
4 × 175 g (6 oz) calves' liver steaks, approx.
    1 cm (½ in) thick
Plain flour, for coating
Cooking oil
Butter
Salt and pepper
Bunch of spring onions, cut into 5 mm (¼ in) pieces

For the Butter Sauce

1 tablespoon chopped rosemary
100 g (4 oz) butter, softened
2 tablespoons white-wine vinegar
1 glass of white wine
100 ml (3½ fl oz) *Chicken Stock* (page 33)
1 tablespoon double cream
Squeeze of lemon juice

For the Red-wine Carrots

2–3 large carrots, peeled
100 ml (3½ fl oz) *Chicken Stock* (page 33)
    or water

Butter
Pinch of sugar
2–3 glasses of red wine

For the Roast Potatoes

2 large Cara potatoes, peeled
Plain flour, for coating
Cooking oil
Butter

For the Red-wine Sauce

2 glasses of red wine
150 ml (¼ pint) *Veal or Beef Jus* (page 34) or
    alternative (page 11)

First, make the butter sauce. Mix the chopped fresh
rosemary with the butter. Refrigerate to set. Once
cold, take 25 g (1 oz) and separate into four small
nuggets. These will be used to fill the kidney.

The kidney can be bought in or out of suet fat.
If bought in, the fat will need to be removed. Now
the inner fat and veins should be cut away carefully,
leaving an open, cleaned kidney. Divide into four.
Season the inside and place a rosemary butter nugget
in the centre of each piece. Wrap the kidney around
the butter, creating four faggot-sized kidneys. If
using pig's caul, squeeze dry and open into a large
net. Cut into four pieces, wrapping each kidney
faggot. Refrigerate until needed.

If pig's caul is unavailable, simply leave the four
kidney pieces without any butter nuggets. Once
roasted on top of the stove the rosemary butter can
then be added, rolling the kidneys to coat them.

For the red-wine carrots, cut the carrots into
thin sticks (6 cm × 5 mm/2¼ × ¼ in). Place the stock
or water and carrots in a saucepan with a knob of
butter and pinch of sugar.

Bring to the simmer and cook for 6–8 minutes
until the carrots are tender. Remove the carrots from
the liquor and keep to one side.

Boil and reduce the cooking liquor by three-
quarters to a syrupy consistency. In a separate pan,
reduce the red wine also by three-quarters. The two
can be mixed together. This is the red-wine liquor
we will now use to re-heat the carrots when needed.

Pre-heat the oven to 200°C/400°F/Gas Mark 6.
Cut two discs (6–7 × 2 cm/2½ × ¾ in) from each Cara
potato. These can now be poached in salted water
until just cooked through. This will take 12–15
minutes. Once cooked, drain and lightly coat with
flour while still warm. Heat 2 mm (a thin layer) of
cooking oil in a frying- or roasting-pan and place the
potatoes in it. Fry until golden brown and crispy.
Turn the potatoes over and repeat to the same stage.

Add a knob of butter and finish by roasting in
the pre-heated oven for 5–6 minutes. Remove and
season with a pinch of salt. The golden crispy
potatoes are ready.

Now heat the white-wine vinegar in a small
saucepan and reduce by half. Add the white wine,
boil and reduce by three-quarters. Add the chicken
stock and reduce by half. This reduction can now be
kept until the sauce is needed. To finish, re-heat the
reduction, adding the double cream. The remaining
rosemary butter can now be whisked in, not allowing
the sauce to boil again. Season with salt and pepper.
Add a squeeze of lemon juice to lift and finish the
sauce.

Now, make the red-wine sauce. Boil and reduce
the red wine by three-quarters. Add the *jus* and cook
for a few minutes. Adjust the seasoning with salt and
pepper. The sauce is ready.

To finish the dish, heat two frying-pans. Season
the kidneys with salt and pepper. Add a drop of
cooking oil to both pans. Place the kidneys in one of
the pans and fry, colouring all around. Cooked on
top of the stove, the kidneys will take approximately
5 minutes, maintaining a slightly pink centre.

Dust the liver with just a little flour and
also begin to pan-fry. Once coloured on one side
(2 minutes), add a knob of butter and turn the liver
over. Continue to cook for a further 2 minutes,
seasoning with salt and pepper.

While the liver and kidneys are cooking, the
carrots can be re-heated in the red-wine liquor.
As they heat, the liquor will reduce, coating the
carrots. Season with salt and pepper.

Heat the red-wine sauce. Once warm, keep to
one side, reducing just 2–3 tablespoons to a thicker

consistency. The sauce can now be brushed over the kidneys and liver to give a rich glaze.

The potatoes can now be placed on the left-hand side of the plates, arranging the red-wine carrot sticks on the right. While arranging the plate, quickly pan-fry the spring onions in a knob of butter, without colour, and season. Place the roasted kidney on top of the roast potato. Spoon 2–3 tablespoons of red-wine sauce over the carrots, placing the liver on top. Now just finish the dish with the spring onions spooned on top of the liver and the rosemary butter sauce around the kidney. The dish is complete.

Note: There are quite a few components to this dish, but if you prepare as much as possible in advance, it becomes quite simple. Here are a few tips on how to make the finishing simpler.
1 Cook and glaze the carrots early with the red-wine reduction. These can now be refrigerated and microwaved when needed.
2 Colour the potatoes on one side only. Finish on the other side in a hot oven when needed.
3 Have both sauces ready, the butter sauce just needing the butter to be whisked in, the separate red-wine glaze reduced and ready.

Pigs' Trotters *Bourguignonne*

This dish is one I dream of becoming the ultimate 'new classic'. Trotters are just amazing to eat. They need some care and attention, and a fair bit of work is involved, but the results merit all that – and more.

Eating pigs' trotters is a very British thing to do. They became part of 'street eating' in the eighteenth century and, in Ireland, used to be a traditional pub food until not so long ago. Crubeens, salted pigs' trotters, are a speciality of Cork.

This trotter dish is well up to date, though. I've taken the *bourguignonne* garnishes from France, usually button onions, mushrooms and bacon, which are served with joints or sautés with a red-wine sauce. Well, I'm doing exactly that here; the difference being that I'm putting the onions, mushrooms and bacon *inside* the actual trotters. These are bound with

a rich pork stuffing also flavoured with *foie gras* (this is not essential). So as you eat this lovely dish, you experience many flavours.

This recipe will fill 6–8 trotters. Ask your butcher to bone the trotters for you. Hind trotters give you a better shape and more trotter. They might need to be singed to remove any hair and then they are best soaked in water for 24 hours. They are best made a day before you wish to eat them, so start the preparation 48 hours in advance. This gives the stuffing time to become firm in the trotters, which will then hold their shape and texture perfectly.

SERVES 6

6 boned pigs' trotters, preferably hind, singed and soaked in cold water for 24 hours

For the Cooking Liquor

Butter
1 onion, chopped
1 carrot, chopped
2 celery sticks, chopped
Sprig of thyme
1 bay leaf
Few black peppercorns
Bottle of red wine (for maximum flavour)
600 ml (1 pint) *Chicken Stock* (page 33)
300 ml (½ pint) *Veal or Beef Jus* (page 34)

For the Stuffing

75–100 g (3–4 oz) *foie gras*, chilled (if unavailable, increase the minced pork quantity)
225 g (8 oz) finely minced lean pork meat, chilled
100 g (4 oz) finely minced pork fat, chilled
1 egg
Knob of butter
2 tablespoons finely chopped shallots

OPPOSITE
Pigs' Trotters Bourguignonne

1 large garlic clove, crushed
1 teaspoon chopped fresh thyme
100 g (4 oz) chicken livers, soaked in milk for
    24 hours
200 ml (7 fl oz) double cream
Splash each of Armagnac and Madeira (or brandy,
    if neither is available)
2–3 tablespoons of thick *jus* (take 5–6 tablespoons
    of cooking liquor and reduce by half before
    chilling and adding)
Salt and pepper

For the Garnish

75–100 g (3–4 oz) button onions
50 g (2 oz) butter
75–100 g (3–4 oz) button mushrooms, quartered
75 g (3 oz) unsmoked bacon or cooked ham, cut
    into 5 mm (¼ in) dice

To cook the trotters, pre-heat the oven to 160°C/ 325°F/Gas Mark 3.

Melt a knob of butter in a braising pan large enough to hold the raw trotters. Add the chopped vegetables, thyme, bay leaf and peppercorns. Cook, allowing to take on a little colour, for 4–5 minutes. Add the red wine, a quarter of the bottle at a time. Reduce by two-thirds before adding more wine, continue to add and reduce until all is added.

The stock and *jus* can now be added, along with the raw trotters. Bring to the simmer, cover with a lid and place in the oven. These can now gently braise for 2½–3 hours until completely tender. To check, simply lift and pinch the trotter skin. This should give and tear very easily. Once cooked, leave to rest in the liquor for 20 minutes.

Butter six large squares of foil. Sit a trotter, open-side up, on each square. They are now ready to fill.

The cooking liquor can now be strained through a sieve. Bring to the simmer and skim off any impurities and also check the consistency and seasoning. The flavour should be quite powerful. Reduce to strengthen and thicken if needed. Once ready, take 10–12 tablespoons of this sauce and boil to reduce by half. This gives you a glossy glaze to paint the trotters with just before serving.

For the stuffing, blitz the *foie gras*, if using, in a food processor and mix with the minced pork meat and fat. Blitz all together for a combined mix. Season well with salt and pepper and add the egg.

The mix is best placed in a stainless-steel bowl or equivalent over a bowl of ice. This will keep the filling firm. Failing that, make sure the food processor is cold, along with all of the ingredients.

Melt a knob of butter in a frying-pan. Once hot, add the chopped shallots, garlic and thyme. Remove the livers from the milk and dry on kitchen paper. Add the livers to the shallots, increase the heat and pan-fry for 2–3 minutes. Leave to cool. These can now also be blitzed and stirred into the pork mix. Now it's time to stir in the double cream a little at a time, mixing well to hold a good consistency. Once all has been added, season again with salt and pepper. Add a splash each of Armagnac and Madeira (or brandy) and pour in the reduced *jus*.

The stuffing is now ready. To test, a spoonful can be poached in lightly simmering water. This will only take 2–3 minutes to cook. From this you can check its seasoning and texture. If very firm, a drop of two more cream can be added, but be careful as too much will spoil the mix.

For the garnish, blanch the button onions in boiling water for 2–3 minutes. Drain and allow to cool naturally. Once cooled, cut each in half.

Melt some of the butter, add the onions, cut-side down, and allow to fry and become golden with tinges of caramelizing. This will take 6–7 minutes. Turn the onions over and continue to cook for another 4–5 minutes. Remove and allow to cool.

After wiping the pan clean, melt another knob of the butter. Once bubbling, add the quartered button mushrooms. Fry until golden brown and

tender. This will take only 4–5 minutes on a fast heat.

On a low heat, melt the remaining butter and add the bacon. This can now just be gently fried, without colour, for 2–3 minutes. (If using cooked ham, just leave in its cooked state.) Once all of the garnish has chilled, fold gently into the stuffing.

Divide and spoon between the trotters. It's best to shape the stuffing cylindrically, creating a shape to fold the trotter skin around. The trotters are best made reasonably plump, keeping the size and shape of the original trotter. Once all are filled, the foil can be rolled around, twisting at either end. For extra firmness, wrap all again with another square of foil.

The trotters are best if now refrigerated for 24 hours.

To serve, steam the trotters for 18–20 minutes. While the trotters are steaming, the sauce and glaze can be re-heated.

Once cooked, allow the trotters to rest for 5 minutes before carefully removing the foil. Brush each with the glaze and present on plates or in large bowls. The sauce can now be poured over or offered separately. These trotters eat like a dream with *Mashed Potato Sauce* (page 125).

Note: If a steamer is unavailable, then sit the trotters in a roasting tray in 5 mm (¼ in) of hot water. These can now be baked in a pre-heated oven at 190°C/375°F/Gas Mark 5, for 15–18 minutes. Leave to rest before serving.

Irish Stew

This famous Irish meat and potato stew is a classic example of the dishes that evolved when most households had only one cooking pot that could be heated over a fire. The stew has a combination of ingredients that would have been fairly ready to hand – some lamb or mutton, lots of onions and, inevitably in Ireland, lots of potatoes.

It is a dish that can be prepared and cooked in many different ways. You can look in a dozen cookery books and you'll find a dozen varying recipes. Some add carrots, others think this is sacrilege. Some put potatoes on the bottom to create a sauce and thicken the juices, and then top with more potatoes. A few recipes include a handful of pearl barley, which would make the dish more substantial. Here's my version for you to try.

SERVES 4

675 g (1½ lb) middle neck of lamb, cut into cutlets
100 g (4 oz) unsalted butter
4 onions, sliced
450 g (1 lb) potatoes, peeled and cut into rough dice
1 garlic clove
1 bouquet garni (1 bay leaf, 1 sprig each of fresh rosemary and thyme tied in a square of muslin or strip of leek) or bouquet garni sachet
1.5 litres (2½ pints) *Chicken Stock* (page 33) or water
175 g (6 oz) carrots, sliced
6 celery sticks, cut into 2.5 cm (1 in) pieces
225 g (8 oz) Savoy cabbage, shredded
Salt and pepper
2 teaspoons chopped fresh parsley, to garnish

Cover the meat with cold water in a large pan and bring to the boil. Drain off the water and refresh the meat in cold water. Drain well.

Melt the butter in a large braising pan and add the sliced onions, half the diced potatoes and the garlic. Add the bouquet garni to the pan and sweat for 2 minutes. Add the lamb cutlets and cover with the chicken stock. Bring the stock to the simmer, cover and cook for 30 minutes. The meat will be half-cooked and the potatoes will have started to purée and thicken the stock.

Add the diced carrots and continue to cook for a further 10 minutes. Add the remaining potatoes and the diced celery and cook for 15–20 minutes. At this stage we do not want to purée the potatoes but just cook them until soft. Add the cabbage and cook for another 2–3 minutes until the meat and vegetables are tender. Season with salt and pepper, remove the bouquet garni and serve in individual bowls or one large bowl. Finish with the chopped parsley. You now have a complete meal.

Boiled Bacon with Pearl Barley and Lentils

After the killing of the pig in the autumn, most households would have a barrel of salted or pickled pork to last throughout the winter. There would also be a barrel of dried beans, and the combination was the dietary mainstay of most of the British throughout the centuries.

There are so many alternative ways of serving boiled bacon. It still eats well with dried beans –

BELOW
Irish Stew

which would have been the broad variety before kidney beans were introduced from America – with other pulses or grains, such as pearl barley and lentils, and even just parsley sauce. It could be made into a winter soup. The bacon can also be served with *Braised Split Peas* (page 117), with just a little stock spooned over. Any leftover stock can be frozen for soup-making, some sauces, or even your next boiled bacon.

SERVES 6–8

1.8 kg (4 lb) unsmoked rolled bacon collar, rind removed
5 carrots
4 onions
2 celery sticks
1 leek
Sprig of thyme
1 bay leaf
1.75–2.25 litres (3–4 pints) *Chicken Stock* (page 33)
75 g (3 oz) pearl barley
1 large swede
2 large parsnips
100 g (4 oz) unsalted butter
1 tablespoon chopped fresh parsley
Salt and pepper
Mashed Potatoes (page 124), to serve

For the Braised Lentils

Butter
1 onion, finely diced
50 g (2 oz) green lentils, preferably *lentilles de Puys*
200 ml (⅓ pint) *Chicken Stock* (page 33) or *Vegetable Stock* (page 36)

Soak the bacon in water for 24 hours before cooking. This will reduce the salt content.

Put the bacon in a large pot. Coarsely chop two of the carrots, 1 of the onions, the celery and leek and add to the pot, with the herbs. Cover with chicken stock, bring to the simmer, skim off any impurities, cover again and cook gently for about 1½ hours until cooked. Allow to rest for 30 minutes in the stock.

To cook the lentils, melt a knob of butter in a small ovenproof braising pan. Add the diced onion

and cook for a few minutes. Pour in the lentils, stirring well. Cover with the stock and bring to a simmer. Cover with a lid and braise in the pre-heated oven for about 30–35 minutes until the lentils are tender and all the stock has been absorbed. If the stock is absorbed before they become tender, simply re-loosen with water. When ready, season with salt and pepper.

Cook the pearl barley in approximately 400 ml (¾ pint) of the cooking liquor for about 15–20 minutes until soft. Meanwhile, cut the remaining carrots and onions, the swede and parsnips into 1 cm (½ in) dice and sweat in half the butter. Add the pearl barley and a little more stock, if necessary, to give a soup consistency. Allow this to simmer for about 15 minutes until all the vegetables are tender. Add the cooked lentils, the remaining butter and the chopped parsley to create a barley, lentil and vegetable stew. Check for seasoning.

To serve, sit the warm mashed potatoes in the centre of the serving plates and spoon some of the stew around. Slice the bacon, allowing two slices per portion, and place on the potatoes. Finish with a spoonful of stock on top of the meat and serve.

Boiled Brisket of Beef and Vegetable Stew

Boiled meat used to be much more common than it is now. Meat that had been salted, as most meats were from the Middle Ages right up until the nineteenth century, had to be boiled (or stewed): cooked in any other way it would be hard and unpalatable. I love the tenderness of boiled meat, and hope that this recipe will reintroduce you to a great, traditionally British, meat-cooking technique.

Brisket is a cut of beef taken from the forequarter. It is normally pickled in brine, which is a combination of salt, saltpetre and water. The beef can be kept in brine for up to ten days. This will help tenderize the cut. If buying brisket already salted, I suggest it is soaked in fresh water for 24–48 hours to release some of the salt flavour.

1 sheep's pluck (lungs, heart and liver)
Chicken Stock (page 33) or water
Carrot, onion, celery and leek, chopped (optional)
6 large onions, finely chopped
25 g (1 oz) unsalted butter or a little cooking oil
175 g (6 oz) pinhead oats
100 g (4 oz) shredded suet
½ teaspoon chopped fresh thyme
½ teaspoon chopped fresh sage
2 teaspoons salt
Pinch of cayenne pepper
Pinch of black pepper
Finely grated zest and juice of 1 lemon
    (optional)
225–450 g (8–16 oz) pig's caul to wrap the haggis
    (page 11, optional, needed if not using
    pudding basins), soaked overnight in cold
    water
Mashed Potatoes (page 124), to serve

If you have difficulty buying a complete sheep's pluck (containing the lungs, heart and liver), then simply buy a sheep's heart, lung and liver separately. These can be cooked in the same way. Wash the pluck, place in a pan and cover with chicken stock or water. (Chicken stock will give you a stronger flavour and more of a jellied finish.) It's best to add some chopped carrot, onion, celery and leek to the stock or water to increase the flavour. The windpipe from the pluck should be left hanging out of the pan to drip into an empty pan. The pluck can now be simmered for 12 hours. Once cooked, leave to cool in the pan, then set in stock overnight. Remove the windpipe. The heart, lungs and liver can now be minced through a medium mincer or chopped; you will need about 1.1 kg (2½ lb) in total. The liver obviously has a very powerful taste; I prefer to use only half to balance the flavours.

The cooking liquor should be tasted for flavour and seasoning. Should it taste a little weak, then simply return to the boil and boil to reduce and increase the depth of flavour. Up to 600 ml (1 pint) of stock will be needed for the haggis mix to give a good moist texture.

The chopped onions can be lightly softened, without colour, in the butter or a drop of oil, then allowed to cool. The pinhead oats can be toasted to a golden brown colour. All the ingredients can now be mixed together, including the meat, herbs, salt, cayenne and pepper, plus the stock to finish the mix. It should be well seasoned, giving a full flavour with a bite from the cayenne pepper. Lemon zest and juice can also be added to this mix to lift the other flavours. Divide the mix into 8–10 portions.

If you are using pig's caul, drain the soaked caul, squeeze out excess water and lay it on a chopping board. Cut into 8–10 evenly sized pieces. Wrap each portion in the caul to make oval shapes. To keep the shape and prevent the caul from splitting, also wrap each portion in buttered foil. If pig's caul is unavailable, then simply wrap each portion in cling film twice, then also in foil.

To cook, simply boil any remaining stock with the addition of water to give enough quantity to cover the haggis. The haggis portions can now be cooked in the simmering liquor for 45–60 minutes. Once cooked, they will keep hot in the stock. Some stock can be strained off and made into a gravy for the haggis. I always like to eat them straight from the stock, the mix being moist enough because of the added stock. Of course, while it was cooking the mashed turnips/swedes will also be on the stove along with mashed potatoes to finish the dish.

Variation

While I was staying in Glasgow and feeling peckish – it was probably 9.30–10.00 p.m. – I decided to pop into a fish and chip shop for a bite to eat. To my surprise I ended up eating the speciality of the house. It was battered deep-fried haggis with curry sauce! Certainly a dish I hadn't tried before and probably what worried me was that I really loved it.

So there's another option, if you have any haggis left over. Once it's cold, just lightly flour, dip in batter (lager mixed with self-raising flour to a thick consistency makes a brilliant batter), and deep-fry until golden. Now just serve a good curry sauce to go with it.

Faggots in Onion Gravy

The word faggot means a bundle, as of twigs for kindling a fire, so almost anything can be brought together to make that bundle. I've made faggots with beef and offal as here, and also with pigeon (*Rich Pigeon Faggot on a Potato Cake with Mustard Cabbage*, page 252).

I usually use the trimmings from cuts of beef when I make these particular faggots. Pig's caul (the lining of a pig's stomach) is the classic wrapping for faggots, and your butcher should be able to get some for you. (It needs to be soaked in cold water for 24 hours before use.) Alternatively, you can fry the faggots without the caul, as for meatballs, but the finish and flavour won't be quite the same.

The best dishes to serve with faggots are *Colcannon* (page 126) or *Mashed Potatoes* (page 124).

SERVES 4

2 onions, finely chopped
1 garlic clove, crushed
½ teaspoon fresh thyme leaves
½ teaspoon chopped fresh sage
½ teaspoon chopped fresh parsley
50 g (2 oz) unsalted butter
150 ml (¼ pint) *Veal or Beef Jus* (page 34)
175 g (6 oz) lean beef rump or topside, well trimmed
175 g (6 oz) ox heart, trimmed
175 g (6 oz) ox kidney, trimmed
175 g (6 oz) lamb's liver, trimmed
Salt and pepper
1 egg
450 g (1 lb) pig's caul, soaked in cold water for 24 hours (page 11)

To Finish

1.2 litres (2 pints) *Veal or Beef Stock* (page 34)
25 g (1 oz) beef dripping
Onion Gravy (page 50)

Cook the chopped onions, garlic and herbs in the butter until soft. Add the veal or beef *jus* and boil to reduce by half. Leave to cool, then allow to set in the fridge.

Mince the meats through a medium cutter. Place all the minced meat in a mixer and beat slowly, adding salt and pepper to taste. The salt will also thicken the meat, giving a gelatinous texture. Add the egg and the reduced, cool onion mix. The faggot mixture is now ready, and is best left chilled for 2–3 hours to set more firmly.

To form the faggots, squeeze any excess water from the caul and cut it into eight 20 cm (8 in) squares. Spoon about 75 g (3 oz) of the faggot mixture into the centre of each square and wrap and turn the caul around the meat to form firm ball shapes.

When you are ready to cook the faggots, warm the veal or beef stock. Fry the faggots in the dripping until brown on all sides, then place them in the stock and simmer very gently for 12–15 minutes until just starting to firm up. Remove the pan from the heat and leave to rest. The faggots can now be allowed to cool, left in the cooking liquor, and chilled. The liquor will set like a jelly and keep the faggots for up to a week in the fridge.

When you want to serve the faggots, warm them gently in the jelly for 15–20 minutes until tender. To serve, lift the faggots from the liquor. Sit the onion gravy on top and serve.

Note: Once cooked, the faggots can be frozen for up to 1 month. The freezing process softens and improves the texture.

Bolognese Sauce or Beef Fillet, Bacon, Chicken Liver and Red-wine *Ragù*

Spaghetti bolognese, which has become so much part of British eating, is a great Italian dish – or is it? In fact, bolognese sauce doesn't really exist in Italy. The only sauce that resembles the British one is the *ragù bolognese*. This is a sauce that must contain at least two meats, beef and pork being the classics. The recipe I'm making here has three meats – beef, bacon and chicken livers.

From reading and researching through many books and recipes, and having the pleasure of eating many huge bowls of spaghetti (with a good glass of red wine to help them along), this recipe has become my favourite. The ingredients work so well together. If you are not a fan of bacon and chicken livers, simply replace them with extra beef. Another extravagant detail, you'll notice, is the use of beef fillet, the most expensive cut of beef. The results are so good that it's money well spent. I use only beef fillet tail pieces, though, which you'll often find are half the price of the prime cut. The meat can be either coarsely minced or shredded by hand, to give a meatier texture.

Please don't be put off by these extras. The recipe can still be made using our everyday minced beef with red wine and tomato passata (passata is Italian for sieved tomatoes, like the French tomato *coulis*, and is available in almost every supermarket). The flavours are full and the consistency is very saucy, rather than just moist mince.

As for pasta to go with this sauce, that's really up to you. Home-made linguine, fettuccine or tagliatelle would be great, but bought spaghetti or other pastas will all suit the sauce perfectly.

The method might sound like a lot of work, but it isn't really: we use only two pans and do a bit of chopping. The result is exceptional and once you've tried it you won't want to make your bolognese any other way or eat any other kind.

SERVES 4–6

175 g (6 oz) chicken livers, cut into rough 1 cm (½ in) dice
Butter
6 rashers of streaky bacon, finely diced
1 large or 2 medium onions, finely chopped
1 large or 2 medium carrots, finely chopped
2 celery sticks, finely chopped
1 large garlic clove, finely chopped or crushed
2–3 glasses of red wine
450 g (1 lb) beef fillet tails/trimmings, coarsely minced or shredded
Olive oil
225 g (8 oz) tomato passata
1 teaspoon tomato purée
6 tomatoes, blanched, skinned and cut into 1 cm (½ in) dice (or a 400 g/14 oz tin of chopped tomatoes, drained of all liquor)

150–200 ml (5–7 fl oz) *Veal or Beef Jus* (page 34)
Salt, pepper and freshly grated nutmeg

Whenever using chicken livers for any recipe it's best to soak them for 24 hours in milk. This will help release excess blood from the livers, making them less bitter. Once soaked, dry on a cloth and cut into 1 cm (½ in) dice.

Melt a knob of butter in a frying-pan, preferably non-stick, and once bubbling add the diced bacon. Fry until golden before transferring to a saucepan.

Now place the onions, carrots, celery and garlic in the frying-pan. The vegetables will lift any bacon flavour left in the pan. Cook for a few minutes until slightly softened and coloured. Add to the bacon. Stir them together and add half a glass of red wine. On a medium–high heat allow this to reduce by at least three-quarters until almost dry. Add another half a glass and continue with the same process until all has been added and reduced.

While the wine is reducing, the beef can be seasoned with the salt, pepper and nutmeg. Heat the frying-pan with some olive oil until very hot. Fry the beef, a handful or two at a time, until well sealed and coloured. Keep to one side. Season the chicken livers and also fry in olive oil very quickly to seal. Also keep separate. Add the passata, tomato purée, half of the diced tomato and the *jus* to the vegetables. Bring to the simmer. The beef can now be added, still leaving the liver separate.

Return to the simmer and cook for 45 minutes. At this point, if the sauce is too thick then simply loosen with water. Add the chicken livers, return to the simmer and cook for a further 15–20 minutes. Add the remaining tomato dice for an extra texture. Re-check the consistency and seasoning, and the bolognese *ragù* is ready.

A spoonful over some tasty buttered pasta with freshly grated Parmesan cheese – you couldn't get more English.

Note: For an even richer finish, add an extra glass of red wine and a dash of Worcestershire sauce. Fresh oregano or basil can be added for a herby *ragù*.

Braised Oxtail

This dish is more than just traditional British, in fact it has become my signature dish. Although it's not possible to buy oxtail at the time of publication, it's so delicious and such a Great British tradition that I wanted to include the recipe anyway, against the day when oxtail is available once again. I find it exciting to cook and even more exciting to eat. You can pick up the tails and eat them with your hands and just dip your bread in the bowl to mop up the sauce. The tails are also very good served with creamy *Mashed Potatoes* (page 124).

SERVES 4–6

4 oxtails, trimmed of fat
100 g (4 oz) beef dripping
225 g (8 oz) carrots, chopped
225 g (8 oz) onions, chopped
225 g (8 oz) celery sticks, chopped
225 g (8 oz) leeks, chopped
450 g (1 lb) tomatoes, chopped
Sprig of thyme
1 bay leaf
1 garlic clove, crushed
600 ml (1 pint) red wine
2.25 litres (4 pints) *Veal Stock* (page 34)
Salt and pepper

BELOW
Bolognese Sauce

For the Garnish

1 carrot, finely diced
1 onion, finely diced
2 celery sticks, finely diced
½ small leek, finely diced
4 tomatoes, skinned, seeded and diced
1 heaped tablespoon chopped fresh parsley

For this recipe, the veal stock should not have been reduced to a sauce consistency (*jus*), as this tends to become too strong when braising the tails. Oxtails can be used in place of veal bones when making the stock, for extra beef flavour.

Pre-heat the oven to 200°C/400°F/Gas Mark 6.

Firstly, separate the trimmed tails between the joints and season with salt and pepper. In a large pan, fry the tails in the dripping until brown on all sides, then drain in a colander. Fry the chopped carrots, onions, celery and leeks in the same pan, collecting all the residue from the tails. Add the chopped tomatoes, thyme, bay leaf and garlic and continue to cook for a few minutes. Place the tails in a large braising pan with the vegetables. Pour the red wine into the first pan and boil to reduce until almost dry. Add some of the stock then pour onto the meat in the braising pan and cover with the remaining stock. Bring the tails to a simmer and braise in the pre-heated oven for 1½–2 hours until the meat is tender.

Lift the pieces of meat from the sauce and keep to one side. Push the sauce through a sieve into a pan, then boil to reduce it, skimming off all impurities, to a good sauce consistency.

While the sauce is reducing, quickly cook the diced garnish carrot, onion, celery and leek in a tablespoon of water until soft. When the sauce is ready, add the tails and vegetable garnish and simmer until the tails are warmed through. Add the diced tomato and spoon into hot bowls, allowing three or four oxtail pieces per portion. Sprinkle with chopped parsley and serve.

See also

Boiled Bacon and Vegetable 'Main-course' Soup
(page 17)
Coarse Pork Pâté (page 275)
Cornish Pasty (page 273)
Home-made Pork Pie (page 280)
Individual Roast Beef with Bitter Onions
(page 232)
*One-piece Roast Pork with Caramelized Apple and
Chestnut Brussels Sprouts* (page 234)
Stilton and Red-onion Salad with Peppered Beef Fillet
(page 99)
Roast Leg of Lamb (page 234)
Roast Rib of Beef (page 236)
Sausagemeat Loaf (page 276)

Sunday Lunch Roast

It was only really in the nineteenth century that taking a meal in the middle of the day – a luncheon – became the norm. And it is probably since then that the Sunday lunch has turned into a Great British institution. Presumably it developed because Sunday was generally a day of rest, when the family could go to church together and then come home and eat together. And in the country renowned for its meat, what better for that lunch than a roast joint of meat?

Originally, roasting meant cooking meat over a fire. This would have been what primitive man did, spearing pieces of his kill with twigs and holding them to or over fire. Roasting was also the most logical process in the days of huge open fires when food was held and revolved at or above the fire by means of a spit. As the meat revolved, the fat in it melted and the meat basted itself. However, this all changed in about the nineteenth century when the enclosed fire – or the domestic oven – was developed. Meat cooked in this way is sometimes said to be baked, rather than roasted, but I don't entirely agree. The meat is exposed to all-round heat but, with good roasting, is always basted during its cooking time. 'Baking' indicates an almost dry form of cooking – and I certainly am not too keen on a dry roast. Whatever the truth, traditionalists and perfectionists have been arguing ever since, but the two terms – roasted and baked – have become virtually interchangeable in relation to oven-cooked meat.

That England became so well known for its roasts was primarily due to the fuel available. England had plenty of trees which, when burned, gave off the high heat necessary for roasting, whilst elsewhere only slower cooking methods, such as simmering or stewing, were possible (done over furze or peat fires). Another reason why roasting became so particularly English lies in agriculture. England's pasture lands are particularly lush because of the mildness of weather and the rain, and this makes lots of grass and hay which in turn makes food animals fat and tasty. The British have also farmed animals for eating at the table from the earliest times, whereas the French, for instance, tend to cook animals that have worked for years on the land, and have become older, tougher and stringier. This partly explains a fundamental difference in culinary styles. The French generally have to bone, roll and braise or stew meats with other ingredients to make them eat

well. The quality of British meat – which I still think is far and away the best in the world – meant that we could, and still do, excel at 'plain roasts'.

Roasting meat in a conventional modern oven is on the surface very straightforward, yet it arouses great controversy – should meat be roasted at high heat, a low heat, or a combination of both? Those in favour of high-heat roasting claim that their meat is the best in flavour and, because of the initial searing, that it has a wonderfully browned outside crust. Lovers of slow-roasts criticize the way in which meat shrinks at higher temperatures, and boast of the tenderness of meat cooked by their favoured process. Fans of the combination method sear their roasts first at a very high temperature, then reduce the heat for the rest of the cooking time.

Nobody is completely right nor completely wrong, for each of the methods is correct if applied to a particular cut of meat. The thing to remember with almost all roasts is to sear and seal the joint before placing in the oven. This will hold in all of its natural juices and flavours, resulting in a far tastier and succulent roast.

A Swedish diplomat, Per Kalm, keen always to comment on British cookery, on one of his visits to England in the 1690s, observed the English at table: 'The Englishmen understand almost better than any other people the art of properly roasting a joint, which also is not to be wondered at; because the art of cooking as practised by most Englishmen does not extend much beyond roast beef and plum pudding.' Well, things have changed since then, as we know – but roasting is still one of the classic Great British ways of cooking, and always will be.

Individual Roast Beef with Bitter Onions

Roast meats were always big joints in the past, placed on the spit and roasted in front of the fire. You can keep the meat here as a whole joint, but occasionally I do like to cut bigger joints into separate portions, as here. Firstly they cook a lot quicker, and it's nice to have your own 'roast'.

It's best to buy a 900 g (2 lb) piece of sirloin. This will ensure a virtually sinew-free cut. You should also trim away any excess fat, keeping the joint lean.

All you need to do now is split the meat lengthways and then each in half again. You now have four mini sirloin joints. The bitter onions give a slightly sweet-sharp flavour and, when eaten with the gravy, balance so well with the roast.

The beauty of this dish is that so few ingredients still result in lots of flavours. The onions can be fried well in advance and then just re-heated.

SERVES 4

Butter
4 large onions, sliced
Pinch of demerara sugar (optional)
4 × 175–225 g (6–8 oz) trimmed individual sirloins
    (as above)
Cooking oil
2 glasses of red wine
300 ml (½ pint) *Veal or Beef Jus* (page 34) or
    alternative (page 11)
Salt and pepper

Melt a knob of butter in a frying-pan and add the onions. With this quantity it may be best to cook in 2–3 batches. Allow the onions to cook fairly rapidly, taking on a deep colour while also becoming tender. As onions cook, the natural sugar content almost caramelizes. English onions generally give the best results. Once all are fried, place in one pan and season with salt and pepper. If, on tasting, they are still slightly too bitter then the demerara sugar can be added. It's important not to add too much or this will leave an artificial finish.

To roast the beef, season each 'joint' and, in a roasting tin, cook on a medium heat in a trickle of oil, fat-side down. As this becomes hot, it will also cook, tenderize and release the fat, so as not to leave a 'raw' taste.

Once well coloured, turn the beef and colour on all sides. The joints can now be roasted to your specification. For a good medium-rare pink finish, roast at 200°C/400°F/Gas Mark 6 for 8–10 minutes. Medium will take 10–12 minutes and well done 12–15 minutes.

Once roasted, it's important to rest the joints for 5–10 minutes; this will relax the meat, giving it a more tender finish.

While the beef is resting, pour off any excess fat from the pan, re-heat and add the red wine. This will lift any flavours. Reduce by three-quarters before adding the *jus*.

Bring to the simmer and cook for a few minutes before straining through a fine sieve. Any excess oils/fat will now sit on top of the sauce and can be spooned off.

To serve, divide the bitter onions between four plates, carve each joint into three and sit either at the side or on top. The red-wine gravy can now either be poured around or served separately.

To go with this dish I like to serve the *Classic Roast Potatoes* on page 238. To make them even richer and finished with a shine they can be brushed with some of the red-wine gravy. It's best to take a third of the sauce and reduce by half. This increases the strength and flavour, leaving a good sticky consistency to brush over.

BELOW
Individual Roast Beef with Bitter Onions

Roast Leg of Lamb

With the introduction of potatoes, daily meals changed to become 'meat with two veg', and long may this continue. It makes for a great Sunday lunch, with a gathering of family and friends enjoying very simple foods. Lamb wasn't part of this tradition until well into the eighteenth century, as sheep were valued primarily for their wool, and it was only occasionally therefore that young sheep, or lamb, was available.

So this is a recipe for a simple leg of lamb with no other flavourings apart from salt and pepper – two of my favourites – but I do give you a few more ideas at the end of the method. There are also plenty of recipes throughout the book for vegetables to accompany the roast.

SERVES 4–6

1 leg of lamb on the bone (usually 1.5 kg/3¼ lb)
Cooking oil
Salt and pepper
300 ml (½ pint) *Chicken Stock* (page 33), or
    600 ml (1 pint) for gravy lovers

Ask your butcher to remove the pelvic bone from the joint. This will help when carving the meat. Pre-heat the oven to 200°C/400°F/Gas Mark 6. Heat a roasting pan with a few tablespoons of cooking oil.

Season the leg with salt and pepper and place in the pan, presentation-side down. This can now be fried, coloured and turned over on a medium heat until completely golden.

Place in the pre-heated oven and roast, basting from time to time, cooking the meat as you like it. Here are the times to watch:
Medium-rare – 15 minutes per 450 g (1 lb) + 15 minutes
Medium – 20 minutes per 450 g (1 lb) + 20 minutes
Well done – 25–30 minutes per 450 g (1 lb) + 25–30 minutes

Once roasted, remove from the oven and leave to rest for 15–20 minutes before carving.

While the lamb is resting, pour away any fat from the tray, leaving in any cooking residue. Heat on top of the stove, adding the chicken stock. Cook and simmer, allowing the stock to reduce by a third. You will now have a very loose gravy full of natural lamb flavours. This can be lightly thickened with arrowroot or cornflour. Either thickener can be loosened with water, or red or white wine.

The lamb is now ready to serve.

Note: *Veal Jus* (page 34) can be used in place of the chicken stock, for an instant, thick gravy.

Variations

Here are some other flavours that can be used to give the lamb flavour an extra dimension.
1   Simply rub the leg with a cut clove of garlic before colouring.
2   Make small incisions across the leg and fill with thin slices of garlic and small sprigs of rosemary.
3   Pour honey over the leg for the last 20 minutes of roasting, basting every 5 minutes to leave a glaze.
4   Mix 2 tablespoons of clear honey with 2 tablespoons of teriyaki marinade and 2 tablespoons of soy sauce. Boil all three together until thick and sticky. Once cooked, brush the leg with the spicy, sticky glaze.
5   Mix 2–3 cloves of crushed garlic with the finely grated zest of 1 lemon and a tablespoon of chopped mint. Cover the leg once coloured and roast. The gravy will also pick up all of these flavours.
6   Brush the leg with redcurrant or mint jelly 10–15 minutes before the end of its cooking time.

One-piece Roast Pork with Caramelized Apple and Chestnut Brussels Sprouts

The relationship between pork and apples is one that has lasted for hundreds of years, and will continue for many more. A pig will always eat windfall apples, if it gets the chance, and the story goes that, in medieval days, the dry sour apple mash left after pressing crab-apples for verjuice would be cooked with a piece of pork. Both of these working together set the tradition, which we have continued.

The pork featured here is cut into individual portions, similar to *Individual Roast Beef with Bitter Onions* (page 232). If you're not sure about cutting the loin, then simply leave as a complete joint. The apples come in a different texture here too. They have been caramelized in halves, giving a more solid texture.

(For the classic *Apple Sauce*, see page 44.) The garnish of apples and Brussels sprouts will work with just about any roast pork – and the sprouts are particularly good served with your Christmas turkey. For an extra garnish, which eats well and creates another interest on the plate, try *Sage Fritters* (page 58).

SERVES 4

900 g (2 lb) pork loin, boned weight, skinned (keep the bones, chopped, to make the gravy)
2 apples, peeled, cored and halved through the middle
300 ml (½ pint) dry cider
Caster sugar
225–350 g (8–12 oz) Brussels sprouts
2 large onions, sliced
Butter
50–75 g (2–3 oz) chopped chestnuts (if using fresh, check cooking times on page 332)
Salt and pepper

For the sauce

Pork bones, chopped
Small bunch sage
200–250 ml (7–8 fl oz) *Chicken Stock* (page 33)
50 g (2 oz) butter, chilled and diced

When buying the loin, it's best to ask for the skin to be removed with a minimum fat content. This will become your crackling. The crackling, apples and gravy can be made well in advance: make all at least 1 hour before roasting.

For the crackling, pre-heat the oven to 200°C/400°F/Gas Mark 6. Score the skin with a sharp knife and season with a good sprinkling of salt. This can now be laid on a wire rack sitting on a baking tray. Bake in the pre-heated oven for 40–50 minutes. During this time, excess fat will run through the wire rack, leaving you with a crispy piece of crackling. The excess fat left in the tin can now be used for roasting the pork loin pieces – no flavours are wasted.

BELOW
One-piece Roast Pork with Caramelized Apple and Chestnut Brussels Sprouts

Place the four apple halves in a saucepan and cover with the cider. Bring to the simmer, cook for 1 minute and allow to cool. During this time the apples will continue cooking. To finish, remove the apples, reserving the cider.

To make the gravy, while the crackling is cooking the chopped pork bones can also be roasted in the oven. At that temperature they should only take 20–30 minutes. (For extra flavour, why not also roast with the bones a mixture of 1 onion, 1 carrot, 1 small leek and a few sticks of celery, all chopped.) Once all are roasted, transfer them to a saucepan. Add the cider from the apples with a few leaves of sage. Bring to the boil and reduce by three-quarters. Now it's time to add the chicken stock and bring to the simmer. The roasted bones will give the stock a deeper colour. Cook for 20–30 minutes, allowing the stock to reduce by a third.

Strain the stock. This can now be thickened by whisking in the butter to create a tasty gravy. It can also be thickened with cornflour loosened with water first. Leave to one side.

Shred the Brussels sprouts. Sweat the sliced onions in a knob of butter for a few minutes, allowing them to soften and take on a golden colour. Remove and allow to cool. While the onions are cooking, blanch the Brussels in boiling, salted water for 30 seconds– 1 minute. Remove them from the pan and allow to cool, refrigerated, on a cloth. These two operations can be done well in advance.

To cook the pork, cut the loin into four mini loins, looking like small but thick sirloin steaks. Season with salt and pepper. Start to colour in a roasting tin on top of the stove on a medium heat, fat-side down (using the pork fat from the crackling). This will now slowly cook away the fat and, at the same time, leave a rich golden colour. Colour the pork completely.

To finish, place the roasting tin in the oven at 200°C/400°F/Gas Mark 6 and cook, fat-side down, for 12–15 minutes. Once cooked, remove from the oven and leave to rest for 12–15 minutes before carving. If you'd prefer to leave the pork loin whole, then simply follow the instructions for the individual loins, leaving it to roast for 30–40 minutes.

While the pork is roasting, finish the apples and sprouts. Melt a knob of butter in a frying-pan, place the apples in it, presentation-side down, and pan-fry until

golden. Turn them over and cook for a further minute or two. To finish, sprinkle with caster sugar and glaze under a hot pre-heated grill. The apples are now golden, glazed and ready to serve.

Melt a knob of butter in a wok or frying-pan. Add the onions, sprouts and chestnuts. Simply fry for a few minutes, seasoning with salt and pepper (a pinch of nutmeg also works well) until hot.

To serve, spoon the stir-fry onto the plates. Sit a glazed apple beside it. Each roast can now be carved into three slices and arranged just falling off the Brussels in a fan shape. Break the crackling into pieces and place it on top. Now just pour the sauce around.

Note: The dish is now complete. If serving it with your Christmas lunch then, obviously, *Classic Roast Potatoes* (page 238) should be on offer. Otherwise, I suggest good, creamy *Mashed Potatoes* (page 124).

Roast Rib of Beef

This book was written when beef was not allowed to be sold on the bone – the classic British way over the centuries. We are told it will return, and I do hope so, because I miss a good roast rib on the bone so much: the beef maintains a much sweeter flavour, and more juices are created to give a better gravy.

Good Scottish beef will always be the best to choose and buy, and the best part of the rib to buy for roasting is the forerib. When buying on the bone (if allowed) you want three ribs. This will weigh approximately 3 kg (8 lb) including bones. The same rib piece can be bought off the bone. Buy it 'oven-ready' (this means the beef will be chined, just leaving the rib bones attached; any bone trimmings can be kept to roast the meat on).

Serve your roast beef with roast potatoes and Yorkshire pudding. A vegetable that goes particularly well is *Parsnip Purée* (from *Steamed and Braised Mallard with Parsnip Tart*, page 261): its creamy texture eaten with the moist and tender rib is sensational (double the quantity for this recipe). Other good accompaniments to a roast rib, and very much along French lines, are *Chips* (page 127) and a simple green salad. Offer a mayonnaise mixed with horseradish cream and a touch of mustard. We know this will work well with the beef and you can also dip your chips in it.

SERVES 8–10

Cooking oil
1 × 3-rib-bone forerib of beef, oven-ready,
    approximate weight 3 kg (8 lb), or a boned
    and rolled rib from the same-sized cut,
    approximate weight 2–2.5 kg/4½–5½ lb)
4 shallots, peeled and roughly chopped
2 garlic cloves, halved
Sprig of thyme
½ bottle of red wine
300 ml (½ pint) *Veal Jus* (page 34)
Salt and pepper

Pre-heat the oven to 190°C/375°F/Gas Mark 5.

Heat a roasting pan with 2–3 tablespoons of cooking oil. Season the beef rib generously with salt and pepper. Place in the hot pan and colour and seal on all sides. Any bone trimmings, if available, can now be placed in the pan, sitting the beef on top. Roast in the pre-heated oven, allowing 15 minutes per 450 g (1 lb), whether on or off the bone, for a medium-rare finish.

It is important to baste the beef every 15 minutes to ensure all-round flavour and seasoning. Half-way through the cooking time, turn the joint over, sprinkling the shallots, garlic and thyme around the pan.

Once the cooking time is complete, remove the beef from the oven and roasting tray. Cover with foil and leave to rest for 20–30 minutes before carving.

Pour any excess fat from the roasting tray, leaving in the shallots, garlic and thyme, which will have collected a lot of beef juices and flavour. Heat the tray on top of the stove and add a third of the wine. This will instantly lift the residue from the pan. Reduce until almost dry. Add another third of the wine, also boiling and reducing until almost dry. Repeat this process with the remaining wine. Add the *jus* and return to the simmer. Cook for 5–10 minutes before pushing through a sieve, extracting the juices from the shallots, garlic and thyme. The red-wine gravy is now ready. Adjust the seasoning with salt and pepper.

After resting, the beef is ready to carve. If serving 'à la meat and two veg', the *Classic Roast Potatoes* (page 238), and almost any two vegetables featured in the book (pages 95–127) will complete your meal.
Note: Chicken or beef stock or water can be used in place of the *jus* to create the gravy. A sprinkling of flour in the roasting pan before adding the liquor will help thicken the sauce.

The recipe for traditional *Horseradish Sauce* to accompany the beef can be found on page 55.

Yorkshire Pudding

Part of probably the most classic and renowned of all Great British dishes – roast beef and Yorkshire pudding. Why Yorkshire? Probably because it was a thrifty cook in the north of England who originally devised a way of utilizing the fat that dripped into a pan under the spit-roasting meat. A batter pudding collecting all of the flavours of the beef fat and juices was a perfect answer. The original Yorkshire would have been 2–3 cm (¾–1½ in) thick, and was turned during its cooking time to give you a crispy topping and base, with the rich pudding inside. It's often still cooked like this today.

The pudding was then cut into squares and served as a course before the roast, with lots of gravy poured over. (The idea was that it might fill you up a bit, so that the roast beef would go round further.) These days Yorkshire tends to be lighter, crisper and quite often cooked in individual moulded trays. They are then served, usually two a portion – but most people will eat even more – *with* the beef, not as a separate course.

The recipe I'm giving here will give you a well risen, crisp pudding. It can be cooked as one thick pudding, but it will need to be turned over halfway through its cooking time. This will also only really work if baking in a roasting tin. Another classic recipe using this batter is, of course, *Toad in the Hole* (page 370). There the batter has been reduced to accommodate the quantity required.

You'll notice I've included an egg white in this recipe, which gives the batter even more of a lift, for a lighter, crisper finish.

MAKES UP TO 24 PUDDINGS

225 g (8 oz) plain flour
Pinch of salt
3 eggs
1 egg white (optional)
300–450 ml (½–¾ pint) milk
Oil, lard or dripping, for cooking

Pre-heat the oven to 220°C/425°F/Gas Mark 7. The quantity will fill 10–12 10 cm (4 in) individual tins, approximately two 12-pudding-mould trays or 1 medium roasting tin, approximately 20 × 25 cm (8 × 10 in). Muffin tins can also be used for even deeper individual puddings.

The batter can be made and used immediately, but I do recommend at least ½–1 hour of resting time. For absolute perfection I usually rest it, refrigerated, for 24 hours and then re-whisk just before baking. Any resting time relaxes the batter, creating a different consistency.

Sift the flour with the salt. Add the eggs and egg white, if using. Whisk in 300 ml (½ pint) of the milk. This will give you a thick batter that works very well. To check for the perfect consistency, simply lift a spoon in and out. The batter should hold and coat the back of a spoon. If it seems to have congealed after resting, then simply add more of the remaining milk until that consistency is found. The batter is now ready to cook.

Oil or grease your chosen tin(s) fairly generously. These can then be heated in the oven until almost smoking. Now it's time to add the batter. For individual tins or mould trays, fill each to almost full. For the medium roasting tray, just add all of the batter. Bake in the pre-heated oven for 25–30 minutes (individuals and mould trays). An extra 5–10 minutes may still be needed for a crispy finish. A roasting tray will take 45 minutes to 1 hour.

Note: The *Onion Gravy* (page 50) is a great accompaniment.

Classic Roast Potatoes

Roast potatoes are a weekly institution in most British families and households. When it's time for that Sunday lunch, it's time for roast potatoes. For the very best results it's important to use the right potato. Almost any potato will roast, but if you love that crispy edge with a light, fluffy and creamy interior, then floury potatoes are needed. I choose between the following four varieties that will always give you the right result –

BELOW
Yorkshire Pudding

ABOVE
Classic Roast Potatoes

Maris Piper, Cara, King Edward or Desirée. To achieve the right finish, these potatoes will take at least 1 hour to cook; for extreme crispiness, cook for 1½ hours.

SERVES 4–6

6–9 medium potatoes (allowing 3 halves each)
Salt
Cooking oil or lard
Plain flour, seasoned

Pre-heat the oven to 200°C/400°F/Gas Mark 6. Peel the potatoes and halve lengthways. The peeled side of the potatoes can now be scraped with a knife to give a smooth domed shape to all halves. Place in a saucepan and cover with cold, salted water. Bring to the boil and then simmer for 5–6 minutes. Drain in a colander and leave to stand for 2–3 minutes before shaking the colander gently. This will begin to break down the edge of the potatoes. These slightly rough edges will become crisp and crunchy during the roasting.

Heat a frying-pan with 5 mm (¼ in) of oil or melted lard. Once it's hot, the potatoes can be lightly rolled in flour, shaking off any excess. Fry the potatoes in the oil, turning occasionally until completely golden brown.

Now transfer the potatoes to a roasting pan. Pour some of the cooking oil into the pan (approximately 2–3 mm/⅛ in deep), sprinkle the potatoes with salt and roast in the oven for 30 minutes before turning in the pan. Roast for another 30 minutes. Remove the crispy roast potatoes from the pan and serve.

A knob of butter can be melted over the potatoes to enrich the crispy roast taste. For an ultra-crispy finish, increase the cooking time to 1½ hours, turning the potatoes in the pan half-way through.

'Banana' Roasts

To make these you need large potatoes. Peel them and cut them lengthways. Shape them to look like bananas by cutting away the edges from top to tail, leaving sharp points, and creating a curved edge in the centre with a knife. Four 'bananas' make one up one portion.

To roast the potatoes, par-boil for 3–4 minutes before draining and allowing them to cool for 10 minutes. Heat olive or cooking oil in a roasting tray or frying pan and colour the potatoes to a golden brown. Before placing in the oven, add a knob or two of butter. The potatoes will take 20–30 minutes to become rich in colour and texture with the points almost burnt. Season with coarse or table salt and serve.

See also

Rack on Black (page 190)
Roast Chicken Legs with Sea Salt and Thyme (page 246)
Roast Grouse (page 247)
Roasted Parsnips (page 95)
Roast Guinness Lamb (page 194)
Roast Partridge with Their own Toasts and Wild Mushrooms (page 255)
Roast Pheasant with Bacon-braised Barley and a Whisky Cream Sauce (page 258)
Slow-honey-roast Belly of Pork (page 184)
Slow-roast Shoulder of Pork, with Pearl Barley and Sage 'Stuffing' (page 209)
Traditional Roast Turkey with Sage, Lemon and Chestnut Stuffing and all the Trimmings (page 327)

Poultry
and Game

'Poultry,' wrote the nineteenth-century French gastronome Brillat Savarin, 'is for the cook what canvas is to the painter. It is served to us boiled, roasted, fried, hot or cold, whole or in pieces, with or without sauce, boned, skinned, stuffed, and always with equal success.' I don't think anyone who cooks would disagree with him, for poultry – chicken especially – is incredibly versatile. Game, too, is one of my favourite ingredients, intense in flavour, and versatile in the ways it can be cooked – and it's very British.

'Poultry is for the cook what canvas is to the painter.'

Brillat Savarin

Wild birds – which we now define as game – would have been an important part of the Britons' early diet, and they ate a wider variety than we would dream of today – seabirds such as guillemots, gannets and puffins, as well as more familiar birds such as ducks, geese, herons, blackbirds, thrushes and so on. Wild ox and wild pig would have been other delicacies, before the idea of domesticating animals was introduced. After this time, primitive man settled to tend his fields and to raise his cattle, sheep, goats and pigs – and, occasionally, his chickens. For it is thought that by late Iron Age the red jungle fowl from India had already been introduced and had become naturalized. This bird had come via Persia, Greece and Rome, and was the ancestor of our domestic chicken, perhaps one of the most important introductions of all.

Many Roman techniques concerning animal rearing became familiar in Britain during their 400 years of occupation. The Romans liked to eat domestic fowl, and reared many more delicate varieties, among them pheasants, peacocks, partridges and guinea fowl, in special enclosures (they did not care for quail, apparently, believing the birds fed on poisonous herbs). They also built unique structures in which wild pigeons could nest and breed – *columbaria* – and these were blueprints for the medieval dovecotes still to be seen near or at the side of very old houses. Three other types of animal were introduced by the Romans for eating, and kept in special quarters near to the kitchen. Rabbits were brought in from Spain (new-born were a particular delicacy), and dormice and snails were fed until they were fat and succulent, the latter too plump to be able to get back into their shells.

Throughout the Middle Ages, poultry and game were important to everyone, although there were many severe game laws which, at different times, forbade most people from hunting birds. The wealthy hunted deer and boar from horseback in specially designated park areas, and their falcons caught wild birds. Trapping rabbits and the native hare was more the province of the peasants and, along with wild birds, probably represented the major fresh meat part of the diet. Chickens were far too valuable as egg layers to be eaten before they were old and stringy, and fit only for the cooking pot (and other meat animals were usually only killed in the autumn). The wealthy, however, could roast their younger, probably better fed – often specially fed – chickens on spits in front of the fire, as they did their large joints of meat or venison. Smaller birds were roasted too, basted with butter and flour or breadcrumbs to protect them from the heat and then served on sops (croûtes) of bread to absorb the juices (much as the partridge – see *Roast Partridge with Their Own Toasts and Wild Mushrooms*, a new British classic, on page 255 – and other game birds still are today). Over the years, thrushes, dotterels, larks, finches, rooks and blackbirds would all have been fattened, roasted and eaten and many were sold in London at shops in the area still known as Poultry (a street in the heart of the City area) from the end of the thirteenth century.

Roast birds in medieval times were served with a black sauce, made with the offal (as we make a

PAGE 240
Roast Pheasant with Bacon-braised Barley and a Whisky Cream Sauce

giblet gravy today), or a white sauce (almonds and spices then, a bread sauce now). Saucing has always been important, and apple sauce for goose, cranberry for turkey, redcurrant or rowan for venison, are very ancient and respected combinations. Older chickens, birds and game meats were also boiled in pottages, the ancestors of our many game stews and game and chicken pudding and pie fillings. British game pies are famous but none so famous – or perhaps infamous – as the Yorkshire Christmas pie once was. This consisted of boned turkey stuffed with a goose, then a chicken, followed by a partridge and a pigeon. These are placed in a thick pie crust and tucked around with chunks of hare, venison, wild birds and masses of butter before being baked. The whole idea sounds pretty awesome and not one I'll jump at trying! Moving into the eighteenth century, game and birds were potted, as was fish, and preserved with melted butter.

Birds, domestic or wild, were for many years a special food, and associated with celebration. They were given as presents during the twelve days of Christmas (perhaps the origin of the 'partridge in a pear tree'). Geese were traditionally roasted and eaten at Michaelmas, probably because the young birds would have eaten well throughout the summer, and become plump ('Christmas is coming, and the goose is getting fat'). However, it is also said that Queen Elizabeth I was eating goose on 29 September 1588, when told of the Spanish Armada's defeat, and decreed that it be eaten on that day thereafter. (Geese were also given as part payment of rent in a bad year, for Michaelmas is one of the farming community's quarter days, when rent was due.)

Large birds such as swans, herons and peacocks were always the centrepiece of feasts, but despite their splendour, they were all rather tough and stringy, so they were soon replaced by the succulent turkey, after its introduction from America in the sixteenth century.

This chapter includes many dishes that will stand as a centrepiece on our dinner tables, certainly not just to look at but, more importantly, to eat and enjoy. Many chicken dishes and cooking methods are featured, along with quite a good selection of game, including quail, grouse, pigeon, partridge, wild duck, venison and hare. While the length of the ingredients lists for many of the recipes in this chapter might seem quite long, most of the ingredients are everyday storecupboard items.

We started with a Brillat Savarin quote, so I thought we'd finish with one too: 'Game,' he writes, 'is a healthy, warming and savoury food, fit for the most delicate palate and easy to digest. In the hands of an experienced cook, game can provide dishes of the highest quality which raises the culinary art to the level of science.'

'Game is a healthy, warming and savoury food, fit for the most delicate palate and easy to digest.'

Brillat Savarin

Chicken Pot-roast with Carrots and Potatoes

Pot-roasting is a style of cooking that has been ignored for far too long. It's really a method of steaming, though in the oven in a pot with a tight-fitting lid.

Many years ago the chicken would have been cooked with lashings of butter to create the steam. Once the bird was cooked, stock would be added to the dish. I'm going to turn that around, and cook the chicken in the steam created by the stock and then finish it with butter.

This extract from Mark Strand's poem, called 'Pot Roast', sums up my feelings nicely – hopefully you'll feel exactly the same.

> I gaze upon the roast,
> that is sliced and laid out
> on my plate
> and over it
> I spoon the juices
> of carrot and onion.
> And for once I do not regret
> the passage of time.

SERVES 4

2 large onions, cut into 1 cm (½ in) dice, or 350 g
    (12 oz) button onions
450 g (1 lb) carrots, peeled
6 medium potatoes
1.6 kg (3½ lb) oven-ready chicken
1 lemon
Olive oil
Bouquet garni of sage and thyme sprigs wrapped
    and tied in leek leaf or muslin
300–600 ml (½–1 pint) *Chicken Stock*
    (page 33)
50 g (2 oz) butter
Salt and pepper
Paprika (optional)

Pre-heat the oven to 200°C/400°F/Gas Mark 6.

The onion choice is really up to you. The button onions do work very well; if using, before adding to the pot-roast, place them in a pan of cold water and bring to the boil. Now refresh in cold water. This will take the rawness and acidity from the onion. Chopped onion will also work with the flavours, but will not need blanching.

The carrots should be quartered lengthways and then cut at an angle into 1–2 cm (½–¾ in) thick pieces.

As for the potatoes, I like to cut them at an angle lengthways from 'corner to corner', then just trim a flat base at the thick ends and the potatoes will stand up in the pan, exposing the tops. These will colour a good golden brown.

To season the chicken, first rub with lemon and then squeeze out the remaining juice and keep it to one side. Now sprinkle with salt, black pepper and paprika, if using. The paprika gives extra flavour to the bird and imparts a pink/red colour. To sprinkle paprika evenly, here's a quick tip: just place ½ teaspoon in a tea strainer and dust across the skin. Heat a large frying-pan with a trickle of olive oil. The chicken can now be fried and coloured all over to a rich golden brown.

Once coloured, sit the bird in a large, deep braising pan. If you don't have a braising pan then use a roasting tin; this can then be covered with foil once all the other ingredients are added. Stand the potatoes around the outside of the chicken, with the bouquet garni. Add half to three-quarters of the stock – this really depends on the size of the dish/tray. The potatoes should be in at least 2.5 cm (1 in) of stock. You might need to add the full 600 ml (1 pint). Brush the potato tops with butter, bring the pot to the simmer and cover with a lid. The dish can now be popped in the pre-heated oven.

After 20 minutes, remove the lid and baste the chicken and potatoes with the stock. Add the carrots and onions and replace the lid. Continue to cook for a further 20 minutes and then baste the bird and potatoes again. The lid can now be left off.

The last 20 minutes of cooking without a lid will help colour the bird and potatoes. During this time, baste once or twice more. After 1 hour total cooking time, the bird will be ready to remove. Cover with foil to keep warm while it relaxes.

The potatoes can now also be removed, brushed with some of the butter and finished under the grill to create a slightly burnt tinge on the tops. Skim excess fat from the remaining liquor and then pour off into a separate dish, keeping the carrots and onions warm in a spoonful or two. You might find the stock will need to be reduced for a more intense flavour. Add the remaining butter for a softer finish. The vegetables (onions and carrots) can now be added. Pour in a teaspoon or two of the lemon juice to lift the flavours and give a very fresh lemon edge.

Divide the chicken into four portions, half a breast with either the thigh or drumstick per portion. Arrange in bowls with three potatoes and a spoonful of carrots and onions. The rich lemony liquor can now be spooned over and the dish served. It's a very tasty dish that gives so many flavours from one pot. Simple but stunning.

Note: An extra touch that also works very well is to finish the liquor with a little chopped fresh sage. Sage and lemon, as we know, work so well together, especially with chicken.

Roast Chicken with Liver-thickened Gravy

This is a simple roast chicken, cooked much as it would have been centuries ago – but in the oven, not on a spit. It almost creates its own gravy in the pan, as the vegetables roasted with it take on all the flavour and juices. Some white wine and chicken stock are added to the pan and reduced. Butter is mixed with the pounded chicken liver and added in turn, which enriches, thickens and flavours the liquids, creating a sauce not unlike the black one served with chicken in the Middle Ages.

For the very best flavour, select a free-range chicken. Chicken livers are mostly included in the giblets of the bird; however, if purchasing an oven-ready bird, you might need to buy the livers separately; most butchers sell them.

SERVES 4

1.5–1.75 kg (3–4 lb) oven-ready and/or free-range chicken
50 g (2 oz) butter, softened
Cooking oil

2 onions, peeled and quartered (root left on)
2 large carrots, peeled and quartered lengthways
4 celery sticks, halved
Sprig of thyme
1 bay leaf
2 glasses of white wine
300 ml (½ pint) *Chicken Stock* (page 33) or water
25 g (1 oz) chicken livers
Salt and pepper

Pre-heat the oven to 190°C/375°F/Gas Mark 5. Brush the chicken with some of the butter and season with salt (using sea-salt, if possible) and pepper. Heat a roasting tin or flameproof casserole dish with a trickle of cooking oil. Lay the chicken breast-side down and colour on a medium heat. Once light golden brown on each breast and leg, remove the bird from the pan. Scatter the vegetables, thyme and bay leaf in the pan. Place the chicken breast-side down on top of the vegetables and roast for 25 minutes. Now the bird can be turned over and basted. Continue to roast for a further 35–40 minutes.

The chicken should now be beautifully roasted, with a good deep golden finish. To test the bird is cooked, press the thigh/drumstick between forefinger and thumb. The flesh should feel tender and give once pressed. Remove the chicken from the pan, cover with foil and leave to rest.

Pour off all the juices from the pan, leaving the vegetables in. Add the white wine to the vegetables, bring to the simmer and allow the liquid to reduce by half.

While the wine is reducing, skim off any fat from the juices saved. These juices can now be added to the pan. Remove the vegetables and reserve. Add the chicken stock or water, bring to the boil and reduce by half. If using water, a stock cube or some stock granules can be added for extra flavour.

While the sauce is being made, sieve or liquidize the raw liver with the remaining butter. This will take on a smooth texture.

Once the sauce has reduced, lower the heat to a simple simmer. Joint the chicken, allowing half a leg and half breast per portion. Arrange on plates with the onions, carrots and celery.

Whisk the liver butter into the simmering gravy. Return to a gentle simmer and strain through a sieve. Spoon the liver gravy over the chicken.

The dish is ready to eat. It really is delicious: the vegetables have become over-cooked, but contain so much flavour from the chicken and the stock it creates. The liver taste doesn't become too strong – it just gives the overall dish a lift.

Note: Once the portions have been cut from the bird, the carcasses can be squeezed into the sauce, releasing even more juices.

Red wine can be used in place of the white. Chopped chives can also be added to the sauce once strained.

Roast Chicken Legs with Sea Salt and Thyme

The sea salt in this recipe is used simply as a seasoning along with the thyme. It gives a crunchy texture to the skin when cooked and, at the same time, sharpens all the other tastes.

The legs can just be served roasted with a green salad, but I like to add further flavourings – the mustard that has always been so popular in British cookery, a little double cream and a squeeze of lemon.

SERVES 4

4 large chicken legs
1 tablespoon olive oil
2 teaspoons coarse sea salt
1 teaspoon fresh thyme leaves
Butter
Squeeze of lemon juice
4 tablespoons double cream or crème fraîche
1 teaspoon English, Dijon or wholegrain mustard
Pepper

Pre-heat the oven to 200°C/400°F/Gas Mark 6.

The thigh bones from the legs can be removed, although this is not essential. If you do wish to take them out for a leaner finish, then simply turn the

legs, skin-side down. Cut along the thigh bone, which will become exposed. Now simply cut either side against the bone, pulling the flesh away. Cut beneath the bone and then twist to remove. The bone may need some help by cutting between the knuckles. The thigh bone is now free.

Heat a roasting or ovenproof frying-pan with the olive oil. Sprinkle the sea salt and thyme over the chicken legs, skin-side up. These seasonings can be lightly pressed onto the skin to keep them attached.

Place the chicken pieces in the pan, skin-side down, and cook on a moderate heat for 5–6 minutes. During the cooking time, add a good knob of butter; this will develop a nutty flavour. Once deep golden in colour, turn the chicken legs over and continue to cook for a further minute or two

BELOW
Roast Chicken Legs with Sea Salt and Thyme

before placing in the pre-heated oven. The legs will now take a maximum of 20 minutes.

Once cooked, remove the pan from the oven and the legs from the pan. Keep them warm. I prefer to leave all residue in the pan, although, for a less buttery finish, it can be poured away. Add a squeeze of lemon juice to the pan, along with a tablespoon or two of water. Bring to the simmer, adding the cream and mustard. Once all is melted, mixed and warm, strain through a tea strainer, over the rich chicken pieces. Check the seasoning and add pepper to taste (you shouldn't need any salt). The chicken is ready to eat.

A bowl of pasta will eat very well with this dish.

Note: For extra thyme flavour, mix together 50 g (2 oz) butter, ½ teaspoon chopped fresh thyme, zest of ¼–½ lemon, salt and pepper. Rub the thyme butter underneath the skin of the chicken pieces. Cook as before.

Roast Grouse

Red grouse (*Lagopus lagopus Scoticus*) are said by many to be the finest game birds in the world. They are unique to Britain, being found only in Scotland and the very north of England. (They are closely related to the willow grouse of Scandinavia and North American grouse and ptarmigans.) Their season runs from 12 August to 10 December. I like to serve the young birds up until the end of October. After that time they seem to be drier in texture. They also need little hanging to develop their flavour – no longer than two or three days, or they become too powerfully gamey in flavour.

Grouse are not usually stuffed, but in Scotland they often mix a few mountain raspberries or rowanberries with butter to put inside the birds. Here, I've used a couple of juniper berries and some thyme for flavouring. The traditional accompaniments for the birds are *Bread Sauce* (page 43) and *Rowan* or *Redcurrant Jelly* (page 386 or 389), all eating very well with the birds. Game chips are also often served, but they do absolutely nothing for me with a roast. The chips become soggy and are quite often straight out of a packet.

When the Glorious Twelfth is here, this recipe comes into its own.

SERVES 4

4 young, oven-ready grouse
4 rashers of streaky bacon
8 juniper berries
4 sprigs of thyme
Cooking oil
1 onion, roughly chopped
1 carrot, roughly chopped
1 celery stick, roughly chopped
1–2 cloves
1 bay leaf
25 g (1 oz) butter
300 ml (½ pint) red wine
300 ml (½ pint) *Chicken Stock* (page 33) or water
Cornflour, loosened with a little red wine (optional)
Salt and pepper
Watercress, to garnish (optional)

Pre-heat the oven to 220°C/425°F/Gas Mark 7. Untie the oven-ready birds and season with salt and pepper inside and out. Wrap over each a rasher of streaky bacon. Place two juniper berries and a sprig of thyme inside each carcass and re-tie.

Heat a little oil in a roasting pan. Add the chopped onion, carrot, celery, cloves and bay leaf. Cook for 10–15 minutes, allowing the vegetables to take on colour and become partially softened. Make space in the pan to lay the birds in on one side. Add the butter and cook for 2–3 minutes. Turn the birds onto the other side and continue to cook for another 2–3 minutes.

Now turn the birds onto their backs and roast in the pre-heated oven for 8–9 minutes. Take the tray from the oven and remove the grouse, allowing them to rest for a minimum of 10 minutes.

Place the baking tray on the stove. Add the red wine and bring to the boil. Allow to reduce by two-thirds. Add the stock or water and return to the boil.

Untie and remove the bacon from the birds. Remove the legs and breasts from the bone, keeping warm to one side. Chop all of the carcasses and add to the roasting pan. The stock must now be reduced by half. During this time the gravy will have picked up all of the roast grouse taste.

Check for seasoning and then strain the sauce through a fine sieve. If you prefer a thicker gravy, then thicken with cornflour, loosened with red wine. A few tablespoons of the gravy can be reduced to a shiny glaze. This can then be brushed over the birds.

Re-warm the grouse in the oven for just a minute or two. The bacon rashers can be crisped under a hot grill. Simply present the grouse on four plates with the bacon rashers, watercress and gravy.

Note: *Classic Roast Potatoes* (page 238) or simple buttered new ones will eat well with this dish, as will *Creamed Cabbage and Bacon* (page 104).

Any grouse bought in November and December are best made into game casseroles or stews (see page 263).

Chicken Fillet 'Steaks' with Chestnut Mushrooms, Sage and Lemon Sauce

A great dish to make for a dinner party, these fillet steaks are guaranteed to shock your friends. They will all be wondering what sort of chicken they came from. The chicken breasts are cut and shaped to look exactly like a beef fillet steak, otherwise known as *tournedos*. It is best to prepare these 24 hours in advance, as this will then give the chicken plenty of time to hold its shape.

The sauce is made to the same recipe as the *Basic White Wine or Champagne Fish Sauce* (page 47). Simply replace the fish stock with chicken stock and include any trimmings from the chestnut mushrooms. A few sage leaves can also be added to help flavour the finished sauce.

This dish eats very well with *Buttered Spinach* (page 113).

6 × 175 g (6 oz) boneless, skinless chicken breasts
3–4 fresh sage leaves, chopped
100 g (4 oz) pig's caul, soaked in cold water
    overnight (page 11, optional)
25 g (1 oz) butter, softened
Salt and pepper

For the Sauce

225 g (8 oz) chestnut or button mushrooms
250 ml (8 fl oz) *Basic White Wine or Champagne Fish
    Sauce* (page 47), made with chicken stock
Lemon juice
2–3 fresh sage leaves, chopped
Salt and pepper

To make the 'fillet steaks' take a large rectangle of foil and top with a similarly sized sheet of greaseproof paper. Brush the paper with butter.

Squeeze excess water from the pig's caul. This can now be totally opened out and laid on top of the buttered paper. (If not using caul, check the Note at the end of the recipe.)

Remove all of the small 'fillets' attached to the underside of the chicken breasts. These can now be diced and blitzed to a purée in a food processor or mincer. Mix with the chopped sage leaves and season with salt and pepper. The breasts can now be cut into strips, roughly the same size as the 'fillets'. Lay the strips side by side on top of the caul, making sure the length is between 20 and 22 cm (8–9 in). This will give you enough to cut into four 'tournedos' fillet steaks. Once all are in place, the sage-flavoured minced chicken can be spread across the top using a wet palette knife. Just a thin layer covering all will guarantee they hold together.

Now roll, keeping the caul on the outside, into a cylindrical shape. Wrap the caul around along with

OPPOSITE
*Chicken Fillet 'Steaks' with Chestnut Mushrooms,
Sage and Lemon Sauce*

the paper and foil. Once rolled, twist the foil at either end. This will give a firmer finish. Refrigerate for several hours, preferably overnight.

Pre-heat the oven to 200°C/400°F/Gas Mark 6. The roll can now be cut into four 'steaks'. Once cut, carefully remove the foil and paper, leaving the caul wrapped around. For extra security, tie one or two lengths of string loosely around.

To cook, melt a knob of the butter in a frying-pan. Season the steaks with salt and pepper. Place in the pan and seal to a golden brown on all sides.

Now place in the pre-heated oven and cook for 10–12 minutes. Once cooked and firm, remove from the oven and leave to rest for 5–6 minutes.

To make the sauce, first trim the stalks from the chestnut mushrooms and use them for the sauce reduction. Slice the mushrooms and sauté in a hot pan with the remaining butter. Season with salt and pepper. Once tender and well coloured, remove from the pan and dry on kitchen paper. Warm the white wine sauce and flavour with lemon juice and chopped sage leaves. The mushrooms can now also be added.

Remove the string from the chicken 'steaks' and present on plates, with the mushroom sauce spooned over.

Note: If pig's caul is unavailable, lay the chicken strips on the paper. Wrap and roll as described. Once set, cut into steaks. These can now be seasoned top and bottom, leaving the foil wrapped around. Cook in the frying-pan sealing the top and bottom. Finish in the pre-heated oven for 12–15 minutes. Once rested, peel away the foil and paper; the 'steaks' will still hold together.

If serving buttered spinach with this dish, the chicken presents very well sitting on top of the green vegetable.

Rabbit Leg Casserole with Marjoram and Mustard

Rabbit and mustard have enjoyed a long-lasting, close relationship in recipes from all over Europe. The flavours work really well together and, with the sweet, herby perfume of the marjoram, the dish is very moreish.

Wild or domestic rabbits can be used if buying the whole animal, but I prefer good, large, plump legs, which finish with a rich moistness. The saddle can be quite dry. The thighbone can be removed if you like, to make the eating a little easier, but it's not essential (see *Roast Chicken Legs with Sea Salt and Thyme*, page 246, for how to do this). Remember to include the bones in the cooking.

It's interesting that when people used to cook goose in the old days, they would put some rabbit legs into the cavity along with flavourings and butter. When cooked, these were given to the children, as they were less rich and more goose was then available to feed hungry men. The dish was known as 'six-legged goose'.

SERVES 4

4 large or 8 small rabbit legs
Plain flour, for dusting
25 g (1 oz) butter
2 large onions, sliced
1 garlic clove, peeled
Good sprig of fresh marjoram
2 glasses of white wine
150 ml (¼ pint) *Chicken Stock* (page 33)
150 ml (¼ pint) double cream
1 tablespoon made English mustard
1 teaspoon chopped fresh marjoram
Salt and pepper

Pre-heat the oven to 190°C/375°F/Gas Mark 5.

Season the rabbit legs with salt and pepper. Lightly dust in the plain flour. Melt the butter in a large frying-pan. Place the legs in the pan and fry to a golden brown, turning over to colour both sides. Add the onions, garlic clove and sprig of marjoram and continue to cook for about 5–6 minutes until the onions have begun to soften.

OPPOSITE
Rabbit Leg Casserole with Marjoram and Mustard

Transfer all to a suitable braising dish. Add the white wine and chicken stock and bring to the simmer. This can now be placed in the pre-heated oven and cooked for 45–50 minutes.

Once cooked, pour through a colander, capturing the cooking liquor in a suitable saucepan. The stock can now be boiled and reduced by half. Add the double cream and simmer for 5–6 minutes. Now add the mustard to finish the sauce. Once whisked in, taste for strength: if you are a big mustard fan, more may be needed for that extra bite. Season with salt and pepper, if necessary. Strain the sauce through a sieve. Discard the sprig of marjoram and garlic clove from the rabbit legs.

Return the legs and onions to the sauce, adding the chopped marjoram to finish the dish.

The casserole is ready to serve. This dish eats very well with greens such as *Buttered Spinach* (page 113). For a complete change, why not serve with buttered noodles?

Note: Button mushrooms (100–150 g/4–5 oz) can be added with the onions for a fuller finish.

Strips of streaky bacon also work well if fried with the onions.

A squeeze of lemon juice is always a great addition to any cream sauce as a lifter – this one included.

Rabbit, Pork and Cider Potato Pie

Rabbit with pork is an old combination in the British tradition, just as rabbit with winter savory is classic in Europe, particularly in France. The combination of all three, moistened with English cider and topped with potatoes instead of pastry, makes for a traditional dish with a fresh outlook.

What I like about this pie is that, once all the ingredients have been added, you don't really have very much more to do, except pop the dish in the oven and leave it for a couple of hours. As the pie slowly cooks it creates its own liquor, which is the sauce for the finished dish.

It's best to use boned rabbit legs and I'm sure your butcher will help you out with this.

SERVES 4–6

4 rabbit legs, boned, bones reserved
300 ml (½ pint) water
600 ml (1 pint) dry cider
450 g (1 lb) pork belly, skinned
4 celery sticks, well washed
1 Granny Smith apple, grated
3 onions, sliced
2 sprigs of savory
2–3 carrots, peeled and cut into 1 cm (½ in)
    thick slices
Small pinch of ground cinnamon
2 bay leaves
2–3 potatoes, peeled and cut into 1 cm (½ in)
    thick slices
25–50 g (1–2 oz) butter
Salt and pepper

Once the rabbit legs have been boned, separate the thigh meat from the drumstick. The bones can now be placed in a saucepan. Pour in the water with half (300 ml/½ pint) the cider and bring to the simmer. This can now be left to cook on a very low simmer while the pie is being put together.

Pre-heat the oven to 180°C/350°F/Gas Mark 4. Slice the pork belly into six slices. The celery, once washed, should be peeled to remove the strings, or just pull them away with the top of a knife. The sticks can now be cut into 1 cm (½ in) pieces, cutting at an angle. These will then spread out more easily.

Mix the grated apple with the sliced onions and season with salt and pepper. Sprinkle a third of the onion mixture in the base of a buttered ovenproof casserole (a round, lidded Le Creuset-style dish is perfect), with 1 sprig of the savory. Half of the sliced celery can now also be added. Season the pork slices and place three in the dish. Lay all of the carrots on top. Season the rabbit leg meats with salt and pepper and place in the dish, pushing all of the ingredients down as you do so.

Scatter with another third of the onions, sprig of savory, cinnamon and the remaining celery. The last three slices of pork belly can now be sat on top.

Now add the remainder of the onions. Strain the cider and water stock, which will have picked up some of the rabbit flavour. Add the remaining neat cider to the stock and pour over the vegetables and meats. The liquor should just reach the same level as the onions. If not then add more water or, for an even richer flavour, use cider. Sit the two bay leaves on top and then overlap the potato slices to cover the surface totally.

Season with salt and divide 25 g (1 oz) of the butter into little knobs and dot around over the potatoes. Bring to the simmer, cover with a lid and place in the pre-heated oven. This can now be left to cook for 1½ hours before removing the lid. The potatoes will have softened and all of the juices strengthened in flavour.

Brush the potatoes with more butter and return to the oven (without the lid) for a further 30 minutes. If, after this time, the potatoes have not coloured, simply increase the temperature of the oven to 200°C/400°F/Gas Mark 6, brush the potatoes with butter once more and cook for a further 15–20 minutes. The pie is now ready and waiting.

It's a good idea to allow the dish to stand for 10 minutes, once removed from the oven, which will allow all the ingredients to relax. Now it's time to serve. The cider will have been mellowed by the stock created from both meats, but will still have its distinctive flavour.

Note: After an hour of the cooking time, it's a good idea to check and lightly press on the potatoes. This will give you a good idea of how much liquor is in the pan. If it appears a lot has been absorbed by the vegetables, simply pour another 150 ml (¼ pint) of water or cider on top. Replace the lid and continue to cook.

Rich Pigeon Faggot on a Potato Cake with Mustard Cabbage

Faggots were extremely popular in the past as a means of using up odd pieces of offal left over after the pig had been killed. They are in a way a sort of cross between a pâté and a sausage, being a pâté mixture bound up in caul fat (all sausages used to be encased in animal entrails) in a sausage shape.

These faggots have a good, gamey, pigeon flavour, bound and balanced with pork and chicken livers, which give the moist texture needed to achieve a succulent finish. It's important, but not essential, to freeze the faggots in their liquor – not a traditional technique, I must admit. However, this breaks the meats down, giving a softer finish. Defrost the quantity required and allow to warm through slowly. You'll then have the richest, moistest faggot you could hope for. So it's best to plan ahead with this dish. This recipe will make approximately twelve faggots. For an ultimate rich flavour, a *Game Stock* (page 34) will be needed. This can be made from the carcasses of the wood pigeons used here.

Serve the faggots with *Potato Cakes* (page 122), or use *The Roast Alternative* (page 123). As for the cabbage, it's just good English green or Savoy, boiled and flavoured with a mustard sauce.

MAKES 12 FAGGOTS

900 ml (1½ pints) *Game Stock* (page 34), made
    from pigeon legs and carcasses
6 wood pigeon breasts (use the legs and carcasses
    from the whole birds for stock)
2 small chicken breasts, skinned
225 g (8 oz) pig's caul, soaked in cold water
    overnight (page 11)
Cooking oil
Salt and pepper

BELOW
Rich Pigeon Faggot on a Potato Cake with Mustard Cabbage

For the Pork Stuffing

175 g (6 oz) pork meat, trimmed (belly or leg
    can be used)
50 g (2 oz) *foie gras* (optional)
75 g (3 oz) pork back fat
75 g (3 oz) chicken livers
1 tablespoon chopped shallots
1 garlic clove, crushed
½ teaspoon lightly chopped thyme leaves
2–3 tablespoons Armagnac or brandy
4 tablespoons Madeira
1 egg white
100 ml (3½ fl oz) double cream (1–2 tablespoons
    more may be needed)
Salt and pepper

For the Pigeon Reduction

Sprig of thyme
2 juniper berries, crushed
½ garlic clove
3 tablespoons Madeira
3 tablespoons port
6 tablespoons pigeon *jus*, made from game
    stock (above)

For the Garnishes (to serve 6)

½ small green or Savoy cabbage, cut into wedges
150 ml (¼ pint) *Mustard Butter Sauce* (page 53),
    using English mustard
Butter
6 *Potato Cakes* (page 122), pan-fried

Reduce 300 ml (½ pint) of the game stock by three-quarters. This will leave you with a thick game *jus* to use for the pigeon reduction.

To make this pigeon reduction, place the thyme, juniper berries and garlic in a small pan along with the Madeira and port. Bring to the boil and reduce by three-quarters before adding the game *jus*. Strain through a sieve and leave to cool.

Remove the skin from the pigeon breasts; these must now be minced twice through a coarse mincer plate. The chicken breasts can be minced once through a fine plate. These will both mince easily, providing the meat is diced and well chilled, along with the mincer.

For the stuffing, the pork meat, *foie gras* (if using), pork back fat and chicken livers can now be minced twice through the coarse plate and once through the fine plate. Or they can be blitzed in a food processor to a fine paste as an alternative to mincing.

Place the shallots, garlic and thyme in a small saucepan with the Armagnac or brandy and Madeira. Bring to the simmer and then reduce until almost dry. Leave to cool.

Working in a bowl over ice, mix the shallots with the pork mixture. Season with salt and pepper and mix in the egg white. The mix will now become quite firm. Stir in the double cream. To check it has the right consistency and flavour, poach a teaspoon of mix in simmering water. After 2–3 minutes, the mousse will be cooked. Now check for seasoning and consistency. The mix should just hold and not be tough or overfirm. If so, then add more double cream, checking until you have a soft cooked consistency. Season with salt and pepper. It's important when testing that the mix is well chilled; if not, the mousse will separate in the pan.

Now the pork mix can be added to the minced pigeon and chicken. Stir in the pigeon reduction and check the seasoning once more. The faggot mix is best left for 2–3 hours to deep-chill and set in the refrigerator. This will make it a lot easier to roll in the caul.

Once set, the mix can now be shaped. Take a good heaped tablespoon and roll by hand, giving you faggots the size of large salad/plum tomatoes.

Squeeze any excess water from the pig's caul and open a quantity across a board. The faggots can now be well wrapped individually, making sure they are totally encased in the caul.

To cook, heat a frying-pan with a little cooking oil. Season the faggots with salt and pepper. These can now be pan-fried until completely sealed and golden. Place the remaining 600 ml (1 pint) of warm stock in a saucepan, carefully add the faggots and simmer very gently for 15–20 minutes. Remove the pan from the stove and allow the faggots to cool in their sauce. Now, for the very best results, sit the faggots in a tray. Strain and pour over the sauce. Freeze six or all of the faggots. It's not essential, but freezing does help the texture.

When you want to re-heat the faggots, defrost and warm, again on a gentle simmer, until heated through. This will take 20–25 minutes. Strain off some of the sauce and skim off any impurities and fat. The sauce will have a rich pigeon flavour. (A splash of red wine might help to liven it up some more.) To give the faggots a shiny glaze, reduce 300 ml (½ pint) of the sauce to a thicker glazing consistency. Some of this can now be brushed over the faggots.

For the garnishes, blanch the cabbage wedges in plenty of well-salted boiling water until just tender. This will take 4–5 minutes. It's important that the cabbage, as with all green vegetables, is boiled with no lid. Refresh in iced water. The part of each wedge required is the outer 3–4 layers, with the stalk/core attached. Cut away the remainder. (The 'waste' cabbage can simply be buttered and served as a vegetable for another dish, or shredded and used in a stir-fry.) Butter and season the outside layers. When you are ready to serve the faggots these can be microwaved for 30–40 seconds.

To present the dish, place a potato cake in the centre of a plate or bowl. Sit the glazed faggot on top. Pour a tablespoon or two of the remaining reduced pigeon sauce over the faggots. Place the cabbage leaves on top, giving an arched shape. Now finish by spooning mustard sauce over the cabbage. The faggots are now ready to serve.

Roast Partridges with Their Own Toasts and Wild Mushrooms

The Romans used to pen and rear partridges, and I expect they roasted them over or in front of the fire, just as we have continued to do in Britain for centuries. The season for partridge runs between 1 September and 1 February. During the nineteenth century partridges were one of Britain's most common game birds. The grey-legged variety is native to Britain, and many years ago it could be found in abundance. Now it has to be bred, and is not so common as the red-legged variety, introduced in the seventeenth century from France. These are reasonably easy to find and larger than the grey-legged, but lack the intense flavour. They are, however, beautiful-looking birds, and a joy to cook and eat.

The history of accompaniments in Britain, as it is everywhere else, is to do with seasons. Partridges are best in autumn, which is when we also find most of our wild mushrooms, so it is almost culinary law that they will go together. For a good combination of flavour and colour, choose a mixture of *trompettes de mort* (black trumpets or trumpets of death), which have a strong earthy flavour; chanterelles or girolles, which are a rich orange colour and have a sort of apricot and pepper nose; morels, which are a rather scarce wild mushroom and only available during the spring months, for a nutty flavour; and *pleurottes* (oyster mushrooms). These last mushrooms are now cultivated, but can still be found wild. They range from an oyster-grey colour through to a yellowish brown. They are best eaten young, for a bitter flavour takes over as they age. Alternatively, you can buy a bag or two of mixed wild mushrooms. It's important, particularly for the *trompettes*, that the mushrooms are well washed.

Dried morels are more readily available and once soaked come back to life very well. The water they have been soaked in can be strained through a sieve or muslin and used as a wild mushroom stock when making the sauce. If using these instead of fresh, 50 g (2 oz) will be sufficient.

The toast base for the bird is an echo of the medieval bread slice or trencher which acted as a plate for pieces of meat or bird (and was later often given to the poor). These toasts are topped with a mix made from the liver and heart of the bird, along with one or two other flavours for a quite delicious finish. The *Game Stock* from page 34 can be used as the sauce. I prefer to cook the stock with no alcohol for this particular dish and add the neat Madeira at the end. I also like to add one more flavour to this dish, but it is expensive – *foie gras*. It's not essential but completely lifts the dish.

A good-quality chicken liver *pâté* or tinned *foie gras* can be substituted if fresh is unavailable. Both *foie gras* and chicken liver *pâté* can be bought loose or tinned from delicatessen counters.

SERVES 4

175 g (6 oz) *trompettes de mort* (black trumpet) mushrooms, or available alternative
175 g (6 oz) chanterelle or girolle mushrooms, or available alternative
75–100 g (3–4 oz) morels (optional)
150 g (5 oz) *pleurottes* (oyster mushrooms), or available alternative
4 plump red-legged partridges, including livers and hearts, preferably barded (covered) with a thin slice of back fat
4 fresh thyme sprigs
1 large garlic clove, quartered
50 g (2 oz) butter
1–2 tablespoons groundnut oil
300 ml (½ pint) *Game Stock* (page 34)
2–3 tablespoons Madeira
Salt and pepper

For the Toasts and Pâté

Butter
2 large shallots, finely chopped
50–75 g (2–3 oz) *foie gras* or chicken-liver *pâté* or tinned *pâté de foie gras*
4 thick slices of granary bread

Pre-heat the oven to 220°C/425°F/Gas Mark 7.

The first task is to prepare the mushrooms – whichever type you're using. For *trompettes de mort*, split the mushrooms lengthways, cutting away the base of the stalk. These must now be washed well, removing the small gritty granules found inside. Wash and rinse carefully two or three times. Leave to drain on a thick cloth.

Large chanterelles or girolles will need to be cut in halves or quarters; small ones can be left whole. Trim away any bruised tops, scraping the stalks and cutting away the base. Wash two or three times before also draining on a cloth.

If using morels, trim away the base of the stalk and split lengthways in half. Again, wash two or three times before draining on a cloth.

For *pleurottes* (oyster mushrooms), cut away the thick stalks. The 'cultivated' variety need not be washed, but instead wiped carefully all over with a cloth. If the mushrooms are large, then simply tear into strips.

Untie the prepared birds, keeping the liver and heart from each to one side. Place a sprig of thyme, piece of garlic, small knob of butter and some salt and pepper in each cavity. Season the outside, replace the piece of back fat and re-tie the partridges.

The livers and hearts can now be chopped coarsely and kept to one side.

For the toasts, melt the butter and add the finely chopped shallots. Cook for a few minutes, without colouring, until softened; remove from the heat and allow to cool. Once cold, mix the chopped livers and hearts with the shallots. If *foie gras* was available, smooth to a purée and add to the mix. If unavailable, add 50–75 g (2–3 oz) of chicken liver or tinned *foie gras pâté*. Season with salt and pepper. The topping for the toasts is now ready.

Heat a roasting pan with some groundnut oil. Place the seasoned birds in the tray on one leg side. Add a knob of butter and cook for 2–3 minutes until well coloured. Turn over onto the other leg and repeat the same cooking time. Now turn each bird breast-side down to seal for a further 2–3 minutes.

Turn onto their backs and roast in the pre-heated oven for 6 minutes. If the birds are particularly plump, roast for an extra 1–2 minutes.

Remove from the oven and place the birds upside-down onto a clean tray or plate, so all juices

OPPOSITE
Roast Partridges with Their Own Toasts and Wild Mushrooms

run into the breasts. Keep the roasting tray with all the juices. Leave the birds to rest for 6–8 minutes.

Spread the toast topping onto the bread using all of the mix, and cut into isosceles triangles (with two sides of equal length). Put the roasting tray on a medium heat and place the triangles, bread-side down, in the sediment and oils left in the pan. Pan-fry the breads for a few minutes, to crisp and absorb all of the flavours. Now remove the breads, sit on a baking tray and finish, topping-side-up, under a medium grill. Toast for a few minutes, heating the mix through.

Heat a large frying-pan or wok. Add a tablespoon of oil and, once very hot, add the chanterelle mushrooms and the morels, if using. Toss in the pan for about a minute before adding the remaining mushrooms. (If using a mixed bag of mushrooms, simply fry them all together.) Add a knob of butter and season with salt and pepper. Cook for 2–3 minutes.

Warm the game stock, adding the Madeira to taste. This sauce holds a very loose consistency. For a slightly thicker sauce and stronger flavour, reduce by half. The sauce is now ready.

The partridges can now be untied, and the fat and the legs removed and trimmed to a neat finish. Remove the breasts. The skin of the breasts can be left on or removed. Squeeze each carcass, allowing all the juices to run through a sieve and into the game sauce for extra flavour.

Place the triangle toasts in bowls or on plates. Point them towards the top of the plate. Sit the two breasts side by side on top of the lower part of the triangle. The legs can now be placed with thigh towards the top, recreating the shape of the bird. Spoon the mixed wild mushrooms around and finish with the sauce, in a reasonably generous quantity, on top of the mushrooms. The dish is now ready to serve.

Note: *Mashed Potatoes* (page 124) are lovely with this dish.
The toast trimmings (left over when cut into triangles) can also be warmed and enjoyed.

Roast Pheasant with Bacon-braised Barley and a Whisky Cream Sauce

Pheasants, probably the most popular sporting birds, are native to Asia, and were spread throughout Europe by the Romans. During the Roman occupation of Britain, pheasants were kept and fed for the chase, much as gamekeepers on large estates do with game birds today. Their season is between 1st October and 1st February, those shot between December and January carrying the best reputation. There are both cock and hen pheasants to choose from. The cock is quite a large bird, and has enough meat for four portions. The hen is smaller, with a much more delicate taste. If using the hen, which I prefer, one bird will give you just two portions.

Pheasants love to eat grains, particularly something like barley, so the association in a dish seemed obvious. The flavour of the barley is lifted by the addition of bacon. For an extra texture I have fried breadcrumbs (a classic accompaniment to roast pheasant), and sprinkled them over the barley, which gives a crispy crunch on the palate. Enriching the cream sauce with whisky, a good combination, is a nod to Scotland where so many pheasants are bred. For maximum taste, it is best to use a single malt rather than a blended whisky.

SERVES 4

2 oven-ready hen pheasants
4 juniper berries, lightly crushed
2 fresh thyme sprigs
Melted butter, for brushing pheasants
Cooking oil
2–3 slices of white bread, crusts removed and crumbed
Salt and pepper

For the Barley

175 g (6 oz) piece of streaky bacon
100 g (4 oz) pearl barley
25 g (1 oz) butter, melted
1 onion, finely chopped
600 ml (1 pint) *Chicken Stock* (page 33)
1 tablespoon chopped fresh parsley

For the Sauce

1 small carrot, roughly chopped

2 shallots, roughly chopped

2–3 cup mushrooms, quartered

8 tablespoons whisky

300 ml (½ pint) *Chicken Stock* (page 33) or water

150ml (¼ pint) double cream

Season the cavity of each bird and place 2 juniper berries and a sprig of thyme inside. Brush the birds with butter and season well with salt and pepper. These can now be refrigerated until needed.

Cut the streaky bacon into 5 mm (¼in) dice. The pearl barley can now be rinsed under a cold tap. Heat the butter in a saucepan. Add the chopped onion and bacon. Cook on a medium heat, allowing the bacon to take on a slight colour. Add the pearl barley and cover with 600 ml (1 pint) of the chicken stock. Bring to the simmer and cook gently for 30–40 minutes, until the barley is tender. During its cooking time the barley will have swollen, becoming soft, absorbing the stock and bacon flavour. While the barley is cooking, the pheasants can be roasted.

Pre-heat the oven to 190°C/375°F/Gas Mark 5. Heat a roasting pan with 2 tablespoons of the cooking oil. Sprinkle the carrot, shallots and mushrooms for the sauce in the pan, leaving enough room in the centre to roast the pheasants. Lay the birds on one side, allowing them to seal and become golden brown. Turn the birds over. Once coloured, turn the birds on their backs and roast in the pre-heated oven for 12–15 minutes. After 12–15 minutes, turn the birds over and continue to roast for a further 15 minutes.

Remove the tray from the oven and place on top of the stove. On a medium heat spoon 6 tablespoons of whisky over the birds. Turn the birds in the pan, so the whisky has covered all. Remove the birds, pouring any juices from inside the cavity into the pan. Leave the birds to rest, breast-side down (this will allow any juices to run into the breasts), for 10–15 minutes.

During the resting time, the sauce can be made. Boil all of the juices, adding the 300 ml (½ pint) of chicken stock (water can replace the stock) and stirring well. The gamey residue will now be lifted from the pan. Allow the stock to reduce by half. Add the double cream and cook on a simmer for 6–8 minutes. This will also slightly reduce, giving a good sauce consistency. Strain the sauce through a sieve, seasoning with salt and pepper. An extra splash of neat whisky can be added, to lift the flavour.

The breadcrumbs can be fried in cooking oil until golden and crispy. Season with a pinch of salt. (The crumbs can be fried in advance and warmed when serving the dish.)

Remove the breasts and legs from the hen birds. Sprinkle the remaining 2 tablespoons of whisky onto the exposed meat of all four portions. The dish is now ready to serve.

Any impurities sitting on top of the creamy whisky sauce can be lifted off with a sheet or two of kitchen roll. Add the chopped parsley to the braised bacon barley and sprinkle with the crispy crumbs.

The presentation of the dish is up to you. The barley and pheasant portions can be served in a large dish, with the sauce offered separately, or all three components can be divided and presented on individual plates.

Note: The vegetables in the roasting pan will have given extra flavour to the sauce. They can be served with the main course, sitting a spoonful underneath the pheasant breasts and legs.

Armagnac can be used in place of the whisky. Armagnac is a classic accompaniment to prunes, in savoury dishes and desserts. Chopped prunes can be added to the cream sauce, and/or some roasted in the pan with the hens.

The roast pheasant can be served with the classic accompaniments to *Roast Grouse* on page 247.

Pheasant is best bought after hanging in feather for 7–8 days. This will give the bird a more gamey flavour, rather than the chicken flavour it's often compared to.

Pressed Guinea Fowl Terrine with Shallots, Mushrooms and Bacon

The Romans introduced the guinea fowl to Britain but, after they left, the bird seemed to disappear as well. Now, fifteen hundred years later, it has been reintroduced from West Africa, but it is only being domestically or commercially reared rather than living naturally as it does elsewhere in Europe.
It is a game bird with the flavour of gamey chicken. It is available all year round but is eaten at its best in early summer.

It is important to keep guinea fowl good and moist, whatever dish you happen to be making with them. The other ingredients here will help achieve just that. I'm using a 1.2 litre (2 pint) terrine mould, which will require two birds. If you are using a 1.75 litre (3 pint) Le Creuset-type terrine, at least three birds will be needed. If a game terrine doesn't seem to be too British, think again. Pressed or potted meats, game and fish became popular in Britain in the eighteenth century, and these were the British equivalent of the French pâté or terrine.

To bone a guinea fowl, simply follow the boning method for chicken, taking the breasts off, skinning and boning the legs. You can also replace the guinea fowl with chicken.

SERVES 10–12

2 guinea fowl, jointed, totally boned and skinned
2 small garlic cloves, crushed
Grated zest of 1 lemon
Small bunch of fresh basil
1 glass white wine
175 g (6 oz) piece of streaky bacon
225 g (8 oz) shallots or button onions, peeled
225 g (8 oz) button mushrooms
10–12 rindless rashers of streaky bacon
1 bay leaf
Salt and pepper

The breasts of the guinea fowl can either be left whole or split into two. Marinate all of the guinea fowl meat with the crushed garlic, lemon zest, basil leaves and white wine. This is best left to marinate overnight to achieve maximum flavour.

Pre-heat the oven to 180°C/350°F/Gas Mark 4.

Cut the piece of bacon into fingers 5 mm (¼ in) thick and blanch in boiling water for a few minutes. The shallots or onions must be blanched twice to take the rawness out of their flavour. Place them in cold water and bring to the boil before refreshing and starting again.

Trim the stalks from the button mushrooms. These can now be poached in water (or chicken stock) for a few minutes until tender.

Line the buttered terrine with the rashers of bacon, slightly overlapping, leaving the ends hanging over the edge of the tin to fold over the filled terrine. If they are short rashers, a few more may be needed to cover the top.

Take the guinea fowl pieces from the marinade and strain the marinade, keeping it to one side.

The guinea fowl, shallots, mushroom and bacon pieces can now be seasoned and layered in the mould in no particular order, keeping a very rustic appearance to the dish. Pack the terrine well, overfilling the mould. Pour the strained marinade over and fold the rashers across the top, tucking in the bay leaf. The terrine can now be wrapped in baking parchment and foil.

Place in a roasting tray of hot water. Cook in the pre-heated oven for 50 minutes to 1 hour. A larger terrine will take 1¼ hours.

Remove from the oven and from the roasting tray. Leave to stand and rest for 30 minutes, before topping with another terrine and a suitable weight. A terrine filled with salt or a bag of sugar will probably be enough. Refrigerate for several hours while pressing, preferably overnight, to guarantee a good finish.

Once pressed, the terrine is ready to turn out and slice.

This dish eats well with a good chutney or relish – home-made *Piccalilli* (page 385) is just perfect.

Steamed and Braised Mallard with a Parsnip Tart

Mallard is a wild duck in season between September and the end of January. It is the largest of the wild duck family, which includes wigeon and teal, and all of them have been eaten in Britain since prehistoric times. You might have to order mallard from your butcher in advance. The recipe can, however, be made using an oven-ready duck, but the cooking time will be longer.

This dish holds many exciting flavours and combinations. The pig's trotter sauce is quite unbelievable to eat, the sticky dice giving so much to the whole experience. This does add quite a lot of work, but it's worth it. If you prefer, the trotters can be omitted. Just serve the duck and parsnip tarts with a gamey red wine sauce.

SERVES 4

2 mallard
1 bottle red wine
1 onion, sliced
2 rashers of streaky bacon, rinded and roughly
    chopped
Few juniper berries
Butter
2 strips of orange peel
Cooking oil
600–900 ml (1–1½ pints) *Game Stock* (page 34),
    reduced to a *jus*, or *Veal Jus* (page 34)
Plain flour, for dusting
1–2 cooked pigs' trotters (page 220), including
    150 ml (¼ pint) trotter-cooking liquor
    (optional)
100 g (4 oz) *Buttered Spinach* (page 113)
Salt and pepper

For the Parsnip Tarts

350–400 g (12–14 oz) *Shortcrust Pastry*
    (page 364), with 1 teaspoon black pepper
Juice of ½ lemon
450 g (1 lb) peeled and cored parsnips, cut into
    2–3 cm (¾–1½ in) pieces
50 g (2 oz) butter
100 ml (3½ fl oz) water
50 ml (2 fl oz) double cream
Salt and pepper

Remove the legs from the mallard (these can be marinated for 24 hours with the red wine, onion, bacon, juniper berries and orange peel). Split each bird in two, cutting away the wishbone and all bones surrounding the breast. The breasts should be left attached only to the breastbone; this will keep their shape during cooking. The breasts can be seasoned with the skin left on and each wrapped individually in cling film with a knob of butter. These can now be kept refrigerated until needed. The mallard carcasses and trimmings can all now be chopped.

Pan-fry the bones in some oil until coloured and place in a saucepan. Fry the onions and bacon in the same pan, lifting any residue. Add to the bones, with the juniper berries and orange peel, before topping with the red wine. Bring to the simmer and reduce by half. Add the game *jus* and bring to the simmer.

Season the mallard legs and dust with flour. Heat a clean frying-pan with a little cooking oil and pan-fry until well coloured on both sides. Place the legs in the game *jus* and simmer gently for 45 minutes–1 hour.

The legs will now be very tender and full of red wine flavour. Remove from the *jus* and trim away any protruding bones from the thighs. Keep to one side. The *jus* can now be strained through a fine sieve. Check the consistency and flavour. The *jus* does not need to be too thick, just full of duck and red wine taste. Season with salt and pepper. The legs can be cooked well beforehand and just re-heated when needed in the *jus*.

To make the pastry cases, follow the recipe on page 364, adding the black pepper to the flour before binding with the butter.

Butter and season four 10 × 2.5 cm (4 × 1 in) pastry rings. Line the rings with pastry, leaving excess pastry hanging over the sides. Line each with greaseproof paper, filling with baking beans or rice. Refrigerate and rest for 15 minutes before baking in a pre-heated oven at 200°C/400°F/Gas Mark 6, for 20–25 minutes until golden. Remove the paper and beans. The over-hanging edge can now be cut away, leaving a straight and neat finish.

For the parsnip purée tart filling, add the lemon juice to the cut parsnips. Melt the butter in a thick-bottomed pan. Once bubbling, add the parsnips and water. Now slowly cook the parsnips until they have become very tender and are breaking down. This will take 25–30 minutes.

Bring the cream to the boil and add to the parsnips. Season with salt and pepper (a pinch of nutmeg can also be added) and liquidize to a smooth purée. For the ultimate smooth finish, push through a fine sieve.

The trotter meat, if using, can now be cut into 5 mm (¼ in) dice. If using trotter liquor (also optional), mix with 150 ml (¼ pint) of the game-and-red-wine cooking *jus*. Check for seasoning. The mallard legs can be re-heated in the remaining game *jus*. From cold they will take at least 30 minutes, on a very gentle heat. This keeps them very moist and tender.

The breasts can now be placed in a hot steamer and cooked for 10–12 minutes. Ten minutes will keep the breasts medium-rare and 12 minutes towards medium. Once cooked, remove from the steamer and leave to rest, still wrapped in cling film, for 5 minutes.

Re-heat the game/trotter sauce and add the diced trotter. The pastry cases can be re-heated in a warm oven.

Microwave or pan-fry the buttered spinach. Spoon between the four tartlets. Top each with hot parsnip purée (which, if made in advance and refrigerated, can also be microwaved), totally filling the tarts. Place the parsnip tarts in the centre of the bowls or plates. Remove the cling film and skin from the breasts, cut away from the bone and carve each into 3–4 slices. Arrange the slices on top of the tarts, leaving enough space to position the legs, which will have taken on a rich colour and glaze from the sauce. Spoon the game/trotter sauce around the tart and serve.

OPPOSITE
Steamed and Braised Mallard with a Parsnip Tart

Note: Any excess parsnip purée should be offered separately. Any remaining game sauce can be frozen. This will last for up to 3 months in the freezer. A sauce packed with flavour, ready to use again.

Game Stew or Pie

For centuries, all sorts of wild birds have been featured in stews and pies – the more common, such as pigeons, partridge, grouse, wild duck, and the less familiar, such as capercaillie, ptarmigan and woodcock. Venison, too, was made into stews and covered with pastry, and venison pasties, made on the same principle as Cornish pasties, have been popular since Tudor times.

This recipe can literally become one or the other. The game, pheasant, partridge and wood pigeon are first going to be slowly braised for 2–2½ hours. This will give the meat a melt-in-the-mouth texture. Once cooked, the stew can be served immediately or be allowed to cool completely before being topped with the puff pastry and baked to create a pie.

For maximum taste, the game should first be marinated for 24 hours. I prefer to take the meat off the bone, apart from the partridge and pheasant drumsticks. I also leave the pigeon legs on the bone.

SERVES 6–8

1 cock pheasant
2 partridges
2 wood pigeons
Pinch of ground allspice
Butter
1.2 litres (2 pints) game *jus* made from *Game Stock* (page 34)
1 tablespoon red-wine vinegar, preferably Cabernet Sauvignon
1 tablespoon redcurrant jelly
Salt and pepper

For the Marinade

4 strips of orange peel
1 teaspoon black peppercorns, lightly crushed
1 teaspoon juniper berries, lightly crushed
1 bay leaf

Bottle of red wine, preferably claret
4 tablespoons brandy
150 ml (¼ pint) port
2 large carrots, peeled and cut into 2 cm (¾ in) cubes
4 celery sticks, cut into 2 cm (¾ in) pieces
225 g (8 oz) button onions, peeled
225 g (8 oz) chestnut or button mushrooms
Sprig of thyme

For the Pie (optional)

450 g (1 lb) *Quick Puff Pastry* (page 365)
1 egg, beaten
Coarse sea salt

Remove the legs and breasts from all birds. The pheasant and partridge legs can be split, taking and boning the thighs from the drumsticks. The drumsticks can now be trimmed and the skin removed. The pigeon legs can simply be trimmed and also skinned. Remove the skin from the breasts. The pheasant breasts can now be cut into three pieces. Cut the partridge breasts in two and leave the pigeon breasts whole.

All the meats can now be placed in a bowl. The carcasses can be used to make the *Game Stock* (page 34).

For the marinade, place the orange peel, peppercorns, juniper berries and bay leaf in a saucepan. Pour on the bottle of red wine and boil until reduced by half. While the wine is reducing, the brandy can be poured over the meats and stirred well so all has been coated. Once the wine has reduced, remove from the stove and add the port. Allow to cool until just warm. Add the chopped vegetables, button onions, mushrooms and thyme to

the meats and then cover with the boiled wine and port. Marinate in the fridge for 24 hours. It is important to turn the game from time to time to achieve maximum flavour.

After 24 hours, pre-heat the oven to 140°C/275°F/Gas Mark 1. Drain the meat and vegetables from the marinade, keeping the wine to one side. Lightly pat the game dry with kitchen paper. Season with salt, pepper and allspice.

Heat a frying-pan with a knob of butter and fry half of the meat, sealing and colouring on all sides. Transfer the sealed meat to a braising pan. Pour a small ladle of the marinade wine into the frying-pan. This will lift all residue and juices. Strain on top of the sealed meat. Wipe the pan clean and repeat the same process, also lifting any flavours with the wine, adding all to the braising pan. The vegetables (from the marinade) can now also be quickly fried in the pan. Add to the meats, pouring the remaining wine on top. Bring to the simmer and pour the game *jus* on top. Return to the simmer. The stew can now be braised in the pre-heated oven, covered with a lid, for 2–2½ hours.

The stew will be beautifully rich and very tender. Remove the orange peel and thyme stalks. The sauce should be of a good consistency. Strain off the sauce and bring to the simmer, skimming off any impurities. If the sauce is too thin, thicken with cornflour or arrowroot loosened with a drop of port. Check for seasoning with salt and pepper.

Warm together the red-wine vinegar and redcurrant jelly and add to the sauce. Pour the finished sauce back over the game and vegetables. The stew is now ready to serve. If you wish to turn it into a pie, leave to cool completely.

Pre-heat the oven to 200°C/400°F/Gas Mark 6. The pastry can now be rolled into a shape large enough to cover the chosen pie dish. Just 350 g (12 oz) may be needed, depending on the size of

OPPOSITE
Marinade for *Game Stew or Pie*

dish used. Brush beaten egg around the edge of the dish. Cut a thin strip of pastry and press around; this will then also be brushed with egg. Having a pastry border to seal the pastry lid on completely will keep the pastry in place, preventing it from shrinking across the top. Press the lid on well, sealing tightly to the pastry border. Brush well with the beaten egg and sprinkle a little coarse sea salt on top. Leave to rest for 15 minutes before baking in the pre-heated oven for 40–45 minutes.

The pastry will now be rich, golden and crispy. It is best to present the whole pie on the table with all the meat and vegetables sealed inside.

Note: If the stew is made into a pie, add enough of the sauce/gravy to cover the meat and vegetables reasonably generously, serving any remaining sauce separately.

Roast Fillets of Hare Wrapped in Ham, with Port and Walnuts

The hare is native to Britain, the one animal that escaped the stringent game laws passed throughout the centuries. A poacher – or a man trying to feed his starving family – could be beheaded or, later, transported, for taking a deer or pheasant, but the hare was always available. Hare as a meat was slightly looked down on by the middle and upper classes, as it was a food of the poor.

A hare is often mistaken for a rabbit. Hare is larger, though, and has two main features that immediately help you tell them apart: the long legs and the length of the ears. The meat is a lot darker than the chicken-like colour of rabbit, and is almost as deep and rich as venison. When buying hare, look for a younger animal, which will be more tender in flavour, and less tough and leathery. Hare doesn't need to be hung for too long: just 2–3 days will be plenty, allowing enough time for the meat to relax.

The ham used in this recipe can be either Parma (an Italian salted and air-dried ham), or Bayonne (a French ham, cured with wine and often slightly smoked). These can be bought loose from delicatessens or in pre-sliced packets. If neither can be found, streaky or back bacon, lightly battered between sheets of cling film to give a thinner slice and prevent shrinkage during cooking, can also be used.

The hare is not going to be marinated in this recipe. Marinating is a lovely process but it can sometimes take over the flavours of the meats. For this dish, I'm looking for the natural flavours of the hare and ham working together.

SERVES 4

2 saddles of hare, filleted, boned and bones chopped
4 slices of Parma or Bayonne ham
Salt and pepper
12 walnut halves, to garnish

For the Sauce

Chopped saddle bones
Walnut oil (or cooking oil)
1 onion, chopped
1 carrot, chopped
2 celery sticks, chopped
1 tablespoon plain flour
300 ml (½ pint) *Chicken* or *Game Stock*
    (page 33 or 34) or water
Sprig of thyme
1 bay leaf
Few juniper berries, crushed
25 g (1 oz) walnuts, chopped
½ teaspoon pink peppercorns or 6 black
    peppercorns, lightly crushed
1 tablespoon red-wine vinegar, preferably Cabernet
    Sauvignon
120 ml (4 fl oz) port
1 teaspoon redcurrant jelly

Pre-heat the oven to 200°C/400°F/Gas Mark 6.

Trim the fillets of any sinews. Lay the Parma or Bayonne ham slices in pairs next to each other, slightly overlapping by 1 cm (½ in), on cling film.

Press two fillets together and place on one of the ham slices. Roll and wrap the fillets well, giving the impression of one good thick loin. Seal in cling film and refrigerate. Repeat the same process with the remaining two fillets.

To make the sauce, fry the chopped bones in a roasting pan on top of the stove, using a tablespoon or two of walnut or cooking oil. Once well coloured, add the chopped vegetables and roast in the pre-heated oven for 20 minutes. Remove from the oven, pouring off any fat from the pan. Sprinkle with the flour, return to the oven and bake for a further 5–6 minutes. The bones and vegetables can now be transferred to a saucepan.

Heat the roasting pan, pouring in the stock or water. This will lift any flavours left in the pan. Add the thyme, bay leaf, juniper berries, chopped walnuts and pink peppercorns to the bones in the saucepan. The red-wine vinegar and port can now also be added; bring to the simmer and reduce by half. Add the stock from the roasting pan and return to the simmer. The stock can now be cooked for 30 minutes on a low simmer. After 30 minutes has passed, pass the stock through a fine sieve. Any impurities or fat sitting on top of the sauce can be lifted using a sheet or two of kitchen roll.

This will give you plenty for the four portions. Add the redcurrant jelly. This sauce will have a good hare flavour but, if too thin, it can be thickened with a pinch of arrowroot or cornflour moistened with port.

For the garnish, use a small, sharp knife to scrape clean each walnut half and cut in half again, giving you 24 pieces.

To roast the hare, unwrap the fillets from the cling film. Three or four strings can now be tied loosely around each pair of fillets and the ham slices.

Heat a roasting pan with some walnut or cooking oil. Season the meat with a twist of pepper. Fry the fillets, colouring the ham all around. This will take 3–4 minutes. Place the tray in the pre-heated oven and cook for 8–10 minutes, keeping the fillets pink. Halfway through the roasting process, turn the fillets over to achieve an even colouring. Remove the fillets from the pan and leave to rest for 5 minutes.

Add the walnut halves to the sauce. The string can now be cut away from the fillets and each piece cut into four, giving two medallions per portion. Spoon the sauce and walnuts around and serve.

This dish will eat very well with any of the following – buttered *Curly Kale* (page 105), *Gratin of Grated Turnips* (page 112) and creamy *Mashed Potatoes* (page 124).

White Pudding

The white pudding as we know it in Britain bears little or no relationship to black pudding; it contains no blood, with oatmeal being the only connection. It is also known traditionally as 'mealie pudding'. Its basic ingredients are oatmeal, beef suet and onions. Not the most exciting of inventions.

The recipe I am including here, however, is more along the lines of the French *boudin blanc*. These have a white-meat base, such as chicken, veal, rabbit or pork. The oatmeal has been replaced with breadcrumbs.

Once poached and cooked, the sausages can be cooled and refrigerated, which means they can be made in advance. When you're ready to eat, simply pan-fry or grill gently, and serve as a starter or main course. *Mashed Potatoes* (page 124) and mustard are good with them, or *Apple Sauce* or *Cumberland Apple Sauce* (page 44 or 47). A simple white pudding salad makes a good starter, with a wholegrain mustard dressing the perfect accompaniment.

MAKES APPROX. 8–10 SAUSAGES

Butter
150 g (5 oz) shallots, finely chopped
175 g (6 oz) chicken breast, diced
175 g (6 oz) pork back fat, diced
100 g (4 oz) lean shoulder of pork, diced
200 ml (7 fl oz) double cream
2 thick slices of white bread, crusts removed and crumbed
2 eggs, beaten
½ teaspoon cornflour
Salt, pepper and freshly grated nutmeg
Sausage skins, enough for 8–10 lengths of 15 cm (6 in)

For the Cooking Liquor

600 ml (1 pint) milk
600 ml (1 pint) water

The sausage skins will have been preserved in salt and will need to be well soaked and rinsed in cold water. These can then be squeezed dry and cut into 15 cm (6 in) lengths. Tie a knot in one end, preparing the skins to be filled.

Melt the knob of butter in a saucepan. Add the shallots and cook, without colouring, until tender. Remove from the heat and allow to cool completely.

Pass the meats and back fat three times through the fine blade of a mincer, or they can be puréed in a food processor and then pushed through a fine sieve.

Warm half the cream and add to the breadcrumbs. Keep at room temperature.

Over a bowl of ice, season the minced meats generously with the salt, pepper and nutmeg. Add 1 egg at a time, mixing it in well. As the egg is being stirred in, the mix will return to a gelatinous form. Add the second egg and re-mix. Add the cornflour

BELOW
White Pudding

to the shallots and stir into the meat. The breadcrumbed cream can now also be stirred into the mix, before adding the remaining double cream. Re-check the seasoning.

The sausage skins can now be filled. This can be achieved simply by using a piping bag and plain nozzle. Place the skin over the nozzle and pull to the knotted end. Pipe the sausage mix and as you do so the skin will fill and extend naturally. Leave up to 4 cm (1¾ in) of excess sausage skin – which then provides space for shrinkage during cooking. Tie the other end.

The sausages can now be pricked in 3–4 places. Season the milk with salt and pour the milk and water into a saucepan. Put the sausages in and heat the cooking liquor, not allowing it to rise above 82°C/180°F. Cook for 15 minutes before removing from the stove and allowing the sausages to cool in the liquor.

The sausages can now be removed from the liquor. If eating immediately, dry and brush with butter before pan-frying gently or grilling until golden brown. Otherwise, the puddings can be refrigerated until needed.

Note: The skin can be removed, if preferred, before pan-frying or grilling. Make an incision with a sharp knife along the length of the sausage. The skin will now easily peel away.

Other flavours can be added to the sausages – freshly chopped herbs (sage or thyme work particularly well), diced sweet peppers, grated lemon zest, mustard seeds and more.

Slow-honey-roast Duck

Domestic ducks were once a very much more familiar sight in Britain than they are today, scratching around in the farmyard alongside the chickens. Many larger houses or villages would have a pond on which ducks could swim, offering another source of fresh meat.

For this recipe I have adopted the slow-roasting cooking method often used in the old days. The duck is basted every so often with honey to give the skin a crisp, golden texture and colour. The duck is

so tender, with such a full flavour, that you just want to eat more and more of it. For this reason, it's best to allow half a duck per person. *Mashed Potato Sauce* (page 125) goes perfectly with this dish.

SERVES 2

1.25–1.5 kg (2½–3 lb) oven-ready duck
1 teaspoon crushed white peppercorns
1 dessertspoon coarse sea salt
5 heaped tablespoons clear honey

Pre-heat the oven to 160°C/325°F/Gas Mark 3. The duck-breast skin should first be scored four or five times, just cutting into the skin itself. Put the duck in a small roasting tray. Sprinkle the peppercorns and the salt over the duck, pushing the salt into the skin. Spoon the honey over the duck, making sure it is completely covered. Place the duck in the oven.

After the first half hour, baste the duck with the honey and duck residue in the roasting tray. Leave to slow-roast for a further 30 minutes. The salt sprinkled over the duck will draw the excess water and fat from the skin itself and this will, obviously, collect in the roasting tray.

After the second half hour, remove the duck from the roasting tray and carefully, from one corner, pour off as much excess fat as possible; it will be sitting on top of the honey in the tray. Replace the duck in the tray, baste with the honey residue and return to the oven. The duck can now be left to slow-roast, basting every 15 minutes for a further hour.

The duck has now been slowly cooked for 2 hours. Remove the duck once more from the tray and again pour off any excess fat. Baste the duck with the honey and return to the oven. During the last half hour of cooking, baste the duck every 5–10 minutes. The honey will now have reduced and become very thick, glazing the duck even more.

OPPOSITE
Slow-honey-roast Duck

After the 2½ hours are up, remove the duck from the oven and tray. If the honey glaze still seems to be a little thin, simply boil it in the tray and reduce it to a thick, coating consistency. Pour over the duck and leave to rest for 15 minutes.

Remove the legs, along with the breasts, making sure they are left whole. Sit the breast and leg for each portion on plates, spooning a tablespoon of honey and any residue over each serving. The slow-roast duck will be well done throughout; the meat will have become very tender and moist, just melting nicely as you eat it.

BELOW
Fillet of Venison Wellington

Fillet of Venison Wellington

This dish is usually associated with fillet of beef, but I've tried it with venison and it works equally well, carrying the extra benefit of a stronger gamey flavour. Venison is one of the healthiest and most nutritious foods available. It may well be a 'red' meat, but it is lower in fat, higher in protein and contains fewer calories than most other red and white meats. Venison is the name given to deer once killed and hung. There are five or six species of deer available in the UK, but the most bought and eaten are roe, fallow or red deer. In France the roe is considered to be the ultimate venison meat (called *chevreuil*) as it is the youngest and the most tender. Fallow deer follows next in popularity in France, but I consider it to be equal to roe. Fallow has a slightly stronger flavour and also gives you a larger saddle fillet, which will still hold a good, pink finish while the pastry case is baking. The largest of the three types of deer meat is red deer. While its taste is still good, it does often require a longer hanging period in order to tenderize the meat. Ask your butcher to bone the venison for you and trim the fillet of all sinew. Also ask for the bones to be chopped, and use them to create a game sauce.

This recipe can, of course, be made using beef fillet. If you decide to go for this, simply increase the cooking time by 15–20 minutes.

SERVES 4

350–450 g (12 oz–1 lb) *Quick Puff Pastry* (page 365)
450–675 g (1–1½ lb) boned loin of venison from a saddle of fallow deer
50 g (2 oz) unsalted butter
4–6 thin *Pancakes* (page 82)
1 egg, beaten
Salt and pepper

For the Stuffing

225 g (8 oz) mushrooms, minced or finely chopped
1 onion, finely chopped
2 smoked back bacon rashers, rinded and finely diced
1 garlic clove, crushed
Pinch of chopped fresh sage
Pinch of chopped fresh thyme

25 g (1 oz) unsalted butter
50 g (2 oz) shelled chestnuts, chopped
25 g (1 oz) fresh white breadcrumbs
1 teaspoon chopped fresh parsley
1 large chicken breast, skinned and minced
     or very finely chopped
1 egg, beaten
Salt and pepper

For the Sauce

Venison bones (optional)
600 ml (1 pint) *Red-wine Sauce* (page 48)
1–2 teaspoons cranberry jelly

To make the stuffing, cook the mushrooms on their own in a pan until almost dry. Cook the chopped onion, bacon, garlic, sage and thyme in the butter for a few minutes without colouring. Leave to cool. Add the chestnuts, breadcrumbs and parsley. Season the chicken with salt and pepper; gradually add the egg and mix until firm to the touch. Stir in the mushrooms and the bacon mixture and check for seasoning. The stuffing can be made well in advance and kept refrigerated until needed.

The sauce can also be made in advance. If you have the venison bones, pre-heat the oven to 220°C/425°F/Gas Mark 7. Roast the bones in the pre-heated oven for about 30 minutes until browned. Add them to the reduction for the red-wine sauce before adding the veal *jus*, then cook in the normal way. Once the sauce has been pushed through a sieve a good venison flavour will have developed. Stir in the cranberry jelly to give a slightly sweeter taste.

Roll out the pastry until large enough to wrap the venison and approximately 3 mm (⅛ in) thick. Leave to rest in the fridge.

Season the venison and fry in the butter in a hot pan until coloured on all sides but not cooked. Leave to cool.

To make the Wellington, lay two or three pancakes along the centre of the pastry and spread three-quarters of the stuffing over to cover them. Place the fillet on top and spread the remaining stuffing over. Fold the pancakes around the meat and lay the other two or three on top. Brush the edges of the pastry with beaten egg and fold over to enclose the meat and stuffing. Trim off any excess pastry and turn the parcel over onto a buttered roasting tray. Leave to rest in the fridge for 30 minutes.

Pre-heat the oven to 220°C/425°F/Gas Mark 7.

Brush the pastry with a little more beaten egg and roast in the pre-heated oven for 20–25 minutes. This will leave the meat still pink inside. Leave to relax for 10–15 minutes.

Now it's time to carve the Wellington. Cut one thick slice or two thinner slices per portion and serve with the rich venison sauce.

Note: A potato accompaniment is not essential for this dish due to the pastry border. However, if you are a potato fan, I suggest serving simple, buttered new potatoes and perhaps some French beans with it.

See also
Roast Chicken Sandwich (page 274)
Traditional Roast Turkey with Sage, Lemon and Chestnut Stuffing and all the Trimmings
(page 327)

Picnics

The *Oxford Dictionary* defines 'picnic' as 'A fashionable social event in which each party present contributed a share of the provisions'. I don't know about you, but I feel the research for this description must have been done many years ago. How times change! Today I see picnics as an eating-out event, the 'hamper' usually provided by one party. Having said that, a picnic does seem to bring family and friends together, with everybody helping prepare the food – so the dictionary could be right.

We think of picnics and food eaten in the open air as one and the same thing, but this was not always so. The origins of the word itself are fairly obscure, but probably derived from the French '*pique-nique*', as the terms appeared around the same time, the late seventeenth century. The Pick-Nick Club was formed by a group of fashionable Londoners, who used to meet in each other's houses, and provide different types of entertainment, as well as selected items of food and drink. The idea obviously spread, because in 1802, *The Times* was obliged to clarify the new fashion: 'A Pic Nic supper consists of a variety of dishes. The Subscribers to the entertainment have a bill of fare presented to them, with a number against each dish. The lot he draws obliges him to furnish the dish marked against it, which he either takes with him in his carriage, or sends by a servant.'

By 1815, only thirteen years later, the concept had become so popular that picnics were given – but out of doors – to celebrate Napoleon's defeat at Waterloo. Since then, picnic has firmly meant a meal taken outside.

But we have always eaten under the sky – people bringing in the harvest eat in the fields, those hunting eat in the woods between drives and, when the fish are not biting, fishermen munch picnics on riverbanks. It is said that Henry VIII and Anne Boleyn ate pasties when they went a-Maying, and Queen Victoria enjoyed some simple foods in the deer forests around Balmoral, washed down by a dram or two. However, these picnic meals were purely for convenience, not taking too much time away from the primary – and most important – object of the expedition, the sport itself. Lady Harriet St Clair, in *Dainty Dishes* (published in 1862), gives the following advice for a shooting breakfast: 'Gentlemen usually prefer eating this about the middle of the day, in the open air, with their fingers, in order that they may lose no time; so it is not generally necessary to send knives and forks or tablecloths; but you must take care, in order not to make them angry, that the luncheon is there at the right time and place.' It's interesting that this 'eating event' was the means of introducing our first 'convenience' foods, provided to fill a gap and not interfere with the main event. The fashionable picnics of today make many appearances at the top events. Whether it's a day at Ascot, Henley Regatta or Glyndebourne, the classic hamper, I'm sure, often takes priority over the actual event.

Other meals away from home were a necessity. When travelling by stagecoach or, later, by railway, edible food was not provided, and could not be relied on at the various stops (then as now, unfortunately), so the answer was to take a home-prepared meal that was portable, in other words a picnic. Charles Dickens would take picnics with him as he travelled around the country giving readings of his works, and railway excursion picnics – travelling by rail to a particular location, laden down with picnic baskets, rugs, parasols, friends and bottles – were hugely fashionable during the Victorian era.

Whatever the reason for the picnic, the food always needs to be portable, and sturdy enough to withstand travel. Surely the original and best picnic dish must be the Great British pie or pasty, meat, vegetables and gravy all contained within their own crispy, crunchy pastry case. Cornish pasties or their Scottish counterpart, Forfar bridies, are perfect, as are the very traditionally British veal and ham or bacon and egg pies, and many others, including sandwiches. In *Jeeves and the Old School Chum* (*Very Good, Jeeves*, P. G. Wodehouse), Bingo waxes lyrical about what Jeeves has packed in the picnic basket: '"There's ham sandwiches," he proceeded, a strange, soft light in his eyes, "and tongue sandwiches and potted meat sandwiches and game sandwiches and hard-boiled eggs and lobster and a cold chicken and sardines and a cake and a couple of bottles of Bollinger and some old brandy…"' Despite this over-abundance, Bertie felt he had to add, '"And if we want a bite to eat after that, of course we can go to the pub."'

You'll find plenty of ideas for your next picnic within this chapter. Creating time to make home-made pork pies and so on is really worth every minute and every mouthful. You feel such pride when presenting a picnic hamper, knowing it contains mostly home-made things – the races at Ascot just wouldn't get a look in! But take warning from something that happened to me many years ago when we were planning a family and friends picnic. One friend rang to ask what sort of sandwiches we should have. I replied ham, cheese, egg, with, you know, tomato, cucumber, pickle, etc. Off we go and lunchtime arrives. We all delve in and find one ham, one cheese, one egg, along with one tomato, one cucumber and one plain pickle! Guess which sandwich that particular friend had to eat…

Another eating-out event is the barbecue. Although not a long-standing element of British eating, it has become a very trendy summer eating habit, one that can provide a good meal at quite a low cost. The barbecue also falls under the picnic heading, but one that provides hot cooked food. The food is transported raw, and cooked over charcoal *in situ*, whether that be on the beach or perhaps in a back garden. It's an idea adopted from our barbecue-mad American, Australian and South African cousins – definitely something to do with the weather! But the basics of cooking in the open air, and over charcoal, are certainly not new. These methods must date from prehistoric times, ever since the discovery of fire.

Whichever you choose, whether picnic or barbecue, I do hope your hamper has room for one of the following recipes.

Cornish Pasty

The pasty has been a staple food in Cornwall for centuries, and often carried different names: tiddy oggy was one and hoggen another, when it didn't contain potato. Almost any food at one time was fitted into the pasty crust, including meat, fish, vegetables, eggs or fruits, sometimes savoury at one end of the pasty, sweet at the other. I'm not sure that those combinations would be accepted today, but I have been offered chocolate pasties before now… I prefer to eat and cook the classic recipe, one that I am sticking close to here.

Legend has it that if a Cornish pasty was dropped 100 feet down a tin mine without the pastry breaking,

a good pasty had landed. Thereafter the pasty could be broken open and the 'meal' enjoyed. I don't suggest you try that with this recipe, but the pastry used here will stay crisp, simply encasing lots of rich and tender flavours.

SERVES 4

750–900 g (1¾–2 lb) *Puff* or *Shortcrust Pastry* (page 365 or 364)
225 g (8 oz) beef skirt or chuck, sliced into very thin strips (approximately 6–8 × 2 cm/ 2–3 × ¾ in)
1 medium potato, peeled and thinly sliced
1 large onion, peeled and thinly sliced
1 small swede, peeled and thinly sliced
25 g (1 oz) butter
1 egg, beaten
Salt and pepper

Roll the pastry between 3 mm and 5 mm (⅛–¼ in) thick. Cut discs approximately 20 cm (8 in) in diameter. Season the meat and vegetables separately with salt and lots of pepper. Melt the butter and trickle over the vegetables. The meat can now be layered to one side of the pastry between individual layers of potatoes, swede and onion, leaving a border of pastry to seal. When laying the final stages, to achieve a better finished shape, carefully arrange the vegetables in a domed fashion.

Brush the border of the pastry with the beaten egg. Fold the pastry over and seal. The edge can now be rolled and pinched from one end to the other, giving a rope effect, or simply cut to your desired shape. Place the pasties on a greased baking tray and brush with more egg. It's now best to refrigerate before baking.

Pre-heat the oven to 200°C/400°F/Gas Mark 6, place the pasties in the oven and bake for 15–20 minutes until golden brown. Now reduce the oven temperature to 180°C/350°F/Gas Mark 4 and continue to cook for 30–35 minutes. The home-made Cornish pasties are now ready to eat.

Pasties for me are best served piping hot, straight from the oven, and if you happen to be in Cornwall, why not have a foaming mug of local 'scrumpy' to go with them?

Note: For an even more peppery flavour, black pepper shortcrust pastry can also be used (page 261).

I also love to eat pasties with either a splash of Worcestershire sauce or a good spoonful of *Piccalilli* (page 385).

The quantity of pastry might seem a lot; however, this is necessary to obtain a securely sealed pasty and make a rope finish, if preferred.

Roast Chicken Sandwich

The Earl of Sandwich (see page 372) would have approved of this – well-seasoned and moist roast chicken sandwiched between slices of good-quality crusty bread, becoming almost a complete meal on its own.

The choice of bread is very important when making any variety of sandwich. I prefer to use an uncut loaf from the granary/wholewheat range. Slices from these breads lend a good texture and taste to help and encourage the filling. You will notice the bread is not buttered in this recipe. Butter has been replaced with the cooking juices for maximum flavour. For the ultimate eating experience, the sandwich is best served warm.

MAKES 4 ROUNDS

1.75 kg (4 lb) oven-ready roasting chicken
50 g (2 oz) butter, softened
1–2 tablespoons cooking oil
8 slices of good-quality bread, preferably granary or wholemeal

BELOW
Roast Chicken Sandwich

Coarse sea salt and pepper
½ iceberg lettuce
4–5 tablespoons home-made *Mayonnaise* (page 49)
    or ready-made mayonnaise, to bind
Squeeze of lemon juice (optional)

Pre-heat the oven to 200°C/400°F/Gas Mark 6. Brush the oven-ready chicken with the butter and season well with salt and pepper. Heat a roasting tray with the cooking oil. Place the chicken on one side in the tray. Cook on a medium heat for 6–7 minutes until taking on a golden colour. Turn onto its other side and repeat.

Now turn the bird on its back, place in the pre-heated oven and roast for 50 minutes. During the cooking time, it is important every 10–15 minutes to baste with the fat and juices in the pan. To check the bird is cooked, pinch the leg between thumb and forefinger: the meat should give, feeling tender. The maximum time the chicken will need is 1 hour.

Remove from the oven and roasting pan and leave to rest for 20–30 minutes. Any fat and juices left in the roasting tray can now be strained into a small bowl through a tea strainer. It's these that I will be 'buttering' the bread with, not wasting a single taste.

After the resting time, remove the legs and their skin, taking the meat from the bones. All of the dark meat can now be shredded with a sharp knife reasonably finely. The juices and fat saved in the bowl can now be stirred together, ready to brush the bread. If there seems to be a lot of fat, then, before mixing, spoon away fat to leave equal quantities of fat and juices. This is purely optional, but does add extra flavour to the sandwich.

Mix the mayonnaise with the shredded leg meat and season with salt and pepper. Brush the slices of bread with fat and cooking liquor. Spoon and spread the shredded meat and mayonnaise mixture onto four of the slices. Shred the iceberg lettuce finely and season with a few granules of coarse sea salt and fresh pepper (a squeeze of lemon juice can also be added to the lettuce for extra bite).

Divide the shredded lettuce between the covered slices. Now the breasts can be carved. Either slice while still on the bone or remove from the carcass before cutting. Lay a few good slices per portion on the lettuce. Sit the other slice of bread on top and the sandwich is made. Apply a little pressure on top and cut into two.

The 'perfect' roast chicken sandwich is ready to serve.

Variation

A quick, lower-fat mayonnaise can be made for a healthier sandwich. The fat/juices on the bread slices will have to be omitted.

Take 140 g (scant 5 oz) of fromage frais (a really low-fat version can be found), 1 teaspoon of Dijon mustard and 1 teaspoon of lemon juice. Mix all three ingredients together, season with salt and pepper and the healthy mayo is made. An egg yolk can be added, for a richer colour and flavour. This recipe can be used in place of any mayonnaise used throughout the book.

Extras for the Sandwich Filling

Any of these can be used, individually or all together, to give a different flavour to the sandwich. Whichever is used, mix with the mayonnaise.

½ small onion, grated
1 teaspoon English, Dijon or wholegrain mustard
1 teaspoon chopped fresh tarragon
2–3 spring onions, finely shredded

Coarse Pork Pâté

There is really very little difference between French pâtés and terrines and English potted meats. The word '*pâté*' means paste, and that is virtually what potted meat is, meat reduced to a paste so that it can be kept in a pot. This recipe borrows from all traditions. It's cooked in a style usually associated with the French confit (meaning 'preserved'). It is then shredded and covered with its own fat, rather like the French *rillettes*, but potted meats were covered with fat too, usually clarified butter, for precisely the same reason – to preserve the meats.

The 450 g (1 lb) of lard is to poach the pork in. Very little of it will actually be used to finish the dish, so please don't be put off.

This recipe has very few ingredients but, once combined for the pâté, they deliver a lot of flavours.

If accompanied by a good home-made chutney (see the Preserves chapter, page 388), and crusty bread or hot toast, you'll have a delicious taste experience.

SERVES 6–8

450 g (1 lb) lard for cooking
900 g (2 lb) skinned and boned pork belly, cut into
    4 pieces
2 garlic cloves, peeled
1 bay leaf
Fresh thyme sprig
150 ml (¼ pint) *Chicken Stock* (page 33, optional)
Salt and pepper

Pre-heat the oven to 180°C/350°F/Gas Mark 4.

Melt the lard in an ovenproof saucepan or dish. Add the four pork pieces, with the garlic, bay leaf and sprig of thyme. Bring to the simmer, cover with a lid and cook in the pre-heated oven for 1–1½ hours.

After an hour has passed, check and pierce the pork with a knife. The meat must be so well cooked that it feels it will almost just fall apart. If not ready, then continue to cook for the last 30 minutes.

Once cooked, remove the meat from the lard and transfer to a bowl. Discard the bay leaf and thyme. The garlic can simply be crushed with the back of a knife and added to the pork pieces.

Shred the pork with a fork. It will eat more smoothly the finer it is shredded.

Strain the fat from the pan and add a tablespoon at a time to the pâté, along with the chicken stock, if using. The stock will guarantee a good moist finish. Five to six tablespoons of each should be more than enough. Season well with salt and pepper.

The pâté will now be quite soft and wet in texture; this is perfect and it will set firm once cold. It's absolutely vital the shredding and finishing of the pâté is carried out while the pork is still warm, when it will absorb all of the juices and flavours.

Now divide between six or eight size-1 (150 ml/ ¼ pint) ramekins or press into a 600 ml (1 pint) dish. Spoon a very little warm fat on top of each, so it is barely covering. This will just seal in all of the flavours and set as a preserving layer. Refrigerated, this pâté will now keep for up to 1 week.

Remove from the fridge 1–2 hours before serving.

This will allow the pâté to come closer to room temperature and be softer to eat.

Note: 50–100 g (2–4 oz) of prunes soaked in Armagnac can be chopped and added to the pâté once shredded. Armagnac also splashed in increases the flavour.

Sausagemeat Loaf

The basic idea of a meatloaf is a very old one. In the Middle Ages, they would pound meats together with spices and other flavourings before stiffening with eggs and breadcrumbs and baking. It is probable that the recipe was taken to America by the Pilgrim Fathers, and it has since come back to Britain as the seemingly uniquely American 'meatloaf'.

A meatloaf is a useful dish as it can be eaten hot or cold, both giving and sharing lots of flavour. It's as a cold dish that it found its way into our picnic hampers. The loaf ingredients can actually be cooked in many different shapes and sizes, known then by different names such as meatballs, 'savoury ducks' or 'faggots'. I use the mixture as the filling for my home-made sausage rolls, see opposite.

I am cooking this loaf in a standard 900 g (2 lb) loaf tin, which can be lined with streaky bacon or the bacon can be simply diced and folded into the rest of the ingredients. If you are using this recipe for your sausage rolls, then the bacon will have to be finely diced and added to the meat mix, or omitted.

SERVES 6–8

10–12 rashers of rindless streaky bacon
350 g (12 oz) pork belly, skinned and boned
175 g (6 oz) lean pork shoulder (or trimmed pigs'
    cheeks, if available)
100 g (4 oz) pork fat
2 onions, chopped or minced
2 slices of white bread, crusts removed, soaked in
    milk
Finely grated zest of 1 lemon
1 egg, beaten
Pinch of ground allspice
Pinch of freshly grated nutmeg
1 teaspoon chopped fresh marjoram or thyme
1 teaspoon chopped fresh sage

Splash or two of Worcestershire sauce
Butter, melted
Salt and pepper

Pre-heat the oven to 180°C/350°F/Gas Mark 4 and select a 900 g/2 lb loaf tin. If lining the loaf tin with the bacon, then simply lay the rashers in, slightly overlapping, leaving the ends hanging over the edge of the tin. The bacon can be stretched using the flat side of a knife, to lengthen. The pork belly, shoulder/cheeks and pork fat can now all be minced through a medium mincer, twice. The bacon should be diced and added to the minced meats, if not used to line the tin.

Obviously, if you are buying all of these products from a local butcher, I'm sure they will look after you and mince them all. They can just be minced once, this will give you a much coarser texture.

If you are mincing the meat yourself, here are a couple of tips to make the job easy. Cut all three meats and the fat into 1–2 cm (½–¾ in) dice. Make sure they and the mincer attachments are very cold. In fact, if on the point of almost freezing, they will just glide through the machine. If minced at room temperature, the meat becomes soft and gets caught. If cut small, the meats can be blitzed in a food processor; it's best not to over-blitz, however, as the meat can become torn. Also process in small quantities; it makes life a lot easier for the machine.

Now mix all of the ingredients, apart from the butter, (squeezing excess milk from the bread), with the meats. This can be made easier by turning in an electric mixer. Check for seasoning, adding Worcestershire sauce to increase the flavour.

Press the mix into the loaf tin evenly and, if lined with bacon, fold the rashers over. Brush with a knob of melted butter and bake in the pre-heated oven for 1½–1¾ hours. Once cooked, the loaf will have come away from the sides of the tin.

Leave to stand for 10–15 minutes before turning out. If cooked for eating cold, then leave to cool in the tin. Once cold, turn out and wrap in cling film until needed.

Note: As a hot dish, the meat loaf goes very well with *Onion Gravy* (page 50) and creamy *Mashed Potatoes* (page 124).
If using the onion gravy, add any juices from the loaf; this saves wasting flavours.

Diced black pudding can also be added to the mix or a small dice of dried apricots works well.
Apple Sauce (page 44) is a good accompaniment.
Any excess mix can be shaped into burgers, pan-fried and eaten with fried onions in a bun.
This quantity of mix will make 20–25 sausage rolls.

Sausage Rolls

Home-made sausage rolls seem to have become an annual event – only made at Christmas time – but they used to form part of afternoon teas and high teas, and are great for a packed lunch or picnic. They are very simple to make and will give you a lot of self-satisfaction as you watch your friends enjoy the end results.

The filling has been made from bought sausagemeat with a few other flavours to help it along. The *Sausagemeat Loaf* mix opposite can also be used, for a totally 'home-made' experience.

BELOW
Sausage Rolls

450 g (1 lb) sausagemeat
1 onion, finely chopped or grated
Finely grated zest of ½ lemon
1 heaped teaspoon of mixed chopped fresh thyme
    and sage
225 g (8 oz) *Quick Puff* or *Flaky Pastry* (page 365)
1 egg yolk, mixed with 2 teaspoons milk
Salt, pepper and freshly grated nutmeg

Pre-heat the oven to 200°C/400°F/Gas Mark 6.

Mix together the sausagemeat, onion, lemon and chopped herbs. Season with the salt, pepper and nutmeg. This can now be refrigerated to firm while the pastry is being rolled.

Roll the pastry thinly (2–3 mm/about ⅛ in) on a floured surface into three long strips approximately 10 cm (4 in) wide.

The sausagemeat can now be moulded, using your hands, into three long sausages, preferably 2.5 cm (1 in) thick. If the meat is too moist, then dust with flour.

Sit each 'sausage' on a pastry strip, 2–3 cm (¾–1½ in) from the edge of the pastry. Brush the pastry along the other side, close to the sausage, with the egg yolk. Fold the pastry over the meat, rolling it as you do so. When the pastry meets, leave a small overlap before cutting away any excess. Once rolled all along, lift them carefully, making sure that the seal is on the base when put down. Cut each into 5 cm (2 in) sausage rolls.

These can now all be transferred to a greased baking sheet. The sausage rolls can be left as they are, or 3–4 cuts with scissors can be made along the top. Brush each with the remaining egg yolk before baking in the pre-heated oven for 25–30 minutes.

Once baked, golden and crispy, remove from the oven and serve while warm. Alternatively, allow the rolls to cool on a wire rack, and keep in a tin or airtight plastic container.

Note: Many additions can be added to the sausage mix. My favourite is to add 50 g (2 oz) of chopped prunes. Take ready-to-eat prunes and cut into a small dice. Soak in a tablespoon of Armagnac (optional) and add to the mix. Pork and prune sausage rolls are simply sensational. Other additions might be chopped spring onions, chopped walnuts or chestnuts. Or boil cider with the onions, reducing until dry. Cool, add and you have pork and cider rolls.

Vegetarian Cheese and Onion 'Sausage' Rolls ⓥ

These are a lovely vegetarian alternative to our very homely *Sausage Rolls* (page 277). They consist of just cheese, onions and pastry. The pastry has been made with the addition of vegetarian suet, giving the 'rolls' a new texture.

Some of the filling might ooze out during the cooking, so the rolls might not have a 'neat' finish, but the flavour is fantastic.

Individual cheese and onion rolls are very handy to serve as part of afternoon tea or a picnic box.

MAKES 8–10 ROLLS

For the Pastry

175 g (6 oz) self-raising flour
Good pinch of salt
75 g (3 oz) shredded vegetarian suet
5–6 tablespoons cold water

For the Filling

175 g (6 oz) strong Cheddar cheese, grated
1 medium onion, finely chopped
Salt and cayenne pepper

Pre-heat the oven to 220°C/425°F/Gas Mark 7.

Sift together the flour and salt. Mix in the suet. Add enough of the cold water to create a pliable dough. Divide the dough into two pieces. On a floured surface, roll into two strips 30 × 10 cm (12 × 4 in). Brush water around the border. Mix together the grated cheese and onion and season with salt and cayenne pepper.

The filling can now be laid onto the two pastry strips up to the moistened edge. Roll up as for two long Swiss rolls, and slice each into four or five slices, giving a total of eight to ten little rolls. Place on a greaseproof or parchment-papered tray, keeping the sealed edge on the base.

Bake in the pre-heated oven for 15–20 minutes until golden brown and crispy. The cheese and onion rolls are delicious served cold but are even better served warm. The cheese is then still soft and sticky.

Note: Lots of other cheeses can be used. The Cheddar can be mixed with half Stilton and the onion replaced with spring onions. Chopped raisins will also eat well with the cheese and onion. Another flavour I like to add is chopped tarragon or just mixed herbs. They all give an extra perfume to the finished rolls.

Gruyère Cheese, Leek and Mushroom Flan ⓥ

This is my favourite flan recipe, one that's full of textures and lots of flavours. Cheddar cheese also works well for this recipe. A tasty accompaniment to offer is the *Spicy Tomato and Mint Relish* (page 381).

SERVES 8–12

1 large onion, sliced
50 g (2 oz) mushrooms, sliced
40 g (1½ oz) unsalted butter
1½ tablespoons groundnut or vegetable oil
1 medium leek, shredded and washed
2 eggs
1 egg yolk
150 ml (¼ pint) double cream or milk
100 g (4 oz) Gruyère or Cheddar cheese, grated
Cayenne pepper (optional)
175 g (6 oz) *Shortcrust* or *Puff Pastry*
    (page 364 or 365)
Salt and pepper

Pre-heat the oven to 180°C/350°F/Gas Mark 4.

Butter a 20 cm (8 in) flan tin or a flan ring and baking sheet.

To start the filling, cook the sliced onion and mushrooms in 1 tablespoon of the butter and ½ tablespoon of the oil for 5–6 minutes until tender. Leave to cool. The shredded leek can now be blanched by plunging into boiling salted water for 1 minute. This will tenderize the vegetable without making it too soggy. After the minute, drain in a colander and allow to cool naturally without running under cold water.

In a basin, beat the eggs and the egg yolk together, then add the cream or milk and leave to one side. Melt the remaining butter and oil together until blended, then leave to cool.

Mix the grated cheese with the eggs and cream and fold in the onion, mushrooms and leek along with the cool butter and oil mixture. Season with salt and pepper and a little cayenne, if using. The mixture can be made the day before it's needed, as it refrigerates very well.

Roll out the pastry and line the flan tin or ring, leaving any excess pastry overhanging the edge; once cooked this can be carefully cut away to give an even finish. Refrigerate and rest for 20 minutes. Line the pastry with greaseproof paper and fill with baking beans or dried rice. Bake blind in the pre-heated oven for 15–20 minutes, then allow to cool. Remove the beans and paper.

BELOW
Gruyère Cheese, Leek and Mushroom Flan

Reduce the oven temperature to 160°C/325°F/Gas Mark 3. Pour the filling mixture into the pastry base and cook in the oven for about 35–40 minutes until the flan just sets. The tart should colour during cooking. If it starts to over-colour, lightly cover with foil or greaseproof paper. The flan is best left to rest for 20–30 minutes before serving as this will help set the texture of the filling, creating a creamy taste.

Home-made Pork Pie

The British have been making pies since at least the Middle Ages. The raised 'coffin' casing was to protect the meat inside from the extreme heat of the fire, and often was not eaten. However, as the art of making pastry developed, many pie recipes did too, and the pork pie is very traditional. It was perfected at Melton Mowbray, and the original recipe used to contain, so I believe, some anchovy essence.

A lot of dishes, such as this one and *Corned Beef* (page 189), sound like hard work, and you might think there is no point in going to all this trouble when there are so many bought varieties available. The reality is that both recipes are relatively simple and there is one thing that eating a bought pie can't give you, and that is the personal satisfaction of knowing you've made it.

The meats I use for this recipe are pork shoulder and back fat. Pork belly can also be used, maintaining the same total weight. The filling must be made before the pastry, as hot water crust has to be moulded while still warm. To finish the pie, a home-made pork jelly can be made using pigs' trotters. Alternatively, home-made chicken stock can be used and set with leaf or powdered gelatine; 25 g (1 oz) per 600 ml (1 pint) stock will guarantee a good setting consistency.

SERVES 8–12

25 g (1 oz) butter
2 large onions, finely chopped
1 teaspoon chopped fresh sage
1 teaspoon chopped fresh thyme
1 teaspoon ground mace
1 teaspoon English mustard powder
1 teaspoon mixed spice
1 kg (2 lb 2 oz) trimmed shoulder pork
     (or pork belly)

175 g (6 oz) pork back fat (or pork belly)
Salt and pepper

For the Jellied Stock

3 pig's trotters or 2 ham hocks
1 onion
1 carrot
2 celery sticks
Few black peppercorns
Sprig of fresh thyme
1 bay leaf
1.8 litres (3 pints) water
25 g (1 oz) gelatine (or 2 leaves), if needed for
     1.2 litres (2 pints) stock

For the Pastry

150 ml (¼ pint) milk
150 ml (¼ pint) water
175 g (6 oz) lard
675 g (1½ lb) plain flour
1 teaspoon salt
1 egg, beaten, to glaze

The mould used for this recipe is a loose-bottomed or spring-clip tin 20 cm (8 in) in diameter and 6.75–7.5 cm (2½–3 in) deep.

First, make the jellied stock. Place all of the ingredients except for the gelatine, in a saucepan and bring to the simmer. Cook for 3 hours, before passing the stock through a sieve.

The stock can now be boiled and reduced to 600–900 ml (1–1½ pints). Once at this stage, test a spoonful or two of the stock, refrigerating until cold and, hopefully, well set. If the jelly is still a little loose, 1 or 2 leaves of gelatine can be added to the stock.

Now make the filling. Melt the butter in a saucepan. Once bubbling, add the chopped onions and cook for a few minutes, without colouring, until beginning to soften.

Remove from the stove and add the sage, thyme, mace, mustard and mixed spice. Leave to cool. While this is cooling, the pork shoulder and back fat can be chopped into 5 mm (¼ in) rough dice. The meat can also be broken down in a food processor or minced coarsely. However, dicing will always maintain the maximum moistness in the meat. Mix the cooked onions with the chopped pork, seasoning well with salt and pepper. Refrigerate until needed.

Now, make the pastry. Pre-heat the oven to 220°C/425°F/Gas Mark 7. Grease the pie mould and place it on a baking sheet. Bring the milk, water and lard to the boil. Sift the flour with the salt into a bowl, leaving a well in the centre. Pour in the boiling lard liquor and stir into the flour to form a dough.

Knead lightly by hand and finish to a smooth dough. Keep a quarter of the pastry warm to one side, then work or roll the rest of the pastry on a lightly floured surface until just large enough to fill the mould and approximately 5 mm (¼ in) thick.

Sit the pastry in the mould and work by hand, gently pushing it out to make it fill to just above the top of the mould. Trim the edges.

Fill the lined mould with the pork filling, packing it in just above the top. Fold the pastry around the top onto the mix and brush with the beaten egg. Roll out the remaining pastry to the same thickness and sit on top of the pie, pressing the edges together and cutting away any excess. Using a 1 cm (½ in) plain metal piping nozzle, cut a cross in the centre, pressing the nozzle in to create a hole and leaving it in place. The pie can now be decorated, if wished, with any pastry trimmings. The border can also be pinched with a fork to give a simple patterned edge. Brush the pie with the beaten egg.

Bake the pie immediately in the hot oven for 30 minutes. The oven temperature can now be reduced to 190°C/375°F/Gas Mark 5 and the pie cooked for a further hour. Once the pie reaches a golden brown stage, gently cover with foil to prevent the pastry from burning.

At this point, the pie can be checked, inserting a skewer through the nozzle. The skewer should be hot and clean when removed. If not, continue to cook for a further 15–20 minutes.

Once cooked, lift the pie from the oven and relax for 15 minutes before removing from the mould. Brush the pastry with the beaten egg. Return to the oven for a further 15–20 minutes until the pie has a golden glaze.

Remove from the oven and allow the pie to rest for 30 minutes. The pie filling will have shrunk slightly during the cooking process, leaving a space to be filled with the jelly.

Using a jug and funnel, pour a little of the jelly stock into the pie. This will be absorbed slowly by the meat, giving it a moister finish. Repeat this process until the pie has cooled. Now refrigerate before adding more cold jelly, and the pie is full. Any remaining jelly can simply be frozen, ready for your next pork pie. Once you've tasted the results, you'll realize it really was worth every minute you put into it.

Note: It's best to make the pork pie at least 48 hours before serving. This will give the filling time to mature, with all the spices impregnating the pork stuffing.

For a richer, golden jelly, the pig's trotters can first be coloured in a hot pan along with the vegetables. Now simply follow the rest of the recipe method.

The home-made *Piccalilli* on page 385 eats very well with this dish.

See also

Arbroath Smokie and Cream Cheese Pâté (page 89)
Boiled and Baked Ham (page 211)
Cheddar Apple Cake (page 344)
Corned Beef (page 189)
Cucumber Sandwiches (page 373)
Egg Sandwiches (page 372)
Haslet (page 212)
Jam Sandwiches (page 374)
Pressed Ox Tongue (page 216)
Scotch Eggs (page 73)
Smoked Salmon Rolls (page 374)
Watercress and Cream Cheese Sandwiches (page 373)

Puddings

This will be a lot of people's favourite chapter, as we all seem to love puddings, and probably eat far too many of them. In Britain we have quite a sweet tooth, and because of that I feel our pudding tradition is second to none. The word pudding should really just be used for foods that are rich and ones that are normally baked or steamed. Many in this chapter fall under this category – *Ale Cake, Steamed Upside-down Pudding, Blackberry and Apple Pudding, Apricot and Almond Pudding* and *Sticky Toffee Pudding*, for instance. The other recipes are 'styled' puddings – trifles, fools, syllabubs, fruit pies, tarts – and should really fall under the desserts title. However, I thought I'd keep them all under the one heading, and so create a total mixture of textures and flavours to excite your tastebuds.

Honey would have been the earliest sweetener in the British diet and it was still used long after sugar – from tropical sugar cane – was introduced. For sugar was originally very expensive and could only be afforded by the rich. Brought in by the spice ships from the fourteenth century onwards, it was considered to be as precious as spices. Like spices, sugar was used in almost every kind of cooking – not just sweet pottages of almond milk, dried fruit and eggs (which had once contained honey), but in meat, poultry and fish dishes too. It was actually used as a kind of spice, possibly to counteract the saltiness of preserved meat or fish, or the acidity of the vinegar or verjuice. (In the Middle Ages, sour flavourings such as verjuice, the juice of unripe grapes, were used a great deal in cooking, before citrus fruits and juices became common.)

When, towards the end of the seventeenth century, the use of spices declined in cooking, the consumption of sugar rose, possibly to compensate for the lack of spice. Sugar had also become much cheaper to buy because it was now being grown in many British colonies and dependencies. Tea, coffee and chocolate were the new drinks of this time and, as they were naturally rather bitter, sugar came to play a great part in their consumption. Because of all this, the eighteenth century is the heyday of the English pudding tradition, which is when the idea of 'dessert' as a separate course originated.

Sweetness also came from fruit, particularly dried. The Romans had brought in many fruit trees, among them apples (as opposed to the native crab apples), pears, plums and cherries, plus many that could only grow well in sheltered places here such as grapes, peaches, apricots and figs. Very few of these were actually eaten raw, because it was believed that raw fruit was bad for your health and digestion. Everything was dried, cooked in pies and other puddings with sugar and spices, and made into preserves. This continued until the eighteenth century. Dried fruits such as raisins were also imported, and used in cooking a great deal by the wealthy. Poorer people ate them in pottages and pies for special occasions such as Christmas.

Most traditional British fruit-filled puddings and cakes are a result of this association of festivity with dried fruit. The multitude of suet puddings which became so popular took over the role of the thick pottages of earlier times, probably providing much the same sort of calorific satisfaction. That they contained meat fat or suet is a reminder of the medieval mixing of savoury and sweet, and the present day mince pie is a classic example – it was once actually made with meat. The rice and milk puddings of today are a sweet version of the medieval frumenty, again cooked in milk. The sweet pie tradition grew from the medieval pastry 'coffins' once containing meats and spices, and the clove in an apple pie is a classic example of this. Bread too, once used as a trencher (plate), and to thicken sauces, played its part in sweet things as well. Many of our most famous and favourite puddings are bread based – summer pudding, queen of puddings, apple charlotte and many more, not forgetting, of course, bread and butter pudding. All the creamy puddings for which we are also famous developed because of our rich dairy produce, and they were included in the 'banquet course' which crowned sixteenth-century feasts.

Menu planning and cooking today have changed so much. Balancing textures and flavours throughout the meal is extremely important, quite often building the eating experience around the grand final course. Sometimes I invite friends round for a drink and a snack and deliberately surprise them. Most expect a savoury dish, but now and again I offer them a chocolate flan, or steamed sponge and custard, or sherry trifle, or bread and butter pudding. This changes the whole evening as it becomes the talking point and everybody feels comfortable eating the pud because it's the only course.

I hope this chapter will give you similar feelings and offer you a good range to choose from.

PAGE 282
Afternoon Tea Pudding (page 320)

Ale Cake with Golden Syrup Cream

Cakes made using ale or beer are a strong part of the British tradition – there's a porter or stout cake in Ireland, for instance. The ale used here can be whatever you choose – a light ale will give you a milder flavour, but a strong stout like Guinness will make it richer.

One of the secrets to eating this cake at its absolute best is to bake it, let it rest and relax for 30–40 minutes, and then serve it just warm. As the syrup cream is spooned on top, it begins to melt, almost turning into a sauce.

MAKES A 15–18 CM (6–7 IN) CAKE

100 g (4 oz) butter, softened
100 g (4 oz) dark soft brown sugar
1 egg, beaten
100 g (4 oz) mixed dried fruit e.g. raisins, currants and sultanas
225 g (8 oz) plain flour
Pinch of ground mixed spice
150 ml (¼ pint) ale
Butter, to grease the tin

For the Syrup Cream

1 tablespoon golden syrup
5 tablespoons double cream

These quantities will fill a 15–18 cm (6–7 in) deep cake tin. Pre-heat the oven to 180°C/350°F/ Gas Mark 4.

Cream together the butter and sugar. Slowly beat in the egg and then fold in the mixed fruits. Sift the flour with the mixed spice and also fold into the cake mix. The ale can now be slowly added until the mix has reached a dropping consistency.

The cake tin can now be greased with butter and the base lined with greaseproof paper. Spoon the cake mix into the tin, smoothing across the top with a palette knife.

Bake in the pre-heated oven for 1 hour before testing with a thin knife, which should come out clean. If not cooked, then continue to bake, testing every 5–10 minutes. The cake should not be dry but just moist.

Once cooked, leave to stand in the tin for 15 minutes before turning out. The cake can now be left to rest for another 15–20 minutes until just warm.

To make the syrup cream, whisk the syrup and cream together to a 'lightly-whipped-cream' stage. These quantities can be multiplied to your choice.

The ale cake is now ready to serve.

Raspberry Cranachan

A Scottish speciality that is often known as cream crowdie. Crowdie was originally a gruel made from oatmeal and water, then the name was applied to fresh cheese (sold as such today). The name then became associated with an oatmeal cream, and raspberries were added. Cranachan was traditionally served at festive times, particularly Hallowe'en, when it contained charms – a ring for marriage, a coin for wealth, a horseshoe for good luck, and so on. These charms can definitely be found in this finished recipe. You'll have a marriage of textures, a wealth of flavours – and good luck to you if you try and eat the lot yourself.

SERVES 4

100 g (4 oz) medium oatmeal
2 tablespoons raspberry jam or 1 tablespoon of Crème de Framboise liqueur (optional)
2 tablespoons water (to loosen the jam)
300 ml (½ pint) double cream
1 dessertspoon caster sugar
2–3 tablespoons (or more) of whisky
175 g (6 oz) fresh raspberries
Icing sugar, to dust

Toast the oatmeal until completely golden brown. Leave to cool. If using the raspberry jam (this can be used to flavour the cream or dribbled through the cranachan) warm together with the water. Once the jam has dissolved, strain through a tea strainer/sieve. This now has a 'jam *coulis*' consistency.

Whisk the double cream, caster sugar and whisky together until lightly whipped. Fold in the toasted oatmeal. Divide half of the raspberries between four glasses. Spoon a little of the 'jam *coulis*', if using, or liqueur, if using, on top of each.

Half-fill each glass with cranachan cream before sitting the remaining raspberries on top. Spoon more 'jam *coulis*' or liqueur on top of the raspberries before topping and finishing with the cranachan mix.

Smooth the top of each cranachan cream. The juicy raspberries have now been set beneath and between the whisky oatmeal cranachan.

To finish, just dust each pudding with icing sugar before serving. The puddings can be eaten immediately or refrigerated until needed. Only dust with icing sugar when ready to eat.

Note: Other fruits can also be used: cooked rhubarb eats beautifully with the oatmeal cream. Oranges can also be used, flavouring the cream with marmalade or an orange liqueur.

BELOW
Raspberry Cranachan

Scottish Fruit Tart with Whisky

This is a typical British tart, its Scottish origins betrayed by the addition of whisky. The enclosing of dried fruit in pastry is very similar to the Scottish black bun, a cake made especially for New Year. And this tart would be perfect for Christmas, New Year, or any time of the year.

If you're not a big fan of whisky it can be omitted from the recipe and replaced with the juice of a lemon. The whisky can be offered separately, served whipped into double cream or custard.

The sweet shortcrust pastry includes the finely grated zest of a lemon, which enhances its flavour and adds to the finished result.

MAKES A 20 CM (8 IN) TART

350 g (12 oz) *Sweet Shortcrust Pastry* (page 364)
Finely grated zest of 1 lemon

For the Filling

100 g (4 oz) soft dark brown sugar
100 g (4 oz) butter
1 tablespoon golden syrup
2 medium eggs, beaten
Grated zest of 1 lemon
100 g (4 oz) currants
50 g (2 oz) sultanas
50 g (2 oz) raisins
50 g (2 oz) walnuts, chopped
2 tablespoons whisky (or juice of 1 lemon)

Once the pastry has been made, with the addition of grated lemon zest, leave to rest for 20 minutes before rolling.

Roll the pastry 2–3 mm (about ⅛ in) thick and line a 20 cm (8 in) flan ring, pressing gently into the edge for a neat finish. Leaving it untrimmed, refrigerate for a further 20 minutes.

Pre-heat the oven to 200°C/400°F/Gas Mark 6. The top edge of the pastry can either be left hanging over during cooking – to trim once baked – or be pressed and trimmed for a 'pinched' finish.

Line the ring with greaseproof paper, fill with baking beans or rice and cook in the pre-heated oven for 15–20 minutes.

Remove from the oven and lift the paper and rice or beans from the case.

For the filling, reduce the oven temperature to 190°C/375°F/Gas Mark 5.

Gently melt the sugar, butter and golden syrup in a saucepan. Remove from the heat and whisk in the beaten eggs. Add the lemon zest, fruits, walnuts and whisky or lemon juice. Mix all together well and spoon into the pastry case.

This can now be baked for 20–25 minutes. Remove from the oven and leave to relax. This tart eats well warm or cold, with pouring/whipped cream, custard or ice cream.

Apricot and Almond Pudding

Apricot and almond trees were introduced to Britain by the Romans and, like figs and peaches, can ripen here in warm, sheltered areas, although apricots are more successful under glass. Almonds were once used, ground or as milk, in many medieval dishes, to thicken and flavour, and here I have combined them in a great pudding.

The apricots are gently cooked, before being placed in a soufflé dish. The sponge, almost like a frangipane mix, but lighter, is spooned on top and then it is baked in the oven. Once cooked the pudding is turned out and topped with the remaining soft cooked apricots.

This dish will eat well with thick cream or custard.

SERVES 6–8

900 g (2 lb) fresh apricots, halved and stoned
Knob of butter
50 g (2 oz) caster sugar
2 tablespoons apricot jam

For the Sponge

3 large eggs, at room temperature
100 g (4 oz) caster sugar
50 g (2 oz) plain flour
175 g (6 oz) ground almonds

Butter and flour an 18–20 cm (7–8 in) soufflé dish. Pre-heat the oven to 190°C/375°F/Gas Mark 5.

Cut each half of apricot into three pieces. Melt a knob of butter in a large saucepan and, once bubbling, add the apricots. Cook and turn for 2 minutes before adding the caster sugar. Continue to cook for a further 2 minutes and then remove from the stove. Add the apricot jam and leave to cool. The apricots are not completely cooked, but will finish their cooking in the sponge.

Spoon two-thirds of the apricots into the base of the buttered and floured soufflé dish.

Break the eggs into a warm mixing bowl, add the sugar and beat until thickened and at a thick

BELOW
Scottish Fruit Tart with Whisky

ribbon (sabayon) stage. Sift the flour with the ground almonds and fold gently into the sabayon. Once completely mixed, spoon over the cooked apricots.

Bake for 35–40 minutes until the top is firm to the touch. Remove from the oven and leave to rest for 10 minutes.

During this resting time, the remaining apricots can be warmed and cooked until tender. Turn the 'soufflé' onto a presentation plate, topping with the warmed apricots.

The pudding is now ready to serve with custard or cream.

Baked Egg Custard Tart

The British have been making custard since someone thought of mixing eggs and milk together over heat. In Tudor times, custard was used as a filling for pastry 'coffins', sometimes with fruit added – in fact the word 'custard' comes from 'crustade', a pastry container or crust.

I have fond childhood memories of baked egg custard tarts, which were always a favourite with me, and tucking into one or two once home from school. Cooking them results in good memories for me and is always enjoyable. Once you've tried this recipe, I'm sure you won't want to forget the experience.

The quantities listed here are an extreme extravagance – lots of egg yolks and cream – but they make for a deliciously rich dessert. The cooking times are a guide. If the tart seems to be almost liquid still, simply continue to cook at the same temperature, checking every 5–10 minutes until set.

All eggs have different strengths, especially when using just yolks. In your own oven and with 'your' eggs the tart could take almost double the time. When checking the tart to see if it's cooked, gently shake the tray. A gentle wobble will indicate that the tart is ready.

At the end of the recipe I have also listed quantities to fill a 25 × 5 cm (10 × 2 in) flan ring (12–16 portions). Another recipe featured in the book that is lovely to eat with the custard tart is *Nutmeg Ice-cream* (page 309).

SERVES 8–12

(makes a 20 cm/8 in tart)

250 g (9 oz) *Sweet Shortcrust Pastry* (page 364)
½ nutmeg, grated, or ½ teaspoon ground nutmeg (optional)

For the Filling

500 ml (18 fl oz) whipping cream
75 g (3 oz) caster sugar
8 egg yolks
Grated nutmeg

To spread the nutmeg flavour throughout the whole dish, when making the sweet shortcrust pastry, grate the nutmeg into the flour before mixing with the other ingredients. Pre-heat the oven to 180°C/350°F/ Gas Mark 4.

Once the pastry has been made, roll out and line a 20-cm (8-in) greased flan ring (any excess pastry can be left hanging over the edge and trimmed once baked, to ensure an even finish). Line with greaseproof paper, rice or baking beans and bake for 15 minutes. Once cooked, remove from the oven, lifting the paper and beans or rice from the case. Turn the oven down to 120°C/250°F/Gas Mark ½.

To make the filling, bring the cream to the boil. Mix together the sugar and egg yolks. Pour the boiled cream onto the egg mixture and stir in well. Pass through a sieve, skimming any froth from the surface.

Pour the custard tart mix into the baked pastry case, grating fresh nutmeg across the surface. Bake for 30–35 minutes until the custard has just set.

Remove from the oven and allow to cool to room temperature before serving.

Note: This dessert eats at its absolute best at room temperature, with the eggs only just holding, and resulting in a soft and creamy texture. If refrigerated, the filling will firm and its full flavour be slightly lost.

Here are the quantities for a 25 × 5 cm (10 × 2 in) flan ring:

350 g (12 oz) *Sweet Shortcrust Pastry* (page 364)
1 whole nutmeg, grated, or 1 teaspoon ground
    nutmeg (optional)

For the Filling

17 egg yolks
1.2 litres (2 pints) whipping cream
190 g (scant 7 oz) caster sugar
Grated nutmeg, for sprinkling

Follow the method for the smaller tart. The cooking time will need to be extended to 45 minutes–1 hour.

OPPOSITE
Baked Egg Custard Tart

Roasted Figs with Brown Sugar Parfait

The Ancient Greeks were convinced the fig was such a healthy fruit that it became a major part of the athletes' diet in the original Olympic games. In Britain, because of our suspicion of raw fruits, figs would always have been eaten cooked, and were most likely valued more as medicine, once thought to cure warts, leprosy, the falling sickness (epilepsy) – and constipation.

Nowadays, we appreciate figs for their all-round usefulness. They hold a flavour and texture that suit many desserts and savoury dishes. In Italy, for instance, the Sicilian fig is classically served raw with *prosciutto* (ham), the rich, soft, fruity flesh complementing the cured slices so well.

Greek athletes might not have eaten this fig recipe, but it is one of the tastiest in the book. The hazelnut tuile biscuits are shaped to sit beneath and above the parfait, giving the figs a base to sit on. It is not essential that you include them in this recipe, but they do provide a crisp texture, balancing with the soft creamy parfait.

SERVES 6–8

For the Figs

12–16 figs (2 per person)
50 g (2 oz) butter
Icing sugar
12–16 flat *Hazelnut Tuiles* (page 356),
    made to the shape of parfait
    (see method)

For the Parfait

4 egg yolks
100 g (4 oz) soft dark brown sugar
3 tablespoons ginger syrup
    (taken from bottled Chinese
    stem ginger)
300 ml (½ pint) whipping cream

For the Port Syrup
(makes 150–200 ml/5–7 fl oz)

150 ml (¼ pint) port
100 g (4 oz) sugar
100 ml (3½ fl oz) water
Juice of 1 lemon

ABOVE
Roasted Figs with Brown Sugar Parfait

Frozen Orange and Espresso Mousse

You will need 6–8 round, square or rectangular stainless moulds. These are approximate sizes for each shape:

Round: 7–8 cm diameter × 2.5 cm deep
(about 3 in diameter × 1 in deep)
Square: 7 × 7 cm × 2.5 cm deep (3 × 3 × 1 in deep)
Rectangle: 7–8 cm × 4–5 cm × 2.5 cm deep
(3 × 2 × 1 in deep)

A terrine can also be used to make the parfait but this will, obviously, take longer to freeze.

To make the parfait, whisk together the egg yolks and sugar in a bowl over simmering water to a sabayon stage (the mix will have doubled in volume with a thick but light consistency). Once at this stage, remove from the heat. The sabayon must now be continually whisked until cool. This is best achieved by transferring to an electric mixer.

While whisking, whip the cream to soft peaks. The ginger syrup can now be added to the cooled sabayon and the whipped cream folded in.

The moulds can be placed on a greaseproof-paper-lined tray and filled with the parfait. Freeze for several hours to set.

To make the port syrup, boil all the ingredients together and cook to a syrup consistency. This can be checked by spooning some syrup onto a saucer. The sauce should hold its consistency.

To roast the figs, pre-heat the oven to 200°C/400°F/Gas Mark 6. Cut the figs in half, brushing each piece with the butter. Place on a baking sheet, cut-side down and roast in the pre-heated oven for 4–5 minutes until soft to the touch.

Remove the figs from the oven, turn them over and dust liberally with icing sugar. These can now be glazed with a gas gun (page 11) or under a hot grill.

To present the dish, remove the parfaits from their moulds using a warm small knife, and sit them on top of a hazelnut tuile biscuit. Top with another biscuit and present on plates. The roasted figs can now be arranged on top of the tuile and the syrup can be drizzled over or around. The dish is now ready to serve.

Ice-creams and iced desserts could not really become part of the British sweet tradition until the nineteenth century, but they then became enormously popular at Edwardian and Victorian dinner parties, particularly in sorbet form.

Here two flavoured mousses, orange and coffee being a very popular duo, are frozen together on top of a coffee sponge base, the latter a texture and flavour borrowed from the *Gâteau Opéra* on page 315. Another borrowing is the rich chocolate ganache topping. The sponge base is a necessity, but the ganache can be replaced with a last-minute dusting of cocoa powder and lots of mixed chocolate shavings.

SERVES 9–12

For the Sponge Base

2 heaped teaspoons coffee granules
2 tablespoons hot water
3 egg yolks
100 g (4 oz) plain chocolate, melted
3 egg whites
65 g (2½ oz) caster sugar

For the Orange Mousse

300 ml (½ pint) double cream
4 tablespoons milk
Finely grated zest of 1 orange
150 g (5 oz) white chocolate, chopped
8 egg yolks
2 tablespoons caster sugar
2 tablespoons sour cream
1½ teaspoons extra grated orange zest
1 tablespoon Grand Marnier

For the Espresso Mousse

300 ml (½ pint) double cream
4 tablespoons milk
50 g (2 oz) finely ground coffee
150 g (5 oz) white chocolate, chopped
8 egg yolks
1 tablespoon caster sugar
2 tablespoons sour cream
1 tablespoon Tia Maria

For the Coffee Syrup (makes 150 ml/¼ pint)

300 ml (½ pint) strong fresh or instant coffee
150 g (5 oz) caster sugar
Splash of Tia Maria liqueur (optional)

This recipe is made in the same form as the *Gâteau Opéra*, using a 25 × 25 cm (10 × 10 in) square or 25 cm (10 in) diameter, loose-bottomed, round cake tin. Pre-heat the oven to 180°C/350°F/Gas Mark 4. Line the base of the cake tin with greaseproof paper and lightly grease.

Dissolve the coffee granules in the hot water. Mix the egg yolks into the coffee, adding the melted chocolate. Whisk the egg whites and sugar to soft peaks and fold into the chocolate mix.

Pour the mixture into the cake tin and bake in the pre-heated oven for 10–12 minutes until just firm. Allow to cool.

To make the orange mousse, pour half of the double cream, the milk and the zest from 1 orange into a saucepan and bring to the boil. Remove from the heat and add the chopped chocolate. Stir until the chocolate has melted.

Whisk the egg yolks and caster sugar together to a thick ribbon (sabayon) stage. Add the chocolate and orange cream mix, and cook in a bowl over

BELOW
Frozen Orange and Espresso Mousse

simmering water until you have a thick-cream consistency. Pass through a fine sieve and whisk until this custard is cool.

Whisk the remaining 150 ml (¼ pint) double cream, the sour cream, ½ teaspoon orange zest and the Grand Marnier to a soft peak. Fold into the cooled orange custard. The mousse can now be spooned on top of the sponge base and frozen.

While the orange mousse is freezing, the espresso mousse can be made. Pour half of the cream, the milk and the ground coffee into a saucepan and bring to the boil. Remove from the heat and add the chopped white chocolate.

Whisk the egg yolks and caster sugar to a thick ribbon (sabayon) stage. Add the chocolate and coffee cream mix and cook in a bowl over simmering water until you have a thick-cream consistency. Pass through a fine sieve and whisk until cool.

Whisk the remaining 150 ml (¼ pint) double cream, sour cream and Tia Maria to a soft peak. Fold into the cooled coffee custard. The espresso mousse can now be spooned on top of the frozen orange mousse.

Return to the freezer until completely set. Once frozen, the mousse can be removed from the tin and topped with a thin layer of chocolate ganache (see *Gâteau Opéra*, page 315). However, for this recipe only half of the quantity will be needed.

To make the coffee syrup, put the coffee and sugar in a pan and bring to the boil. Cook until reduced by half. Allow to cool. For a liqueur coffee syrup, add a splash of Tia Maria.

It is best to cut and portion the mousse while still frozen, using a hot knife (return the portions you're not serving to the freezer until needed). Before serving, remove from the freezer and leave refrigerated for 15–20 minutes. This takes the completely frozen texture from the dessert, giving a slightly softer touch, without losing the frozen edge. Serve with the coffee syrup, warm or at room temperature.

This dessert also eats very well with *Bitter Chocolate Sauce* (page 323) or pouring cream. Nine to twelve portions is quite a large recipe; however, the ingredient quantities cannot be reduced without spoiling the consistency and texture of the mousses.

Warm Port and Fig Broth with Cream Cheese Ice-cream

Apicius, the great Roman gourmet, preserved figs in honey, and force-fed figs and mead (a honey wine) to his pigs to fatten them and improve the flavour of the meat. The combination of port and figs here, in a fruit-soup dessert, is a delicious one, the luxury fruit cooked in the imported fortified wine that has become so associated with Britain.

The two work together so well with cream cheese ice-cream to finish the dish that I'm sure you won't need to be force-fed.

SERVES 6

For the Broth (makes about 600 ml/1 pint)

8 fresh figs (Black Mission), quartered
300 ml (½ pint) port
250 ml (8 fl oz) water
20 g (scant 1 oz) sugar
½ cinnamon stick
2 teaspoons lemon juice

For the Cream Cheese Ice-cream

400 ml (14 fl oz) whipping cream
50 ml (2 fl oz) milk
4 egg yolks
60 g (generous 2 oz) caster sugar
175 g (6 oz) cream cheese

To Serve

6–9 fresh figs, halved
Port Syrup (page 289, optional), or 25 g (1 oz) butter and 25 g (1 oz) icing sugar

First, make the ice-cream. Boil together the cream and milk. While the cream is heating, whisk together the egg yolks and sugar until they form thick ribbons. You can do this using a food processor, electric mixer or an electric hand whisk.

Beat the cheese until smooth. Pour the boiled cream and milk onto the cream cheese, stir until smooth, and then mix with the whisked egg yolks.

Cook in a bowl over simmering water, stirring until the custard coats the back of a spoon. (Do not let it boil or the eggs will scramble.) Strain through a sieve. Leave to cool, stirring from time to time to prevent a skin from forming.

Once cooled, churn in an ice-cream machine, in two batches if necessary. (If you don't have an ice-cream machine, see Note, page 309.) Each will take approximately 20 minutes, to the point of thickening and increasing in volume. It is important not to churn until frozen as this will curdle the mix, leaving a slightly grainy texture.

Pour the ice-cream into a container and place it in the freezer to finish setting. Repeat the same churning process for the second batch.

Now make the broth. Place all of the broth ingredients in a saucepan. Bring to the simmer and cook slowly until the quantity has reduced by a third.

Remove the cinnamon stick, pour into a liquidizer and blend until smooth. Pass through a fine sieve. The broth is now ready.

Two or three fig halves will be plenty per portion for the fig garnish. There are two methods for cooking the garnishes.
1. Remove the stalks from the figs and place in the port syrup (it is best to make the syrup slightly looser than mentioned in the recipe). Simmer for a few minutes until the figs have become tender.
2. Butter the fig halves and place on a baking sheet, face-side down. Bake in a pre-heated oven at 200°C/400°F/Gas Mark 6, for 4–5 minutes before removing from the oven. Turn the figs and dust with icing sugar. These can now be glazed with a gas gun, (page 11) or under a hot grill.

To present the dish, warm the broth and spoon into bowls. Place 2–3 fig halves in each bowl. Shape the cream cheese ice-cream (creating a scroll or using a scoop), and present on the warm figs or in a separate bowl.

Note: *Fig Rolls* (page 360) go very well with this dish.

Iced Vanilla Parfait with Nutmeg Clotted Cream and Caramelized Apples

Vanilla and nutmeg are two flavours used in bread and butter pudding, and that dessert was the inspiration behind this parfait. The beauty of serving ice-cream such as a parfait as the main part of a dessert is that it can be prepared, made and frozen well in advance. The caramelized apples can also be made in advance, just warming them through when you are ready.

Using vanilla pods will give a natural flavour, with the small black seeds running through the mix. If unavailable, replace with 2–3 teaspoons of vanilla essence.

Here, I'm making the parfait in a terrine or loaf tin, but you can make individual parfaits. Another way of presenting the parfait is to set and freeze it in teacups. The apples can then be presented on top with the cream.

SERVES 6

6 egg yolks
175 g (6 oz) caster sugar
2 vanilla pods, split and scraped, or 2–3 teaspoons of vanilla essence
450 ml (¾ pint) double cream
150 ml (¼ pint) clotted cream
Freshly grated nutmeg
3 Granny Smith's or Golden Delicious apples
Butter
Demerara or caster sugar

Line a 1.2 litre (2 pint) terrine or loaf tin or six 6 × 6 cm (2½ × 2½ in) rings with cling film or greaseproof paper.

Whisk together the egg yolks, sugar and vanilla seeds or essence in a bowl over simmering water until doubled in volume, at a thick ribbon (sabayon) stage. Remove from the heat and continue to whisk until cool (this can be done in an electric mixer).

Lightly whip the double cream until at a soft peak stage. Fold into the sabayon and pour into the lined mould or individual rings. The parfait can now be frozen until set. The freezing process will take a minimum of 2–3 hours.

The split vanilla pods, if using, can be cut into thin long strips. These will then be used to decorate the dish.

Finely grate between ¼ and ½ teaspoon of nutmeg into the clotted cream (more can be added for nutmeg fans). Refrigerate to set the cream, making it easier to shape.

Peel the apples and cut into quarters. Cut away the core and split each quarter in two. This now gives you 24 apple wedges, 4 per portion.

Place the wedges in cold water and bring to the boil. Drain and dry the apples. When ready to serve, these can be pan-fried in melted butter, adding a teaspoon or two of the chosen sugar; this will begin to caramelize. Add 1–2 tablespoons of water, turning the caramel into a thick syrup.

Another method is to dust the wedges with caster sugar (icing sugar can also be used) and caramelize under a hot grill or using a gas gun (page 11), when serving the dessert.

To serve the parfait, turn out the rings and place apple wedges on each plate with the nutmeg clotted cream, shaped between two spoons or into scrolls.

Note: A sponge base can be used in the individual moulds or be placed on top of the terrine. Once turned out of the terrine, the sponge becomes the base. The sponge base from the *Sherry Trifle* recipe (page 312) can be used for this purpose. Simply spread the sponge mix 1 cm (½ in) deep onto a suitably sized baking tin or tray.

Cranberry and Walnut Tart

Cranberries are actually native to Europe, although they are more associated with America. They have become the traditional accompaniment, in sauce form, to our roast Christmas turkey. Another popular use is in a relish or chutney, normally served with game birds, pies and venison.

The sharp bite the fresh fruit has when served with savoury dishes also lends itself well to these walnut tarts, the base of which resembles the sticky sweet pecan pie, gooey flavours we all love. The tart is also garnished with cranberries warmed in orange juice and their own jelly.

SERVES 6

225 g (½ lb) *Sweet Shortcrust Pastry* (page 364)
    (450 g/1 lb will be needed for individual
    rings)
40 g (1½ oz) butter
100 g (4 oz) caster sugar
50 g (2 oz) light soft brown sugar
50 g (2 oz) dark soft brown sugar
175 g (6 oz) golden syrup
1 teaspoon vanilla essence
Pinch of salt
2 whole eggs
1 egg yolk
100 g (4 oz) cleaned walnuts, scraped and lightly
    chopped (halved or quartered)
100 g (4 oz) fresh cranberries
Icing sugar, sifted, to decorate

For the Cranberry Compote

225 g (8 oz) fresh cranberries
Juice of 1 orange
50 g (2 oz) caster sugar
1–2 tablespoons cranberry jelly

This recipe will fill a 17–20 cm (7–8 in) flan ring or six 9 cm (3½ in) diameter individual tartlet tins.

Pre-heat the oven to 200°C/400°F/Gas Mark 6. Line the pastry case or cases with the sweet pastry, greaseproof paper and baking beans or rice.

Blind-bake in the pre-heated oven for 20 minutes. Remove from the oven and leave to cool. Turn the oven down to 160°C/315°F/Gas Mark 2½.

Melt the butter in a saucepan, allowing it to reach a nut-brown stage. Mix together the caster sugar, light and dark soft brown sugar and golden syrup. This can now be stirred into the nut-brown butter off the heat.

The vanilla, salt, whole eggs and yolk can now also be added. Allow the mix to cool. Once cooled,

spoon into the tart case(s). Mix together the chopped walnuts and the cranberries and sprinkle over the tart(s). Bake in the pre-heated oven for 40–45 minutes for the large tart and just 20 minutes for individual ones. Leave to rest before removing from the flan ring or tartlet tins.

The tarts are best served warm, but will also eat well cold.

To make the compote, place the cranberries, orange juice and sugar in a saucepan and bring to a simmer. Lift the cranberries from the pan.

Add the jelly to the liquor and bring to the simmer. The consistency needs to be syrupy: the sauce can either be reduced or more jelly added to achieve this. Allow to cool slightly before mixing with the cranberries.

The cranberry compote will eat at its best served warm. To serve, dot small spoonfuls of compote around the rim of the plate and sift over a little icing sugar.

Note: Vanilla ice-cream (see *Nutmeg Ice-cream,* page 309) or bought) eats very well with this dish.

Steamed Lemon Sponge with Easy Lemon Sauce

This recipe belongs to Marguerite Patten and was the first pudding I cooked at the age of thirteen. I followed the recipe from her book *Puddings and Desserts,* which was published in 1963. The book belonged to my mother originally, but I am pleased to say it's mine now.

This recipe is a great example of how classic recipes will never die. Almost thirty years on and it cooks and tastes just sensational. Thank you for the

OPPOSITE
Cranberry and Walnut Tart with Vanilla Ice-cream

recipe, Marguerite, and also for the inspiration it gave me to want to cook – I've never looked back.

This recipe will fill a 1.2 litre (2 pint) pudding basin.

SERVES 6–8

225 g (8 oz) butter
175 g (6 oz) caster sugar
Zest and juice of 2 lemons
4 eggs
225 g (8 oz) self-raising flour, sifted
Pinch of salt

For the Easy Lemon Sauce

Zest and juice of 2 lemons
Water
50 g (2 oz) caster sugar
1 heaped tablespoon arrowroot mixed with
 1 tablespoon of water

You will need a 1.2 litre (2 pint) pudding basin (preferably plastic), buttered and floured.

To make the sponge, cream together the butter, sugar and lemon zest until light and fluffy. Add the eggs one at a time until mixed well. Mix together the flour and salt and beat into the sponge mix. Add the lemon juice. Spoon into the prepared bowl, cover lightly with buttered foil and place in a hot steamer for 1¼–1½ hours.

The sauce can be made just 5 minutes before the sponge is ready. Pour the juice from the lemons into a measuring jug and top up with water to 300 ml (½ pint). Pour into a saucepan with the zest and caster sugar and bring to the boil. Once boiling, whisk in the arrowroot. Return to a simmer and allow to cook for 2–3 minutes.

Once the sponge is cooked, remove from the steamer and stand for a few minutes. Remove the foil and turn out onto a plate, squeezing the plastic bowl to help it along. Pour some of the sauce over. Cut into portions and offer the remaining sauce separately.

Steamed Upside-down Blackberry and Apple Pudding

Steamed puddings are direct descendants of the puddings that used to be wrapped in pudding cloths and suspended in the cooking pot. Apples have always been a favourite ingredient, and their combination with blackberries – which are around at the same time of the year – is very traditional. The marriage usually appears in pies, where the fruits are encased in sweet pastry, but here I have steamed a light lemon and cinnamon sponge on top of the fruits. Once cooked, the pudding is turned out upside-down. I always save some of the 'topping' to finish the dish, making the dessert even fruitier.

SERVES 6

4 green dessert apples, peeled, cored and quartered
Butter
50 g (2 oz) caster sugar
225 g (8 oz) blackberries, washed
1 tablespoon blackberry jam

For the Sponge

100 g (4 oz) unsalted butter
150 g (5 oz) caster sugar
4 eggs
1 egg yolk
200 g (7 oz) self-raising flour
¼ teaspoon ground cinnamon
Finely grated zest of 1 lemon
1–2 tablespoons of milk, if needed

Butter and flour a 900 ml (1½ pint) pudding bowl or six 150 ml (¼ pint) bowls.

Halve each apple quarter, giving eight wedges per apple. These can now also be halved, cutting through the middle, creating pieces, rather than thin slices.

Melt a knob of butter in a saucepan, adding the apples and caster sugar. Cook for 2–3 minutes before adding the blackberries and blackberry jam. Stir in and remove from the heat. Leave to cool.

To make the sponge, beat the butter and sugar together until almost white and the sugar has dissolved. This stage can be easily achieved in an electric mixer.

Beat together the eggs and egg yolk. These can now be slowly poured in while the butter is whisking. Mix in completely until light and fluffy.

Sift the flour with the cinnamon and fold in, with the lemon zest, until completely incorporated, adding the milk as necessary to create a dropping consistency.

Spoon half of the apple and blackberry mix into the pudding bowl(s). Top with the pudding mix and cover with greaseproof paper or tin foil, with a fold in the centre to create space for the rising pudding. Place in a steamer or on a trivet in a saucepan, and steam. Individual puddings will take 35–40 minutes and a large pudding 1–1¼ hours. Top up with water as necessary during cooking.

BELOW
Steamed Upside-down Blackberry and Apple Pudding

Once cooked, remove from the steamer and leave to rest for 5 minutes before turning out. During this resting time the remaining blackberry and apple mix can be re-heated. This will soften both fruits.

Once the sponge has been turned out, spoon the extra fruits on top, allowing them to tumble onto the plate.

This pudding, as with almost all steamed sponges, will eat well with pouring cream or custard.

Sticky Toffee Apple Pudding

Toffee apples were always a Guy Fawkes Night treat when I was a child. The crunchy boiled sugar surrounding the apple was so moreish. These days I'm not sure I could eat one of those, but the toffee flavour does work well with apples, so here is a recipe giving you exactly that.

The toffee flavour can be as sticky as you want it to be. This is created by dark soft brown sugar cooking and caramelizing around the outside of the suet sponge, while the apples cook inside.

SERVES 6

For the Suet Pastry

175 g (6 oz) self-raising flour
Pinch of salt
75 g (3 oz) beef or vegetable suet
150 ml (¼ pint) water or milk
50 g (2 oz) unsalted butter
25–50 g (1–2 oz) dark soft brown sugar

For the Filling

675 g (1½ lb) Bramley apples, peeled and quartered
50 g (2 oz) butter
75 g (3 oz) light soft brown sugar
2–3 tablespoons lemon juice

To make the pastry, sift together the flour and salt. Add the suet, stirring in the water or milk. The dough can now be worked and mixed, creating a smooth consistency. Wrap and rest for 20 minutes.

Spread the butter around a 900 ml (1½ pint) pudding basin and sprinkle with the dark brown sugar. The more sprinkled, the stronger the toffee flavour will be. Roll out three-quarters of the pastry and line the basin.

Halve the apple quarters once more into eight slices per apple. These can now also be halved to shape into rough chunks.

Melt the butter. Once bubbling, add the apples and cook for 1–2 minutes. Add the sugar and lemon juice and remove from the stove. Leave to cool. Once cooled, spoon the apples into the pudding basin.

Roll the remaining quarter of the pastry and place on top of the pudding, sealing the edges well. This can now be covered with folded greaseproof paper and foil and tied with string if necessary. Steam over boiling water for 1½–1¾ hours, topping up the hot water if necessary.

Once cooked, remove from the steamer and rest for 5 minutes before carefully turning out.

The sticky toffee apple pudding is now ready to serve and eats very well with custard, thick cream or vanilla ice-cream.

Syllabub

One of our most famous British sweets, related to a number of others such as posset, flummery and Atholl Brose. The original syllabub was a mixture of fresh milk and a still sweet wine popular in Britain in Elizabethan times, imported from Sillery, a *grand cru* village in Champagne. The milk was squeezed straight from a cow into a bucket of 'Sille' wine, creating a fine froth. 'Bub' was Elizabethan slang for a bubbling drink, hence 'sille bub'.

Syllabub was drunk rather than eaten at first. It is said that Charles II was so fond of it that he kept cows in St James's Park so that if he got thirsty while walking, the cows could be milked directly into a bowl of wine!

Recipes for syllabub haven't changed much from the original; they still use lemon, sugar, whipped cream and sweet wine, sherry or brandy – depending on which part of the country you come from, as there are many different versions. The mixture is left to sit for several hours, by which time the alcohol and cream will have separated, creating the classic syllabub consistency.

SERVES 4–6

½ bottle of sweet white wine or 150 ml (¼ pint) sweet sherry
50 g (2 oz) caster sugar
Peeled rind and juice of 2 lemons
4 tablespoons brandy
300 ml (½ pint) double cream

If using the sweet wine, bring to the boil with the sugar and reduce by half. Once reduced, remove from the stove and add the lemon rind. Once cool, add the lemon juice and brandy, cover with cling film and leave to stand for several hours or, for an even stronger flavour, overnight. If using sweet sherry, follow the above method, but without reducing by half, only warming through before adding the rind.

Once infused, strain through a sieve. The double cream can now be whisked, pouring the wine in slowly until all has been absorbed. It is important to keep the cream softly whipped. Spoon into glasses and chill for several hours. You may find the wine syrup will almost separate from the cream, sitting in the bottom of the glass.

This dessert then almost eats and drinks like an Irish coffee, with the thick cream on top.

Note: This syllabub eats very nicely with fresh raspberries placed in the bottom of the glasses. The fruits then become marinated with the sweet wine and brandy.

Jam Roly-poly

This is a classic example of a British steamed pudding made with suet, but it is rolled with a filling, rather than being cooked in a pudding bowl. If this became a favourite during your schooldays, I think it stays with you for life. The gooey texture of suet sponge absorbing and oozing strawberry jam, to be finished with the flavour of fresh vanilla custard: need I say more? Here is the recipe.

SERVES 6

225 g (8 oz) self-raising flour
1 teaspoon baking powder
Pinch of salt
Finely grated zest of 1 lemon or orange (optional)
150 g (5 oz) vegetarian or beef suet
100–150 ml (3½–5 fl oz) milk
150–175 g (5–6 oz) strawberry jam
Custard Sauce (page 324), to serve

Sift together the self-raising flour, baking powder and pinch of salt. Add the grated zest of lemon or orange, if using, along with the suet, and work to a breadcrumb consistency.

The milk can now be added, a little at a time, until a soft texture has formed, but do not allow to become sticky. Wrap in cling film and allow to rest for 20–30 minutes.

The suet dough can now be rolled into a rectangle, approximately 30 × 20 cm (12 × 8 in). Spread the jam onto the paste, leaving a clear 1 cm (½ in) border.

The border can now be brushed with water or extra milk before rolling. Pinch at either end to seal the jam inside. The roly poly can now be wrapped very loosely in greaseproof paper, followed by loose foil. Tie at either end.

The pudding can now be steamed for 2 hours, topping up the water during the cooking time. Once cooked, unwrap, slice and serve with the custard.

Note: The orange or lemon zest is an optional extra, but either adds an extra flavour and bite to the dish. Orange marmalade, lemon curd or mincemeat can also be used as the filling in place of the jam.

Baked Raspberry Puddings

The raspberry is one of our greatest soft fruits, and it grows best in Scotland, both wild and cultivated. Raspberries used to be eaten in crumbles and pies, never raw as we would today, and here I have used them in a baked pudding. Baked puddings were introduced in the early seventeenth century as an alternative way of cooking the traditional pudding mixture other than boiling it in a pudding bag. It tended to be more of a rich man's method, as the fuel for ovens was more expensive than that for one cooking pot.

These puddings are baked in individual size-1 soufflé dishes. These are larger than the standard size-1 (150 ml/¼ pint) ramekins. The beauty of this recipe is that it's so easy to make: all the ingredients (bar the raspberries) are blitzed in a food processor, poured into the moulds and baked – it couldn't be simpler.

SERVES 4

225 g (8 oz) fresh raspberries
4 eggs
50 g (2 oz) plain flour
50 g (2 oz) ground almonds, or hazelnuts
25 g (1 oz) butter, melted
65 g (scant 3 oz) caster sugar
150 ml (¼ pint) double cream
Finely grated zest of 1 lemon
Icing sugar, for dusting

Pre-heat the oven to 190°C/375°F/Gas Mark 5 and butter four size-1 soufflé dishes.

Blitz all the ingredients (bar the raspberries) together in a food processor until smooth. Warm the soufflé dishes in the oven. Once warmed, divide the raspberries between the dishes and pour the pudding mix on top.

BELOW
Jam Roly-poly

Bake immediately for 30–35 minutes (maximum 40 minutes) until golden brown. The mix will have almost souffléd in the dishes, creating a light sponge. Remove from the oven and dust each with icing sugar.

The dessert can now be served with lightly whipped cream or a lemon custard (see Variation on *Custard Sauce*, page 324).

Note: Many other fruits can be used in this dessert, particularly mixed red summer berries.

Strawberry Cheesecake Swiss Roll

The sponge for Swiss roll is normally a basic Genoise, where a thick frothy texture is created with the eggs and sugar (sabayon) before folding in the flour. This recipe is a little different, separating the eggs, then whisking the whites to a meringue consistency and folding into the cake mixture at the last minute. The texture is lovely to eat but, when rolling, the cold sponge does sometimes crack. But that's the beauty of home-made dishes – the flavours must come first, and who minds if the sponge is broken?

SERVES 6–8

Strawberry Jam (page 387), for spreading
Icing sugar, for dusting

For the Sponge

4 large eggs
50 g (2 oz) caster sugar
50 g (2 oz) plain flour

For the Cream

15 g (½ oz) caster sugar
100 g (4 oz) full-fat soft cream cheese
150 ml (¼ pint) double cream, lightly whipped

For this recipe you will need an 18 × 28 cm (7 × 11 in) Swiss roll tin, buttered and lined with greaseproof paper. Pre-heat the oven to 180°C/350°F/Gas Mark 4.

Separate the eggs into two bowls. The yolks can now be mixed with the caster sugar and whisked to a thick (sabayon) consistency. Sift the flour into the egg-yolk mix and fold in.

Whisk the egg whites to a soft peak stage. Add a few tablespoons to the egg yolks, beating in well. The remaining whisked whites can be gently folded into the sponge mix.

Pour into the lined tin and bake in the pre-heated oven for 12–15 minutes. Once cooked, remove from the oven and cover with a damp cloth to prevent the sponge from drying and cracking.

The cheesecake cream can now be made while the sponge cools. Beat the sugar into the cream cheese until the sugar has dissolved and creamed. Gently fold in the lightly whipped double cream. The cream can now be refrigerated for 20–30 minutes, to firm it slightly.

Once the sponge has cooled, remove the cloth. Place a sheet of greaseproof paper on a small chopping board and place on top of the sponge. Now simply turn the sponge tray over and lift off carefully. If the greaseproof paper lining the tin is still attached to the sponge, carefully pull away.

The strawberry jam can now be spread onto the sponge, leaving a 1 cm (½ in) clear border.

Spoon cheesecake cream on top and then carefully roll using the greaseproof paper. Remove the paper and lightly dust with icing sugar.

The strawberry cheesecake Swiss roll is now ready to serve.

Note: Freshly scraped vanilla can be added to the cheesecake mix for a fuller and fresher flavour.

Gooseberry Sherbet

Fruit-flavoured water ices, known as 'sorbets' to the French and 'sherbets' to the Arabs, have been known since the thirteenth century. They were invented by the Chinese, brought to Europe by Marco Polo, and perfected by the Italians. Apparently the first water ices in England were created by Charles I's Italian chefs, but it took another few centuries before sorbets or ice-creams became common in the British tradition.

However, sherbets are not the same as sorbets. A sorbet is made from fruit purée mixed with sweet stock syrup and that's basically it, while a sherbet uses those ingredients plus milk and egg white, which give it a fizzy-like finish. Almost any other fruit, fresh or frozen, can replace the gooseberries.

SERVES 4–6

450 g (1 lb) fresh or frozen gooseberries
250 ml (8 fl oz) stock syrup (see Note)
250 ml (8 fl oz) milk
1 teaspoon lemon juice
1 egg white

Wash the fresh gooseberries, put them in a saucepan with the stock syrup and bring to a simmer. Cover and cook gently for 3–4 minutes or until the fruit is tender. Remove from the heat and leave to cool. Now purée the gooseberries in the syrup and strain them through a sieve. Stir in the milk and lemon juice, then pour the mixture into an ice-cream machine and begin to churn. It will take between 20–25 minutes to reach a thick, almost setting stage. When ready, whisk the egg white to soft peaks and add it to the mix. Store the sherbet in the freezer until needed – or eat it straight away.

Note: If you do not have an ice-cream maker, freeze the sherbet before adding the egg white, whisking every so often to break the ice crystals. Once it has frozen, put it into a food processor and blitz it to a purée. Then fold in the beaten egg white and re-freeze.

For a stock syrup, bring 300 ml (½ pint) water and 225 g (8 oz) caster sugar to the boil. Simmer for a few minutes until the sugar has completely dissolved and thickened the water. Cool and keep refrigerated. This makes 450 ml (¾ pint).

RIGHT
Gooseberry Sherbet

Rhubarb Tart

Rhubarb is native to northern Asia, and did not reach Britain until the sixteenth century. It was used medicinally at first, and was not valued as a food until at least the eighteenth century.

Home-made fresh fruit tarts are so seductive, the juicy fresh fruits sitting on top of a good home-made pastry cream – *crème pâtisserie* in French – in a crisp pastry case. They really are very special to eat. For rhubarb I like to use sweet shortcrust pastry. This gives the crumbly texture needed to balance against the cream and soft texture of the fruit.

The pastry case and cream will work as a lovely base for a tart made with almost any fruit – fresh raspberries, blackberries, strawberries, as well as any pre-cooked fruits (apricots, damsons, gooseberries, plums and so on).

SERVES 6–8

300–350 g (10–12 oz) *Sweet Shortcrust Pastry*
 (page 364)
750–900 g (1¾–2 lb) fresh rhubarb
60–75 g (2¼–3 oz) caster sugar

For the Pastry Cream
(makes approx. 500 ml/17 fl oz)

4 egg yolks
75 g (3 oz) caster sugar
Salt
25 g (1 oz) cornflour
300 ml (½ pint) milk

1–2 vanilllla pods, split and scraped,
       or 2–3 teaspoons vanilla essence
35 ml (1¼ fl oz) double cream
25 g (1 oz) unsalted butter

Pre-heat the oven to 220°C/425°F/Gas Mark 7.

Roll the pastry on a floured surface to approximately 3 mm (⅛ in) thick, and use it to line a flan ring of 20–25 cm (8–9 in) diameter and 2.5–3.5 cm (1–1½ in) deep. To guarantee a clean finish with no shrinking of the pastry, it's best to have any excess hanging over the edge of the ring. (Once baked, this can be cut away with a sharp knife.) Prick the base of the pastry with a fork, and refrigerate for 20 minutes before baking.

Line the pastry case with greasepoof paper and baking beans or rice. Blind-bake in the oven for 20–25 minutes until golden and crispy. Remove from the oven, taking out the beans or rice and paper, trim the overhanging pastry and leave to cool. Reduce the oven temperature to 180°C/350°F/Gas Mark 4.

To prepare the rhubarb, first peel it if slightly tough and stringy. Now cut it into 2–3 cm (¾–1¼ in) sticks and place in a roasting tray. Sprinkle with the sugar, place in the oven, and cook for 10–15 minutes or until tender. Remove from the oven and leave to cool. The rhubarb can now be carefully spooned from the tray, and any juices brought to the boil and reduced to a syrupy consistency. The rhubarb is now ready to use.

For a different finish, stand the cooked rhubarb on a baking tray, lightly dust with icing sugar and glaze under a hot grill or with a gas gun (page 11). This will give the fruit slightly burnt, bitter-sweet tinges, creating another flavour and colour. Leave to cool.

Meanwhile, make the pastry cream. Cream together the egg yolks and caster sugar in a bowl. Add a small pinch of salt and the cornflour. Bring the milk to the boil with the split and scraped vanilla pod (or essence) and pour onto the egg-yolk mixture. Return the mixture to the pan, bring back to the simmer and cook for a few minutes, making sure it doesn't boil. Add the double cream and butter and then pass through a sieve. Press a piece of greaseproof paper or cling film onto the surface to prevent a skin from forming. Leave to cool. The fresh, vanilla-tasting pastry cream is ready to use. (Grated fruit zests can be added to the milk for a different flavour.) You will need approximately 400 ml (14 fl oz); the remainder will last well in the fridge for 3–4 days.

When all the tart components are cold, the tart can be assembled. Spread the pastry cream into the flan ring, and fill to approximately 1 cm (½ in) deep. Now sit the fruit on top, either carefully arranged on the cream or merely spooned over in a more rustic fashion. Brush the syrup over the rhubarb for a more flavoursome finish. The tart is now ready to enjoy, with the tender fruits and rich cream balanced by the crumbly pastry.

Note: Try using custard powder instead of cornflour for an even more intense flavour,

The quantities for this pastry cream recipe can be halved for a shallow mould. Once cooled, any remaining cream can be refrigerated for 3–4 days, or used as a base for individual fruit tartlets.

Queen of Puddings

This is also known as Manchester Pudding. It is another combination of custard ingredients and breadcrumbs and, significantly, Mrs Beeton calls it Queen of Bread Puddings. You could use breadcrumbs as here, or some vanilla sponge and jam, which is a delicious variation. What you can't do without, though, is the meringue topping. This is a really sweet pudding, the one you want to eat plenty of but quite often regret afterwards.

OPPOSITE
Rhubarb Tart

600 ml (1 pint) milk
Grated zest of 1 lemon
50 g (2 oz) unsalted butter
50 g (2 oz) caster sugar
100 g (4 oz) fresh white breadcrumbs
6 egg yolks, beaten
4 tablespoons *Strawberry Jam* (page 387)

For the Meringue

4 egg whites
225 g (8 oz) caster sugar

Pre-heat the oven to 180°C/350°F/Gas Mark 4 and butter six 7.5 cm (3 in) soufflé dishes or one 1.75 litre (3 pint) soufflé dish.

Bring the milk and zest to a boil in a pan, remove from the heat and leave to stand for 15 minutes. Remove the zest and add the butter and sugar. Bring back to a simmer and remove from the heat. Stir in the breadcrumbs and allow to cool slightly. Add the yolks to the mix. Pour it into the soufflé dish(es) and stand them in a roasting tray three-quarters full of hot water. Bake for 30–40 minutes until set. When the puddings have just set, remove from the oven and the water bath and leave to rest for 10 minutes.

Increase the oven temperature to 230°C/450°F/Gas Mark 8. Divide the jam between the tops of the puddings. To make the meringue, whisk the egg whites with the sugar until they form firm peaks. Pipe or spoon the meringue over the top of the puddings and return them to the hot oven, or place under a pre-heated grill, for about 6–8 minutes until golden brown. The queen of puddings is now ready to serve.

Variation

Baked vanilla sponge (see *Lemon and Vanilla Sponge Cake*, page 341)
Strawberry Jam (page 387)
4 eggs
75 g (3 oz) caster sugar
300 ml (½ pint) milk
300 ml (½ pint) double cream
1 vanilla pod, split (optional)

For the Meringue

4 egg whites
225 g (8 oz) caster sugar

Pre-heat the oven to 160°C/325°F/Gas Mark 3 and prepare six 7.5 cm (3 in) soufflé dishes or one 1.75 litre (3 pint) soufflé dish.

Split the sponge into three layers and sandwich together again with the strawberry jam. Cut into 1 cm (½ in) squares and divide between the soufflé dishes or arrange in the base of the large dish.

Whisk the eggs and sugar together and add the milk, cream and the scraped-out insides of the vanilla pod, if using. Strain through a sieve and pour on top of the sponge sandwich. Sit the moulds in a roasting tray three-quarters filled with hot water and cook in the pre-heated oven for 30–40 minutes until the custard has just set. Remove from the oven and the water bath and leave to rest.

Increase the oven temperature to 230°C/450°F/Gas Mark 8.

To make the meringue, whisk the egg whites with the sugar until they form firm peaks. Pipe or spoon the meringue over the top of the puddings and return them to the hot oven for about 6–8 minutes until golden brown.

Now you have two ways of making this pudding: it's up to you to decide which one to try.

Bread and Butter Pudding

Yet another variation on custard, bread and butter pudding has become one of our classics. It was always a good way of using up stale bread with milk, sugar and eggs, but this would often result in an overcooked, dry and tasteless pud, which left it with a bad name. This recipe will give you quite a different dish, something with an almost sponge-like texture with thick fresh custard oozing out between

OPPOSITE
Bread and Butter Pudding

the layers. I'm using just egg yolks and half milk and double cream, which is obviously a little more expensive to make, but once you've tried it you'll never want to make it any other way.

SERVES 6–8

12 medium slices of white bread
50 g (2 oz) unsalted butter, softened
8 egg yolks
175 g (6 oz) caster sugar
1 vanilla pod or a few drops of vanilla essence
300 ml (½ pint) milk
300 ml (½ pint) double cream
25 g (1 oz) sultanas
25 g (1 oz) raisins

To Finish

Caster sugar

Grease a 1.75 litre (3 pint) pudding basin with butter.

First, butter the bread, remove the crusts and cut in half diagonally, creating triangles. Whisk the egg yolks and caster sugar together in a bowl. Split the vanilla pod, if using, and place in a pan with the milk and cream or add the vanilla essence. Bring the milk and cream to the simmer, then sieve onto the egg yolks, stirring all the time. You now have the custard.

Arrange the bread in layers in the prepared basin, sprinkling the sultanas and raisins in between layers. Finish with a final layer of bread without any

fruit on top as this tends to burn. The warm egg mixture may now be poured over the bread and cooked straightaway, but I prefer to pour the custard over the pudding then leave it to soak into the bread for 20 minutes before cooking. This allows the bread to take on a new texture and have the flavours all the way through.

Pre-heat the oven to 180°C/350°F/Gas Mark 4.

Once the bread has been soaked, place the dish in a roasting tray three-quarters filled with warm water. Lightly cover with buttered foil and place in the pre-heated oven. Cook for about 20–30 minutes until the pudding begins to set. Because we are using only egg yolks, the mixture cooks like a fresh custard and only thickens; it should not become too firm.

When ready, remove from the water bath, sprinkle liberally with caster sugar to cover, and glaze under the grill on medium heat. The sugar will dissolve and caramelize and you may find that the corners of the bread start to burn a little. This helps the flavours, though, giving a bittersweet taste, and certainly looks good. The bread and butter pudding is now ready to serve and when you take that first spoonful and place it in a bowl you will see the custard just seeping from the dish. You now have a new British classic at its best.

Note: Freshly grated or ground nutmeg can be sprinkled between the layers for an extra spicy flavour.

Bread and Butter Pudding Ice-cream

You all know how close bread and butter pudding is to me, so turning it into an ice-cream may seem a little out of character, but not at all. When eating this ice-cream you feel you capture all of the original recipe's flavours.

The ice-cream is finished with caramelized Melba toast, which represents the crispy glazed topping of the classic hot pudding.

SERVES 6–8

For the Ice-cream

250 ml (8 fl oz) whipping cream
250 ml (8 fl oz) milk
25 g (1 oz) raisins
25 g (1 oz) sultanas
1 vanilla pod, split
¼ teaspoon freshly grated nutmeg

For the Crumbs

100 g (4 oz) fresh white breadcrumbs
40 g (1½ oz) demerara sugar

For the Custard

6 egg yolks
50 g (2 oz) caster sugar

To Serve

Caramelized Melba toasts (see Note opposite)
Custard Sauce (page 324, optional)

Pre-heat the oven to 180°C/350°F/Gas Mark 4.

Bring all of the ingredients for the ice-cream to a simmer. Remove from the heat and allow to infuse for 20–30 minutes.

Meanwhile, mix the crumbs with the demerara sugar and spread on a baking sheet. Roast for approximately 10 minutes, then remove the tray from the oven. The crumbs and sugar will have begun to solidify: break them down again into crumbs and return to the oven for a further 5 minutes. Remove from the oven and break to a crumble. Leave to one side.

Cream together the egg yolks and sugar. Remove the vanilla pod from the cream mixture and strain the cream onto the yolks. Keep the dried fruit to one side. Whisk the egg mixture with the cream and return it to the saucepan, or a bowl over simmering water, and cook the custard over a low heat until it thickens and coats the back of a spoon. Add the reserved fruit and allow to cool.

Once cool, stir the crumbs into the mix. Now churn the ice-cream in an ice-cream maker for 20–25 minutes until it has thickened and increased in volume. Pour it into a bowl and allow it to finish setting in the freezer.

To serve, sit a triangle of caramelized Melba toast on top of a scroll of the ice-cream. You could also trickle a little custard sauce around it, to represent the custard that flows out of a baked bread and butter pudding when cut.

Note: Use 7.5 × 3.5 cm (3 × 1¾ in) rings to make individual ice-creams.

This ice-cream can also be made without an ice-cream machine. Once ready for churning, place the mix in a large bowl and freeze until well thickened. Now whip to keep a blended consistency, re-freeze and repeat this process every 15–20 minutes until almost set. Leave to freeze completely.

To make caramelized Melba toasts, toast medium-sliced bread on both sides. Then remove the crusts and split the slice through the middle. Scrape away the crumbs and cut each piece into two triangles. Dust heavily with icing sugar and sit them at the bottom of a grill on a low setting. The sugar will slowly caramelize and the bread will toast. Once they are golden with burnt tinges of sugar, your Melbas are ready.

White Chocolate Coffee Ice-cream

Coffee and chocolate were introduced at about the same time to Britain, and coffee in particular became a passion, with coffee houses opening all over London (actually the origin of many of the present-day London men's clubs). Both white chocolate and ice-cream are much later inventions, but the combination is one that works so well, with the infusion of the fresh coffee beans working behind the white chocolate.

This is lovely to eat on its own or served as an accompaniment to almost any chocolate dessert, in particular the *Gâteau Opéra* on page 315.

MAKES 600 ML (1 PINT)

50 g (2 oz) whole fresh coffee beans
150 g (5 oz) white chocolate, chopped
550 ml (18 fl oz) milk
4 egg yolks
40 g (1½ oz) caster sugar

To achieve the maximum flavour from the beans, place them in an airtight container with the white chocolate. Keep in a warm place for 24 hours and the coffee flavour and nose will be absorbed by the chocolate.

Bring the milk to the boil. While heating, whisk the egg yolks with the sugar until thick, frothy and falling from the whisk in thick ribbons. Pour the milk onto the egg 'sabayon' and cook in a bowl over simmering water, stirring well until the 'custard' is beginning to thicken. Pour over the chocolate and coffee beans, stir until the chocolate has melted, allow to cool and strain through a sieve. The ice-cream mix can now be churned in an ice-cream maker, in two batches if necessary, not allowing it to freeze completely. A thick, creamy consistency will be enough; this will guarantee a smooth, silky finish.

This process will take 20 minutes per batch. Pour the ice-cream into a suitable container and put in the freezer to finish setting. If you don't have an ice-cream maker, see Note for previous recipe.

Nutmeg Ice-cream

Nutmeg is a spice that has had a long relationship with Britain's cooking – bread and butter pudding immediately comes to mind. Here I've used it in an ice-cream, and it will work well with many dishes, from something as simple as a baked apple to my *Baked Egg Custard Tart* on page 288.

If you substitute a fresh vanilla pod (or a few drops of vanilla essence) for the nutmeg, you will have a wonderful vanilla ice-cream.

MAKES 750–900 ML (1¼–1½ PINTS)

300 ml (½ pint) double cream
300 ml (½ pint) milk
1 nutmeg, freshly grated
6 egg yolks
175 g (6 oz) caster sugar

Mix together the cream and milk in a saucepan. Add the grated nutmeg and bring slowly to the boil. While the cream mix is heating, whisk the egg yolks and sugar together until pale and light. Pour on the hot cream and stir until well blended. Cook in the bowl over a pan of simmering water, stirring, until the custard coats the back of a spoon. (Do not let it boil, or the eggs will scramble.) Strain through a sieve, then leave to cool, stirring from time to time to prevent a skin from forming.

You will need to churn the ice-cream in an ice-cream maker in two batches. Pour in the first half and churn for 20 minutes until it has thickened and increased in volume. Repeat with the second batch. It's important not to churn it until it is completely frozen or it will take on a curdled, slightly grainy texture. Pour the ice-cream into a container and put it in the freezer to finish setting. This will guarantee a lovely silky-smooth consistency.

Note: If you don't have an ice-cream maker, see Note, page 309.

Clotted Cream Ice-cream

Clotted cream is a speciality of Devon, Cornwall and Somerset. The warm, very fresh milk is left to sit in a wide pan until the cream – which is lighter than the rest of the milk – rises, then is heated very slowly until the cream has formed a crinkled layer on top of the milk. This cream is carefully skimmed off and enjoyed by all as part of the British tradition of cream tea, with scones and jam.

Here, I've used the richness of clotted cream in an ice-cream, which is the one used in the *Afternoon Tea Pudding* on page 320. That's a pudding that everybody should try, warm griddle scones topped with toffeed strawberries and a scoop of this ice-cream – a new experience. The ice-cream also eats very well with all summer fruits, and with our classic *Summer Pudding* (page 313), as well as any hot steamed sponges.

MAKES APPROX. 750 ML (1¼ PINTS)

375 ml (13 fl oz) milk
125 g (4½ oz) caster sugar
5 egg yolks
125 ml (4½ fl oz) clotted cream

Bring the milk to the boil. Whisk together the caster sugar and egg yolks until they are rich, thick ribbons (sabayon). This can be easily achieved in a food processor or electric mixer. Pour on the hot milk and stir well. This can now be cooked in a bowl over a pan of simmering water, stirring, until the custard coats the back of a spoon. Remove from the heat, adding the clotted cream.

Once cold, churn the ice-cream in an ice-cream maker in two batches, if necessary, allowing approximately 20 minutes for each. The ice-cream will now have increased in volume, holding a thicker consistency. Repeat the same process for the next batch. It's important not to churn it until it is completely frozen or it will take on a curdled, slightly grainy texture. Pour the ice-cream into a container and put in the freezer to finish setting.

Note: The quantity of clotted cream can be increased to give you a richer flavour.

If you don't have an ice-cream maker, see Note, page 309.

Bakewell Tart Ice-cream

The historic Bakewell tart is said to have originated at the Rutland Arms in Bakewell, Derbyshire. Some claim it was created by an Italian cook, for the almond filling is very similar to a frangipane, but the British had just as much experience in baking with ground almonds. It is a cross between a cake and pudding, and can be served for dessert or for afternoon or high tea. It was quite a challenge to simulate that taste in an ice-cream – but it works. All the flavour is here. Crisp pastry tartlets, raspberries bound in their own *coulis*, almond ice-cream and just a touch of lemon water icing – the Bakewell classic in a completely new form.

SERVES 6

½ × *Sweet Shortcrust Pastry* (page 364)
225 g (8 oz) fresh raspberries
150 ml (¼ pint) raspberry *coulis* (see Note opposite)

300 ml (½ pint) double cream
300 ml (½ pint) milk
100 g (4 oz) ground almonds
8 egg yolks
125 g (4½ oz) caster sugar
50 ml (2 fl oz) Amaretto (almond liqueur)

For the Lemon Water Icing

Finely grated zest and juice of ½–1 lemon
100–150 g (4–5 oz) icing sugar

Preheat the oven to 200°C/400°F/Gas Mark 6 and grease six 10 cm diameter × 1–2.5 cm deep (4 × ½–1 in) tartlet tins.

First, make the ice-cream. Bring to the boil the cream, milk and almonds. Whisk the egg yolks, sugar and Amaretto until ribbons form. Pour the cream mixture over the eggs and cook in a bowl over simmering water until it coats the back of a spoon. Leave to cool. Then strain through a sieve, and churn in an ice-cream machine for 20–25 minutes. When it has thickened and increased in volume, pour into a container and freeze until set.

While the ice-cream is churning, roll the pastry to 3 mm (⅛ in) thick and use it to line the tartlet tins. Then line the pastry cases with greaseproof paper and baking beans and blind-bake for 15–20 minutes, until crispy and golden. Leave to cool.

Make the lemon water icing just before you assemble the tarts by whisking the lemon juice and zest into the icing sugar. Strain out the zest if you prefer a smoother finish.

To build the tart, pipe or drizzle a little lemon icing across the plate, then spoon a little into the base of each pastry case. Sit the cases in the centre of the plates on top of the icing. Stir together the raspberries and the *coulis*, then divide, either warmed or left cold, between the tartlets. Now scroll or scoop the almond ice-cream on top of the raspberries. Drizzle with more icing.

Note: To make a raspberry *coulis*, place 450 g (1 lb) fresh raspberries, 100 g (4 oz) icing sugar, 85–150 ml (3–5 fl oz)

water and a squeeze of lemon juice in a saucepan. Heat gently for 5 minutes. Remove from the heat and blend in a food processor to a purée, then strain through a fine sieve.

Fresh raspberries in *coulis* can be replaced with good-quality raspberry jam.

Sticky Toffee Pudding Ice-cream

Sticky toffee pudding is in the premier dessert division, and this variation on the theme is right up there with the stars. I serve it straight, in a bowl or glass, with a toffee sauce poured over, just like the classic hot pudding.

SERVES 6–8

500 ml (17 fl oz) double or whipping cream
500 ml (17 fl oz) milk
200 g (7 oz) dates, chopped
12 egg yolks
100 g (4 oz) caster sugar
1 × 394 g tin condensed milk, made into toffee (see Note)
250 g (9 oz) dried sugar dates (see Note), chopped into small dice

Boil the cream and milk with the chopped dates. Whisk the egg yolks and sugar until they form ribbons. Pour the boiled cream onto the egg mixture and whisk it in. Cook over a pan of simmering water until it coats the back of a spoon.

Add the softened condensed-milk toffee, stirring until it is well mixed in. Leave to cool, then pass through a sieve and discard the dates. Now churn the mixture in an ice-cream maker until it has thickened almost to setting point.

For the last few turns in the machine, add the dried sugar dates. Pour into an airtight container and put in the freezer to finish setting. It goes beautifully with toffee-cream sauce (see Note), or melted rich sweet bought toffees. Any sauces are best served warm.

Note: This ice-cream makes a brilliant accompaniment for crumbles, pies and steamed puddings. Or even serve with the pudding itself (page 299).

If you can't get the dried sugar dates, which are available in some delicatessens, replace with Medjool dates.

To make toffee from condensed milk, simply put a completely unopened tin of condensed milk in a deep saucepan, cover with cold water, bring to the boil and boil for 3 hours. Keep the tin totally covered with water. After 3 hours, remove the pan from the heat and allow the tin to cool while still immersed. The toffee is now ready for use but can be kept refrigerated until the expiry date on the tin. When you open it you will find a rich golden-brown toffee just waiting to be eaten.

For a toffee-cream sauce, simply whisk in some double or single cream – about 250 ml (9 fl oz) per 200 g tin of toffeed condensed milk.

BELOW
Sherry Trifle

Sherry Trifle

The name 'trifle' actually comes from the word meaning something of little importance, and it was applied to the pudding in around the sixteenth century, when sweet things were served as part of a 'banquet' course, and all had rather frivolous names. In the beginning, custard was poured over wine-soaked macaroons or ratafia biscuits, covered with a syllabub. The recipe has taken on many variations over the years but, as with most other things, I like good old-fashioned simplicity, and my recipe here has plenty of taste and texture, without all the extras.

There are two options for making the custard layer in this dessert. For a simple packet variety, follow the recipe here. For an entirely home-made version, use the *Pastry Cream* recipe featured on page 305.

SERVES 4

For the Sponge

3 eggs
75 g (3 oz) caster sugar
75 g (3 oz) plain flour
40 g (1½ oz) unsalted butter, melted

For the Syrup

125 g (4½ oz) caster sugar
150 ml (¼ pint) water
3–4 tablespoons sweet sherry, to taste

For the Custard Sauce

600 ml (1 pint) milk
50 g (2 oz) custard powder
50 g (2 oz) caster sugar

For the Filling and Topping

Strawberry Jam (page 387) or raspberry jam
150–300 ml (¼–½ pint) double cream,
    whipped, to taste

Pre-heat the oven to 190°C/375°F/Gas Mark 5 and grease and line a 20 cm (8 in) flan tin or flan ring and baking sheet.

To make the sponge, whisk the eggs and sugar in a bowl over a pan of hot water until the mixture has doubled in bulk and is light and creamy. Remove from the heat and continue to whisk until cold. Gently fold in the flour and melted butter. Pour the mix into the lined flan tin or ring and bake in the pre-heated oven for 15 minutes. Turn out and allow to cool.

To make the syrup, boil the sugar and water together for about 2 minutes to a syrup, then add the sherry – more than the amount listed for a stronger flavour.

To make the custard sauce, mix some of the milk with the custard powder in a pan. Bring the remaining milk to the boil in another pan. Pour this onto the custard powder, whisking all the time. Return to the heat and bring back to the boil. While stirring, the sauce will thicken. Add the sugar, cover with buttered greaseproof paper and allow to cool.

Split the sponge in half horizontally and spread jam on both pieces. Place one half in a bowl and soak with half the sherry syrup. Sit the other sponge on top and again soak with sherry syrup. Pour the custard on top and allow to set in the fridge. When set, spoon the whipped cream on top (the quantity is up to you) and serve.

Note: You can also make individual trifles in 10 cm (4 in) soufflé dishes. Bake little sponges to fit, or cut to fit, and assemble in exactly the same way.

Spotted Dick

Spotted Dick – also known as Spotted Dog or Plum Bolster – is a typical example of an early roly-poly boiled pudding made with suet (the relic of the savoury). I've never been quite sure about the name, but always very sure about the taste. It was one of those puddings I would look forward to at school when it came to lunchtime. The moist dough dotted with currants or raisins and topped with loads of custard (usually lumpy) was a real treat. Here's a modernized recipe for you to enjoy. The pud can be served with thick cream or custard

and also eats very well drizzled with honey or golden syrup.

SERVES 6–8

300 g (10 oz) plain flour
10 g (⅓ oz) baking powder
150 g (5 oz) shredded suet
75 g (3 oz) caster sugar
100 g (4 oz) currants
Finely grated zest of 1–2 lemons
185–200 ml (6–7 fl oz) milk

Mix together all the dry ingredients with the currants and lemon zest. Pour in 185 ml (6 fl oz) of the milk and stir together, adding more milk if necessary to give a binding/dropping consistency. The wetter the mix, the moister the sponge. Roll the mix into a 15–20 × 5 cm diameter (6–8 × 2 in) cylinder, wrap it in buttered greaseproof paper, with a fold to allow space for the sponge to rise, and tie the paper at both ends. Put it in a hot steamer and cook for about 1 hour.

Remove the paper and slice the pudding into portions. I find it's best to cut the slices approximately 2.5 cm (1 in) thick for a good texture.

Spotted Dick goes very well with *Custard Sauce* (page 324).

Note: Why not try replacing 50 g (2 oz) of flour with 50 g (2 oz) of cocoa, and add some chocolate chips and orange zest? Or replace the sugar and half the milk with 5–6 tablespoons of golden syrup.

Summer Pudding

Another Great British pudding using bread, but it originated much later than the others, during the eighteenth century. It was called 'hydropathic pudding' at first, because it had been designed for nursing-home patients not allowed the rich pastry desserts of the time.

I've listed quantities and varieties of fruits below but, of course, the beauty of this dish is that the choice of berries is entirely your own, so use what is easily available. You need about 1.4 kg (3 lb) of soft fruit altogether. If there is a lot of the fruit mix left over, it can be kept for a few days and served as it is with ice-cream or cream.

SERVES 8–10

Approx. 1.4 kg (3 lb) mixed soft fruit e.g.
    raspberries, strawberries, tayberries,
    loganberries, blackberries, redcurrants,
    blackcurrants and/or blueberries
2 tablespoons *crème de framboise* liqueur (optional)
1 loaf of white bread, thinly sliced
Clotted or whipped cream, to serve

For the Raspberry Purée

450 g (1 lb) fresh or frozen raspberries
50 g (2 oz) icing sugar

For the Sugar Syrup

300 ml (½ pint) water
175 g (6 oz) caster sugar

Lightly butter a 1.5 litre (2½ pint) basin or eight 150 ml (¼ pint) moulds. Trim and wash all the fruits and leave to drain.

To make the raspberry purée, simply blitz the berries and sugar together in a blender and then push through a sieve.

BELOW
Summer Pudding

To make the sugar syrup, simply boil the water and sugar together for a few minutes to a clear syrup. Leave to cool.

Mix half of the raspberry purée with the sugar syrup and bring to the simmer. Add the fruits and *crème de framboise*, if using, to the sauce, then remove from the heat and leave to rest. The fruits should have all softened but will still have kept their shape. When cool, pour some of the syrup into a separate bowl.

Remove the crusts from the bread and cut each slice into three, keeping a disc shape for the base. Dip these in the reserved raspberry syrup and line the basin or moulds with the soaked bread, overlapping slightly with each slice. When the basin or all the moulds are lined, fill with the fruits and a little of the sauce and cover with more bread. Cling film the top and cover with a plate, pressing down with a weight, and leave in the fridge for a few hours, or preferably overnight.

Mix the remaining raspberry sauce with a little of the remaining pudding juices until you have a sauce consistency. Turn out the summer pudding(s) onto a plate (or plates) and spoon the finished raspberry sauce over them. Decorate with some of the remaining fruit mix, sauce and clotted or whipped cream.

Gâteau Opéra

A French name and a French concept, but I couldn't resist including this gâteau, which is a chocoholic's dream, with lots of layers and lots of chocolate.

There are quite a few ingredients involved but it's all relatively simple to put together. It's made in a 25 cm (10 in) square cake tin and served as a dessert, but it can be made in a large round tin and presented as a cake.

A scroll of white chocolate and coffee ice-cream sits on top of the cake and a trickle of coffee syrup is used to finish the dish.

The sponge cake is going to be cooked in three separate 25 cm (10 in) square tins. This will ensure that each sponge is equal in thickness and with a smooth finish. The sponges will then be stacked in the cake tin, spreading the ganache and cream in between. If you only have the one tin, then bake in three loads. Each sponge will take only 12 minutes to bake.

SERVES 9–12

For the Chocolate Sponge

4 heaped teaspoons coffee granules
85 ml (3 fl oz) hot water
9 egg yolks (3 per sponge)
275 g (10 oz) strong plain chocolate, melted
9 egg whites (3 per sponge)
185 g (generous 6 oz) caster sugar

For the Chocolate and Hazelnut Ganache

375 g (13 oz) plain chocolate, chopped
225 ml (7½ fl oz) double cream
4 tablespoons Frangelico hazelnut liqueur (optional)
100 g (4 oz) Nutella hazelnut paste
4 egg yolks
50 g (2 oz) caster sugar
225 ml (7 fl oz) double cream, whipped to soft peaks

For the Coffee Buttercream

2 medium eggs
150 g (5 oz) caster sugar
4 tablespoons water
150 g (5 oz) softened butter, at room temperature
1 dessertspoon strong coffee flavouring (Camp)

For the Finishing Ganache

200 g (7 oz) plain chocolate
100 g (4 oz) unsalted butter
50 ml (2 fl oz) double cream

For the Coffee Syrup

300 ml (½ pint) strong fresh or instant coffee
150 g (5 oz) caster sugar

To Serve

White Chocolate Coffee Ice-cream (page 309)

Pre-heat the oven to 180°C/350°F/Gas Mark 4. Grease and flour three 25 cm (10 in) square, loose-bottomed baking tins.

For the sponge, dissolve the coffee granules in the hot water and remove from the heat. Beat the egg yolks into the coffee, then stir in the melted chocolate.

Whisk the egg whites and caster sugar to a soft-peak, meringue stage. Fold the meringue into the chocolate mix. Divide equally between the three baking tins (or spoon on just a third if only one tray is available). Bake in the pre-heated oven for 12 minutes. Allow to cool. Remove the sponge and line a cake tin with greaseproof paper. One of the sponges can now be placed in the base.

Now make the chocolate and hazelnut ganache. Melt together the chocolate, unwhipped double cream, liqueur (if using), and Nutella.

Whisk the egg yolks and sugar together until the mixture trails off the whisk in ribbons. Stir the egg into the chocolate, then gently fold in the whipped cream. Leave it to cool, stirring occasionally until it has reached a spreading consistency.

For the coffee buttercream (this is the second spread to fill the gâteau, working with the chocolate hazelnut ganache), whisk the whole eggs in an electric mixer to a ribbon (sabayon) stage.

Boil the sugar and water together to a 'soft ball' stage – 117°C/240°F. Once at this temperature, pour into the egg sabayon and continue to whisk until cool (room temperature).

The softened butter can now be added gradually, with the coffee flavouring, to finish the buttercream.

To assemble the gâteau, divide the chocolate ganache into two, along with the buttercream. Spread the first half of the chocolate on the cake in the tin.

Refrigerate to set a little before spreading the first half of the buttercream on top. Also refrigerate to set.

Another sponge can now be laid on top of the buttercream. Repeat the same process – chocolate, buttercream and sponge – remembering to leave it to set between each spread. Refrigerate to set.

Now make the finishing ganache. This will be used to spread across the top of the gâteau, giving it a smooth, chocolatey, shiny finish. Make sure all the ingredients are at room temperature before you start, to prevent it from separating.

Melt the plain chocolate and butter together gently. Stir in the double cream. This can now be cooled to a spreading consistency, before topping the cake. Leave to set.

BELOW
Gâteau Opéra with
White Chocolate Coffee Ice-cream

Finally, make the coffee syrup. Boil the coffee and sugar together and reduce by half. Cool to room temperature and the syrup is ready.

Remove the tin and the Gâteau Opéra is now ready to serve as a cake or dessert. It is best eaten close to room temperature, keeping the creams smooth. For desserts, the gâteau can be cut into 9–12 squares. Place the squares on plates and top each with a scroll of white chocolate coffee ice-cream and a trickle of coffee syrup.

Note: When spreading the creams on the sponges, a thickness of only 5–6 mm (¼ in) of each per layer will be needed. The buttercream can be used to cover and fill almost any other cake.

Any ganache not used in this gâteau can be rolled into balls and dusted with cocoa powder or dipped in melted chocolate, making the mix into home-made chocolates.

The sponges, once cooled slightly, can be lightly rolled between sheets of cling film, keeping the thickness to 5–6 mm (¼ in), to make them completely flat and smooth. It is not essential but, if prepared and finished in this way, trim the edges to fit the tin size.

For an extra touch, add a ready-made chocolate pencil.

Burnt Cream or Crème Brûlée

Of the two names, the French sounds a lot tastier than the English but apparently, burnt cream has been made in England since about the seventeenth century. As its basis is the good old British custard, it could be much older than that. The caramelized sugar topping was said to have been invented by a chef at Trinity College, Cambridge.

It can be served cold (refrigerated), but I really do believe that the best way to eat burnt cream is at room temperature. The custard is just at setting point and releases its full vanilla flavour. If refrigerated, it tends to set completely, becoming over-chilled and not releasing its full flavour. Anyway, the choice is yours.

SERVES 6

8 egg yolks
50 g (2 oz) caster sugar
600 ml (1 pint) double cream
1 vanilla pod, split, or a few drops of good
    vanilla essence
Icing sugar

Pre-heat the oven to 180°C/350°F/Gas Mark 4.

Mix the egg yolks and sugar together well in a bowl. Bring the cream to the boil with the vanilla pod, if using. Remove the vanilla pod and scrape the insides into the cream. Or add the vanilla essence. Now whisk the cream into the egg yolks and sugar. Sit the bowl over a pan of hot water and heat until the custard begins to thicken, stirring all the time. It should have the consistency of single cream. It is now ready for the next stage.

Divide the custard between six 7.5 cm (3 in) ramekins or moulds. Sit these in a roasting tin and add warm water until it comes three-quarters up the sides of the moulds. Finish in the oven until just setting, about 20–30 minutes. To test, remove one of the moulds from the water after 20 minutes and shake gently. There should still be slight movement in the centre of the custard. If it is still runny, put it back in the oven and check after another 5 minutes. Remove from the oven and allow to cool. I prefer to eat these at room temperature, so I don't put them in the fridge.

To finish the *brûlées*, once cooled and set, sprinkle them liberally with icing sugar. If you have a gas gun (page 11), this is great for achieving a quick and even glaze. If not, then colour them under a pre-heated hot grill, having the moulds as close as possible to the heat. As the sugar is heating, it will bubble and start to colour. More sugar may need to be added and then continue to colour until deep golden brown. The *brûlées* are now ready to serve.

Variation

You can make chocolate *brûlées* by simply adding grated chocolate to the mix before putting it into the ramekins. About 100 g (4 oz) of good-quality plain chocolate should be enough for this recipe – but, of course, if you prefer it stronger, just add some more. The *brûlées* can be glazed with icing sugar, but I think they are better when topped with chocolate shavings.

Nutty Apple Crumble

Jane Grigson suggested that crumbles may have originated in America, the idea of a streusel cake topping having been taken there by Austrian Jewish immigrants. This may be so, but cooked fruit topped with something such as pastry or breadcrumbs is familiar in the British tradition. Wherever and whenever it originated, the crumble is very much part of British taste history, and is a particular favourite served as part of our Sunday lunch with lots of home-made custard.

This crumble has a new feature and twist. The crumble topping is going to be cooked separately, which gives it a very crunchy finish. Almonds are also included for a coarse nutty crunch. The apple filling is simple – Bramleys, a knob of butter, sugar and, to give another flavour, the finely grated zest of a lemon. A pinch of cinnamon can also be added to either the apples or the crumble.

SERVES 6

For the Apples

900 g (2 lb) Bramley apples
25 g (1 oz) butter
50 g (2 oz) caster sugar
Finely grated zest of 1 lemon

For the Crumble

100 g (4 oz) butter
175 g (6 oz) plain flour
75 g (3 oz) demerara sugar
50–75 g (2–3 oz) nibbed almonds

Pre-heat the oven to 200°C/400°F/Gas Mark 6, if cooking the crumble immediately.

To make the crumble topping, rub the butter into the flour. Once it has a breadcrumb texture, add the sugar and almonds. The mix can now be re-rubbed until it becomes coarse and lumpy. Sprinkle onto a baking tray and bake in the pre-heated oven for about 15–20 minutes, turning occasionally.

It should now be crunchy and golden. Once at this stage, remove from the oven and leave to cool.

This can now be kept in an airtight container and used whenever needed. It will stay fresh for up to 48 hours.

Any fruit filling can now be cooked, cooled and re-heated with this topping.

To cook the Bramleys, peel and quarter the apples, and cut each quarter into three wedges. Remove the core and cut each wedge in half, giving you chunky pieces. Melt the butter in a large saucepan and, once bubbling, add the apple pieces. Cook for a few minutes and then add the caster sugar and lemon zest. Cook the apples on a medium heat until softened and tender. This will release some of the apple juices, giving a sweet apple purée surrounding the chunks. The cooking time will be between 10 and 15 minutes (20 if the chunks are particularly big).

Spoon into a buttered 1.5 litre (2½ pint) serving dish. This can now be left to cool or topped immediately with the chunky crumble topping and finished in the pre-heated oven for 15–20 minutes. If allowed to cool, when needed, simply spoon the crumble on top and bake for up to 30 minutes. The apples can also be simply microwaved and topped with the warmed crumble mix.

This dessert eats at its best with fresh *Custard Sauce* (page 324) or pouring cream.

Note: The almonds can be omitted from the recipe.

Blancmange

The word 'blancmange' derives from the French *blanc-manger*, meaning 'white food'. The dish was first recorded in the fourteenth century in a cookery book compiled by chefs working for Richard II. It was then a bland pottage or soup, containing minced boiled capon, sugar, cooked rice and almond milk, and was decorated with red aniseeds or blanched almonds. The recipe changed over the years, as did the name, and by the seventeenth century, as with so many British desserts, the blancmange had become sweet, losing all its savoury connections, apart from the setting agent, the stewed calf's foot (nowadays, of course, we use commercial gelatine).

Here is a basic recipe, but many other flavours can be added to create new tastes and textures. For instance, hazelnuts are often used to replace the almonds, and you could add chocolate or raspberry purée for a completely different type of flavour.

SERVES 4

300 ml (½ pint) milk
Thinly peeled rind of 1 lemon
50 g (2 oz) caster sugar
50 g (2 oz) ground almonds
3–4 leaves gelatine, soaked in cold water
60 ml (2½ fl oz) brandy
300 ml (½ pint) whipping cream
1 vanilla pod (optional)

If using the vanilla pod to increase the blancmange flavour, split lengthways and place in the milk with the lemon peel. Bring the milk to a simmer, remove from the stove, add the sugar and the almonds and leave to stand and infuse for 1 hour.

Once infused, pass the milk through a sieve. The vanilla pod can now be scraped, adding the rich vanilla seeds to the sweetened lemon milk. The soaked gelatine leaves can now be warmed in a few tablespoons of the milk. Once dissolved, add to the blancmange base. The brandy can now also be added to the milk. With the gelatine cooling, the mix will begin to thicken.

Once at a cold stage, but not set, lightly whip the cream and fold into the mix. The blancmange can now be spooned into four 150 ml (¼ pint) pudding basins or size-1 ramekins. Refrigerate for 2–3 hours until completely set before turning out, if using the pudding basins.

The blancmange is ready to eat. Holding a fresh lemon and almond flavour, this dessert can quite happily be eaten on its own. For a richer finish, a warm (or cold) raspberry *coulis* (see Note to *Bakewell Tart Ice-cream*, page 311) will make the perfect accompaniment. Raspberries have always held a very close relationship with lemon and almonds, so this sauce works very well with it.

To go with this and help presentation, fresh raspberries can be added to the dish.

Note: The gelatine quantity is listed as 3–4 leaves. Three will give you a gentler and softer setting, the dessert only just holding its own weight. Four will obviously guarantee the hold, but the blancmange will not eat with such a melting consistency.

Raspberry *coulis* can also be added to the mix, creating a fresh fruit flavour and colour. Simply follow the recipe omitting half of the milk quantity and replacing it with the raspberry *coulis*. Now the raspberry blancmange can be finished as instructed in the above method.

When using the fresh scraped vanilla pod in the blancmange, while setting, the seeds will fall to the base of the moulds. When set and turned out the blancmange is presented with a black speckled top. The vanilla flavour still runs through the complete dessert and, with this finish, it looks as good as it tastes.

BELOW
Blancmange

Afternoon Tea Pudding

Afternoon tea is a uniquely British institution (see page 366), and a Cornish cream tea is too, so I decided to combine the ideas here in a pudding. Warm scones, clotted cream and strawberry jam are everybody's favourite, but announcing that that is what you are having for pudding at your next dinner party might make the guests wonder if you have had one or two glasses too many. But when the dessert is presented, they will be delighted with the result: a griddle scone topped with warmed sweet strawberries and clotted cream ice-cream.

SERVES 4–6

450 g (1 lb) fresh strawberries
50 g (2 oz) icing sugar
3 tablespoons water
25 g (1 oz) butter
1 dessertspoon demerara sugar (optional)

To Serve

1–2 warm *Griddle Scones* per portion
(page 362)
Clotted Cream Ice-cream (page 310)

Chop 100 g (4 oz) of the strawberries and place in a saucepan with the icing sugar and water. Bring to the simmer and cook for 4–5 minutes before pushing through a sieve. This is a strawberry sauce to roll the fruits in once pan-fried. A teaspoon or two of strawberry jam can also be added while simmering. This will give the sauce a richer flavour.

The remaining strawberries, if small, can be left whole, or halve them.

Melt the butter and, once bubbling, add the fruits. Cook on a relatively high heat for 1–2 minutes, warming through and allowing to soften slightly.

The demarara sugar, if using, can now be added. This will caramelize, giving you toffeed strawberries. Pour in the sieved strawberry sauce and then they are ready to serve.

The warm griddle scones can now be presented on plates, topped with the strawberries and clotted cream ice-cream. This dish looks absolutely delicious and is very moreish. The plate can be decorated with a dusting of icing sugar and a sprig of mint to create colour.

Note: Almost any fruit can be used in this recipe. All summer fruits – raspberries, blackberries and so on – will work well. Fresh plums, apricots, peaches and more will also eat beautifully with the clotted cream ice-cream.

Rhubarb and Apple Charlotte

No one is quite sure why this eighteenth-century British pudding is called a charlotte. It was probably to honour the new bride of George III, Charlotte Sophia of Mecklenburg-Strelitz. Tender fresh fruits are surrounded by a casing of crisp, baked bread slices. It's traditionally made with apples alone, but I have added rhubarb for extra flavour. The rhubarb is slightly cooked before the pudding is baked, which allows the juices to run and mix with the fruits, turning into a rhubarb syrup/sauce to offer with the crispy finished charlotte.

Fresh cream, custard or ice-cream will all eat well with this dish.

SERVES 6

450 g (1 lb) stale bread (approx. 12–18 slices)
Softened butter, for spreading

For the Fruit Filling

450 g (1 lb) fresh rhubarb
50 g (2 oz) butter
75 g (3 oz) caster sugar
3 green dessert apples

Pre-heat the oven to 220°C/425°F/Gas Mark 7 and have ready six 7–8 × 5 cm (3–3½ × 2 in) individual metal pudding or dariole moulds or a 12.5 × 6–7 cm (5 × 2½–3 in) cake tin.

OPPOSITE
Rhubarb and Apple Charlotte

Cut six bread discs to fit the bases of the moulds, and six to fit the tops (if using a large mould, just cut one of each).

Cut away the crusts of the remaining slices and slice into approximately 3 cm (1 in) fingers.

Butter all of the bread on one side only. Place a disc, butter-side down, in the base of each mould. The fingers can now be laid, butter-side against the mould, slightly overlapping all the way round.

To make the fruit filling, peel the rhubarb, if stringy, and cut into 1 cm (½ in) chunks. Melt half of the butter in a large saucepan and, once bubbling, add the rhubarb. Turn the fruit pieces in the pan for 1 minute before adding 50 g (2 oz) of the caster sugar. Continue to cook for a further minute. The rhubarb can now be strained in a colander or large sieve, allowing the sweet juices to collect in a bowl.

While draining the rhubarb, the apples can also be prepared. Peel, core and cut each fruit into eight wedges. The wedges can now be cut in half, leaving chunky pieces.

Melt the remaining butter in a saucepan, adding the apples once bubbling. Cook for 2 minutes before

adding the remaining sugar. Continue to cook for 1–2 minutes. Leave to cool.

The rhubarb will have now drained. Take a quarter of the actual fruit pieces and mix with the juices collected. These can now be brought to a simmer and cooked until tender. Once tender, liquidize and push through a sieve. You now have a fresh rhubarb syrup to serve with the charlottes.

Once both fruits have cooled, gently mix together. It is best now to taste for sweetness. If the flavour is too tart, a sprinkling of caster or icing sugar can be added. (A pinch of ground cinnamon can also be added.)

Divide the mix between the charlottes, then top with the lids. Any excess bread at the sides should be folded over, to keep the lids in place.

For individual charlottes, bake in the pre-heated oven for 20 minutes; a large charlotte will take twice as long – 40–45 minutes.

Once cooked, turn out the charlottes onto plates to reveal the crispy golden finish. Spoon the rhubarb syrup around and serve.

BELOW
Baked Apple with Dates and Walnuts

Baked Apples with Dates and Walnuts

Until fairly recently, raw fruits were looked upon with some suspicion, as they were considered to be unwholesome. Most fruits from the sixteenth century onwards were cooked, and served with digestive spices – even the humble apple. The old-fashioned baked apple is a classic example, and it's a good basic idea that just needs a little help. Usually it's an apple scored around the middle, cored, filled with sugar, butter and a pinch of spice, and then cooked with a little water until tender. Here I've given it a little more.

Dates, walnuts and apples are a lovely combination. I have also added grated apple to the mix, which helps bind the other flavours. My favourite dates to use are the Californian-grown Medjools. These are dried dates with a thick wrinkled flesh and a buttery toffee flavour. They are more expensive, but worth every penny.

SERVES 4

3 large dessert apples (Golden Delicious or
    Granny Smith)
25 g (1oz) light soft brown sugar
6–8 dates, preferably Medjool
10 walnut halves, scraped clean and roughly
    chopped
Pinch of ground cinnamon
25 g (1 oz) butter

Optional Extras

2 tablespoons crème fraîche or double cream
1 egg yolk
Calvados, to taste

Pre-heat the oven to 200°C/400°F/Gas Mark 6.

Split two of the apples horizontally through the middle. The halves can now be cored. Place in a buttered ovenproof dish, sprinkle with a little of the sugar and bake in the pre-heated oven for 10 minutes.

While baking, the remaining apple can be peeled, cored and coarsely grated. The dates can now be split and stoned before being cut into thin strips.

Mix together the grated apple, dates and chopped walnuts, adding the pinch of cinnamon. The optional extras, if using, can now also be added to the mix. A good splash of Calvados (a tablespoon or two) will be plenty for this quantity.

Spoon into and on the par-baked apples. Sprinkle with the remaining sugar and top each with a knob of the measured butter. Lower the oven temperature to 180°C/350°F/Gas Mark 4. Finish baking for a further 25–30 minutes. During the baking, apple juices mingling with the sugar can be used to baste the apples, to intensify the full flavour.

Once cooked, remove from the oven, trickling each with the natural sweetened juices. Extra-thick cream will be all the apples need to complete the dish.

Bitter Chocolate Sauce

Chocolate recipes began to appear in cookery books at the beginning of the eighteenth century, but they used the raw material rather than the processed. The sweet and bitter chocolates we enjoy today did not appear until at least 100 years later, made at first by Mr Fry and then by Mr Cadbury.

This sauce goes very well with all sorts of puddings, in particular sorbets and ice-creams.

MAKES APPROX. 500 ML (17 FL OZ)

300 g (10 oz) bitter dark chocolate, chopped
150 g (5 oz) unsalted butter
75 ml (3 fl oz) double cream

Place all of the ingredients together in a bowl over simmering water until the chocolate has completely melted. Stir well. This sauce must be served warm.

Note: This recipe also works using plain or milk chocolate.
Single cream can be used to replace the double cream, and the quantity doubled for a richer finish.

Custard Sauce or *Crème Anglaise*

Eggs and milk have always been freely available in Britain, so their early combination in a smooth, sweet sauce whether to be poured or baked (in moulds in pastry), was perhaps inevitable. Custard, the king of the classic British sweet sauces, is the ideal accompaniment to baked or steamed puddings, stewed fruit, sweet pies and tarts and so on. The French so associated custard with the English that they distinguished it with the name *crème anglaise*.

This fresh custard sauce can act as a base for many different flavours such as lemon, orange, rum and coffee. You must only ever serve it warm, not boiled, as boiling will scramble the egg yolks in the cream mix. The fresh vanilla is optional and can be omitted when using other flavours.

The quantity for this recipe can also be halved.

MAKES 750 ML (1¼ PINTS)

8 egg yolks
75 g (3 oz) caster sugar
1 vanilla pod, split (optional)
300 ml (½ pint) milk
300 ml (½ pint) double cream

Beat the egg yolks and sugar together in a bowl until well blended. Scrape the insides of the vanilla pod, if using, into the milk and cream, add the pod too, and bring to the boil. Sit the bowl over a pan of hot water and whisk the cream into the egg yolks and sugar. As the egg yolks cook, the custard will thicken. Keep stirring until it starts to coat the back of a spoon, then remove the bowl from the heat and the pod from the custard. Serve warm or cold. Stir the sauce occasionally until cool, to prevent a skin forming, or cover with greaseproof paper while it cools.

The custard can also be brought back up to heat over a pan of hot water, but must never boil. If that happens, the sauce will separate.

Variations

For a lemon custard, add the zest of 2 lemons to the milk and cream when heating. Once the custard has thickened, add the juice of 1 or more lemons, to taste. Strain through a sieve.

For an orange custard, add the zest of 2 oranges as for the lemon custard, but no juice. Why not try a few drops of Grand Marnier or Cointreau instead?

For a rum custard, add rum to taste at the end of the cooking process, and a spoonful or two of coconut milk for an extra flavour.

For a coffee custard, replace the vanilla pod with 2 teaspoons of freshly ground coffee. Once the custard is ready, strain it through a sieve.

BELOW
Baked Rice Pudding

Baked Rice Pudding

Most of the traditional, nursery-style milk puddings are Victorian, but many have their origins in much earlier dishes. The grain puddings, such as tapioca, sago and rice, have developed from the wheat frumenty of the fourteenth century so, like many other sweet dishes, were originally savoury. It took a while for rice to be accepted but, once it was, it was baked with milk, butter and spices for a rich rice pudding that is little different from the classic of today. Street vendors in the eighteenth century would sell bowls of grains boiled to a jelly and then served with some sugar, spice and butter. The natural jellied liquid of boiled grains is still the basis of many local recipes, including the Welsh *llymru*, which was anglicized to 'flummery'. Another version was Atholl Brose, a strong and delicious oat-based liqueur popular at New Year in Scotland.

This is a very basic recipe, but it holds a lot more than plain basic flavour, and with it you can be as sensible or naughty as you like. The pudding can be made with all milk. As you can see, I've been a little extravagant and used half single cream. The single can be replaced by double cream for an even richer finish. The cream content, whether double or single, can be halved and substituted with extra milk. For a very thick baked rice pudding the cooking time can be taken as far as 2–2½ hours, but the time quoted here keeps the rice slightly looser and, I think, more enjoyable.

SERVES 4–6

100 g (4 oz) short-grain pudding rice
450 ml (¾ pint) milk
450 ml (¾ pint) single cream
50 g (2 oz) caster sugar
25 g (1 oz) butter, unsalted
Freshly grated nutmeg

Pre-heat the oven to 180°C/350°F/Gas Mark 4 and butter a 1.5 litre (2½ pint) pudding or pie dish. Wash the rice and place in the pie dish. Warm the milk and cream together and pour over the rice. Sprinkle the sugar over the rice and stir in. Dot with the butter and grate fresh nutmeg over the top. Bake for 10 minutes. After the 10 minutes reduce the oven temperature to 150°C/300°F/Gas Mark 2 and bake for a further 1 hour 20 minutes–1 hour 30 minutes.

The pudding will now have a golden brown topping, with rich creamy rice pudding underneath. This eats beautifully with a dollop of home-made fruit ice-cream.

See also

Apple and Blue Cheese Tart or Pie (page 67)
Christmas Pudding (page 333)
Christmas Pudding Scotch Pancakes (page 334)
Rich Warm Chocolate Cake (page 349)
Tuile Biscuits (page 356)
Warm Spiced Pineapple Cakes (page 394)

A Festive Christmas

We are in December and the big annual event is upon us. It's that part of the year when we all spend far too much money and usually invite too many guests to the lunch, cramming everybody around the table. The kitchen looks like a bomb has hit it and a row has normally started. Well, I hope the recipes here, accompanied with some tips and hints on how to attack the day, will take all that pressure away and leave you with just lots of flavours to enjoy. Before we get to those points, how did Christmas begin? Here's a brief history.

December has been a time for celebration since the very earliest days, and for many peoples. In northern Europe, the heathen Scandinavians worshipped their gods, Odin and Thor among them, and celebrated the winter solstice in a feast that lasted for twelve days. Our Christmas word 'Yule' comes from the name of this festival. In southern Europe, the Romans held their Saturnalia in December, an orgy of feasting and drinking in honour of the god Saturn (god of agriculture and vegetation), when gifts were exchanged. As Christianity spread throughout Europe during the first centuries after Christ, converts were persuaded to dedicate their winter festival to Him instead of to their pagan gods – one reason why the arbitrary date of 25 December became His supposed birth date.

And since then, 25 December and the 'twelve days of Christmas' have been important in the Christian calendar, although many of the traditions associated with our Christmas still have their roots in pagan practices. The Yule cake stems from the Norse tradition of offering sweet cakes to the gods, and the burning of a Yule log in the hearth, and even perhaps the lighting of spirit poured over Christmas pudding, are relics of early fire worship. Bringing greenery such as holly and mistletoe into the house is a reflection of pagan tradition as well, although the prickly holly soon came to symbolize the Crown of Thorns. All this worried the Church, which wanted Christmas to be a time of religious fasting and reflection instead of a time of apparently irreligious feasting and revelry. In fact, when the Puritans came to power in 1642, they actually 'banned' Christmas! They believed that the spices and fruits included in traditional festive foods such as mince pies and puddings inflamed passions.

With the Restoration in 1660, Christmas became a time of feasting again in England and elsewhere. But in Scotland the influence of the religious reformer, John Knox, was so great that Christmas was not properly recognized until as late as the 1950s. (A Scottish friend of mine remembers her father going to work on Christmas Day, for the Scots' major celebration was and still is New Year, or Hogmanay.) It wasn't until the Victorian era that Christmas became as it is today, and Prince Albert was very influential in this, introducing many German ideas. He popularized Christmas trees decorated with symbols such as apples (the 'fruit of the Tree of Knowledge') and candles, the forerunners of our present-day electric lights. Christmas cards, crackers and Father Christmas became features of the festival at this time, although Christmas cakes, puddings and mince pies had long existed, relics of the celebratory pottages and pies, packed with dried fruits and spices, of centuries before.

The main food feature of early Christmases used to be brawn, a jellied loaf that was usually made from a wild boar's head. Swans, cranes and peacocks were also eaten by the rich on feast days, but they were notoriously tough, and it must have been a relief when the fleshier and more tender turkey was introduced from the Americas in the sixteenth century. This large bird soon became popular. Large flocks were reared in the grain-rich region of East Anglia – as they are today – and marched to London, the main turkey market, often wearing small shoes to protect their feet. Until then, farmyard geese had been a more common celebratory food. They too were taken to London on foot, but they had their feet tarred, as they could not be shod – thus the expression 'to shoe a goose', meaning a waste of effort (or a wild goose chase).

Stuffings using breadcrumbs, shredded meat, herbs and spices had been part of the British tradition since very early on, so the newfangled turkey was treated in the same way as other birds. A sharp sauce had long been associated with birds, both domestic and wild, and while goose had its apple or sorrel sauce, turkey soon became associated with cranberries, probably an American influence (although wild cranberries are native to Europe). The lightly spiced bread sauce eaten with Christmas turkey – and also with game birds – is a direct reflection of the medieval habit of thickening sauces with breadcrumbs.

Then there's the Christmas pud, of course, which which is a direct descendant of the Great British pottage via the classic British steamed pudding. This particular type of pudding is thought to have become associated with Christmas because George I – who was later known as the 'pudding king' (and sung about in the nursery rhyme, 'Georgie-Porgie, pudding and pie') – is said to have had it at his first Christmas meal in this country. During the Victorian era, alcohol was added, as well as trinkets (similar to *Twelfth Night Cake*, page 343), and butter sauces, spiked with rum, port or brandy, became traditional accompaniments.

So now you know a little of the Christmas history, let's move on to the cooking for the actual event. Cooking lunch for maybe up to a dozen family and friends can cause stress that we really don't need. So how do we make the event an easy one? As with all cooking, the answer lies in the preparation, and, of course, in keeping the dishes simple to make as well as amazing to eat. The recipes in the following pages are all classics we love, but I have given them a twist. The flavours are like pulling a Christmas cracker: there's something in there to excite you and take you by surprise.

IMPORTANT CHRISTMAS POINTS TO REMEMBER
Before the Day

1 It's best to serve a cold starter (if offering a three-course menu) that can be prepared at least 24 hours in advance.

2 The stuffing for the turkey can be made up to 48 hours in advance, with the turkey 'filled' and perhaps a roulade made – the remainder of the stuffing rolled in buttered foil – 24 hours in advance.

3 Turkey stock made from giblets or veal *jus* can be made well in advance.

4 All vegetables can be prepared on Christmas Eve.

5 If making home-made cranberry sauce, this can be made several weeks in advance and kept refrigerated.

6 Any brandy or rum butters can be made well in advance and frozen.

7 Home-made rum sauce or custard can be made in advance or on the day.

On Christmas Day

1 Pre-cook vegetables such as carrots, French beans, broccoli, cauliflower or Brussels sprouts in the morning. These can be refreshed in iced water, buttered, seasoned and placed in covered serving dishes. Microwave to re-heat when needed. Or plunge into boiling water to re-heat (about 1 minute) and then season and butter.

2 If using, make the *Home-made Bread Sauce* (page 43).

3 The roast turkey can be topped with bacon slices, which will crisp beautifully during the roasting time.

4 Thirty to forty minutes before the turkey has finished cooking, place the roast potatoes in the oven.

5 When cooked, remove the turkey from the oven and roasting pan. Cover with foil and leave to rest for 30 minutes.

6 Place the parsnips in the oven once the turkey's removed (they usually take 20–30 minutes). The potatoes can also continue to cook during the 30 minutes' resting time.

7 Meanwhile, finish the gravy in the roasting pan using the prepared stock or alternative.

8 Cook the chipolata sausages and bacon.

9 Re-heat vegetables and sauces when needed.

10 The main course is ready to serve with little panic.

11 The Christmas pudding can be microwaved in portions, or steamed for 2 hours previously.

Happy Christmas eating!

Traditional Roast Turkey with Sage, Lemon and Chestnut Stuffing and all the Trimmings

Here we have the biggest 'roast' of the year. The secret to success with a roast turkey is keep it simple and, of course, moist and juicy. Quite often I hear that the bird has been roasted for up to 6 hours, or even throughout the night! It's purely because of the size and volume of the bird that we like to cook 'safely' and just leave it for another hour to be sure.

A 1.6 kg (3½ lb) chicken will only take 50–60 minutes to roast. Multiply that by three and you have a 4.5 kg (10 lb) turkey. We don't need a calculator to work out the rest. However, most people will, as I've said, roast for twice that time, leaving you with a dry and coarse texture to the meat. For a 4.5–5.4 kg (10–12 lb) bird, the cooking time is 3–3½ hours and, if you're a little nervous, then 4 hours maximum.

So that's the main point over with; the rest is all about organized trimmings: good crispy bacon rashers, pork chipolatas, the chestnut stuffing (this one is also flavoured with lemon and apple to increase tastes and textures) and a good gravy to finish the whole experience.

I've also included a recipe for home-made cranberry sauce. If you're not a huge fan of cranberries, you can just add a teaspoon or two of cranberry jelly to the gravy for a sweeter finish – the flavour works very well. And, of course, you can serve the roast with *Bread Sauce* (page 43).

So here's the recipe for our main event.

SERVES 6–8

For the Cranberry Sauce

450 g (1 lb) fresh cranberries
100 g (4 oz) caster sugar
Juice of 2 large oranges
½ teaspoon very finely chopped shallots
1 glass port

For the Turkey

4.5–5.4 kg (10–12 lb) fresh turkey, oven-ready
50 g (2 oz) butter
1 small onion (optional)
Salt and pepper

For the Stuffing

Butter
2 large onions, finely chopped or grated
Grated zest of 2 lemons (juice may also be needed)
1 heaped tablespoon chopped fresh sage
675 g (1½ lb) good-quality pork sausagemeat
100–175 g (4–6 oz) roasted chestnuts, chopped
    (page 332)
2 apples, grated
100 g (4 oz) fresh white breadcrumbs
2 eggs
Turkey liver (optional)
Salt, pepper and ground mace

For the Gravy

½–1 oz plain flour (optional)
600 ml (1 pint) turkey stock, made from fried or
    roasted giblets boiled in water and reduced,
    or *Chicken Stock* (page 33) or 450 ml (¾ pint)
    Veal Jus (page 34) or alternative (page 11)
Butter

For the Garnishes

Rashers of streaky bacon
Chipolata sausages

The cranberry sauce can be made at least two or three weeks in advance. Simply place all the ingredients in a pan and bring to a simmer. Cook gently for 10–15 minutes until the cranberries are just beginning to break. Once cooked, refrigerate until needed. Heat gently before serving.

The stuffing is best made 24 hours in advance, which will give the mix time to relax and the flavours to mingle. The other reason is, of course, so that you can have the turkey 'stuffed' and ready for cooking on the day.

OPPOSITE
Traditional Roast Turkey

Melt a knob of butter and cook the chopped or grated onions, for a few minutes until they begin to soften. Add the lemon zest and sage and remove from the heat and allow to cool. Once cooled, add the onion to the sausagemeat along with the chestnuts, apples and breadcrumbs. Season with salt, pepper and a good pinch of mace. The eggs can now also be added as the binder, to hold all together. Check for seasoning.

It's now time to taste the stuffing. If the lemon has been lost among all of the other flavours, then add a squeeze or two of the juice to open all the tastes. If the turkey liver is going to be added, then cut it into dice and quickly pan-fry in a knob of butter. Leave to cool before folding into the mix. The turkey neck can now be filled with the stuffing, folding any excess skin under. This not only helps flavour the bird but also helps keep it in a good shape.

Before stuffing, here's a quick tip on how to improve the flavour of your roast. Gently release the skin from the breast and push extra seasoned and softened butter between the meat and skin. As the turkey roasts, the butter melts. After filling the neck, pull the skin underneath and seal with a cocktail stick or two. Any remaining stuffing can either be wrapped and rolled in buttered foil or spooned into a suitable ovenproof dish. These can be baked for 20–30 minutes, while the turkey is roasting.

If using the onion to cook with the bird, then simply quarter and place it inside the carcass. The turkey can now be cling filmed and refrigerated until the big day.

To roast the turkey, a 4.5 kg (10 lb) bird will take 3 hours and every 900 g (2 lb) in weight on top of that will need a further 30 minutes (for example, a 6.5 kg/ 14 lb bird will take 4 hours). The bird will then need to rest for 30 minutes. This will relax the meat, making it even more tender and, at the same time, gives you a free oven to finish roasting potatoes and parsnips. Turkey, covered with foil, can be left to rest for up to 45 minutes and still retain its heat.

Pre-heat your oven to 200°C/400°F/Gas Mark 6. If you plan on eating at 1.30 p.m., then, for a 6.5 kg (14 lb) bird you will need to pop it in at 9.00 a.m. (or 8.45 a.m. for extra roasting and free oven time), which gives you extra sleeping time!

Sit the turkey in a large roasting tin, brush the breast with butter and season with salt and pepper.

The rashers of bacon can either be cooked separately (see below) or they can be arranged on top of the bird at this point (or both). Place the tin in the oven and cook at this temperature for 30 minutes. After the half-hour has passed, baste with the fat that has melted in the pan. The breast and legs will have taken on a golden tinge. Cover the turkey completely with foil and reduce the oven temperature to 180°C/350°F/Gas Mark 4. The bird should now be basted every 20 minutes until half an hour before the end of its cooking time, when you should also start roasting your potatoes. At this point, remove the foil and bacon (this can be crisped separately) and continue to cook and baste to a rich, deep golden finish. To check the bird is cooked, pinch the thigh/leg and if it 'gives' the turkey is definitely ready.

Place the turkey on a large presentation plate and totally cover with foil (to retain the heat).

The fat can now be poured carefully from the tin and used to roast the parsnips or pan-fry the sprouts. (It can also be refrigerated and kept to stir-fry your turkey paella or risotto on Boxing Day.)

While the turkey is resting, finish cooking the vegetables, along with the chipolatas and bacon. The quantities of these two ingredients are really up to you. The minimum you need is 1 rasher and 1 sausage per person. It's always popular, however, to have extra for second helpings.

The chipolatas can be cooked in the turkey fat poured from the roasting tin, which will give even more flavour and help enhance the finished taste. They can be either grilled, roasted or pan-fried to a golden brown. It's best to cook the sausages during the resting time of the roast turkey, as they only take about 15 minutes.

There's a choice for cooking the bacon too: the rashers can either be grilled until crispy or laid over the turkey breasts to protect the bird during cooking. This also contributes to the finished flavour, as the bacon fat melts over the skin.

If the bacon is still a little soft after it has been removed from the turkey, just place it on a baking tray and finish in the oven or under a hot grill.

To make the gravy to a thick sauce consistency, once the fat has been poured off, add the flour if not using veal *jus* (using 25 g/1 oz will give you a thicker finish) and stir into the sediment left in the roasting tin. Now add the stock. Bring to a simmer and cook gently for a few minutes. Season with salt and pepper and strain through a sieve. This can now be finished with a knob of butter just before serving.

The turkey will have rested to a warm stage, and the meat will be totally relaxed, moist and tender. The turkey is now at its best, served with a hot gravy.

Note: Using a 6.5 kg (14 lb) bird will allow second helpings for 6–8 people.

There are two other ways to make gravy. You can add turkey stock (made from frying or roasting the giblets) or chicken stock to the residue taken from the roasting tray to make a basic gravy. Or you can simply add veal *jus*/gravy or alternative (page 11) to the roasting tray.

Roast Loin of Pork with an Apricot and Sage Stuffing

This roast is a good alternative to the classic Christmas turkey. The loin is filled with a moist, slightly sweet and savoury stuffing in keeping with the style of Christmas lunch dishes. But, to be honest, I eat this at any time of the year.

Stuffing a pork joint totally changes its texture and provides a beautiful moist centre which can so often become drained of all its juices, particularly during roasting. The loin is best bought on the bone and 'French-trimmed', which means that you can tell how many portions you have by the number of bones neatly exposed above the meat.

For this recipe I'm using a six-bone joint, which will give you the same number of very generous portions. It's also important to ask your butcher to remove the 'chine' bone. This is the central piece that connects the joint to the opposite loin. Once this has been removed, you will be able to cut between each bone without any problems.

Another feature of this recipe is the finished glaze. The rind skin is removed and cooked separately to provide the crackling. Once the loin is nearly roasted (approximately 15–20 minutes before the end of its cooking time), honey is spooned over and basted every 5 minutes. As the loin cooks, the honey thickens to a deep caramel colour, leaving a rich glaze over the joint.

The residue in the pan can also be used to flavour the gravy.

SERVES 6

1 × 6-bone loin of pork, 'French trimmed'
(see recipe intro), with skin removed for the
crackling
4 rashers of streaky bacon or back bacon
2–3 tablespoons cooking oil
Salt and pepper
Plain flour, for dusting
100 g (4 oz) lemon honey

For the Stuffing

50 g (2 oz) chicken livers
4 shallots or 1 onion, finely chopped
300 ml (½ pint) dry cider
50 g (2 oz) wild or button mushrooms, cut into
small dice
Butter
Cooking oil
225 g (8 oz) pork belly (including 50 g/2 oz of
belly fat or pork sausagemeat), finely minced
or blitzed in a food processor
2 eggs
75 g (3 oz) ready-to-eat dried apricots, cut into
5 mm (¼ in) dice
5–6 sage leaves, chopped
50 g (2oz) fresh white breadcrumbs

For the Gravy or Cream Sauce

Glass of white wine or 150 ml (¼ pint) cider
150–300 ml (¼–½ pint) *Veal Jus*/gravy (page 34),
(or 150 ml (¼ pint) *Chicken Stock* (page 33)
plus 150 ml (¼ pint) double cream)

The chicken livers are best bought 24 hours in advance and left to soak in milk. This draws the bitter flavour from the livers, giving them a fresher taste. Once soaked, dry on kitchen paper.

Pierce the loin through the centre of the meat and from end to end using a long, sharp carving knife. Make this cut approximately 5 cm (2 in) deep, creating a passage to fill with the apricot and sage stuffing. Now refrigerate until needed.

For the stuffing, place the shallots or onion in a saucepan with the cider. Bring to the boil and allow to reduce until almost dry. Leave to cool.

The mushrooms can now be quickly pan-fried in a small knob of butter until softened. Season with salt and pepper and leave to cool.

Heat a frying pan with a little cooking oil. Once hot, add a knob of butter and fry the livers for 1–2 minutes on each side, seasoning them with salt and pepper. Leave to cool. Once cold, the livers can either be finely chopped or blitzed in a food processor. If you are mincing your own pork, also mince the livers, using a fine mince plate. Place the minced pork in a bowl that is sitting over a bowl of ice. This helps to keep the meat firm and makes it easier to mix. Season with salt and pepper before mixing in the chicken livers. Add one egg at a time, mixing thoroughly. The mixture should be bound together and firm

Now mix in the cold shallots, mushrooms and apricots along with the chopped sage and breadcrumbs. Check for seasoning, adding more if necessary.

Pan-fry a spoonful of the mix (like a mini-burger) to check that the flavour is right for you. Fill a piping bag with the mix, making sure it has a piping hole at least 5 cm (2 in) diameter. Insert the tip of the piping bag into the cut at one end of the loin and squeeze until the cavity becomes full. It's best to be as generous as possible to give a good quantity of the filling. Any excess stuffing can be rolled in buttered foil, creating a log shape, and baked for just 20–25 minutes in the oven. You'll have extra stuffing to offer with the dish.

Place 2 rashers of bacon over each end of the loin and tie with string to hold them in place. The fat on the loin can be scored with a sharp knife before gently tying between each bone to keep its neat cylinder shape. Once filled, the loin is best refrigerated for a few hours before roasting.

Pre-heat the oven to 200°C/400°F/Gas Mark 6.

To roast, heat a large roasting tray with the cooking oil. Season the joint with salt and pepper. Once hot, seal either end of the loin in the pan, giving a golden brown finish. (To prevent the bacon from sticking to the pan, lightly dust both ends in plain flour.) Next seal and colour the fat side on a medium heat. Once totally golden brown, turn onto the bones, place in a pre-heated oven, and roast for 50 minutes–1 hour, basting with the fat in the pan every 10–15 minutes. The skin removed for crackling can simply be scored with a sharp knife, salted well, placed in a separate tray and put directly into the oven. As the loin is roasting, the crackling will become very crisp.

For the last 15–20 minutes of the roasting time, remove the loin from the oven, pouring away any excess fat. Return the loin to the pan and cover the golden brown joint with the lemon honey. Continue to roast, basting every 5 minutes. The honey will become thicker and sit on the joint to give it a rich glaze.

Remove the pork from the pan and leave to rest. The roasting tray can now be heated on top of the stove, boiling any honey left on the base. As this reduces without burning and becomes even thicker, spoon some over the resting loin. Now add the white wine or cider to the pan and mix well with any sediment left in the base. Add the *jus*/gravy, if using, and bring to a simmer. Skim away any fat from the sauce, season with salt and pepper and strain through a fine sieve. The gravy is now ready.

If you're making a cream sauce rather than a gravy, add the chicken stock once the cider has reduced. Boil and reduce by half before adding the cream and bringing to a simmer. Season and strain, and the sauce is then ready.

It's important that the pork has at least 15–20 minutes' resting time before you remove the string and carve between the bones. The rich, moist stuffing will be revealed as you cut through the first slice. It not only looks sensational, but tastes it too. The stuffed loin can now be served offering the gravy or cream sauce separately.

Note: Two wonderful accompaniments to serve with this dish are *Hazelnut Mashed Potatoes* (page 126) and *Grilled Baby Leeks* (page 97).

Chestnuts

It's Christmas time, and we're shopping in Oxford Street in London. As we approach a small street brazier, coals aglow, our noses pick up that classic savour of roasted chestnuts. It's odd that we rarely cook them at home just to eat, only using them in our chestnut stuffings. But here we are trying to carry far too many carrier bags, and these wonderful eats suddenly take

priority. The first bite (once peeled) releases a slightly bittersweet taste, but the texture then becomes tender all the way through.

When buying these nuts to cook, make sure to choose rich and shiny ones with a good weight to guarantee a better result. It's also an idea to buy a few more than needed – there always tends to be one or two duds, however well selected. They're in the shops in the autumn and winter – when the nuts mature – which is why they've probably become associated with Christmas. If picking them yourself in the country, be sure to choose sweet chestnuts, which come in a casing with long, very prickly spines (like a sea-urchin). The horse chestnut – which produce the conkers kids play with on the end of string – comes in a casing with shorter, stubbier spines.

Chestnuts can be cooked by two basic methods – boiled or roasted. Whichever you choose, the first job is to make a slit/cross into the shell on two sides of the chestnut, cutting through the skin surrounding the flesh, which has a bitter taste.

To roast and cook completely, arrange on a baking sheet, sprinkle with a little water and cook for 15 minutes in an oven pre-heated to 200°C/400°F/Gas Mark 6. Or pre-heat the grill to hot and grill for about 15 minutes.

To boil, simply cover the chestnuts with cold water, bring to the boil, and cook for 5–6 minutes. Turn the heat off, and leave the chestnuts to sit in the liquid.

Peeling roasted or boiled chestnuts is very easy if the chestnuts are still warm, so just remove a few at a time and peel. The skin surrounding the flesh must also be removed. Now they are ready to use in the stuffing on page 329, or perhaps with the Brussels sprouts in the recipe on page 106.

If all of this seems to be hard work, then I suggest you use dry vacuum-packed chestnuts from France. These should be available from most supermarkets or delicatessens. Once opened, there's no peeling, just chopping.

Other chestnuts available for savoury dishes or puddings are tinned, unsweetened purée; tinned, sweetened purée/*crème de marrons*; sweet and rich *marrons glacés*; and tinned chestnuts in syrup – another *marrons glacés* variety.

Christmas Pudding

Fairly heavy puddings have always been eaten in Britain, and were part of culinary tradition. A plum pudding – the original title for Christmas pudding, containing lots of prunes (rather than plums) – was as essential to many people as roast beef. It was the German kings in Britain who really popularized puddings such as these, and Prince Albert made them part of the Christmas feast.

In medieval times, a pudding called 'hackin' was made from meat, usually shin of beef, stewed together with raisins, currants, prunes, sugar, spices, claret and lemon juice. This was thickened with either sago or breadcrumbs. All of these flavours were mixed and cooked in pig's or sheep's gut. I promise this recipe is nothing like that. In the seventeenth century, puddings began to be cooked in pudding cloths and, by the nineteenth century, the meat had disappeared, although the suet remained.

The traditional day for making the pudding was the 30th November – St Andrew's Day or Stir-up Sunday. (The latter name comes from the Anglican prayer book reading for that day: 'Stir up, we beseech Thee, O Lord...'.) Everyone in the family would have a stir of the mix, from east to west, in honour of the wise men who travelled in that direction. I prefer to make my puddings around August (or even earlier). This gives them more time to mature. I leave the mixture raw for anything up to a week, refrigerated, stirring from time to time. Once cooked, the puddings must be left in a cool place until the big day.

MAKES 3 x 900 G (2 LB) PUDDINGS

225 g (8 oz) plain flour
1 teaspoon baking powder
225 g (8 oz) fresh white breadcrumbs
225 g (8 oz) shredded suet
100 g (4 oz) ground almonds
500 g (1 lb 2 oz) soft dark brown sugar
1 teaspoon ground mixed spice
½ teaspoon grated nutmeg
½ teaspoon cinnamon
175 g (6 oz) stoned prunes
175 g (6 oz) carrots, peeled
750 g (1¾ lb) mixed currants, sultanas and raisins
50 g (2 oz) chopped mixed peel
2 apples, peeled, cored and roughly chopped
Juice and grated zest of 1 orange
Juice and grated zest of 1 lemon
5 eggs
100–150 ml (4–5 fl oz) rum
4 tablespoons black treacle
4 tablespoons golden syrup
300 ml (½ pint) stout

Sift the flour with the baking powder. Add the breadcrumbs, suet, ground almonds, soft dark brown sugar and spices. Mince the prunes and carrots together through a medium plate and add to the mix, with the dried fruit, mixed peel, apples and lemon and orange zest. Beat the eggs and stir into the pudding mix, with the lemon and orange juice, rum, treacle, golden syrup and stout. You should now have a pudding mixture of approximately 3 kg (7 lb) in total weight. It will have a reasonably moist and loose texture but if it appears dry, add some more stout and rum. Then taste it to check for full flavour and richness. If it's bland, add some more spices to liven it up. Now the uncooked mix can be refrigerated for up to a week to mature.

To cook the puddings, butter and lightly flour three 900 g (2 lb) pudding basins. Fill each three-quarters full with the mix, top with a circle of greaseproof paper and then cover with baking parchment, muslin or foil and tie it on firmly, leaving a fold to give the pudding room to rise. Steam over boiling water for 4–6 hours (6 hours will make the puddings even richer). Don't forget to top up the water from time to time.

Leave the puddings to cool before refrigerating or storing them in a cold, dark place.

To serve the puddings, on the Big Day they will need a minimum of 1 hour of steaming (preferably 1½–2, which will make them richer), to return them to a tender pudding texture. I like to serve rum or brandy-flavoured *Custard Sauce* or *Crème Anglaise* (page 324) with Christmas pudding, along with lots of pouring cream – well, it is Christmas!

Christmas Pudding Fritters with Cranberry Ice-cream

After a generous serving of the Christmas lunch starter and main course, the rich fruity pudding always ends up being just a thin slice. So what do we do with the remaining two-thirds or half of the pudding? Well, here's the answer: turn them into crispy fritters. The cranberry ice-cream is also a great extra because it uses up the jar that wouldn't otherwise get finished. This is a wonderful pudding made from simple Christmas leftovers. Offering hot, crispy fritters with home-made ice-cream is the perfect present for any guest.

The number of servings depends on the quantity of pudding left over.

Leftover Christmas pudding

For the Cider Batter
(to coat a maximum of 20 fritters)

225 g (8 oz) self-raising flour, sifted
50 g (2 oz) caster sugar
300 ml (½ pint) cider
Cooking oil, for frying

For the Cranberry Ice-cream (to serve 4–6)

Approx. 200 g (7 oz) leftover cranberry sauce
200–250 g (7–9 oz) carton or tinned ready-made custard
150 ml (¼ pint) double cream, lightly whipped to soft peaks

Whisk the cranberry sauce into the custard. Gently fold in the whipped cream and place in a container suitable for freezing. This can now be placed in the freezer for 3–4 hours, after which the ice-cream is ready.

Pre-heat the cooking oil to 180°C/350°F/Gas Mark 4. An electric fryer is best used for safe temperature control.

For the fritters, break down the leftover pudding and roll into balls approximately 2 cm (¾ in) in diameter. Roll in a little of the flour and pierce with cocktail sticks.

Mix together the sifted flour with the caster sugar. Whisk in the cider, and the batter is made. Dip the balls into the thick batter and gently lower 6–8 at a time into the oil, allowing the batter to soufflé and float. Once

golden and crispy, the fritters are ready to take out. Drain on kitchen paper. Three fritters should be ample per portion. Fry more if needed and serve with a scroll of the home-made cranberry ice-cream.

Christmas Pudding Scotch Pancakes

This pudding idea is not a classic yet, but I hope it will become one for the future.

These pancakes contain all of the Christmassy flavours, but have a much lighter finish than a conventional pudding. They can be made a few hours in advance, while the turkey is roasting, and then re-heated in the oven, or microwaved.

The beauty of this dish is that you can eat as many or as few pancakes as you like. I suggest four to five per portion. Along with the 'cakes' we'll have a vanilla and raisin syrup, rum-flavoured custard and lots of extra-thick cream.

This recipe will give you 25–30 pancakes.

SERVES 5–6
For the Pancake Batter

350 g (12 oz) self-raising flour
1 teaspoon ground mixed spice
75 g (3 oz) currants, sultanas and raisins (more can be added for a fruitier flavour)
40 g (1½ oz) glacé cherries, chopped
20 g (scant 1 oz) mixed peel, chopped
40 g (1½ oz) unsalted butter
225 ml (7½ fl oz) milk
3 eggs
150 g (5 oz) caster sugar
Butter or oil, for frying
Pinch of salt

For the Vanilla and Raisin Syrup

100 g (4 oz) raisins
150 ml (¼ pint) water
50 g (2 oz) caster sugar
Juice of 1 lemon
1 vanilla pod, split

To Decorate

Icing sugar, sifted
Holly leaves

To Serve

Rum custard (see Note)
Extra-thick cream

Sift the flour, adding the spice, fruits, glacé cherries and mixed peel. Melt the butter and whisk into the milk with the eggs, sugar and pinch of salt. Whisk into the flour mix and the batter is ready.

To cook the pancakes, heat a non-stick frying-pan and brush with butter or oil. The batter can now be spooned, using a tablespoon, into the pan, allowing 1 spoon per pancake. These will only take approximately 2–3 minutes before they are ready for turning over. To help time the turning, look for small bubbles appearing on the surface. This tells you they are ready to turn. Once turned, cook for 2 minutes before removing from the pan. In a large pan, 4–6 pancakes can be cooked at the same time. Once all are cooked, keep covered with a tea towel as this prevents them from becoming dry.

To make the vanilla and raisin syrup, simmer all the ingredients together and cook for 10 minutes. Remove the vanilla pod and blitz to a purée. Push through a sieve. The pod can now be scraped and the vanilla seeds added to the syrup. The syrup is now ready.

To serve, warm the pancakes and stack into a tower on each plate, allowing four to six per portion. Spoon warm rum custard around, if serving, and drizzle the warm raisin syrup over the top. Now just finish with a spoonful of thick cream. The plate can now be decorated with a dusting of icing sugar (to create the snow effect) and a holly leaf. The Christmas pudding pancakes are now ready to serve.

Note: If you have family or friends who are not big fans of dried fruit, then keep some of the batter plain and just serve Scotch pancakes with rum custard.

The lemon juice in the vanilla and raisin syrup can be replaced with rum or brandy for an even richer Christmas finish.

For a quick rum custard, just warm tinned or carton custard and flavour with rum. Simple, quick, easy and tasty. To loosen it slightly, add a little single or whipping cream.

I'm using extra-thick cream for this recipe, but clotted, whipped or just pouring cream can be used.

BELOW
Christmas Pudding Scotch Pancakes

Christmas Cake

Christmas cake is a prime example of the type of British enriched bread or cake made over the centuries for celebrations – it's packed with dried fruits, nuts and other flavours, including a number of spices. Christening cakes, wedding cakes and, at one time (before the advent of novelty cakes), birthday cakes all used to be made on the same basic principles.

This is one of those fruit cakes that holds such a moist richness it becomes very moreish, and, once you have tasted it, I think you might find yourself cooking it for more than one celebration a year.

MAKES ONE 20 CM (8 IN) CAKE

225 g (8 oz) unsalted butter
225 g (8 oz) soft brown sugar
250 g (9 oz) plain flour
½ teaspoon ground mixed spice
½ teaspoon ground cinnamon
Pinch of salt
4 large eggs
50 g (2 oz) ground almonds
50 g (2 oz) chopped almonds
Juice and finely grated zest of 1 lemon
Finely grated zest of 1 orange
2 tablespoons marmalade
1 tablespoon black treacle
4 tablespoons brandy
500 g (1 lb 2 oz) currants
200 g (7 oz) sultanas
200 g (7 oz) raisins
75 g (3 oz) glacé cherries
50 g (2 oz) mixed candied peel
Brandy, to finish

For this recipe, you will need a 20 cm (8 in) round or square cake tin. The tin should be double- or even treble-lined with greaseproof paper; this helps prevent the cake from burning during its cooking time.

Pre-heat the oven to 140°C/275°F/Gas Mark 1.

Cream together the butter and soft brown sugar until creamy, light and pale. Sift together the flour, spices and salt. Beat the eggs together and then work in a little at a time into the fluffy butter and sugar. It's important to add slowly; this then makes sure the eggs are emulsified with the butter and will not curdle. If the mix begins to curdle then sprinkle some of the flour in. This will stop the mix from separating completely.

The sieved flour and ground almonds can now be gently worked into the mix. Add the chopped almonds, zests, marmalade, black treacle, lemon juice and brandy. To finish, fold in the fruits and mixed peel.

The Christmas cake mix can now be spooned into the lined cake tin, spreading evenly. Bake in the pre-heated oven for approximately 4–4½ hours.

After the first 30 minutes, cover the top of the cake with a double thickness of greaseproof paper. This will help prevent the top of the cake from becoming too dark. Pierce the paper to release the steam created.

To test the cake is cooked, press the centre; if it feels slightly springy and does not hold the impression, then your cake is ready. Another way to test is to insert a small knife or skewer. The cake should be moist but with no raw mix showing.

Once cooked remove from the oven and leave to stand in the tin for 45 minutes before turning out on to a wire rack and leaving to cool.

Once it's cool, make small holes in the cake with a skewer or small knife and trickle a spoonful or two of brandy on top. This will be nicely absorbed by the cake, giving a richer and moister finish. It's best now to wrap the cake in greaseproof paper and keep in a tin or plastic container. The brandy-soaking can be repeated every 4–5 days. This will give the cake time to absorb the brandy flavour and mature, making it richer than ever.

The cake eats beautifully as it is, but can, of course, be finished in the classic way with marzipan and icing.

Home-made Mincemeat and Mince Pies

This is Delia Smith's recipe, so many thanks to her for allowing me to quote it. It really is the best I've ever tasted and, as she says, once you've made it and tried it, you'll never again revert to shop-bought.

Mincemeat and the small pies made with it are echoes of the savoury-sweet pies of medieval times, and used actually to be made with shredded meat. This continued right up until quite recently – one of Mrs Beeton's recipes for mincemeat called for 450 g (1 lb) of beef and a pint of brandy. Nowadays, all that we are left with in a savoury sense is the beef suet (you can also buy vegetarian suet now).

Mince pies have always been a favourite of mine – well, at least since making them with this mincemeat. You can make a half-quantity if you prefer.

MAKES APPROX. 2.75 KG (6 LB)

For the Mincemeat

450 g (1 lb) Bramley apples, cored and chopped small (no need to peel them)
225 g (8 oz) shredded suet
350 g (12 oz) raisins
225 g (8 oz) sultanas
225 g (8 oz) currants
225 g (8 oz) whole mixed candied peel, finely chopped
350 g (12 oz) soft dark brown sugar
Juice and grated zest of 2 oranges and 2 lemons
50 g (2 oz) whole almonds, cut into slivers
4 teaspoons mixed ground spice
½ teaspoon ground cinnamon
Nutmeg, grated
6 tablespoons brandy

For the Mince Pies

Sweet Shortcrust Pastry (page 364)
Milk, for brushing
Icing or caster sugar, to decorate

All you do is combine the above ingredients, except for the brandy, in a large mixing bowl, stirring them and mixing them together very thoroughly indeed. Then cover the bowl with a clean cloth and leave the mixture in a cool place overnight for 12 hours, so the flavours have a chance to mingle and develop. After that pre-heat the oven to 120°C/225°F/Gas Mark ¼,

cover the bowl loosely with foil and place it in the oven for 3 hours.

Then remove the bowl from the oven and don't worry about the appearance of the mincemeat, which will look positively swimming in fat. This is how it should look. As it cools stir it from time to time; the fat will coagulate and instead of it being in tiny shreds it will encase all the other ingredients. When the mincemeat is quite cold, stir in the brandy. Pack in clean, dry jars, cover with wax discs and seal. It will keep in a cool, dark cupboard indefinitely, but it is best eaten within a year of making.

To make mince pies, line small tartlet cases or Yorkshire pudding trays with thin discs of the sweet shortcrust pastry. Spoon in some mincemeat, a tablespoon or two depending on the size of the tin. Brush the edges of the pastry with milk, then top with pastry lids. Chill before baking.

Pre-heat the oven to 200°C/400°F/Gas Mark 6. Brush the tops of the pies with milk, and bake for 25–30 minutes, depending on size. Once golden, crisp and cooked, remove and allow to rest for 5 minutes before placing on a wire tray to cool. The pies can be sprinkled with caster sugar during their last 5 minutes in the oven, or dusted with icing sugar once cooled.

The mincemeat traditionally includes three spices to symbolize the gifts brought to Jesus by the three kings. Once, pies were made in an oval shape to represent the manger. And if you eat twelve pies between Christmas Day and Twelfth Night, you will ensure a whole twelve months of good fortune.

Note: Vegetarians can make this mincemeat happily, using vegetarian suet.

See also

Bread Sauce (page 43)
Buttered Brussels Sprouts (page 106)
Classic Roast Potatoes (page 238)
Creamy Bubble and Squeak Soup with Crunchy Bacon (page 29)
Roast Parsnips (page 95)

Cakes,
Sweetened Breads
and Baking

Although there are not many famous
breads in Britain, the number of
traditional enriched breads, cakes and
biscuits is immense. Why this should
be so, I'm not quite sure, but it could
have something to do, once again,
with our national sweet tooth. In fact
it's said we liked sweet things so much
that we had to invent an extra meal at
which to enjoy them – what we call
afternoon tea.

The first breads would have been hard and flat, made from the local ground grain, and baked on hot flat hearthstones by the fire. The flat metal griddle or girdle, which is suspended over the fire, is an example of this method. The word is thought to come from the name for hot stones in the Celtic language, *greadeal*, and the use of the implement is common to all the Celtic countries, from northern France to Ireland and Scotland. Today, the northern bannock or oatcake is the nearest equivalent to that earliest type of bread.

Quite early on, the leavening or raising power of 'barm', consisting of fermented liquor containing airborne yeasts, was discovered, and so a lighter bread could be baked, either directly on hot hearthstones or in the hot air under a clay dome set over the stones, the earliest oven. Ovens, however, were not common, and for centuries small, plain, yeasted and non-yeasted breads continued to be the most common. The much later sweetened descendants of these are drop scones, pancakes, crumpets, muffins and the Welsh pikelets.

Breads of this type were still made at home. For breads which needed to be baked in an oven, doughs would have to be taken to the manorial oven or to a public baker. The rich would have white breads, made from the finest wheat flour. This was the 'manchet', for eating, whereas the 'trencher' (a slice of bread used as a plate) would be of less fine brown bread. These trenchers were always a few days old, so would have been fairly hard, thus more able to absorb fats and liquids. By the end of the sixteenth century, wooden and metal plates had been introduced – as well as the fork – so the trencher 'plate' was discontinued. Bread was still used, though, as sops in the bottom of soup or as sippets, little pieces of bread or toast arranged on top of or around a dish. Breadcrumbs, too, were added – and still are – to sauces as a thickener, and to sausages, stuffings, drinks and desserts.

The poor, however, would have to make do with the husks of wheat in their inevitably coarser brown bread, or use other local grains such as rye and barley. These both contained much less natural gluten than wheat so were dense, dark and hard, making a much less digestible product.

For special occasions from the Middle Ages on, basic doughs were often enriched by honey, spices or dried fruits, and these mark the beginnings of tea breads, loaves and buns – as well as cakes. In later years, eggs and butter were often added to the dough, the beaten eggs allowing enough air to be incorporated without the addition of yeast. When chemical raising agents were introduced in the nineteenth century, many yeast-raised doughs were abandoned.

As far as biscuits are concerned, the earliest were rusks, pieces of baked bread put back into the oven to dry out. Later, finer mixtures would be used and baked in an oven or dried. Biscuits like these, cut into animal and human shapes, were known as 'fairings' because they were sold at local fairs.

The baking tradition in Britain seems to have always been at its strongest in the north and west, and in Ireland. This may be because these areas were furthest from outside influences, including France and elsewhere, and recipes and traditions were able to be retained. High tea, for instance, demands a variety of baked goods, and high tea is a tradition that is quite rare in the south. But the fuel needed for baking was at one time more plentiful in the north than in the south, and this may be another contributing factor. The glory of English cakes, however, is entirely due to the gentry's adoption of the new meal, afternoon tea (see page 366 for how it began and recipes for the occasion). Sticking to this chapter you'll find many flavours and 'classic' cakes such as parkin, simnel, lardy and Twelfth Night, all included alongside many others.

Happy baking!

PAGE 338
Home-made Malt Loaf (page 350)

Lemon and Vanilla Sponge Cake

Sponges were made with vigorously beaten eggs and sugar, and flour. They date from before the nineteenth century, when chemical raising agents were introduced. The Victorians added butter to a sponge mix, resulting in the Victoria sponge recipe. This is a combination of many old methods, giving a lighter and softer finish to the cake, which is just perfect to offer for afternoon tea. The lemon and vanilla are wonderful flavours together, and the rich but light finish is a dream to eat. The sponge can also be made into cup cakes.

The top is glazed with lemon 'water icing', just lemon juice mixed with icing sugar and spooned over the top. Another way to make the experience extra lemony is to split the cake in two and fill with lemon curd. The curd can have its strong flavour softened by folding in a tablespoon of lightly whipped cream.

MAKES ONE 20 CM (8 IN) CAKE OR 18–22 LITTLE CAKES

1 vanilla pod, split lengthways and scraped
6 eggs
175 g (6 oz) caster sugar (preferably flavoured with vanilla)
175 g (6 oz) plain flour, sifted
50 g (2 oz) butter, melted
Finely grated zest of 2 lemons
Juice of 1 lemon

For the Icing

1 tablespoon lemon juice
6 tablespoons icing sugar

For this recipe, you will need a 20 cm (8 in) diameter, deep, round or square cake tin, lined with buttered greaseproof paper; or make 18–22 little cakes in paper cases. Pre-heat the oven to 200°C/400°F/ Gas Mark 6.

Scrape all of the vanilla seeds from the pod. Add to the eggs, with the caster or vanilla sugar in a bowl over a pan of hot water. Whisk until the mix has at least doubled in volume, making sure the hot water does not come in contact with the bowl. The yolks and sugar will now be thick, light and creamy. Remove the bowl from the heat and continue to whisk until cold, thick and forming ribbons.

Lightly fold in the flour, melted butter, lemon zest and juice. Pour the mix into the cake tin or cake cases and bake for 25–35 minutes for the large cake or 12–15 minutes for the small. Test with a skewer, which will come out clean when the sponge is ready. Remove from the oven and allow to rest in the tin for 10–15 minutes, before turning out and sitting, base-down, on a wire rack. Leave to cool.

To make the icing, warm the lemon juice and pour into a bowl. Mix the icing sugar a tablespoon at a time into the juice until the mixture begins to coat the back of a spoon. More icing sugar can be added for a thicker finish. The icing can now be spooned on top of the cake(s).

Note: If filling with lemon curd, it's best to split and fill the sponge before icing.

If using paper cake-cups, place them in individual Yorkshire pudding tins for best results.

BELOW
Lemon and Vanilla Sponge Cakes

Simnel Cake

Simnel is a traditional British cake made during Lent, and for a while became associated with the fourth Sunday of that period – Mothering Sunday. Many years ago, young women away from home, probably in service, were allowed home to visit their parents on that day, and would take this cake with them as a gift. It's basically a rich fruit cake baked with a layer of marzipan running through it, and topped with almond paste too. Traditionally it is then garnished with eleven small marzipan balls arranged in a circle on top of the cake, which are lightly toasted to a golden brown. These balls represent the eleven faithful disciples.

MAKES A 20 CM (8 IN) ROUND CAKE

225 g (8 oz) plain flour
1 teaspoon ground mixed spice
½ teaspoon ground cinnamon
Pinch of salt
175 g (6 oz) butter
175 g (6 oz) light brown soft sugar
3 eggs, beaten
1 tablespoon golden syrup, warmed
175 g (6 oz) sultanas
175 g (6 oz) currants
50 g (2 oz) glacé cherries, chopped
50 g (2 oz) mixed peel, chopped
2–3 tablespoons brandy

BELOW
Simnel Cake

Milk, if necessary
600 g (1 lb 5 oz) marzipan
1 tablespoon warmed apricot jam, strained
1 egg, for glazing

This recipe will need a 20 cm (8 in) diameter, deep, round cake tin, greased and double-lined with greaseproof paper. Pre-heat the oven to 170°C/325°F/Gas Mark 3.

Roll 200 g (7 oz) of the marzipan into a 20 cm (8 in) disc.

Sift the flour with the dried spices and salt. Cream together the butter and soft brown sugar until light and fluffy. The eggs can now be poured from a jug slowly while being beaten into the butter mix. Add the golden syrup, with the sifted flour. Add all of the fruits and brandy. The cake mixture should not be too loose. If very thick, soften with milk. Spoon half the cake mix into the lined tin. Smooth completely flat, making sure there are no air bubbles. Place the marzipan disc on top. Pour on and smooth the remaining cake mix.

Because of the long cooking time it's best to wrap and tie brown paper around the tin. The cake can now be baked in the pre-heated oven for 1½–2 hours. After 1½ hours, check every 10 minutes by pressing in the centre; the cake should feel firm when it's ready. (The cake should not be tested with a skewer. This will simply lift the warm marzipan and give the impression the cake is not cooked.) When the cake is done, remove from the oven and rest for 30 minutes. Turn the cake out onto a wire rack. The cake must be absolutely cold before topping with more marzipan.

Once cold roll another 200 g (7 oz) of marzipan into a 20 cm (8 in) disc. Brush the top of the cake with the warm, strained apricot jam. Place the marzipan disc on top and trim around for a neat finish. The top can now be score-marked for a criss-cross pattern or left plain. Brush with some of the beaten egg and colour under a pre-heated grill to a light golden brown.

The remaining 200 g (7 oz) of marzipan can now be shaped into eleven small balls. Place the balls on a baking sheet, brush with egg and also glaze under the grill. Sit the balls on top and the simnel cake is ready. The cake can now be left as it is or finished with a ribbon tied around it and some small marzipan flowers or leaves arranged on top. Happy Easter!

Twelfth Night Cake

Twelfth Night, 6 January, is the last night of the Christmas feast, and long ago there were always festivities before the work of the New Year began in earnest. This cake – very like a Christmas cake, in fact – was made as part of the celebration, and often a bean would be inserted into the mixture. Whoever was given the slice containing this was named King of the Bean, which meant good luck was theirs for the coming year.

The cake is usually covered with royal icing, but I prefer to keep it plain or top it with a fondant icing, the recipe included here. This whole recipe is very quick and easy to make. I've also added chopped dates to give the mixture a fuller fruit flavour. It's not essential to include these; simply replace their weight with extra dried fruits.

MAKES A 20 CM (8 IN) CAKE

175 g (6 oz) butter
175 g (6 oz) caster sugar
3 eggs, beaten
175 g (6 oz) plain flour
¼ teaspoon ground cinnamon
¼ teaspoon freshly grated nutmeg
175 g (6 oz) currants
175 g (6 oz) sultanas
175 g (6 oz) dates, preferably Medjool, chopped
50 g (2 oz) blanched almonds, chopped
4 tablespoons brandy

For the Fondant

50 ml (2 fl oz) warm water
350 g (12 oz) icing sugar, sifted

This recipe requires a 20 cm (8 in) round or square cake tin. The tin needs to be greased and double-lined with greaseproof paper. Pre-heat the oven to 170°C/325°F/Gas Mark 3.

Cream the butter and sugar together until light and fluffy. Pour the beaten eggs from a jug a little at a time, mixing them into the sweet butter.

Stir in the flour and spices, followed by the fruits and chopped almonds. Mix all together well, adding the brandy.

Spoon the mix into the cake tin, smoothing and levelling the top. The cake can now be baked in the pre-heated oven for 1 hour. If the cake is not quite ready, this can be checked by inserting a skewer or small sharp knife; once almost totally clean, the cake is ready. If not, return to the oven and cook for a further 30 minutes. It's important to keep an eye on the cake while it's cooking. If it's becoming dark, cover with foil. This will prevent it from burning.

Leave for 20–30 minutes to relax in the tin before turning out and leaving to cool.

For the fondant icing, sift the icing sugar into a large bowl. Stir in the warm water a little at a time until the sugar has reached a thick, coating, fondant consistency.

Most cakes are decorated on the base, turning it over for that flat finish. This cake is best left sitting on its base, with the fondant poured and spread on top. I like to see the fondant just falling around the sides and not completely covering the cake.

Note: *Classically, the top is decorated with glacé cherries and angelica.*

Cheddar Apple Cake

Cheddar is one of our most famous British cheeses, and often, particularly in the north, it is baked in pies along with apples. This recipe, however, is from the West Country, so try to use a good mature Cheddar from that region. It's not a thick cake, more the depth of Italian *focaccia* bread. Once it is baked, the cheese is sprinkled on top and then the cake is returned to the oven or the cheese melted under the grill. It's quick and easy to make and is best eaten while still warm, with the cheese at its sticky best. But you can also serve it at teatime or take it on a picnic. The quantity of cheese is up to you. The more is melted on top, the richer the cake.

MAKES AN 18–20 CM (7–8 IN) CAKE

225 g (8 oz) self-raising flour
Pinch of salt
Pinch of freshly grated nutmeg
100 g (4 oz) butter
225 g (8 oz) grated, peeled apple (approx.
    2 apples, preferably Granny Smith's
    for their 'tart' bite)
25 g (1 oz) sugar
1 small egg (½ large egg), beaten
50–100 g (2–4 oz) Cheddar cheese, grated

This can be baked in an 18–20 cm (7–8 in) cake tin or flan ring. Grease the tin and pre-heat the oven to 180°C/350°F/Gas Mark 4.

Sift the self-raising flour with the salt and nutmeg. Rub the butter into the flour, creating breadcrumbs. Mix the apples with the sugar and stir into the flour. Add the beaten egg and mix to a dough.

This can be rolled to fit in the tin, or transfer the dough to the tin and press into the edges; the mix should be 2–3 cm (¾–1¼ in) thick. Place in the pre-heated oven and bake for 40–50 minutes until just firm.

The grated cheese (quantity to suit personal taste) can now be sprinkled on top and returned to the oven to melt, or finished under the grill. Allow to cool slightly, serving just warm.

Note: Fresh herbs can be added to the cake mix. Chopped sage or tarragon are two flavours that will work well with cheese and apples. A dessertspoon of either will be enough.

OPPOSITE
Chocolate Treacle Sandwich

Chocolate Treacle Sandwich

Sandwich cakes can be the most basic of sponge cakes, just held together with jam and whipped cream. Delicious they are too, but this recipe, Scottish in origin, I believe, gives a lot more. The addition of cooking oil and black treacle makes it very moist and rich. (In Ireland, a chocolate sandwich cake is made with mashed potatoes.)

I'm filling the cake with a chocolate butter cream. To balance the richness of this cake, I've also added a layer of lightly whipped fresh cream. Extravagant to the point of indulgence.

MAKES A 20 CM (8 IN) CAKE

For the Sponges

175 g (6 oz) plain flour
50 g (2 oz) cocoa powder
1 heaped teaspoon baking powder
1 heaped teaspoon bicarbonate of soda
2 tablespoons black treacle
2 eggs
75 g (3 oz) caster sugar
150 ml (¼ pint) milk
150 ml (¼ pint) vegetable oil

For the Chocolate Filling

175 g (6 oz) plain or milk chocolate, chopped
80 ml (3 fl oz) double cream
25 g (1 oz) butter

For the Cream Filling

150 ml (¼ pint) double cream, lightly whipped

For this recipe you will need two 20 cm (8 in) sandwich cake tins, the bases lined with greaseproof paper and then buttered and floured. Pre-heat the oven to 170°C/325°F/Gas Mark 3.

Sift together the flour, cocoa powder, baking powder and bicarbonate of soda. Add all the other sponge ingredients and whisk to a smooth consistency.

Divide the mix between the two tins and bake in the pre-heated oven for 20–25 minutes. Once cooked, and just becoming firm, remove from the oven and leave to rest for 10 minutes before turning out and cooling on wire racks.

To make the filling, melt the chopped chocolate with the double cream in a bowl over a pan of warm water. Once melted, add the butter and remove from the heat.

As this mix cools it will also thicken. It can now be spread onto the base sponge, before being topped with the lightly whipped cream and then the remaining sponge. The chocolate treacle sponge is ready to serve.

Sally Lunn Cake or Bread

Sally Lunn is a famous teacake that's yeast based, taking on a sweet loaf look. The name is said to come from the lady herself, a pastry chef from Bath who, in the eighteenth century, sold the cakes on the street. Another story says the cake was French in origin, and that when its name, 'Soleil Lune', 'the sun and moon', was cried in the streets, the people in the West Country took it as 'Sally Lunn'. Who knows?

One thing I do know and have found is that there are many different recipes. I've tried more than I can remember. In the West Country, one of the

favourite spices is saffron, and this is included in most of the recipes. Florence White's *Good Things in England* (1932) says that the cake should only be made with clotted cream, never butter. That must prove it's a West Country recipe. The simplicity of this recipe is one of its pluses: it's quick and easy to make. Once cooked, the cake is split into three and finished with clotted cream, the cake left still warm.

So here is the recipe. It's made with lemon zest to add another flavour, or mixed spice. I quite like to make it with both. The one change I have made is to use dried yeast in place of fresh. It's easily obtainable, but if you have fresh, the method of use is included after the recipe.

MAKES A 15 CM (6 IN) ROUND CAKE

1 teaspoon sugar
2 tablespoons warm milk (tepid)
1 teaspoon dried yeast
225 g (8 oz) plain flour
1 teaspoon salt
Good pinch of ground mixed spice (optional)
Finely grated zest of 1 small lemon
120 ml (4 fl oz) double cream, at room temperature
2 eggs, beaten

To Glaze

1 tablespoon milk
1 tablespoon sugar

If Filling the Cake

Softened butter and/or clotted cream

All you will need for this recipe is a 15 cm (6 in) round cake tin 7–8 cm (2½–3 in) deep. If you have a non-stick pan, simply grease it. If not, then it's best to use greaseproof paper and grease the paper.

Stir the teaspoon of sugar into the warm milk. Sprinkle in the dried yeast. Leave to stand for 10–15 minutes until a thick froth (2 cm/¾ in deep) has formed.

Sift together the flour, salt and mixed spice, if using. Add the grated zest of the lemon. The yeast mixture, double cream and eggs can now all be added. This will now have a thick batter consistency, just firm enough to form a 'bun' shape.

Once the batter or dough has been shaped into a suitable ball/bun, place in the prepared tin. Cover and leave in a warm place until it has risen to the top of the tin. This will take 1–1½ hours. Pre-heat the oven to 200°C/400°F/Gas Mark 6.

The cake can now be baked in the oven. This should take just 15–20 minutes until it has a rich golden colour. Boil together the milk and sugar for the glaze and, while the cake is still in its tin, brush the top. This will leave a rich shine. Leave to settle for 5–10 minutes and then remove from the tin. The traditional way to finish the Sally Lunn is to split it into three and spread with clotted cream or butter. Reassemble and serve while still warm.

To be honest, it's best to leave it as a baked 'bun'; once sliced, you can help yourself to the butter or cream. It's very important to eat it on the day. After that, the texture becomes very dry and it is best toasted and then buttered.

Note: To use fresh yeast, this recipe will need just 10 g (⅓ oz). Simply crumble and stir into the warm milk and sugar. Once at a smooth liquid stage it's ready to use.

Lardy Cake

If you happen to be on a diet, lardy cake will be your worst nightmare, for it's a delicious bread dough flavoured with lots of sugar, mixed spice and rolled around pork fat. It's traditionally made in Wiltshire, probably because it's a pig-rearing county and there was always plenty of lard. It was made as a special celebration cake, usually at harvest time. It's lovely to

BELOW
Lardy Cake

offer at teatime, and must really be eaten, to taste at its best, within 48 hours of making.

The cake is usually made with lard alone, but I've used half butter. Don't be put off by the thought of eating a pork-fat cake, as the butter does balance the taste. Lardy cake is certainly something you couldn't make too often, but when you do you'll wish you'd made two. Simply double the recipe and freeze one cake, well wrapped in cling film, for up to a month.

Elizabeth David says that lardy cake, like cigarettes, should carry a Government health warning. She's not far wrong, but the warning should be followed by my words of advice: 'Please try at least once.'

MAKES A 20 CM (8 IN) CAKE

1 teaspoon dried yeast
120 ml (4 fl oz) milk, warmed
1 teaspoon sugar
225 g (8 oz) plain flour
¼ teaspoon salt
1 teaspoon ground mixed spice
1 egg, beaten
Flour, for dusting
100 g (4 oz) lard, chilled and diced
100 g (4 oz) butter, chilled and diced
100 g (4 oz) sugar
50 g (2 oz) currants
50 g (2 oz) sultanas

This recipe requires a 20 cm (8 in), round, deep, greased cake tin.

Stir the yeast into the warm milk and teaspoon of sugar. Leave for 10–15 minutes in a relatively warm place until a thick, frothy consistency is achieved.

Sift the flour, salt and mixed spice together in a mixing bowl. Make a well in the centre. Mix in the yeast, along with the beaten egg, to form a sticky dough.

Dust a surface with flour and knead the dough for a good 10 minutes until a smooth, elastic dough is achieved. Return to the bowl, dust with flour and leave to double in volume. This will take approximately 1 hour in a fairly warm place.

The dough can now be knocked back and placed on a fresh floured surface. This can now be rolled into a rectangle, approximately 25 × 15 cm (10 × 6 in). Separate the lard, butter, 100 g (4 oz) sugar and fruits into three equal mixed quantities. Sprinkle one of the quantities across the top two-thirds of the rectangle. Fold over the uncovered third onto the middle piece. Now fold the remaining third on top. This makes a three-layered square dough sandwich. Now it's best to press down and seal the exposed edges with a rolling pin. Turn the sandwich once to the left and re-roll into the rectangular shape, repeating the same sprinkling of fats and fruits and folding. Turn left once more and repeat for the last time.

The finished layered dough can now be rolled slightly larger to fill the cake tin. Place the dough in the tin, folding the corners under so it fits. Cover with a damp tea-towel and leave to rise until doubled in size. This will take 50–60 minutes. Pre-heat the oven to 200°C/400°F/Gas Mark 6.

The dough can now be scored with a sharp knife, crossing through the middle to create several diamonds. Bake in the pre-heated oven for 25–30 minutes until golden brown.

Once cooked remove from the oven and turn out onto a wire rack. Leave upside-down so the melted fats can distribute themselves through the cake. The lardy cake is now ready to serve.

Note: The maximum cooking time for the cake will be 35 minutes.

When making the layered dough, if, by the second turn, it seems to be too warm and the lard and butter are too soft, then refrigerate for 15 minutes before re-rolling.

If you want to use fresh yeast, the recipe will need just 10 g (⅓ oz). Simply crumble and stir into the warm milk and sugar. Once at a smooth liquid stage, it's ready to use.

OPPOSITE
Rich Warm Chocolate Cake

Rich Warm Chocolate Cake

Established in the late seventeenth century in London, 'chocolate houses' were only for drinking chocolate. It wasn't until much later, in the nineteenth century, that chocolate was made into bars and used commonly in cooking.

I prefer to serve this chocolate cake as a dessert served warm with extra-thick cream rather than as an afternoon-tea cake, but it can be eaten as both.

It is best to use a good bitter plain chocolate to achieve the maximum taste.

MAKES AN 18–20 CM (7–8 IN) CAKE

225 g (8 oz) strong bitter chocolate
100 g (4 oz) unsalted butter
100 g (4 oz) caster sugar
3 eggs, separated

25 g (1 oz) plain flour, sifted
Pinch of salt

Grease and line an 18–20 cm (7–8 in), loose-bottomed cake tin. Pre-heat the oven to 180°C/350°F/Gas Mark 4.

Chop the bitter chocolate and mix with the butter and sugar in a stainless steel bowl. Melt together over a bowl of softly simmering water. Once melted, remove from the heat. The chocolate needs to be at a warm room temperature.

The egg yolks can now be forked together and then slowly added to the chocolate. Whisk the egg whites to soft peaks. Fold the sifted flour and salt into the chocolate mix before whisking in a quarter of the egg white. The remaining egg white can now be gently folded in.

Pour into the lined cake tin, making sure it is smoothed evenly into the tin. Bake in the oven for 30–35 minutes until firm.

Leave to stand in the tin for 15–20 minutes before carefully removing. The warm chocolate cake is now ready to serve.

Thick pouring cream or a good scoop of vanilla ice-cream will eat very well with this dish. For chocolate lovers, the rich *Bitter Chocolate Sauce* (page 323) can also be offered.

Home-made Malt Loaf

Slices of malt loaf topped with lots of butter are a great favourite of mine. Malt loaf is one of those Great British traditions that we never seem to make at home, but always keep the ready-made in store to go with a hot drink for elevenses or afternoon tea.

This recipe is using a malt extract. This gives a very rich flavour, and also maintains a moist finish. Two-thirds extract can also be mixed with a third black treacle.

This is a loaf that needs to mature to reach the moist texture we all know exists in a malt loaf. Once cooked and cold, it should be wrapped in baking parchment and kept for a minimum of 2–3 days in an airtight container. Here's the recipe.

MAKES A 900 G (2 LB) LOAF

8 tablespoons malt extract
75 ml (3 fl oz) hot strong tea
175 g (6 oz) wholemeal self-raising flour
Good pinch of ground mixed spice
75 g (3 oz) raisins
75 g (3 oz) sultanas
1 egg

Butter a 900 g (2 lb) loaf tin and line it with greaseproof paper. Pre-heat the oven to 140°C/275°F/ Gas Mark 1.

Mix the malt extract with the hot tea and leave to cool. Place the flour with the mixed spice in a

bowl along with the fruits, egg and malty tea. Mix well together before spooning into the lined loaf tin.

Bake in the pre-heated oven for 1¼–1½ hours. Pierce with a skewer and, once it can be removed clean, then the loaf is ready. Leave to stand for 10 minutes in the tin before turning out onto a wire rack. Once cold, wrap and pack as explained in the recipe introduction.

Please have the patience to wait for this loaf. The first buttered slice is worth waiting 2–3 days for.

Note: As an optional extra, include the grated zest of ½ orange.

Parkin

This is a type of gingerbread that is made in the north of England and Scotland, and includes a proportion of oatmeal as well as treacle and golden syrup. There are a number of forms but, generally, in England, it is made into large cakes, in Scotland, small cakes and biscuits. The history of the name is not known – it may have just come from somebody's family name.

In Yorkshire parkin is eaten on Bonfire Night, 5 November. Apparently, Guy Fawkes was a Yorkshireman, and a dialect calendar published 300 years after his execution in 1606 states: 'Th' children's all lukkin' forrad to th' plot an' parkin.' I wonder…

MAKES A 20 CM (8 IN) SQUARE CAKE

100 g (4 oz) self-raising flour
Pinch of salt
2 teaspoons ground ginger
½ teaspoon ground nutmeg
½ teaspoon mixed spice
75 g (3 oz) medium oatmeal
175 g (6 oz) dark syrup (or 100 g/4 oz golden
    syrup and 50 g/2 oz black treacle)
100 g (4 oz) butter
100 g (4 oz) soft brown sugar
1 egg, beaten
2 dessertspoons milk

This parkin mix will need a 20 cm (8 in) square cake tin. Pre-heat the oven to 140°C/275°F/Gas Mark 1.

Sift together the self-raising flour, salt, ginger, nutmeg and mixed spice. Mix in the oatmeal.

The dark syrup (or golden syrup and black treacle), butter and sugar will now have to all be melted in a saucepan together. This can be made easier by first sitting the pan on the scales and weighing it. Now add the dark syrup or golden syrup and treacle. This saves a lot of sticky transferring. Now just add the weighed sugar and butter. Heat together, only allowing all to melt and not simmer or boil.

Stir the syrup mix into the dry mix and blend together. Add in the egg and milk to create a soft, almost pouring consistency. Pour the mixture into the greased tin. Bake in the pre-heated oven for 1¼ hours until firm in the centre.

Once cooked, leave to stand in the tin for 30 minutes before turning out. Once cooled, the parkin can be served straight away. However, if kept in an airtight tin the cake will, like a good wine, mature with age. It should be left for a minimum of 2 weeks, when a whole new texture will have been created; for best flavour, leave for 3 weeks.

Note: The grated zest of 1 orange can be added to the mix, giving a slightly tangy finish.

BELOW
Parkin

Lemon Syrup Loaf

This deliciously lemony and golden syrupy loaf is a classic example of an enriched bread which is now served as a tea bread. It is very simple to make and even more tasty to eat, which is why it very rarely lasts longer than the day on which it has been baked!

MAKES A 900 G (2 LB) LOAF

175 g (6 oz) unsalted butter
175 g (6 oz) caster sugar
3 eggs
225 g (8 oz) self-raising flour
Finely grated zest of 1 lemon
2 tablespoons milk
6 tablespoons lemon juice
3 tablespoons golden syrup

For this recipe you will need a 900 g (2 lb) loaf tin, buttered and lined with greaseproof paper. Pre-heat the oven to 180°C/350°F/Gas Mark 4.

Cream together the butter and sugar until light and fluffy. Lightly beat the eggs and slowly whisk into the butter mix.

Sift the flour and fold in, with the lemon zest. Fold in the milk and then half the lemon juice.

Spoon into the lined tin and spread level. Bake in the pre-heated oven for 45–50 minutes until firm to the touch.

Warm together the remaining lemon juice and golden syrup. Remove the cake from the oven and pierce several holes in the top with a skewer. The lemon and golden syrup can now be slowly spooned over, allowing it to be absorbed by the sponge.

Once all has been added and the sponge has cooled, remove from the tin. The cake is now ready to serve. The loaf can be sprinkled with icing sugar to create a sweet dusted topping.

Note: It may seem as though a lot of liquid is being added when pouring over the lemon and syrup; however, once cool, this will give a moist/sticky finish to the cake.

Banana and Golden Syrup Loaf

Bananas were one of the fruits carefully and competitively cultivated in early greenhouses by the gentry in the mid eighteenth century – along with pineapples, guavas, mangoes and so on. It was only when steamships could speed the highly perishable fruit to its destination that people in general began to know them. Our first shipments of bananas – from the Canaries – docked in 1882. One of the banana shipping companies was started by a Mr Fyffe, and the name is familiar to us still.

This is a very simple recipe, and a great way of using up any over-ripe bananas. The golden syrup flavour working with them makes the loaf even richer, with a wonderful soft texture.

MAKES A 900 G (2 LB) LOAF

225 g (8 oz) self-raising flour
100 g (4 oz) butter, softened
4 ripe bananas, mashed
50 g (2 oz) dark soft brown sugar
4 tablespoons golden syrup
4 eggs

This recipe will fill a buttered and greaseproofed 900 g (2 lb) loaf tin. Pre-heat the oven to 180°C/350°F/Gas Mark 4. Then simply mix all of the ingredients together until well combined.

Spoon into the lined tin and bake in the pre-heated oven for 50–55 minutes. The loaf can be tested by piercing with a skewer. The loaf will be cooked when the skewer is removed clean.

Remove from the oven and rest in the tin for 10 minutes before turning out and allowing to cool.

Note: For a nutty finish, 50 g (2 oz) of chopped walnuts, hazelnuts or pecan nuts can be added to the above recipe.

OPPOSITE
Banana and Golden Syrup Loaf

Hot Cross Buns

The origin of the hot cross bun is unknown, but some say it dates from early, even pagan, times, when the small round shape represented the sun, the cross dividing it into four parts for the seasons. Breads bearing crosses were commonplace, though, right up until the Reformation in the sixteenth century, usually to guard against evil spirits and bad luck. In the Middle Ages the strongest and most effective bread was that made on Good Friday. It was suspended from the ceiling to guard the household until the next Easter. Perhaps it was this Good Friday loaf that began the Easter association of the bun with a cross on it.

Whatever the case, hot cross buns have now become an annual treat. And I'm delighted because I love them straight from the oven, hot and sticky, or toasted and dripping with butter.

A piping bag with a small plain tube (1 cm/½ in diameter) will be needed to pipe the cross.

MAKES APPROX. 12 BUNS

50 g (2 oz) caster sugar, plus 1 teaspoon
125 ml (4 fl oz) water, warmed
125 ml (4 fl oz) milk, warmed
1 tablespoon dried yeast
450 g (1 lb) plain flour
1 teaspoon salt
1 heaped teaspoon ground mixed spice
50 g (2 oz) currants
50 g (2 oz) mixed peel
50 g (2 oz) melted butter
1 egg, beaten

For the Cross

4 tablespoons plain flour
1 tablespoon caster sugar
3–4 tablespoons water

For the Sticky Glaze

2 tablespoons sugar
2 tablespoons water

Stir the teaspoon of caster sugar into the warm water and milk. Add the dried yeast, cover and leave in a warm place until a thick frothy surface (about 2 cm/¾ in deep) has appeared. This will take about 15–20 minutes.

Sift the flour, salt and mixed spice into a warm bowl, adding the 50 g (2 oz) of sugar, currants and mixed peel. Make a well in the centre and pour in the melted butter, egg and yeast milk/water. Stir to mix and work by hand to a sticky dough.

Now knead and work the dough on a clean surface until smooth and elastic. This will take 8–10 minutes. Place the dough in a clean bowl, cover with a damp tea-towel and leave to rise in a warm place for 45–60 minutes until doubled in volume.

Now knock back the risen dough to its original size. The mix can now be divided into 12 and shaped into nice round buns. Place the buns on a greased baking sheet (two sheets may be needed), leaving a good distance between each for rising. Now cover again with the tea-towel and leave to rise once more for 35–45 minutes until doubled in volume. Pre-heat the oven to 220°C/425°F/Gas Mark 7.

While the buns are rising, the piping dough can be made. Mix the flour with the sugar and water to a smooth paste. This can now be placed in the piping bag with the plain tube.

Remove the towel from the buns and, with the back of a small knife, mark the cross on each bun. The piping dough can now be piped in the indentation in each bun.

Place the buns in the pre-heated oven and cook for 15–18 minutes, until they are golden brown and, when tapped underneath, sound hollow.

While the buns are cooking melt the sugar for the sticky glaze in the water over a low heat. As soon as the buns are removed from the oven, brush with the glaze for a shiny, sticky finish. Place on a wire rack to cool, that's if there are any left by then!

Note: If you prefer to use fresh yeast, 25 g (1 oz) will be needed. Simply crumble the yeast into a small bowl and cream with the warm milk and water. Now continue as per the recipe, adding the melted butter.

OPPOSITE
Hot Cross Buns

Tuile Biscuits

Even though 'tuile' is a French name, biscuits such as these did exist in the British tradition. Wafers were 'biscuits' made in an iron mould held over the fire on a long handle, and were often rolled into a curl after baking. These were the predecessors of the modern British brandy snap, a biscuit virtually indistinguishable from the tuile. (Interestingly, wafer irons were taken to America by the first settlers, and the American waffle tradition was born.)

Tuiles are often used as containers for serving ice-cream or sorbet, and are also served as petits-fours. They can be made in almost any shape – a basic curved disc, leaf, swan, triangle, twist and many more. (Use a stencil cut from an ice-cream tub lid.) For a large circular tuile you will need a 10–12 cm (4–4¾ in) diameter disc. For petits-fours, a 6–8 cm (2½–3 in) disc will be just right.

To shape a tuile into a cup, sit the warm biscuit in, or over the outside of, a cup. For a curved shape, lay it over a rolling pin.

Tuiles will stay crisp for up to 48 hours if they are kept in an airtight container. Any mix not used immediately will keep, if refrigerated, for 7–10 days.

Basic Tuile Biscuits

MAKES 15–18 LARGE OR 30–35 SMALL TUILES

2 egg whites
75 g (3 oz) icing sugar, sieved
50 g (2 oz) plain flour, sieved
50 g (2 oz) unsalted butter, melted

Pre-heat the oven to 180°C/350°F/Gas Mark 4.

Place the egg whites in a bowl. Add the sieved icing sugar and whisk for 10–15 seconds. Add the flour, gently pour in the melted butter and mix to a smooth paste.

To cook the tuile biscuits, spread the mix, using your shaped stencil if needed (see introduction left), on baking parchment, leaving space between each for them to spread. Bake for 8–10 minutes until golden brown and beginning to bubble on the tray. Remove from the oven and complete shaping while the tuiles are still warm. Once cold and crisp they are ready to eat.

Hazelnut Tuiles

MAKES APPROX. 16 LARGE OR 30 SMALL TUILES

2 egg whites
25 g (1 oz) caster sugar
125 g (4½ oz) plain flour
125 g (4½ oz) ground hazelnuts
1½ tablespoons hazelnut oil

Pre-heat the oven to 180°C/350°F/Gas Mark 4.

Lightly whisk the egg whites and caster sugar to a froth. Add all of the remaining ingredients and mix to a paste. Spread as described in the basic recipe (left) and bake for 5–8 minutes until light golden. Remove from the oven and complete shaping while still warm.

Sesame Seed and Orange Tuiles

MAKES 5–6 LARGE OR 10–12 SMALL TUILES

4 tablespoons orange juice
25 g (1 oz) sesame seeds
50 g (2 oz) caster sugar
25 g (1 oz) plain flour
Finely grated zest of 1 orange

Pre-heat the oven to 180°C/350°F/Gas Mark 4.

Bring the orange juice to the boil and reduce by half. Leave to cool.

Once the juice has cooled, mix all the ingredients together. Spread and cook as for the basic recipe (see left), shaping while still warm.

Brandy Snap Biscuits

MAKES 40–45 BISCUITS

125 g (4½ oz) unsalted butter
125 g (4½ oz) light soft brown sugar
125 g (4½ oz) golden syrup
4 teaspoons lemon juice
125 g (4½ oz) plain flour
1 teaspoon ground ginger

Pre-heat the oven to 190°C/375°F/Gas Mark 5.

Place the butter, sugar, golden syrup and lemon juice in a saucepan and stir over a moderate heat until the butter melts and the sugar has dissolved. Remove the pan from the heat. Sift the flour and ginger into the pan and mix to a smooth paste. Allow the mixture to cool completely.

Roll into balls the size of a 2 pence piece and press them onto a greased baking tray. Keep a good distance between each one or you will finish up with one vast brandy snap. Bake for 8–10 minutes. Allow the brandy snaps to relax for a few seconds, then mould them to the shape required (see introduction, page 356). If the snaps cool before you can shape them all, pop them back into the oven to warm through again.

Gingerbread Biscuits

Ginger was one of the most common spices available in Britain, so it was used a lot in many regional specialities such as *Parkin* (page 350), which is actually a form of gingerbread. Gingerbread was first made as a biscuit, baked slowly until crisp, and cut into various shapes. The cake type of gingerbread developed only in the eighteenth and nineteenth centuries, when leavens (raising agents), such as bicarbonate of soda, were introduced.

These biscuits taste delicious if you add some chopped pecan nuts or dates – or both. If you are using dates or nuts, simply stir them in with the evaporated milk.

MAKES APPROX. 20 BISCUITS

225 g (8 oz) plain flour
¼ teaspoon salt
2 teaspoons bicarbonate of soda
1 heaped teaspoon ground ginger
½ teaspoon ground cinnamon
50 g (2 oz) unsalted butter
100 g (4 oz) soft brown sugar
100 g (4 oz) golden syrup
1 tablespoon evaporated milk

Sift together the flour, salt, soda and spices. Heat the butter, sugar and syrup until dissolved. Leave to cool. Once cooled, mix into the dry ingredients with the evaporated milk to make a dough. Chill for 30 minutes.

Pre-heat the oven to 190°C/375°F/Gas Mark 5 and grease two baking sheets.

Roll out the biscuit dough to about 5 mm (¼ in) thick and cut into fingers, circles or even gingerbread men. Place on the baking sheets, allowing a little space to spread. Bake in the pre-heated oven for 10–15 minutes. Remove from the oven. Leave to cool slightly on the baking sheet before transferring to a wire rack.

Note: An additional teaspoon of ginger can be added for a stronger ginger flavour. Gingerbread men often enjoy being 'dressed' with currant eyes and buttons.

Cheddar and Pecan Cheese Biscuits

Flavoured with grated Cheddar and rolled in chopped pecan nuts, these cheese biscuits would be perfect to serve with your cheese course or to enjoy with other cheese accompaniments – grapes, apples, celery, and so on. The pecan nuts give the biscuits an added crunch.

100 g (4 oz) Cheddar cheese, grated
100 g (4 oz) butter
½ teaspoon cayenne pepper
150 g (5 oz) plain flour
50 g (2 oz) chopped pecan nuts

Pre-heat the oven to 180°C/350°F/Gas Mark 4.

Cream together the Cheddar cheese and butter. Add the cayenne pepper and flour, mixing to a firm dough. The mix can now be rolled into a log, approximately 5 cm (2 in) in diameter and rolled to coat in the chopped pecan nuts. Refrigerate to firm.

The log can now be cut into round or oval slices (3 mm/⅛ in thick).

Place the biscuits on a baking sheet lined with parchment or greaseproof paper. Bake in the pre-heated oven for 12–15 minutes. Leave to cool slightly before transferring to a wire rack.

Stilton and Sesame Seed Biscuits

Again, a very British cheese mixed with sesame seeds to make a pungent cheese biscuit for a savoury snack or to accompany a cheeseboard. Almost any other cheese can be grated and used to flavour the biscuit.

MAKES APPROX. 40 BISCUITS

100 g (4 oz) plain flour
100 g (4 oz) butter
¼ teaspoon cayenne pepper
100 g (4 oz) Stilton cheese, grated
25–50 g (1–2 oz) sesame seeds

Pre-heat the oven to 180°C/350°F/Gas Mark 4.
Rub the flour, butter and cayenne together.

OPPOSITE
Cheddar and Pecan Cheese Biscuits and
Stilton and Sesame Seed Biscuits

Add the grated Stilton cheese and mix to a firm dough. Roll into a log, approximately 5 cm (2 in) in diameter, and then roll in the sesame seeds. Refrigerate to firm the log.

Once chilled and set, cut into discs or oval shapes approximately 3 mm (⅛ in) thick. Place on a baking sheet covered with parchment or greaseproof paper and bake in the pre-heated oven for 12–15 minutes.

Leave to cool for a few minutes on the tray before transferring to a wire rack. The biscuits are now ready to eat.

Shortbread Biscuits

Shortbread is a delicious and buttery example of the rich Scottish baking tradition. There are various regional types, most famously, perhaps, the 'petticoat tails' of Edinburgh, a round cake cut into wedges to resemble the hooped petticoats of long ago. Shortbread is perfect for afternoon tea, and is often featured, along with Atholl Brose, an oatmeal drink, and black bun, a rich dried fruit cake encased in pastry – and, of course, whisky – at Hogmanay or New Year celebrations.

MAKES 16–24 BISCUITS, DEPENDING ON SIZE

225 g (8 oz) unsalted butter
75 g (3 oz) caster sugar
350 g (12 oz) plain flour
15 g (½ oz) cornflour

Pre-heat the oven to 180°C/350°F/Gas Mark 4 and grease and line a baking sheet.

Cream together the butter and sugar until the sugar has dissolved into the fat. Sift the flour and cornflour together and work into the butter mix. Roll out the dough to approximately 5 mm (¼ in) thick and, using a pastry cutter, cut into biscuits. Alternatively, cut the dough into shortbread fingers. Place on the baking sheet and bake in the pre-heated oven for 20–25 minutes until golden brown. Leave to cool on a wire rack. The biscuits eat very well when sprinkled with caster sugar.

Variation

Lightly roll the shortbread mix about 1–2 cm (½–¾ in) thick and 20 cm (8 in) in diameter and place it in a flan ring. Mark it into eight pieces and prick all over with a fork before cooking. It will take about 30–35 minutes to bake in the pre-heated oven.

Fig Rolls

Dried figs were introduced many centuries ago to Britain, and were used in many medieval pottages and in sweet and savoury pies. Fig rolls are a more recent marrying of dried fig purée and pastry, a great friend to a mug of tea, or to accompany a dessert.

This is not quite the classic biscuit, though. Here the fig purée still runs through the centre but there are two different biscuit pastes to wrap it in. One is flavoured with ground almonds while the second contains soft brown sugar, two different textures, both complementing the rich fig filling.

MAKES APPROX. 15 BISCUITS

For the Filling

200 g (7 oz) ready-to-eat dried figs
150 ml (¼ pint) water
50 g (2 oz) dark soft brown sugar
50 g (2 oz) dry sponge fingers, crushed or crumbled

For the Brown-sugar Dough

250 g (9 oz) plain flour
¾ teaspoon baking powder
90 g (3½ oz) light soft brown sugar
125 g (4½ oz) butter
1 egg
1 tablespoon milk (optional), to finish
3 teaspoons caster sugar (optional), to finish

For the Almond Dough

375 g (13 oz) ground almonds
185 g (generous 6 oz) caster sugar
185 g (generous 6 oz) icing sugar
2 eggs
2 teaspoons lemon juice

First, make the filling. Place the figs in a saucepan with the water, bring to a simmer and cook for 10 minutes. Add the sugar and continue to cook until the liquid has almost evaporated. Purée the mix and allow it to cool. Then stir in the sponge-finger crumbs. Roll it into a log 30 cm (12 in) long. To make handling easier, cut into two 15 cm (6 in) pieces.

Make the brown-sugar dough next. This is the outside dough and it needs to chill for 30 minutes before use. Rub together the flour, baking powder, sugar and butter to a breadcrumb texture. Add the egg and mix to a dough. Wrap it in cling film and chill for 30 minutes.

Now make the almond dough. Mix together the ground almonds and the sugars. Beat an egg, add it with the lemon juice to the almond mix and work to a firm paste. Dust the work surface with icing sugar and roll the paste 30 cm (12 in) long and wide enough to roll round the fig log. Beat the remaining egg and brush the paste. Cut into two 15 cm (6 in) pieces. Place a fig log on top of each and roll. Chill.

OPPOSITE
Fig Rolls

Lightly flour the work surface and roll the brown-sugar dough to 30 cm (12 in) long and wide enough to cover the first dough. Again, cut it into two 15 cm (6 in) pieces. Brush each piece with the remaining egg and sit a wrapped fig roll on top. Cover the roll with the dough. Press the rolls slightly to take on the classic shape, then cut, making seven or eight biscuits from each. Press a fork on top of each and draw it across to create a channel effect. Refrigerate for 15–20 minutes. Pre-heat the oven to 180°C/350°F/Gas Mark 4.

Leave the biscuits plain or brush with milk and sprinkle with caster sugar. Bake for 20–25 minutes. Remove from the oven and cool on wire racks.

Golden Oatcakes

Oatcakes – also known as bannocks – are a typical example of the earliest types of bread cooked in Britain – flat and hard, shaped and cooked on the hearthstone or on a flat griddle. Once they were made with oats and water alone. I've added some golden syrup, which gives the biscuits a golden edge, and a delicious toffee flavour.

The oats used here are rolled oats. These have been steamed and then flattened mechanically, making them quicker to cook. (Porridge made with rolled oats will only take 10–12 minutes to make, for instance.) They are very good for biscuits, hence their use here. The rolled oats can be replaced with jumbo oats for a coarser and nuttier finish.

MAKES 10–14 BISCUITS

100 g (4 oz) butter
2 tablespoons or 50 g (2 oz) golden syrup
50 g (2 oz) demerara sugar
½ teaspoon bicarbonate of soda
50 g (2 oz) self-raising flour
225 g (8 oz) rolled oats

Pre-heat the oven to 180°C/350°F/Gas Mark 4.
Melt the butter, golden syrup, sugar and bicarbonate

of soda in a saucepan over a gentle heat. It's important this is not allowed to get too hot, just melting.

Sift the self-raising flour into a bowl and mix with the rolled oats. Pour the syrupy butter into the bowl and mix well.

The biscuit mix can now be shaped and rolled into 10–14 balls. Place on a greased baking tray and flatten with your hand, then cook in the pre-heated oven for 12–15 minutes. Once golden brown and firm, remove from the oven and transfer to a wire rack. Leave to cool before storing in an air-tight container.

Note: These are lovely biscuits to offer at teatime, coffee-time – any time. They are also an alternative accompaniment to ice-creams.

Home-made Crumpets

Crumpets fit into the category of tea cakes, and appeared in the later seventeenth century. The name is thought to come from the Middle English *crompid*, meaning to bend or curl into a curve, which is what home-made crumpets tend to do. They are very closely related to the Welsh version, now known as 'pikelet', which is still found in the Midlands, the west of England and Wales. Muffins are also related, but few exist now in the British tradition – although they are, of course, very popular in America (where we took them). And they are not too different from drop or girdle/griddle scones.

Toasted crumpets are a favourite in my home, particularly with my sons, Samuel and George. But it's never at teatime, although that's when I remember having them. If they want crumpets – and it's always toasted with lashings of butter and huge dollops of jam, washed down with a big mug of tea – it has to be for breakfast.

Watching that famous 'bubbled' look develop in the pan is quite amazing. And to eat them straight from the pan with lots of butter is a very 'melting' experience. Whether it be for breakfast or afternoon tea, here's the recipe.

MAKES APPROX. 20 CRUMPETS

450 g (1 lb) plain flour
15 g (½ oz) salt
15 g (½ oz) fresh yeast
600 ml (1 pint) warm water

Sieve together the flour and salt. Mix the yeast with a few tablespoons of the warm water. Whisk three-quarters of the remaining warm water into the flour and then add the yeasty liquid. Cover and leave in a warm place until the mixture has risen. Once risen, check the consistency. If the batter is very thick, loosen with the remaining water. The batter should now be left to stand for 8–10 minutes.

Warm a non-stick frying-pan on a low heat. Grease some crumpet rings or small tartlet rings and rub the pan with butter.

Place the rings into the frying-pan and pour in some of the batter until half-full (5 mm–1 cm/ ¼–½ in deep). Cook on a low heat until small holes appear and the top has started to dry. The base of the crumpet will now be golden and it can be turned over and cooked for a further minute. The crumpets are now ready for lots of melting butter.

Note: The crumpets can be cooked without turning: simply cook until the tops are completely dry.

The finely grated zest of 1 lemon can also be added to the batter, to give a lemon bite.

If fresh yeast isn't available, use 2 teaspoons dried yeast. Mix with the flour and salt, add the water and leave to rise as above.

Griddle Scones

These are great to eat at Sunday teatime with butter, jam and cream. They take no time to make and very little to cook, and we all seem to have these ingredients sitting in our cupboards. This recipe will give you about 20 scones – of course, you can halve the recipe, but I'm sure you'll eat 20. The other plus is the great variety of scones you can make by adding other flavours. I like to make them with the finely grated zest of lemon, but

ABOVE
Home-made Crumpets

orange or lime can also be used. Chopped apple can be added with a pinch of ground cinnamon, or you can even make them Christmassy with the addition of glacé fruits. They can also be eaten as a pudding with fresh fruits and creamy sabayons – or in the Afternoon Tea Pudding on page 320. And one last tip – eat them as soon as possible.

MAKES APPROX. 20 SCONES

450 g (1 lb) self-raising flour, plus extra for
    dusting
Pinch of salt
50 g (2 oz) unsalted butter, plus extra for frying
50 g (2 oz) lard
175 g (6 oz) currants or sultanas
Grated zest of 1 lemon
100 g (4 oz) caster sugar
2 eggs
2–4 tablespoons milk

Sift and mix the flour with the salt, then rub in the butter and lard. Fold in the currants or sultanas, lemon zest and sugar. Make a well in the centre and add the eggs and milk, mixing in the flour to form a soft dough. The dough can now be rolled out to 1 cm (½ in) thick and cut into 6 cm (2½ in) rounds, or moulded by hand into 1 cm (½ in) thick individual scones.

    Heat a frying-pan or griddle and cook over a medium heat in a little butter for 5 minutes on each side until golden brown. The scones are now ready to eat.

Variation

The scones eat very well with griddle strawberries. These are simply strawberries cooked on a grill plate, giving a slightly bitter, burnt tinge that is then balanced with a dusting of icing sugar. I like to eat these with crème fraîche to finish the dish.

    For a richer scone, use 100 g (4 oz) unsalted butter instead of 50 g (2 oz) lard.

Shortcrust Pastry and Sweet Shortcrust Pastry

The first pastries in England were probably hot-water crust, but a variety was used over the years. Both of the pastries here share a basic method: the difference is the sugar. Use the unsweetened, obviously, in savoury tarts and flans; the sweetened in open fruit tarts and other sweet pastries. The latter pastry contains sugar, but it also differs in that I've added an extra egg yolk for a richer finish. You could use water instead, but I'm giving you the recipe with the maximum flavour. Either caster or icing sugar can be used, but I have found that icing sugar gives a richer, smoother consistency. The choice is yours.

FOR SHORTCRUST PASTRY (MAKES 400 G/14 OZ)

225 g (8 oz) plain flour
Pinch of salt
150 g (5 oz) cold butter, chopped
1 whole egg
25 ml (1 fl oz) water

FOR SWEET SHORTCRUST PASTRY (MAKES 450 G/1 LB)

225 g (8 oz) plain flour
Pinch of salt
150 g (5 oz) cold butter, chopped
75 g (3 oz) caster or icing sugar
1 egg yolk
1 whole egg

For the basic shortcrust pastry, sift the flour with the salt. Rub the flour and butter together to a crumble texture. Add the egg and water together and mix briefly to a smooth dough. Wrap in cling film and refrigerate for 30–60 minutes before rolling and using.

    To make the sweet pastry, sift the flour with the salt. Quickly rub in the butter in a bowl or cold work surface until the mixture resembles crumbs. Stir the sugar into the flour mixture, then add the egg yolk and egg. Work everything together and refrigerate for 30–60 minutes before using.

Note: When blind-baking any pastry-lined flan case or ring, line with greaseproof paper or foil and fill with baking beans or rice. This applies to all the pastry recipes.

    For a different flavour, add the finely grated zest of 1 lemon to the flour mix for a lemon crust, or the seeds from a vanilla pod. You could even use both.

Quick Puff or Flaky Pastry

We might think that puff pastry is a French invention, but the British were making rich butter pastes – flour mixed with butter, sugar, rose-water and spices, then interleaved with more butter – in the sixteenth century. It was given the name puff pastry in 1605, and was used mainly in the making of sweet tarts and the precursors of vol-au-vents.

Making puff pastry in the traditional way cannot really be beaten. This recipe, however, is a lot quicker and does bring you very close to it. The resultant pastry can be used in any recipe needing puff pastry. Any not used will freeze very well.

MAKES 750 G (1¾ LB)

300 g (11 oz) butter, chilled
450 g (1 lb) plain flour
1 teaspoon salt
200–250 ml (7–8 fl oz) cold water

Cut the chilled butter into small cubes. Sieve the flour with the salt. Add the butter, gently working into the flour but not totally breaking down. Add the water, mixing to a pliable dough, still with pieces of butter showing.

Turn onto a floured surface and roll as for classic puff pastry, into a rectangle (approximately 45 × 15 cm/18 × 6 in). Fold in the right-hand one-third and then fold in the left-hand side on top. Leave to rest for 20 minutes. The pastry now needs to be rolled three times in the same fashion, resting it for 20 minutes between each turn.

The quick puff/flaky pastry is now ready to use.

Note: A richer version of this pastry can be made with a higher butter content and with the addition of the juice from 1 lemon. Just follow the above recipe, only adding 175–225 ml (6–7½ fl oz) of water with the juice.
Good puff pastry can also be bought.

See also

Christmas Cake (page 336)
Home-made Mincemeat and Mince Pies (page 336)
Home-made Pork Pie (page 280)
Saffron Bread (page 397)
Sausage Rolls (page 277)
Vegetarian Cheese and Onion 'Sausage' Rolls (page 278)

Afternoon Tea and High Tea

This is a tradition that has 'British' written all over it. It features a wonderful selection of light and tasty eats, with warm scones, home-made jams and classic clotted cream dominating the show. Afternoon tea, like the savoury course, is a way of eating that is completely unique to Britain. There are a number of reasons for its 'invention'.

The first is the introduction to Britain of the new drink, tea, in the late sixteenth century. Catherine of Braganza, the wife of King Charles II, is said to have been very enthusiastic about tea-drinking. Tea then was mostly green tea from China and, during the next 200 years or so, it was to take over in popularity from home-brewed ale and the other imported drinks, coffee and chocolate. At first, tea was a drink for the rich, as the leaves were not cheap (one reason for all the rather expensive tea accessories – silver teapots, caddy spoons, sugar tongs and so on). It was drunk at breakfast, and after dinner, and later was the drink of choice at the new pleasure- or tea-gardens which opened in and around London (most famously at Vauxhall, Ranelagh and Marylebone) in the late eighteenth century. It wasn't until the mid nineteenth century, when it was planted in India and later Ceylon (Sri Lanka), that tea, by now usually black, became cheaper and more available to all. Some people were horrified by the amount of tea drunk by all classes, and considered it a harmful drug. A commentator in the late 1750s wrote: 'When will this evil stop? ... Your very *Chambermaids* have lost their bloom, I suppose by *sipping tea*.' It is actually thought that milk began to be put in tea in order to dilute the effects of tea and its tannin. However, tea-drinking had by now become the national habit – and it's still with us.

Another reason concerns the changing pattern of mealtimes. Before the seventeenth century, lives and mealtimes were dominated by the sun. People rose and breakfasted at sunrise, ate a dinner – the main meal of the day – some hours later, and then supped before going to bed not long after the sun set. Following the introduction of oil lamps, wealthier people could extend their days, getting out of bed later, and staying up for longer at night. Breakfast was taken later in the morning, and the dinner hour began to slide from about midday towards evening, the distance between them becoming longer and longer.

As lunch did not exist as a separate meal, there was a need for the occasional snack. It was hunger, apparently, that drove Anna, the seventh Duchess of Bedford, to order some mid-afternoon slices of bread and butter, as well as macaroons and other small cakes and biscuits. Her friends learned of her new habit, approved, and by the mid nineteenth century, afternoon tea had become a fashionable and popular way of eating and entertaining. The choice of foods became wider, with sandwiches enclosing thin slices of cucumber, potted meats or fish (or Gentleman's Relish, for the men), tiny sausage rolls, muffins, rich fruit or seed cakes, and biscuits.

The working population, however, still had their dinner around midday, and the meal they ate when work was finished, from five to seven o'clock, became known as 'high tea'. It was followed, at around ten in the evening, by 'supper'. High tea was fairly substantial, consisting of dishes that could be cooked slowly all day while the householders were at work, or of foods that could be cooked quickly on returning from work. Irish stew and Lancashire hotpot are examples of long-cooked dishes. Quicker dishes might include chops, bacon, sausages, toad in the hole, preserved fish, salads, pies and cold or potted meats with pickles. These would be followed by bread, butter and a variety of sweet cakes, all washed down with plenty of tea. Supper would consist of tea, bread and butter, perhaps some cheese, and a few small cakes. Because of high tea and supper, both of which survive mostly now in the north of England and Scotland, it is said that many regional baking and other local specialities have been preserved rather than lost.

Afternoon tea was a meal to be enjoyed at home, and was a leisurely affair. High tea was more a meal of necessity, but it too was home-based. 'At homes' started off as tea parties, and various other 'meals' based on tea came into being, such as family tea, nursery tea, then church teas and sporting teas. The strawberries and cream associated today with teatime at Wimbledon and other sporting venues have their origin in the 'subtleties' served at the tea-gardens in the Georgian era. And the height of the tea craze must surely have been the *thé dansants* – 'dancing teas' – enjoyed in many hotels in Edwardian times, and now being reintroduced, I believe. In the late nineteenth century, the first public snack and sandwich bars and tea-rooms opened, both in Glasgow. Thackeray was to describe these new phenomena as '… fifty separate ways of spoiling one's dinner'.

This chapter might not give you fifty ways, but it does give lots of nice ways of spoiling your dinner. These recipes all suit that time of eating, and would be good at many other times, too, whether you are looking for a substantial high tea or a lighter afternoon tea. They range from some hearty, hot and savoury dishes that are very much in the 'high tea' tradition, such as the *Cumberland Sausages* (page 368) and *Toad in the Hole* (page 370), to more delicate and 'ladylike' morsels such as *Cucumber Sandwiches* (page 373), among others. When trying these recipes, I do hope you'll find all the reasons how and why this occasion has stayed with us for so long. Enjoy the Great British tradition of teatime.

Pork Sausages

The word 'sausage' actually comes from the Latin, *salsicius*, prepared by salting, which in turn comes from *salsus*, meaning 'salted'. As a food, sausages have been around in Britain since Roman times. The Anglo-Saxons developed their own varieties, and the Normans introduced their French ideas, among them the pure pork sausage, the black pudding, made with blood, and the *andouille*, an entrail sausage known in England as chitterlings.

More or less every country in the world has a variety of sausages on offer, both fresh and dried or smoked, but what about the Great British sausage? We have a number of choices – the Yorkshire, Oxford, Cumberland, Cambridge and the country pork sausage – and we eat them for breakfast, lunch, high tea and dinner. At first our sausages would have been dried, and then possibly smoked, but now we tend only to eat them fresh.

This is my recipe for pork sausages. I'm using the classic cut associated with sausages, the shoulder, but I've also added pork cheek, which has a wonderfully lean texture and a good pork taste. Since first putting this recipe together, I've tried replacing the meat and pork fat with just a piece of pork belly. This works well, because pork belly has a good but not excessive

fat content. If you take 1 kg (2¼ lb) of pork belly and mix it with an extra 150–200 g (5–7 oz) pork fat, you will have a perfect balance for a good pork sausage.

The sausage skins should be readily available from most butchers. The skins will have been salted; this preserves them, keeping them fresh. Before using, soak in cold water, preferably running water. To be completely sure of cleaning and taking out all the salt flavour, run the tap water through the actual skin. Now dry with a cloth before using.

I also always cut 25 cm (10 in) lengths of skin, tying a knot in one end before filling. This will then leave you with 5–8 cm (2–3 in) spare. During cooking, this will shrink around the filling, but, due to the excess, will not burst.

MAKES APPROX. 16 SAUSAGES

900 g (2 lb) boned and rinded shoulder of pork
4 pigs' cheeks, trimmed (optional)
225 g (8 oz) rinded pork back fat
1 onion, very finely chopped
25 g (1 oz) unsalted butter
¼ teaspoon chopped fresh thyme
¼ teaspoon chopped fresh sage
1 garlic clove, crushed (optional)
Pinch of ground mace
2 slices of white bread, crusted and crumbled
1 egg, beaten
Worcestershire sauce
Salt and pepper
About 4 metres (4½ yards) sausage skins, well
    washed
25–50 g (1–2 oz) lard, for frying

Mince the shoulder, cheeks and back fat (or belly and fat) through a medium mincer. This will give you a medium-coarse finish. If you prefer a finer sausage and smoother texture, then pass through the mincer once or twice more. Refrigerate the meats. To make mincing easier, always cut up the meats and fat quite finely before mincing. Also make sure they are well chilled; they will then mince very quickly and easily.

Sweat the chopped onion in butter with the herbs and garlic (if using) for 2–3 minutes until soft. Leave to cool. Once cold, the onion can be mixed with the pork meat. Season with salt, pepper and the ground mace.

Add the breadcrumbs and egg. A few drops of Worcestershire sauce can now be added to finish the sausage mix, being careful not to overdo it, as the Worcestershire sauce can become the most predominant flavour.

I always make a small sausage 'burger' and pan-fry it at this stage. This will tell you if you have the right flavour, in particular with the seasonings and mace.

Now it's time to fill the skins, while the sausage mix is at this temperature and workable. Here's a tip for filling. Use a 1 cm (½ in) plain tubed piping bag. Only half-fill the bag. This gives you more control. If it's overfilled, you can almost break your hand trying to squeeze the meat from it.

Take the skin and pull back to the knot, sit over the end of the piping tube and squeeze. Once the skin has been filled to the size of a standard sausage, remove the bag, and make sure to push the sausage meat further in to give a good, plump shape. Push out any air left in the remaining skin and then tie at the end. Repeat the process with the remaining sausages. It's best to rest the sausages in the fridge for at least 30 minutes before cooking.

The sausages can be grilled or pan-fried. I prefer to pan-fry. With this cooking method you have total control of the heat. Melt the lard in a warm frying-pan. Lay the sausages in the pan and fry gently, letting them take on a golden edge. The excess skin will quickly shrink around the sausage. Extreme heat will burst the sausage. I never prick the sausage skin – I really can't see any point in it. The casing is there to hold all of those flavours and juices in. If released, the meat will be left very dry.

Beautifully, slowly cooked sausages will take 15–20 minutes. Well worth waiting every second.

These sausages will eat very well with your breakfast, lunch or dinner. I can't resist eating home-made sausages (or any sausages for that matter) with *Mashed Potatoes* (page 124) and *Onion Gravy* (page 50). Another great accompaniment is *Braised Split Peas* (page 117).

Note: The shoulder and cheeks can be replaced with 1.1 kg (2 lb 6 oz) of pork belly, reducing the pork fat quantity to be added to 150–200 g (5–7 oz).

Cumberland Sausage

This is probably one of the most famous of British sausages, thought to be the meatiest of them all. Some butchers in Cumberland actually claim they are made with 98 per cent pork. But there are a number of people who feel that the real Cumberland has long gone. The sausages were once made from a special breed of pig and they say its last sow died in 1960.

The most instantly recognizable feature of Cumberland sausage is that it is not twisted into individual sausages, but made in long lengths, sometimes several feet long, and traditionally rolled like a Catherine wheel. You buy by the length, rather than weight, which is twisted and then cut off for you. Another speciality of the sausage is its seasoning, which is made up of several spices: 1 per cent ground cayenne pepper, 1 per cent ground nutmeg, 24 per cent ground white pepper, and 74 per cent fine salt, to be precise. For every 450 g (1 lb) of meat, you will need 15 g (½ oz) of this seasoning.

If you are going to have a go at these, it's probably best just to pipe two or three long sausages and roll into Cumberlands. These can then be pan-fried, grilled or baked.

MAKES 2–3 GOOD-SIZED CUMBERLANDS

450 g (1 lb) lean shoulder pork, cut into rough dice
250 g (9 oz) pork belly, rind removed, cut into rough dice
125 g (4½ oz) rindless pork back fat, cut into rough dice
100 g (4 oz) white breadcrumbs
1 teaspoon chopped fresh thyme
1 teaspoon chopped fresh sage
1 teaspoon chopped fresh rosemary
2–3 metres (2–3 yards) sausage skins, soaked and washed in water
Butter, lard or cooking oil, for frying

OPPOSITE
Cumberland Sausage

2 teaspoons salt
1 teaspoon ground white pepper
Pinch of freshly grated nutmeg
Pinch of cayenne pepper

The meats can be minced to your choice. The Cumberland sausage has always come in different textures, depending on where it has been made.

For a good medium texture, mince once through a coarse disc, and then through a medium disc. This will have broken the texture just a little more, giving it a finer consistency. Mix in the breadcrumbs, seasonings and herbs.

The skins are ready to be filled. The easiest way is to follow the method used for *Pork Sausages* (page 367), using a piping bag and tube. Once made, refrigerate for at least 30 minutes before cooking.

To bake, pre-heat the oven to 180°C/350°F/Gas Mark 4. Brush the sausages with butter and place in a roasting tray. The sausages can now be baked for 25–35 minutes, basting with the butter. Once ready, cut into portions.

To pan-fry, heat a frying-pan with a knob of lard or drop of cooking oil. Place the sausages in the pan once warm. This can now be gently fried until golden (this will take 12–15 minutes). Turn the Cumberlands over and cook for a further 8–10 minutes.

To grill, brush with butter and place under a medium-hot grill. Cook for 8–10 minutes on each side and then serve.

A good bowl of *Mashed Potatoes* (page 124) and classic *Apple Sauce* (page 44) will eat very well with this dish. Or there's also a recipe for *Cumberland Apple Sauce* (page 47), that has an extra spicy touch, just perfect for this recipe.

Note: Individual, smaller-sized sausages can also be made.

Toad in the Hole

It's not known when batter puddings – Yorkshire pudding is the most famous – developed, but it must have been inspired by economy. During spit-roasting, a pan was put below the animal or bird to catch the juices and fats, and these were used to baste the roast.

Sometimes these fats were used to cook smaller food items, and it must only have been a matter of time before a batter was poured in to make a crisp wrapping for the meat, and to make the meat go further. The recipe for Yorkshire pudding was first written down in a cookery book in 1737 (see page 237 for mine), although it had probably long existed, and toad in the hole must have developed afterwards.

The original toad in the hole wasn't made with sausages, but strips of fresh or leftover meat. Sausages were substituted at some point, and they have become the classic of today. The toad can be baked in a roasting tray, baking dish, or individual tins of about 10 cm (4 in). If making individual toads, there may be some batter left over, so just bake it in separate tins for extra Yorkies.

You can use any sausages you like. The home-made *Pork Sausages* on page 367 are excellent, or choose good-quality bought pork, lamb or beef sausages.

SERVES 4

8 sausages
4 tablespoons cooking oil or lard/dripping

For the Batter

175 g (6 oz) plain flour
Pinch of salt
1 egg
1 egg white
250–300 ml (8–10 fl oz) milk

You need four 10 cm (4 in) individual tins – it's best to use tins 2 cm (¾ in) deep – or a small roasting tin or ovenproof dish. Pre-heat the oven to 220°C/425°F/Gas Mark 7.

The batter can be made as far ahead as 24 hours. This gives it time to relax totally and changes the consistency; when using, just quickly re-whisk. However, this is not essential; the timing is up to you – in fact, the batter can be made and instantly used, but I do suggest a minimum rest of 30 minutes.

OPPOSITE
Toad in the Hole

Sift the flour with the salt. Add the egg and egg white. The egg white will give extra lift to the batter. Whisk in 250 ml (8 fl oz) of the milk; this will give you a very thick batter. To check the correct consistency, simply lift a spoon in and out: the batter should hold and coat the back of a spoon. If it seems to have congealed, add the remaining milk. The batter is now ready to use or rest. If resting, check the consistency again before use, adding a little extra milk if required.

If using small tins, put a little of the cooking oil/fat in a frying-pan and divide the rest of the oil/fat between the small tins. Heat these in the oven. The sausages can now be quickly fried for a minute or two to seal in the flavour and begin to colour. Then transfer to the individual tins, ready for the batter.

If using a roasting tin or ovenproof dish, simply heat half of the oil/fat and colour the sausages on top of the stove, adding the remaining oil/fat.

To cook the toad in the hole, the fat should be very hot and almost at a smoking stage with the sausages in. Pour in the batter mix to come three-quarters of the way up the sausages. Place in the pre-heated oven and bake individual toads for 20–25 minutes, until well risen and rich in colour. Large toads in a roasting tray or ovenproof dish should be cooked for 35–45 minutes.

The toads are now ready to serve. For me, the best accompaniment is *Onion Gravy* (page 50). I like to spoon some into the cooked individual toads or just ladle over the portions of the large toad on the plates.

Instead of gravy, some good fried onions also eat well. Just take a large sliced onion and pan-fry in a trickle of oil for 8–10 minutes until well coloured, with little tinges of burnt. Add a good knob of butter and a pinch of demerara sugar. Cook for a further minute or two before seasoning with salt and pepper.

The onions are now ready to serve. The perfect accompaniment to toad in the hole is simply buttered garden peas or good mushy peas.

Mini Toad in the Holes

Here's an alternative toad in the hole dish. These are simple to make and great to serve as canapés at a party.

1 × batter recipe (page 370)
Butter
3 onions, finely chopped
1 tablespoon demerara sugar
Glass of red wine
450 g (1 lb) pork sausages
Salt and pepper

You will need 3 non-stick mini-muffin trays with 12 'compartments'.

Follow the recipe on page 370, using the same batter quantity and cooking method. Once the puddings are cooked, remove from the oven and keep warm. Heat a frying-pan or wok. Add a knob of butter and, once bubbling, the chopped onions. Shallow-fry until deep brown in colour. Add the sugar and red wine, bring to the boil and reduce until almost dry. Season with salt and pepper.

Remove the skin from the sausages and mix the meat together. This can now be rolled into small balls, 1–2 cm (¼–¾ in) in diameter. Now shallow-fry them for just a few minutes until completely golden brown.

Make a hole in the Yorkshire puddings and spoon a little onion into each. Place the hot sausage balls on top, leaving a domed finish. The canapés are ready.

Note: To make 36–40 mini toads, follow the *Yorkshire Pudding* recipe (page 237) for the increased batter quantity.

Egg Sandwiches Ⓥ

Sandwiches are said to have been invented when the eighteenth-century Earl of Sandwich could not bear to leave the gaming tables to eat, and ordered his dinner to be brought to him. Some meat slices arrived between two slices of bread and a new form of British eating was born. Sandwiches are actually a very British idea, and they have become very popular eating for packed lunches, picnics and afternoon tea.

Egg sandwiches are, without question, one of the most popular features of afternoon tea. I'm not quite sure why; maybe because it's one of those fillings we rarely make at home. They are best made with thinly sliced white or brown bread – a thicker slice of bread is likely to allow the bread flavour to dominate that of the egg. Hard-boiled egg can be bound with mayonnaise, which moistens the texture. If the eggs have been soft-boiled (see below), the creamy yolk will be enough.

For a very soft egg yolk, place eggs in cold water and then boil for 4–5 minutes. Run under cold water for 3–4 minutes and then peel and fork to a spreadable consistency for a very creamy finish.

MAKES 4 ROUNDS OF SANDWICHES

4 hard-boiled eggs (page 81)
Salt and pepper
1–2 tablespoons *Mayonnaise* (page 49, or bought)
8 thin slices of white or brown bread

There's no butter listed in the ingredients; without the mayonnaise, however, some butter, softened to ensure a very thin spread, will be needed to give a creamy finish.

Fork the eggs to break down the whites, mixing them with the yolks. Forked too finely, the eggs lose texture and do not balance the mayonnaise enough. Once broken down to a medium stage, season with salt and pepper. Add the mayonnaise and spread onto four slices of the bread, not right to the edges, as these will be cut away with the crusts and that is just a waste of tasty egg. Top with the remaining slices.

Cut away the crusts and quarter from corner to corner, creating four small triangles. The sandwich can also be cut into three or four fingers.

Another egg-sandwich ingredient that's classic is mustard and cress. Mustard and cress are the very thin stalks and leaves from sprouted mustard seeds. These can be added to the sandwich, giving a warm bite to the total flavour. If not using cress, try adding ½–1 teaspoon of Dijon mustard to the mayonnaise. English mustard can be too strong for the egg flavour.

Note: If you are entertaining with these home-made egg sandwiches, it's best to make at least one and half times or even twice as many as you expect to need – everybody loves them and always finds room for more.

Anchovy is another flavour added to eggs for sandwiches. Take 2–3 tinned fillets and crush them to a paste. Then mix with the mayonnaise or butter before spreading.

Watercress and Cream Cheese Sandwiches Ⓥ

Watercress, with its peppery fresh flavour, was popular for afternoon tea – and nursery, family and high teas as well – and here I have mixed it with cream cheese for a moist and tasty sandwich filling.

MAKES 4 ROUNDS OF SANDWICHES

1 bunch of watercress, picked into small sprigs
25 g (1 oz) butter, softened
100 g (4 oz) cream cheese
8 thin slices of wholemeal or brown bread
Squeeze of lime or lemon juice
Salt and pepper

The watercress can be completely picked, just using the leaves, but I prefer the bite and texture gained by including the stalks. It's best to rinse the leaves before picking. Any water left on can then be easily shaken away.

Mix the softened butter with the cream cheese and spread onto the eight slices.

Add a squeeze of lime or lemon to the watercress, season with salt and pepper and divide between four slices. Top with the remaining slices, cut away the crusts and divide each round into four triangles.

Cucumber Sandwiches Ⓥ

Cucumber, sliced very thinly, is a familiar and traditional sandwich filling, made famous by the lack of cucumbers in Oscar Wilde's *The Importance of Being Earnest*. The butter can be replaced with the healthy *Mayonnaise* (see Variation, page 49). A very thin spread is all that will be needed.

MAKES 4 ROUNDS OF SANDWICHES

Butter, for spreading
8 thin white or brown bread slices
40–48 thin slices of peeled cucumber
Salt and pepper

Butter each slice of bread. It's best to work the butter to a creamy consistency to ensure a thin spread.

The cucumber needs to be sliced 20–30 minutes before the sandwiches are going to be made. Once sliced, sprinkle ¼ teaspoon of salt onto the cucumber. Mix among the slices and place them in a stainless-steel colander or sieve. It's important not to use aluminum – this will just give a metallic taste caused by a reaction with the salt. Leave to stand, so excess water will be 'drained' from the cucumber.

After 20–30 minutes, taste one of the slices. They should not be over-salty and so should not need to be rinsed; if too salty for your taste, however, then quickly rinse under cold water, shaking off well. Lay the slices slightly over-lapping on top of four of the bread slices. Season with a twist of pepper and top with remaining bread. Remove the crust and cut into squares, triangles or fingers.

Note: The seed centre of the cucumber can also be removed. Take ½ small cucumber, peel and halve lengthways. Now slice thinly and salt, drain and finish as above.

For an extra 'bite' in a cucumber sandwich, add a few drops of vinegar – malt, white or red wine can all be used – to the cucumber before placing on the bread.

Smoked Salmon Rolls

Rolls were used to contain sandwich fillings from quite early times – bridge rolls were actually 'invented' for bridge players who, like the Earl of Sandwich, couldn't bear to leave the table. The rolls here, however, are pieces of bread rolled up around a spicy filling of smoked salmon and horseradish.

MAKES 4 SANDWICH ROLLS

4 slices of thin brown bread
4 slices of smoked salmon
½ quantity healthy *Mayonnaise* (see Variation, page 49) or softened butter
¼–½ teaspoon creamed horseradish

To make the bread even thinner, roll each slice with a rolling pin. Now cut the crusts off. Add the horseradish cream to the mayonnaise and spread onto each slice, not quite to the edge for a neater finish. Place a slice of smoked salmon on top of each and then roll as for a

mini swiss roll. These can now be served as they are or sliced into 1 cm (½ in) 'Catherine wheel' pieces.

Jam Sandwiches ⓥ

One last sandwich we should not forget is the Great British Jam Sandwich. If you use one of the home-made preserves from the next chapter (page 386–390), the idea – probably long a favourite at nursery teas – won't appear so old-fashioned.

Just take medium-sliced white bread, lightly spread it with softened butter and spoon the jam across, before topping with the other slice. Cut the crusts off and serve.

Note: Here's an idea that was used a lot during our *nouvelle cuisine* days of the 1970s and 1980s. If making strawberry jam sandwiches, lightly twist some fresh black pepper on one of the buttered slices before finishing the sandwich. It's not a bad combination, a little fiery bite to excite the strawberries. It would certainly be a bit different to offer strawberry jam sandwiches *au poivre*.

Jam Omelette ⓥ

The British dishes nearest to the French omelette, introduced to England in about the late sixteenth century, were more like scrambled eggs in concept. Later, though, the omelette as made in France became known, and various savoury versions became popular in Victorian and Edwardian times, including *Omelette Arnold Bennett* (page 71).

Sweet omelettes were liked as well, and home-made jam was the favourite filling. If you're ever stuck for an idea, or just fancy eating something sweet and quick to make, then you have found the perfect sweet snack. Once made and turned out, the omelette is dusted with icing sugar and grill-marked with a hot skewer to garnish and give a bitter-sweet flavour. A large dollop of extra-thick cream (always a nice extra) spooned on top adds the final touch.

MAKES 1 OMELETTE

3 eggs, beaten
15 g (½ oz) butter
1 tablespoon *Strawberry Jam* (page 387), warmed
Icing sugar

The skewers can be heated on the ring used for cooking the omelette. Obviously, a gas stove will give you the open flame to heat the skewers. If you have an electric cooker, place the skewers under a hot grill.

Warm a 15–20 cm (6–8 in) omelette pan on the stove. While the pan is warming, crack the eggs into a bowl and whisk with a fork.

Once the pan is hot, add the butter. As the butter melts and becomes bubbly, pour the eggs into the pan. They will take only 3–4 minutes to cook.

To keep the omelette light, keep the eggs moving by shaking the pan and stirring them with the fork. This will prevent them from sticking and colouring. (A golden brown omelette basically means it has been over-cooked. The natural yellow of the eggs gives you the most tender finish to the dish.) You will soon have a scrambled look and consistency to the eggs.

Allow to set on the base for 5–10 seconds, remove from the heat before spooning the warmed jam into the centre. The eggs will still be moist and not completely set in the centre. Holding the pan at a downward angle, slide and tap the omelette towards the edge, folding it over as you do so. Turn out onto a plate and shape under a cloth to give a cigar shape. Dust generously with icing sugar and mark a criss-cross pattern with the hot skewers.

The omelette is now ready to eat, filled with strawberry jam and holding a souffléd texture. This makes it a dream to eat, with every mouthful melting.

BELOW
Jam Omelette

Home-made Scones ⓥ

Although most of us think that scones are Scottish – the Stone of Scone, for instance – the word apparently comes from the Dutch word *Schoonbroot*, or 'beautiful bread'. They have become one of the most popular afternoon and high tea small cakes, and form part of yet another British speciality, the cream tea. Straight from the oven, and still warm, they are spread with home-made preserves and then topped with clotted cream. Wonderful!

MAKES 8–10 SCONES

225 g (8 oz) self-raising flour
1 teaspoon baking powder
Pinch of salt
25 g (1 oz) caster sugar
50 g (2 oz) unsalted butter
150 ml (¼ pint) milk
1 egg, beaten, or plain flour, for brushing or dusting

Pre-heat the oven to 220°C/425°F/Gas Mark 7.

Sift together the flour, baking powder and salt into a bowl. Stir in the sugar, add the slightly softened butter and rub quickly into the flour, creating a fine breadcrumb consistency. Add the milk, a little at a time, working to a smooth dough. This is now best left to rest for 10–15 minutes before rolling.

Roll on a lightly floured work surface until 2 cm (¾ in) thick. Using a 5 cm (2 in) pastry cutter, cut the dough, using one sharp tap and not twisting the dough as you cut. Twisting the scone mix will result in an uneven rising.

Once cut, the scones can be either brushed with the beaten egg for a shiny glaze, or dusted with the flour for a matt finish.

Place the scones on a greased baking tray and bake in the pre-heated oven for 10–12 minutes until golden brown. Allow to cool slightly, and serve while still warm.

OPPOSITE
Home-made Scones

Note: An extra 50 g (2 oz) of butter can also be added to give a richer finish.

50 g (2 oz) of mixed sultanas and currants can be added for fruity scones. The sugar can be omitted for plain savoury scones. 50 g (2 oz) of grated Parmesan or Cheddar cheese can be added, with a good pinch of English mustard, for home-made cheese scones. Freshly chopped thyme can also be added to savoury scones.

Once the scones have been cut, any trimmings can be worked together and re-cut until all of the mix has been used.

See also

Banana and Golden Syrup Loaf (page 352)
Cauliflower Cheese with Crispy Parmesan Crumbs (page 68)
Cheddar Apple Cake (page 344)
Chocolate Treacle Sandwich (page 345)
Cornish Pasty (page 273)
Griddle Scones (page 362)
Home-made Malt Loaf (page 350)
Home-made Pork Pie (page 280)
Lardy Cake (page 347)
Lemon and Vanilla Sponge (page 341)
Lemon Syrup Loaf (page 352)
Parkin (page 350)
Strawberry Jam (page 387)
Saffron Bread (page 397)
Sally Lunn Cake or Bread (page 346)
Sausage Rolls (page 277)
Shortbread Biscuits (page 359)
Simnel Cake (page 342)
Vegetarian Cheese and Onion 'Sausage' Rolls (page 278)
Welsh Rarebit (page 178)

Preserves
and Pickles

Until a few hundred years ago, people
in Britain – and all over the world –
relied on preserved food in order to
be able to survive the winter months.
Perhaps the earliest known form of
preservation was *chuño*, the 'freeze-
drying' of potatoes by the Incas in
Chile, some 1000 years ago.
Meat animals in northern Europe
would have to be killed in autumn, for
there was little fodder on which to
feed them over winter. Some of the
meat – of cattle, sheep and pigs –
would be eaten fresh, but the bulk
would be salted, brined and/or smoked
to preserve it. Our Great British bacon
tradition is a direct result of this form
of preservation.

Fish, too, were preserved by salting and smoking, not just for winter, but to allow them to be transported inland from the coast.

Vegetables and fruit were less easy to preserve but it is from these foods that the most common and popular Great British preserves today are descended. Pulses could be dried, as could grains, and from early times these were life-sustaining in winter pottages. In Tudor and Stuart times, vegetables, herbs and nuts were pickled to provide winter salads, garnishes and flavourings for meat and fish. Mushrooms, cucumbers and beetroot, as well as parts of flowers and vegetables – among them borage and violet flowers, nasturtium leaves, samphire and broom buds – were pickled in verjuice, the medieval forerunner of vinegar. It was made from the sour juice of unripe grapes or crab apples (although the flavour of verjuice is thought to have resembled a sharp cider more than it did vinegar). A mushroom pickle, made with a variety of spices, might be the ancestor of our present-day mushroom ketchup, for the liquid was sometimes used as much as the vegetable because of its piquancy. Following the development of trade with India, and later the influence of the years of the Raj, vegetable and fruit chutneys and other Indian pickles became popular as an accompaniment to meat, and many recipes were invented and copied. I've included home-made *Piccalilli* (page 385) and *Mango Chutney* (page 388) in this chapter.

Many dried fruits were imported from abroad for the puddings and pies that are so much part of the British tradition. That fruit were not dried much in Britain is probably due to the fact that traditional fruit-growing areas did not have much cheap fuel, and this could be the reason for the development of the British tradition of preserving fruit in sugar, as jams, marmalades and jellies.

Fruits were also brandied and candied, and boiled to thick pastes with sugar: these were cut into cubes, rolled in powdered sugar, and eaten as a Turkish delight might be today. These pastes were also served as fruit cheeses or 'marmalades' to accompany meats. Quince was the favourite, or original, marmalade, the idea introduced from Portugal, but many other fruits were used. Citrus fruits were not used until later, and even then the marmalade had to be cut with a knife rather than lifted on a spoon. Softer sets of fruit and sugar became popular in Elizabethan times, and were known by the slang word 'jam'. Fruits were also preserved in fruit curds and butters, pickles, sauces and vinegars. When you think of how short a season most fruits have, the workers in their stillrooms must have been very, very busy.

Making home-made pickles and jams brings so much sense of achievement and self-satisfaction. Watching the preserves develop in the pan is very exciting, with the texture and taste changing all the time as the ingredients bubble. I love giving and receiving different flavoured jams and pickles as presents. You know the products are home-made and somehow no bought products will ever match them. So this chapter can hopefully help you with your Christmas list.

PAGE 378
Spicy Tomato and Mint Relish (page 381)

Spicy Tomato and Mint Relish

Relishes are really quick pickles, and are great with all kinds of meat. This tomato relish suits lamb in particular. Serve it with roast lamb instead of redcurrant jelly or mint sauce. It also eats well with *Shepherd's Pie Fritters* (page 185).

For a tomato relish with the flavour of apples working behind it, simply omit the mint. This now becomes a great favourite for roast pork.

MAKES 450–600 ML (¾–1 PINT)

Butter
1 onion, finely diced
1 garlic clove, crushed
Pinch of ground mixed spice
1 Granny Smith apple, peeled and diced
2 tablespoons sherry or white-wine vinegar
1 tablespoon demerara sugar
1 tablespoon tomato purée or ketchup
10 tomatoes, blanched, seeded and flesh diced or
       1 × 400 g (14 oz) tin of chopped tomatoes,
       drained
1 teaspoon chopped fresh mint
Dash of Worcestershire sauce
Dash of Tabasco sauce
Salt and pepper

Melt a knob of butter and, once bubbling, add the chopped onion and garlic. Cook for a few minutes until softened. Add the mixed spice and apple and cook for a further minute. Add the vinegar and sugar and bring to the boil. Reduce until almost dry. Add the diced tomatoes along with the ketchup or purée (ketchup will help the acidity and spicy finish). Cook for a few minutes. Season with salt, pepper, Worcestershire sauce and Tabasco and remove from the heat. Stir in the chopped mint. Drain the relish in a sieve, saving all of the tomato juices. These can now be reduced to a thick syrup consistency. This will help strengthen the flavour of the chutney. Once reduced, add to the relish. This relish will eat well slightly warmed or cold. It will keep for a week if refrigerated.

Note: To sterilize the jars, place them in a large saucepan, cover with cold water, bring to the boil and boil for 15 minutes. Carefully remove and leave to dry. Once the jars have been filled, covered and sealed, you can sterilize again: sit the jars on a wire rack or cloth in a large pan and almost cover them with water. Bring to the boil and boil for 15 minutes. Remove from the pan, dry and cool.

Pickled Limes

Limes were introduced to Britain in the late seventeenth century, and their juice quickly became popular, used in punches. They were also pickled; the particular pickling mixture here is Indian in influence, using green chillies, mustard seeds, ginger, star anise and fenugreek.

Star anise is a star-shaped 'pod', the fruit of an evergreen tree related to the magnolia that grows wild in China and Japan. Within each of the star's petals a small oval, light brown seed is found, and these seeds are what is needed here, although the whole star pod is fragrant, carrying a strong smell of aniseed mixed with liquorice.

Fenugreek also should be mentioned. This is a seed used in most curry powders. The leaves are also used, fresh or dried, in Indian cookery. Fenugreek is an ancient herb and was originally used medicinally by the Greeks and Egyptians. It's a member of the pea and clover family. The seeds are found in tiny pods, and they are small, square shaped and a dusty yellow colour. To capture their curry-like flavour they must always be roasted, making sure they do not burn, which will make them taste very bitter.

These pickled limes are featured in the trout dish on page 145, mixed with pan-fried new potatoes, but they can also be served with curries or added to stir-fried spicy chicken. To capture the full flavour and to preserve the limes, the recipe must be made at least 4 weeks before using.

MAKES A 450 G/800 ML (1 LB/1½ PINT) JAR

6 limes, washed and cut into 6 wedges, trimming
       away any central excess pith from each wedge
50 g (2 oz) salt
1 tablespoon yellow mustard seeds
1 teaspoon fenugreek seeds

Seeds from 2 star anises
4 small fresh green chillies, split, seeded and finely
  chopped
100 g (4 oz) light muscovado sugar
1 tablespoon ground ginger
4 tablespoons water

In a stainless-steel colander (aluminum will not work due to a reaction from the citrus fruit and salt), sprinkle the limes with the salt. Place over a bowl, cover and leave to stand for 24 hours.

Place the mustard seeds, fenugreek, star anise seeds and chillies in a frying-pan and dry-roast on top of the stove on a medium heat. Cook until the seeds begin to colour and pop.

Pour off the water/liquor from the limes and place the fruit in a saucepan. Add the sugar, ginger and water. Bring to the boil and cook until the sugar has dissolved.

Mix the lime wedges with the dry-roast spices and chillies. Pack them into a sterilized jar (see Note, page 381), making sure the limes are pressed in together firmly. Pour the sugar mixture on top, covering the limes as much as possible.

Seal the jars and leave in a cool place, or refrigerate, for at least 4 weeks before using. The limes will keep, refrigerated, for a minimum of 6 months.

Pickled Damsons

Damsons are related to plums, and grow well all over Britain. They have traditionally been made into jams, cheeses and pickles because rarely do they ripen enough to eat in the hand. They bring back memories of my scrumping days. The problem was I just didn't know what to do with them. They often ended up in an apple and damson crumble or pie.

They hit the shelves of greengrocers during the months of September and October, so that's the time to make this recipe. The pickled fruits eat well with cold or warm ham, game and pies (especially pork pies), served cold or, better still, just slightly warmed.

This recipe is made with red-wine vinegar, but white-wine, cider or malt vinegar can also be used. The fruits can be marinated in the vinegar overnight to increase the flavour, but to appreciate the taste they should be pickled at least 2–3 weeks in advance.

All the 'spices' – cinnamon, ginger, lemon, orange and cloves – are flavoursome extras. These flavours will give you a better result. A substitute for them is allspice: replacing all of these flavourings with half a dozen lightly crushed berries will give a similar flavour.

MAKES APPROX. 3 KG (7 LB)

2 kg (4½ lb) damsons
300 ml (½ pint) red-wine vinegar
1 kg (2¼ lb) preserving sugar
Walnut-sized piece of fresh root ginger
Peeled rind of ½ lemon
Peeled rind of ½ orange
Piece of cinnamon stick
3–4 cloves

Remove the stalks from the damsons and then wash and prick with a fork. Peel and halve the piece of ginger, if using, and tie in muslin cloth, along with the other spices (including orange and lemon rind). Place the spice bag in a large saucepan along with the vinegar and sugar. Bring to the boil, stirring until the sugar has dissolved. Once at this syrup stage, add the damsons and bring to a simmer. Cook gently for 2–3 minutes, making sure the damsons are not broken, but becoming tender.

Remove the fruits carefully with a slotted spoon and arrange on trays to cool.

While the damsons are cooling, return the syrup to the boil. This will now need to be kept boiling for 5–8 minutes, until thickened and syrupy.

Place the fruits in warm, sterilized jars (see Note, page 381). While the syrup is still hot, strain on top of the damsons. Cover with lids and leave to cool. The pickled fruits should now be kept in a cool dark place for a minimum of 2–3 weeks before using. Once opened, these will keep, refrigerated, for a minimum of 6 months.

Note: This recipe can also be used with plums. The plums can be left whole or halved with stones removed. If they have been halved, once added, return to the simmer/boil and remove from the syrup straight away. This prevents the plums from becoming too broken.

Plum or Damson Cheese

This is a highly traditional way of making a very thick sweet fruit purée. There's no 'cheese' included in the recipe at all. The dish just seems to have adopted the name through its consistency. It's basically a very thick, solidly set purée. Once made and set in suitable jars – ones that will release the jelly whole – it's left to mature for 6 months and over. Most will last for up to 2 years. When served, the jelly is just turned out of the jar and sliced. This will then be served with anything from buttered toast for tea to cream cheese as a dessert. In the eighteenth century, fruit cheeses were eaten by themselves with a fork, or were served with cold meats, rather as we would serve a chutney or relish nowadays.

The quantity of fruit is greatly reduced with the cooking. In many old recipes, 450 g (1 lb) of preserving sugar is boiled with the same weight of fruits. This, when cooked to the 'cheese' stage, loses most of its fruit flavour, becoming intensely sweet. Depending on the fruit, 100–175 g (4–6 oz) of sugar per 450 g (1 lb) fruit is plenty, and you are left then with a good intense fruit taste.

MAKES 1.2 KG (2½ LB)

2 kg (4½ lb) plums or damsons
500 g (1 lb 2 oz) preserving sugar

The plums or damsons must first be baked in a slow oven (150°C/300°F/Gas Mark 2) until softened, for approximately 50–60 minutes. Transfer to a saucepan and bring to a soft boil. Cook for a few minutes until the juices are thickening. Take off the heat and remove the stones. The fruits can now be pushed through a sieve.

Add the preserving sugar to the sieved fruits and bring to the boil. Allow to cook and reduce until very thick, making sure the fruits do not stick. To test the right consistency, pull a spoon across the base of the pan. For a cheese, the trail of fruit from the spoon must stay and be left clear. At this stage the fruits may have started to crystallize around the edge of the pan. If it is at a thick-cream stage but still too soft to hold a trail, the fruit purée can be removed and set in jars, but it will finish with a softer texture, and hence it is known as a 'fruit butter'.

Once thick enough, lightly brush the inside of sterilized, suitable jars (see Note, page 381) with groundnut oil; the 'cheeses' will then turn out easily. Pour the purée in, cover and leave to cool. As mentioned in the recipe introduction, the jars should be left for at least 6 months (even up to 2 years), refrigerated, before opening. Once opened, the cheese will last about a month, refrigerated.

Pickled Shallots or Onions

These must have been one of the earliest and, if we think how popular they are today, perhaps the best-loved of all pickles. They are a perfect accompaniment to cold meat and you can't have a traditional 'ploughman's' of bread and cheese without a pickled onion.

Shallots hold a fuller flavour than onions, but both will give good results. It's important that, whichever is chosen, they are all the same size.

Shallots or onions can be pickled hot or cold. The hot method will take less time to make and infuse to get the pickled results. Cold pickling, however, will give a crisper finish. I'll give you both methods to play with; both are very tasty and moreish. I'm also using cider vinegar, as the flavour works very well with the oniony taste, but it is more expensive. White-wine or malt vinegar will both give a good basic flavour.

Cold Pickling

2.4 litres (4½ pints) water
225 g (8 oz) salt
1 kg (2¼ lb) small shallots or onions, skin left on
600 ml (1 pint) spiced vinegar (page 385)

Mix together half of the water with half of the salt. The shallots or onions can now be left to stand, unpeeled, in this brine for a minimum of 12 hours.

The shallots or onions can now be drained and peeled. Place in a fresh brine, using the remaining quantities of water and salt. These should now be left to stand for 3 days.

Drain and place in sterilized pickling jars (see Note, page 381). Pour the cold vinegar and spices on top, making sure they are covered (more vinegar can be added if needed.) Cover, seal and, for the best results, leave for 3 months before eating. Once opened, they will last for up to a year, refrigerated.

Hot Pickling

1 kg (2¼ lb) small shallots or onions, unpeeled
100 g (4 oz) salt
600–900 ml (1–1½ pints) spiced vinegar (see right)

Bring the shallots to the boil in plain water and cook for 2–3 minutes. Drain and peel. Sprinkle and roll in the salt and leave to dry-marinate for 24 hours.

After 24 hours, wash the onions well. Cover with the spiced vinegar and bring to the boil. Cook for 6–8 minutes before spooning the shallots into sterilized jars (see Note, page 381). Pour the spicy vinegar on top and cover. These will be best eaten after a minimum of 2 weeks to 1 month. Once opened, they will last for up to a year, refrigerated.

OPPOSITE
Piccalilli with *Boiled or Baked Ham* (page 211)

SPICED VINEGAR (MAKES 600 ML/1 PINT)

600 ml (1 pint) cider vinegar
1 teaspoon mustard seeds
1 heaped teaspoon allspice berries
8 cloves
8 black peppercorns
½ cinnamon stick
½ teaspoon coriander seeds

Place all in a saucepan and bring to the boil. This can now be used immediately for 'hot pickling' or left to cool for 'cold pickling'.

Piccalilli

A recipe of 1694 has the title 'pickle lila, an Indian pickle', and details vegetables preserved in a brine and vinegar sauce flavoured with spices, among them mustard seed and turmeric. It's still much the same today, and is very easy to make. There are also any number of variations that you can try – different vegetables, mustards and vinegars.

This pickle eats wonderfully with cold meats, pâtés, cold pies and terrines. It also eats particularly well with oily fish, such as mackerel and herrings; its acidity works against the oils and leaves a good, clean taste.

MAKES APPROX. 1.25 KG (3 LB)

1 cauliflower
3 large onions
8 large shallots or 16 onions
1 cucumber
600 ml (1 pint) white-wine vinegar
300 ml (½ pint) malt vinegar
¼ teaspoon chopped dried chilli
350 g (12 oz) caster sugar
50 g (2 oz) English mustard powder
25 g (1 oz) ground turmeric
3 tablespoons cornflour
Salt and pepper

Cut the cauliflower into small florets. Peel and cut the shallots or onions into 1 cm (½ in) dice. Place in a bowl, sprinkle with 25 g (1 oz) of salt and leave to stand for 24 hours. Afterwards, rinse in cold water and dry.

Peel and de-seed the cucumber and cut it into 1 cm (½ in) dice. Sprinkle with a little salt and leave to stand for 10–15 minutes. Rinse in cold water, then dry and add to the shallots or onions and cauliflower.

Boil the two vinegars together with the chilli and then leave to cool for 30 minutes. Strain through a sieve and discard the chilli.

Mix together the sugar and remaining dry ingredients in a bowl. When the vinegar is cool, mix a little of it with the dry ingredients. Bring the bulk of the vinegar back to the boil, pour into the sugar mixture, and whisk until it is all blended together. Bring this mixture back to the boil and cook for 3 minutes, then simply pour over the vegetables and mix well. Leave to cool. The piccalilli is now ready and can be put into sterilized jars (see Note, page 381). Serve at once or keep refrigerated for up to a month.

Lobster or Shellfish Oil

This oil takes 2 weeks of infusing before you have a result – but it's worth it. The olive oil holds a rich colour and flavour from the lobster, and is a wonderful finish to many dishes featured, such as *Lobster Omelette 'Thermidor'* (page 75) and *Lobster Bisque Soup* (page 23). Once made, infused and strained, the oil will keep for several months, refrigerated.

MAKES 300 ML (½ PINT)

350 ml (12 fl oz) olive oil
1 small carrot, chopped
1 small fennel bulb (or ½ medium), chopped
1 celery stick, chopped (optional)
2 shallots, chopped
350–450 g (12 oz–1 lb) crushed lobster shells
85 ml (3 fl oz) brandy

½ tablespoon chopped fresh flatleaf parsley
½ tablespoon chopped fresh tarragon
1 garlic clove, crushed
1 teaspoon tomato purée
1 small sprig of thyme
1 bay leaf
1 star anise
2–3 coriander seeds, crushed

Warm 2 tablespoons of the olive oil in a large saucepan. Add the chopped carrot, fennel, celery (if using) and shallots. Cook until just softening.

Heat a frying-pan until piping hot. Add a touch of olive oil and quickly fry the lobster shells until they have taken on a fuller and rich red colour.

Add the brandy, flambé and reduce until almost dry. The lobster shells can now be transferred to the saucepan with the vegetables and cooked for 3–4 minutes. Add all the remaining ingredients, including the rest of the olive oil. Stir well and gently cook over a low heat for 1½–2 hours. Leave to cool.

Pour into a suitable container, cover, refrigerate and infuse for two weeks. After the fortnight, re-warm and pass through a fine strainer, preferably including muslin to leave you with approximately 300 ml (½ pint) of rich red lobster oil. Once opened, the oil will keep refrigerated for several months.

Note: Crab or langoustine oil can also be made using the above recipe.

Rowan Jelly

The scarlet berries of the rowan, a tree that grows in the north of England and Scotland, make a jelly that is a traditional accompaniment or 'tracklement' for game, particularly roast grouse and venison (pages 247 and 270). The berries have a sour–sweet flavour that works very well with most game birds. They are often mixed with crab-apples, which helps with the setting of the jelly. If using apples, simply add a third in weight to the berries. Rowanberries have a short season and are rarely available in the shops but can be picked for free wherever they grow wild.

Strawberry Jam

MAKES 750–900 G (1¾–2 LB)

2 kg (4½ lb) ripe rowanberries
Approx. 1.2 litres (2 pints) water
450 g (1 lb) preserving sugar to every 600 ml
(1 pint) of juices

Place the picked rowanberries in a deep pan, adding just enough water to cover them. Bring to the boil and cook until softened. This should take just 10–15 minutes; any more and the flavour of the fruit can become bitter.

To extract the maximum flavour, lightly mash the fruits and then strain through a fine sieve or muslin/jelly bag. It's best to allow the fruits to drain naturally (if so, leave for 24 hours). However, the jelly bag can be helped along immediately with a squeeze, also allowing a little of the purée through, which will leave you with a slightly more cloudy finish.

Whichever method chosen, once completely drained, measure the quantity of juice. Add to it 450 g (1 lb) of preserving sugar per 600 ml (1 pint). I normally prefer to reduce the sugar quantity to 350 g (12 oz). This gives you a less sweet flavour to the fruit. However, rowanberries have a fairly low pectin content, and consequently do not gel so easily. You can try it with less sugar, but it will take longer to boil and reduce.

Once the preserving sugar has been added to the juice, bring to the boil and cook until it reaches a good jelly point. This will normally take approximately 20 minutes. It's best to check every 5–6 minutes, by taking a tablespoon of the 'jam' on a saucer and refrigerating. Once set, the jelly is ready and can be poured into hot, sterilized jars (see Note, page 381).

This jelly lasts between 2 and 3 months, improving in flavour from week to week.

Note: When boiling the jelly, any impurities rising to the top should be skimmed off.

While the berries are at their first and second stages of cooking, fresh herbs can be added. Thyme, marjoram or savory all work very well. Simply tie a good healthy sprig in muslin; this can now be added and used in both stages. Discard once the jelly is ready to set.

Britain is famous for its strawberries, so I have chosen to make my base jam using these lovely, flavoursome fruits. Other soft fruits, such as raspberries, blackberries, cherries, tayberries and blackcurrants, can also be used.

The recipe also works with some of the larger soft fruits, including ripe plums, peaches and apricots. Most of these hold a medium quantity of pectin, the natural substance found in the cells of fruit, which is released by the natural acids also present in the fruit, and by cooking the fruit in sugar. The sugar also helps the setting of the jelly.

The proportion of sugar to fruit is important in jam-making. The normal ratio is equal quantities of each, which helps the pectin to reach its setting point and preserves the jam. However, I often feel this can lead to a very sweet jam with a minimal fruit flavour. By reducing the sugar to three-quarters of the fruit quantity, the fruit flavour becomes more apparent and still gives the jelly finish. The sugar can also be reduced to half the fruit quantity. This then creates a

BELOW
Strawberry Jam

thick syrup rather than a jam, but does work well with many dishes because of the strong fruit flavour.

Whatever quantity of sugar used, I suggest you work with a jam sugar. This is one that contains pectin and guarantees a jellied finish. Any jams made with the reduced sugar quantity should always be kept refrigerated, giving the jam a longer life.

Small soft fruits, such as raspberries and blackberries, can be left whole, or half the quantity lightly mashed to give a thicker finish to the jam. Larger berries should be cut or mashed, while small ones should be left whole. Plums, apricots and peaches are best cut into large wedges.

Two methods follow, each giving great results.

MAKES 1.5 KG (3¼ LB)

1 kg (2¼ lb) fresh strawberries
Finely grated zest and juice of 1 lemon
1 kg (2¼ lb) or 750 g (1½ lb) or 500 g (1lb 2 oz)
    jam sugar (containing pectin)

Method 1

Mash half the quantity of fruits in a large saucepan. Add the lemon zest, juice, sugar and remaining fruits and bring to the boil. (It's important to use a large saucepan because this allows the jam to boil rapidly without boiling over.) The jam can now be cooked for 3–4 minutes for a fairly loose consistency. If you prefer a jellied-style jam, boil for 8–10 minutes. Skim away any frothy impurities as it cooks. Once cooked, leave to cool slightly before spooning into suitable containers or sterilized jars (see Note, page 381).

Method 2

Place the sugar, zest and juice in a large pan and bring to a simmer. Add the fruits (left whole if not too big) and stir in carefully. Bring the mix to the boil and cook for 3–4 minutes for a loose consistency. If you prefer a jellied-style jam, boil for 8–10 minutes. Skim off any impurities. You now have a good, rich, shiny jam with the strawberries still holding their shape. Leave to cool slightly before spooning into containers or sterilized jars (see Note, page 381).

Mango Chutney

When mango pickles were first introduced to Britain, the idea was copied, and we used cucumbers, peaches and melons in an attempt to recreate the flavours. After the years of the Raj, we could import the necessary mangoes, and now there's no excuse not to try to make it yourself.

This is a chutney I love to spoon onto a good spicy curry. Curries have become a way of British life, so I thought I would include this recipe. Naturally, the mango chutney is the thing you buy and quite often the curry is the thing that you make. Next time you order a take-away, at least this part of it will be home-made.

MAKES APPROX. 1.75 KG (4 LB)

6 mangoes, not too ripe
450 g (1 lb) soft light brown sugar
2 teaspoons ground mixed spice
Good pinch of ground turmeric
½ teaspoon cayenne pepper
3 cooking apples, peeled, cored and chopped
2 onions, finely chopped
4 garlic cloves, finely crushed with 1 teaspoon salt
750 ml (1¼ pints) malt vinegar
50 g (2 oz) finely grated fresh root ginger

Peel the mangoes and then cut either side of the stone, giving you two thick slices of the fruit. Cut the opposite ends of the mango away from the edge of the stones. Any remaining fruit should be scraped off into a bowl. Cut the large fruit slices into thick strips or chunks. Stir the sugar, mixed spice, turmeric and cayenne into the mango. This is now best left for a good few hours to marinate.

Next, place all the ingredients together in a large saucepan. Bring to the simmer and cook for 1½ hours, stirring from time to time, for even cooking and to prevent it from sticking. The mango will have become soft and cooked through, leaving a thick syrup. If the chutney seems to be too thin, simply increase the heat, reduce and stir to a 'drier' consistency. Leave to rest for 20–30 minutes, before ladling into sterilized preserving jars (see Note, page 381).

These can now be cooled and kept in a cool place. The chutney can be eaten just days after cooking, but is best left for several weeks to mature. Once opened, it will last for up to 3 months, refrigerated.

Home-made Redcurrant Jelly

Redcurrant jelly and mint sauce are two flavours and accompaniments usually offered with lamb. They are very traditional, coming from the idea that you serve a meat with something it may have fed on or that grew nearby. Dorothy Hartley in *Food in England* is even more specific, saying redcurrant should be served only with valley mutton, as the berry's flavour is too strong for the more delicate mountain mutton. For me, this home-made redcurrant jelly goes well with all mutton and lamb dishes.

MAKES 750–900 G (1½–2 LB)

1.5 kg (3 lb) freshly picked redcurrants
350 g (12 oz) preserving sugar for every 600 ml
    (1 pint) juice

Place the redcurrants in a saucepan and barely cover with water. Bring to the boil and then reduce the heat and simmer for 25–30 minutes, until the currants have become overcooked and mushy.

Leave to strain through a fine sieve or muslin bag into a bowl and allow to drain naturally. This will take all of the flavour and colour from the fruit. After several hours, when the dripping has stopped, measure the quantity of juice. For every 600 ml (1 pint) of juice, add 350 g (12 oz) of preserving sugar. (Normally, the quantity is 450 g/1 lb sugar to 600 ml/1 pint of juice but I find this too sweet and sickly. Redcurrants have a high pectin level, and with preserving sugar, 350 g/12 oz will be plenty.) Boil the sugar with the juices and simmer for 10 minutes. The jelly is now ready to pour into sterilized hot jars (see Note, page 381). Once cold, the jelly will set. Once opened, it will keep refrigerated for up to 6 months.

Note: The flavour can be changed slightly with the addition of the grated zest of 1 orange and 2–3 tablespoons of port. This will give you an even richer jelly with an orange tang.

Candied Oranges

This is basically candied orange peel, cooked in a sweet syrup to calm the bitter flavour of the pith and zest. I'm using it as a garnish for the *Scallops with Grilled Black Pudding à l'Orange* (page 147), but it can be used in many other dishes, sweet and savoury.

MAKES 2 ORANGES

2 oranges, each cut into 8 wedges
200 ml (7 fl oz) water
225 g (8 oz) caster sugar

Once the wedges have been cut, the flesh can be trimmed off, leaving just the pith and outside zest.

Place the orange zest 'petals' in a saucepan, cover with cold water and bring to the boil. Once at boiling point, drain off and refresh the orange peel under cold water.

Repeat the same process, until they are blanched five times.

Bring the measured water and caster sugar to the boil. Add the 'petals' and poach gently for 1½ hours. Leave to cool in the syrup. Left steeped in the cooking syrup, the oranges will last for several months.

To use as a garnish, cut the orange into 3 mm (⅛ in) dice.

Note: The candied oranges can be used in many dishes. Dice and add to a steamed sponge, flavour a bread and butter pudding, garnish a mousse or sprinkle over ice-cream.

Orange Marmalade

The best oranges to use, for their strong bitter flavour and high pectin content, are Seville, in season from late December/early January until late February. However, almost any orange and other citrus fruit – lemon, lime, grapefruit – can be used in this recipe.

How did marmalade get its name? There are several stories. Until the seventeenth century, a fruit preserve was made from quince, known in Spain and Portugal as *marmalada* and *marmelo*, hence the name 'marmalade'. Later, oranges took the place of quince, but the name stayed the same. Another story I read was about the voyage of Mary, Queen of Scots, from France to Scotland to claim her throne. She was seasick, and one of her maids, who was making a dish of bitter oranges for her, said, '*Marie est malade,*' which sounds a bit like marmalade. Who knows?

The pectin in citrus fruits is held in the pith and pips, so we shouldn't throw them all away. The sugar content in marmalade is double that of the fruit, to balance the bitterness of the peel.

MAKES 1.25–1.5 KG (2¼–3½ LB)

450 g (1 lb) oranges
Juice of 1 lemon
1.2 litres (2 pints) water
900 g (2 lb) granulated sugar or preserving sugar

Wash and scrub the oranges to remove any artificial colouring. Halve them and squeeze out the juice into a large pan, keeping any pips and membrane. Now cut the orange shells in half and cut away and discard the pith. How conscientiously you do this really depends on how bitter you prefer your marmalade to be. Put the pips and membrane in a piece of muslin and tie it into a bag. Cut the peel into thin or thick strips and place it in a saucepan with the orange and lemon juice and the water. Tie the bag to the pan handle and submerge it in the water.

Bring it to a simmer and cook for 1–1½ hours, until the peel is tender and the liquor has reduced by half. Remove the muslin bag, squeezing out any juices, and discard it. Add the sugar and stir over a low heat until it has dissolved. Now bring the marmalade to the boil, skimming away any impurities and stirring from time to time. Cook for 10 minutes. While the marmalade is boiling, chill a side plate, for testing the setting point.

After 10 minutes has passed, spoon a little marmalade onto the plate and chill. It should jellify and wrinkle when moved with a spoon but, if it does not, continue to boil for a further 5 minutes, and then re-test. Remove from the heat and skim off any impurities. Leave to stand for 15–20 minutes. Stir it to spread the peel, then ladle into sterilized jars (see Note, page 381). Cover and seal. Store in a cool, dark place. Once opened, it can be kept refrigerated for up to 6 months.

Note: For a 'warmer' taste, 50–60 ml (2–2½ fl oz) of brandy, whisky, Cointreau or Grand Marnier can be added at the end of the cooking time. Or why not put in 50–75 g (2–3 oz) of freshly grated ginger with the orange peel, for a spicy finish'?

OPPOSITE
Orange Marmalade

Spices and Flavourings

There are few native British spices, although spices themselves have been used by the British since very early times – coriander seeds, from a Mediterranean plant, were found at a Bronze Age site. The Romans introduced many spices vital to their cooking, as they did herbs, among them pepper, ginger and mustard. After the Norman Conquest, more spicing ideas were introduced, both French and Arab, and the returning Crusaders, too, would have brought back many of the spices they encountered in the East. These included cinnamon, cassia (Chinese cinnamon), cardamom, nutmeg, mace and cloves, and all were incorporated, in sometimes alarming amounts, into medieval cooking, along with other imports such as almonds, almond milk and dried fruits. So you can see that foods from all those years ago were not as basic as their image has led us to believe. But these spices and herbs were not just used in cooking, they played a very big part in medicinal products too.

It has been claimed that this early British passion for spices developed because of the need to disguise too salty or off flavours, creating very pungent tastes. However, those that could afford to buy spices – for they were very expensive for a long time – would have been frequently able to eat fresh meat and fish. It is more likely that they simply enjoyed the taste the spices could give, or that it was fashionable (I like to think it was the former). The quality of the spices would not have been of the best, either, after long travel from their countries of origin – their 'noses' and strength in flavour would have diminished. It is likely that many medieval dishes that would be very hot today using *fresh* spices, would have been merely piquant or tasty then.

London was the centre of the spice trade in Britain, and very early on – around 1180 – the trade was organized by the Guild of Pepperers. In the fourteenth century this, one of the first London guilds, became the guild of Grossers or Grocers (from *grossarii*, dealers who buy and sell in the gross). Wealthy people all over the country used spices in the majority of their cooking – in soups, pies, sauces, meat and fish dishes, and in puddings, both sweet and savoury. In *Food and Drink in Britain*, C. Anne Wilson describes a typical recipe for stewed beef: it 'recommends the addition of cinnamon, cloves, maces, grains of paradise, cubebs, minced onions, parsley, sage and saffron. The stew was thickened with bread steeped in broth and vinegar, with extra salt and vinegar added at the last for good measure. The final instruction, "and look that it be poignant enough", seems redundant.' I'd certainly agree with that – you wouldn't need to be searching for flavours.

Imported spices remained expensive for a very long time, although pepper and ginger were quite common (perhaps one reason why dried ginger is used in many regional British cakes and biscuits). Mustard was cheap and popular, because it could be cultivated in this country – primarily in East Anglia, where, much later, a Norwich mustard company was founded by one Jeremiah Colman (thank you, Jeremiah, it's delicious). It was used in many sauces, and served with fresh and salted fish and meat, and brawn. Saffron, too, was planted in East Anglia, where it gave its name to a town, Saffron Walden, and is the one thing that hasn't changed its price – just as expensive then as it is now.

The discovery of the New World in the sixteenth century brought chillies, vanilla and allspice to Europe and eventually to Britain, and they too were incorporated into much British cooking. Some spices were now sold as mixtures – hot or mild, as you might buy curry powder – and a type of pre-prepared curry powder was in fact available in the late eighteenth century, although curries were not to become a British passion until after the days of the Raj. A number of spices were used whole – cinnamon and nutmegs, for instance – and the clove-pierced onion so vital for our bread sauce was in use by the 1660s, a borrowing from the French, one which we have continued for many years.

As spices diminished in price after the seventeenth century – mainly due to the wider cultivation and availability – it seems that spices began to lose their importance in the cooking of northern Europe. Pickles, preserves, desserts/puddings, cakes and biscuits still relied on them to a certain extent, but they were not added automatically to every meat or fish dish. That sugar was now cheap, too, may well have played a part in this. In fact, the spiced liquid from pickles was often used instead of the spices themselves and, at the end of the eighteenth century, the first bottled sauces were sold commercially, the origin perhaps of our British passion for tomato ketchup, brown sauce and, the most famous of all, Worcestershire sauce.

In these last few years of the twentieth century, we British actually seem to have returned to our medieval tastes, and we are now familiar with and cooking with a huge choice of spices. Many of these we know from Indian recipes and restaurants, a reminder of the years the British spent on the subcontinent. But we are also playing host to many other nationalities and their particular spices and flavours – Thai lemongrass, for instance – and a number of these are being enthusiastically incorporated into a new style of 'Great British' cooking. But whenever cooking with spices, it's important to take a note from the early lessons. For me, spices should be used to lend a flavour, helping the main ingredients, but never used to mask and spoil a natural taste.

Curry Powder

Mixtures of ground spices were able to be bought as long ago as the eighteenth century, although they were expensive. Nowadays there are many good-quality curry powders and pastes available, all carrying different strengths to suit the curry of your choice. But this is one that I use quite a lot. As I've said about cooking generally, there's nothing like making it yourself. This will give you a well-flavoured medium-hot curry.

MAKES ABOUT 25 G (1 OZ)

2 teaspoons cumin seeds
2 teaspoons cardamom pods or seeds
1 tablespoon coriander seeds
½ teaspoon ground ginger
½ teaspoon ground turmeric
½ teaspoon paprika
½ teaspoon chilli powder
¼ teaspoon ground cloves

The cumin, cardamom and coriander can all be 'roasted', as for *Garam Masala* (page 396). Simply place in a dry frying-pan over a medium heat and roast until they colour and become aromatic. Leave to cool. They can now be ground to a powder in a coffee grinder or blender. Shake through a fine sieve or tea-strainer and mix with all of the remaining spices. This powder will keep well in an airtight container in a dark place.

Curry Cream Sauce

I use this sauce for *Smoked Eel Kedgeree* (page 162), and also for *Curried Eggs* (page 396). The curry powder is the home-made one on the left, but it can be replaced with a bought medium-hot powder, such as Madras.

MAKES APPROX. 500–600 ML (17 FL OZ–1 PINT)

Knob of butter
1 large onion, finely chopped
2 garlic cloves, crushed
1 tablespoon curry powder (left) or ready-made Madras curry powder
300 ml (½ pint) *Chicken* or *Vegetable Stock* (page 33 or 36)
300 ml (½ pint) double cream
150 ml (¼ pint) coconut milk
Squeeze of lime juice (optional)
Salt

Melt the knob of butter and add the chopped onion and garlic. Cook on a medium heat, without colouring, for 5–6 minutes. Add the curry powder and continue to cook for a further 6–8 minutes, stirring occasionally. Add the vegetable or chicken stock and bring to the simmer. Allow the sauce to cook on a fast simmer, reducing the stock by half. This will increase its total flavour. Add the double cream and return to the simmer. This can now be cooked for 10–15 minutes. Add the coconut milk, bring to the simmer and the sauce is ready. Season with salt, adding a squeeze of lime, if using, to lift the total taste. Once cooked, strain through a sieve for a smooth sauce.

Note: To cut down the cream by half, simply simmer the stock, but do not reduce. Instead take 1 teaspoon of arrowroot and moisten with a tablespoon or two of the cream. Whisk the arrowroot into the stock and return to the simmer. It's best to use single cream here, as the sauce will be thickened from the arrowroot. Cook as per the recipe, finishing with the coconut milk and squeeze of lime.

For a slightly sweet finish, a tablespoon of *Mango Chutney* (page 388) can be added. If limes are unavailable, substitute them with lemon juice.

This recipe gives you a mild sauce; 1½–2 tablespoons of curry powder can be used for a hotter finish.

Curried Eggs

During the years of the Raj, many local culinary concepts came to be adopted by British households. The memsahibs, the British wives of the men serving in the tropical subcontinent, would attempt to get Indian cooks to make dishes in the Anglo-French style so prevalent at home but, inevitably, spices and other less familiar ingredients would creep in. The taste for these adaptations was acquired, and brought back to Britain, where Mrs Beeton was to devote a whole chapter in one of her books to the art of Indian cooking.

European curries bear little resemblance to the Indian originals. Indian curry was a sauce (the Hindi word *kari* means 'sauce') working as a relish, not a complete dish. Its purpose was to lift and enhance bland foods, such as rice or wheat pancakes, known as chapattis. It was almost used as tomato ketchup is used by us today, as an extra flavour to lift tastes. A pre-medieval 'curry' might have consisted of aubergine, onions and probably lentils, flavoured with cardamom, cumin, coriander and turmeric. If you wanted it hotter, then there might be the addition of white pepper and mustard seeds. Whatever the case, most would have been diluted with coconut milk or yoghurt. The hot chillies included in today's curries were not, in fact, introduced to India from tropical America until the sixteenth century. So in this recipe we are using a *kari* sauce, made with the 'modern' chilli flavour.

The eggs, classically, are served with plain boiled rice. This always works well, but a good braised rice will give you even more flavour.

SERVES 4

8 medium eggs
600 ml (1 pint) *Curry Cream Sauce* (page 393)
1 dessertspoon chopped fresh coriander (optional)

Pre-heat the oven to 180°C/350°F/Gas Mark 4. Boil the eggs for 7–8 minutes. These can now be run under cold water for a few minutes. Shell carefully and split in half lengthways. They can now be laid in an ovenproof dish.

OPPOSITE
Warm Spiced Pineapple Cakes

Bring the curry sauce to a fast simmer, reduce by a quarter to thicken slightly and pour over the eggs. Cover with foil and bake in the pre-heated oven for 15–20 minutes.

Once warmed through, remove the foil and, if using, sprinkle with the chopped coriander. Serve with rice of your choice.

Note: To lift the rice or sauce, why not add a spoonful of raisins for a sweeter finish?

Warm Spiced Pineapple Cakes

Pineapples may not seem particularly British but, in the eighteenth century, English gardeners led Europe in pineapple growing. The gentry competed with each other to raise them in 'stove houses', buildings heated by Dutch stoves, the ancestors of our modern greenhouses. The public became so passionate about the fruit that wrought-iron gates and fences were topped with pineapple shapes, which can still be seen to this day. But pineapples did not become truly common until the late nineteenth century, when steamships brought the fruit from the West Indies.

Pineapples always make me think of the Caribbean, anyway, and two of the spices being used originate from there – allspice from Jamaica and nutmeg from Grenada. Once the pineapples have been cut into discs to fill the moulds, any trimmings can be chopped and made into a sorbet (recipe provided on page 396). The pineapple sorbet is an optional extra but does bring a lively contrast of flavours and textures, and uses up all the pineapple trimmings too. I have also included a pineapple caramel sauce just to dribble over the dessert. So there are lots of different flavours and textures to enjoy.

SERVES 8–10

2 medium pineapples, peeled
Groundnut oil, for frying
Caster sugar for caramelizing

For the Sponges

125 g (4½ oz) Brazil nuts
250 g (9 oz) butter
1 tablespoon clear honey
150 g (5 oz) plain flour

½ teaspoon salt

½ teaspoon baking powder

½ teaspoon each of ground cinnamon, nutmeg,
    freshly grated ground ginger, ground allspice,
    ground black pepper

200 g (7 oz) sugar

6 egg whites

For the Pineapple and Caramel Sauce
(makes about 300 ml/½ pint)

125 g (4½ oz) sugar

85 ml (3 fl oz) water

50 ml (2 fl oz) double cream

85 ml (3 fl oz) pineapple juice

For the Pineapple Sorbet (optional)

225 g (8 oz) pineapple trimmings

150 ml (¼ pint) stock syrup (page 312), replacing
    the water with bought pineapple juice

Juice of ½ lemon

White rum, to taste (optional)

This recipe will fill eight to ten 7.5 × 5 cm (3 × 2 in) individual rings or one large 25 cm (10 in) square or round, loose-bottomed cake tin.

The pineapple is going to be cut into discs to fit the individual moulds. This is best achieved by cutting either side of the core, giving two large half-cylinders to cut from. There will, obviously, be some flesh left on the core, which can be cut away and chopped, to use in the sorbet mix.

Once the 'sides' have been cut from both fruits, the individual cutters can be used to cut discs through the thickness of the half-cylinders. These can be cut into 1 cm (½ in) thick slices; 4–5 discs will be needed from each half-cylinder. Any trimmings can now be chopped for the sorbet mix. If using one large cake tin, discs can still be cut or simply halve through the centre of the pineapples, cutting lengthways and removing the core. Now cut into enough half-moon slices to fill the bottom of the tin.

The discs can now be pan-fried in a little oil on one side only, creating a golden caramel finish. Once starting to colour, add a pinch or two of caster sugar to finish the caramelizing of the fruits. Place caramel-side down, in the individual rings or cake tin. Leave to cool.

Pre-heat the oven to 160°C/325°F/Gas Mark 3 and toast the Brazil nuts before rubbing off the skins. Blitz the nuts to a ground texture in a food processor. Then place the butter in a saucepan over a medium heat, melting and cooking until lightly brown in colour. At this stage, remove from the heat and stir in the honey. Sift the flour, salt, pepper, baking powder and all the spices together. Add the sugar and Brazil nuts, stirring in the honey butter.

Whisk the egg whites to a soft-peak stage and fold into the pudding mix.

Pour the mix onto the caramelized pineapples and bake in the pre-heated oven for 35–40 minutes. The puddings will be just firm to the touch. If baking a large pudding, the cooking time will be extended by 10–15 minutes.

They are now turned upside-down out of their moulds or tin, to show the caramelized pineapple slices. They can also be allowed to cool, refrigerated and then microwaved when needed. They will keep for 2–3 days, if refrigerated.

To make the sauce, first boil the sugar and water together until they reach a golden caramel colour. The double cream and pineapple juice can also be boiled and then poured onto the caramel. Mix well before straining through a sieve. The sauce is ready to serve.

To make the sorbet, chop all the pineapple trimmings and place in a saucepan with the syrup. Bring to a simmer and cook for a few minutes until the pineapple has softened. Add the lemon juice and rum to taste, if using. Allow to cool before churning in the ice-cream machine (see Note, page 309). The freezing process will take 20–30 minutes.

To serve, re-heat the pudding(s) if necessary. Spoon the sauce around or over the dessert and place a scoop of pineapple sorbet, if using, on the side.

Note: These quantities can be halved, to make just 4–5 individual cakes or to fill a 17–18 cm (6½–7 in) tin.

Garam Masala

Garam masala was a mixture of spices put together originally to 'spice' people up. This lifted the body and prepared you for a hard winter and work. It was quite a hot spice and helped set people's appetites in India for hot dishes. It has since become a very varied mixture of spices for different dishes, some hotter than others.

The spice mixture does not have to be used just in Indian curry dishes, but will liven up vegetarian risottos, pancakes, ratatouille, lentils and most tomato-based dishes, as well as cream and yoghurt sauces. This recipe is a combination that should suit all of these. Once made, keep in an airtight container in a dark place and use when wanted. Of course, you can buy garam masala ready-made, but the aromatic smell and flavour when you've made it yourself is wonderful.

MAKES ABOUT 50 G (2 OZ)

2 tablespoons coriander seeds
2 tablespoons cumin seeds
1 teaspoon cardamom seeds
1 cinnamon stick
2 bay leaves
1 tablespoon black peppercorns
2 teaspoons cloves
½ teaspoon freshly grated nutmeg
¼ teaspoon ground mace
¼ teaspoon ground ginger

Dry-roast all the ingredients, except the nutmeg, mace and ginger, in a dry pan over a medium heat until they darken slightly and become aromatic. Leave to cool, then add the remaining spices and grind to a powder in a coffee grinder or blender. Store in an airtight jar.

Saffron Bread

Saffron's rich, orange-coloured strands are the stigmas of *Crocus sativus*, the saffron crocus. Saffron is the most highly flavoured and expensive spice in the world. While writing this book, the price ranged from £65 to £75 per 25 g (1 oz). This makes it several hundred pounds per 450g (1 lb). The reason for this expense is that each plant will contribute just three stigmas. It's harvested by hand, and to make up 25 g (1 oz), 13,000 stigmas are needed.

This is a spice that has been with us since many centuries before Christ, and it has been used not just as a flavouring but also in perfume, medicine and dyeing. It's thought that saffron was introduced to Britain by the Romans (as were so many other herbs and spices), and it was the Arabs who re-introduced the spice to medieval Europe. The word saffron actually comes from the Arabic for 'yellow'.

Saffron for some time was quite an important crop in England. The town of Saffron Waldon in Essex grew the crocuses whose stigmas produce the spice, as well as Stratton in Cornwall, until just a hundred or so years ago. In the fifteenth century, anybody 'abusing' the spice in Germany would have been burned and buried.

Most of the world's saffron today comes from Spain, where it grows on the flat, central plains of La Mancha. The stigmas are put through a grading process that's based on length (the best are up to 5 cm/2 in) and on depth and strength of colour. Powdered saffron can also be found. This is a cheaper product and must be looked at carefully. To help its colouring, turmeric is often added. Any box, tin or packet carrying a Selecto label will always be a safe bet.

Because of its strength, recipes using saffron need very little. To get the best results, the strands must first be infused with warm water. Many old recipes will tell you to do this 24 hours in advance. This really isn't necessary. It's best to take the amount required and pour a little hot water (1–2 tablespoons) on top. This can now be left to steep and infuse for 1 hour. A quicker alternative is to break the threads down using a mortar and pestle. Pour on the warm water and leave for 10–15 minutes. However, leaving it to steep for 1 hour will always give stronger results.

This is a sweet tea-loaf-type bread, best served sliced and spread with butter, fresh or toasted.

MAKES A 900 G (2 LB) LOAF OR
2 × 450 G (1 LB) LOAVES

1 teaspoon saffron strands
2 tablespoons warm water
4 teaspoons dried yeast
150 ml (¼ pint) warm milk
75 g (3 oz) sugar
450 g (1 lb) plain flour
½ teaspoon salt
¼ teaspoon ground cinnamon
¼ teaspoon freshly grated nutmeg
175 g (6 oz) butter, diced
175 g (6 oz) mixed dried fruits
50 g (2 oz) mixed peel, chopped

The saffron should first be steeped in the 2 tablespoons of warm water, as explained in the introduction.

Stir the dried yeast into half the milk then add 1 teaspoon of the sugar. This can now be left to froth. It's important the froth is good and thick (2 cm/¾ in deep) before using. This will take approximately 5–10 minutes.

Sift the flour, salt and spices together in a mixing bowl and rub in the butter. Add the remaining sugar and all dried fruits and mixed peel. Make a well in the centre, pouring in the yeast and saffron mixture (the saffron strands can be strained off, but I prefer to add the lot for maximum taste).

Mixing by hand, gradually bring and mix the flour into the liquids. As you are mixing, add the remaining milk until a good soft dough (but not too sticky) is formed. The dough can now be kneaded for 10–15 minutes to give an elastic, smooth finish. Cover with a damp tea-towel and leave in a warm place to rise. For this bread mix, the rising time will be up to 3–4 hours.

Once doubled in size, knead and knock back the dough. This can now either be placed into the well greased 900 g (2 lb) loaf tin or split in two and divided between the two 450 g (1 lb) loaf tins.

Cover and leave to double in size once more. This will take 2–3 hours.

Pre-heat the oven to 190°C/375°F/Gas Mark 5. Bake the large loaf for 50–60 minutes and the 2 small loaves for 40–50 minutes.

To check the bread is done, tap on the base; a hollow sound will tell you it's ready. Now remove from the tin and cool on a wire rack.

Note: The bread can be given a shiny finish by boiling a tablespoon of sugar with a tablespoon of milk. As soon as the bread is out of the oven, brush with the glaze.

If fresh yeast is available, take 25 g (1 oz) and crumble into the sugar and milk as for dried yeast. This, once stirred, will become thick and smooth – ready to use in the recipe.

OPPOSITE
Saffron Bread

See also

Gingerbread Biscuits (page 357)
Iced Vanilla Parfait with Nutmeg Clotted Cream (page 294)
Lemon and Vanilla Sponge (page 341)
Mango Chutney (page 388)
Nutmeg Ice-cream (page 309)
Parkin (page 350)
Piccalilli (page 385)
Pickled Limes (page 381)
Spicy Scrambled Eggs (page 81)
Spicy Smoked Haddock Saffron Soup (page 18)

Bibliography

British Cookery, Lizzie Boyd (ed.), Christopher Helm, 1976

Complete Home Cookery Book, Mrs Stanley Wrench, Associated Newspapers (1941)

The Cookery of England, Elizabeth Ayrton, André Deutsch Ltd, 1975

The Cooking of the British Isles, Glynn Christian, Sainsbury's, 1991

The Cook's Encyclopaedia, Tom Stobart, B.T. Batsford Ltd, 1980

Cuisine of the Sun, Roger Vergé, translated by Carol Conran, Macmillan Publishers Ltd, 1979

Delia Smith's Complete Cookery Course, BBC Worldwide Ltd, 1989

English Food, Jane Grigson, Macmillan Publishers Ltd, 1974

Farmhouse Cookery, The Reader's Digest Association Ltd, 1980

Food and Drink in Britain, C. Anne Wilson, Penguin Books Ltd, 1984

Food in England, Dorothy Hartley, Macdonald, 1954

Food in History, Reay Tannahill, Penguin Books Ltd, 1988

Herbs, Roger Phillips and Nicky Foy, Pan Books, 1983

Herbs: A Connoisseur's Guide, Susan Fleming, W.H. Smith, 1990

The Herb and Spice Book, Sarah Garland, Frances Lincoln Ltd, 1979

Irish Traditional Cooking, Darina Allen, Kyle Cathie Ltd, 1995

Jane Grigson's Fruit Book, Penguin Books Ltd, 1983

Jane Grigson's Vegetable Book, Penguin Books Ltd, 1980

Larousse Gastronomique, Larousse, 1938

The Little Potato Book, Susan Fleming, Piatkus Books, 1987

The Memsahib's Cook Book, Rhona Aitken, Piatkus Books, 1989

Mrs Beeton's All About Cookery, Ward Lock, 1911

North Atlantic Seafood, Alan Davidson, Penguin Books Ltd, 1980

An Omelette and a Glass of Wine, Elizabeth David, Robert Hale Ltd, 1984

On Food and Cooking, Harold Mcgee, Allen and Unwin, 1986

Puddings and Desserts, Marguerite Patten, Paul Hamlyn, 1963

The Rich Tradition, Elizabeth Luard, Bantam Press, 1994

Scottish Regional Recipes, Catherine Brown, Molendinar Press, 1981

Seeds of Change, Henry Hobhouse, Sidgewick & Jackson, 1985

Seven Centuries of English Cooking, Maxine de la Falaise, Grove Press, 1973

A Taste of History, English Heritage in association with British Museum Press, 1993

A Taste of Scotland, Theodora Fitzgibbon, Pan Books, 1970

Wild Food, Roger Phillips, Pan Books, 1983

Index